T.O. 1F-111A-1

Reproduction for nonmilitary use of the information or illustrations contained in this publication is not permitted without specific approval of the issuing service. The policy for use of Classified Publications is established for the Air Force in AFR 205-1.

LIST OF EFFECTIVE PAGES

INSERT LATEST CHANGED PAGES. DESTROY SUPERSEDED PAGES.

NOTE: The portion of the text affected by the changes is indicated by a vertical line in the outer margins of the page. Changes to illustrations are indicated by miniature pointing hands, shading, or legend.

TOTAL NUMBER OF PAGES IN THIS PUBLICATION IS 296, CONSISTING OF THE FOLLOWING:

Page No.	Issue
*Title	18 Aug 67
*A	18 Aug 67
*SS Flyleaf 1	18 Aug 67
*OS Flyleaf 1	18 Aug 67
*TCTO Flyleaf 1	18 Aug 67
TCTO Flyleaf 2 Blank	Original
i thru ii	Original
iii	7 Apr 67
*iv thru v	18 Aug 67
vi	7 Apr 67
*1-1	18 Aug 67
1-2 thru 1-3	Original
1-4 thru 1-5	7 Apr 67
*1-6 thru 1-7	18 Aug 67
1-8 thru 1-9	7 Apr 67
*1-10 thru 1-14B	18 Aug 67
*1-15 thru 1-16B	18 Aug 67
*1-17	18 Aug 67
1-18 thru 1-19	7 Apr 67
*1-20 thru 1-25	18 Aug 67
1-26 thru 1-28A	7 Apr 67
1-28B Blank	7 Apr 67
1-29	7 Apr 67
*1-30	18 Aug 67
1-31	Original
*1-32 thru 1-34	18 Aug 67
1-35	7 Apr 67
*1-36	18 Aug 67
1-36A	7 Apr 67
1-36B Blank	7 Apr 67
*1-37 thru 1-38	18 Aug 67
*1-38A Added	18 Aug 67
*1-38B Blank Added	18 Aug 67
*1-39 thru 1-40	18 Aug 67
1-41	7 Apr 67
*1-42 thru 1-48	18 Aug 67
*1-48A Added	18 Aug 67
*1-48B Blank Added	18 Aug 67
*1-49 thru 1-52	18 Aug 67
*1-52A Added	18 Aug 67
*1-52B Blank Added	18 Aug 67
*1-53 thru 1-56	18 Aug 67
*1-56A thru 1-56B Added	18 Aug 67

Page No.	Issue
*1-57 thru 1-59	18 Aug 67
1-60	Original
*1-61 thru 1-62	18 Aug 67
*1-62A Added	18 Aug 67
*1-62B Blank Added	18 Aug 67
1-63	7 Apr 67
*1-64 thru 1-66	18 Aug 67
1-67	Original
1-68	7 Apr 67
*1-69 thru 1-70	18 Aug 67
1-70A	7 Apr 67
*1-70B	18 Aug 67
1-70C	7 Apr 67
*1-70D	18 Aug 67
*1-71 thru 1-76	18 Aug 67
1-76A	7 Apr 67
1-76B Blank	7 Apr 67
*1-77 thru 1-80B	18 Aug 67
*1-80C Deleted	18 Aug 67
*1-80D Blank Deleted	18 Aug 67
*1-81 thru 1-98	18 Aug 67
*1-98A thru 1-98B Added	18 Aug 67
*1-99 thru 1-104	18 Aug 67
1-105	7 Apr 67
1-106	Original
*1-107	18 Aug 67
1-108	Original
*1-109 thru 1-112	18 Aug 67
1-112A	7 Apr 67
1-112B Blank	7 Apr 67
1-113	Original
*1-114	18 Aug 67
1-115 thru 1-117	7 Apr 67
*1-118	18 Aug 67
1-119	7 Apr 67
*1-120	18 Aug 67
*1-120A Added	18 Aug 67
*1-120B Blank Added	18 Aug 67
*1-121 thru 1-124	18 Aug 67

Page No.	Issue
1-125	7 Apr 67
*1-126	18 Aug 67
1-127 thru 1-129	Original
1-130	7 Apr 67
*1-131 thru 1-134	18 Aug 67
*2-1 thru 2-2	18 Aug 67
2-3	Original
*2-4 thru 2-6	18 Aug 67
*2-6A thru 2-6B Deleted	18 Aug 67
*2-7 thru 2-20	18 Aug 67
*2-21 thru 2-23 Added	18 Aug 67
*2-24 Blank Added	18 Aug 67
*3-1	18 Aug 67
3-2	7 Apr 67
*3-3 thru 3-4A	18 Aug 67
3-4B Blank	7 Apr 67
*3-5 thru 3-12A	18 Aug 67
3-12B Blank	7 Apr 67
*3-13 thru 3-20	18 Aug 67
*3-21 Added	18 Aug 67
*3-22 Blank Added	18 Aug 67
4-1	Original
4-2 Blank	Original
*5-1 thru 5-12	18 Aug 67
*5-12A Added	18 Aug 67
*5-12B Blank Added	18 Aug 67
*5-13 thru 5-14	18 Aug 67
*5-14A thru 5-14B Deleted	18 Aug 67
*5-15 thru 5-18	18 Aug 67
*5-18A thru 5-18D Deleted	18 Aug 67
*5-19 thru 5-24	18 Aug 67
*5-25 Added	18 Aug 67
*5-26 Blank Added	18 Aug 67
*6-1 thru 6-6	18 Aug 67
*6-7 thru 6-20 Added	18 Aug 67
*7-1 thru 7-6	18 Aug 67
7-7 thru 7-8	7 Apr 67
*Index 1 thru Index 10	18 Aug 67

F-111 AARDVARK PILOT'S FLIGHT OPERATING INSTRUCTIONS
ISBN #9781940453316
COPYRIGHT ©2014 PERISCOPE FILM LLC
WWW.PERISCOPEFILM.COM

*The asterisk indicates pages changed, added, or deleted by the current change.

ADDITIONAL COPIES OF THIS PUBLICATION MAY BE OBTAINED AS FOLLOWS:

USAF ACTIVITIES.—In accordance with T.O. 00-5-2.

TABLE OF CONTENTS

SECTION I	description & operation	1-1
SECTION II	normal procedures	2-1
SECTION III	emergency procedures	3-1
SECTION IV	crew duties	(Not Applicable)
SECTION V	operating limitations	5-1
SECTION VI	flight characteristics	6-1
SECTION VII	all weather operation	7-1
APPENDIX I	performance data	(See T.O. 1F-111A-1A)
	alphabetical index	1

SCOPE.

This manual contains the necessary information for safe and efficient operation of the F-111A. These instructions provide you with a general knowledge of the airplane, its characteristics, and specific normal and emergency operating procedures. Your experience is recognized, and, therefore, basic flight principles are avoided. Instructions in this manual are for a crew inexperienced in the operation of this airplane. This manual provides the best possible operating instructions under most circumstances. Multiple emergencies, adverse weather, terrain, etc. may require modification of the procedures.

PERMISSIBLE OPERATIONS.

The Flight Manual takes a "positive approach" and normally states only what you can do. Unusual operations or configurations are prohibited unless specifically covered herein. Clearance must be obtained before any questionable operation, which is not specifically permitted in this manual, is attempted.

HOW TO BE ASSURED OF HAVING LATEST DATA.

Refer to T.O. 0-1-1-4A which is issued weekly and devoted solely to the listing of all current Flight Manuals, Safety Supplements, Operational Supplements, and Checklists. Its frequency of issue and brevity assures an accurate, up-to-date listing of these publications.

ARRANGEMENT.

The manual is divided into seven fairly independent sections to simplify reading it straight through or using it as a reference manual.

Note
Performance data normally included in Appendix I is contained in Classified Supplement 1F-111A-1A.

SAFETY SUPPLEMENTS.

Information involving safety will be promptly forwarded to you by Safety Supplement. Supplements covering loss of life will get to you within 48 hours by TWX, and those covering serious damage to equipment within 10 days by mail. The title page of the Flight Manual and the title block of each Safety Supplement should be checked to determine the effect they may have on existing supplements. You must remain constantly aware of the status of all supplements. Current supplements must be complied with, but there is no point in restricting your operation by complying with a replaced or rescinded supplement.

OPERATIONAL SUPPLEMENTS.

Information involving changes to operating procedures will be forwarded to you by Operational Supplements. The procedure for handling Operational Supplements is the same as for Safety Supplements.

CHECKLISTS.

The Flight Manual contains only amplified checklists. Abbreviated checklists are issued as separate documents, see the back of the title page for the date of your latest checklist. Line items in the Flight Manual and checklists are identical with respect to arrangement and checklist number. Whenever a Safety Supplement affects the checklist, write in the applicable change on the affected checklist page. As soon as possible, a new checklist page, incorporating the supplement will be issued. This will keep handwritten entries of Safety Supplement information in your checklist to a minimum.

HOW TO GET PERSONAL COPIES.

Each flight crew member is entitled to personal copies of the Flight Manual, Safety Supplements, Operational Supplements, and Check Lists. The required quantities should be ordered before you need them to assure their prompt receipt. Check with your supply personnel — it is their job to fulfill your Technical Order requests. Basically, you must order the required quantities on the appropriate Numerical Index and Requirement Table (NIRT). Technical Orders 00-5-1 and 00-5-2 give detailed information for properly ordering these publications. Make sure a system is established at your base to deliver these publications to the flight crews immediately upon receipt.

FLIGHT MANUAL BINDERS.

Looseleaf binders and sectionalized tabs are available for use with your manual. These are obtained through local purchase procedures and are listed in the Federal Supply Schedule (FSC Group 75, Office Supplies, Part 1). Check with your supply personnel for assistance in procuring these items.

WARNINGS, CAUTIONS, AND NOTES.

The following definitions apply to "Warnings", "Cautions", and "Notes" found throughout the manual.

Operating procedures, techniques, etc., which will result in personal injury or loss of life if not carefully followed.

```
CAUTION
```

Operating procedures, techniques, etc., which will result in damage to equipment if not carefully followed.

Note

An operating procedure, technique, etc., which is considered essential to emphasize.

YOUR RESPONSIBILITY — TO LET US KNOW.

Every effort is made to keep the Flight Manual current. Review conferences with operating personnel and a constant review of accident and flight test reports assure inclusion of the latest data in the manual. However, we cannot correct an error unless we know of its existence. In this regard, it is essential that you do your part. Comments, corrections, and questions regarding this manual or any phase of the Flight Manual program are welcomed. These should be forwarded through your Command Headquarters to ASD, Wright-Patterson AFB, Ohio, Atten: ASZO.

AIRPLANE DESIGNATION CODES.

Major differences between airplanes covered in this manual are designated by number symbols which appear in the text or on illustrations. Symbol designations for individual aircraft, and groups of aircraft are as follows:

⑲	65-5701	㊴	66-021
⑳	65-5702	㊵	66-022
㉑	65-5703	㊶	66-023
㉒	65-5704	㊷	66-024
㉓	65-5705	㊸	66-025
㉔	65-5706	㊹	66-026
㉕	65-5707	㊺	66-027
㉖	65-5708	㊻	66-028
㉗	65-5709	㊼	66-029
㉘	65-5710	㊽	66-030
㉙	66-011	㊾	66-031
㉚	66-012	㊿	66-032
㉛	66-013	51	66-033
㉜	66-014	52	66-034
㉝	66-015	53	66-035
㉞	66-016	54	66-036
㉟	66-017	55	66-037
㊱	66-018	56	66-038
㊲	66-019	57	66-039
㊳	66-020		

♦ "through" or "and on".

Changed 7 April 1967

GLOSSARY

AA GUN	Air-to-Air Gunnery
AA RKT	Air-to-Air Rocketry
A/B	Afterburner
AC	Aircraft Commander
ac	Alternating Current
ADF	Automatic Direction Finder
ADI	Altitude Director Indicator
AFC	Automatic Frequency Control
AFRS	Auxiliary Flight Reference System
AG GUN	Air-to-Ground Gunnery
AI	Airborne Intercept
AILA	Airborne Instrument Low Approach
AIPD	Airborne Intercept Pulse Doppler
AIR FF	Air Freefall
AIR RET	Air Retard
ALT CAL	Altitude Calibration
ALT HLD	Altitude Hold
ALTM	Altimeter
ALT REF	Altitude Reference
AMI	Airspeed-Mach Indicator
ANT CAGE	Antenna Cage
ANT TILT	Antenna Tilt
ATF	Automatic Terrain Following
ATT GYRO	Attitude Gyro
AUX ATT	Auxiliary Attitude
AUX NAV	Auxiliary Navigation
AVVI	Altitude-Vertical Velocity Indicator
AYC	Adverse Yaw Compensation
B/C	Biological/Chemical
BDHI	Bearing Distance Heading Indicator
BNDTI	Bomb Nav Distance Time Indicator
CADC	Central Air Data Computer
CCM	Counter-Counter Measures
CCW	Counterclockwise
CIR	Circular
CKT	Circuit
CMDS	Countermeasures Dispenser Set
CMRS	Countermeasures Receiver Set
COM	Common
COMP	Compass
cps	Cycles Per Second
CRS SEL NAV	Course Select Navigation
CW	Clockwise
DBT	Dual Bombing Timer
dc	Direct Current
DEST	Destination
DG	Directional Gyro
DISP	Dispenser
DIV BOMB	Dive Bombing
EBL	Emergency Boom Latching
EPR	Engine Pressure Ratio
FDC	Flight Director Computer
FLSC	Flexible Linear Shaped Charges
FOD	Foreign Object Damage
FTC	Fast Time Constant
FW	Forward Warning
GHz	Gigahertz
GND/GRD	Ground
GND MAN	Ground Manual
GND VEL	Ground Velocity
GRD FF	Ground Freefall
GRD RET	Ground Retard
HF	High Frequency
HOM	Homing
HSI	Horizontal Situation Indicator
IF	Intermediate Frequency
IFF	Identification Friend or Foe
IFIS	Integrated Flight Instrument System
ILS	Instrument Landing System
INPH	Interphone
I/P	Identification of Position
iRT	Infrared Track
IRS	Infrared Search
IRU	Inertial Reference Unit
ISC	Instrument System Coupler
JETT	Jettison
LCOSS	Lead Computing Optical Sight System
LEV BOMB	Level Bombing
LNCH	Launch
LOF BOMB	Loft Bombing
LSB	Lower Side Band
LSTC	Low Speed Trim Compensation
MACH HLD	Mach Hold
MAG VAR	Magnetic Variation
MAN CRS	Manual Course
MAN FIX	Manual Fix
MAN HDG	Manual Heading
MED	Medium
MFC	Manual Frequency Control
MIC	Microphone
MI/DIA	Miles/Diameter
MON	Monitor
MR	Milli-radian
MRT	Modulator-Receiver Transmitter
MSMA	Maximum Safe Mach Assembly
NC	Navigation Computer
NORM	Normal
NWS/AR	Nosewheel Steering/Air Refueling
OMO	Omni Warning Open
OMS	Off, Monitor, Safe
OMT	Omni Warning Threat
OVRD	Override
p	Pilot
PP/PRES POS	Present Position
pph	Pounds Per Hour
PPI	Plan Position Indicator
psi	Pounds Per Square Inch

Changed 18 August 1967

RAT	Ram Air Turbine	TAS	True Airspeed
REC	Receive	TBC	Trackbreaker Chaff
REF ENGAGE	Reference Engage	TF	Terrain Following
RHAWS	Radar Homing and Warning System	TFR	Terrain Following Radar
RKT	Rocket	TIT	Turbine Inlet Temperature
RPM	Revolutions Per Minute	T.O. & LAND	Takeoff and Land
RT	Receiver-Transmitter	T/R	Transmit/Receive
SIF	Selective Identification Frequency	TRANS	Transmit
SIT	Situation Display	TTI	Total Temperature Indicator
SLC	Side Lobe Cancellation	UHF	Ultra High Frequency
SMDC	Shaped Mild Detonating Cord	USB	Upper Sideband
SP	Stabilization Platform		
STAB AUG	Stability Augmentation		
STBY	Standby		
STC	Sensitivity Time Control		

The F-111A

Section I
Description & Operation

SECTION I
DESCRIPTION & OPERATION

TABLE OF CONTENTS.

	Page
The Airplane	1-1
Engines	1-6
Oil Supply System	1-16
Fuel Supply System	1-16A
Electrical Power Supply System	1-24
Hydraulic Power Supply System	1-32
Pneumatic Power Supply Systems	1-33
Landing Gear System	1-33
Tail Bumper System	1-39
Nose Wheel Steering System	1-39
Brake System	1-39
Aircraft Arresting System	1-40
Aerodynamic Deceleration Equipment	1-41
Wing Flaps and Slats	1-41
Wing Sweep System	1-43
Flight Control System	1-43
Autopilot System	1-55
Central Air Data Computer System	1-57
Maximum Safe Mach Assembly	1-58
Auxiliary Flight Reference System	1-58
Pitot-Static System	1-61
Instruments	1-62
Bombing-Navigation System	1-71
Armament System	1-81
Tactical Air Navigation System	1-89
Instrument Landing System	1-90
Radar Altimeter System	1-91
Terrain Following Radar	1-92
IFF System	1-97
Attack Radar	1-98
Lead Computing Optical Sight System	1-105
Penetration Aids	1-107
Communication Equipment	1-107
Lighting System	1-112
Canopy	1-114
Air Conditioning and Pressurization Systems	1-115
Oxygen System	1-123
Crew Module Escape System	1-125
Miscellaneous Equipment	1-131

THE AIRPLANE.

The F-111A is a two place (side-by-side) long range fighter bomber built by General Dynamics, Fort Worth Division. The airplane is designed for all-weather supersonic operation at both low and high altitude. Mission capabilities include: long range high altitude intercepts utilizing air-to-air missiles and/or guns; long range attack missions utilizing conventional or nuclear weapons as primary armament and close support missions utilizing a choice of missiles, guns, bombs and rockets. An automatic low altitude terrain following system enhances penetration capability. Power is provided by two TF-30 axial-flow, dual-compressor turbofan engines equipped with afterburners. The wings, equipped with leading edge slats and trailing edge flaps, may be varied in sweep, area, camber, and aspect ratio, by the selection of any wing sweep angle between 16 and 72.5 degrees. A selective forward wing sweep provides takeoff and landing capabilities at minimum speeds. For all other regimes the wings are manually swept in accordance with desired mach number. This feature provides the airplane with a highly versatile operating envelope. The empennage consists of a fixed vertical stabilizer with rudder for directional control, and a horizontal stabilizer that is moved symmetrically for pitch control and asymmetrically for roll control. Stability augmentation incorporates triple redundant features which enhance system reliability. The tricycle-type forward retracting landing gear is hydraulically operated. The main landing gear consists of a single common trunnion upon which two wheels are singly mounted, and contains but one extending/retracting/locking system which ensures symmetrical main gear operation. Also ground loads imposed upon the gear tend to extend the drag strut to the locked position. Stores are carried in a fuselage-enclosed weapons bay and externally on both pivoting and fixed wing-mounted pylons. The fuel system incorporates both inflight and single point ground refueling capabilities. See figure 1-1 for airplane general arrangement.

AIRPLANE DIMENSIONS.

Length (overall including pitot static boom) — 75 feet, 6.5 inches
Wing span (wings swept) — 32 feet
Wing span (wings extended) — 63 feet, 0.0 inches

Height (to top of vertical tail) — 17 feet, 1.4 inches
Refer to Section II for turning radius and ground clearance dimensions.

Changed 18 August 1967

Section I
Description & Operation

T.O. 1F-111A-1

General Arrangement Diagram

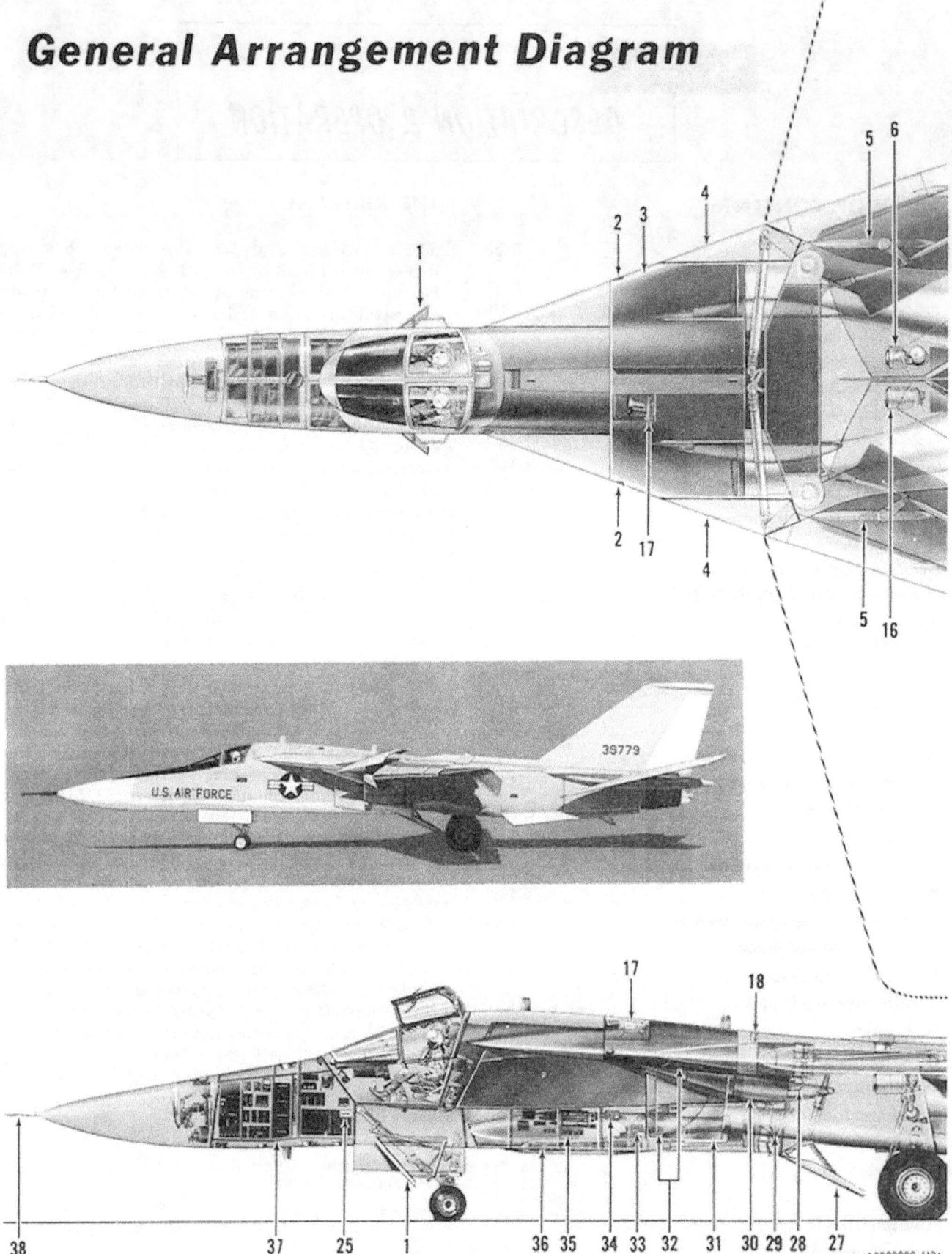

Figure 1-1. (Sheet 1)

T.O. 1F-111A-1

**Section I
Description & Operation**

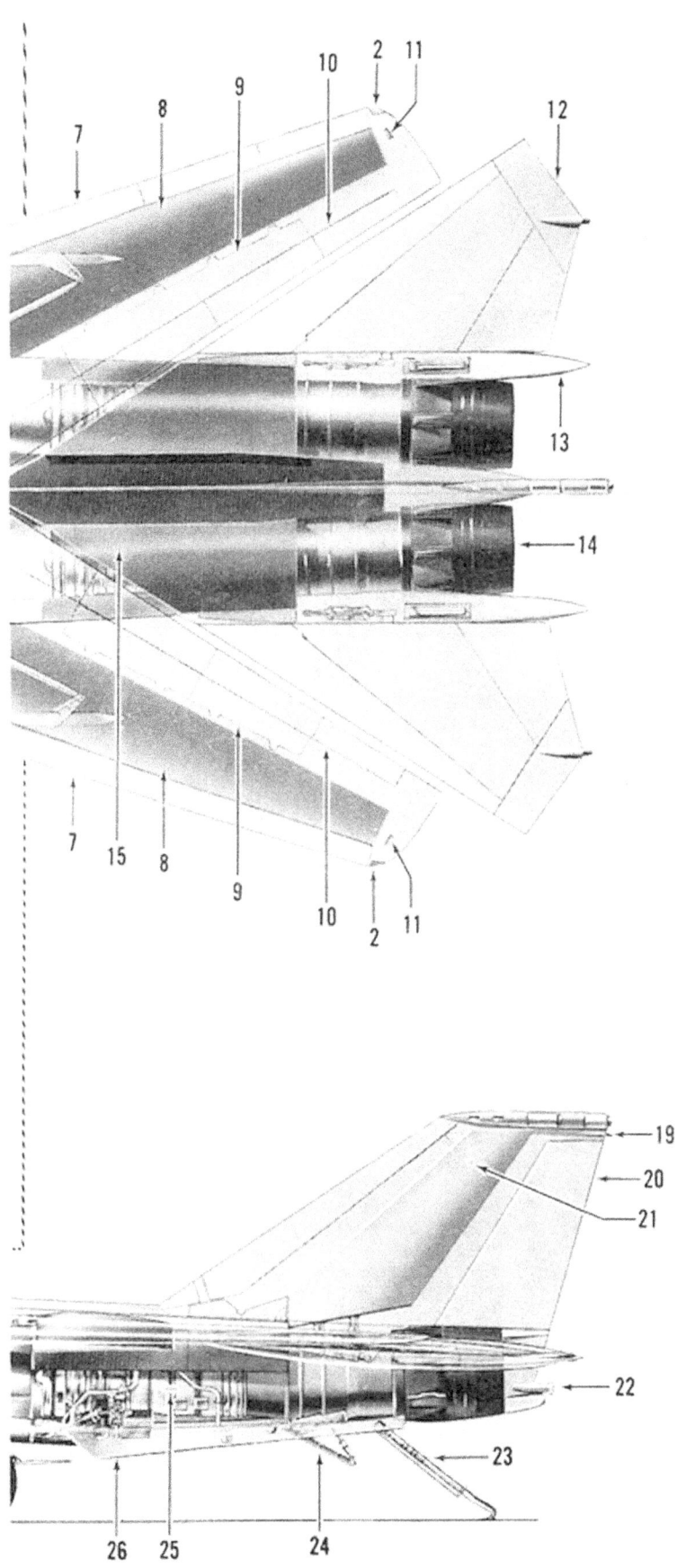

1. Entrance Ladder and Step.
2. Wing Position Lights.
3. Forward Fuel Tank.
4. Rotating Glove.
5. Pivoting Pylons.
6. Primary Hydraulic System Reservoir.
7. Slats.
8. Wing Fuel Tanks.
9. Spoilers.
10. Wing Flaps.
11. Wing Formation Lights (Upr & Lwr).
12. Horizontal Stabilizer.
13. Speed Bumps.
14. Engines.
15. Aft Fuel Tank.
16. Utility Hydraulic System Reservoir.
17. Air Refueling Receptacle.
18. Anti-Collision Lights (Upper & Lower).
19. Tail Position Light.
20. Rudder.
21. Fuel Vent Tank.
22. Fuel Dump Outlet.
23. Arresting Hook.
24. Tail Bumper.
25. Fuselage Formation Lights (4).
26. Strake (2).
27. Forward Landing Gear Door/Speed Brake.
28. Air Conditioning System Cooling Air Intake.
29. Translating Cowl.
30. Spike.
31. Splitter Vane.
32. FOD Doors.
33. Fuel System Precheck Selector Panel.
34. Single Point Refueling Adapter Receptacle.
35. Aft Electronic Equipment Bay.
36. Weapons Bay.
37. Forward Electronic Equipment Bay.
38. Pitot Static Probe.

Figure 1-1. (Sheet 2)

Section I
Description & Operation

T.O. 1F-111A-1

Crew Station General Arrangement (Typical)

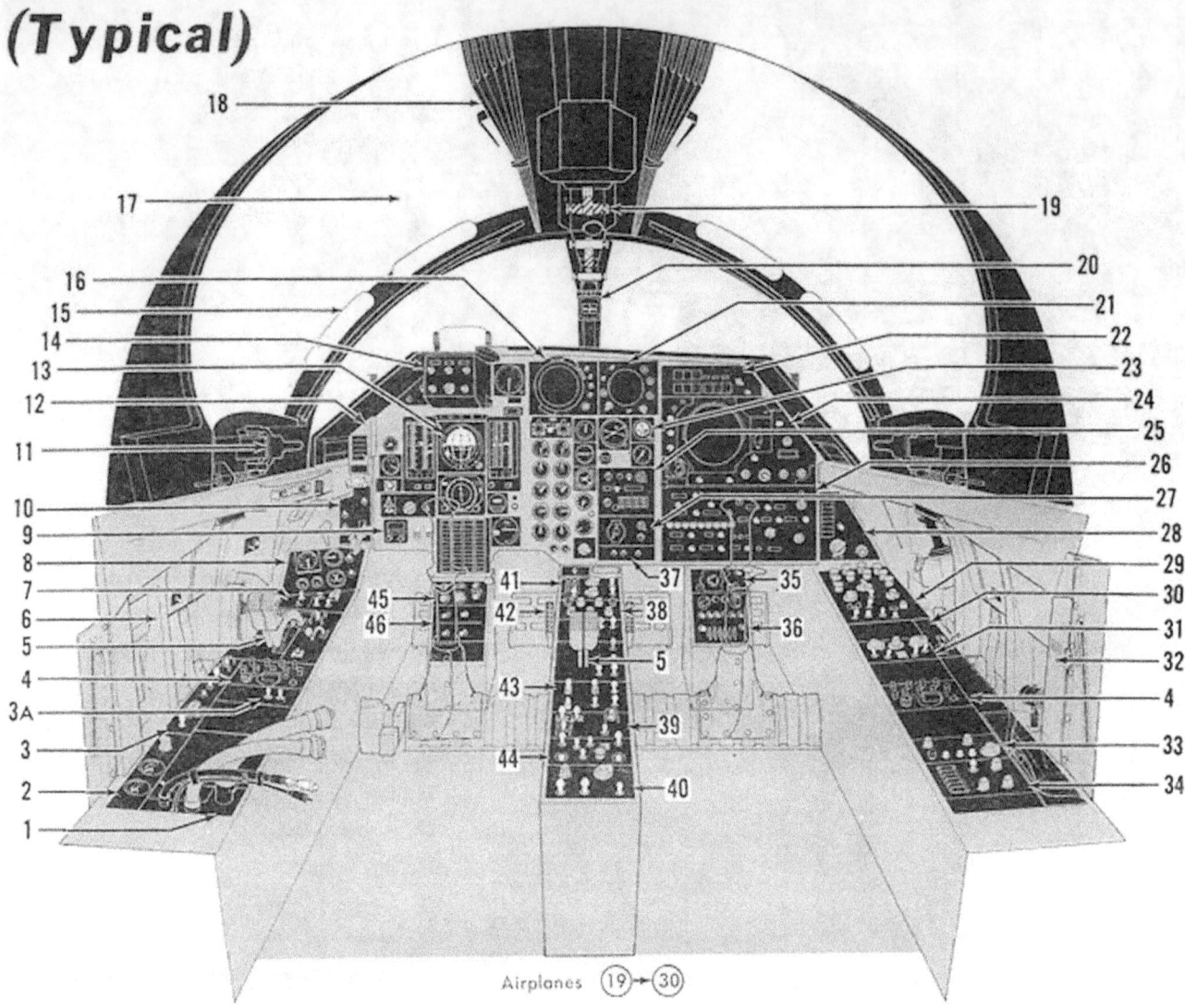

Airplanes 19 → 30

1. AC Oxygen-Suit Control Panel (See fig. 1-58).
2. Electrical Power Test Panel (See fig. 1-11).
3. Flight Control Switch Panel (See fig. 1-23).
3A. Engine Panel
4. Interphone Panel (2) (See fig. 1-50).
5. Throttle Panel (2) (See fig. 1-5).
6. Left Sidewall (See fig. 1-19).
7. Miscellaneous Switch Panel (See fig. 1-36).
8. Auxiliary Gage Panel (See fig. 1-15).
9. Dual Bombing Timer (See fig. 1-33).
10. Landing Gear Control Panel (See fig. 1-16).
11. Internal Canopy Latch Handle (2).
12. Left Main Instrument Panel (See fig. 1-6 & 1-6A).
13. Integrated Flight Inst's (See fig. 1-28A).
14. LCOS Control Panel (See fig. 1-46).
15. Mirrors (4).
16. TFR Scope Panel (See fig. 1-38).
17. Canopy.
18. Thermal Curtain (2).
19. Canopy Center Beam Assembly.
20. Magnetic Compass.
*21. RHAW Scope Panel.
*22. RHAW Panel.
23. Right Main Instrument Panel (See fig. 1-28).
24. Attack Radar Scope Panel (See fig. 1-44).
25. UHF Radio Control Panel (See fig. 1-49).
26. Bomb Nav Control Panel (See fig. 1-30).
27. TACAN Control Panel (See fig. 1-34).
28. Nuclear Weapons Control Panel (See fig. 1-32).
29. Armament Select Panel (See fig. 1-31).
30. Radio Beacon Set.
31. Attack Radar Control Panel (See fig. 1-42).
32. Right Sidewall (See fig. 1-55).
*33. CMRS Control Panel.
*34. CMDS Control Panel.
35. ILS Control Panel (See fig. 1-35).
36. IFF Control Panel (See fig. 1-39).
37. Antenna Select Panel (See fig. 1-40).
38. TFR Control Panel (See fig. 1-37).
39. Auxiliary Flight Cont Panel (See fig. 1-22).
40. Air Conditioning Control Panel (See fig. 1-53).
41. Fuel Control Panel (See fig. 1-8).
42. Ejection Handles (2).
43. Autopilot/Damper Panel (See fig. 1-24).
44. Electrical Control Panel (See fig. 1-10).
45. Compass Control Panel (See fig. 1-26).

Figure 1-2. (Sheet 1)

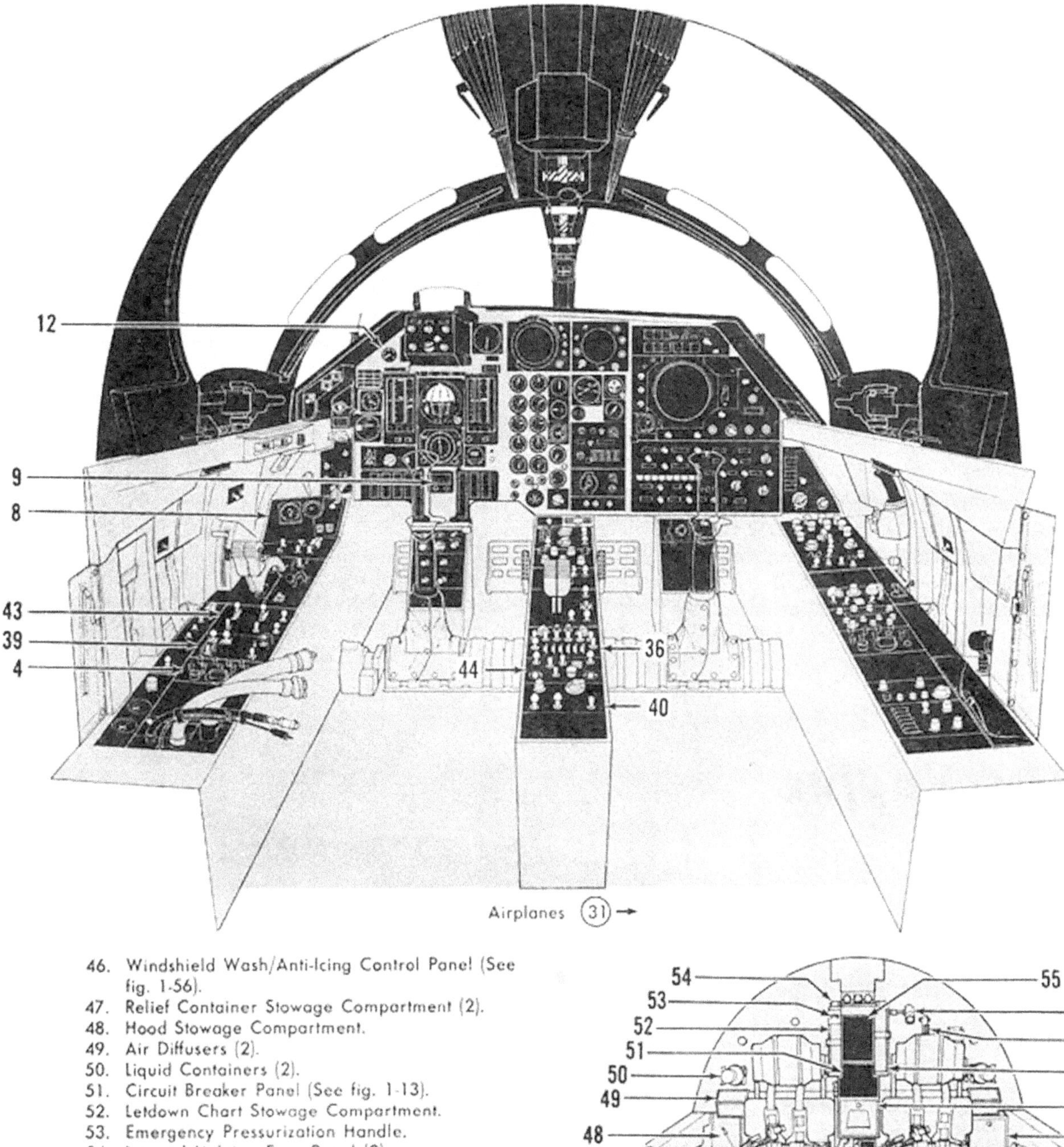

T.O. 1F-111A-1

Section I
Description & Operation

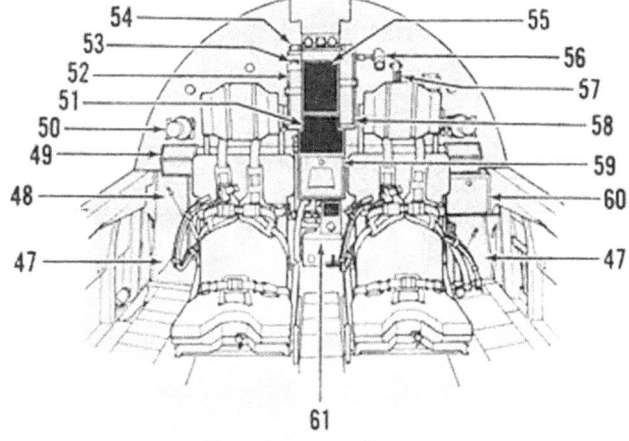

Airplanes (31) →

46. Windshield Wash/Anti-Icing Control Panel (See fig. 1-56).
47. Relief Container Stowage Compartment (2).
48. Hood Stowage Compartment.
49. Air Diffusers (2).
50. Liquid Containers (2).
51. Circuit Breaker Panel (See fig. 1-13).
52. Letdown Chart Stowage Compartment.
53. Emergency Pressurization Handle.
54. Internal Lighting Fuse Panel (2).
55. Lighting Control Panel (See fig. 1-51).
56. Utility Light.
57. Left Canopy Detach Handle.
58. Letdown Chart Holder Stowage Compartment.
59. Ground Check Panel (See fig. 1-25).
60. Food Stowage Compartment.
61. Pilot's Oxygen-Suit Control Panel (See fig. 1-58).

*See T.O. 1F-111A-1B.

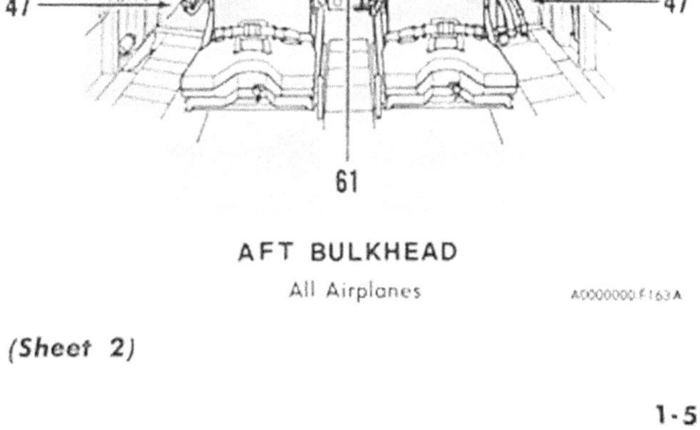

AFT BULKHEAD
All Airplanes

Figure 1-2. (Sheet 2)

Changed 7 April 1967

1-5

Section I
Description & Operation

AIRPLANE WEIGHT.

The aircraft operating weight is approximately 44,285 pounds. This weight includes two crewmembers (430 lbs), engine oil (159 lbs), unusable fuel (250 lbs), cooling water (229 lbs), and oxygen (25 lbs). For specific aircraft weight, refer to the associated handbook of Weight and Balance Data, T.O. 1-1B-40.

FLIGHT CREW.

The flight crew consists of two pilots seated side-by-side. The crew member assigned to the left crew station normally serves as aircraft commander. The pilot at the right crew station, in addition to his normal pilot duties, operates the offensive and defensive equipment associated with the controls at that station.

ENGINES.

The airplane is powered by two Pratt and Whitney TF-30-P-1 or -P-3 sixteen-stage axial flow turbofan engines equipped with afterburners. See figure 1-3. The engines are mounted side by side in the fuselage and are interchangeable. The sea level, standard day thrust rating of the engine is in the 10,000 pound class in military power and in the 18,000 pound class in afterburner. Provisions are made for starting the engines with an external pneumatic ground starter cart. Also the left engine has the capability of being started without the aid of ground support equipment by means of a pyrotechnic cartridge. With either engine operating, the other engine can be started by using bleed air from the operating engine. Electrical power is supplied for the engine igniter plugs by an engine-driven alternator. Each engine is supplied a flow of air through a separate inlet duct located below the intersection of the wing and fuselage. An automatically controlled, movable spike is used in each inlet duct to control airflow to the engines. Additional engine inlet air is provided during ground operation and at low airspeeds through openings in the outboard side of each nacelle, when the translating cowls are in the extended position. Splitter vanes are used at the front of the inlet ducts to remove the low energy air from the fuselage and the lower surface of the wing glove, thus preventing boundary layer air from disturbing engine inlet air. These features allow optimum engine performance throughout a wide range of airplane operating conditions. Air from the inlet of each engine is routed through a single duct for both the basic engine section and the fan section. Three compressor stages provide the initial pressurization of the air flowing into the engine and into the fan duct. The fan duct is a full-annular duct which directs

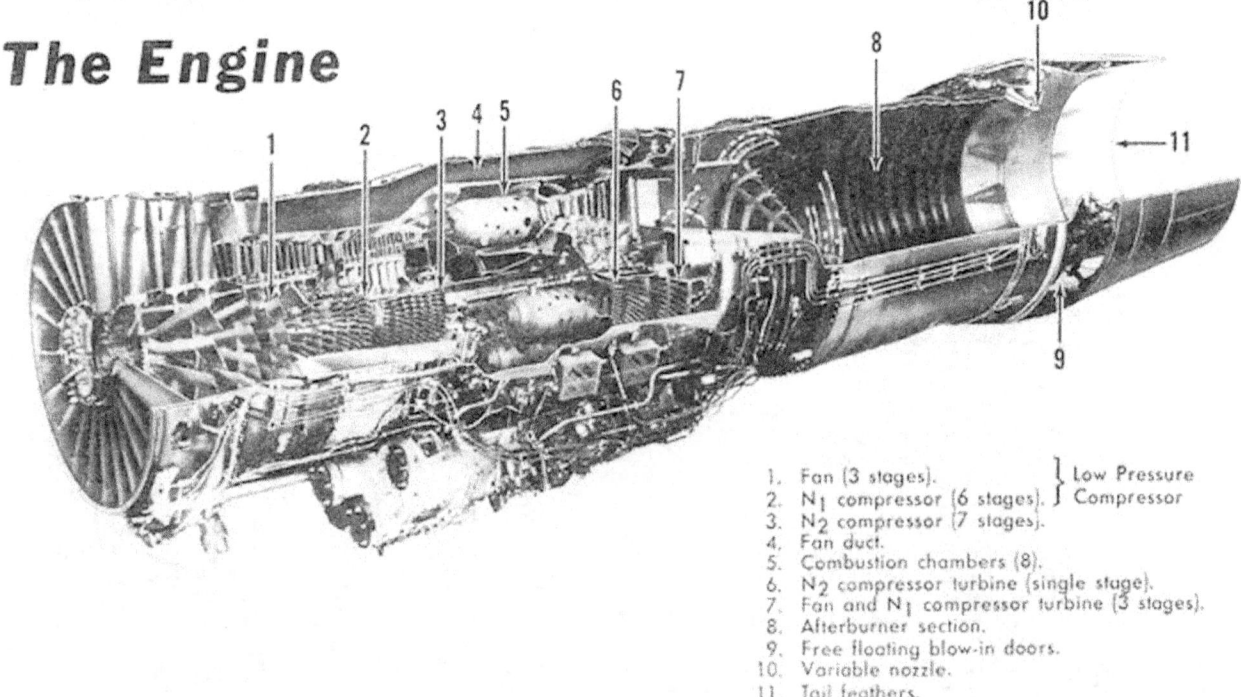

The Engine

1. Fan (3 stages). ⎫ Low Pressure
2. N_1 compressor (6 stages). ⎭ Compressor
3. N_2 compressor (7 stages).
4. Fan duct.
5. Combustion chambers (8).
6. N_2 compressor turbine (single stage).
7. Fan and N_1 compressor turbine (3 stages).
8. Afterburner section.
9. Free floating blow-in doors.
10. Variable nozzle.
11. Tail feathers.

Figure 1-3.

flow aft to join the engine airflow coming from the turbine discharge. The fan air develops a significant portion of total engine thrust. Engine air is compressed by 9 stages of the low pressure compressor (N1) of which three stages are the fan, and 7 stages of the high pressure compressor (N2). The air is then diffused into the combustion section which contains 8 combustion chambers. The turbine section of the engine consists of a single-stage turbine to drive the high pressure compressor and a three-stage turbine to drive the low pressure compressor. The turbines are mechanically independent of each other. High pressure compressor speed is indicated by a tachometer. Speed of the low pressure compressor is not monitored except by an overspeed caution lamp. After leaving the turbine section of the engine, the air is joined with the fan air in the afterburner section. Bleed air from the engine compressors is used for cockpit and equipment bay air conditioning and pressurization, hydraulic system pressurization, fuel tank pressurization, hydraulic oil cooling, engine vortex destroyers, generator/CSD cooling, ground oil cooling, and windshield rain removal. Also, hot bleed air is used for engine inlet and guide vane anti-icing (Refer to "Anti-Icing and Defog Systems", this section).

ENGINE FUEL CONTROL SYSTEM.

Each engine fuel control system (figure 1-4) automatically provides optimum fuel flow for any throttle setting. This system responds to several engine operating parameters and makes it unnecessary to adjust the throttle in order to compensate for variations in inlet air temperature, altitude or airspeed. The engine fuel system consists of a two-stage engine-driven fuel pump, fuel control unit, flowmeter, filter, a pressurizing and dump valve, nozzles, and a fuel-oil heat exchanger. Fuel from the tanks is routed through the flowmeter to the centrifugal stage of the engine fuel pump, through a filter, and back to the gear stage of the pump. Bypass valves route fuel past the filter or first pump stage in event of failure of these components. The second pump stage delivers fully pressurized fuel to the fuel control unit which provides metered fuel flow through the fuel-oil heat exchanger to the fuel pressurizing and dump valve. This dual function valve directs the fuel through the primary and secondary fuel manifolds to eight fuel nozzles which spray the fuel into the eight engine combustion chambers. When the fuel pressure drops during engine shutdown, the fuel pressurizing and dump valve automatically opens and drains the primary fuel manifold.

Fuel Control Unit.

The engine fuel control unit is a hydromechanical device incorporating an engine-driven, flyball-type speed governor. The control unit consists of a fuel metering system and a computing system which operates as a function of throttle setting, main combustion chamber pressure, high pressure rotor N2 speed, compressor inlet pressure, compressor inlet temperature, and flight mach number which is provided from the CADC. The metering system selects the rate of fuel flow to be supplied to the engine in response to the throttle setting. However, metering sections are regulated by the fuel control computing system which monitors the various engine operating parameters. Fuel enters the fuel control through a filter that is provided with a springloaded bypass. Fuel metering is accomplished by maintaining a constant pressure across a variable valve area which is controlled by the computing system. The constant pressure is maintained by means of a pressure regulating bypass valve. This valve consists of a servo-operated valve and a springloaded valve. Normally, the servo maintains constant valve regulation; but in the event of servo malfunction, the spring valve alone will provide adequate regulation. Deviations from the desired metering pressure are sensed in the valve regulating unit which varies the bypass flow area, thereby restoring the desired pressure by returning excess fuel to the pump inlet.

ENGINE AFTERBURNERS.

The afterburner (A/B) augments engine thrust by injecting fuel into the engine exhaust stream in the afterburner section where it is ignited by a hot streak ignition system. Operation is controlled by the throttle. When the throttle is moved forward within the afterburner range, the afterburner fuel control pressurizes the afterburner first fuel manifold, (zone 1) schedules light-off flow, and activates the variable nozzle system. This system senses a pressure change and controls the exit area of the afterburner exhaust nozzle. Six free-floating, blow-in doors are located near the aft end of the afterburner. These doors open any time outside air pressure is greater than pressure inside the duct, allowing outside air to enter, thus increasing the total engine thrust. The trailing edge of the afterburner consists of free-floating leaves which reduce drag at the aft end of the engine by directing the exhaust gases into the slipstream with minimum turbulence.

Afterburner Fuel System.

The afterburner fuel system (figure 1-4) consists of the following major components: an exhaust nozzle pump, an afterburner fuel pump, an afterburner fuel control unit with integral exhaust nozzle control, and fuel spray rings. Fuel from the tanks flows through the flowmeter to the afterburner fuel pump. The exhaust nozzle pump is supplied fuel from the boost stage of the engine main fuel pump. The exhaust nozzle pump supplies fuel to the afterburner fuel control until a predetermined fuel flow rate is exceeded. At this flow rate, the afterburner fuel pump inlet is opened and begins to supply fuel to the afterburner fuel control unit.

Section I
Description & Operation

T.O. 1F-111A-1

Engine Fuel System

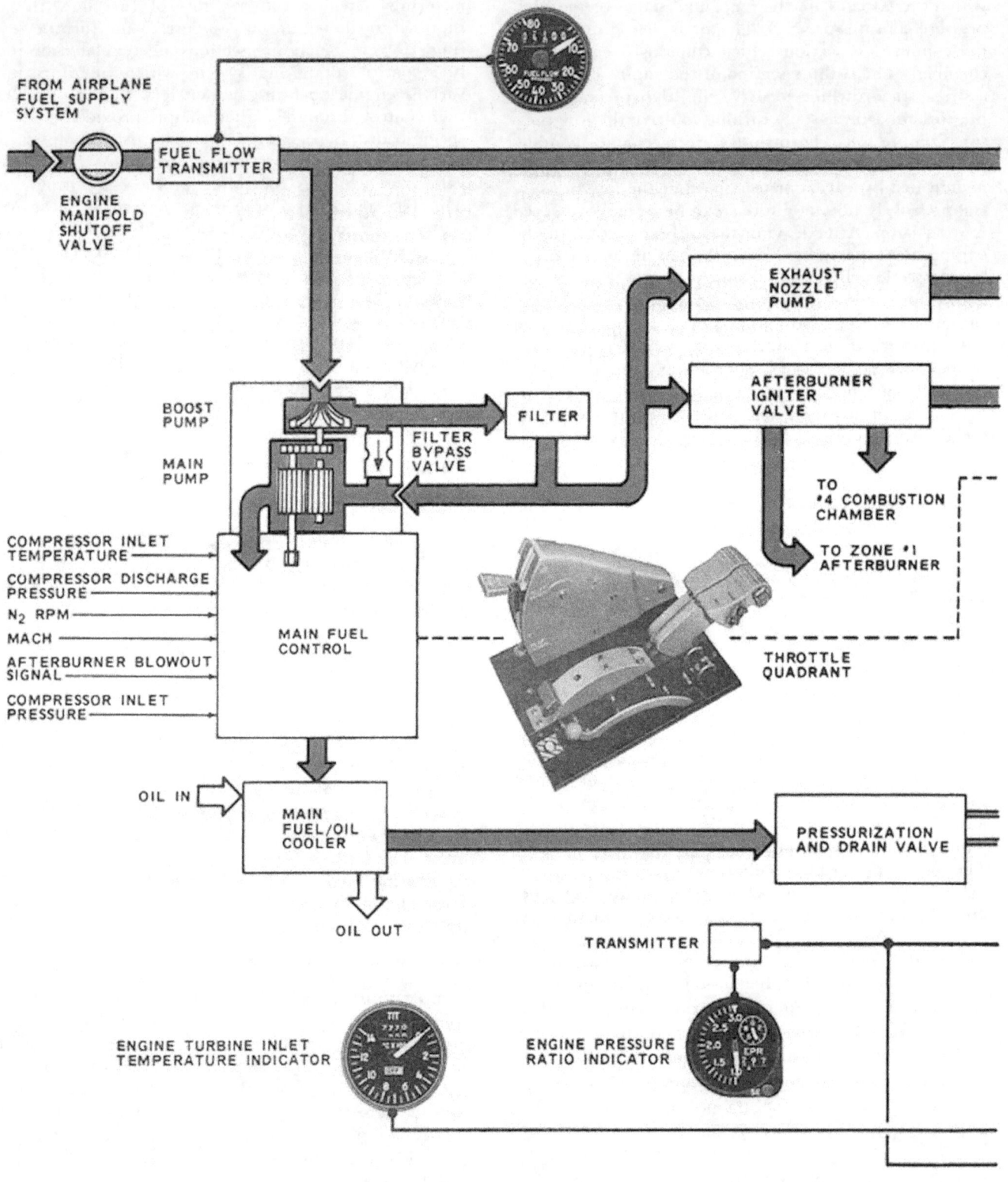

Figure 1-4. (Sheet 1)

T.O. 1F-111A-1

Section I
Description & Operation

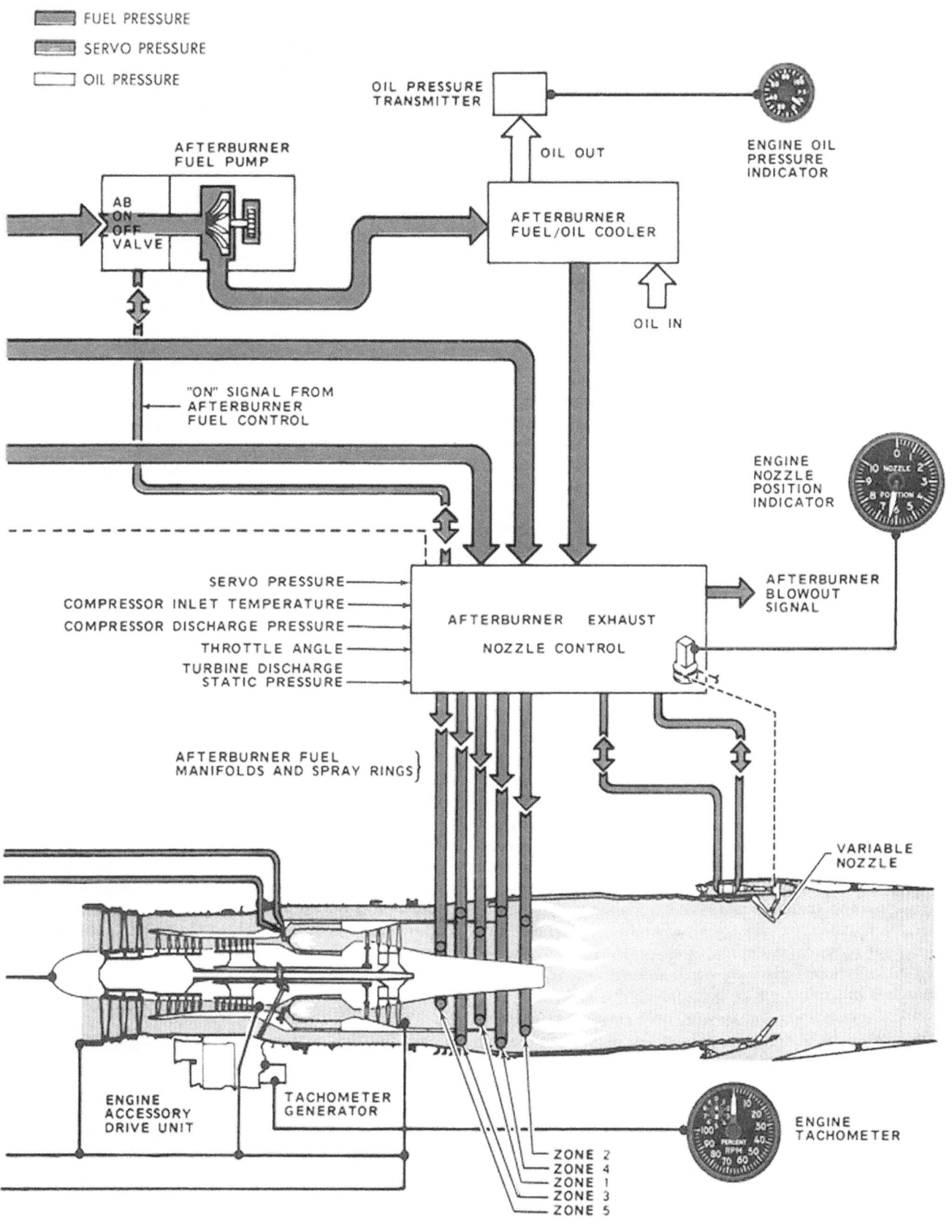

Figure 1-4. (Sheet 2)

Changed 7 April 1967

1-9

Fuel from the afterburner pump passes through a fuel-oil cooler before entering the afterburner fuel control unit. This unit includes a computer and a high pressure flow section. Fuel is then directed to the spray rings where it is atomized and ignited in the afterburner combustion chamber. Five zones of afterburning can be selected through the afterburner fuel control unit which schedules fuel to the spray rings in the various zones of the afterburner as a function of throttle setting. When the throttle is advanced for afterburner initiation and when high pressure compressor speed exceeds approximately 80 percent rpm, the afterburner initiation valve schedules light-off fuel flow until afterburner light-off occurs, as sensed by the exhaust nozzle control.

Afterburner Ignition.

The function of the afterburner ignition system is to provide a means of igniting fuel in the afterburner combustion chamber to initiate afterburner operation. When the system is actuated, fuel from the afterburner fuel system is injected into the aft end of No. 4 engine combustion chamber, thereby creating a local excessively rich fuel-air mixture. This mixture results in a longer flame which burns past the turbines to provide hot streak ignition for a second injection of fuel into the engine in the vicinity of the turbine exhaust section. This second hot streak continues aft and ignites the fuel that is injected into the afterburner combustion chamber.

ENGINE INLET SPIKES.

Engine inlet air velocity is regulated throughout the entire aircraft speed range in order to maintain maximum engine performance. This regulation of the air inlet velocity is accomplished by a movable spike located in the inlet of each engine. Each spike is a quarter circle, conical-shaped, variable diameter body that is independently movable forward and aft. The spikes are located in each air intake at the intersection of the wing lower surface and the fuselage boundary plate. Position and shape of the spikes are changed automatically to vary the inlet geometry and to control the inlet shock wave system. Local air pressure changes due to variations in inlet local mach and diffuser exit mach number are measured by sensors in the spike control unit. Signals from the control unit operate hydraulic actuators which are powered by the utility hydraulic system to position the spike fore and aft (extend or retract) and adjust the spike cone angle by contracting and expanding the spike as required. In the event the system malfunctions, a pneumatic override is provided to position and lock the spike full forward and fully contracted. An electronic anti-icing system prevents ice formation on the sensors. Refer to "Anti-Icing and Defog System" this section.

ENGINE TRANSLATING COWLS.

During ground operation and low speed flight, an additional amount of air is required to prevent compressor stalls when power settings of over 75 percent are used. This additional air is provided by extension of translating cowls which form the leading edge of each inlet duct. When a cowl is in the extended position, an opening is exposed aft of the cowl in the engine inlet duct to provide a path for additional outside air to the engine. The translating cowl system consists of a movable cowl on each engine, two flip-flap type cowl position indicators, an amber cowl caution lamp, a red cowl warning lamp and two switches for manually opening or closing the cowls. On airplanes ⑲ ♦ ㉚ which have been modified by T.O. 1F-111A-766, the cowls are opened or closed by electric actuators and there are no provisions for automatic cowl operation.

> **CAUTION**
>
> To prevent overheating the electrical motors, the translating cowls on airplanes ⑲ ♦ ㉚ should not be operated more than two complete cycles within a 10 minute period.

On airplanes ㉛ ♦ and those airplanes modified by T.O. 1F-111A-804 the cowls are actuated by hydraulic pressure from the utility hydraulic system. An additional switch is provided in this configuration for operation of a pneumatic back-up system to open the cowls in the event of hydraulic system failure. During normal operation the cowls are automatically controlled as a function of speed and altitude, however, they can be opened manually.

VORTEX DESTROYERS.

The ingestion of foreign objects into the engine is prevented by an aerodynamic screen of engine bleed air, which is directed down and outboard beneath each inlet through vortex destroyer air jets. The vortex destroyers serve to prevent the formation of vortexes below the inlet, thereby preventing foreign objects from being entrained in a vortex and sucked into the engine. When the weight of the airplane is on the landing gear a ground safety switch, located on the landing gear automatically activates the vortex prevention air screen.

ENGINE VARIABLE EXHAUST NOZZLES.

The variable nozzle system incrementally opens and closes the engine exhaust nozzle for afterburner modulation. The control is a hydromechanical computing device that determines and sets the nozzle area required to maintain a desired turbine pressure ratio during afterburner operation. The nozzle position is scheduled by the throttle setting and governed by turbine pressure ratio. The nozzle is closed for all ranges of non-afterburner operation except for ground engine idle at which time it is positioned fully open for minimum thrust. The nozzle closes when either throttle is advanced 3 degrees above IDLE. If afterburner blowout occurs, the blowout signal valve is actuated, and the nozzle closed. In addition, the afterburner fuel selector valve closes off fuel flow to all afterburner zones, and a signal is directed to the engine main fuel control to reduce fuel flow to the main combustion chamber. When the nozzle has moved to the closed position, the blowout signal is removed. Afterburner operation can again be initiated; however, the throttle must first be moved to a nonafterburning position.

ENGINE IGNITION SYSTEM.

The functions of the engine ignition system are to provide a means of initiating combustion in the combustion chambers during the starting cycle and to provide a means for furnishing an engine ignition source in the event of a flameout. Each engine has a dual main ignition system including two ignition exciters, two igniter plugs, an ignition alternator, and an automatic restart switch. The alternator is engine driven and is capable of providing sufficient energy to both exciters of the ignition system for ground starting or for windmill starts during all flight conditions. Ignition alternator voltage is stepped up by transformer and capacitor circuits within the exciters to provide ionizing voltage for the igniter plugs. The alternator incorporates two independent current generating circuits for increased reliability. The automatic restart circuit energizes the ignition system in the event of a combustion chamber flameout by sensing the rate of change of burner pressure. Engine ignition is accomplished by the two spark igniters located in the lower combustion chambers (No. 4 and No. 5) of each engine. Advancing the throttle more than 3 degrees from OFF position actuates the throttle ignition switch for that engine. This action provides ignition when the engine start switch is in PNEU or CARTRIDGE. Electrical ignition is cut off when the ground start switch returns to OFF. This normally occurs when the starter centrifugal cutout switch, opens on the last engine to be started. Ignition is also cut off when the throttle is retarded to less than approximately 3 degrees from OFF position.

ENGINE STARTING SYSTEM.

Several means are provided for starting the engines. The left engine can be started by pyrotechnic cartridge, both engines can be started by external pneumatic pressure, and once either engine is running the remaining engine can be started by pneumatic crossbleed from the operating engine. The left engine is equipped with a cartridge-pneumatic starter to provide the flexibility of operation without ground support equipment. The right engine is equipped with a pneumatic starter only. Electrical power required for starting can be obtained from either an external ground source or the airplane battery. When starting the left engine with the cartridge, the cartridge is ignited by placing the ground start switch to CARTRIDGE and lifting the left throttle out of the OFF position. When starting the engines with a pneumatic source, either external or crossbleed, placing the ground start switch to PNEU and lifting the left or right throttle out of the OFF position opens the starter pressure shutoff valve, on the engine being started, and allows pneumatic pressure to drive the respective starter. After a pneumatic start the ground start switch will return to OFF when the centrifugal cutout switch in the starter on the second engine started opens. On P-1 engines this will occur at 36 to 39 percent on the left engine and at 43 to 46 percent on the right engine. On P-3 engines this will occur at 38 to 41 percent on the left engine and at 45 to 48 percent on the right engine. This breaks the starter control circuit and allows the starter pressure shutoff valve to close, shutting off the pneumatic pressure. Two spare cartridges are carried in the main landing gear wheel well. An engine start counter, located in the left forward equipment bay, separately records the number of cartridge and pneumatic starts for each engine.

ENGINE CONTROLS AND INDICATORS.

Throttles.

A set of throttles (7, figure 1-5), is provided for both the aircraft commander and the pilot. The respective left and right throttles in each set are mechanically linked together. Each throttle provides thrust setting adjustment for its respective engine. Throttle friction for both sets of throttles is controlled by means of the friction lever located adjacent to the left set. Moving the lever toward INCR increases throttle friction, and moving the lever toward DECR decreases the friction. Force required to move the throttles varies from approximately 5.0 pounds when the friction lever is in the full DECR position to 15.0 pounds when the friction lever is in the full INCR position. Both sets of throttles have positions marked OFF, IDLE, MIL, and MAX AB, respectively. Only the aircraft commander's throttles can be raised to go into or from the OFF position. The pilot's throttles cannot be used for engine starting or shutdown. When the aircraft commander's throttles are lifted to move them out of the OFF position, the throttle starter switches are actuated. If the ground start switch is in the CARTRIDGE position, the left engine starter cartridge is automatically fired. If the ground start switch is in the PNEU position the starter pneumatic pressure shutoff valves on both engines are opened to allow starting by pneumatic pressure. Movement of either set of throttles past approximately three degrees forward of OFF activates the engine ignition system. An adjustable detent at the MIL position provides a means of readily selecting this position. The left throttle of the aircraft commander's set includes a cage-gyro switch for caging the LCOS gyros. The right throttle of each set includes a microphone switch and a speed brake switch.

Engine Ground Start Switch.

The engine ground start switch (11, figure 1-5), located on the pilot's throttle panel, is a three position switch

Changed 18 August 1967

Section I
Description & Operation

T.O. 1F-111A-1

marked PNEU, OFF and CARTRIDGE. The switch is solenoid held in the PNEU and CARTRIDGE positions and is spring-loaded to and locked in the OFF position. The switch toggle must be pulled out before it can be moved to either PNEU or CARTRIDGE. Placing the switch to either the PNEU or CARTRIDGE position supplies power to arm the throttle start switches. With the switch in the PNEU position lifting either throttle out of the OFF position allows electrical power from the respective throttle start switch to open the starter pressure shutoff valve on the engine being started. With the switch in the CARTRIDGE position lifting the left throttle out of the off position allows electrical power from the throttle start switch to fire the left cartridge. A centrifugal cutout switch in the starter of the last engine started will open the circuit to the solenoid holding the engine ground start switch and it will return to OFF.

Air Start Buttons.

Two airstart pushbuttons (6, figure 1-5), one located on the aircraft commander's and pilot's throttle panels, respectively, provide a means of obtaining ignition for air starting the engines. The buttons are marked AIR START. When either airstart button is depressed, the airstart timer relay actuates and allows ignition generator power to operate the ignition exciters for both engines. The relay will remain energized for approximately 55 seconds after the airstart button is released, thereby providing ignition for this length of time.

Ignition Cutoff Switch.

The ignition cutoff switch (9, figure 1-25), located on the ground check panel, is labeled GRD IGNITION and has two positions marked NORM and OFF. When the switch is in OFF, a relay, which deactivates the engine electrical ignition system for both engines by grounding the ignition alternator output, is energized. When the switch is in the NORM position, the relay is deactivated and the ignition circuits are not grounded through this relay.

Translating Cowl Switches. 19 ♦ 30

Two translating cowl switches (12, figure 1-5), located on the center console are provided for opening or closing the translating cowls. The switches are labeled L COWL and R COWL for the respective cowl and have two positions marked OPEN and CLOSE. Placing either switch to the OPEN or CLOSE position will

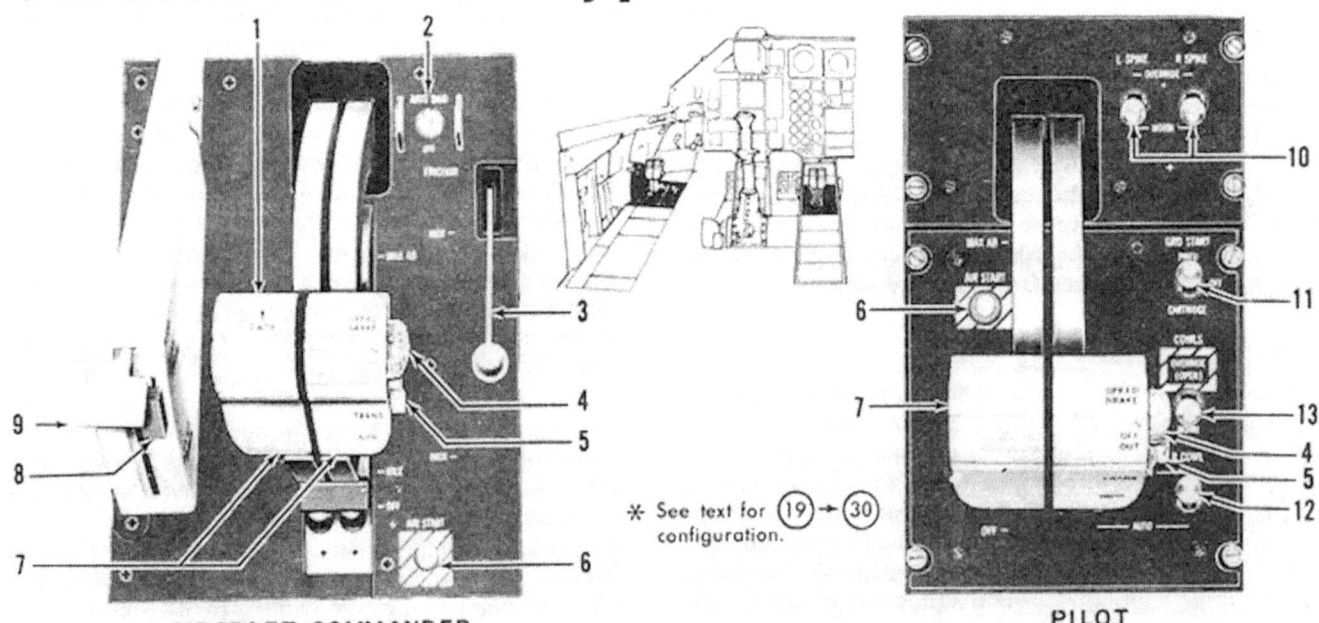

Figure 1-5.

1-12 Changed 18 August 1967

Engine Panel

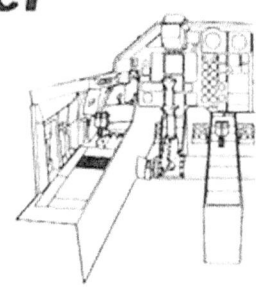

cause the respective cowl to drive to the position selected by the switch. The switches are the lock lever type which must be pulled out to change position.

Translating Cowl Switches.

Two translating cowl switches (12, figure 1-5), located on the center throttle panel, are provided for the manual or automatic control of the cowls. The switches are labeled L COWL and R COWL and have two positions marked OPEN and AUTO. The switches are the lock lever type which must be pulled out to change position. The OPEN position provides for manually opening the cowls regardless of other conditions. With the switches in the AUTO position the position of the cowls is automatically controlled as a function of speed and altitude. The cowls will automatically open when either or both of the following conditions occur: (1) Mach is less than 0.44 or (2) airspeed is less than 255 KIAS and altitude is less than 9,000 feet. The cowls will automatically close when either or both of the following conditions occur: (1) Mach is greater than 0.50 and no automatic open signal is present or (2) should the primary mach signal source fail to close the cowls at 0.50 mach they will close on an independent signal from the spike system, before the aircraft exceeds 0.90 mach.

Translating Cowl Test Switches.

Two translating cowl test switches (5A, figure 1-25) located on the ground check panel are provided for ground checking the operation of the translating cowl system. The switches are labeled L COWL and R COWL for the respective cowl and have two positions marked NORM and HI MACH. The switches are held in the NORM position when the door to the ground check panel is closed. Placing both switches to the HI MACH position, with the translating cowl switches in AUTO will close the cowls. When the switches are returned to NORM the cowls will open. The switches are also used in conjunction with the flight control master test switch and CADC test switch for cowl systems checkout.

Translating Cowl Emergency Override Switch.

The translating cowl emergency override switch (13, figure 1-5), located on the center throttle panel, is a two position lock lever switch marked OVERRIDE (OPEN) and NORM. With the switch in the NORM position utility hydraulic system pressure is provided to actuate the cowls. When the switch is placed to the OVERRIDE (OPEN) position pneumatic pressure will drive the cowls open. This position is used only in the event of a utility hydraulic system failure or if the cowls cannot be opened by any other means. The switch must be pulled out of the lock before it can be moved from either position. The functions of the switch are disarmed at speeds above mach 0.50.

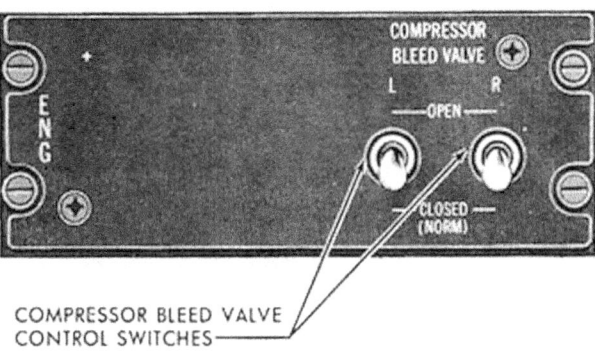

Figure 1-5A.

Mach Trim Test Switch.

The mach trim test switch (3, figure 1-25) located on the ground check panel, has two positions marked NORM and TEST. The switch is springloaded to the NORM position. Holding the switch to the TEST position will check operation of the engine mach lever on the fuel control unit.

Compressor Bleed Valve Control Switches.

Two engine compressor bleed valve control switches (figure 1-5A), are located on the engine panel. The switches are labeled COMPRESSOR BLEED VALVE with an L and R for the respective engine. Each switch has two positions marked OPEN and CLOSED (NORM). At speeds above mach 1.6 the switches are placed to the OPEN position to bleed air from the engine compressor to prevent compressor stalls.

Compressor Bleed Valve Control Switches.

Two engine compressor bleed valve control switches (7A, figure 1-15), located on the auxiliary gage panel, provide automatic or manual control of the engine compressor bleed valves to aid in the prevention of compressor stalls. The switches are labeled COMPRESSOR BLEED with an L and R for the respective engine.

Section I
Description & Operation

T.O. 1F-111A-1

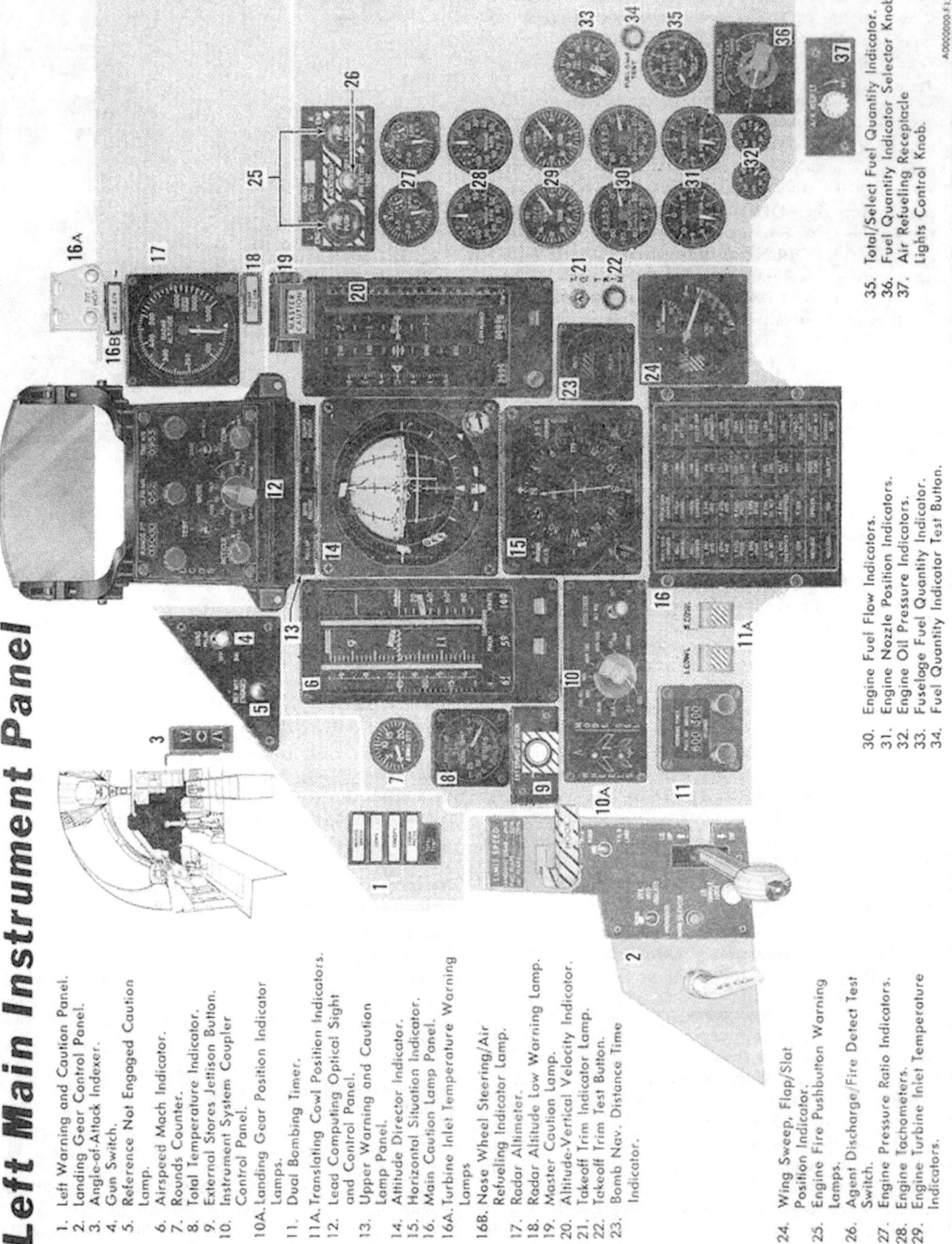

Left Main Instrument Panel

1. Left Warning and Caution Panel.
2. Landing Gear Control Panel.
3. Angle-of-Attack Indexer.
4. Gun Switch.
5. Reference Not Engaged Caution Lamp.
6. Airspeed Mach Indicator.
7. Rounds Counter.
8. Total Temperature Indicator.
9. External Stores Jettison Button.
10. Instrument System Coupler Control Panel.
10A. Landing Gear Position Indicator Lamps.
11. Dual Bombing Timer.
11A. Translating Cowl Position Indicators.
12. Lead Computing Optical Sight and Control Panel.
13. Upper Warning and Caution Lamp Panel.
14. Attitude Director Indicator.
15. Horizontal Situation Indicator.
16. Main Caution Lamp Panel.
16A. Turbine Inlet Temperature Warning Lamps.
16B. Nose Wheel Steering/Air Refueling Indicator Lamp.
17. Radar Altimeter.
18. Radar Altitude Low Warning Lamp.
19. Master Caution Lamp.
20. Altitude-Vertical Velocity Indicator.
21. Takeoff Trim Indicator Lamp.
22. Takeoff Trim Test Button.
23. Bomb Nav. Distance Time Indicator.
24. Wing Sweep, Flap/Slat Position Indicator.
25. Engine Fire Pushbutton Warning Lamps.
26. Agent Discharge/Fire Detect Test Switch.
27. Engine Pressure Ratio Indicators.
28. Engine Tachometers.
29. Engine Turbine Inlet Temperature Indicators.
30. Engine Fuel Flow Indicators.
31. Engine Nozzle Position Indicators.
32. Engine Oil Pressure Indicators.
33. Fuselage Fuel Quantity Indicator.
34. Fuel Quantity Indicator Test Button.
35. Total/Select Fuel Quantity Indicator.
36. Fuel Quantity Indicator Selector Knob.
37. Air Refueling Receptacle Lights Control Knob.

Figure 1-6.

Changed 18 August 1967

Left Main Instrument Panel

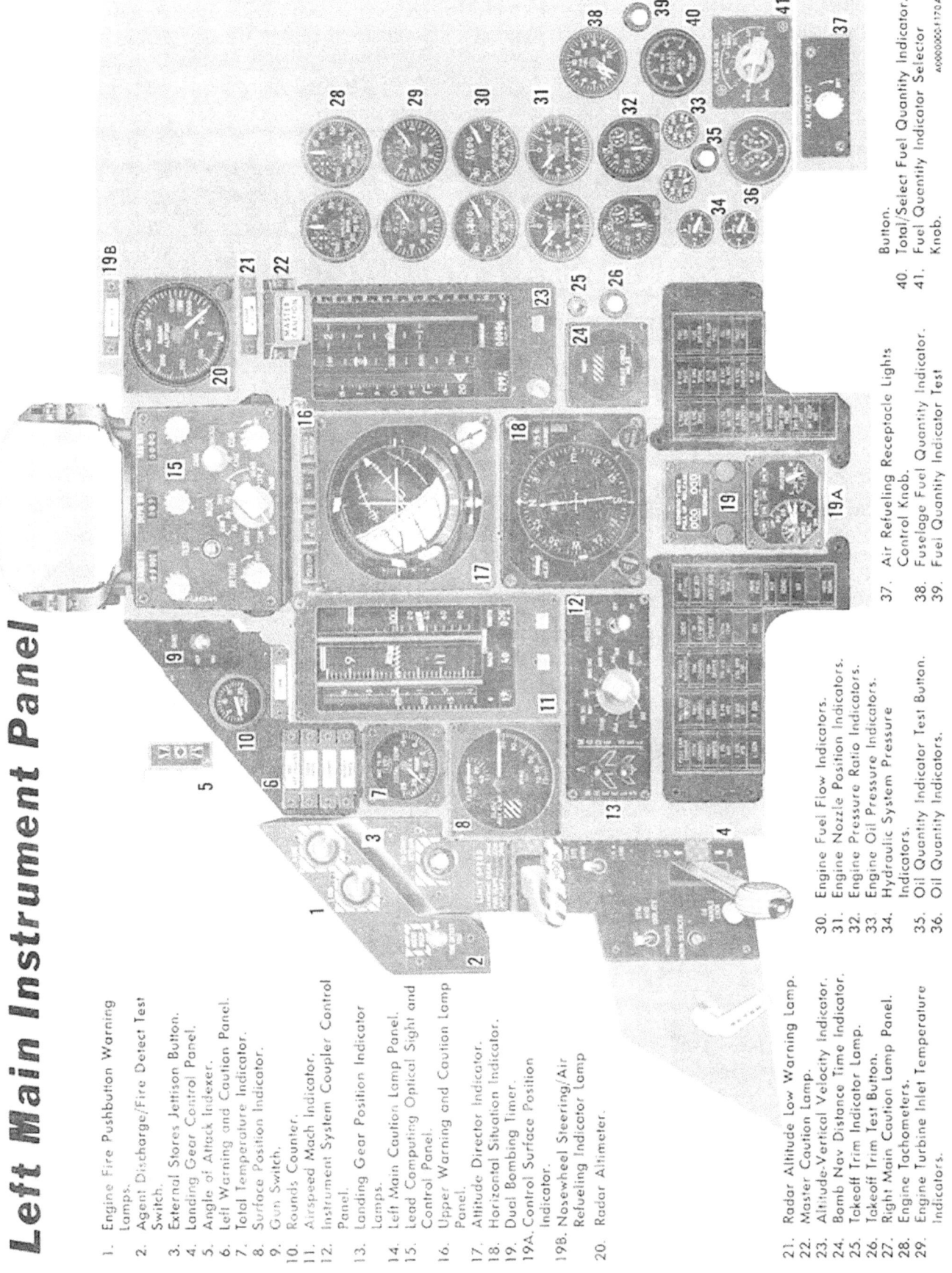

1. Engine Fire Pushbutton Warning Lamps.
2. Agent Discharge/Fire Detect Test Switch.
3. External Stores Jettison Button.
4. Landing Gear Control Panel.
5. Angle of Attack Indexer.
6. Left Warning and Caution Panel.
7. Total Temperature Indicator.
8. Surface Position Indicator.
9. Gun Switch.
10. Rounds Counter.
11. Airspeed Mach Indicator.
12. Instrument System Coupler Control Panel.
13. Landing Gear Position Indicator Panel.
14. Left Main Caution Lamp Panel.
15. Lead Computing Optical Sight and Control Panel.
16. Upper Warning and Caution Lamp Panel.
17. Attitude Director Indicator.
18. Horizontal Situation Indicator.
19. Dual Bombing Timer.
19A. Control Surface Position Indicator.
19B. Nosewheel Steering/Air Refueling Indicator Lamp.
20. Radar Altimeter.
21. Radar Altitude Low Warning Lamp.
22. Master Caution Lamp.
23. Altitude-Vertical Velocity Indicator.
24. Bomb Nav Distance Time Indicator.
25. Takeoff Trim Indicator Lamp.
26. Takeoff Trim Test Button.
27. Right Main Caution Lamp Panel.
28. Engine Tachometers.
29. Engine Turbine Inlet Temperature Indicators.
30. Engine Fuel Flow Indicators.
31. Engine Nozzle Position Indicators.
32. Engine Pressure Ratio Indicators.
33. Engine Oil Pressure Indicators.
34. Hydraulic System Pressure Indicators.
35. Oil Quantity Indicator Test Button.
36. Oil Quantity Indicators.
37. Air Refueling Receptacle Lights Control Knob.
38. Fuselage Fuel Quantity Indicator.
39. Fuel Quantity Indicator Test Button.
40. Total/Select Fuel Quantity Indicator.
41. Fuel Quantity Indicator Selector Knob.

Figure 1-6A.

Each switch has three positions marked AUTO, OPEN and CLOSE. The switches are locked in each position and must be pulled out before they can be moved. With the switches in AUTO the compressor bleed valve on each engine will automatically open when one or more of the folowing conditions occur:

- Power settings are below MIL when the airplane is on the ground.
- Speed is greater than mach 0.44 and angle of attack is greater than 14 degrees.
- Power settings are below MIL and speed is greater than mach 1.1.
- Speed is greater than mach 1.6.

The CLOSE position of the switches is provided to override the automatic open signal for ground check out of the system. The OPEN position of the switches is provided to open the valves in the event the automatic feature fails.

Foreign Object Damage (FOD) Prevention Door Switch.

The FOD prevention door switch (6, figure 1-23), located on the flight control switch panel, is labeled FOD and has two positions marked EXTEND and RETRACT. A cover has been mounted over the switch to deactivate it. On airplanes 🆔 ♦ the switch has been deleted.

Spike Control Switches.

Two spike control switches (10, figure 1-5), located on the pilot's throttle panel, are labeled L SPIKE and R SPIKE respectively. The switches are lever lock type switches with two positions marked OVERRIDE and NORM. In the NORM position the spikes are automatically controlled to maintain maximum engine performance. When either switch is positioned to OVERRIDE, pneumatic pressure is applied to the spike actuator to move the spike to the full forward and fully contracted position. The switch must be pulled out of the lock before it can be moved from either position.

Spike Test Buttons.

Two spike test buttons (2, figure 1-25), located on the ground check panel, are provided to check operation of the spikes. The buttons are marked L SPIKE and R SPIKE. Depressing and holding either button will cause the respective spike to move to the full aft, fully expanded position. The spike caution lamps will light while the spikes are in transit. When the buttons are released the spikes will move to the full forward, fully contracted position.

Engine Tachometers.

Two engines tachometers (28, figure 1-6 or figure 1-6A), located on the left main instrument panel, indicate the percent of RPM of the high pressure compressor (N2) in each engine. Each tachometer main dial is graduated from 0 to 100 percent rpm in increments of 2 percent, the subdial is graduated from 0 to 10 percent in increments of 1 percent.

Compressor Bleed Valve Position Indicators. 🆔 ♦

A flip-flop type compressor bleed valve position indicator (7B, figure 1-15), located on the auxiliary gage panel, is provided to indicate the positions of each engine compressor bleed valve. When power is off the indicator shows crosshatched. When power is on the following indications are provided:

- NONE — Neither valve open
- BOTH — Both valves open
- LEFT — Left valve open (right valve closed)
- RIGHT — Right valve open (left valve closed).

Engine Fuel Flow Indicators.

Two engine fuel flow indicators (30, figure 1-6 or figure 1-6A), located on the left main instrument panel, show fuel flow for each engine in pounds per hour. The indicators are calibrated from 0 to 80,000 pph in increments of 2000 pph. A digital readout of fuel flow is displayed on the face of the indicator. This readout shows fuel flow to the nearest 50 pph.

Engine Nozzle Position Indicators.

Two engine nozzle position indicators (31, figure 1-6 or figure 1-6A), located on the left main instrument panel, show nozzle position. The indicators are calibrated from 0 (smallest nozzle area) to 10 (largest nozzle area). The indicators use 115 volt ac power from the essential ac bus.

Engine Oil Pressure Indicators.

Two engine oil pressure indicators (32, figure 1-6 or 33, figure 1-6A), located on the left main instrument panel, indicate engine oil pressure in pounds per square inch. The indicators are calibrated from zero to 100 psi in increments of 5 psi. The oil pressure indicating system operates on 26 volt ac which has been reduced by a transformer which has an input of 115 volts ac from the ac essential bus.

Engine Pressure Ratio Indicator.

Two engine pressure ratio (EPR) indicators (27, figure 1-6 or 32, figure 1-6A), located on the left main instrument panel, indicate the ratio of turbine discharge pressure to engine inlet pressure. The main dial of each indicator is calibrated from 1.0 to 3.0 in 0.1 increments. A smaller circular dial (subdial) on the indicator face is calibrated in 0.01 increments for precise reading. A set button on the lower right of each indicator permits movement of a reference pointer on the perimeter of the indicator to serve as an index for computed EPR. The precise EPR position of the reference pointer is displayed by a digital readout window on the indicator face. 115 volt ac power to the indicators is supplied from the essential ac bus.

Engine Turbine Inlet Temperature Indicators.

Two engine turbine inlet temperature (TIT) indicators (29, figure 1-6 or figure 1-6A), located on the left main instrument panel, show turbine inlet temperature in degrees centigrade. The indicator dials are graduated from 0 to 1400 degrees in 50 degree increments. In addition, a digital readout of turbine inlet temperature in 1 degree increments is displayed. Power to the TIT indicators is supplied from the 28 volt dc engine start bus. A flag marked OFF appears on the face of the indicator when power to the indicator is interrupted.

Turbine Inlet Temperature (TIT) Hot Caution Lamps.

A TIT hot caution lamp for each engine (16A, figure 1-6) is located on the left main instrument panel just above the radar altimeter. The lamps are provided to indicate an engine over temperature condition. When engine temperature exceeds 1111°C (—8° +0°) the corresponding lamp will light and remain on until the temperature is reduced to below this value. On airplanes 31 ♦ the lamps are located on the main caution lamp panel (figure 1-29A).

Spike Caution Lamps.

Two amber spike caution lamps, one for the spike in each engine inlet, are located on the main caution lamp panel (figure 1-29 or 1-29A). When lighted, the letters L ENG SPIKE and R ENG SPIKE, respectively are visible. A spike caution lamp lights when the aircraft mach number is less than 0.3 and the respective spike is not full forward and fully contracted. When the spike control switch is placed to OVERRIDE the spike caution lamp will light and remain on until the spike has reached the full forward and fully contracted position. During spike self test the lamps will light until the spike has reached its full aft and full expanded position. The lamps operate on 28 volt dc electrical power from the essential dc bus.

Translating Cowl Position Indicators.

Two translating cowl indicators (11A, figure 1-6), located on the left main instrument panel, indicate the position of the translating cowls. The indicators are labeled L COWL and R COWL for the respective cowl. When the cowls are full open the indicators display the word OPEN. When the cowls are in transit the indicators will show cross hatched. With the cowls closed the indicators will display the word CLOSED. On airplanes 31 ♦ the indicators are located on the auxiliary gage panel (8, figure 1-15).

Translating Cowl Caution Lamp.

An amber translating cowl caution lamp (figures 1-29 and 1-29A), located on the main caution lamp panel will light if either translating cowl is not fully closed at speeds above mach 0.50. When the lamp lights the word COWL is visible. The lamp operates on 28 volt dc power from the essential dc bus. On airplanes 31 ♦ the lamp is also used to indicate a loss of redundancy in the automatic open commands.

Translating Cowl Warning Lamp.

A red translating cowl warning lamp (figures 1-29 and 1-29A) is provided on the left main instrument panel to warn the crew when either cowl is not fully open and (a) mach is below 0.35, or (b) the landing gear handle is in the down (DN) position. In addition, on airplanes 31 ♦ the lamp will light when mach is below 0.44 for more than 15 seconds or when the landing gear emergency release handle has been pulled. When the lamp lights the letters COWL will be visible. The lamp operates on 28 volt dc power from the essential ac bus.

WARNING

Any time the translating cowl warning lamp lights during flight, check airspeed. If below mach 0.35 position the cowl switches to OPEN. On airplanes 19 ♦ 30 do not cycle the cowl switches in an attempt to open the cowls. Such action may result in closing the cowls and subsequent loss of engine power. On airplane 31 ♦ attempt opening the cowls with the alternate system. If one or both cowls cannot be opened, follow the appropriate emergency landing procedure in Section III.

Foreign Object Damage (FOD) Prevention Door Caution Lamp.

The FOD prevention door caution lamp (figure 1-29 or 1-29A), located on the main caution lamp panel, has been deactivated. On airplanes 31 ♦ the lamp has been deleted.

Engine Oil Hot Caution Lamps.

The two engine oil hot caution lamps are located on the main caution lamp panel (figure 1-29 or 1-29A). When the oil temperature of either engine exceeds 245°F, the associated lamp will light. When lighted, the following letters will be visible in the lens of the respective lamp: L ENG OIL HOT; and R ENG OIL HOT.

ENGINE FIRE DETECTION AND EXTINGUISHING SYSTEM.

Engine fire detection is provided by sensing elements routed throughout each engine compartment. Should a fire or overheat condition occur the rise in temperature is detected by the sensors which light the respective left or right engine fire warning lamp. Shutoff valves are provided to isolate fuel and hydraulic fluid from the affected engine. After the shutoff valves are closed fire extinguishing agent can be discharged into the affected engine compartment to put out the fire. The extinguishing agent is contained in a single container with a separate discharge valve for each engine. Self test features are incorporated in the system for maintenance checks and troubleshooting.

Fire Pushbutton Warning Lamps.

Two fire pushbutton warning lamps (25, figure 1-6 or 1, figure 1-6A), labeled L ENG and R ENG, are located on the left main instrument panel. When a fire is indicated by a warning lamp, depressing either button will close the engine fuel shutoff valve and utility and primary hydraulic system shutoff valves to the respective engine and will arm the extinguishing agent discharge valve to the affected engine. Depressing the button again will open the fuel shutoff valve and disarm the fire extinguisher agent discharge valve; however, the hydraulic shutoff valves will remain closed. The buttons are covered by frangible covers to prevent inadvertent actuation and provide a visual indication that the buttons have been actuated.

Agent Discharge/Fire Detect Test Switch.

The agent discharge/fire detection test switch (26, figure 1-6 or 2, figure 1-6A), located on the left main instrument panel, is a three position switch marked AGENT DISCH, OFF and FIRE DETECT TEST. The switch is spring loaded to the OFF position. Holding the switch to the AGENT DISCH position will discharge fire extinguishing agent into the engine compartment of the engine selected after depressing the affected engine fire pushbutton warning lamp. Holding the switch to the FIRE DETECT TEST position will light both fire warning lamps if the fire detection system is operational.

Fire Detection System Ground Test Switches.

Two fire detection system ground test switches (17, figure 1-25), located on the ground check panel, are labeled R ENG and L ENG. The switches have three positions marked CONTROL BOX, NORM and ELEMENT. The switches are spring loaded to the NORM (center) position and are used to ground check the system circuitry during maintenance or troubleshooting.

ENGINE OPERATION.

The following paragraph, containing information pertinent to engine operation, will aid in the evaluation and correction of engine malfunctions. For a detailed discussion of Engine Stall Characteristics refer to Section VI.

Afterburner Control Malfunction.

In the event an afterburner fails to shut down when the associated throttle is retarded to MIL, move the throttle to IDLE. If this corrects the problem, normal operation of the engine up to MIL power may be restored, however; do not advance throttle beyond MIL. If retarding the throttle to IDLE does not correct the malfunction, shut the engine down. Following such an afterburner shut down, the engine may be restarted, but it is recommended that throttle settings above MIL be avoided for remainder of the flight.

Engine Acceleration.

Engine acceleration time is severely affected by the amount of compressor discharge air being bled from the engine and by outside temperature. The engine may require 15 to 30 seconds to accelerate from idle to military when full bleed is taken from one engine during ground operation. In flight this effect is minimized but during final approach for landing, engine acceleration may require as much as 10 to 15 seconds to increase thrust from idle to military with full bleed from the accelerating engine.

OIL SUPPLY SYSTEM.

Each engine is equipped with an oil supply system which consists of an oil tank, a main supply pump, six scavenger pumps, a deoiler, two filters, an overboard breather pressurizing valve, a pressure valve, and three oil coolers (air-oil, fuel-oil, and afterburner fuel-oil). The air-oil cooler operates with engine bleed air. Oil is fed to the main oil supply pump from the oil tank. It is then pumped in series through the two filters, the air-oil cooler, fuel-oil cooler, and afterburner fuel-oil cooler. Oil flow through the fuel-oil coolers is controlled by temperature and pressure sensing bypass valves. The oil is then directed to the engine bearings and to the accessory gearbox. Scavenger pumps return the oil to the oil tank. Capacity of the tank is five gallons, four gallons of which are usable. For oil quantities and specification, see figure 1-62, Servicing Diagram.

Engine Oil Quantity Indicator.

The engine oil quantity indicator (5, figure 1-15), located on the auxiliary gage panel, is a dual indicating instrument with two displays labeled L and R for the left and right engine respectively. Each display is graduated from 0 to 16 in one quart increments. A pointer for each display provides an indication of the number of quarts of oil remaining in each oil tank. The indicator operates on 115 volt ac power from the left main ac bus. On airplanes ❸❶ ♦ the engine oil quantity indicator is located on the left main instrument panel (36, figure 1-6A).

Engine Oil Quantity Indicator Test Button.

The engine oil quantity indicator test button (4, figure 1-15), located on the auxiliary gage panel beside the oil quantity indicator, provides a means of checking the indicator. When the button is depressed and held the pointers will drive to predetermined values of 5 quarts on the left display and 5.7 quarts for the right display. When the button is released the pointers will return to their previous indications. On airplanes ❸❶ ♦ the engine oil quantity indicator test button is located on the left main instrument panel (35, figure 1-6A).

Oil Low Caution Lamp.

An oil low caution lamp, (figure 1-29 or 1-29A), located on the main caution lamp panel, lights any time the oil level in either the left or right engine oil supply tank drops to four (4) quarts usable oil remaining. When the lamp is lighted the letters OIL LOW are visible.

FUEL SUPPLY SYSTEM.

The fuel supply system (figure 1-7), consists of a forward and aft integral fuselage tank, two integral wing tanks, an integral vent tank, and the associated fuel pumps, controls, and indicators. During normal operation, the left engine receives fuel from the forward fuselage tank, and the right engine receives fuel from the aft fuselage tank. Fuel from the wing tanks is transferred to the fuselage tanks before being delivered to the engines. The fuel system employs ten fuel pumps, of which six deliver fuel to the engine and four are used to transfer fuel from the wing tanks to the fuselage tanks. Provisions are made for inflight refueling of the internal and external fuel tanks from a boom-type tanker aircraft. Single-point refueling is

Section I
Description & Operation

T.O. 1F-111A-1

Fuel Quantity Data (Typical)

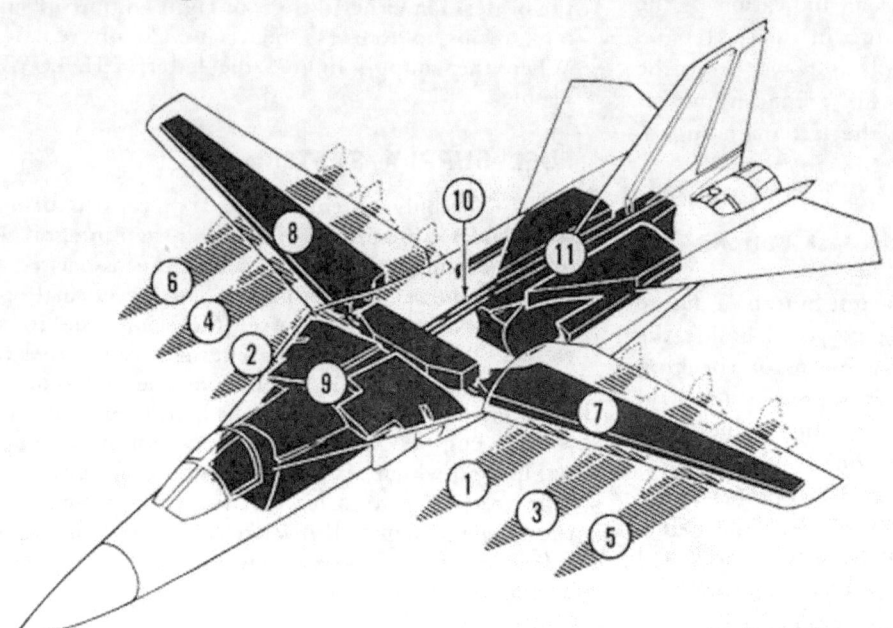

NOTE:
Weights based on JP-4 fuel at 6.5 pounds per gallon. (Std Day Only).

		U.S. GALLONS AND POUNDS			
		USABLE FUEL		FULLY SERVICED	
		GALLONS	POUNDS	GALLONS	POUNDS
1	LEFT INBOARD PYLON TANK	458.9	2,983	463.5	3,013
2	RIGHT INBOARD PYLON TANK	458.9	2,983	463.5	3,013
3	LEFT CENTER PYLON TANK	458.9	2,983	463.5	3,013
4	RIGHT CENTER PYLON TANK	458.9	2,983	463.5	3,013
5	LEFT OUTBOARD PYLON TANK	458.9	2,983	463.5	3,013
6	RIGHT OUTBOARD PYLON TANK	458.9	2,983	463.5	3,013
7	LEFT WING INTERNAL TANK	376.9	2,450	379.2	2,465
8	RIGHT WING INTERNAL TANK	376.9	2,450	379.2	2,465
9	FORWARD FUSELAGE TANK	2,851.7	18,536	2,851.7	18,536
10	FUEL LINES	36.5	237	52.8	343
11	AFT FUSELAGE TANK	1,427.1	9,276	1,442.3	9,375
	TOTAL —	7,822.5	50,847	7,886.2	51,262

Figure 1-6B.

provided for ground servicing and is accomplished through a standard ground refueling receptacle on the left side of the fuselage. All tanks are equipped with refuel automatic shutoff valves. Gravity refueling can be accomplished through filler caps in the wings and fuselage. For fuel tank capacities, refer to figure 1-6B.

FUEL TANKS.

The forward fuselage tank extends from the aft bulkhead of the crew module to the bulkhead forward of the main wheel well. The forward tank is divided into three separate bays; F-1, F-2, and the reservoir tank (trap tank). The bays are interconnected by standpipes and one-way flow flapper valves. The flapper valves allow fuel to flow from F-1 into F-2 and from F-2 to the reservoir. The reservoir tank is an integral part of the forward tank and retains 2538 pounds of fuel after all other fuel has been used. A float switch in the reservoir tank lights the FUEL LOW caution lamp when fuel remaining drops below approximately 2300 pounds. The aft fuel tank extends from aft of the main gear wheel well to a bulkhead at the rear of the fuselage structure. The aft tank is divided into two bays, A-1 and A-2. Each wing has an integral fuel tank that extends from the wing pivot structure to near the wing tips. The wing tanks cannot feed fuel directly to the engines. To use wing tank fuel, the fuel must first be transferred to the fuselage tank. A vent tank located in the vertical fin is provided for fuel expansion and for venting the fuselage and wing tanks.

FUEL PUMPS.

There are ten fuel pumps in the fuel system that operate on 115 volt, three phase, 400 cycle ac power. The six fuselage fuel pumps are dual inlet booster pumps, and the four wing fuel pumps are single inlet transfer pumps. Booster pumps 1 and 3 are in bay F-2, 2 and 4 are in the reservoir tank, and 5 and 6 are in bay A-1. Transfer pumps 7 and 9 are in the left wing, and transfer pumps 8 and 10 are in the right wing. Pumps 3, 4, 5 and 6 are the primary engine feed pumps, and 1 and 2 are standby engine feed pumps. Number 1 boost pump is a standby pump and operates continuously with the engine feed selector switch in any position except OFF. When not needed for engine fuel supply, the fuel provided by pump 1 is circulated into the reservoir tank through a pressure relief valve. The number 2 standby pump is energized by a pressure sensing switch whenever the manifold pressure falls below 16.1 psi above tank pressure.

ENGINE FUEL SUPPLY SYSTEM.

The engine fuel supply system controls the sequence of fuel flow to the engines and the transfer of fuel between the fuselage fuel tanks. The engine fuel supply system, when functioning in the automatic engine feed mode, maintains a predetermined fuel quantity difference between the forward fuel tank and the aft fuel tank in order to control the airplane center of gravity. There are four modes of engine fuel feed (AUTO, BOTH, FWD and AFT) which are controlled by the engine feed selector knob on the fuel control panel. The first mode (AUTO) is a feed condition in which the left engine receives fuel from the forward tank and the right engine receives fuel from the aft tank. In this mode a fuel differential between the forward and aft tank is automatically monitored and maintained by the gaging system. The second mode (BOTH) of operation is the same as the first mode except that the fuel differential between forward and aft tanks is not maintained by the gaging system. The third and fourth modes (FWD and AFT) are those in which both engine fuel manifolds can be fed by either the forward or aft tank alone.

FUEL TRANSFER.

In order to use the fuel in the wing internal tanks, it must be transferred to the fuselage tanks. The forward and aft refuel valves will open during transfer operation any time the tank is not full. Refuel valves cannot be controlled from the cockpit. The activation of the fuel transfer system is controlled by the fuel transfer switch on the fuel control panel. The fuel level in the fuselage tanks is maintained by float valves which open or close refuel valves. If AUTO engine feed is selected, an 8200 ($\pm$400) pound fuel differential is maintained between the forward fuselage tank and the aft fuselage tank, with the greater amount being in the forward tank. This differential is maintained by an automatic transfer of fuel from the aft tank to the forward tank when the differential is less than 8200 pounds. If the differential is greater than 8200 pounds, the aft fuel pumps are shut off and fuel is used from the forward tank until the differential is re-established. When transferring from the external tanks and wing tanks the fuel pump low pressure indicator lamps should be used in conjunction with the fuel quantity indicator to determine when the particular tank is empty. When emptying the wing tanks, the wing transfer fuel pump low pressure indicator lamps may not light simultaneously depending on wing sweep angle. With the wings forward the outboard transfer pumps will run out of fuel ahead of the inboard pumps. With the wings aft the reverse will occur.

FUEL PRESSURIZATION AND VENT SYSTEM.

The fuel pressurization system air is obtained from the engine compressor bleed line and is used to provide pressure for the fuel tanks. The system maintains a pressure between 5.0 and 6.0 psig in the tanks by means of the fuel tank vent and pressurization control valve. Should the fuel tank pressure approach 6.0 psig, the vent valve opens to vent the excess air overboard through the vent/dump outlet located at the lower aft end of the fuselage. If the pressure decreases, the valve controls air into the tank to maintain pressure.

Section I
Description & Operation

T.O. 1F-111A-1

Fuel Supply System

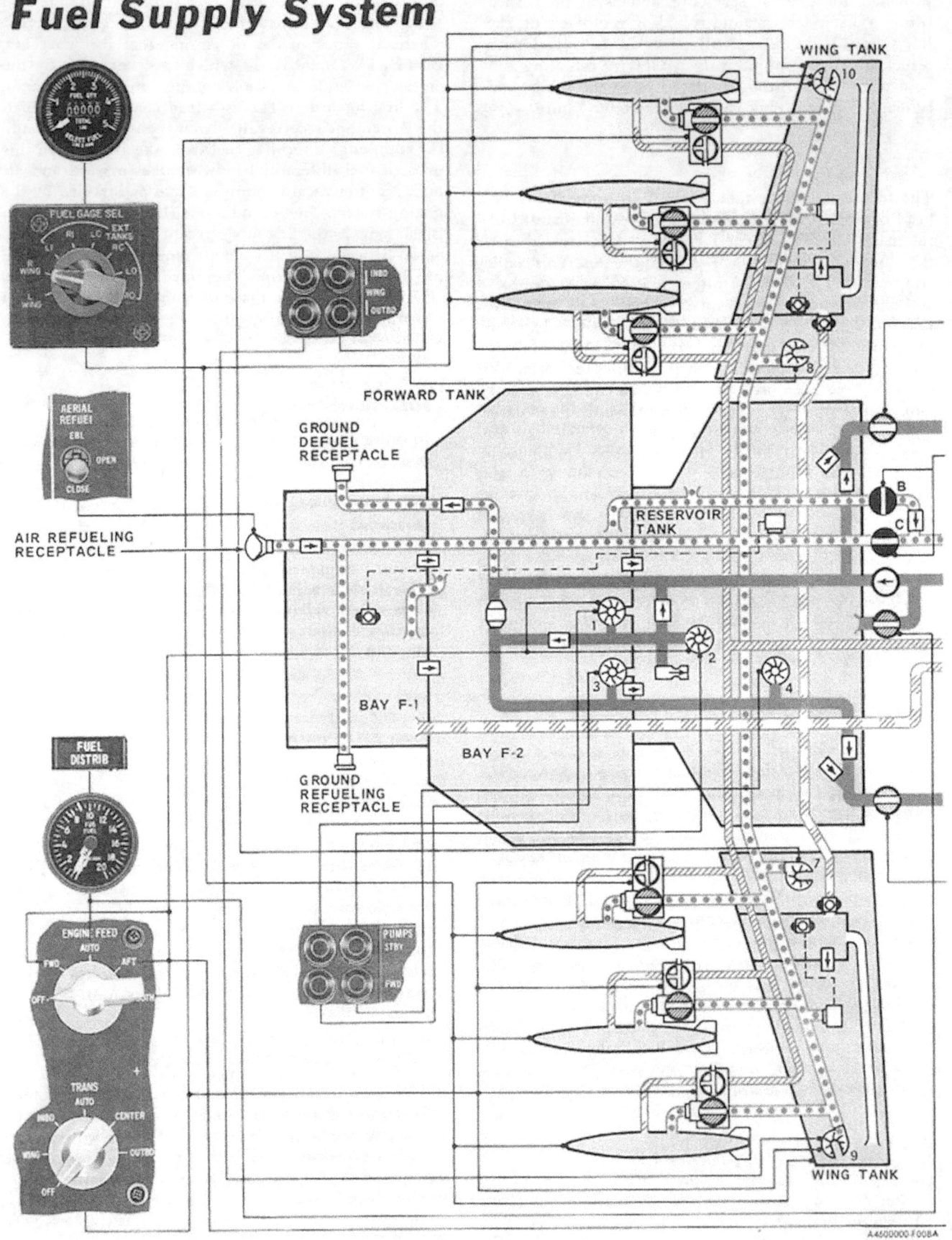

Figure 1-7. (Sheet 1)

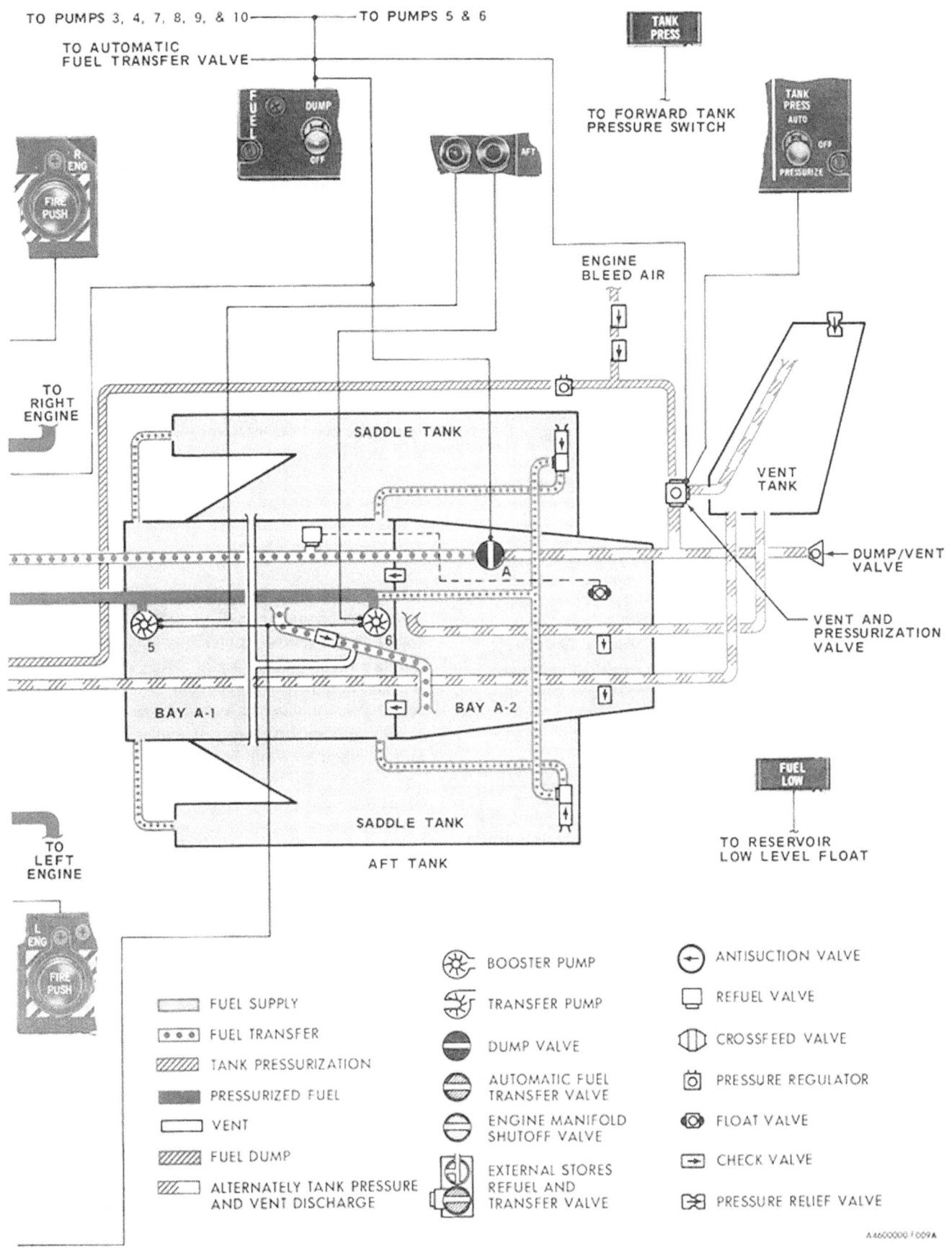

Figure 1-7. (Sheet 2)

FUEL DUMP SYSTEM.

The airplane is equipped with a fuel dump system capable of dumping fuel at a rate of 2300 pounds per minute minimum. During dumping operation, all fuel is automatically transferred to the forward fuselage tank. Fuel tank pressure then forces the fuel overboard through the fuel dump line. All fuel except that in the reservoir tank can be dumped. The fuel dump outlet is located between and aft of the engines directly beneath the rudder.

Note

- Fuel dumping should normally be accomplished with engines at MIL power or less. If dumping operation is necessary during afterburner operation, the fuel may ignite behind the airplane. This should cause no concern however, since the fire will be behind the airplane. Other aircraft in the immediate vicinity should be advised to stay well clear during dumping operations.

- To eliminate prolonged fuel dripping from the fuel dump outlet after dumping is discontinued, the fuel system may be momentarily depressurized to clear residual fuel from the fuel dump lines. (This will happen automatically when the landing gear is extended for landing.)

AIR REFUELING SYSTEM.

The airplane is equipped with an air refueling system capable of receiving fuel from a flying-boom type tanker aircraft. The system consists of a hydraulically actuated receptacle and slipway door, a signal amplifier, and the associated controls and indicators. Hydraulic pressure for operation of the receptacle and its latch mechanism is supplied by the utility hydraulic system. The receptacle is located on top of the fuselage immediately aft of the crew module. When the receptacle is extended, a mechanical linkage retracts the aft end of the slipway door into the fuselage forming a slipway into the receptacle. When retracted, the upper surface of the receptacle and the slipway door join to form a surface flush with the fuselage skin. The refueling receptacle is equipped with two lamps located one on each side. As the receptacle extends, the lamps will light the receptacle and the slipway area. During normal refueling operations, the refueling boom enters the receptacle and is automatically latched in place by a hydraulically actuated latching mechanism. In the event the boom fails to latch automatically an emergency boom latch (EBL) switch is provided to latch the boom in place. When the boom is latched in place, fuel flows through the receptacle and the refuel manifold into the fuel tanks at a rate of approximately 5100 to 5800 pounds per minute. As the tanks are filled, float operated valves automatically close the tank refueling valves shutting off flow to the tanks. As the last tank is filled, a disconnect signal is automatically sent to the boom latching mechanism to disconnect the boom, thus stopping fuel flow. A disconnect signal can be manually initiated at any time during refueling by either receiver pilot or by the tanker boom operator. If a disconnect cannot be made by other methods, a brute force pull-out can be safely accomplished.

SINGLE POINT REFUELING SYSTEM.

The airplane is equipped with a single point refueling system which enables all airplane fuel tanks to be pressure filled simultaneously from a single refueling receptacle. During ground refueling operations, fuel flows through the refueling receptacle and refueling manifold into the fuel tanks. As each tank fills, a float operated valve automatically closes the refuel valve stopping flow to the tank. The single point refueling receptacle is located on the left side of the fuselage forward of the engine air intake.

GRAVITY REFUELING.

Gravity refueling is accomplished through filler caps in the top of the wing and fuselage. There is one filler cap in each wing on the trailing edge near the fuselage. There are five filler caps in the fuselage. One for F-1, F-2 and A-2 tanks and two for A-1 tank. Plug in type static ground receptacles for grounding the airplane during gravity refueling are provided under each wing and adjacent to the filler caps on the top of the fuselage. Each receptacle is marked GROUND HERE for identification.

FUEL SYSTEM CONTROLS AND INDICATORS.

Engine Feed Selector Knob.

The engine feed selector knob (2, figure 1-8), located on the fuel control panel, is a rotary, five-position detent switch marked OFF, FWD, AUTO, AFT, and BOTH. When the knob is rotated to OFF, all fuel boost pumps are de-energized. When the knob is rotated to FWD, boost pumps 1, 3, and 4 are energized, and boost pump 2 is placed on standby. In this configuration, both engines are fed from the forward fuel tank. When the knob is rotated to AUTO, boost pumps 1, 3, 4, 5 and 6 are energized, and boost pump 2 is on standby. In this configuration the left engine receives fuel from the forward tank and the right engine receives fuel from the aft tank with a differential of 8200 pounds automatically maintained between the two tanks. When the knob is rotated to AFT position, boost pumps 1, 5, and 6 are energized, boost pump 2 is on standby, and both engines are fed from the aft fuselage tank. When the knob is rotated to BOTH, boost pumps 1, 3, 4, 5, and 6 are energized and boost pump 2 is on standby. In this configuration the left engine is fed from the forward fuselage tank, and the right engine is fed from the aft fuselage tank. Fuel distribution will be maintained if fuel flow to each engine is equal, however the 8200 pound differential between tanks is not maintained by the gaging system.

Fuel Transfer Knob.

The fuel transfer knob (5, figure 1-8), located on the fuel control panel, is a six-position rotary switch marked WING, INBD, AUTO, CENTER, OUTBD, and OFF. When the knob is in the OFF position, all fuel transfer functions are off. When the knob is rotated to WING, four transfer pumps, two in each wing tank, are energized; and fuel is transferred from the wing tanks to the fuselage tanks. The INBD, CENTER, and OUTBD positions of the knob are for transferring fuel from external tanks when installed. The AUTO position automatically sequences the transfer of fuel from the outboard, center, and inboard external tanks and the wing tanks in that order. If an external tank is not installed, the sequence of transfer remains the same except the missing tank is skipped.

Fuel Dump Switch.

The fuel dump switch (6, figure 1-8), located on the fuel control panel, is a two position switch marked DUMP and OFF. When the switch is in the OFF position, dump valves A and B are closed and C is open. When the switch is positioned to DUMP, dump valves A and B are opened, C is closed, the automatic transfer valve is opened, the tanks are pressurized and fuel booster pumps 5 and 6 and fuel transfer pumps 7, 8, 9, and 10 are energized, thereby transferring fuel from the wing and aft tanks to the forward tank to be dumped. The fuel tanks will pressurize when the dump switch is in DUMP regardless of the position of the fuel tank pressurization selector switch, the landing gear, or the air refueling door.

Fuel Tank Pressurization Selector Switch.

The fuel tank pressurization selector switch (4, figure 1-8), located on the fuel control panel, is a three-position, lever-lock toggle switch marked AUTO, OFF, and PRESSURIZE. When the switch is positioned to AUTO, the fuel tanks are pressurized, except when the landing gear is down, or the aerial refueling door is open. When the switch is placed to OFF, the pressurization airflow to the tanks is turned off and the tanks are vented. When the switch is placed to PRESSURIZE and pressurization air is available, fuel tank pressurization is maintained with the landing gear down or the refuel door open.

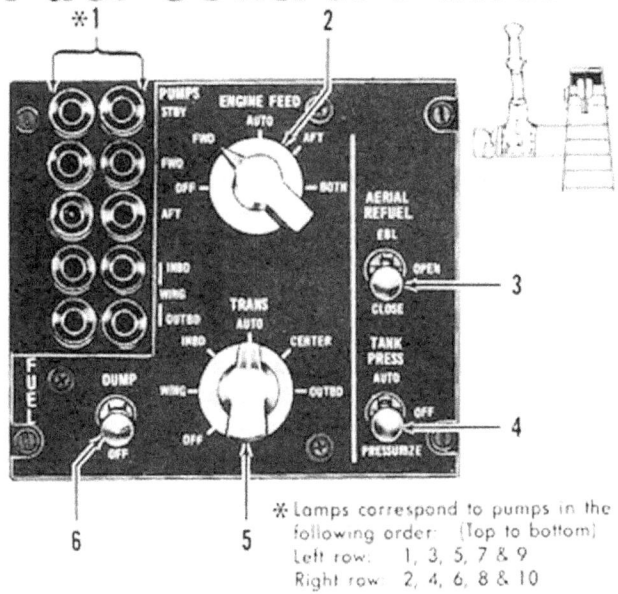

* Lamps correspond to pumps in the following order: (Top to bottom)
Left row: 1, 3, 5, 7 & 9
Right row: 2, 4, 6, 8 & 10

1. Fuel Pump Low Pressure Indicator Lamps.
2. Engine Feed Selector Knob.
3. Air Refuel Switch.
4. Fuel Tank Pressurization Selector Switch.
5. Fuel Transfer Knob.
6. Fuel Dump Switch.

Figure 1-8.

Air Refueling Switch.

The air refueling switch (3, figure 1-8), located on the fuel control panel, is a three position lever lock toggle switch marked EBL, OPEN and CLOSE. When the switch is positioned to OPEN, hydraulic pressure is directed to the refueling receptacle actuating cylinder to extend the receptacle and retract the fairing door. Positioning the switch to CLOSE will cause the refueling receptacle to retract. The EBL (emergency boom latch) position is used in the event that the automatic latching feature of the receptacle fails to latch the boom in place. Positioning the switch to EBL will provide a signal directly to the hydraulic latching mechanism through a boom contact switch in the receptacle, bypassing the signal amplifier. This will cause the hydraulic latching actuators to latch the boom in place. When the switch is in EBL, the automatic disconnect signal will not be available to unlatch the boom at completion of refueling. The boom must be manually disconnected by depressing and holding the nose wheel steering and air refuel button located on either control stick grip. Upon release of the button, the nose wheel steering air refueling indicator lamp will light to indicate a disconnect. If a disconnect cannot be made by other methods, a brute force pull-out can be safely accomplished. Electrical power is supplied to all external tank refuel valves when the switch is in the OPEN or EBL position.

Nose Wheel Steering/Air Refuel Buttons.

The nose wheel steering/air refuel buttons (4, figure 1-21), located one on each control stick grip, are labeled NWS and A/R DISC. The air refueling function of the button provides a means of manually disconnecting the air refueling boom. Depressing this button, on either control stick grip, will interrupt power to the boom latching mechanism causing it to unlatch. For a description of the NWS function of the buttons, refer to "Nose Wheel Steering System," this section.

Precheck Selector Valves.

Four precheck selector valves, one for each internal fuel tanks, are located on a recessed panel just aft and below the single point refueling receptacle. The valves are provided to functionally test the refuel valves. The valves are labeled FWD (forward tank), AFT (aft tank), L WG (left wing tank), and R WG. The fwd and aft tank valves are labeled SEC, REFUEL, and PRI. The PRI and SEC positions check the primary and secondary floats respectively as described above. The wing tank selector valves at the precheck selector panel are marked REFUEL and CK (check). In addition to the valves at the precheck panel, there is a selector valve in each wing tank. This valve appears as a rod with a screwdriver slot flush with the lower surface of the wing. This valve is marked PRI and SEC and is used to select the float valve in the wing tank to be checked when the selector at the refuel station is in the CK position.

Position Lights/Stores Refuel Battery Power Switch.

The position lights/stores refuel battery power switch (5, figure 1-25), located on the ground check panel, has three positions marked POS LIGHTS, NORM and STORES REFUEL. Placing the switch to the STORES REFUEL position will supply battery power to the external fuel tank fuel valves for single point ground refueling. A float switch in the external tank will break the circuit and shut off the flow of fuel when the tank is full. Placing the switch to NORM deenergizes the circuit. The switch is mechanically held in the NORM position when the ground check panel door is closed. For a description of the POS LIGHTS position of the switch refer to Lighting System, this section.

Fuel Quantity Indicator Test Button.

The fuel quantity indicator test button (34, figure 1-6 or 39, figure 1-6A), located on the left main instrument panel, is provided to test the fuselage fuel quantity and total/select fuel quantity indicators. When the test button is depressed each of the three pointers and the total fuel digital counter will drive to the following indications: Forward and aft tank pointers, 2000 ± 400. Select tank pointer, 2000 ± 100. Total fuel digital counter, 2000 ± 1250. The indicators will either increase or decrease to the 2000 pound reading depending on the quantity of fuel in the tanks. A normal confidence check of fuel quantity indicator operation may be made by depressing the test button long enough to observe movement of the pointers and counter. When the button is released the pointers and counter will return to their original readings.

Fuel Quantity Indicator Selector Knob.

The fuel quantity indicator selector knob (36, figure 1-6 or 41, figure 1-6A), located on the left main instrument panel, has eight positions marked L WING, R WING, LI (left inboard external tank), RI, LC (left center external tank), RC, LO (left outboard external tank) and RO. Placing the knob to the desired tank enables reading the amount of fuel remaining in that tank on the total/select fuel quantity indicator.

Total/Select Fuel Quantity Indicator.

The total/select fuel quantity indicator (35, figure 1-6 or 40, figure 1-6A), located on the left main instrument panel, provides indications of total fuel in all tanks and the fuel remaining in individual wing or external pylon tanks. The indicator is graduated from zero to 5 (times 1000 pounds) in increments of 100 pounds and has a pointer and a five digit counter. The pointer will read the fuel remaining in the wing or external tank as selected by the fuel quantity indicator selector knob. The counter continuously reads the total fuel remaining in all tanks. Due to fuel quantity indicating system tolerance it is possible to have a small amount of fuel remaining in the wing tanks when the select fuel indicator reads empty. The fuel pump low pressure indicator lamps for the wing transfer pumps provide the most positive indication that the wing tanks are completely empty. The select fuel quantity indicator circuit uses a single compensator sensor which is located in the aft fuel tank. If the aft tank is emptied while there is fuel in one or more of the wing or external tanks, the uncovering of the compensator will cause the select gage indications to read erroneously high.

Fuselage Fuel Quantity Indicator.

The fuselage fuel quantity indicator (33, figure 1-6 or 38, figure 1-6A), located on the left main instrument panel, indicates the amount of fuel remaining in the forward and aft fuselage tanks and the amount of fuel differential between the two tanks. The indicator is graduated from zero to 20 (times 1000 pounds) in 500 pound increments. The indicator has two pointers marked F (forward) and A (aft) for the forward and aft tanks. When operating in automatic engine feed, the A pointer will be maintained approximately 8200 pounds below the F pointer. In this position the F pointer will be between two dot indices on the outer scale of the indicator. The two dots indicate the point at which aft to forward fuel transfer will occur to maintain the 8200 pound fuel differential. Two bar indices outboard of the dots indicate the point at which the fuel distribution caution lamp will light to indicate the fuel differential between the forward and aft tanks is out of tolerance. The indices move with the A pointer and thus provide a ready reference of fuel differential when operating in manual engine feed.

Fuel Manifold Low Pressure Caution Lamps.

Two amber fuel manifold low pressure caution lamps (figure 1-29 or 1-29A), are located on the main caution lamp panel. The letters R FUEL PRESS or L FUEL PRESS are visible when the respective lamp is lighted. The applicable lamp lights any time the fuel pressure in the right or left fuel manifold is less than 15.5 psi.

Fuel Low Caution Lamp.

The amber fuel low caution lamp (figure 1-29 or 1-29A), located on the main caution lamp panel, lights any time fuel in the reservoir tank is less than 2350 ($\pm$235) pounds. Fuel quantity indication will be between 1700 and 3000 pounds in the forward tank when the lamp lights. When the lamp is lighted, the letters FUEL LOW are visible.

Fuel Pump Low Pressure Indicator Lamps.

Ten green lamps (1, figure 1-8), located on the left side of the fuel panel, are fuel pump low pressure indicator lamps. When a fuel pump is energized, whether by automatic or manual tank selection, and the pump is not generating at least 3.5 psi, the corresponding green lamp lights. The uppermost two lamps are for the standby booster pumps in the forward tank. The next two lamps are for the forward fuselage tank booster pumps. The next two lamps are for the aft fuselage tank booster pumps. The next two lamps reflect the wing inboard transfer pumps, and the lower two lamps are for the wing outboard transfer pumps. The fuel pump low pressure indicator lamps may not light simultaneously depending on wing sweep angle. With the wings forward the outboard transfer pumps will run out of fuel before the inboard pumps. With the wings aft the reverse will occur.

Fuel Tank Pressurization Caution Lamp.

The amber fuel tank pressurization lamp (figure 1-29 or 1-29A), located on the main caution lamp panel, lights when fuel tank air pressure drops below approximately 3.5 ($\pm$.5) psi during flight with the landing gear and the air refueling receptacle retracted. The lamp also lights any time the fuel tanks are pressurized and the landing gear or air refueling receptacle is extended. When the lamp lights the letters TANK PRESS are visible.

Fuel Distribution Caution Lamp.

The amber fuel distribution caution lamp (figure 1-29 or 1-29A), located on the main caution lamp panel, is provided to indicate when the fuel distribution between the forward and aft tanks is out of tolerance. The lamp is operative only when the engine feed selector knob is in AUTO and will light when the differential between the forward and aft tanks is less than 7600 ($-$200) pounds or more than 10,000 ($-$200) pounds. When lighted, the letters FUEL DISTRIB are visible.

Nose Wheel Steering/Air Refueling Indicator Lamp.

The nose wheel steering and air refueling indicator lamp (16B, figure 1-6 and 19B, figure 1-6A), located on the left main instrument panel, is labeled NWS A/R. For air refueling, the lamp provides an indication when the air refueling circuitry is set to receive the refueling boom. As the receptacle extends into place, the lamp will light. When the boom is latched in the receptacle, the lamp will go out. When the boom disconnects, the lamp will again light. For a description of the NWS function of the lamp, refer to "Nose Wheel Steering", this section.

Fuel Tank Pressure Gage.

The tank pressure gage, located adjacent to the single point refueling receptacle is provided to monitor tank pressure during ground refueling. The gage is graduated from 0 to 15 psi, in 0.5 psi increments.

FUEL SYSTEM OPERATION.

Automatic Fuel System Management.

Normal fuel system management is accomplished by positioning the engine feed selector switch to AUTO and the fuel transfer switch to AUTO. This establishes a mode of operation whereby fuel is automatically transferred in sequence from the external tanks and wing fuel tanks to the fuselage fuel tanks. The remaining fuel in each tank, other than the fuselage tanks, may be monitored at any time by positioning the fuel gage selector switch to the desired tank position and observing the indication on the select fuel quantity indicator.

Manual Fuel System Management.

In the event that either the automatic engine feed or automatic fuel transfer modes of operation become inoperative or manual control of the fuel system is desired, several alternate modes of fuel flow control may be selected.

Manual Engine Fuel Supply. When the engine feed selector switch is in the FWD, AFT, or BOTH position, the automatic fuel distribution system between the forward and aft fuselage fuel tank is inoperative. If a change in fuel distribution between the forward and aft fuselage tanks is needed, it is obtained by alternately switching from BOTH to FWD or AFT as necessary. The relative fuel levels will be indicated on the fuselage fuel indicator.

Section I
Description & Operation

T.O. 1F-111A-1

Manual Fuel Transfer. If the automatic fuel transfer mode should become inoperative or manual transfer of fuel is desired, the fuel transfer knob may be positioned to OUTBD, CENTER, INBD, or WING as necessary. During a normal manual transfer of fuel, the fuel transfer knob is positioned first to OUTBD (outboard pylon tank) and the fuel quantity indicator selector knob is positioned to EXT TANKS—LO or RO. It will be necessary to periodically switch the fuel quantity indicator selector knob back and forth between LO and RO to monitor the fuel level in each outboard pylon tank. When the fuel quantity gage indicates that both tanks are empty, the fuel transfer knob is positioned to CENTER and the fuel quantity indicator selector knob is positioned to EXT TANKS—LC or RC. When the center pylon tanks are empty, the inboard pylon tanks are selected. After the inboard pylon tanks are emptied the fuel transfer knob is positioned to WING and the fuel quantity indicator selector knob is positioned to L WING or R WING. During fuel transfer from the wings and external tanks there is a tendency for more of the fuel to be transferred to the forward tank. This tendency normally has no effect on the fuselage tank fuel distribution since this tank is maintained full during the transfer operation. If the fuel levels in the fuselage tanks are lowered before the wing and external fuel is transferred, AUTO engine feed should be used to achieve the proper differential between the forward and aft tanks. However, when operating in AUTO engine feed, distribution is corrected by burning fuel from the forward tank and during low fuel consumption rates, the fuel distribution caution lamp may light indicating excessive fuel in the forward tank.

Fuel Dumping.

During fuel dumping operations it should be noted that the automatic center-of-gravity control will not operate normally. If the engine feed selector knob is in AUTO during dumping, the No. 5 fuel pump in the aft tank will shut off when the 8200 pound fuel differential is exceeded. The No. 6 pump will continue to run. Assuming that fuel is also being transferred from the wing tanks, the forward fuselage tank will remain nearly full while the aft fuselage and wing tanks are emptying. This will cause the center-of-gravity to gradually shift forward. When the wing tanks are emptied, fuel from the forward fuselage tank will be dumped at a faster rate than that being transferred from the aft fuselage tank. This will cause the center-of-gravity to shift aft until the 8200 pound fuel differential is reestablished. From this point until the aft fuselage tank is empty, the No. 5 fuel pump in the aft tank will cycle on and off to maintain the 8200 pound fuel differential.

Air Refueling.

For air refueling system operation, refer to Section II.

Single Point Refueling.

For single point refueling procedures refer to Strange Field Procedures, Section II.

ELECTRICAL POWER SUPPLY SYSTEM.

The electrical power supply system provides 115 volt, three-phase, 400 cycle ac power and 28 volt dc power. Two ac generator drive assemblies, one mounted on each engine, supply ac power. Two transformer rectifier units provide 28 volt dc power. (See figures 1-9 and 1-12.)

ALTERNATING CURRENT POWER SUPPLY SYSTEM.

AC power is supplied by two 60 kva generating systems. Each generator is driven by a constant-speed drive assembly which regulates generator frequency at 400 cycles per second. Voltage regulation and system protective functions are performed by generator control units. There are three ac buses: a left main ac bus, a right main ac bus, and an essential ac bus. During normal operation, the right generator supplies power to the right main ac bus, and the left generator to the left main ac bus and the essential bus. Each generator is connected to its associated bus with multiple wire generator feeders. Power transfer contactors located near the main ac buses are used to switch the buses from one generator to another. Each main ac bus is normally individually powered and isolated from the other. The power contactors provide a bus tie function automatically in the event of a generator failure. If a fault or malfunction occurs causing an undervoltage, overvoltage, underfrequency, or overfrequency, the associated ac generator control unit removes the generator from the bus. Undervoltage or overvoltage de-excites the generator and disconnects it from the bus. Underfrequency or overfrequency does not de-excite the generator but disconnects it from the bus. If a malfunction is corrected, the generator may be reconnected to the bus by positioning the generator switch to OFF and then back to ON. If a malfunction causing an excessive amount of heat occurs in the constant-speed drive (CSD) unit, a thermal device in the unit automatically decouples the drive from the engine. Once decoupled, the drive cannot be recoupled during flight. An emergency generator with a 10 kva output is provided to generate electrical power in the event of failure of both main ac generators. The emergency generator is driven by a hydraulic motor which receives power from the utility hydraulic system. In the event of loss of both primary generating systems, a solenoid-operated valve is deenergized, allowing hydraulic pressure to operate the emergency generator. A pin can be inserted in the valve to prevent emer-

1-24

Changed 18 August 1967

gency generator operation during ground maintenance checks. Emergency generator power is applied to the ac and dc essential buses and to the 28 volt dc engine start bus.

Generator Switches.

The two generator switches (1, figure 1-10), located on the electrical control panel, are lever-lock type toggle switches with positions marked OFF, ON, and TEST. In the OFF position, the generator is not excited; the power contactor is open; and the generator system is reset.

Note

If a generator is de-excited while connected to the bus, it will not automatically reset, even though the fault condition is cleared. The generator switch must be positioned to OFF to reset the system.

Positioning the switch to ON will excite the generator and connect it to its respective ac bus. In the TEST position the generator will be disconnected from its bus and will be excited. The TEST position can be used to check generator operation without connecting it to a bus.

Section I
Description & Operation

T.O. 1F-111A-1

AC Electrical Power Supply System

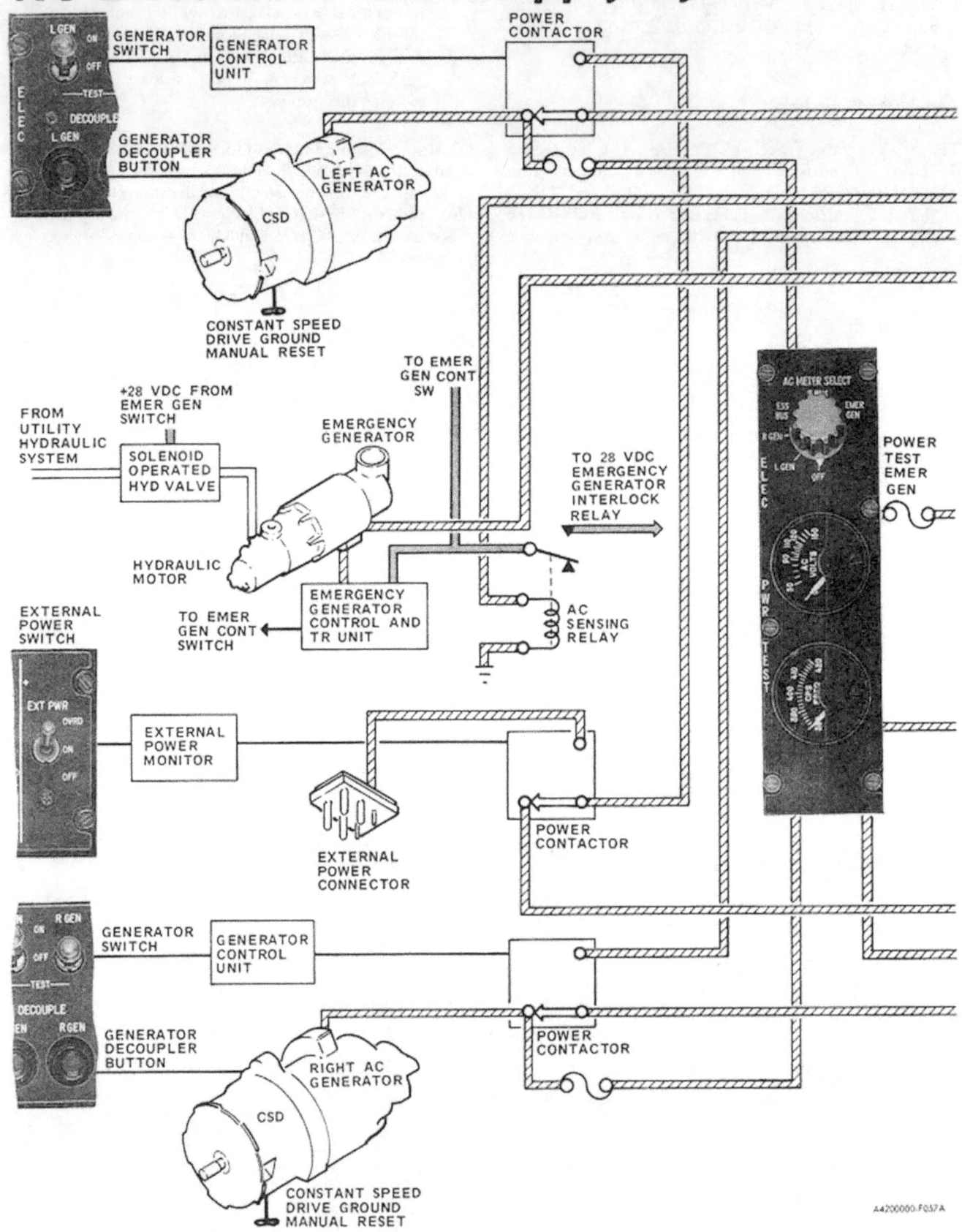

Figure 1-9. (Sheet 1)

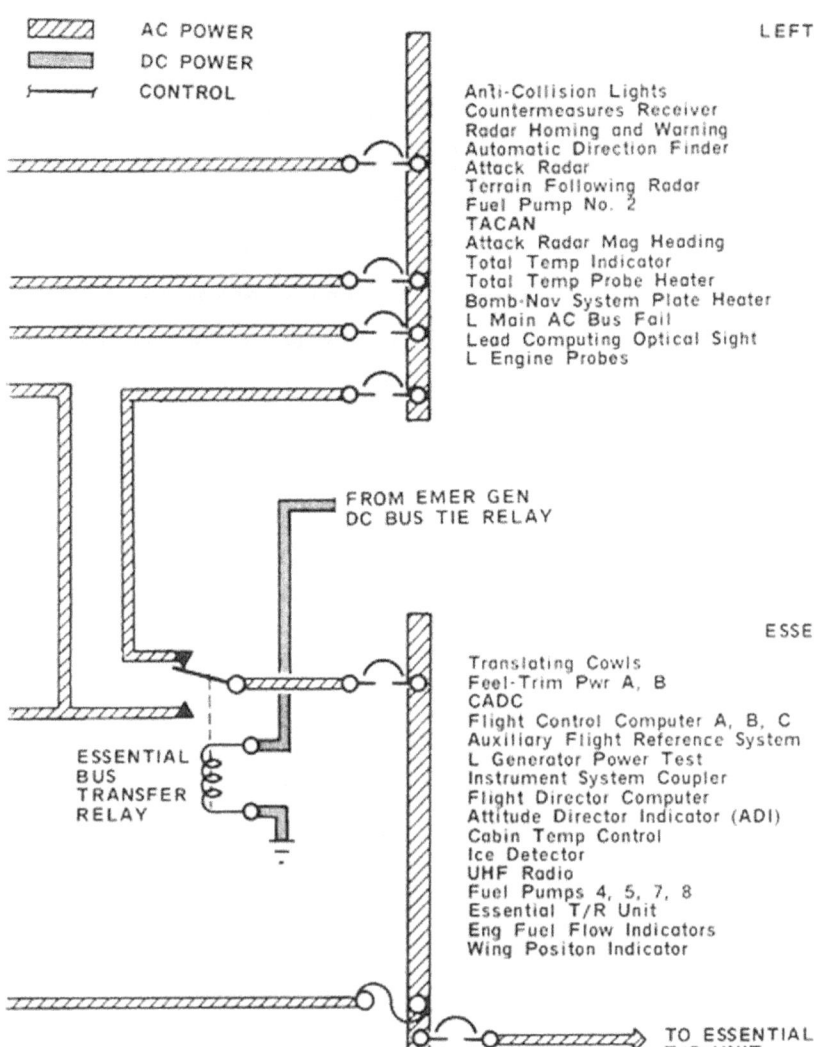

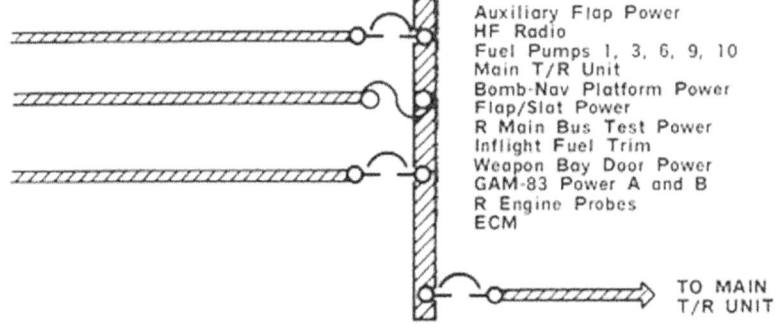

Figure 1-9. (Sheet 2)

Section I
Description & Operation

T.O. 1F-111A-1

Electrical Control Panel

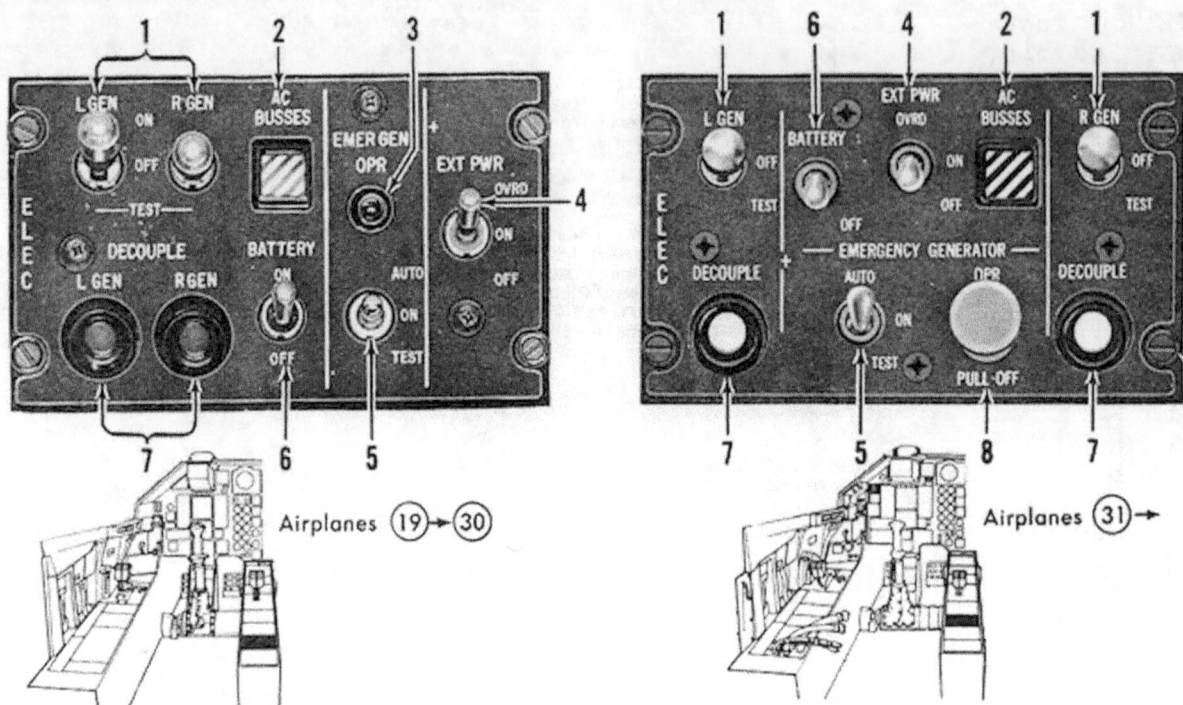

1. Generator Switches.
2. Electrical Power Flow Indicator.
3. Emergency Generator Indicator Lamp.
4. External Power Switch.
5. Emergency Generator Switch.
6. Battery Switch.
7. Generator Decouple Pushbuttons.
8. Emergency Generator Indicator/Cutoff Button.

Figure 1-10.

Generator Decouple Pushbuttons.

The generator decouple pushbuttons (7, figure 1-10), located on the electrical control panel, are provided to actuate the constant-speed drive decoupler. When a pushbutton is depressed, the constant-speed drive will be decoupled. Once decoupled, the constant-speed drive cannot be reconnected during flight.

Electrical Power Flow Indicator.

The electrical power flow indicator (2, figure 1-10), located on the electrical control panel, is a flip-flop type indicator labeled AC BUSSES and displays the various bus configurations. If both buses are receiving power from their respective generator, the indicator will display NORM, indicating that the buses are isolated from each other and are operating normally. If only one generator is providing power for both buses, the indicator will display TIE. When the emergency generator is operating and supplying power to the ac essential bus, the indicator will display EMER. When ground power is connected to the airplane and supplying power to the ac buses, the indicator will display TIE. When there is no ac power being applied to the airplane, the indicator will display a crosshatched surface.

Emergency Generator Switch.

The emergency generator switch (5, figure 1-10), located on the electrical control panel, is a toggle switch having positions marked ON, AUTO, and TEST. When the switch is in the ON position, the hydraulically driven emergency generator is operating, but not connected to the essential ac bus unless all ac power is lost. In the AUTO position, if all ac power is lost, the emergency generator hydraulic valve will open, the emergency generator will operate, and the ac essential bus transfer relay will be energized, thereby connecting the emergency generator to the essential ac bus.

Note

In the event that the emergency generator does not come on within 3 seconds, manually place the switch to the ON position.

When the switch is in the TEST position, the emergency generator operates and the emergency generator indicator lamp lights. The TEST position will not connect the emergency generator to the essential ac bus.

The TEST position also opens the dc bus tie contactor to provide a method of checking operation of the two 28 volt dc converters. If the main and essential dc buses remain energized, both converters are operating and the electrical power flow indicator will display a crosshatch. If either converter has failed and the battery switch is ON, the power flow indicator will cycle or operate erratically.

Emergency Generator Indicator/Cutoff Push Button 31

The emergency generator indicator/cutoff push button, (8, figure 1-10) located on the electrical control panel, provides a means of de-exciting the emergency generator. The push button is marked OPR (operate) and PULL OFF. When the button is depressed the emergency generator will come on the line and supply power to the airplane systems whenever both engine driven generators fail. Should this occur a green indicator lamp in the button will light. When the emergency generator is supplying power pulling the button out will de-excite the emergency generator and shut off its power output.

External Power Switch.

The external power switch (4, figure 1-10), located on the electrical control panel, is a toggle switch having positions marked OFF, ON and OVRD. In the OFF position, external power cannot be supplied to the airplane ac buses. In the ON position with neither engine operating, external power supplies total airplane power. With the left engine operating, the left main ac generator will supply total airplane electrical load, and external power is disconnected from the ac buses. With only the right engine operating, the right main ac generator supplies power to the right main ac bus, and external power feeds the left main ac and essential buses. Associated with the external power is a power monitor which measures external power voltage, frequency and phase sequence. Should any one of these parameters be out of tolerance, the monitor prevents closing of the external power contactor. When the external power switch is in the OVRD position, the external power monitor circuit is bypassed, thus allowing external power which is out of voltage and frequency tolerance to be applied to airplane buses. The override position does not override external power with improper phase sequence.

This page intentionally left blank.

Electrical Power Test Panel

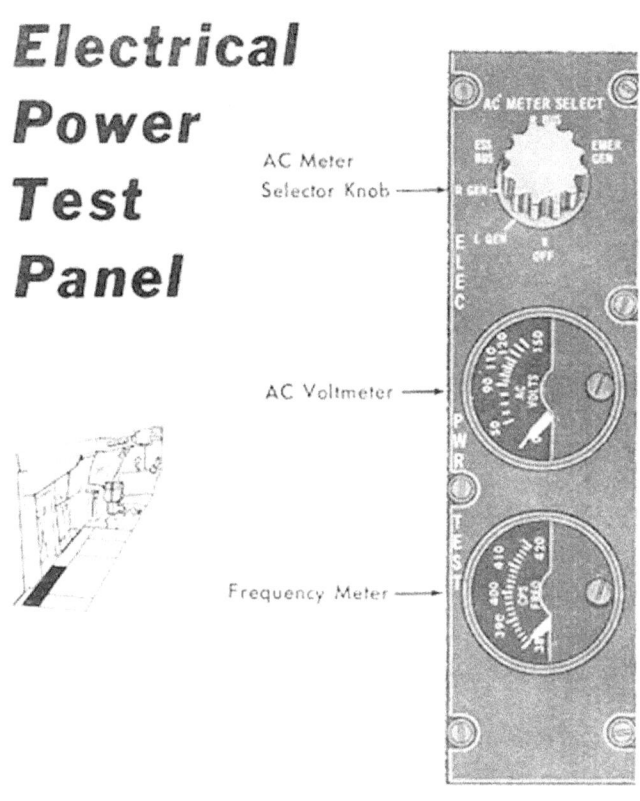

Figure 1-11.

AC Meter Selector Knob.

The ac meter selector knob (figure 1-11), located on the electrical power test panel, has six positions marked OFF, L GEN, R GEN, ESS BUS, R BUS, and EMER GEN. When the switch is rotated from OFF to any one of the other positions, the frequency meter and ac voltmeter display the frequency and voltage of the bus or generator selected.

Emergency Generator Indicator Lamp. ⑲ ♦ ㉚

The green emergency generator indicator lamp (3, figure 1-10), located on the electrical control panel, lights when the emergency generator is operating. The lamp receives power from the emergency generator through the emergency generator control unit.

Generator Caution Lamps.

Two amber generator caution lamps (figure 1-29 or 1-29A), are located on the main caution lamp panel.

Either lamp lights when the respective generator is disconnected from the ac bus. When lighted, the letters L GEN are visible in the left lamp and R GEN in the right lamp.

Frequency Meter.

The frequency meter (figure 1-11), located on the electrical power test panel, displays frequency in cycles per second (cps) of the various buses and generators as selected by the ac meter selector switch. The frequency meter is graduated from 380 to 420 cps in increments of 2 cps.

AC Voltmeter.

The ac voltmeter (figure 1-11), located on the electrical power test panel, displays voltages of the various buses and generators as selected by the ac meter selector switch. The ac voltmeter is graduated from 0 to 150 volts. Above 50 volts, the meter graduations are in increments of 5 volts and below 50 volts the graduations are in increments of 10 volts.

DIRECT CURRENT POWER SUPPLY SYSTEM.

DC electrical power is provided by two 28 volt dc transformer-rectifier units and a 24 volt battery. There are three dc buses: a main dc bus, an essential dc bus, and an engine start bus. The essential dc bus is divided into two separate buses, one located in the forward equipment bay and one located in the crew module on the aft console (figure 1-13). The essential buses are electrically connected. During normal operation, the main dc bus section receives power from the main transformer-rectifier unit which is connected to the right main ac bus. The essential dc bus and the engine start bus receive power from the essential transformer-rectifier unit which is connected to the essential ac bus. A bus-tie contactor connects the essential dc bus to the main dc bus during normal operation. Normally the outputs of the two transformer-rectifier units supply the total dc load in parallel.

Battery Switch.

The battery switch (6, figure 1-10), is located on the electrical control panel. The two position switch is marked OFF and ON. Positioning the switch to ON connects the engine start bus to the airplane 24 volt battery, provided the essential dc bus is not energized. If the essential dc bus is energized, the battery is connected to the main dc bus through the battery charger circuit. When the battery switch is positioned to OFF, the engine start bus is connected to the essential dc bus, and the battery charger circuit is disconnected from the main dc bus.

Section I
Description & Operation

T.O. 1F-111A-1

DC Electrical Power Supply System

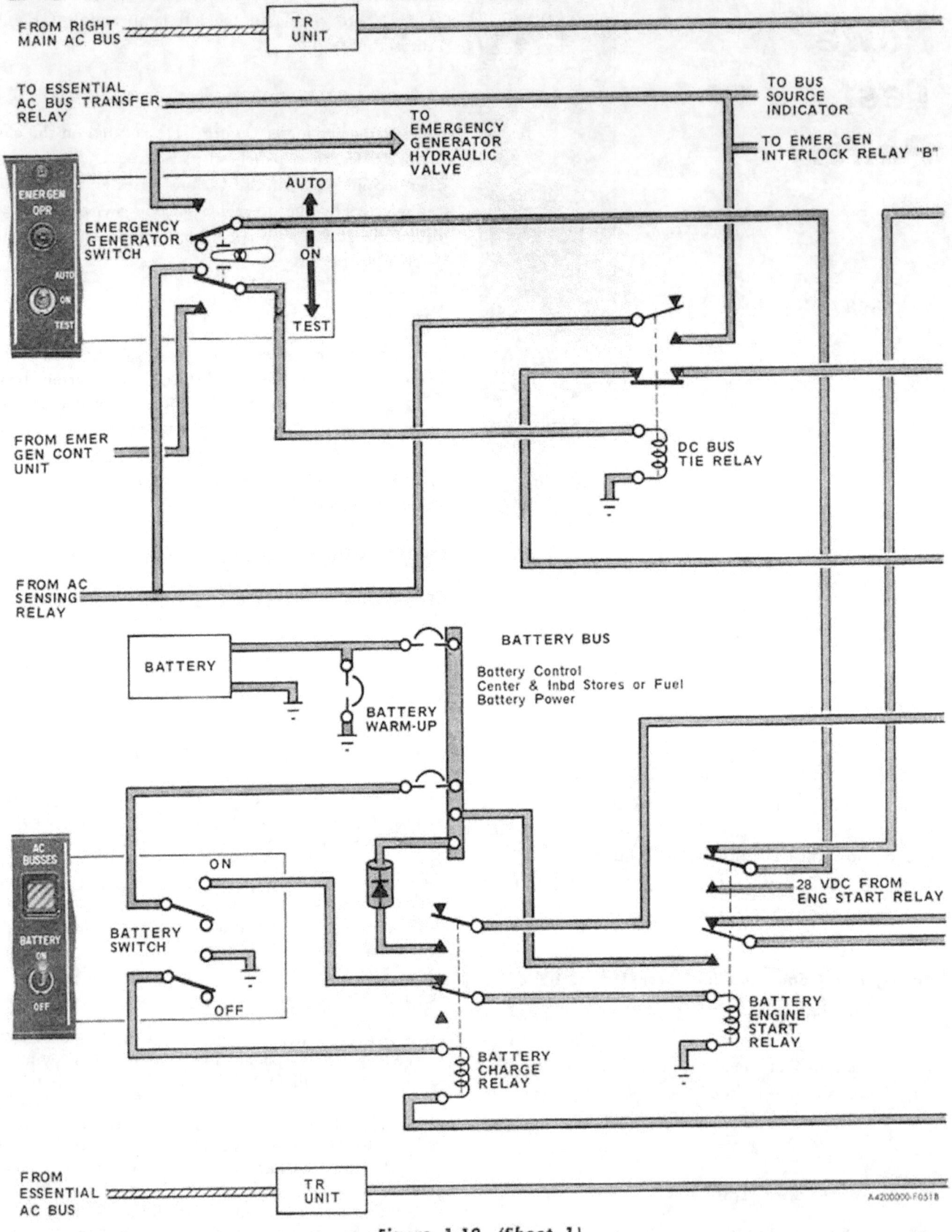

Figure 1-12. (Sheet 1)

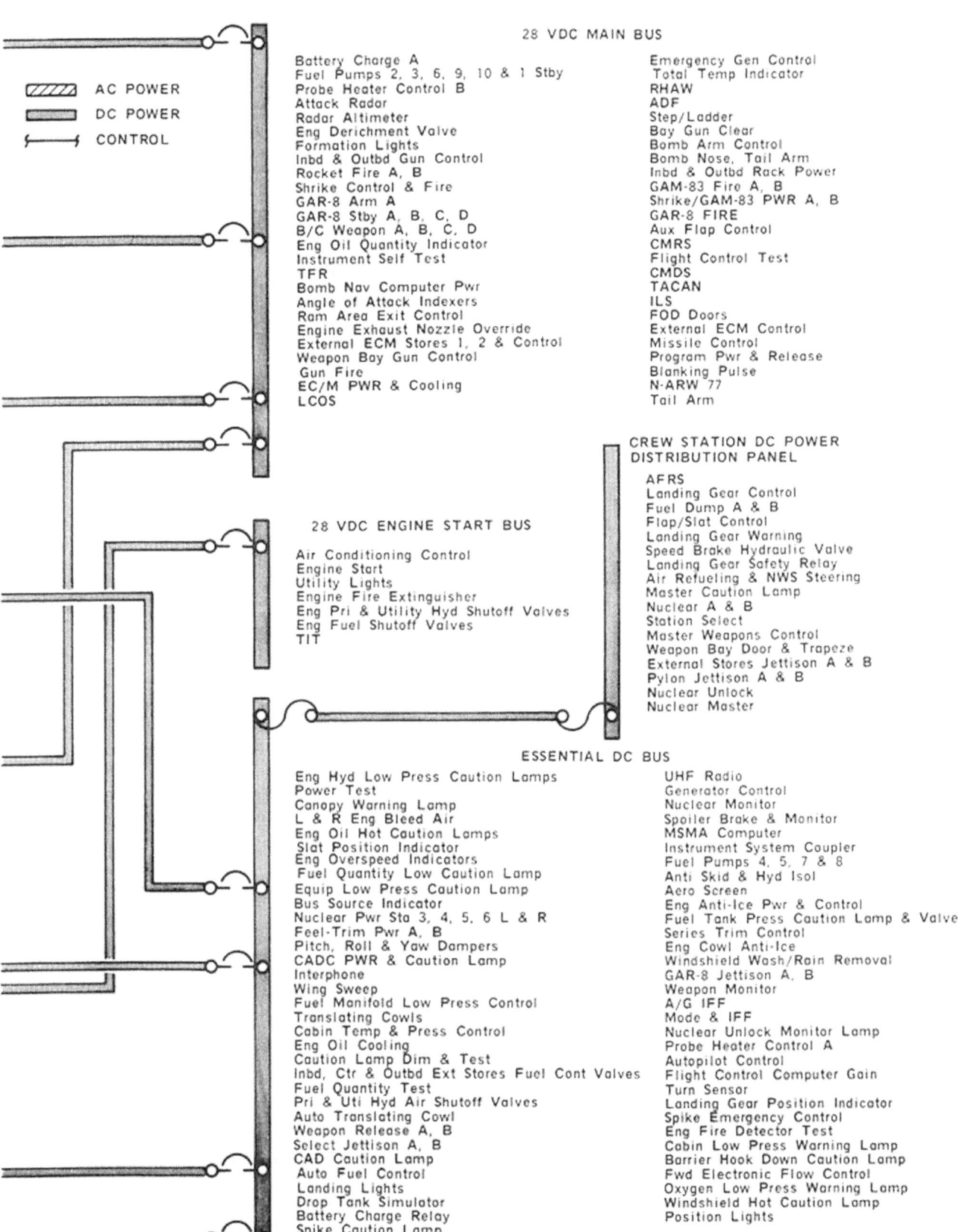

Figure 1-12. (Sheet 2)

Section I
Description & Operation

Circuit Breaker Panel

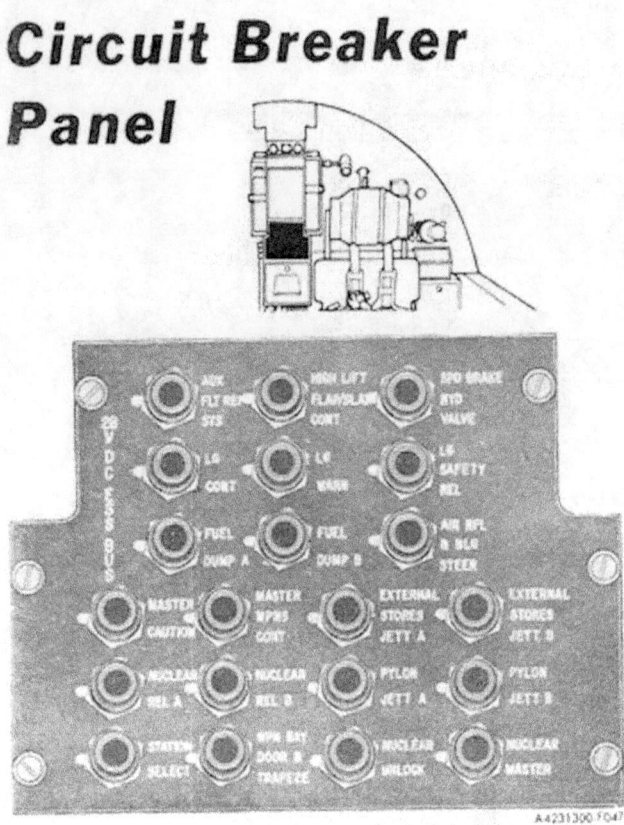

Figure 1-13.

HYDRAULIC POWER SUPPLY SYSTEM.

Hydraulic power is supplied by two independent, parallel hydraulic systems designated as the primary and utility systems (figure 1-14). Both systems operate simultaneously to supply hydraulic power for the flight controls and wing sweep. If one or the other system should fail, either system is capable of supplying sufficient power for wing sweep and flight control operation. In addition to supplying wing sweep and flight control hydraulic power, the utility system also supplies power for operation of the landing gear, tail bumper, nose wheel steering, wheel brakes, speed brakes, flaps, air inlet control, weapons bay doors, trapeze, and emergency electrical generator. Hydraulic pressure for each system is supplied by two engine-driven, variable delivery pumps. To assure hydraulic pressure in the event of single engine failure, one pump in each system is driven by the right engine, and one pump in each system is driven by the left engine. Pressurized accumulators are installed in the system to supplement engine-driven pump delivery during transient hydraulic power requirements. Each system has a piston-type reservoir for hydraulic fluid storage that also acts as a surge damper for return line pressures. These reservoirs are pressurized with nitrogen to insure critical pump inlet pressure for all operating conditions. Hydraulic pressure of each system is displayed on the left console. Low pressure caution lights for each of the four pumps are displayed on the caution light panel. An automatic isolation valve reserves all utility power output for flight control and wing sweep operation by isolation of the other utility functions in the event of a primary system failure. Normal isolation is accomplished 30 seconds after the landing gear, flaps and slats are retracted to depressurize those functions of the utility hydraulic system used only during take-off, landing, and ground operation.

HYDRAULIC PUMPS.

Four variable delivery pumps are employed. Normal power for the primary and utility systems is provided by two engine-driven pumps in each system. One pump in each system is driven by each engine. The pumps are each rated at 42.5 gpm, 5800 rpm, and 3100 ($\pm$50) psi.

HYDRAULIC ACCUMULATORS.

Eight accumulators, three in the primary hydraulic system and five in the utility hydraulic system, are provided. Each system has two accumulators for the horizontal stabilizer and one for the autopilot damper servos. The utility system has two accumulators for the wheel brake system. See figure 1-62 for servicing data.

HYDRAULIC FLUID RESERVOIRS.

Both primary and utility hydraulic reservoirs are floating piston, air-oil separated type using air pressure on one side of the piston to maintain hydraulic pressure on the other. Pneumatic pressure is supplied from pneumatic storage reservoirs located on the forward end of each hydraulic reservoir, and, as an alternate source, from the engine bleed air system. A pressure operated hydraulic relief valve prevents over pressurization by venting excess fluid overboard when reservoir pressure exceeds 135 psi. Steady-state fluid flow is passed through the reservoir to maintain reservoir warmth and to remove air from the fluid. During high flow rates, the fluid is bypassed around the reservoir and cooler loop directly to the pumps by means of the suction bypass valve. A 15-micron bypass type filter is located upstream of the reservoir. The reservoir also acts as a surge damper for return line impulse pressures. See figure 1-62 for servicing data.

HYDRAULIC COOLING SYSTEM.

Cooling is provided by an air-to-hydraulic heat exchanger and a fuel-to-hydraulic heat exchanger in each hydraulic system. The controls are arranged so that the cooling medium is air only at low speeds, fuel and air at intermediate speeds, and fuel only at high speeds.

Changed 18 August 1967

HYDRAULIC ISOLATION VALVE.

An isolation valve is incorporated in the utility system to provide automatic and normal isolation of certain functions of the utility system. In the event of loss of pressure in the primary system the valve will automatically reserve all utility power output for flight control and wing sweep operation by isolating all other utility system functions. Normal isolation occurs 30 seconds after the landing gear, flaps and slats are retracted, to isolate those portions of the utility system used only during takeoff and landing. This adds a measure of protection in the event a leak develops in a remote part of the utility system.

UTILITY HYDRAULIC SYSTEM ISOLATION SWITCH.

The utility hydraulic system isolation switch (8, figure 1-16), with positions marked NORM and PRESSURIZE, is located on the landing gear control panel. The NORM position functions in conjunction with the landing gear, flaps and slats. Thirty seconds after the gear, flaps and slats are fully retracted the following systems are isolated from the utility system:

- Landing gear
- Flaps and slats
- Nosewheel steering
- Brakes

Positioning the switch to PRESSURIZE supplies utility hydraulic pressure to these systems.

HYDRAULIC PRESSURE INDICATORS.

Two 0-4000 psi pressure indicators (6 and 7, figure 1-15), one each for the primary and utility systems, are located on the auxiliary gage panel. Pressure is measured mechanically and transmitted electrically by pressure transmitters in the system pressure lines. On airplanes ㉛ ♦ the hydraulic pressure indicators are located on the left main instrument panel (34, figure 1-6A).

LOW PRESSURE CAUTION LAMPS.

Four amber low pressure caution lamps, energized by pressure switches in each pump pressure line, are located on the main caution lamp panel (1-29 or 1-29A). These lamps light when the individual pump output pressure falls below 500 (±100) psi. When lighted, the following letters will be visible in the respective lamp lenses: L PRI HYD; L UTIL HYD; R PRI HYD; and R UTIL HYD.

HYDRAULIC FLUID OVERHEAT CAUTION LAMPS.

Two hydraulic fluid overheat caution lamps, one for each system, are located on the main caution lamp panel (1-29 or 1-29A). A lamp lights when the hydraulic fluid temperature of the associated system exceeds 240±10°F (110±6°C). When lighted, the following letters will be visible in the respective lamp lenses: PRI HOT; and UTIL HOT.

PNEUMATIC POWER SUPPLY SYSTEMS.

There are four independent pneumatic power supply systems which provide pressure for emergency operation of the landing gear, spike system, translating cowls (on airplanes ㉛ ♦) trapeze, and for pressurization of the hydraulic reservoirs. Pressure for emergency extension of the landing gear is provided by a pneumatic reservoir located in the main landing gear wheel well. Each spike and translating cowl (㉛ ♦) is provided with a separate pneumatic reservoir located in the main landing gear wheel well. Each trapeze is provided with a separate pneumatic reservoir located in the weapons bay. Two pneumatic reservoirs, one for each hydraulic system reservoir, provide pneumatic pressure for hydraulic system operation. For a functional description of each pneumatic system, refer to the associated system descriptions, this section. For servicing information on the pneumatic systems, see figure 1-62.

LANDING GEAR SYSTEM.

The landing gear is tricycle-type, forward retracting, and hydraulically operated. The main landing gear consists of a single common trunnion upon which two wheels are singly mounted. This arrangement of the main landing gear provides symmetrical main landing gear operation. Fusible metal, thermal pressure relief, plugs are incorporated in the main landing gear wheels to relieve tire pressure in the event of maximum performance braking. The nose landing gear has two dual-mounted wheels. The landing gear system is normally powered by the utility hydraulic system. A pneumatic system is provided as an alternate (emergency) means of extending the gear in the event the normal system fails. The nose landing gear retracts into the nose wheel well, and the main landing gear retracts into a fuselage well.

MAIN GEAR.

Three hydraulic actuators are provided for operation of the main landing gear. A single-acting linear actuator retracts the main landing gear. Two double-acting linear actuators, one for an uplock and one for a downlock, are provided to lock the landing gear in the retracted or extended position. There are two main landing gear doors. The aft door is mechanically linked to the main landing gear and opens and closes with movement of the gear. The forward door, which also serves as the speed brake, is hydraulically operated. A mechanical connection between the main landing gear and the speed brake selector valve causes the main landing gear door to open and close in the proper sequence during landing gear operation. A ground safety

Section I
Description & Operation

T.O. 1F-111A-1

Hydraulic Power Supply System (Utility)

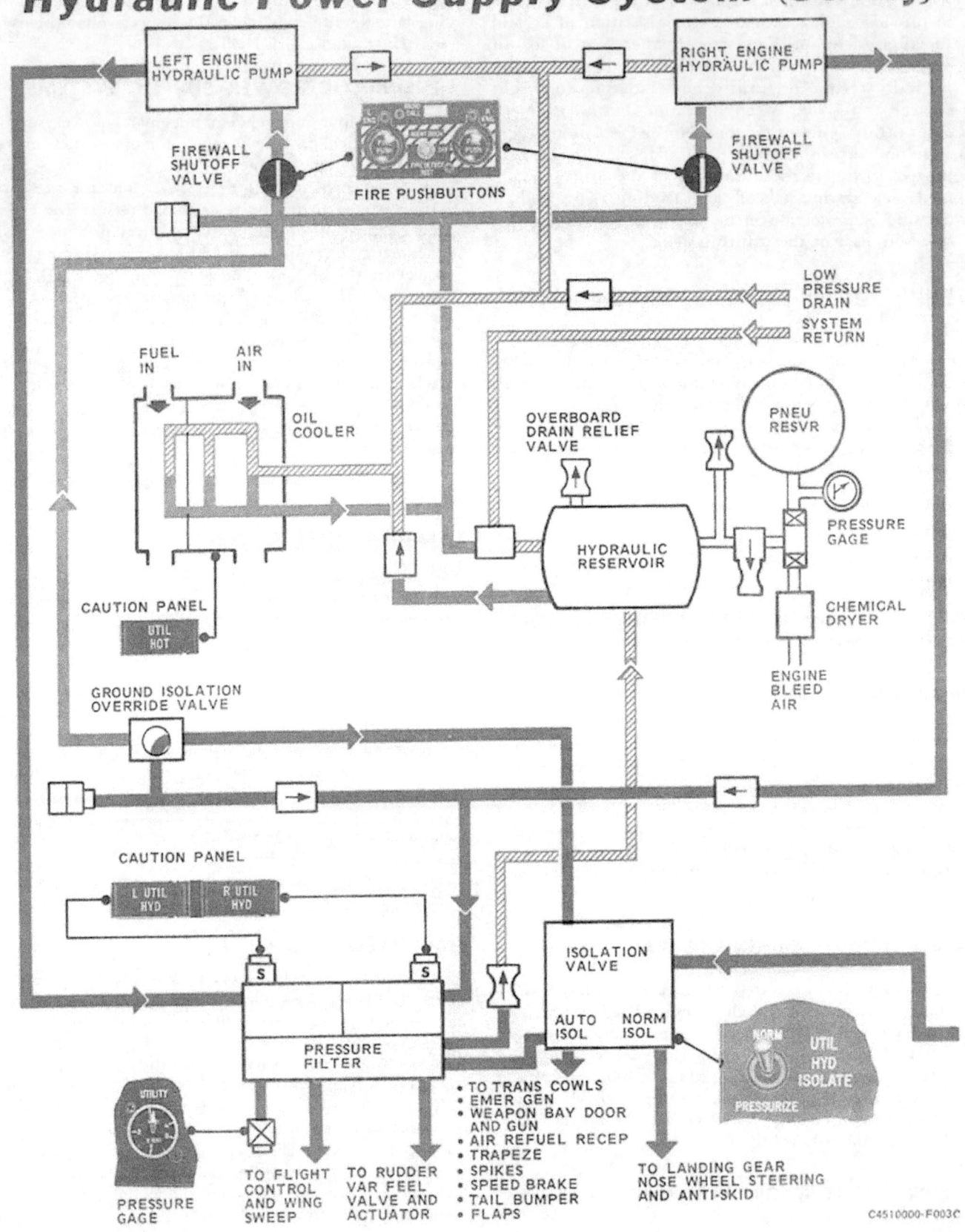

Figure 1-14. (Sheet 1)

T.O. 1F-111A-1

Hydraulic Power Supply System (Primary)

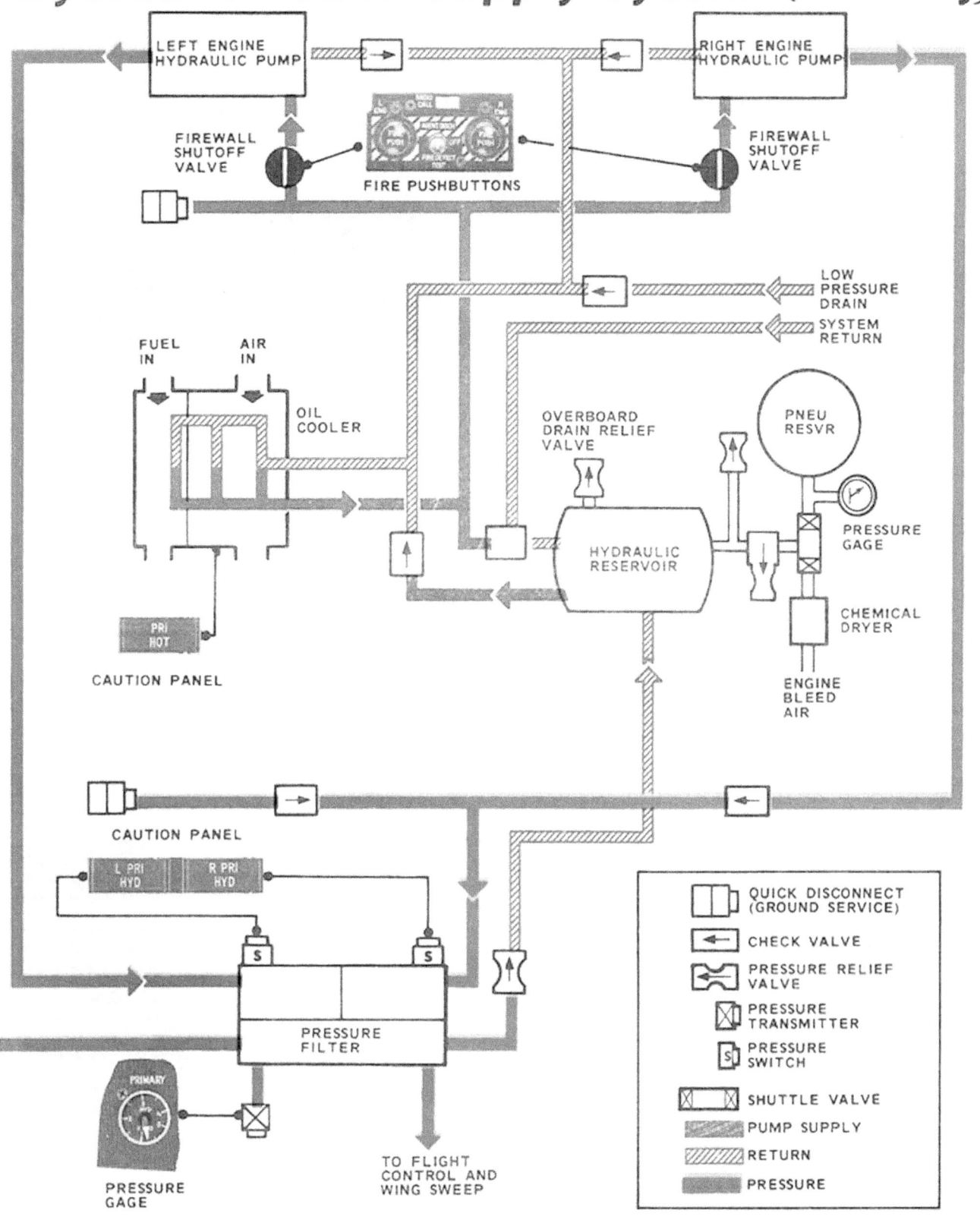

Figure 1-14. (Sheet 2)

Section I
Description & Operation

T.O. 1F-111A-1

Auxiliary Gage Panel

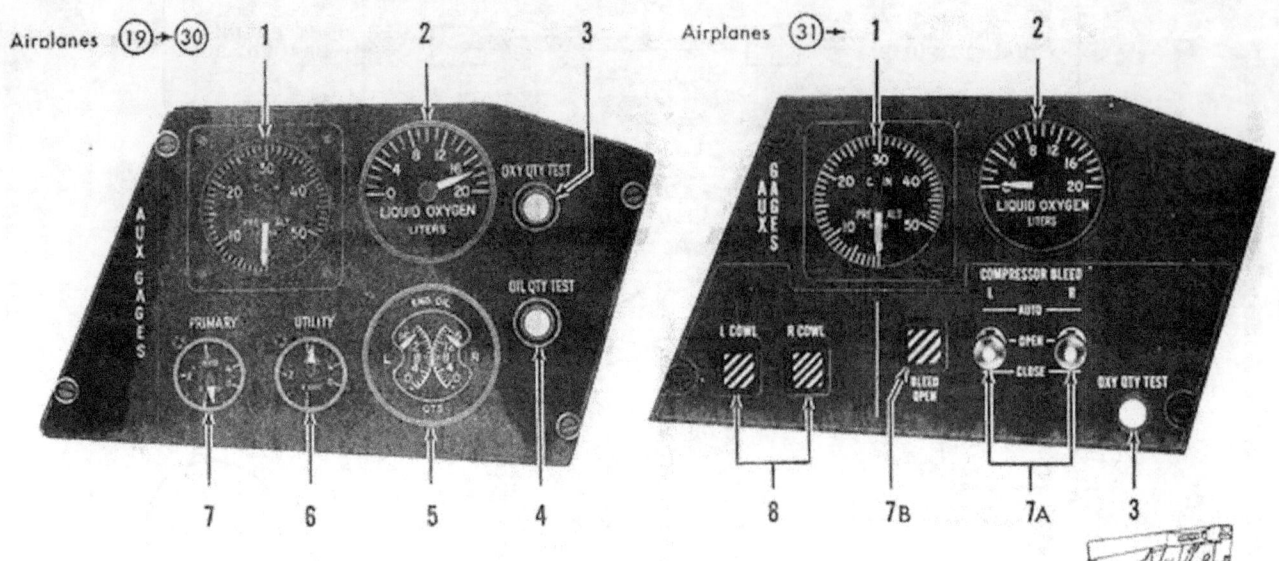

1. Cabin Altitude Indicator.
2. Oxygen Quantity Indicator.
3. Oxygen Quantity Indicator Test Button.
4. Oil Quantity Indicator Test Button.
5. Oil Quantity Indicators.
6. Utility Hydraulic Pressure Indicator.
7. Primary Hydraulic Pressure Indicator.
7A. Compressor Bleed Valve Control Switches
7B. Compressor Bleed Valve Position Indicator
8. Translating Cowl Position Indicators.

Figure 1-15.

switch, located on the lateral trunnion beam, prevents normal gear retraction while the airplane is on the ground.

NOSE GEAR.

Three hydraulic actuators are provided for operation of the nose landing gear and nose wheel well doors. A single-acting actuator retracts the nose landing gear. An uplock actuator locks the nose landing gear in the retracted position and also, through linkages, opens and closes the two nose wheel well doors. A downlock actuator locks the nose landing gear drag strut when the nose landing gear is extended.

LANDING GEAR CONTROLS AND INDICATORS.

Landing Gear Handle.

The landing gear handle (3, figure 1-16), located on the landing gear control panel, has two positions marked UP and DN. The handle has a gear unsafe warning lamp in the end. Moving the handle to the UP or DN position will cause the following actions to occur.

Landing Gear Control Panel

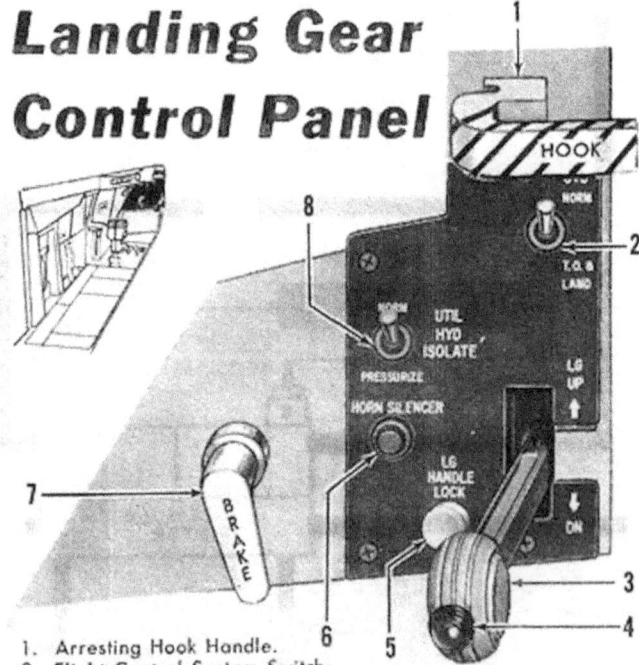

1. Arresting Hook Handle.
2. Flight Control System Switch.
3. Landing Gear Handle.
4. Landing Gear Warning Lamp.
5. Landing Gear Handle Lock Release Button.
6. Landing Gear Warning Horn Silencer Button.
7. Auxiliary Brake Handle.
8. Utility Hydraulic System Isolation Switch.

Figure 1-16.

Changed 18 August 1967

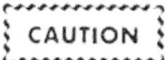

CAUTION

Once a selection of the landing gear handle has been made (UP or DN), do not reposition the handle until the gear has completed its cycle to the selected position. In event the speed brake control valve sticks, repositioning the landing gear handle while the gear is in transit could result in interference between the gear and door. A sticking door control valve will not affect normal or emergency gear extension.

Gear Up

When the handle is moved to the UP position, an electrical signal actuates a solenoid-powered valve, sending hydraulic pressure to the nose gear downlock actuator, nose gear retract actuator, nose gear uplock door actuator, and the speed brake door actuator. The nose gear unlocks and retracts. When it is almost retracted, it mechanically triggers the nose gear uplatch which then locks the gear up and closes and locks the doors. The main gear forward door (speed brake) actuator extends the door. When the door is sufficiently open to allow the main gear to retract, a linkage from the door opens a valve which sends hydraulic pressure to the main gear downlock actuator, main gear retract actuator, and the uplock actuator. The gear then unlocks and retracts. When it is almost retracted, it mechanically triggers the uplatch which locks the gear up and also actuates a valve to close the speed brake door.

Gear Down

When the handle is moved to the DN position, an electrical signal actuates a solenoid-powered valve, sending hydraulic pressure to the nose gear uplock actuator, nose gear downlock actuator, and the speed brake door actuator. The nose gear uplock actuator unlocks and drives the nose gear doors open and locked, at which time the nose gear is allowed to free fall (extend) against the snubbing of its retract actuator. When the gear is almost extended, the downlock actuator drives it fully extended and locked. The speed brake door actuator opens the door until the door clears the main gear. A linkage then actuates a valve

This page intentionally left blank.

to pressurize the main gear uplock actuator and downlock actuator. The uplock opens, allowing the gear to free fall (extend) against the damping of its retract actuator. When the gear is extended, the downlock actuates. This causes the speed brake door actuator to position the door in the partially retracted (trail) position.

The landing gear handle is locked in the DN position by a spring loaded electrical solenoid when the weight of the airplane is on the landing gear. A landing gear safety switch controls 28 volt dc power to the solenoid. The weight of the airplane compresses the shock strut and opens the safety switch which breaks the circuit to the solenoid. When the solenoid is deenergized, the solenoid extends a mechanical lock holding the landing gear handle in the DN position. Removing the weight from the landing gear closes the safety switch on the landing gear and energizes the solenoid. The energized solenoid retracts the lock and frees the landing gear handle.

Landing Gear Handle Lock Release Button. The landing gear handle lock release button is located on the landing gear control panel (5, figure 1-16). The button must be depressed to release the landing gear handle from the up position to lower the gear. Normally, it is not necessary to depress the button when retracting the gear since the gear handle is locked in the down position by a solenoid which will release the handle as the weight of the airplane comes off the gear on takeoff. Should the solenoid malfunction, depressing the button will release the handle to allow gear retraction.

WARNING

Any time it is necessary to depress the landing gear handle lock release button to move the handle to the UP position, the crew member should immediately suspect a malfunction of the landing gear ground safety switch. A failure of this switch, which left it in the closed position, would render ineffective the AUTO position of the fuel tank pressurization switch and cause all spoilers to remain armed even with the landing gear retracted. If a malfunction of the landing gear safety switch is suspected, the fuel tank pressurization switch should be placed to PRESSURIZE and the spoiler switch to OFF.

Landing Gear Emergency Release Handle.

The landing gear emergency release handle (10, figure 1-28), located on the right main instrument panel, is provided to extend the landing gear in the event the normal hydraulic system fails. When the handle is pulled pneumatic pressure is directed to simultaneously open the speed brake door and unlock the nose and main gear uplocks. The gear will free fall to the extended position, then pneumatic pressure will actuate the nose and main gear downlocks and retract the speed brake door to the trail position. Once the gear has been extended by the emergency method it cannot be retracted. The speed brake door may fail to retract to the trail position. This will be indicated by the landing gear handle warning lamp remaining on after the gear is extended and locked. Should this occur, pushing the handle back in will relieve the pressure in the system and allow the air load to push the speed brake door to the trail position.

CAUTION

As the airplane slows down after landing, the weight of the door and lack of air load will cause the door to extend and drag the ground. Stopping the airplane as soon as possible will prevent extensive damage to the door.

Landing Gear Warning Horn.

The landing gear warning horn provides an audible signal in the crew members' headsets when an unsafe landing gear condition exists. The horn sounds when all of the following conditions exist: The nose and main landing gear are not down and locked and/or speed brake door is not in trail position, indicated airspeed is below 160 ($\pm$12) knots, airplane altitude is less than 10,000 ($\pm$350) feet, and one or both throttles are set below minimum cruise setting. The malfunction and indicator lamp test button located on the lighting control panel may be used to test the landing gear warning horn. The warning horn may be silenced by depressing the horn silencer button adjacent to the landing gear handle (6, figure 1-16).

Landing Gear Position Indicator Lamps.

A planform silhouette of the airplane having two green indicator lamps is located on the left main instrument panel (10A, figure 1-6 or 13, figure 1-6A). The lamps are positioned to represent the nose and main landing gear. When the landing gear is down and locked, the lamps are lighted. In-transit positions of the landing gear and unsafe landing gear conditions are indicated by lighting of the red warning lamp in the landing gear handle knob. A safe up-and-locked landing gear condition is indicated when both the green indicator lamps and the red warning lamp are off.

Section I
Description & Operation

T.O. 1F-111A-1

Ground Safety Locks and Safety Pins

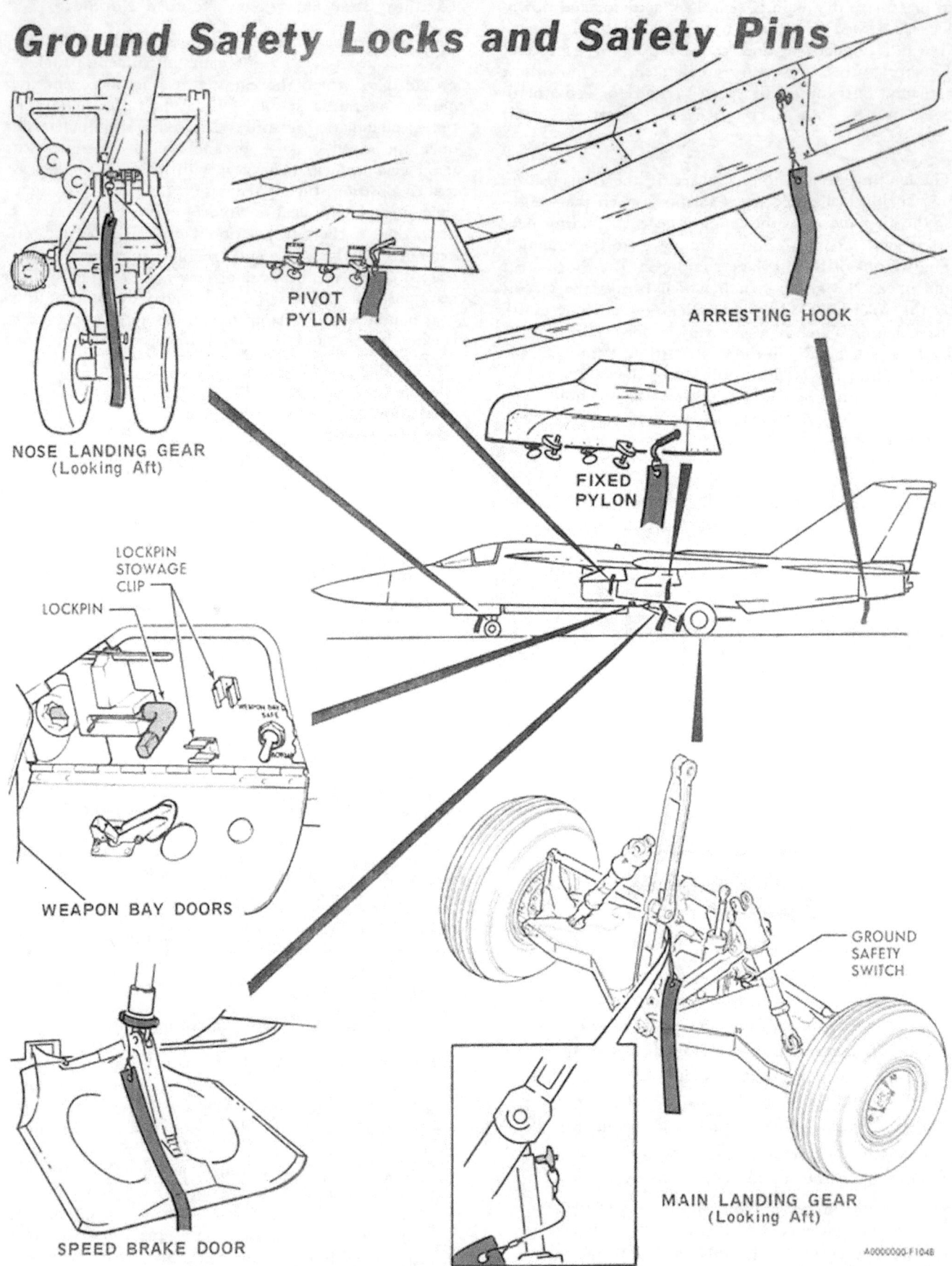

Figure 1-17. (Sheet 1)

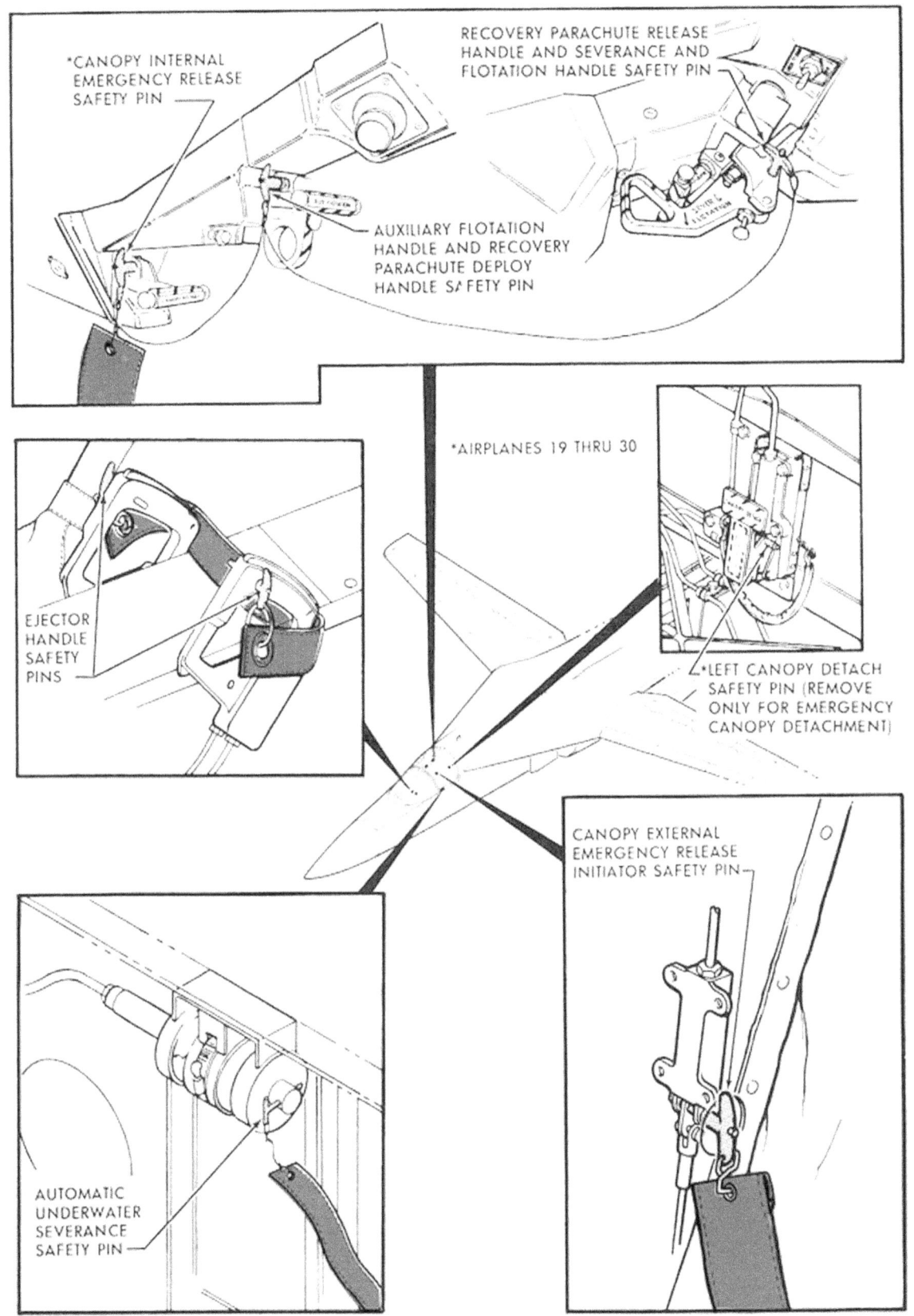

Figure 1-17. (Sheet 2)

This page intentionally left blank.

TAIL BUMPER SYSTEM.

The tail bumper protects the control surfaces, engines, and portions of the airframe from damage that might occur if the tail inadvertently contacts the ground during ground handling. The tail bumper also provides limited protection during overrotation on take-off and during landings. In flight, the tail bumper is held in the fully retracted position by hydraulic pressure in the tail bumper lift cylinder. The hydraulic pressure is ported to the tail bumper lift cylinder from the speed brake control valve. When the landing gear is extended and the speed brake returns to trail position, the lift cylinder pressure is relieved and the tail bumper is extended by the pneumatic action of the tail bumper dashpot. The dashpot, which functions as the impact shock absorber, has its own separate reservoir that is charged with compressed nitrogen. Retraction of the landing gear allows hydraulic pressure to again be ported to the tail bumper lift cylinder to retract the bumper and hold it in this position.

NOSE WHEEL STEERING SYSTEM.

The nose wheel steering system provides directional control of the airplane for taxiing and during takeoff and landing. The system is electrically engaged, hydraulically actuated and controlled by the rudder pedals. Hydraulic pressure is supplied from the utility hydraulic system. When the system is energized, movement of the rudder pedals at either crew station is mechanically transmitted through a system of push-pull rods to a hydraulic steering actuator which turns the nose wheels. A mechanical linkage at the actuator provides a nonlinear increase in steering angle, as the pedals are displaced, to prevent overcontrolling. Maximum deflection of the rudder pedals steers the nose wheels 40 degrees either side of center. The steering system automatically centers the nose gear during retraction. Nose wheel shimmy damping is accomplished by restricting the displacement of hydraulic fluid in the steering actuator. The flight control system switch must be in the T.O. & LAND position or the rudder authority switch must be in the FULL position to permit sufficient rudder pedal travel for steering. Power for engaging the system is furnished from the 28 volt dc essential bus.

Note

Nose wheel steering will be inoperative if the landing gear is extended using the landing gear emergency release handle.

NOSE WHEEL STEERING/AIR REFUEL BUTTONS.

A nose wheel steering/air refuel button (4, figure 1-21), is located on each control stick grip. The buttons are labeled NWS and A/R DISC. With the weight of the airplane on the gear, depressing either button actuates a holding relay to engage the system. The button can then be released and the system will remain engaged until the button is again depressed and released to open the relay and disengage the system. The button receives 28 volt dc power from the essential bus. For a description of the A/R DISC function of the buttons refer to "Fuel Supply System," this section.

NOSE WHEEL STEERING/AIR REFUELING INDICATOR LAMP.

A green nose wheel steering/air refueling indicator lamp labeled NWS/A/R is located on the left main instrument panel (16B figure 1-6 and 19B, figure 1-6A). The lamp will light when the nose wheel steering system is energized. For a description of the A/R DISC function of the lamp, refer to "Fuel Supply System", this section. The lamp receives power from the 28 volt dc essential bus.

BRAKE SYSTEM.

Each main landing gear wheel is equipped with a hydraulically operated multiple disc brake. Pressure for operation of the brakes is supplied by the utility hydraulic system for normal operation and by two hydraulic accumulators in the event of utility hydraulic system failure. Anti-skid control, automatic braking during landing gear retraction, and an auxiliary brake are provided. Normal brake operation is controlled by conventional brake pedals, each mechanically connected to brake metering valves. The brake hydraulic system is a dual-normal type, separated into two circuits. Each circuit operates independently of the other. One circuit operates one half of the pressure pistons on the left brake and one half the pressure pistons on the right brake. The other circuit operates the other half of the pistons on each brake. During normal operation of the brakes, pressure is metered to the brakes from both hydraulic circuits in proportion to applied force on the brake pedals. Full braking effectiveness is achieved with approximately 60 percent of full brake pedal travel. If one hydraulic circuit becomes inoperative, the brake system can provide sufficient increased pressure to the operative circuit for 90 percent of normal braking effectiveness. This is accomplished by application of greater than normal brake pedal travel and slightly higher pedal force. The dual-normal type brake hydraulic system provides emergency brake operation automatically; therefore, actuation of an emergency brake control handle is not required. Two hydraulic accumulators are provided in the system to supply brake system pressure in the event of failure of the utility hydraulic system. Each accumulator is precharged and supplies pressure to only one of the individual brake circuits. Fully charged accumulators will provide 10-14 full-pressure brake applications or one full-pressure brake application with 32 anti-skid cycles. A priority valve, which limits the quantity of fluid which can be displaced from the brake accumulator through the brake metering valves by actuating the brake pedals, is included in each hydraulic circuit. If the brake accumulators are not replenished as fluid is displaced by repetitive brake applications or by anti-skid cycling, the priority valves will close when accumulator pressure has been reduced to approximately 1000 psi.

CAUTION

Do not actuate the brake pedals inflight. When utility hydraulic pressure is isolated from the brake system there is no way to replenish the brake accumulators. If the utility hydraulic system fails after the brake accumulators are bled off to below 1000 psi there will be no braking available with the brake pedals on landing.

When accumulator pressure is 1000 psi, sufficient fluid volume for 5-10 auxiliary brake applications is remaining. After the priority valves close, the remaining fluid can be utilized only by pulling the auxiliary brake handle. No braking action can be achieved by actuating the brake pedals.

ANTI-SKID SYSTEM.

Anti-skid control is provided for normal braking. Solenoid operated valves in each brake and anti-skid control valve assembly function to release brake pressure in response to electrical signals received from the anti-skid control system as impending wheel skids are detected. The solenoid valves will reapply brake pressure upon being de-energized after the wheel returns to normal speed.

Anti-Skid Control Switch.

The anti-skid control switch (2, figure 1-5), is located on the aircraft comander's throttle panel and labeled ANTI-SKID. The switch has two positions, one marked OFF and an unmarked ON (up) position. Placing the switch to ON will provide anti-skid control during normal braking. With the switch in OFF, anti-skid control will not be available and brake pressure will be in direct response to pedal pressure.

Anti-Skid Caution Lamp.

An amber caution lamp labeled ANTI-SKID is located on the main caution lamp panel (figure 1-29 or 1-29A). The lamp will light when the anti-skid switch is in the ON position and a malfunction has caused the anti-skid system to become deenergized. On airplanes ㉛ and those modified by T.O. 1F-111A-514 the anti-skid caution lamp will light anytime the landing gear is down and the anti-skid switch is not in the ON position. When the lamp is lighted, anti-skid control is not available and braking will be in direct response to pedal pressure.

AUXILIARY BRAKE HANDLE.

The auxiliary brake handle (7, figure 1-16), labeled AUX BRAKE, is located on the landing gear control panel. When the handle is pulled out, a mechanical linkage opens a selector valve which admits pressure from the hydraulic accumulators directly into the brake lines downstream of the brake control valve. The primary function of the auxiliary brake control handle is to apply the brakes while the airplane is parked. The auxiliary brake control can be used to set the brakes for engine run-up. A secondary function of the auxiliary brake control is to serve as a supplemental emergency brake in the event that accumulator pressure is reduced sufficiently to cause the priority valves to close and prevent normal brake application by pedal actuation. Brake pressure cannot be metered by the auxiliary brake handle. The total accumulator pressure is ported directly to the brake cylinders, bypassing the metering valves and the anti-skid valves. Therefore, the auxiliary brake handle should not be pulled while the airplane is in motion except when braking cannot be achieved by pedal actuation.

CAUTION

Pulling the auxiliary brake handle while the airplane is moving will cause the wheels to lock and result in tire skidding or blowout.

BRAKE HYDRAULIC HAND PUMP.

A hydraulic handpump, located in the main landing gear wheel well, is provided to replenish brake accumulator pressure during ground handling operation.

AIRCRAFT ARRESTING SYSTEM.

The arresting hook system provides for emergency arrestment of the airplane. The system consists of an arresting hook, arresting hook dashpot, a dashpot air bottle, an uplock latch, arresting hook controls, a pressure gage, and an air filler valve. Except for the controls the arresting hook components are located in the lower aft end of the fuselage tail cone.

ARRESTING HOOK HANDLE.

The arresting hook handle (1, figure 1-16), located on the landing gear control panel, is connected to a low friction push-pull type mechanism contained in a flexible metal housing. The handle is labeled HOOK on diagonal stripes. The mechanism provides a direct mechanical linkage from the handle to the arresting hook uplatch mechanism in the tail cone. The arresting hook is released by grasping the handle and pulling aft. The total travel of the handle from retract to extend position is approximately four inches. Approximately one second is required for the arresting hook to extend. The hook must be raised manually to its stowed position.

ARRESTING HOOK CAUTION LAMP.

The amber arresting hook caution lamp, labeled HOOK DOWN, is located on the main caution lamp panel (figure 1-29 or 1-29A). The caution lamp lights to indicate hook down position only.

AERODYNAMIC DECELERATION EQUIPMENT.

SPEED BRAKE.

The speed brake, which also serves as the main landing gear forward door, is provided as an aid to deceleration during flight. The speed brake is hydraulically operated and may be used as a speed brake only when the landing gear is up and locked. For operation of the speed brake as a landing gear door refer to "Landing Gear System" this section.

Speed Brake Switches.

A three-position speed brake switch (4, figure 1-5), marked IN, OFF, and OUT is located on the right throttle at each crew station. The switches are thumb actuated and slide forward (IN) and aft (OUT). The aircraft commander's switch is detented in all positions. The pilot's switch is spring loaded to OFF from both the IN and OUT positions and will override the aircraft commander's switch. When the pilot's switch is released to OFF, the speed brake will move to the position selected by the aircraft commander's switch. The speed brake switches are activated to allow operation of the speed brake by a switch on the landing gear uplock when the landing gear is retracted.

GROUND ROLL SPOILERS.

Deceleration during ground roll is aided by symmetrical extension of the flight control spoilers which reduces aerodynamic lift and allows maximum effectiveness of the wheel brakes.

Ground Roll Spoiler Switch.

The ground roll spoiler switch (8, figure 1-19), located on the crew module left sidewall, has positions BRAKE and OFF. If the weight of the airplane is on the landing gear and both throttles are in IDLE, positioning this switch to BRAKE will cause the flight control spoilers to extend. Under the same conditions placing the switch to OFF will retract the spoilers. With the spoiler switch positioned to BRAKE, if the airplane weight is removed from the landing gear or if either throttle is advanced out of IDLE, the spoilers will automatically retract.

WING FLAPS AND SLATS.

WING FLAPS.

The wing flaps are full span, multisection Fowler-type flaps. Each wing flap is divided into five sections. The four outer sections, designated as the main flaps, are mechanically connected and operate as one unit. The inboard section, designated as the auxiliary flap, operates independently from the main flaps. The main flaps are powered by a single hydraulic motor which is connected to a gearbox located in the fuselage section. The hydraulic motor and gearbox assembly drive a torque shaft which is connected through gearboxes to mechanical actuators attached to the flaps. An electric motor mounted on this same gearbox provides an emergency mode of operation in the event of a utility hydraulic system failure. The auxiliary flap actuators are disabled when either the wing sweep angle switch senses more than 16 degrees wing sweep or when the wing sweep handle is at a position greater than 16 degrees. Also, a mechancal interlock locks the flap and slat handle in the UP position when either the wing sweep angle is greater than 26½ degrees or when the wing sweep handle is at a position greater than 26½ degrees. Asymmetrical flap travel is prevented by an asymmetry device. When the asymmetry device senses asymmetrical flap travel, a signal is sent to close the flap drive control valve and to engage torque shaft brakes which stop travel of the flaps. Once the flap drive control valve has been closed and the torque shaft brakes are engaged by this method, the flaps cannot be extended or retracted by either the normal or emergency mode. Integral with each main flap section is a mechanically controlled vane. As the flap extends downward the vane is positioned by a mechanical linkage to provide the proper airflow through the space between the flap leading edge and the spoiler trailing edge. The auxiliary (inboard) flaps are independently operated by electrical actuators. There is no mechanical connection between the auxiliary flaps since there is no necessity to prevent unsymmetrical operation. The main flap hydraulic motor receives pressure from the utility hydraulic system. The auxiliary flap actuators receive 115 volt ac power from the right main ac bus.

WING SLATS.

Each wing is equipped with a leading edge slat. Each slat is divided into four sections which are connected and operate as one unit. The slats operate in conjunction with the main flaps and are connected to the main flap drive assembly by flexible drive shafts. On the extend cycle, the slats will extend to the full down position before the main flaps start to extend. On the retract cycle, the flaps will fully retract before the slats start to retract.

ROTATING GLOVES.

The outboard edges of the wing gloves, adjacent to the wing inboard leading edges are equipped with movable surfaces to allow full forward movement of the inboard slats. These surfaces are called rotating gloves. (4, figure 1-1). A door forms the lower surface of each rotating glove. Each rotating glove and its associated door are operated by a mechanical actuator and linkage which is connected to the slat drive flexible shaft. When the slats are extended, the rotating gloves automatically rotate (leading edge down and trailing edge up) and the doors open to allow full extension of the slats.

Flap and Slat Handle.

The flap and slat handle (9, figure 1-5), located on the aircraft commander's throttle panel, has three positions marked UP, SLAT DOWN, and FLAP DOWN. A manually operated gate (8, figure 1-5), located between the SLAT DOWN and FLAP DOWN areas, must be released before the handle can be moved from one area to another. When the handle is moved from UP to any position in the SLAT DOWN area, a mechanical linkage opens the flap drive control valve, directing hydraulic pressure to the flap drive motor. The flap drive assembly rotates the flexible shafts connected to the slat drive mechanism to position the rotating glove and to extend the slats to a position corresponding to handle position. Moving the handle down to the gate will cause the slats to fully extend. When the gate is released and the handle is moved into the FLAP DOWN area, the flap drive assembly will rotate the flexible shafts connected to the main flap actuators, extending the main flaps to a position corresponding to handle position. The flaps can be set at an infinite number of positions between full up and full down. The flap and slat drive assembly is so designed that it will not extend the flaps until the slats are fully extended. On airplanes ㉛ ↧ a detent position is provided in flap handle travel to aid in selecting the 15 degree flap position. When the handle is moved down to a position corresponding to 28 degrees or more of flaps, a contact closes providing electrical power to the auxiliary flap actuators. Full down position of the flap and slat handle will provide 37.5 degrees of flap deflection. The retraction cycle sequence is just the opposite from the extension cycle. Moving the handle from the full FLAP DOWN position to the full UP position will first cause the flaps to retract and then the slats to retract. It should be noted that at no time will the flaps extend until the slats are fully extended nor will the slats retract until the flaps are fully retracted regardless of flap and slat handle position. Normal extension or retraction of the flaps and slats takes approximately 12 seconds.

Flap and Slat Switch.

The flap and slat switch (1, figure 1-22), located on the auxiliary flight control panel, has two positions marked EMER and NORM. When the flap and slat switch is in the NORM position, the flaps and slats are actuated normally by use of the flap handle. When the switch is in EMER, the flaps and slats may be extended or retracted electrically by holding the emergency flap and slat switch to EXTEND or RETRACT as applicable and the flap drive control valve is closed, disabling the flap drive motor. The EMER position is used in the event of utility hydraulic system failure.

Emergency Flap and Slat Switch.

The emergency flap and slat switch (2, figure 1-22), located on the auxiliary flight control panel, has positions marked EXTEND and RETRACT and is spring loaded to the center unmarked OFF position. The switch is provided as an emergency method of operating the main flaps and slats in the event of a utility hydraulic system failure. Operation of the flaps and slats using this switch is identical to that when using the flap and slat handle except that electric power is used to operate the flap drive motor instead of hydraulic power. It should be noted that the emergency flap and slat switch does not control the auxiliary flaps since the auxiliary flap actuators are energized only when the flap and slat handle is positioned to more than 28 degrees.

Note

Emergency flap extension or retraction takes approximately 80 seconds at 180 KIAS. This time will vary with airspeed.

Flap and Slat Position Indicators.

The flap and slat position indicators are a part of the wing sweep, flap/slat position indicator (24, figure 1-6 or 8, figure 1-6A), located on the left main instrument panel. The indicators display main flap position in degrees and slat and auxiliary flap position in a window as either UP or DN (down). When the slats or auxiliary flaps are in transit or when electrical power is turned on a crosshatch is displayed in the indicator window.

WING SWEEP SYSTEM.

The variable sweep wings are moved to and held in position by two hydraulic, motor-driven, linear actuators. The actuators are mechanically interconnected to insure positive synchronization (figure 1-18). The left actuator is furnished power by the primary hydraulic system, and the right actuator is furnished power by the utility hydraulic system. In the event of failure of either hydraulic system, the remaining system, by utilizing the load transfer capability of the mechanical interconnect will still provide wing actuation. However, actuation under this condition will be at a reduced rate commensurate with actuator loading. Wing position is controlled by a closed loop mechanical servo system in response to an input signal from the wing sweep handle. The maximum rate at which the wings extend or retract is controlled by flow-limiting devices in the hydraulic lines. Directional reversal, due to aerodynamic loads, is prevented by the nonreversing (Acme-type) threads in the actuator. The wing sweep handle is locked in the 16 degree position by a solenoid operated latch whenever the auxiliary flaps are out of the zero position. Also, a mechanical interlock prevents the wing sweep handle from being moved past the 26½ degree position when either the flap and slat handle is out of the UP position or the main flaps are out of the fully retracted position.

WING SWEEP CONTROL HANDLE.

The wing sweep control handle (5, figure 1-19), is shaped like a pistol grip and is spring loaded to a stowed position under the canopy sill on the left side of the crew module. Teeth in the top of the handle lock it to serrations in the handle support, when it is stowed, to prevent inadvertent movement. To adjust wing sweep, the handle must be rotated to the vertical position to unlock it; then it can be moved forward or aft as necessary. The handle is mechanically linked to the wing sweep control valve. The handle is pulled aft to sweep the wings aft and pushed forward to sweep the wings forward. As the handle is moved an index mark on the wing sweep position indicator follows the handle position to assist in selecting the desired wing sweep position.

WING SWEEP HANDLE LOCKOUT CONTROLS.

Two wing sweep handle lockout controls (6, figure 1-19), one labeled FIXED STORES and the other labeled WEAPONS, are located just above and aft of the wing sweep control handle. When either control is moved forward, the word ON is visible, and a latch extends which prevents aft movement of the wing sweep handle past the latch. When either control is moved aft, the word OFF is visible and the latch retracts. The fixed stores lockout control, when ON, prevents the wing sweep handle from being moved aft past the 26 degree position. This is the sweep angle at which the fixed pylons and stores are in a streamlined configuration. The weapons lockout control restricts aft movement of the wing sweep handle to 55 degrees. This is the wing sweep angle past which, certain weapons on the inboard pivot pylons would strike the fuselage. The wing sweep handle lockout controls restrict aft movement of the wing sweep handle only. Forward motion is unrestricted.

WING SWEEP HANDLE 26 DEGREE FORWARD GATE.

A wing sweep handle 26 degree forward gate (4, figure 1-19), located above the wing sweep handle, is provided to stop forward motion of the wing sweep handle at 26 degrees. The gate is thumb-actuated and is spring loaded to the latched position. Depressing the gate will retract a latch, allowing the wing sweep handle to be moved forward past the 26 degree position.

WING SWEEP POSITION INDICATOR.

The wing sweep position indicator (24, figure 1-6 or 8, figure 1-6A), is a part of the wing sweep, flap/slat position indicator located on the left main instrument panel. The indicator displays the wing position in degrees and is graduated in 2 degree increments from 16 to 72 degrees. An index mark at 26 degrees provides a reference for selecting this position. A movable index on the outside of the scale is provided to assist in setting the wing sweep handle to the desired position. The angle of wing sweep is monitored by a transmitter which mechanically follows the change in wing position and converts this information to an electrical signal which drives the wing sweep indicator pointer.

FLIGHT CONTROL SYSTEM.

The flight control system (figure 1-20), provides control of the airplane by movement of the primary control surfaces. The primary control surfaces consist of a pair of movable horizontal stabilizers, rudder, and spoilers. Movement of the control surfaces is controlled by the control stick and rudder pedals. Rate gyros and accelerometers, in conjunction with electronic computers and damper servoactuators provide continuous automatic damping about the three axes of the airplane. Separate channels of mechanical linkage control hydraulic servo actuators, which produce control surface movement. Yaw control of the airplane is accomplished by deflection of a rudder surface located on the trailing edge of the vertical stabilizer. Pitch attitude of the airplane is controlled by symmetrical deflection of the horizontal stabilizer surfaces. Roll attitude is controlled by asymmetrical deflection of the horizontal stabilizer surfaces. When the wing sweep angle is less than 45 degrees, roll control is aided by action of two spoilers on top of each wing. The stability augmentation system employs triple-redundant sensors, electronic circuitry and electro-hydraulic dampers. The pitch and roll damper gains are continuously set by a self-adaptive system to the

Section I
Description & Operation

T.O. 1F-111A-1

Wing Sweep and Pylon System

1. Wing Sweep Control Handle.
2. Wing Sweep Actuators.
3. Wing Sweep Control Box.
4. Wing Sweep Control Valve.

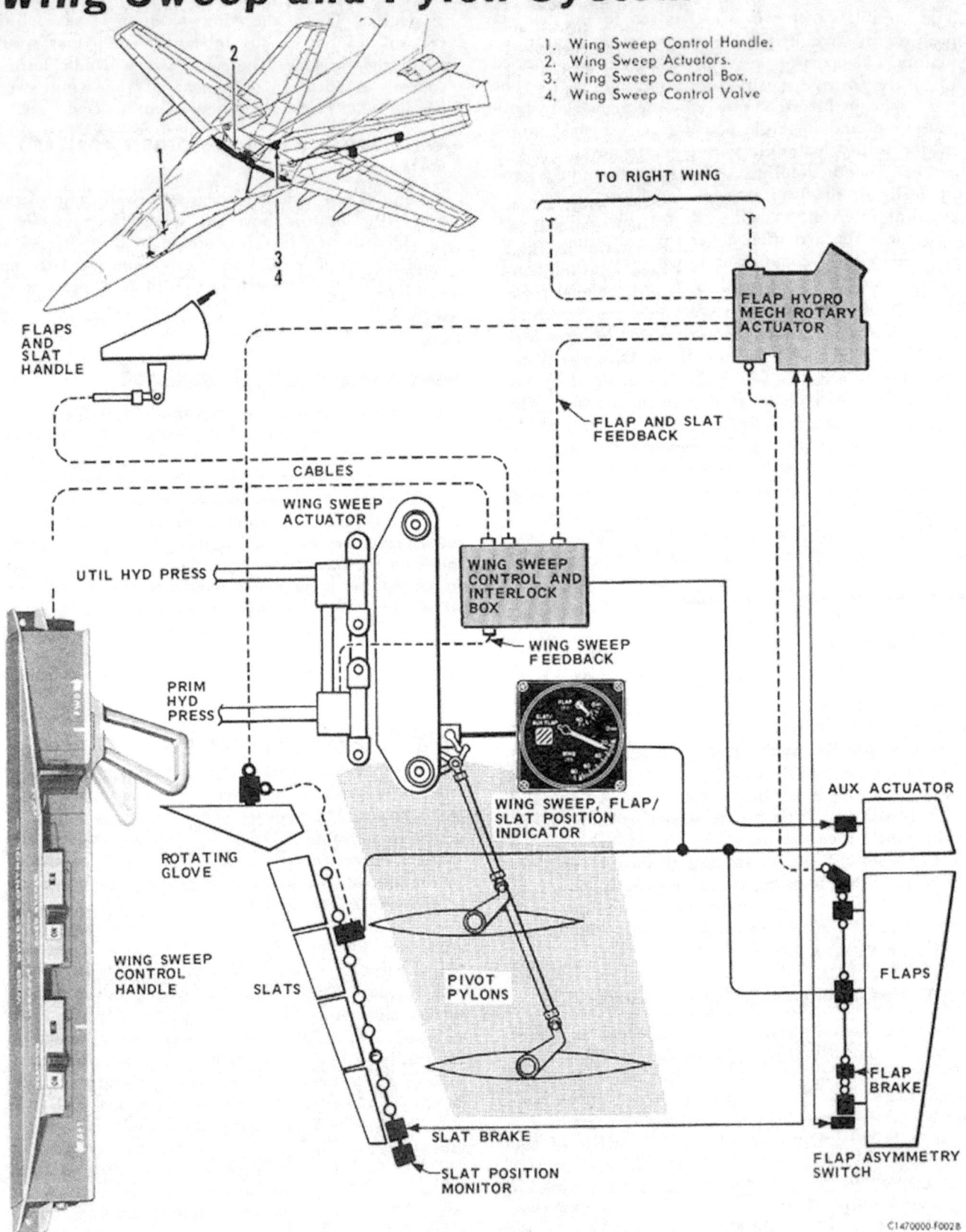

Figure 1-18.

Left Sidewall

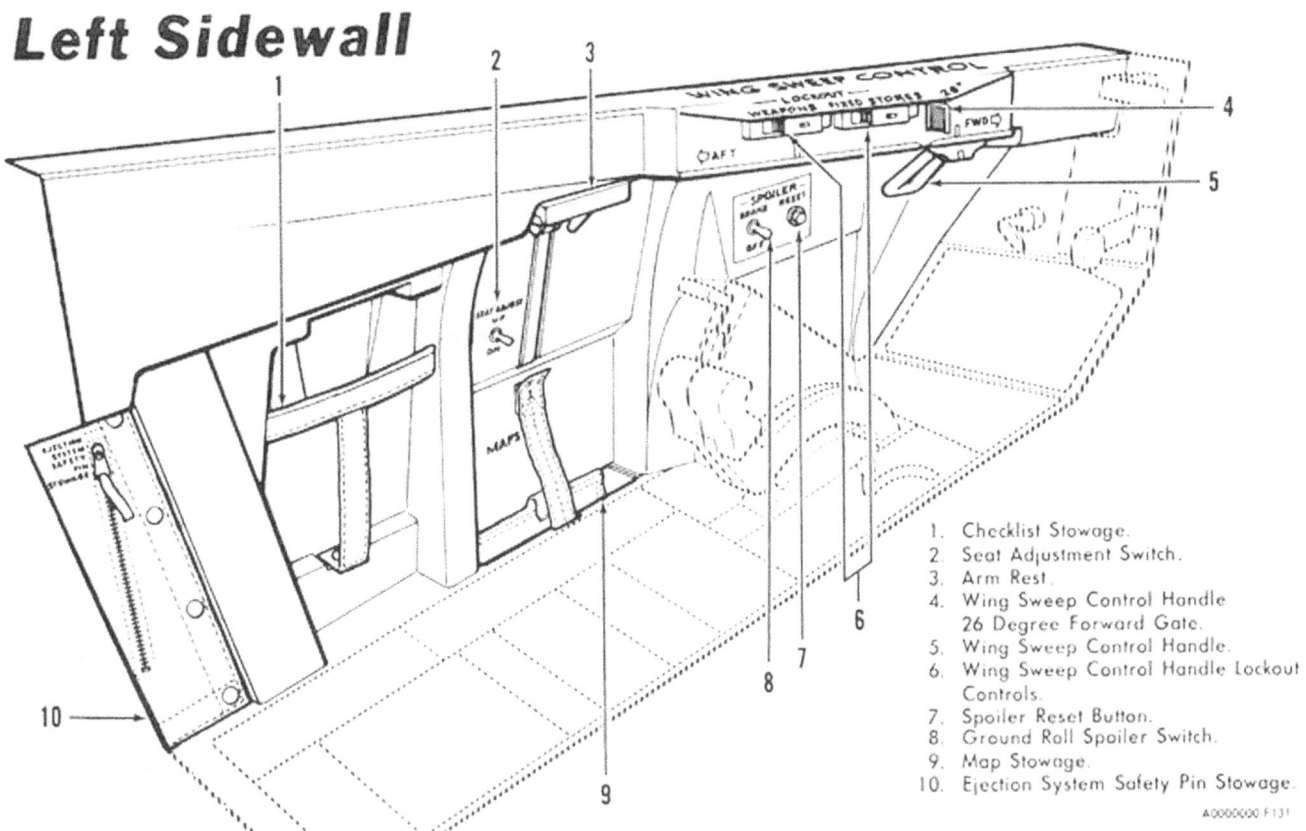

1. Checklist Stowage.
2. Seat Adjustment Switch.
3. Arm Rest.
4. Wing Sweep Control Handle 26 Degree Forward Gate.
5. Wing Sweep Control Handle.
6. Wing Sweep Control Handle Lockout Controls.
7. Spoiler Reset Button.
8. Ground Roll Spoiler Switch.
9. Map Stowage.
10. Ejection System Safety Pin Stowage.

Figure 1-19.

optimum value for the flight condition. Command augmentation, through the pitch and roll dampers, augments the pilot inputs to provide a near constant relationship between control force and aircraft response. Automatic failure detection and correction, as well as self-test features, are provided in the system. The flight control system functions in conjunction with the terrain following radar (TFR) to provide the capability of automatic terrain following. Signals from the TFR, control the pitch axis of the flight control system through the pitch damper to maintain the airplane at a preselected altitude above the terrain. When operating in either automatic or manual terrain following, a failure in the TFR will generate a 2g pull up signal to the pitch damper. For description of the TFR refer to "Terrain Following Radar," this section.

PITCH CHANNEL.

Manual control of the aircraft in pitch is achieved by fore and aft movement of the control stick. This movement is transmitted along the pitch channel push-pull tubes and bellcranks to the left and right horizontal stabilizer actuator control valves. These control valves control the flow of hydraulic fluid to the actuators, thus causing the horizontal stabilizers to move symmetrically. Stick throw is limited by mechanical stops to prevent interference with the seat and control panel knobs. With the series trim actuator at zero, these stops allow the pilot to command 25 degrees trailing edge up and 10 degrees (15 degrees on airplanes 31 ♦) trailing edge down elevator motion of the horizontal stabilizer. The pitch command input limits are set at the input to the pitch-roll mixer which limits the sum of manual inputs, series trim inputs, and damper servo inputs to 25 degrees trailing edge up and 10 (15 degrees on airplanes 31 ♦) degrees trailing edge down motion of the horizontal tail. Since airloads on the surfaces are not transmitted back to the controls, artificial feel has been incorporated into the system to give the pilot the desired feel. The artificial feel is provided by a spring in parallel with the mechanical linkage. With the pitch damper off, total stick travel from neutral to full aft is 7 inches and from neutral to full forward is 2.8 inches (4.2 inches on airplanes 31 ♦). The force required to move the stick from neutral to full aft, ranges from the initial breakout force of 1.7 pounds to a force of 65 pounds (or to a force of 43 pounds on airplanes 31 ♦). The force required to move the stick from neutral to full forward, ranges from 1.7 pounds to 36 pounds (or to 57 pounds on airplanes 31 ♦).

Section I
Description & Operation

T.O. 1F-111A-1

Flight Control System Schematic

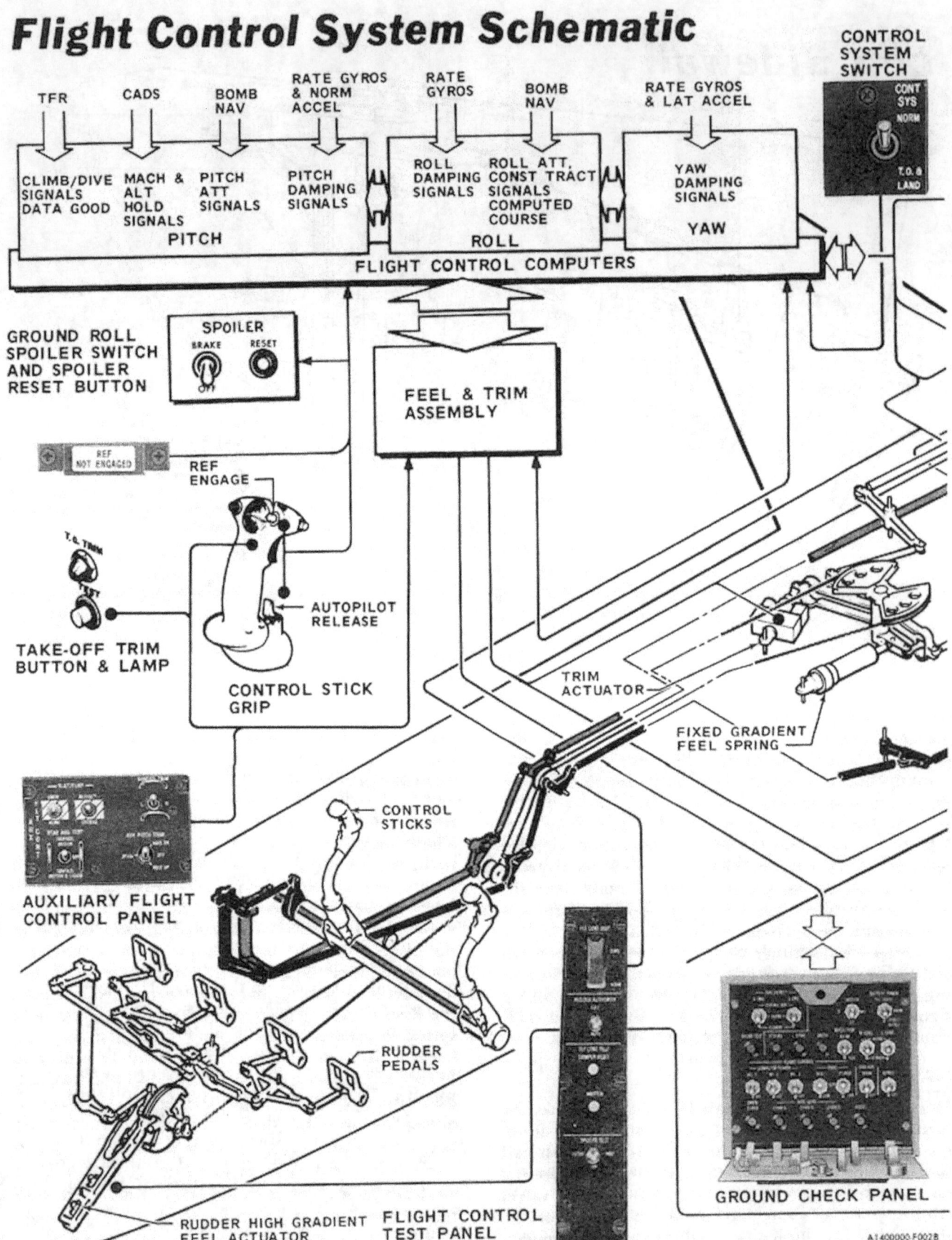

Figure 1-20. (Sheet 1)

T.O. 1F-111A-1

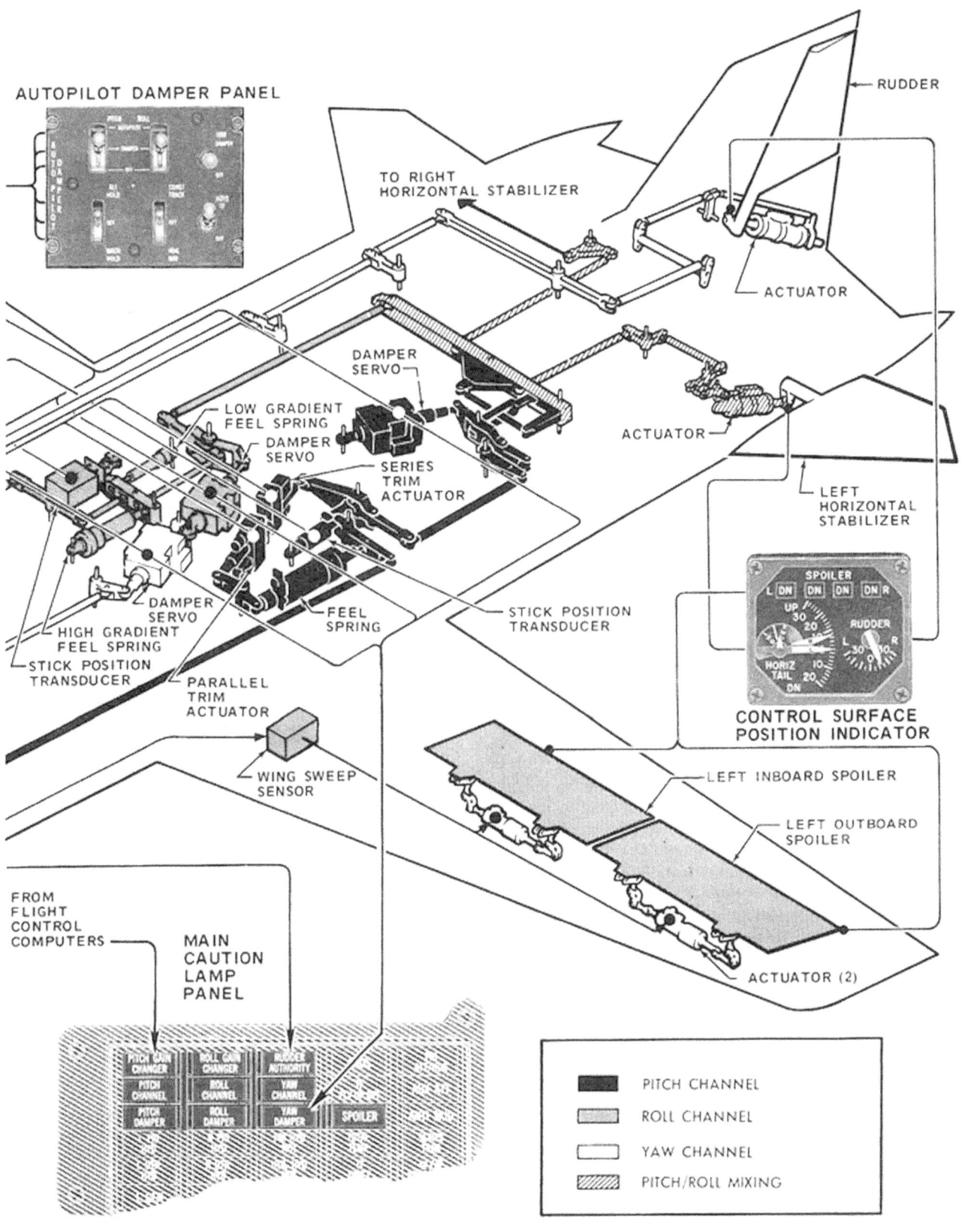

Figure 1-20. (Sheet 2)

Section I
Description & Operation

ROLL CHANNEL.

Lateral movement of the control stick is transmitted along the roll channel push-pull tubes and bellcranks to the horizontal stabilizer actuator control valves. This motion operates the horizontal stabilizer actuators in opposite directions, causing an asymmetrical movement of the horizontal stabilizers. Stick displacement is limited by stick stops to ±8 degrees of differential horizontal stabilizer motion. Stick travel from neutral to hardover is 4.8 inches. The stick forces and surface displacement in the roll channel are nonlinear with respect to stick travel. Differential horizontal stabilizer command, which consists of damper servo commands and stick commands, is limited to ±8 degrees of differential motion by mixer stops in the pitch-roll mixer. As the stick is moved laterally from neutral, the stick forces increase from a breakout force of 1.2 pounds to a force of 15 pounds at one half the total stick travel (2.4 inches). At this point a force detent is encountered and the total command to the horizontal stabilizer is 2 degrees of differential horizontal stabilizer motion. Force to the stick must be increased from 15 pounds to 23 pounds to pass the force detent. From this point to hardover, the stick force increase is linear to the maximum of 31 pounds. When the wings are forward of 45 degrees, roll control is aided by action of two spoilers on the top of each wing. Each spoiler surface is actuated by a hydraulic servo actuator. The outboard pair of spoiler actuators is supplied pressure by the utility hydraulic system. The inboard pair of spoiler actuators is supplied pressure by the primary hydraulic system. The actuators receive their command signals from the stick position transducers located in the roll channel linkage. Lateral movement of the control stick causes the stick position transducers to generate command signals which are sent through the wing sweep sensor assembly to the spoiler actuators. Both commanded spoilers extend to a maximum of 45 degrees at the stick force detent. The spoiler extension is in non-linear proportion to stick displacement. The spoilers are operable only when the wing sweep angle is between 16 degrees and 45 degrees. When the wing sweep angle is between 45 and 47 degrees, the spoiler command signals are zeroed and the spoilers are locked down. Between 47 and 49 degrees, the hydraulic supply to the spoilers is cut off. A spoiler monitor is provided in the roll channel to deactivate and lock down either pair of spoilers should one of that pair of spoilers malfunction. If a spoiler inadvertently extends without being commanded and the aircraft starts a roll, the pilot would apply an opposite stick command to maintain wings level. Simultaneous extension of spoilers on each wing will cause the monitor, through a voting process, to cut off hydraulic pressure to the malfunctioning spoiler and its mate on the opposite wing. This action will retract and lock the pair of spoilers in the down position and cause the spoiler caution lamp to light. Flight is continued using the remaining pair of spoilers and asymmetrical horizontal tail operation for roll control. The spoiler monitor may be reset by depressing a spoiler reset button. This will cause the spoiler caution lamp to go out and will restore hydraulic pressure to the pair of spoilers that is locked down. If the malfunction still exists, the faulty spoiler will again extend and the previous sequence of events will be repeated. One attempt to reset a faulty spoiler is sufficient. In the event a spoiler extends because of a failure while roll autopilot is engaged, the wings must be held level by the pilot. Roll autopilot does not move the control stick and the pilots control stick corrective motion will be required to operate the monitor. When the pilot moves the control stick to hold wings level, the monitor will vote and the failed spoiler will be locked down as previously described. For deceleration during ground roll, the flight control spoilers are used as ground roll spoilers. In which case, they are controlled with the ground roll spoiler switch (refer to "Aerodynamic Deceleration Equipment," this section).

YAW CHANNEL.

Manual control of the aircraft in yaw is achieved by using conventional rudder and rudder pedals. Movement of the rudder pedals is transmitted to the rudder actuator control valve by a combination of control cables, push-pull tubes, and bellcranks. The control valve controls the flow of hydraulic fluid to the rudder actuator. The actuator moves the rudder in the direction commanded by the rudder pedal movement. Rudder authority is either of two configurations: 30 degree authority or 7½ degree (11¼ degree on airplanes ③) authority. In one configuration, rudder pedal travel is approximately 2½ inches, full pedal force is 86 pounds, and full rudder command is 30 degrees. In the other configuration, full rudder pedal travel is approximately one inch, and full rudder command is 7½ degrees (11¼ degrees on airplanes ③). Rudder authority configuration is determined by the position of either the control system switch (and slat position on airplane ③) or the rudder authority switch. Rudder breakout force is approximately 17 pounds and approximately 86 pounds is required to achieve the available pedal travel.

PITCH-ROLL MIXING.

Combined roll and pitch movements of the control stick are transmitted by the linkage of their respective channel to pitch-roll mixer assembly where they are combined and converted into left and right horizontal stabilizer actuator command signals. The mixer pitch channel input stops are set at 25 degrees up and 10 degrees (15 degrees on airplanes ③) down symmetrical horiozntal stabilizer command. The mixer roll channel input stops are set at ±8 degrees of differential horizontal stabilizer command. Therefore, the combined mixer stops limit individual actuator commands to 33 degrees up or 18 degrees (25 degrees on airplanes ⬛ ♦) down. However, the horizontal actuators are limited to 30 degrees trailing edge up and 15 degrees trailing edge down. Some of the excess horizontal stabilizer actuator command will be absorbed as overtravel within the valve spool when the pilot is commanding full pitch and roll. Any channel input command in excess of the pitch-roll mixer input stops will result in limiting of control stick motion.

STABILITY AUGMENTATION.

The stability augmentation system is triple redundant in that each pitch, roll, or yaw command generates three redundant signals. Each of the pitch, roll, and yaw channel electronics incorporates three signal selectors. Whenever a pitch, roll, or yaw command is generated, each of the three signal selectors for the particular channel, analyzes each of the three redundant signals. Through a process of majority logic voting, the signal selectors select the middle value signal and send three like signals to the appropriate damper servo. Should one of the three signals to the selectors become erroneous, the middle valve of the two good signals will be selected and three signals like it sent to the damper servo. Of the three signals sent to the damper servos, one is used by the damper as a model or standard against which the other two are compared. Should one of these signals be erroneous, it will be voted out by the damper logic circuitry.

Command Augmentation.

The effectiveness of the control surface varies with the flight conditions. At low speed and high altitude several degrees of elevator are required to command one g while at high speed and low altitude it may take less than a degree. Since stick force and surface movement are directly related to stick motion an unaugmented system will require heavy stick forces at low speed and very light forces during high speed low altitude flight. The "feel" would then vary continuously with flight conditions. The command augmentation system augments the control stick command through the damper. The damper moves directly proportional to the stick input (for a particular gain). This damper input is then reduced proportional to the resulting airplane response. At a flight condition where the control surface effectiveness is high the aircraft response will be large and the damper contribution will be reduced greatly. Likewise, in a low response flight condition, the damper contribution will not be reduced as much. The surface motion will then vary with flight conditions so that the resulting airplane response will always be very nearly the same for the stick force. The continuously adapting gain helps the system to approach the ideal of a constant stick force and aircraft response relationship.

Low Speed Trim Compensation. ⬛ ♦

A low speed trim compensation (LSTC) system is incorporated into the flight control system to provide increased low speed stability when flying the airplane in the landing configuration. The system is referenced at 9 degrees angle of attack and is activated when the slats are extended. As angle of attack is increased above 9 degrees, a signal is automatically sent to displace the pitch damper down. For a decrease in angle of attack the damper movement is up. Damper movement is one degree for each degree of angle of attack. The signal is faded into the damper gradually to reduce engage or disengage transients. The pilot must offset this damper movement with stick command in order to hold one g flight. The result is a more apparent change in stick force with speed variation

This page intentionally left blank.

(angle of attack) in the landing configuration. The system can be turned off by placing the flight control disconnect switch to the OVRD position.

Adverse Yaw Compensation. 31

An adverse yaw compensation (AYC) system is incorporated into the flight control system to enhance coordination in turns when flying the airplane in the landing configuration. The system is activated when the slats are extended. When the system is activated side slip angle, washed out yaw rate and roll rate signals are sent to the yaw damper. The roll rate signal gain increases proportionally to angle of attack and moves the rudder in the direction of the roll command. The side slip angle signal moves the rudder in the direction required to return side slip angle to zero. The system can be turned off by placing the flight control disconnect switch to the OVRD position.

Self-Adaptive Gain System.

The self-adaptive gains system continuously varies the gain of the signals sent to the pitch and roll damper servos, as flight conditions and aircraft configuration change, to optimize airplane response. Aircraft response is sensed and through the gain changer logic the gain is varied to optimize damping. Elevator effectiveness is affected by many variables such as mach, altitude, wing angle, gross weight, center of gravity, and external stores. A gain increase will compensate for reduced elevator effectiveness by giving more elevator for the same command thereby holding the aircraft response and damping nearly constant. The damping sensor and gain changer logic network are triple-redundant and the middle value gain is selected to gain adjust the three signals in the appropriate channel. The pitch and roll gains are reset to minimum when their respective damper switches are turned off. When the damper is turned on the gains may require as much as 7 minutes (2 minutes on airplanes 31) to increase to the optimum value. During this time the aircraft response and damping may be noticeably reduced. The pitch and roll gains are locked at the optimum value when in the take off and landing configuration. In very smooth air, on airplanes 31, the aircraft response to external disturbances is small so the sensor outputs are supplemented by a low amplitude pulse to improve gain changer performance.

Artificial Stall Warning System. 31

The artificial stall warning system shakes the rudder pedals to provide additional warning that the airplane is approaching a stall. The system is automatically activated when the airplane exceeds 19 ($\pm$1) degrees angle of attack with the slats extended.

TRIM.

Yaw Trim.

Yaw trim is accomplished by an electrically driven actuator which mechanically positions the rudder linkage. Since the yaw trim actuator is in series with the rudder linkage, there is no movement of the rudder pedals as trim is applied. Yaw trim is controlled by either of two rudder trim switches, one located on the auxiliary flight control panel and one located on the flight control test panel. Hardover yaw trim that will not respond to either of the rudder trim switches will require about 80 pounds of rudder pedal force to hold the rudder centered. In event of such a malfunction, the rudder authority switch is used to increase rudder pedal authority and reduce the required force to approximately 30 pounds.

Roll Trim.

Roll trim is accomplished through the roll damper servo. Roll trim command signals operate roll trim relays in the feel and trim assembly. The relays supply 26 volts ac to the roll trim integrator motor for manual control. The output of the roll trim integrator supplies a signal which is summed with the roll rate in the roll computer and sent to the roll damper servo which positions the horizontal stabilizer. Therefore roll trim commands a given roll rate rather than a given amount of control surface displacement. Since the output of the roll damper servo is in series with the roll channel linkage, the control stick does not move as trim is applied. Roll trim is controlled by trim buttons located on each control stick.

Pitch Trim.

Pitch Trim Series (Autotrim). Pitch series trim is incorporated into the system to automatically return the pitch damper to neutral, when operating in stability augmentation, to provide full damper authority at all times and to prevent damper disengage transients. Movement of the control stick sends command augmentation signals to the pitch damper causing the damper to displace. Damper displacement from neutral causes a slow movement of the series trim in the same direction. The series trim then replaces long term damper commands to the horizontal stabilizers allowing the pitch damper (and control stick) to return to and operate about neutral. Pitch damper motion for stability augmentation is too rapid to produce a significant change in the series trim position. The series trim is most effective in neutralizing pitch damper response to long term pilot commands during turns, speed changes and wing sweeping.

Manual Pitch Trim. Manual pitch trim is accomplished by either a pitch trim series actuator or a pitch trim parallel actuator. Pitch trim command signals operate pitch trim relays in the feel and trim assembly, thus supplying 115 volts ac to one of the pitch trim actuators. Output of the pitch trim parallel actuator causes the control stick to move as trim is applied. Output of the pitch trim series actuator does not cause the control stick to move. Manual pitch trim

Section I
Description & Operation

T.O. 1F-111A-1

is controlled by either a trim button on the control stick or by an auxiliary pitch trim switch (series trim) on the auxiliary flight control panel. The pitch trim configuration changes as a function of positions of the pitch damper switch, auxiliary pitch trim switch, and the control system switch. The configurations are as follows:

1. The pitch parallel trim actuator drives to neutral and is locked when:

    a. The pitch damper is off or:

    b. The auxiliary pitch trim switch is out of the stick position.

2. The pitch series trim actuator stops at its present position and no longer keeps the damper at neutral when:

    a. The pitch damper is turned off or:

    b. The control system switch is in T.O. & LAND or on airplanes ㉛ ♦ when the switch is in NORM and slats are extended.

When using the auxiliary pitch trim switch with the pitch damper on, pitch trim is applied by electrically positioning the pitch damper. The pitch trim series actuator is used for trim when the pitch damper is off by use of the stick trim button.

FLIGHT CONTROL SYSTEM CONTROLS AND INDICATORS.

Control Sticks.

The two control sticks, one located at each crewmember's station, are mechanically interconnected. Each stick grip (figure 1-21), contains a trim button, weapon release button, reference engage button, aerial refuel and nose wheel steering button, a gun trigger and an autopilot release lever. The control sticks also serve as a means of actuating the crew module bilge/flotation bag inflation pump. Refer to "Crew Module Escape System," this section.

Rudder Pedals.

Rudder control is provided by two sets of rudder pedals, one set located at each crewmember's station. The two sets of rudder pedals are mechanically interconnected and in addition to controlling the rudder, each pedal operates the respective wheel brake in the conventional manner.

Trim Button.

A trim button (2, figure 1-21), located on each control stick grip, is provided to control trim in the pitch and roll axes. The button has positions marked LWD, RWD, NOSE UP, NOSE DOWN, and is spring-loaded to the center unmarked OFF position. Moving the but-

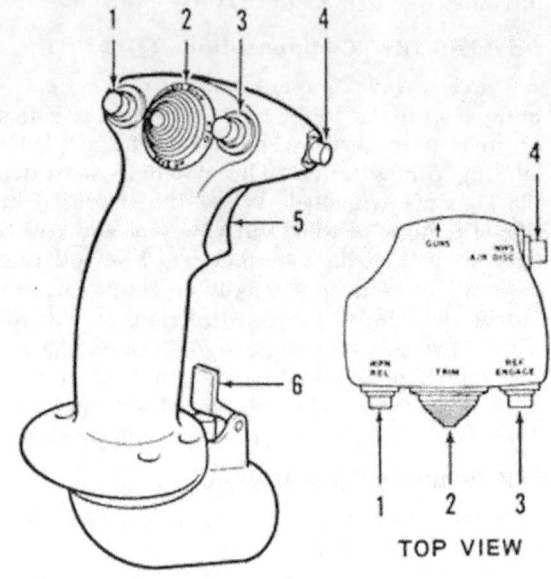

Control Sticks

1. Weapon Release Button.
2. Trim Button.
3. Reference Engage Button.
4. Aerial Refuel and Nose Wheel Steering Button.
5. Gun Trigger.
6. Autopilot Release Lever.

Figure 1-21.

ton to NOSE UP or NOSE DOWN causes the pitch trim actuator to position the horizontal stabilizer surfaces symmetrically with trailing edge either up or down as selected. Moving the button to LWD or RWD causes the roll damper servo to position the horizontal stabilizer surfaces asymmetrically as selected. The aircraft commander's trim button can always override the pilot's trim button control. Maximum travel of the horizontal stabilizer using the trim button is 10 degrees up and 8 degrees down through the parallel trim with the pitch damper on. Maximum command for roll trim using the trim button is equivalent to 32 degrees roll rate per second. The resultant horizontal stabilizer travel is, that travel required at the particular flight conditions to cause the airplane to roll at 32 degrees per second.

Auxiliary Pitch Trim Switch.

An auxiliary pitch trim switch (4, figure 1-22), with positions marked STICK, NOSE DN, NOSE UP, and OFF, is located on the center console. The switch is provided to control the pitch trim series actuator. When the switch is in the STICK position, pitch trim signals can be commanded only by the trim buttons on the control sticks. When the switch is held in NOSE DN or NOSE UP position, the pitch trim series actua-

1-50

Changed 18 August 1967

Auxiliary Flight Control Panel

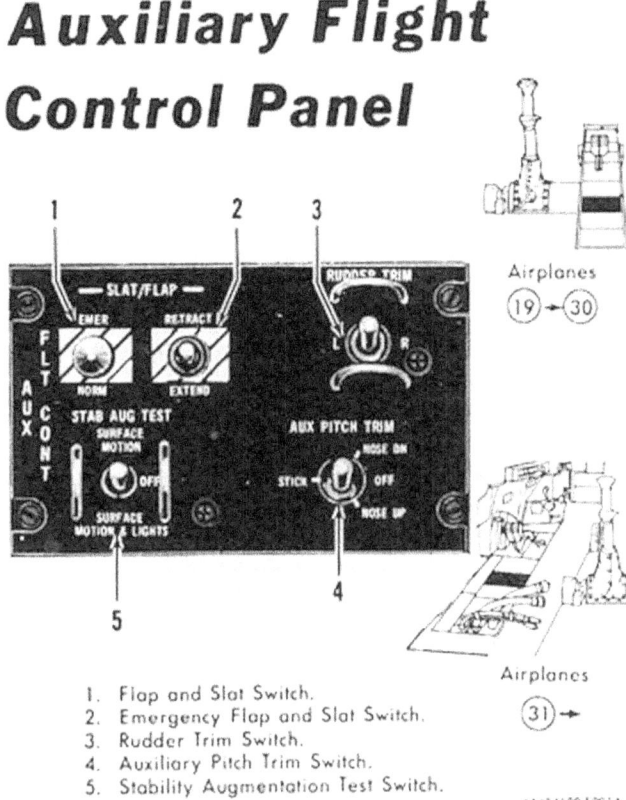

1. Flap and Slat Switch.
2. Emergency Flap and Slat Switch.
3. Rudder Trim Switch.
4. Auxiliary Pitch Trim Switch.
5. Stability Augmentation Test Switch.

Figure 1-22.

tor and the pitch damper move the horizontal stabilizer symmetrically as selected until the switch is released to OFF or the limits are reached. With the switch in the OFF, NOSE DN, or NOSE UP position, the trim buttons on the the control sticks are inoperative. When the switch is not in the STICK position, the roll trim command is zero and roll trim cannot be commanded from the control stick trim button.

Rudder Trim Switches.

Two rudder trim switches (3, figure 1-22 and 1, figure 1-23), located on the flight control switch panel and auxiliary flight control panel respectively, are provided for rudder trim control. The switches have positions marked L and R and are spring-loaded to the center unmarked OFF position. Holding either switch in L or R causes the rudder trim actuator to drive the rudder in the selected direction until the switch is released to OFF or a maximum deflection of 7½ degrees (11¼ degrees on airplanes ③① ♦) is reached. On airplanes ③① ♦ the rudder trim switch (1, figure 1-23), located on the flight control switch panel, has been deleted.

Takeoff Trim Test Button.

The takeoff trim test button (22, figure 1-6 or 26, figure 1-6A), is located on the left main instrument panel.

When the button is depressed, the takeoff trim relay is energized; the pitch parallel trim and yaw trim actuators are driven to 0 degrees; the roll trim integrator is synchronized so that the output to the roll damper is zero; the auxiliary pitch trim integrator is driven to a null; and the pitch trim series actuator is driven to a noseup position of 3.8 degrees.

Autopilot/Damper Switches.

Three switches, one each for the pitch, roll, and yaw channels, are located on the autopilot/damper panel. The pitch and roll damper switches (1, figure 1-24) are three position switches marked AUTOPILOT, DAMPER and OFF and are solenoid held in the AUTOPILOT and OFF positions and are spring-loaded to the DAMPER position. The yaw damper switch (2, figure 1-24) is a two position switch marked DAMPER and OFF. It is solenoid held in the OFF position and is spring-loaded to the DAMPER position. Placing any of the switches to DAMPER turns the respective damper on. The pitch and roll channels come on with the automatic gain at a low value and then begin setting the correct gain for that flight condition. Placing either the pitch or roll switch to AUTOPILOT will engage autopilot attitude stabilization. Placing a

Flight Control Switch Panel

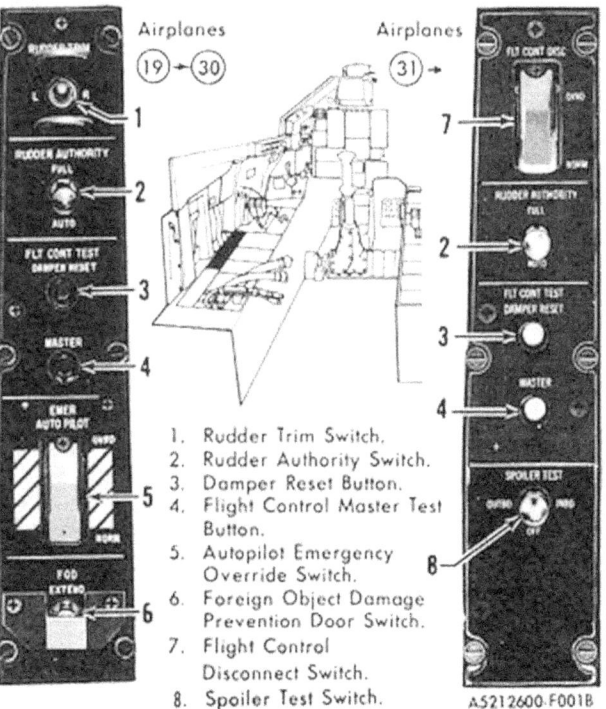

1. Rudder Trim Switch.
2. Rudder Authority Switch.
3. Damper Reset Button.
4. Flight Control Master Test Button.
5. Autopilot Emergency Override Switch.
6. Foreign Object Damage Prevention Door Switch.
7. Flight Control Disconnect Switch.
8. Spoiler Test Switch.

Figure 1-23.

Section I
Description & Operation

T.O. 1F-111A-1

Autopilot Damper Panel

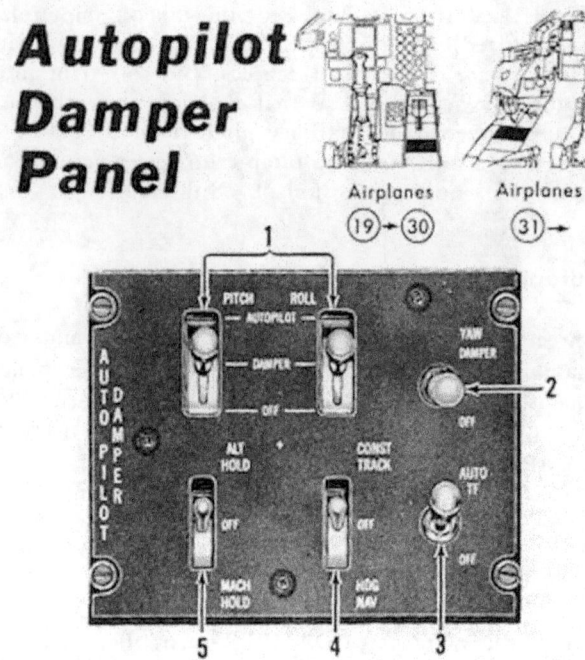

1. Pitch and Roll Autopilot Damper Switches.
2. Yaw Damper Switch.
3. Auto Terrain Following Switch.
4. Constant Track/Heading Nav Selector Switch.
5. Altitude Hold/Mach Hold Selector Switch.

Figure 1-24.

switch to OFF disengages the damper system of the respective channel and causes the respective damper caution lamp to light. These switches are also used to engage the autopilot. For description of that function, refer to "Autopilot System," this section.

Auto Terrain Following Switch.

The auto terrain following (auto TF) switch (3, figure 1-24), located on the autopilot/damper panel, is a two position lever lock switch marked AUTO TF and OFF. The switch is locked in the OFF position and must be pulled out to move from OFF to AUTO TF. When the switch is in the OFF position and either TFR channel mode selector knob is in the TF position, the airplane must be flown manually using the pitch steering commands on the ADI and LCOS to hold the terrain clearance selected on the TFR terrain clearance knob. With the switch in the OFF position the reference not engaged lamp will remain on. When the switch is placed to the AUTO TF position and either TFR channel mode selector knob is in the TF position signals from the TFR will control the pitch damper to automatically hold the airplane on the terrain clearance setting selected by the TFR terrain clearance knob. With the switch in AUTO TF the reference not engaged lamp will go out.

Note

When auto TF is selected at least one TFR channel must be in the TF mode or the fly-up off caution lamp and the reference not engaged lamp will light.

Should the TFR fail with the switch in either the OFF or AUTO TF position, the TF failure warning lamp will light, a 2g (incremental) fly-up signal will be sent to the pitch damper and the pitch steering bars on the ADI and LCOS will indicate a fly-up command. The fly-up signal can be interrupted by depressing and holding the auto-pilot release lever. The malfunctioning TRF channel must be turned off to get rid of the fly-up signal when operating with the auto TF switch in the OFF position. If the auto TF switch is in the AUTO TF position it must be placed to OFF before turning off the malfunctioning TFR channel to get rid of the fly-up signal. For additional information on the auto TF switch refer to "Terrain Following Radar," this section.

Damper Reset Button.

The damper reset button (3, figure 1-23), located on the flight control switch panel, is a momentary pushbutton switch labeled DAMPER RESET. When the button is depressed, the pitch, roll and yaw damper caution lamps and their respective channel caution lamps on the main caution lamp panel will go out and the dampers and their respective electronic channels will be simultaneously reset to accept inputs for logic voting. If a malfunction is present at the time the reset button is released, the appropriate caution lamps will light.

Rudder Authority Switch.

The rudder authority switch (2, figure 1-23), located on the flight control switch panel, has positions marked FULL and AUTO. When the switch is in AUTO, full rudder authority of 30 degrees either side of center is available provided the flight control system switch is in T.O. & LAND or rudder authority of 7½ degrees either side of center if the control system switch is in NORM. On airplanes 31 ♦ when the rudder authority switch is in the AUTO position, full rudder authority of 30 degrees either side of center is available when the control system switch is in the T.O. & LAND position or NORM position and the slats are extended. With the switch in AUTO and the control system switch is in NORM with the slats retracted, 11¼ degrees of rudder either side of center is available. When the rudder authority switch is in the FULL position, full rudder authority is available regardless of the position of the control system switch in either configuration.

Changed 18 August 1967

Flight Control System Switch.

The flight control system switch (2, figure 1-16), located on the landing gear control panel, is a two position switch marked T.O. & LAND and NORM. When the switch is placed in the T.O. & LAND position the following occurs: the rudder variable authority actuator moves to the 30 degree authority position, the TFR fly-up signals to the pitch damper are locked out, the pitch and roll computer gains are driven to preset values (roll gain—100 percent, pitch gain—30 percent), and the pitch series trim actuator is locked. The T.O. & LAND position is used when the airplane is in the take off or landing configuration with landing gear down and wing slats and flaps extended. When the switch is placed to the NORM position the following occurs: the pitch damper will respond to TFR fly-up signals, the pitch and roll gains are automatically determined by the flight control computers as flight conditions change, the pitch series trim actuator is unlocked and the rudder authority actuator moves to the 7½ degree position. The NORM position is used during inflight operations when the airplane is in the clean configuration with landing gear, slats and flaps retracted. On airplanes ❸❶ ♦ the NORM position is used at all times and the position of the slats determines which set of functions are available. With the slats extended all of the takeoff and land functions are automatically provided. With the slats retracted all of the inflight (clean configuration) functions are provided except rudder authority is 11¼ degrees left or right of center. On these airplanes the T.O. & LAND position is used only in the event of malfunction.

WARNING

On airplanes ❶❾ ♦ ❸⓪ a malfunction in the flight control computer, caused by a grounded circuit, can produce a 2 "g" fly-up command to the pitch damper. This can occur with the flight control system switch in T.O. & LAND or NORM and no lamp indications will result. The TFR does not have to be on. The fly-up may be offset by forward stick movement, manual trim or by turning the pitch damper OFF.

Flight Control Master Test Button.

The flight control master test button (4, figure 1-23), located on the flight control switch panel, provides a source of power to the flight control test switches and buttons on the ground check panel, to the CADC test switch on the ground check panel, to the stability augmentation test switch on the auxiliary flight control panel and to the spoiler test switch on the flight control switch panel. Depressing the button closes a switch, thus allowing power to be applied to the flight control test switches and buttons. When the button is released, these switches and buttons are inoperable.

This page intentionally left blank.

Stability Augmentation Test Switch.

The stability augmentation test switch (5, figure 1-22), located on the auxiliary flight control panel, is a three position switch marked SURFACE MOTION, SURFACE MOTION & LIGHTS with an unmarked center OFF position. This switch, when used in conjunction with the control system switch and the flight control master test button, provides a means of ground checking the stability augmentation system. With the flight control system switch in NORM and the master test button depressed, selecting the following positions of the stability augmentation test switch will obtain the results as indicated:

Note

Takeoff trim must be set immediately prior to performing both portions of this check.

1. SURFACE MOTION:
   a. Right horizontal stabilizer trailing edge moves full down
   b. Left stabilizer trailing edge moves down slightly
   c. Rudder trailing edge moves right then left.
2. SURFACE MOTION & LIGHTS:
   a. Same horizontal stabilizer motion as items 1(a) and (b) above.
   b. Rudder trailing edge moves right and back to neutral.
   c. Three (3) damper and three (3) channel caution lamps light
   d. The roll and pitch gain changer caution lamps will light.

Spoiler Reset Button.

The spoiler reset button (7, figure 1-19), located on the crew module left sidewall, is a momentary pushbutton labeled SPOILER RESET. The button is provided to reset the spoiler monitor in the event that a malfunction has caused a pair of spoilers to be voted out and locked down. If a pair of spoilers has been locked down and the spoiler caution lamp is lighted, depressing the spoiler reset button will cause the caution lamp to go out and the spoiler circuitry to be reset to accept signals from the spoiler transducers. If the malfunction still exists the faulty spoiler will again extend and the corrective control stick motion will cause the spoilers to again lock down and the spoiler caution lamp to light.

Spoiler Test Switch.

The spoiler test switch (8, figure 1-23), located on the flight control switch panel, is a three position switch marked OUTBD, OFF and INBD. The switch is used in conjunction with the flight control master test button to ground check the operation of the spoilers. With the switch in OUTBD, depressing the master test button will cause the outboard pair of spoilers to extend momentarily and then lock down and the spoiler caution lamp will light. Depressing the spoiler reset button or placing the spoiler test switch to OFF will return the spoilers to operation and the spoiler caution lamp will go out. The INBD position of the switch is used to make the same check of the inboard spoilers. If the spoiler switch is moved from OUTBD to INBD (or vice versa) before the reset button is depressed the first pair of spoilers lock down will be returned to operation, however the caution will remain on.

Computer Power Switches.

The computer power switches (16, figure 1-25) labeled NO 1, NO 2, and NO 3 are located on the ground check panel. When any one of the switches is placed in the UP position, activating power is applied to the selected branch in each pitch, roll, and yaw computer. The switches are held in this position when the door to the panels is closed.

Damper Servo Button.

The damper servo button (15, figure 1-25), labeled DMPR SERVO, is located on the ground check panel. When the damper servo, rate gyro channel B and channel C buttons and flight control test master switch are depressed and held, the electrical power to valve No. 1 on each damper servo is interrupted, resulting in an electrical command signal from each computer, causing the damper servos to vote hydraulically. This causes the pitch, roll, and yaw damper and channel caution lamps to light.

Rate Gyro Test Buttons.

The rate gyro test buttons (CHAN A, CHAN B, and CHAN C) (14, figure 1-25), are located on the ground check panel. When two or more of the buttons are depressed in conjunction with the flight control master test button, the respective rate gyros are torqued, resulting in a predetermined displacement of the primary flight control surfaces. The CHAN A button, when depressed, torques the "A" gyros in the pitch, roll, and yaw channels. The CHAN B and CHAN C buttons, when depressed, torque their respective gyros.

Control Surface Position Indicator.

The control surface position indicator (19A, figure 1-6A), located on the left main instrument panel, is composed of three separate sets of indicators which provide indications of the positions of the spoilers, rudder and horizontal tail (horizontal stabilizer). The position of the spoilers is indicated on four flip-flop type indicators, two for the left and two for the right spoilers. When the spoilers are retracted the letters DN appear in each indicator. As the spoilers extend the indicators become blank. Rudder position is provided by a pointer on a scale, 30 degrees (L) left or (R) right of zero. The scale is graduated in 5 degree increments. The position of the horizontal stabilizers

Section I
Description & Operation

T.O. 1F-111A-1

Ground Check Panel

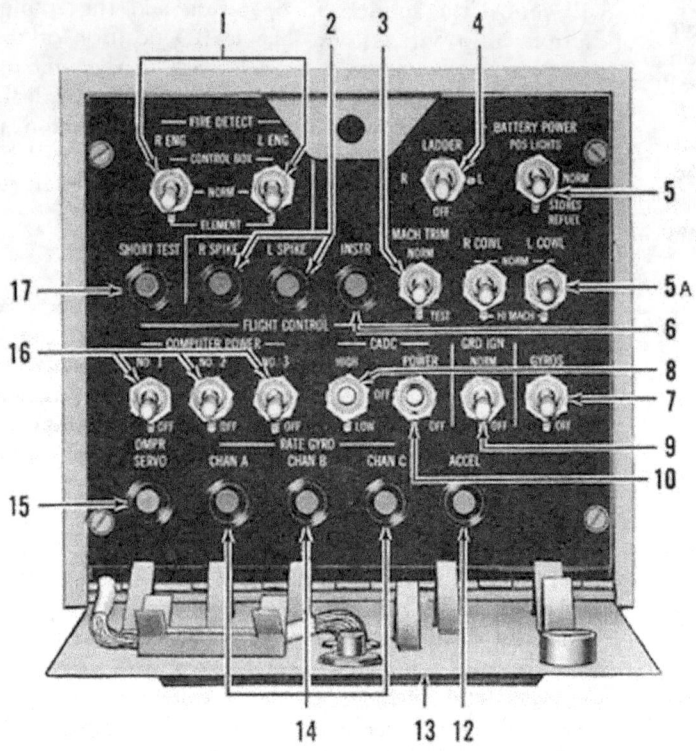
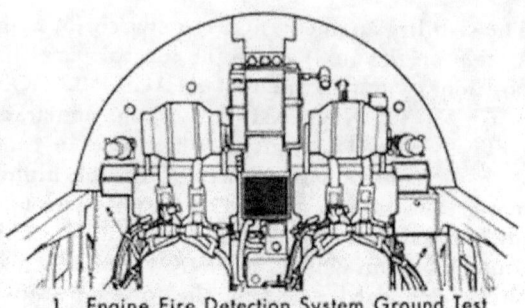

1. Engine Fire Detection System Ground Test Switches (2).
2. Spike Ground Check Switches (2).
3. Mach Trim Test Switch.
4. Entrance Ladder Switch.
5. Position Lights/Stores Refuel Battery Power Switch.
5A. Translating Cowl Test Switches.
6. Instrument Test Switch.
7. AFRS Power Switch.
8. CADC Test Switch.
9. Ignition Cutoff Switch.
10. CADC Power Switch.
11. Deleted.
12. Accelerometer Test Button.
13. Ground Check Panel Access Door.
14. Rate Gyro Test Buttons (3).
15. Damper Servo Button.
16. Computer Power Switches (3).
17. Engine Fire Detection System Short Test Button.

Figure 1-25.

is indicated by two pointers, marked L and R, on a scale, 30 degrees up and 20 degrees down. The scale is graduated in 2 degree increments. An index mark mounted on the axis of the left pointer provides indications of left or right wing down (LWD or RWD) against a scale mounted on the axis of the right pointer. In this manner asymmetric stabilizer position indications also provide left or right wing down indications.

Takeoff Trim Indicator Lamp.

A takeoff trim indicator lamp (21, figure 1-6 or 25, figure 1-6A), located on the left main instrument panel, is provided to indicate when the horizontal stabilizer and rudder are in the proper trim position for takeoff and the auxiliary pitch trim integrator is zeroed. When the takeoff trim button is depressed and all affected surfaces reach their proper position, the lamp lights. When the takeoff trim button is released, the lamp goes out.

Roll, Pitch, and Yaw Channel Caution Lamps.

Three amber caution lamps, one each for the roll, pitch, and yaw channels, are located on the main caution lamp panel (figure 1-29 or 1-29A). Lighting of any one of the lamps indicates that a malfunction has been sensed in the computer of the respective roll, pitch or yaw channel. Since the electronics in each channel is triple redundant, lighting of one of these caution lamps indicates that one of the three sets of electronics is in error (passive first failure) and does not indicate a complete failure.

Roll, Pitch, and Yaw Damper Caution Lamps.

Three amber caution lamps, one each for the roll, pitch, and yaw dampers, are located on the main caution lamp panel (figure 1-29 or 1-29A). Lighting of any one of the lamps indicates that a malfunction has been sensed in its respective damper. Since each damper has two active valves and a model valve, lighting of one of the caution lamps does not indicate a complete damper failure.

Flight Control Spoiler Caution Lamp.

The flight control spoiler caution lamp, located on the main caution lamp panel (figure 1-29 or 1-29A), is provided to indicate when a malfunction in the spoiler circuitry has occurred causing a symmetric pair of flight control spoilers to be locked down. On airplanes ❸❶ ♦ the lamp is also used in conjunction with the spoiler test switch when ground checking spoiler operation. Refer to spoiler test switch this section.

1-54
Changed 18 August 1967

Roll and Pitch Gain Changer Caution Lamps.

Two amber gain changer caution lamps, one each for the roll and pitch gain changer, are located on the main caution lamp panel (figure 1-29 or 1-29A). Lighting of either of these lamps indicates that a portion of the triple redundant gain setting in the respective channel is in error. Depressing the damper reset button will reset the lamp for a temporary error. Since the gain changer circuitry in each channel is triple redundant, lighting of one of these caution lamps indicates that one of these three sets of electronics is in error and does not indicate a complete failure. On airplanes ❸❶ ♦ the lamps also indicate a disagreement between the position of the control system switch and slats and the configuration of the flight control system. This will occur when the landing gear handle is in the DN position and the flight control system is not in the take off and land configuration or when the slats are retracted and the flight control system is in the take off and land configuration.

Rudder Authority Caution Lamp.

An amber rudder authority caution lamp (figure 1-29 or 1-29A), is located on the main caution lamp panel. Lighting of the lamp indicates the rudder authority actuator is not in the position commanded by the control system switch. On airplanes ❸❶ ♦ the lamp will also light if rudder authority does not switch to full when the slats are extended or to 11¼ degrees when the slats are retracted with the control system switch in the NORM position.

AUTOPILOT SYSTEM.

The autopilot system consists of electronic circuitry that, in conjunction with the primary flight control system, controls the aircraft during the four modes of autopilot flight. The autopilot system receives input signals from other systems and computes command signals to the pitch and roll dampers to control the aircraft. The autopilot modes are attitude stabilization, mach hold, altitude hold, heading nav, and constant track. Incompatible autopilot mode selection is prevented by circuit interlocks. Attitude stabilization is normally in effect when the autopilot is engaged. Attitude stabilization will hold the aircraft at the reference roll and/or pitch attitude until selection of another autopilot mode or until pilot initiation of control stick steering. The aircraft may be manually maneuvered at any time by use of control stick steering without disengaging the autopilot. During operation of the autopilot, the control stick will not follow the movement of the surfaces. Pitch autopilot disengage transients are reduced by the pitch series trim actuator. Engage transients are prevented by continuous synchronization of the pitch and roll attitude input signals so that their commands to the dampers are zero at the time of autopilot engagement.

ATTITUDE STABILIZATION MODE.

The attitude stabilization mode is the initial control mode established when the autopilot is engaged. Attitude stabilization can be engaged in either or both the roll and pitch channels. Attitude reference signals are received by the pitch and/or roll computers from the bomb nav system. Resultant signals from the pitch and/or roll computer then control the pitch and/or roll damper position, thus holding the aircraft at the reference attitude existing at the time of autopilot engagement; however, roll angles of less than 3 (±1) degrees will result in a wings level attitude command upon engagement of this mode. If the constant track mode is selected, the roll damper will control the aircraft according to the new reference. However, when the constant track mode is discontinued, the autopilot will revert back to attitude stabilization and will maintain the attitude that existed at the time of disengagement. For example, if pitch and roll autopilot are engaged with the aircraft in a twenty-degree bank, this bank angle will be held. If the constant track mode is then selected, the aircraft will respond by returning to the selected ground track. The original pitch attitude will continue to be controlled by attitude stabilization and will remain unchanged. If the constant track mode is subsequently discontinued, the autopilot will revert back to attitude stabilization in roll. The pilot may change the attitude stabilization pitch and roll references at any time by using control stick steering on airplanes ❶❾ ♦ ❸❶. The mode selector knob on the bomb nav control panel must be in one of its primary modes. The autopilot emergency override switch (flight control disconnect switch ❸❶ ♦) must be in NORM to engage the autopilot.

MACH HOLD MODE.

The mach hold mode maintains constant mach. In this mode, throttle position is fixed and mach is controlled by aircraft pitch attitude through operation of the horizontal stabilizer surfaces. Upon engagement of this mode, a mach reference is set up in the central air data computer (CADC). Any deviation of mach from this reference results in an error signal being sent to the pitch computer from the CADC. If mach increases above the reference, the resulting mach error signal will command a nose up attitude through the pitch damper causing the aircraft to return to the referenced mach number. An opposite command is used for a decrease in mach.

ALTITUDE HOLD MODE.

The altitude hold mode automatically maintains constant altitude. Upon engagement of this mode, an altitude reference is established in the central air data computer (CADC). Any deviation in altitude by the aircraft results in an altitude error being fed to the pitch computer from the CADC. If the aircraft altitude increases above the reference, the resulting altitude error signal will command a nose down attitude through the pitch damper until the desired altitude is obtained. An opposite command is given for a decrease in altitude.

CONSTANT TRACK MODE.

The constant track mode maintains the airplane on a constant ground track. When this mode is engaged, the existing ground track is sensed in the bomb nav system and is set up as a mode reference. Any deviation from this reference by the aircraft results in an error signal being sent from the bomb nav system to the roll computer. The roll computer, in turn, sends a command to the roll damper, correcting the deviation.

HEADING NAVIGATION MODE.

When operating in the heading (nav) navigation mode the roll computer receives steering error signals from the bomb nav system to steer the airplane to a preset destination set into the bomb nav system destination counters. The steering error signal is obtained by comparing the actual ground track with the computer course from present position to destination. The computed course may be either great circle or short range (direct), depending on the position of the bomb nav mode selector knob. The roll computer, in turn, sends commands to the roll damper to turn the airplane to fly to the destination. The error signal is displayed on the ADI by selecting the NAV position with the instrument system coupler mode selector knob.

CONTROL STICK STEERING.

When any autopilot mode is engaged, including basic attitude stabilization, the reference controlling the aircraft can be disengaged by use of control stick steering. Control stick steering is activated in the pitch channel by applying a force greater than 1.7 pounds, in a forward or aft direction, to the top of the control stick. This mode is activated in the roll channel by applying a force of 1.3 pounds laterally to the control stick. When this force is applied in either or both channels, the reference or references are disengaged. The reference not engaged lamp will light, and the pilot can maneuver the aircraft to a new reference. When the force to the control stick is reduced below 1.7 pounds in the pitch channel or 1.3 pounds in the roll channel, attitude stabilization will automatically reengage in the affected channel or channels provided the attitude limits are not exceeded, and the reference not engaged lamp will go out. The reference engage button must be depressed to reengage sub-modes. The attitude limits are ± 30 degrees in pitch and ± 60 degrees in roll. Should these limits be exceeded in one or both channels, attitude stabilization will not re-engage in that channel until its attitude angle is reduced to less than

its limit. In addition, the roll channel cannot be engaged if either the pitch attitude is greater than ± 30 degrees or the yaw damper is turned OFF.

CONTROLS AND INDICATORS.

Computer Power Switches.

Three computer power switches (16, figure 1-25), located on the ground check panel, control electrical power for autopilot and certain flight control system operations. (Refer to "Flight Control System," this section). The autopilot is normally ready to engage after the power switches are placed in the ON position and the stabilized platform of the bomb nav system is properly erected.

Autopilot/Damper Switches.

Two autopilot/damper switches (1, figure 1-24), one each for pitch and roll, are located on the autopilot/damper panel. The switches have three positions marked AUTOPILOT, DAMPER, and OFF and are solenoid held by 28 volt dc power in the AUTOPILOT and OFF position and are spring-loaded to the DAMPER position. If while operating in the AUTOPILOT or OFF positions, this 28 volt dc holding power is lost, the switches will return to the DAMPER position. The switches operate independently of each other. When the switches are in the AUTOPILOT position, attitude stabilization is engaged and the airplane will maintain constant attitude. When the switches are moved to DAMPER or OFF, all other mode switches will move to OFF and the airplane will then revert to pilot-controlled flight. The pitch autopilot switch will return to DAMPER when the auto TF switch is positioned to AUTO TF. For additional information on these switches, as related to control of the roll and pitch dampers, refer to "Flight Control System," this section.

Constant Track/Heading Nav Mode Selector Switch.

The constant track/heading nav mode selector switch (4, figure 1-24) located on the autopilot/damper panel, is a three position switch marked CONST TRACK, OFF and HDG NAV. The switch is solenoid held by 28 volt dc power to CONST TRACK or HDG NAV and is spring-loaded to OFF. When the switch is placed in the CONST TRACK position and the reference engage button is depressed, the airplane will be held on a constant ground track. When the switch is placed in the HDG NAV position and the reference engage button is depressed, the airplane will be held on the course to the destination set in the bomb nav system. The switch will not latch in the CONST TRACK or HDG NAV positions unless the roll autopilot/damper switch is in the AUTOPILOT position. If while operating in CONST TRACK or HDG NAV position, 28 volt dc power to the holding solenoid is lost, the switch will return to the OFF position. The reference not engaged lamp will not light for this malfunction. When the switch is positioned to OFF, the autopilot will discontinue controlling the airplane in a constant track or heading nav mode and will revert to attitude stabilization in the roll channel.

Altitude Hold/Mach Hold Selector Switch.

The altitude hold/mach hold selector switch (5, figure 1-24), located on the autopilot/damper panel, is a three position switch marked ALT HLD, OFF, and MACH HLD. The switch is solenoid held by 28 volt dc power to ALT HLD or MACH HLD and is spring-loaded to OFF. When the switch is in the ALT HLD position and the reference engage button is depressed, the autopilot will control the airplane to maintain the altitude present at the time the mode was engaged. When the switch is positioned to MACH HLD and the reference engage button is depressed, the autopilot will control the airplane to maintain the mach number present at the time of mode engagement. The switch will not latch in either ALT HLD or MACH HLD position if the pitch autopilot/damper switch is not in AUTOPILOT position. Selection of AUTO TF position on the auto terrain following switch is incompatible with altitude hold or mach hold mode and will cause the switch to move to the OFF position. If while operating in MACH HLD or ALT HLD positions, 28 volt dc power to the holding relay is lost, the switch will return to the OFF position. The reference not engaged lamp will not light for this malfunction.

Reference Engage Buttons.

A reference engage button (3, figure 1-21), marked REF ENGAGE is located on each control stick grip. When any autopilot mode is selected, other than attitude stabilization, one of the reference engage buttons must be depressed before the mode will engage. Either button may be used to engage the autopilot.

Autopilot Release Lever.

The autopilot release lever (6, figure 1-21), located at the base of the stick grip, permits either pilot to disengage certain functions of the autopilot without removing his hand from the stick. Depressing the lever will return the autopilot/damper switches to DAMPER. This disengages all autopilot functions and places the airplane under pilot control. When the airplane is being flown on TFR the 2g climb command that is generated, should the TFR fail, can be interrupted by depressing the autopilot release lever. The command will reappear, however, when the lever is released unless the TFR system is turned off.

Autopilot Emergency Override Switch.

The autopilot emergency override switch (5, figure 1-23), located on the flight control switch panel, has positions marked NORM and OVRD. The switch is guarded to the NORM position. If the switch is positioned to OVRD, certain inputs are removed from the roll and pitch damper systems. These signals are roll and pitch autopilot commands, roll trim commands, pitch damper trim inputs and the TF fly-up signal. The switch disconnects these command signals from the roll and pitch damper channels and causes the reference not engaged caution lamp to light. On airplanes 31 ♦ plus T.O. 1F-111A-518, the switch is labeled FLT CONT DISC (flight control disconnect) and the location of the switch is changed on the flight control switch panel (8, figure 1-23). On these airplanes the OVRD position also turns off low speed trim and adverse yaw compensation. The positions and functions of the switch remain unchanged.

Reference Not Engaged Caution Lamp.

The reference not engaged caution lamp (5, figure 1-6), located on the left main instrument panel, will light under the following conditions:

- When the autopilot/damper switches are in the AUTOPILOT position and control stick steering is being used.

- When any autopilot mode (altitude hold, mach hold, constant track or heading nav) is selected and the reference engage button has not been depressed.

Note

The use of control stick steering after any autopilot mode has been engaged will result in the mode being disengaged and the lamp will light and remain on until the reference engage button is depressed again.

- When either TFR channel mode selector knob is in the TF position and the auto TF switch is OFF. When the auto TF switch is in AUTO TF and neither TFR channel mode selector knob is in the TF position.

- When the emergency autopilot switch (flight control disconnect switch 31 ♦) is placed to the OVRD (override) position.

On airplanes 31 ♦ the letters REF NOT ENGAGED are visible in the face of the lamp when lighted.

AUTOPILOT OPERATION.

Engaging the Autopilot.

1. Bomb nav mode selector knob—Primary mode. The bomb nav system must be in a primary mode for autopilot operation.
2. ADI—Check for normal indications.
3. Attain a safe altitude and trim the airplane to the desired attitude.

Note

Autopilot operation cannot be engaged at attitudes exceeding ±30 degrees in pitch and ±60 degrees in roll.

4. Pitch, roll autopilot/damper and yaw damper switches—DAMPER.

    Check that all dampers are operating properly.

5. Flight instrument reference select knob—PRI.
6. Roll and pitch autopilot/damper switches—AUTOPILOT.
7. Reference not engaged caution lamp—Out. Check that the reference not engaged caution lamp goes out with no force applied to the control stick.

Selecting the Autopilot Control Modes.

After the autopilot is initially engaged in attitude stabilization, the pilot may select a single control mode or a combination of compatible modes by means of the mode switches on the autopilot/damper panel. A mode affecting the pitch channel (mach hold or altitude hold) may be selected simultaneously with a mode affecting the roll channel (constant track or heading nav). However, two modes in the same channel cannot be selected simultaneously.

Note

The autopilot will stabilize on the desired reference mach or altitude more rapidly when the initial conditions of power and attitude are established prior to engaging the respective mode. After the engage transients have subsided the autopilot should hold altitude within ±60 feet and speed within ±0.01 mach under all conditions.

The following procedures are for selecting each control mode after attitude stabilization has been engaged.

Selecting the Mach Hold Mode. Manually maneuver the aircraft to achieve the desired mach number.

1. Mach hold/altitude hold switch—MACH HLD.
2. Reference engage button—Depress.
   If it is desired to increase or decrease the reference mach number, it will be necessary to disengage this mode while the desired change to airspeed is made.

Selecting the Altitude Hold Mode. Manually maneuver the aircraft to the desired altitude by using control stick steering.

1. Mach hold/altitude hold switch—ALT HLD.
2. Reference engage button—Depress.
   If it is desired to increase or decrease the reference altitude, use control stick steering to maneuver the aircraft to the new reference and depress the reference engage button.

Selecting the Constant Track Mode. Manually maneuver the aircraft until it is following the desired ground track.

1. Constant track switch—CONSTANT.
2. Reference engage button—Depress.
   If it is desired to change course, use control stick steering to maneuver the aircraft until the new ground track is established. Release the force to the stick and depress the reference engage button.

Selecting the Heading Nav Mode.

1. Destination counters—Set.
2. Fix mode TARGET selector button—Depress.
3. Instrument system coupler mode selector knob —NAV.
4. Constant track/heading nav mode selector switch—HDG NAV.
5. Reference engage button—Momentarily depress.
   If a steering error is present when the reference engage button is depressed this will result in an immediate bank correction.

Disengaging the Autopilot.

To disengage all autopilot functions and place the aircraft under pilot control, either depress the autopilot release lever or place the pitch and roll autopilot/damper switches to DAMPER. In either case, all the switches will move to OFF.

CENTRAL AIR DATA COMPUTER SYSTEM (CADC).

The airplane is equipped with a central air data computer system which provides aerodynamic intelligence to various control systems. The system consists basically of an electromechanical computer which processes raw data from the angle-of-attack transducer, pitot-static probe, and a temperature sensor probe located on the right side of the fuselage above the nose wheel well. The computer utilizes the following raw data: indicated static pressure, pitot pressure, total temperature, and indicated angle of attack. When this data reaches the computer, it is transformed into electrical signal outputs through an arrangement of transducers, mechanical linkage, and servo repeaters. The central air data computer is equipped with a failure monitoring system which continually monitors the computing functions. Should a computing function fail, a CADC caution lamp (CADS caution lamp on airplanes 🛈 ♦) on the main caution lamp panel will light. If a computing function should fail, which affects the pressure altitude or indicated airspeed displays on the integrated flight instrument system, a warning flag will appear on the associated instrument. In addition, mach, angle-of-attack, and pressure altitude data good signals are supplied from the CADC monitor system to be used as failure monitor interlocks for terrain following radar, and the flight director computer system respectively. The computer requires

115 volt ac and 28 volt dc power. Listed below are the various airplane systems served by the air data computer system, followed in parentheses by the computer outputs which go to the systems:

1. Altitude-vertical velocity indicator (pressure altitude and vertical velocity).
2. Airspeed mach indicator (mach number, indicated airspeed, true wing angle of attack).
3. Maximum safe mach assembly (pressure altitude, mach number, true air temperature).
4. Flight control system (angle of attack, incremental mach number and incremental LOG static pressure).
5. Translating cowl (mach number).
6. Engine fuel control unit (mach number).
7. Deleted.
8. Spike caution lamp (mach number).
9. Bomb nav system (pressure altitude, pressure altitude rate, true airspeed).
10. True airspeed indicator (true airspeed).
11. Lead computing optical sight (pressure altitude, total pressure, true airspeed).
12. Terrain following radar (true body angle of attack, true airspeed).
13. Angle-of-attack indexer (true wing angle of attack).
14. Environmental control (indicated airspeed, true air temperature).
15. Deleted.
16. Flight director (incremental pressure altitude and pressure altitude).
17. Landing gear warning (indicated airspeed, pressure altitude).
18. Marker beacon (pressure altitude).

CADC POWER SWITCH.

The CADC power switch (10, figure 1-25), with positions POWER and OFF, is located on the ground check panel. When the switch is in the OFF position, no aircraft power is supplied to the CADC or the maximum safe mach assembly. Also the CADC caution lamp (CADS caution lamp on airplanes ③① ▶) will light and the OFF warning flags in the airspeed indicator and altimeter will appear. When placed in the POWER position 115 volt, 400 cycle, single phase ac power is supplied to the CADC and the maximum safe mach assembly.

CADC TEST SWITCH.

The CADC test switch (8, figure 1-25), with positions HIGH, OFF, and LOW, is located on the ground check panel. The switch is spring-loaded to the OFF position. The switch, when used in conjunction with the flight control master test button, activates a self test system in the CADC. The normal system inputs are disconnected from the CADC, and a set of pre-selected test inputs are fed into the CADC. The HIGH position of the switch is used in conjunction with the pitot heater switch to ground check the total temperature probe pitot heater. Normally this switch is used by the flight crew only during functional or acceptance check flights.

MAXIMUM SAFE MACH ASSEMBLY.

The maximum safe mach assembly (MSMA) receives mach number, pressure altitude and true air temperature signals from the central air data computer and wing sweep position from the wing sweep sensor and provides outputs to the maximum safe mach bar on the airspeed mach indicator and to the reduce speed warning lamp. The MSMA computes the maximum continuous safe mach of the airplane regardless of whether the limitation is due to structural loading limitation or temperature and provides a signal to the maximum safe mach indicator. It also continuously compares the airplane mach number to the maximum safe mach, computed as a function of structural load limit, and provides a signal to light the reduce speed warning lamp when the airplane reaches maximum allowable speed. The MSMA utilizes 115 volt ac power from essential ac bus through the central air data computer power switch and 28 volt dc power from the essential dc bus. A power failure to the MSMA will cause the CADS caution lamp to light.

AUXILIARY FLIGHT REFERENCE SYSTEM (AFRS).

The auxiliary flight reference system (AFRS) provides standby or backup attitude and directional information. The system consists of a number of electronic packages which receive, compute, and transmit gyroscopic attitude and directional reference signals. Basic components of the system include vertical and directional gyros, a coupler, a compass controller, and a remote compass transmitter (flux valve). The vertical gyro is unlimited in roll but is limited to ±82 degrees in pitch. Any change in airplane attitude with respect to the vertical reference is detected by the vertical gyro and electrically transmitted to the standby attitude indicator at all times and to the attitude director indicator when the system is operaing in the auxiliary mode. The directional gyro and the flux valve operate together as the compass set to provide heading signals for the BDHI at all times and to the HSI and the ADI when the system is operating in the auxiliary mode. The AFRS compass operates in three modes; slaved, DG (directional gyro) and compass. In the slaved mode, the system is basically a directional gyro slaved to the remote compass transmitter. This mode is designed for use at latitudes up to 70 degrees. In the polar regions, the direction of the earth's magnetic field becomes more vertical rather than horizontal to such an extent that the slaved mode is not reliable and the DG mode should be used. In the DG mode, the system is freed from the remote compass transmitter and operates as a free gyro indicating an arbitrary gyro heading. In the DG mode, apparent drift due to earth rotation is corrected. The random drift (precession rate) of the gyro in the DG mode will not exceed ±1 degree per hour. This mode may be used at all latitudes but is most useful when operating in the polar regions or when the magnetic field is weak or distorted. The compass (COMP) mode, provides unstabilized compass heading. The purpose of this mode is to permit continued operation of the AFRS in the event of a malfunction of the gyros. The AFRS operates on 115 volt ac power from the ac essential bus and 28 volt dc power from the dc essential bus.

FLIGHT INSTRUMENT REFERENCE SELECT SWITCH.

The flight instrument reference select switch (1, figure 1-36), located on the miscellaneous switch panel, has two positions marked PRI and AUX. Placing the switch to the PRI (primary) position supplies pitch, roll and heading information from the bomb nav system to the following subsystems, as applicable.

- Autopilot
- Attitude Director Indicator
- Horizontal Situation Indicator
- Flight Director Computer
- Terrain Following Radar
- Lead Computing Optical Sight
- Attack Radar

Placing the switch to the AUX (auxiliary) position supplies pitch, roll and heading information from the AFRS (auxiliary flight reference system) to all the above subsystems except autopilot and the attack radar which gets roll information only.

AUXILIARY FLIGHT REFERENCE SYSTEM POWER SWITCH.

The auxiliary flight reference system power switch (7, figure 1-25), located on the ground check panel, has positions GYROS and OFF. Placing the switch to GYROS supplies power to the AFRS, the BDHI, and the standby attitude indicator. Placing the switch to OFF de-energizes these components.

AFRS GYRO FAST ERECT BUTTON.

The auxiliary flight reference system gyro fast erect button (6, figure 1-36), located on the miscellaneous switch panel, provides a means for fast erection of the AFRS. The button is labeled ATT GYRO FAST ERECT. During initial turn on of the system (initial erection), the gyro will automatically erect at the fast rate. If re-erection is required after initial erection due to the limits of the gyro being exceeded, fast erection may be accomplished by depressing and holding the fast erect button until the attitude indicators return to normal. During initial erection or when the fast erect button is depressed the AUX ATT lamp on the main caution lamp panel will light, the OFF flag on the standby attitude indicator will come into view and, if the flight instrument reference select switch is in the AUX position, the OFF flag on the ADI will come into view. During initial erection or whenever the fast erect button is depressed, the displacement gyroscope erects at a rate of approximately twelve (12) degrees per minute.

COMPASS MODE SELECTOR KNOB.

The compass mode selector knob (5, figure 1-26), located on the compass control panel, is used to select the mode of operation of the auxiliary flight reference system compass. The knob has three positions marked SLAVED, COMP, and DG. When the SLAVED mode is selected, gyro-stabilized magnetic heading from the remote compass transmitter is provided. In the DG mode, the remote compass transmitter information is removed from the system and the system operates as a free gyro indicating an arbitrary gyro heading. In the COMP mode, the compass heading is obtained directly from the remote compass transmitter without stabilization by the directional gyro and is used in event of an attitude malfunction of the auxiliary flight reference system.

Note

When moving the knob from the SLAVED position to COMP the compass cards on the HSI and BDHI and the altitude sphere of the ADI will rotate off the heading and immediately return. This is normal. When moving the knob from COMP back to the SLAVED position the compass cards of the HSI and BDHI and the attitude sphere of the ADI will rotate off the heading but will not return until the heading set knob is depressed and held to null the synchronization indicator.

Compass Control Panel

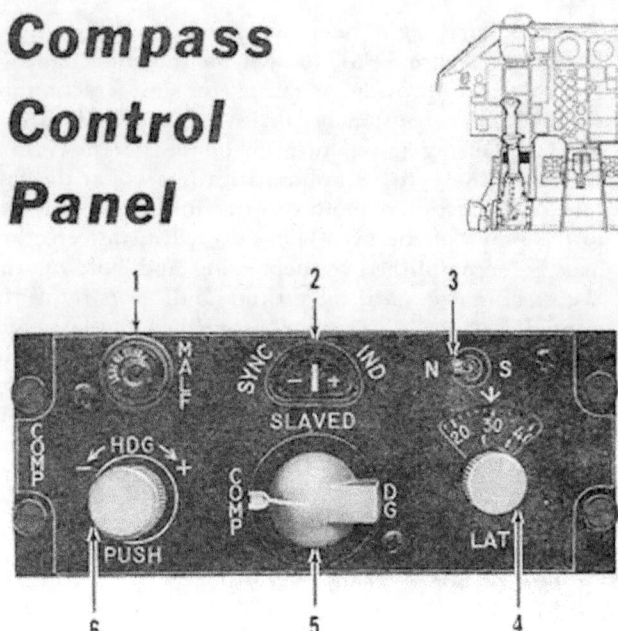

1. Heading Malfunction Caution Lamp.
2. Synchronization Indicator.
3. Hemisphere Selector Switch.
4. Latitude Correction Knob.
5. Compass Mode Selector Knob.
6. Heading Set Knob.

Figure 1-26.

LATITUDE CORRECTION KNOB.

The latitude correction knob, located on the compass control panel (4, figure 1-26), is marked with latitudes from 0 degrees to 90 degrees. Setting the knob to the latitude at which the flight is being made determines the rate of gyro drift correction when operating in DG mode and improves heading accuracy when operating in SLAVED mode.

HEADING SET KNOB.

The heading set knob (6, figure 1-26), located on the compass control panel, provides a means of rapidly synchronizing the AFRS gyro with the remote compass transmitter when operating in the SLAVED mode, and to set in desired heading on the BDHI when operating in the DG mode. When the compass is operated in the SLAVED mode, fast synchronization is accomplished by depressing and holding the knob depressed until the synchronization indicator on the compass control panel becomes centered. When the compass is operated in the DG mode, system heading is changed by depressing and turning the knob to the right to increase the heading and left to decrease the heading.

The rate of heading change is determined by the amount the knob is turned. When the compass is operated in the COMP mode, the system continuously tracks the remote compass transmitter and it is not necessary to use the knob.

HEMISPHERE SELECTOR SWITCH.

The hemisphere selector switch (3, figure 1-26), located on the compass control panel, has two positions marked N (North) and S (South). The switch must be positioned to the correct hemisphere in which the airplane is operating to provide the proper polarity of the earth's rate correction.

SYNCHRONIZATION INDICATOR.

The synchronization indicator, located on the compass control panel (2, figure 1-26), indicates whether or not the AFRS gyro and remote compass are synchronized. During operation in the SLAVED mode the pointer will normally fluctuate slightly when the compass set is synchronized with the gyro. Should the compass get out of synchronization, the pointer will deflect toward either the plus or minus sign on the face of the indicator. The heading set knob must be depressed and held until the pointer is centered to synchronize the system. The indicator is de-activated when operating in the DG or COMP modes.

AUXILIARY ATTITUDE (AUX ATT) CAUTION LAMP.

The auxiliary attitude caution lamp, (figure 1-29), located on the main caution lamp panel, will light if attitude information from the AFRS becomes unreliable. The lamp will also light during initial erection and when the fast erect button is depressed. When lighted, the amber letters AUX ATT are visible. Should the lamp light and remain on, the flight instrument reference select switch should be positioned to the PRI position. The standby attitude indicator will be unreliable when the lamp is lighted.

HEADING MALFUNCTION CAUTION LAMP.

An amber heading malfunction caution lamp (1, figure 1-26), located on the compass control panel, is provided to indicate that the AFRS heading is unreliable. A push-to-test circuit is provided to check the lamp.

AUXILIARY FLIGHT REFERENCE SYSTEM OPERATION.

The AFRS gyro, which provides auxiliary roll and pitch information, is limited to 82 degrees in pitch.

Climbing or diving the airplane at angles greater than 82 degrees may cause large errors in pitch and roll indications. Therefore, after executing such maneuvers the fast erect button on the miscellaneous control panel should be depressed and held until attitude indications return to normal. If this is not accomplished, the gyro will erect to a normal position at a rate of 5 degrees per minute. The directional gyro is limited to 85 degrees in pitch. Exceeding this limit may induce large heading errors. These errors are readily detectible by observing the synchronization meter on the compass control panel when operating the compass in the slaved mode. Manual re-synchronization of the compass can be accomplished by depressing the heading set knob to center the synchronization pointer between — and +. If manual synchronization is not accomplished, the directional gyro will slave to the synchronized position at a rate of 1.5 degrees per minute.

PITOT-STATIC SYSTEM.

The airplane is equipped with a single pitot-static system which provides pitot and static pressures required for operation of standby instruments and the central air data computer (CADC). The system consists of the pitot-static tube, mounted on an adapter installed on the forward tip of the radome, and the tubing required for connection to the operating components. The tubing includes two sets of drains, and a static

Allowable Differences Between Primary and Standby Instruments

AIRSPEED DIFFERENCE TOLERANCES

Airspeed— Knots	Altitude — Feet				
	Sea Level	10,000	20,000	30,000	40,000
200	+ 11 − 11	+ 12 − 10	+ 12 − 10	+ 12 − 10	+ 13 − 9
300	+ 17 − 15	+ 18 − 14	+ 19 − 13	+ 20 − 12	+ 19 − 13
400	+ 24 − 18	+ 25 − 17	+ 26 − 16	*	+ 23 − 19
500	+ 31 − 21	+ 33 − 19	*	+ 28 − 24	+ 26 − 26
600	+ 34 − 18	*	+ 28 − 24	+ 26 − 26	+ 26 − 26

ALTITUDE DIFFERENCE TOLERANCES

Airspeed— Knots	Altitude — Feet				
	Sea Level	10,000	20,000	30,000	40,000
200	+ 105 − 95	+ 200 − 160	+ 310 − 240	+ 460 − 330	+ 730 − 450
300	+ 140 − 60	− 255 − 105	+ 420 − 130	+ 685 − 105	+ 985 − 195
400	+ 220 + 20	+ 405 + 45	+ 690 + 140	*	+ 855 − 325
500	+ 405 + 205	+ 700 + 340	*	+ 655 − 135	+ 590 − 590
600	+ 690 + 490	*	+ 565 + 15	+ 395 − 395	+ 590 − 590

NOTES: 1. Enter tables at primary instrument readings to obtain upper and lower limits on differences.
2. Subtract standby reading from primary reading to obtain difference (may be negative).
3. Do not interpolate across heavy lines.
4. * Check not recommended at this condition.
5. Difference limits include indicator and CADC tolerances, and standby instrument position error.
6. Primary and standby altimeter set to 29.92 for the checks.

Figure 1-27.

system manifold just forward of the instrument panel. Connections of both pitot and static pressures are made at the CADC unit and at the standby airspeed indicator. The other standby instruments, the altimeter, and the vertical velocity indicator are connected only to the static system. The pitot-static probe is equipped with a heating element for anti-icing. Refer to "Anti-icing and Defog Systems" this section. For pitot-static system instrument error and difference between primary and standby instruments, see figure 1-27. It will be noted that a relatively large difference exists between the primary and secondary instrument readings on this figure. This is because the standby instruments are provided with uncorrected data from the pitot static system while the primary instruments are provided with data from the CADC which compensates for pitot-static system errors.

INSTRUMENTS.

The instruments consist of the total temperature indicator (TTI), true airspeed (TAS), standby instruments and the integrated flight instrument system (IFIS).

TOTAL TEMPERATURE INDICATOR.

The total temperature indicator (8, figure 1-6 or 7, figure 1-6A), located on the left main instrument panel, provides indications of aerodynamic heating. The indicator is an electrical resistance type instrument that uses a remote temperature sensing probe, an amplifier and a motor to position the indicator pointer. The temperature sensing probe is equipped with a heating element for anti-icing. Refer to "Anti-Icing and Defog System" this section. The face of the indicator is graduated in 10 degree increments from —50 degrees to +250 degrees centigrade, with a critical temperature index mark of 153.3 degrees and a maximum temperature index mark at 214.3 degrees. A digital readout counter in the face of the indicator, marked SEC TO GO, indicates the time remaining for operation in the critical temperature range between 153.3 and 214.3 degrees. The counter will start to drive down from 300 seconds toward zero and an amber total temperature caution lamp will light when the critical temperature of 153.3 degrees is reached. The counter will continue to drive until one or more of the following conditions are met: until it reaches zero; until the temperature is reduced below 153.3 degrees, or until the maximum temperature index of 214.3 degrees is reached. When the maximum temperature index is reached or when the counter drives to zero, a red reduce speed lamp will light. The counter will reverse and drive back to 300 seconds any time the temperature falls below 153.3 degrees. If the reduce speed warning lamp is on, it will go out as the counter starts to drive back. The total temperature caution lamp will go out when the counter has driven back to 300 seconds. An OFF flag will appear in the face of the indicator when power is removed from the instrument or when the amplifier output signal varies from the temperature probe input signal by 10 to 12 degrees C. The indicator operates on 115 volt ac power from the essential ac bus.

Total Temperature Caution Lamp.

The total temperature caution lamp (1, figure 1-6), located on the left main instrument or on the main caution lamp panel (figure 1-29A), will light any time the airplane is operated above the critical temperature of 153.3 degrees centigrade. When lighted, the words TOTAL TEMP appear on the lamp face. Once lighted the lamp will remain on until the total temperature counter has reversed and driven back to 300 seconds.

Reduce Speed Warning Lamp.

The reduce speed warning lamp (figure 1-29), located on the left main instrument panel, functions in conjunction with the total temperature indicator to indicate that the airplane has flown for at least 300 seconds in the critical temperature range of from 153.3 to 214.3 degrees centigrade or that the maximum temperature index of 214.3 degrees has been reached or exceeded. When lighted the words REDUCE SPEED are visible in red on the face of the lamp. If the lamp was lighted due to the expiration of 300 seconds in the critical temperature range it will remain on until the temperature is reduced to below 153.3 degrees and the total temperature counter has reversed and started to drive back to 300 seconds. If the lamp was lighted upon reaching the maximum temperature index of 214.3 degrees as the counter was driving to zero it will go out as soon as the temperature is reduced below 214.3 degrees. The lamp also functions in conjunction with the maximum safe mach assembly, refer to "Airspeed-Mach Indicator" this section.

TRUE AIRSPEED INDICATOR.

The true airspeed indicator (4, figure 1-28), located on the right main instrument panel, provides a digital readout of true airspeed. The instrument displays true airspeed on a servo-driven 4-digit counter within the range of 40-1750 knots. The indicator is operated by electrical signals from the CADC.

STANDBY INSTRUMENTS.

The standby instruments include the airspeed indicator, altimeter, vertical velocity indicator, magnetic compass, attitude indicator and bearing distance heading indicator (BDHI). These instruments provide backup indications in the event of failure of the integrated flight instrument system. Position error must be applied to the airspeed and altimeter reading to obtain correct readings. Refer to Appendix I, Part I.

Airspeed Indicator.

The airspeed indicator (2, figure 1-28), located on the right main instrument panel, is operated by pitot and static pressures direct from the pitot-static system. The instrument is graduated from 0.6 to 8 times 100 knots.

Altimeter.

The altimeter (13, figure 1-28), located on the right main instrument panel, is a barometric type which operates on static pressure direct from the pitot-static system. A barometric pressure set knob located on the left corner of the instrument provides a means of adjusting the barometric scale on the instrument.

Vertical Velocity Indicator.

The vertical velocity indicator (5, figure 1-28), located on the right main instrument panel, provides rate of climb and descent information. The instrument operates on static pressure from the pitot-static system.

Magnetic Compass.

The magnetic compass (figure 1-2), located on the windshield center beam, provides magnetic heading information. A deviation correction card for the compass is located below the center of the glare shield.

Attitude Indicator.

The attitude indicator (12, figure 1-28), located on the right main instrument panel, provides backup attitude information in the event of malfunction or failure of the attitude director indicator. The indicator displays pitch and roll information on an attitude sphere in

This page intentionally left blank.

Right Main Instrument Panel

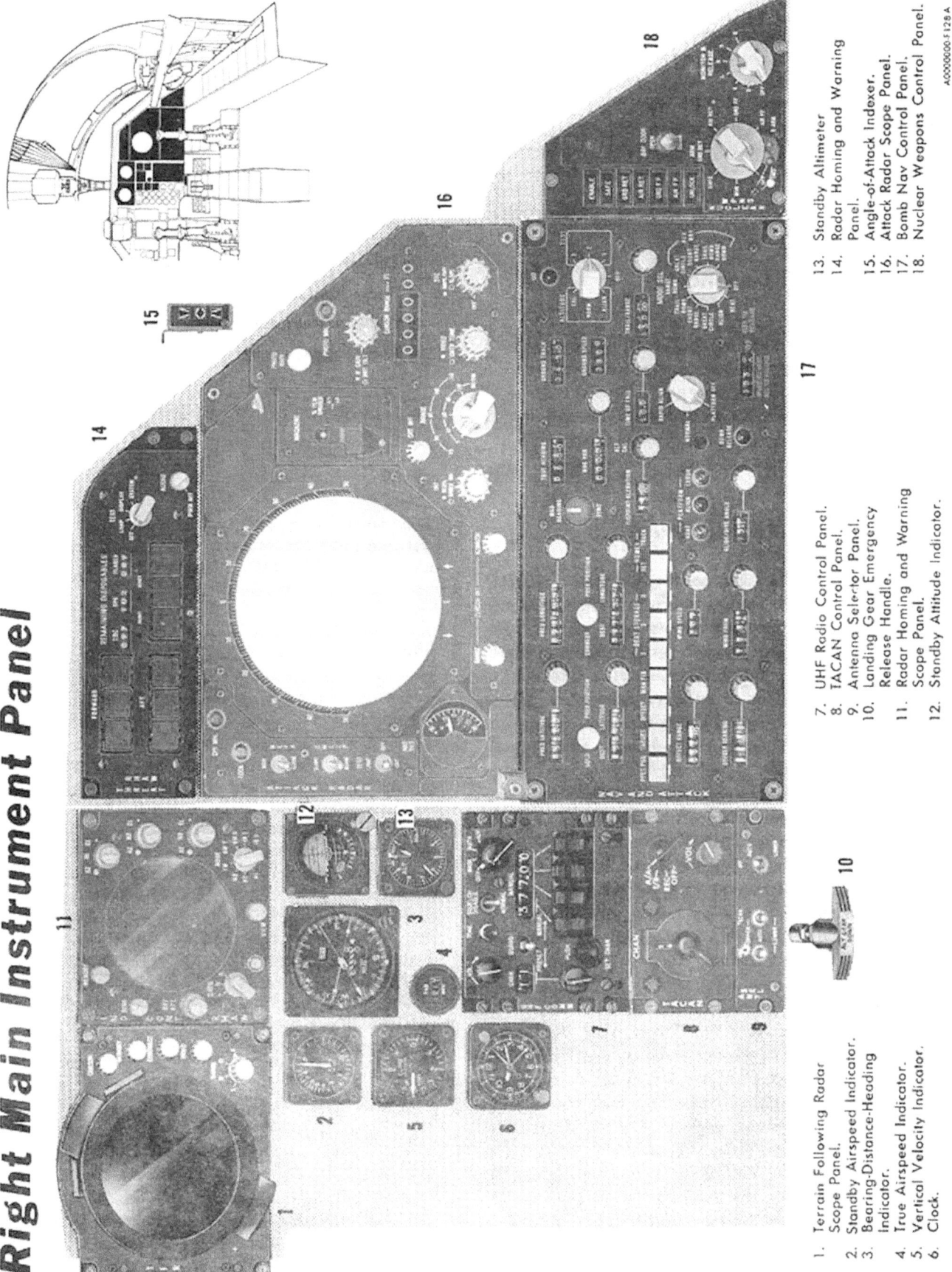

Figure 1-28.

1. Terrain Following Radar Scope Panel.
2. Standby Airspeed Indicator.
3. Bearing-Distance-Heading Indicator.
4. True Airspeed Indicator.
5. Vertical Velocity Indicator.
6. Clock.
7. UHF Radio Control Panel.
8. TACAN Control Panel.
9. Antenna Selector Panel.
10. Landing Gear Emergency Release Handle.
11. Radar Homing and Warning Scope Panel.
12. Standby Altitude Indicator.
13. Standby Altimeter
14. Radar Homing and Warning Panel.
15. Angle-of-Attack Indexer.
16. Attack Radar Scope Panel.
17. Bomb Nav Control Panel.
18. Nuclear Weapons Control Panel.

relation to a miniature aircraft. Pitch and roll signals are received from the auxiliary flight reference system (AFRS). The indicator receives 115 volt ac power from the ac essential bus. In the event of power failure or an AFRS malfunction, an OFF warning flag will appear on the lower left face of the indicator. A pitch trim knob on the lower right side of the instrument is provided to adjust the attitude sphere to the proper pitch attitude.

CAUTION

The attitude warning flag will not appear with a slight electrical power reduction or failure of other components within the system. Failure of certain components can result in erroneous or complete loss of pitch and bank presentations without a visible flag.

Bearing-Distance-Heading Indicator.

The bearing-distance and heading indicator (BDHI) (3, figure 1-28), is located on the right main instrument panel. The instrument is a remote type heading indicator with a rotating compass card. Automatic direction finding (ADF) and TACAN bearing information is displayed by means of pointers. A synchro driven range indicator is provided which receives signals from the TACAN set. Range of the distance display is 0 –999 nautical miles. A red and black striped range warning flag partially obscures the range indicator when distance-to-station signals are too weak or there is a loss of lock-on to TACAN distance signals. Magnetic heading of the airplane is shown by the index at the top of the instrument and the compass card. A pointer designated as number one is servo driven and receives signals from a TACAN coupler. Bearing information is read from the compass card under the pointer tip. A pointer designated as number 2 is also servo driven and, when required, receives signals by selection from the ADF set. When ADF signals are desired, the function selector knob on the UHF radio control panel is positioned to ADF. When deenergized, the pointer is positioned concurrent with the number one pointer and rotates with it. The BDHI receives heading information from the auxiliary flight reference system (AFRS). The set index knob located on the lower right side of the indiactor is used to set the heading index to a desired magnetic heading. Once set, the index rotates with the compass card. A flag marked OFF will appear in the window when the BDHI is not energized or when power is not available to the compass card.

INTEGRATED FLIGHT INSTRUMENT SYSTEM.

The integrated flight instrument system takes outputs from the following systems and integrates them into usable displays on the integrated flight instruments.

- Central air data computer (CADC)
- Auxiliary flight reference system (AFRS)
- Instrument landing system (ILS)
- Tactical air navigation system (TACAN)
- Terrain following radar (TFR)
- Radar homing and warning system (RHAWS)
- Bomb nav system
- Attack radar system
- Radar altimeter
- Lead computing optical sight system (LCOSS)
- Dual bombing timer (DBT)
- Shrike

The primary components of the system are the integrated flight instruments; consisting of the airspeed-mach indicator (AMI), altitude-vertical velocity indicator (AVVI), attitude director indicator (ADI) and horizontal situation indicator (HSI), a flight director computer (FDC) and an instrument system coupler (ISC). The four integrated flight instruments are grouped together on the left main instrument panel to provide actual and command flight and navigational information in a clear concise manner. Altitude, airspeed, acceleration, mach, vertical velocity, and angle of attack are displayed on moving tapes on the AMI and AVVI. The ADI and HSI display attitude, heading and navigational information from various other systems in the airplane. The lead computing optical sight (LCOS) command steering bars operate in conjunction with the system to provide the same pitch and bank steering commands as the ADI. The instrument system coupler accepts inputs from other airplane systems and channels them through the flight director computer for display on the ADI, LCOS and HSI. The system incorporates self test features to check reliability and isolate malfunctions. The system operates on 115 volt and 26 volt ac power from the essential ac bus and 28 volt dc power from the essential dc bus.

Airspeed Mach Indicator.

The airspeed mach indicator (AMI) (figure 1-28A), located on the left main instrument panel, provides remote reading vertical presentations of angle of attack, "g" acceleration, mach and airspeed on vertical moving scales. Readout windows below each moving scale present digital values for "g" acceleration, mach, and airspeed. Slewing switches for setting reference mach and airspeed markers are located on the bottom of the indicator. Signals for operation of the various scales are provided from the central air data computer and remote accelerometer. In the event of a malfunction or power failure a spring-loaded OFF warning flag will appear across the face of the mach scale. Presentations on the face of the indicator are from left to right.

Note

The airspeed indicated on the airspeed mach indicator has been calibrated for pitot-static system errors by the CADC and therefore is actually KCAS (knots calibrated airspeed). However, this air speed is referred to as KIAS (knots indicated airspeed) throughout this manual since it is read directly from the instruments.

Angle-of-Attack Indicating System.

The angle-of-attack indicating system provides an indication of the angular position of the wing chord in relation to the airplane flight path. This indication is used for approach speed monitoring and to warn of an approaching stall. The system includes a vane type transmitter, indicator, and two sets of indexers. The indicator and indexers are electrically slaved to the sensor vane transmitter. In flight, the vane, which is located on the left side of the fuselage, will align itself with the airflow. Rotation of the vane generates an indicated angle-of-attack signal to the central air data computer. The central air data computer converts the signal to true wing angle-of-attack and sends this signal to the angle-of-attack indicator and also lights the appropriate angle-of-attack indexer. A damper assembly prevents rotational overshoot and flutter of the vane due to turbulence. Vane anti-icing is provided by means of a 115 volt ac heating element in the leading edge of the vane. The heating element receives power from the left main ac bus and is controlled by the pitot heat switch.

Angle-of-Attack Indicator. The angle-of-attack indicator, located on the airspeed-mach indicator, indicates in degrees the angular position of the wing chord in relation to the airplane flight path. The vertically moving tape displays angle of attack from minus 10 degrees to plus 25 degrees. The angle-of-attack indicator is operated by means of synchro signal received from the central air data computer.

Angle-of-Attack Indexer. An angle-of-attack indexer (3, figure 1-6, or 5, figure 1-6A, and 15, figure 28) is located on either side of the glare shield. Each indexer consists of 3 red lamps arranged vertically. The low speed symbol (top V-shaped lamp) lights when the angle of attack exceeds 10.5 degrees. The on speed symbol (center donut-shaped lamp) lights between 11.0 and 9.0 degrees. The high speed symbol (bottom inverted V-shaped lamp) will light when the angle-of-attack is less than 9.5 degrees. The indexer lamps function only when the landing gear is in the down position. A dimming rheostat, located on the side of the indexer controls the intensity of the lamps which receive 28 volt dc power from the main dc bus.

Accelerometer. The accelerometer located adjacent to the angle-of-attack indicator, provides normal G (load factor) information. The G forces being sustained by the aircraft are continuously shown by the acceleration scale read against a fixed index line. The tape scale is graduated from -4 to $+10$ Gs. The presentation on the digital readout is from 0.0 to 9.0 G's. The accelerometer and readout window are actuated by electrical signals from the remote accelerometer.

Mach Indicator. The mach scale in the center of the airspeed-mach indicator indicates true mach number which is shown on a moving scale and is read against the fixed index. The scale is calibrated in hundredths and shows numbers in tenths from 0.4 through 3.5. At speeds below mach 0.4, the scale will continue to read 0.4. The moving scale is operated by electrical signals from the CADC. A command mach marker and command mach readout window indicate manually selected command mach. The command mach marker remains at the top or bottom of the display column until the selected command mach comes into view on the mach scale, at which time it will synchronize and move with the scale. The selected true mach is numerically displayed in the command mach readout window at all times. Command mach setting is controlled manually by the command mach slewing switch under the command mach readout window. When selecting a command mach number, slewing speed is proportional to the amount the slewing switch is displaced from its normal center position. The maximum allowable mach is indicated by a diagonally-striped maximum allowable mach marker which normally rests at the bottom of the mach scale. When maximum allowable speed is approached, the marker will climb toward the fixed index line. The maximum allowable mach marker will show on the scale depending on the airplane configuration, air density, and temperature. The maximum allowable mach marker is operated by electrical signals from the maximum safe mach assembly (MSMA).

Airspeed Indicator. The airspeed scale on the right column of the airspeed-mach indicator indicates airspeed on a moving scale read against a fixed index. The scale is calibrated in 10 knot increments and displays numerals at each 20 knot interval from 100 to 200 knots and each 50 knot interval from 200 through 1000 knots. At speeds below 50 knots, the scale will continue to read 50. The airspeed scale is operated by electrical signals from the CADC. If there is an airspeed signal failure from the CADC, the IAS monitoring flag marked OFF will appear across the airspeed scale. A command airspeed marker and a command airspeed readout window below the scale indicates selected command airspeed. Command airspeed setting is controlled by the command airspeed slewing switch under the command airspeed readout window. When selecting a command airspeed, slewing speed is proportional to the amount the slewing switch is displaced up or down from the center position. Once the command airspeed is set into the command airspeed readout window, the command airspeed marker remains at the top or bottom of the display column until the selected command airspeed comes into view on the moving scale, at which time it will synchronize and move with the reading on the scale. This will be the same reading as shown in the readout window.

Note

If the slewing switch is moved to the detented position on the right, the command airspeed marker will align with the fixed index and continuous digital presentation of the airspeed will then be displayed on the moving scale and in the readout window.

Altitude-Vertical Velocity Indicator.

The altitude-vertical velocity indicator (AVVI) (figure 1-28A), located on the left main instrument panel, provides remote reading presentations of altitude and vertical velocity on vertical moving scales. Readout windows across the bottom of the indicator present digital readout of barometric pressure and command altitude. A barometric pressure set knob and command altitude slewing switch are also located on the bottom of the indicator. Signals for operation of the moving scales, markers and readouts are provided from the CADC. A spring-loaded OFF warning flag will appear across the face of the coarse altitude scale in the event of malfunction or power failure to the indicator. The barometric pressure reading is set by a knob marked BARO located on the lower left corner of the indicator and is numerically displayed in the barometric pressure readout window above the knob.

Note

A mechanical failure within the altitude-vertical velocity indicator may not cause the flag to appear even though the indicator reading will be unreliable. If a failure is suspected, rely on the standby altimeter using the position error shown in Appendix I, Part I. The radar altimeter also may be used since it provides an absolute indication of distance above the terrain at altitudes below 5000 feet.

Presentations on the face of the indicator are from left to right as follows:

Vertical Velocity Indicator.

The vertical velocity indicator is located on the left side of the altitude-vertical velocity indicator. The instrument indicates climb or dive velocities from 0 to 1500 feet per minute by means of a moving index pointer to the right of a vertical fixed scale. The scale is graduated in increments of one hundred feet from 0 to 1.5 thousand. When the vertical velocity exceeds this scale the pointer index will move to the top or bottom of the instrument to a readout window where a moving scale, graduated in thousands of feet from 2 to 40 thousand feet per minute, will indicate the rate of climb or descent. The instrument receives information from the CADC.

Vernier Altimeter.

The altitude scales in the center of the altitude-vertical velocity indicator indicate aircraft pressure altitude which is read on the altitude scale against a fixed index line. The vernier scale is calibrated in 50 foot graduations and indicates each hundred foot level from 0 to 1000 feet. The coarse scale is calibrated in 500 foot graduations and indicates each thousand foot level from -1000 through $+120,000$ feet. Both the vernier and coarse scales are operated by electrical signals from the CADC. A command altitude marker and the command altitude readout window below the scale indicate manually selected command altitude. The command altitude numerals are controlled manually by the command altitude slewing switch under the command altitude readout window. When selecting a command altitude, slewing speed of the command marker and readout window numerals is proportional to the amount the slewing switch is displaced from center. The command altitude remains at the top or bottom of the display column until the selected command altitude comes into view on the altitude scale, at which time it will synchronize and move with the scale. The selected command altitude is numerically shown in hundreds in the altitude readout window at all times.

Gross Altimeter.

The gross altimeter located on the right side of the altitude-vertical velocity indicator is a thermometer-type altitude index which shows aircraft altitude against a gross altitude scale. It is operated by electrical signals from the CADC. The gross altitude scale is calibrated in thousands of feet and numerically indicates 10,000 foot levels from 0 to 120,000 feet. Command altitude is indicated by a double line command altitude marker and is simultaneously shown and operated in conjunction with the command altitude marker on the vernier altimeter.

Attitude Director Indicator.

The attitude director indiactor (ADI) (figure 1-28A), located on the left main instrument panel, is a remote indicating instrument which displays attitude, heading, turn and slip, glide slope deviation, "g" deviation, and bank and pitch steering information. The indicator

T.O. 1F-111A-1

Section I
Description & Operation

Integrated Flight Instruments

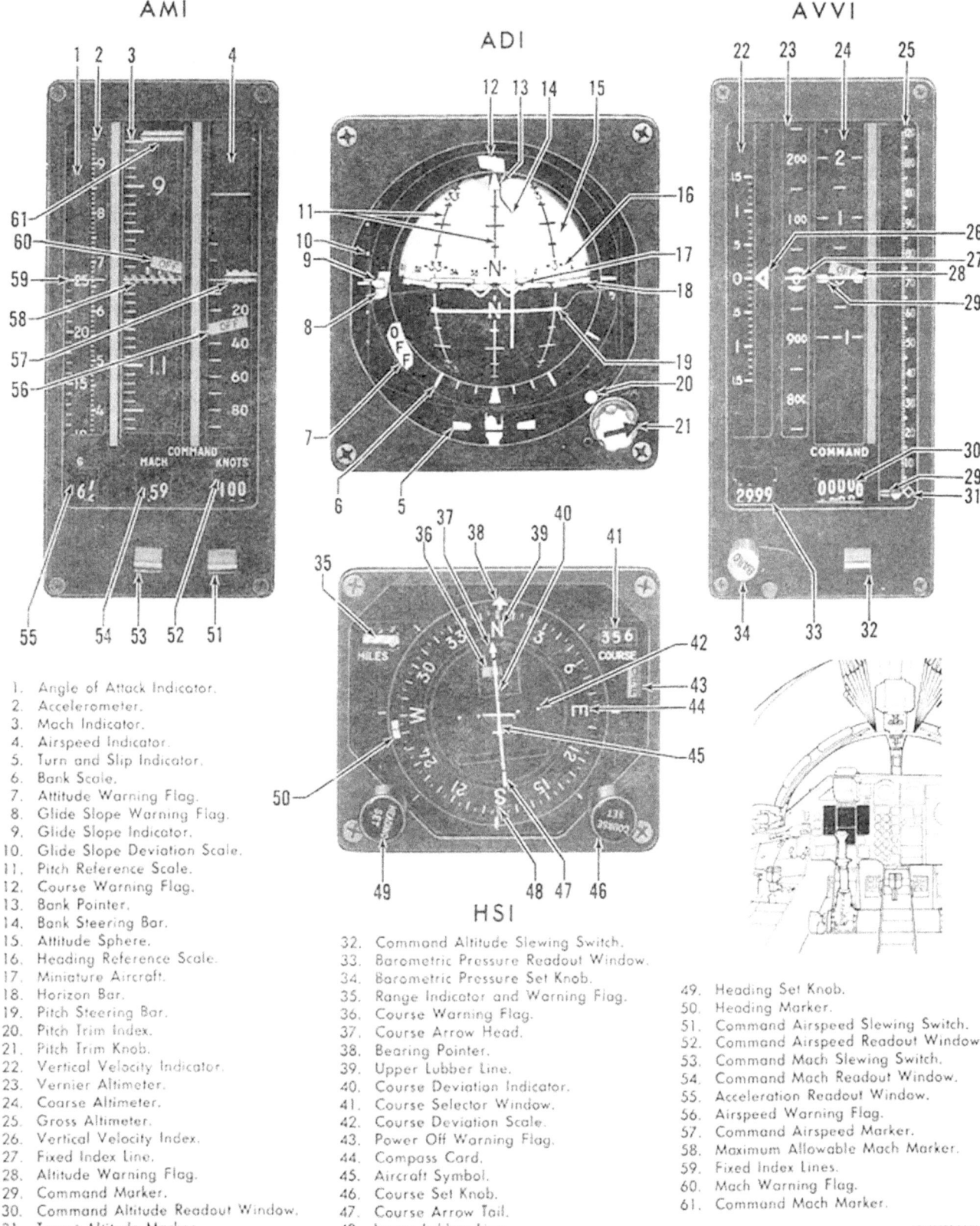

1. Angle of Attack Indicator.
2. Accelerometer.
3. Mach Indicator.
4. Airspeed Indicator.
5. Turn and Slip Indicator.
6. Bank Scale.
7. Attitude Warning Flag.
8. Glide Slope Warning Flag.
9. Glide Slope Indicator.
10. Glide Slope Deviation Scale.
11. Pitch Reference Scale.
12. Course Warning Flag.
13. Bank Pointer.
14. Bank Steering Bar.
15. Attitude Sphere.
16. Heading Reference Scale.
17. Miniature Aircraft.
18. Horizon Bar.
19. Pitch Steering Bar.
20. Pitch Trim Index.
21. Pitch Trim Knob.
22. Vertical Velocity Indicator.
23. Vernier Altimeter.
24. Coarse Altimeter.
25. Gross Altimeter.
26. Vertical Velocity Index.
27. Fixed Index Line.
28. Altitude Warning Flag.
29. Command Marker.
30. Command Altitude Readout Window.
31. Target Altitude Marker.
32. Command Altitude Slewing Switch.
33. Barometric Pressure Readout Window.
34. Barometric Pressure Set Knob.
35. Range Indicator and Warning Flag.
36. Course Warning Flag.
37. Course Arrow Head.
38. Bearing Pointer.
39. Upper Lubber Line.
40. Course Deviation Indicator.
41. Course Selector Window.
42. Course Deviation Scale.
43. Power Off Warning Flag.
44. Compass Card.
45. Aircraft Symbol.
46. Course Set Knob.
47. Course Arrow Tail.
48. Lower Lubber Line.
49. Heading Set Knob.
50. Heading Marker.
51. Command Airspeed Slewing Switch.
52. Command Airspeed Readout Window.
53. Command Mach Slewing Switch.
54. Command Mach Readout Window.
55. Acceleration Readout Window.
56. Airspeed Warning Flag.
57. Command Airspeed Marker.
58. Maximum Allowable Mach Marker.
59. Fixed Index Lines.
60. Mach Warning Flag.
61. Command Mach Marker.

Figure 1-28A.

includes an attitude sphere, turn and slip indicator, pitch and bank steering bars, miniature aircraft, glide slope indicator, warning flags and a pitch trim knob. The attitude sphere displays pitch, bank and heading in relation to the miniature aircraft. These signals are received directly from either the bomb nav system stabilization platform or the auxiliary flight reference system depending on the position of the flight instrument reference select switch. The pitch reference of the attitude sphere to the miniature aircraft may be adjusted with the pitch trim knob. The turn and slip indicator, located in the bottom of the ADI, receives turn signals directly from a remotely located rate-of-turn transmitter and is designed for a 4 minute turn. Pitch and bank steering commands from other systems are processed by the instrument system coupler and routed through the flight director computer to the pitch and bank steering bars and glide slope deviation indicator. (Refer to "Instrument System Coupler Mode Selector Knob" and "Instrument System Coupler Pitch Steering Mode Switch," this section, for ADI indications during various modes of operation). An OFF warning flag indicates loss of power to the ADI or an AFRS malfunction, other warning flags indicate the loss of signal to the bank steering bar and loss of signal to the glide slope deviation indicator.

CAUTION

The attitude warning flag will not appear with a slight electrical power reduction or failure of other components within the system. Failure of certain components can result in erroneous or complete loss of pitch and bank presentations without a visible flag.

The ADI operates on 115 volts ac power from the essential ac bus.

Horizontal Situation Indicator.

The horizontal situation indicator (HSI) (figure 1-28A), located on the left main instrument panel, is a remote indicating instrument which displays course, heading, distance and bearing information. The indicator includes a compass card, course and heading set knobs, course arrow, to-from indicator, lubber lines, bearing pointer, course deviation indicator and scale, range indicator and course selector windows, warning flags and an aircraft symbol. The compass card is servo driven and receives magnetic heading signals directly from either the bomb nav system or auxiliary flight reference system depending on the position of the flight instrument reference select switch. Airplane heading or its reciprocal are read under an upper and lower lubber line. The aircraft symbol is fixed and is oriented to the nose of the airplane. A heading set knob is provided to set a heading marker to the desired heading. Once it is set the marker rotates with the compass card. A course set knob is provided to set the course arrow and digits in the course selector window to the desired course. Once set, the arrow will rotate with the compass card. The shaft of the course arrow provides course deviation indications. The reciprocal course may be read off the tail of the arrow. An unreliable course signal or loss of the course signal to the indicator will cause a warning flag to appear in the upper center of the indicator. The bearing and distance to TACAN stations are displayed by the bearing pointer and range indicator window. Loss of the TACAN signal or an unreliable signal will cause a range warning flag to appear in the range indicator window. Loss of power to the HSI will cause an OFF warning flag to appear on the right side of the instrument. (Refer to "Instrument System Coupler Mode Selector Knob," this section, for HSI indications during various modes of operation). The HSI operates on 115 volt ac power from the ac essential bus.

Instrument System Coupler Pitch Steering Mode Switch.

The instrument system coupler pitch steering mode switch, located on the instrument system coupler control panel (10, figure 1-6 or 12, figure 1-6A), is a three position switch marked ALT REF (altitude reference), OFF and TF (terrain following). The switch is solenoid held in either the ALT REF or TF position, when used with a compatible position of the instrument system coupler mode selector knob. When the switch is placed in the ALT REF position, pitch steering commands, referenced to the pressure altitude at the time the switch is engaged, will be displayed on the pitch steering bars on the attitude director indicator (ADI) and lead computing optical sight (LCOS). The ALT REF position is compatible with all positions of the instrument system coupler mode selector knob except AIR/AIR, however, when making an ILS or AILA approach the switch will automatically return to OFF when the glide slope is intercepted. When the switch is placed to the TF position pitch steering commands referenced to the altitude setting of the terrain following radar will be displayed on the pitch steering bars on the ADI and LCOS. The TF position is compatible with all positions of the instrument system coupler mode selector knob except ILS, AILA and AIR/AIR. However, with the knob in CRS SEL NAV, NAV and SHRIKE position, the switch will return to OFF when a pull-up signal is generated by the armament system.

Instrument System Coupler Mode Selector Knob.

The instrument system coupler mode selector knob, located on the instrument system coupler control panel (10, figure 1-6 or 12, figure 1-6A) has twelve positions. Nine positions of the knob are activated and are marked ILS, AILA, TACAN, CRS SEL NAV, NAV, MAN CRS, MAN HDG, AIR/AIR and SHRIKE. Three unmarked positions provide space for the installation of new equipment. The knob must be depressed to change positions. The knob positions provide the following functions:

● The ILS (instrument landing system) position provides the capability of flying ILS approaches to runways equipped with localizer and glide slope transmitters. Localizer steering commands are displayed by the bank steering bars on the attitude indicator (ADI) and lead computing optical sight (LCOS) and course deviation information is displayed on the course deviation indicator of the horizontal situation indicator (HSI). Pitch steering commands will be displayed on the pitch steering bars on the ADI and LCOS if the pitch steering mode switch is in the ALT REF position. When the glide slope beam is intercepted the pitch steering mode switch, if on, will return to OFF and glide slope steering commands will then be displayed on the pitch steering bars on the ADI and LCOS and glide slope deviation will be displayed on the glide slope deviation indicator on the ADI.

Note

Once the glide slope is intercepted, a glide slope deviation of more than two dots as measured on the glide slope deviation scale will cause the pitch steering bar on the ADI to drive out of view and remain out of view until a correction is made to bring the glide slope indicator back within the two dot deviation scale.

With the radar altimeter operating and set for a minimum altitude penetration, the pitch steering bars on the ADI and LCOS will indicate a fly-up command and the radar altitude low warning lamp will light when the airplane penetrates the set altitude. If a pull-up is then initiated the fly-up command can be terminated and the warning lamp will go out when the airplane is above the minimum penetration altitude setting as follows: (1) By momentarily depressing the instrument system coupler mode selector knob or by placing the knob to another mode. (2) By placing the instrument system coupler pitch steering mode switch to ALT REF when level off altitude is reached. In the event an ILS approach or AILA is begun from above 5000 feet absolute altitude the radar altitude low warning lamp will light and the pitch steering bars on the ADI and LCOS will indicate a fly-up command when the airplane decends through 5000 feet. In this case the fly-up command can be terminated and the lamp will go out by taking the action as in (1) above. For ILS procedures refer to Section VII.

● The AILA (airborne instrumental low approach) position provides the capability of making instrument letdowns and approaches to runways not equipped with ground based letdown systems. The bomb nav and attack radar systems furnish simulated localizer and glide slope information to provide the same indications on the ADI, LCOS and HSI as when using the ILS position. For AILA procedures refer to Section VII.

● The TACAN (tactical air navigation) position provides the capability of making instrument approaches and flying a selected course to or from a TACAN station. Course steering commands are displayed on the bank steering bars on the ADI and LCOS and course deviation information is displayed on the course deviation indicator and bearing pointer on the HSI. Distance from the TACAN station is displayed in the range indicator window on the HSI. The bearing pointer will indicate the magnetic bearing to the station.

● The CRS SEL NAV (course select navigation) position provides the capability of approaching a bomb nav system computed destination along a manually selected course other than the most direct route. This may be used to avoid weather, obstacles or sensitive enemy areas. The pilot sets the HSI course arrow and course selector window to the desired course using the course set knob. This establishes a course error signal to the bomb nav system to provide a steering command to the bank steering bars on the ADI and LCOS and course deviation information to the course deviation indicator on the HSI.

● The NAV (basic navigation) position provides course information from the bomb nav system when it is used in any one of four modes of operation. When the bomb nav mode selector knob is in either the GREAT CIRCLE, SHORT RANGE, BOMB TRAIL or BOMB RANGE positions, course steering commands to a destination set into the bomb nav system are displayed by the bank steering bars on the ADI and LCOS and course deviation is displayed on the course deviation indicator on the HSI. If the bomb nav system is inoperative, course information can be obtained from the auxiliary flight reference system (AFRS) by placing the bomb nav mode selector knob to AUX NAV in one of the above positions. Distance to destination or time/distance to target and mode position of the bomb nav mode selector knob are displayed on the bomb nav time distance indicator (BNTDI). This mode is also used in conjunction with the heading navigation mode of autopilot operation. For further information refer to AUTO PILOT this section.

● The MAN CRS (manual course) position provides the capability of flying a manually selected course instead of a bomb nav system computed course. This position can be utilized to fly a constant course while taking a fix, changing destination or working a navigation problem. The desired course is set in the course selector windows of the HSI.

Section I
Description & Operation

T.O. 1F-111A-1

Warning, Caution and Indicator Lamps

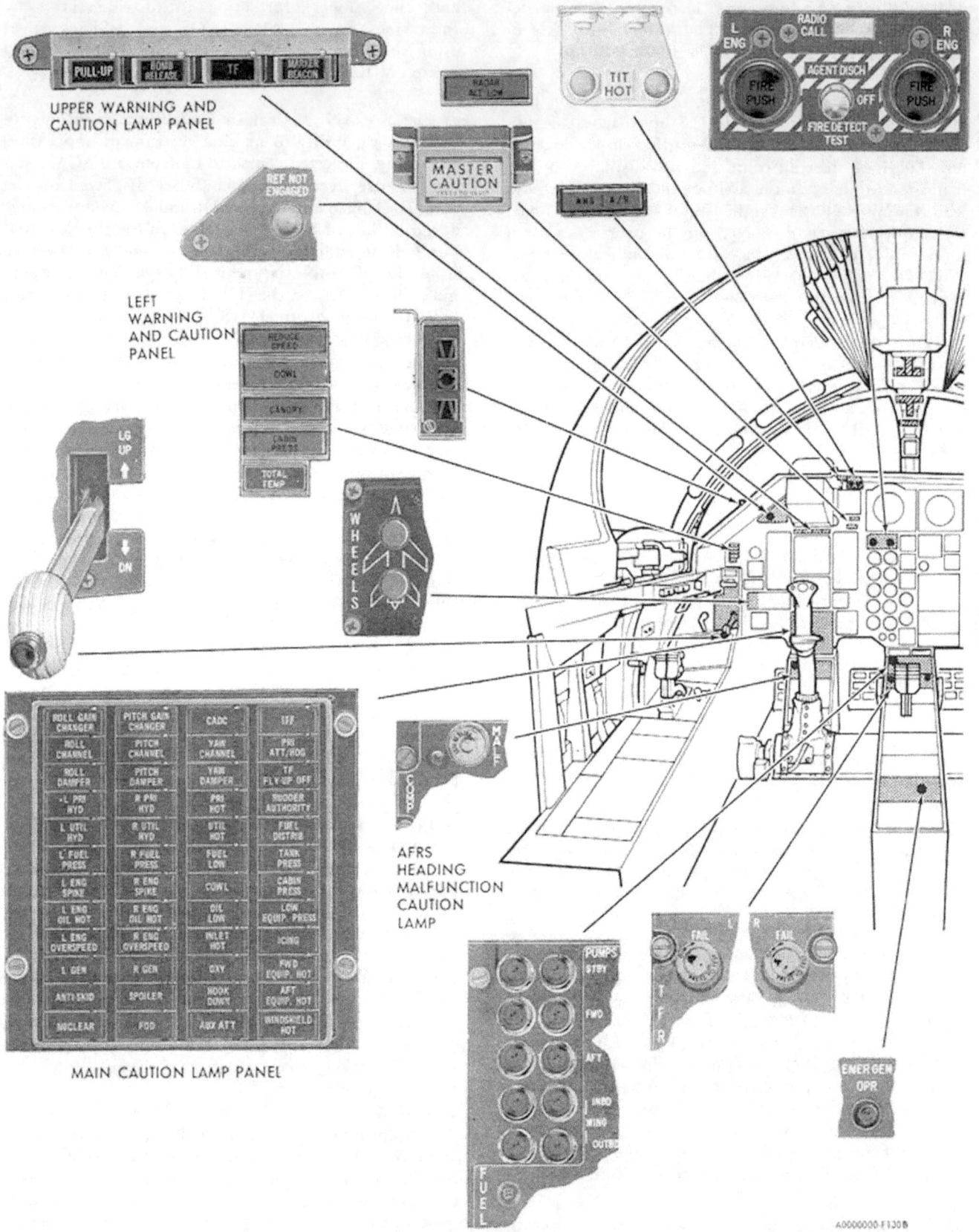

Figure 1-29. (Sheet 1)

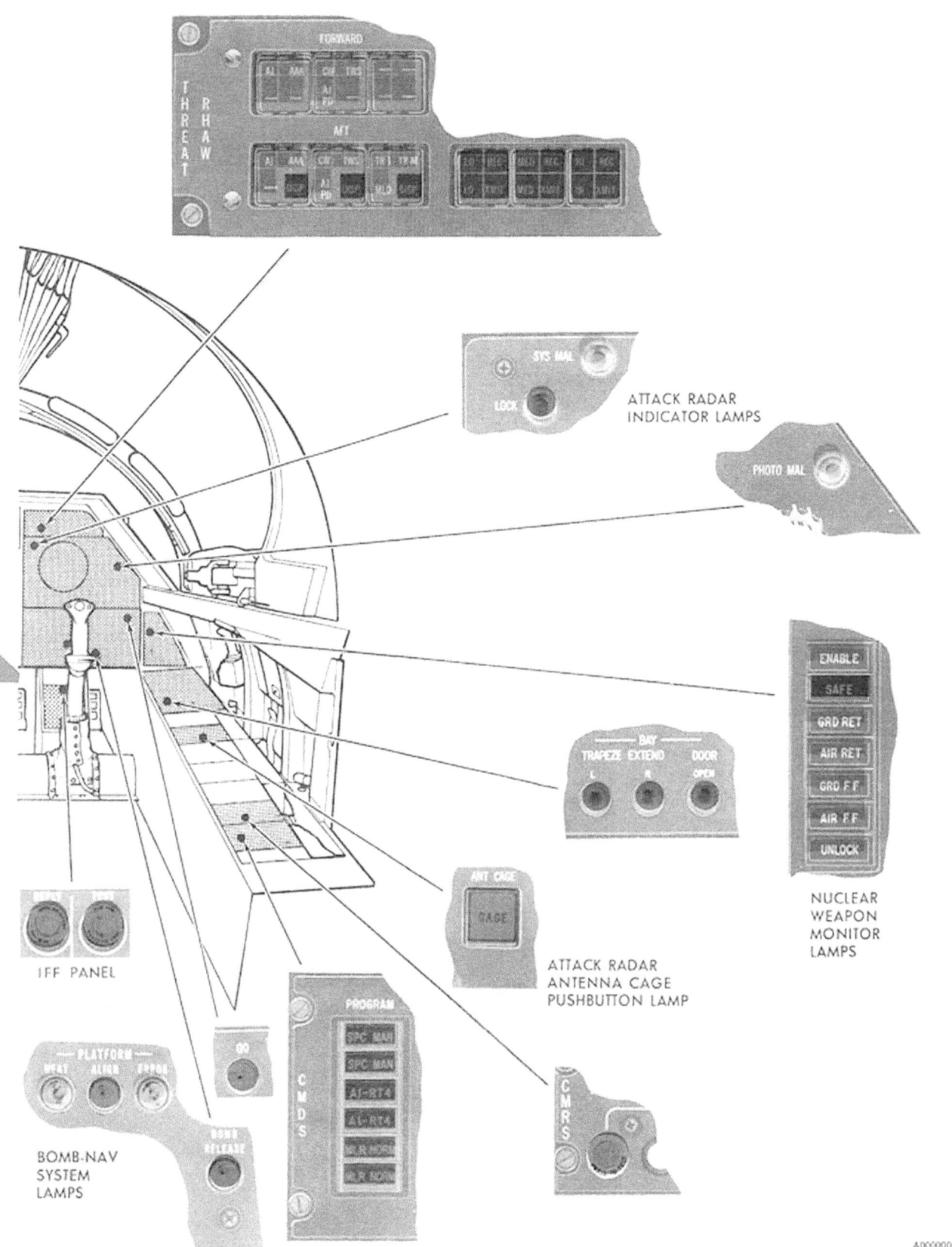

Figure 1-29. (Sheet 2)

Section I
Description & Operation

T.O. 1F-111A-1

Warning, Caution and Indicator Lamps

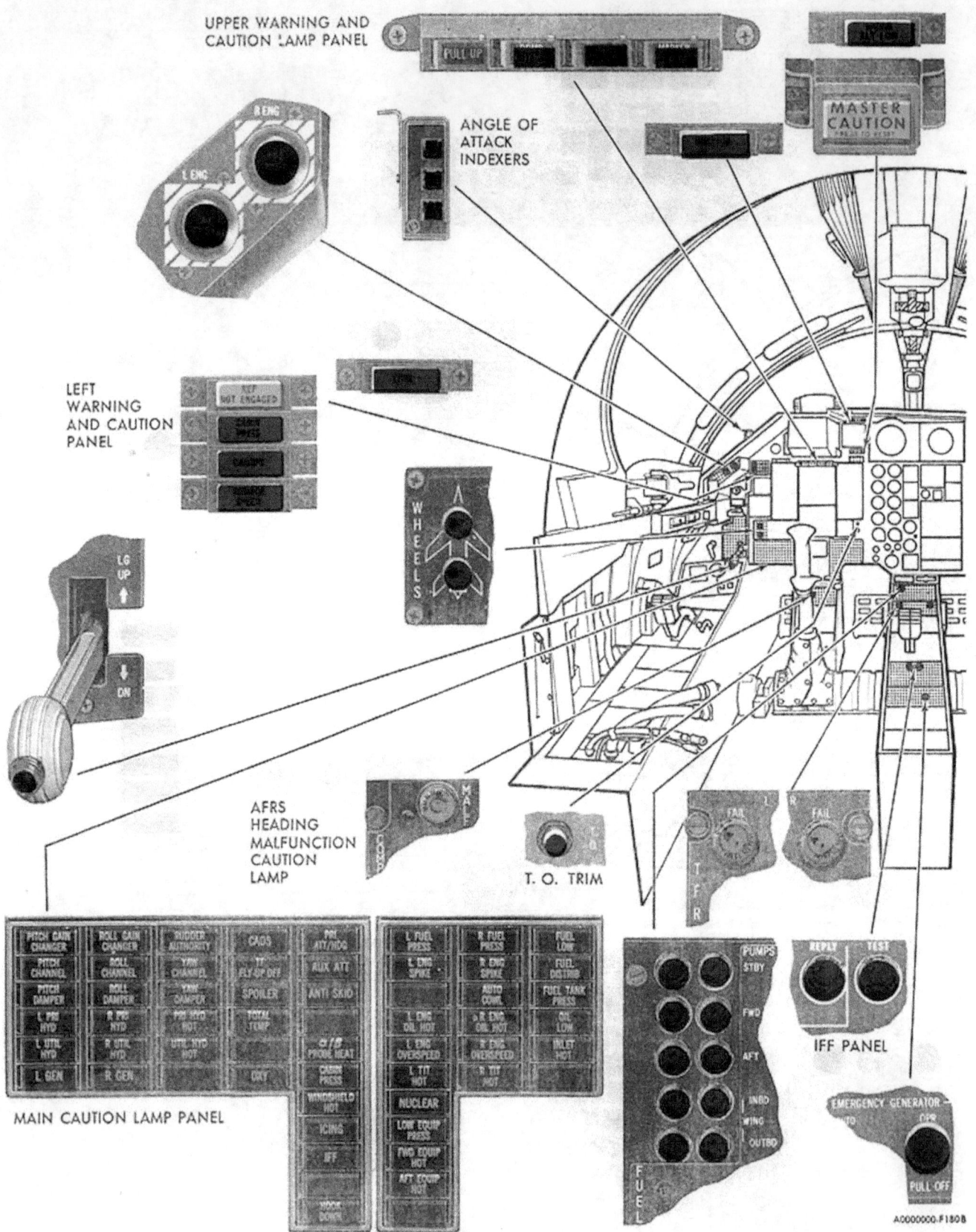

Figure 1-29A. (Sheet 1)

T.O. 1F-111A-1

Section I
Description & Operation

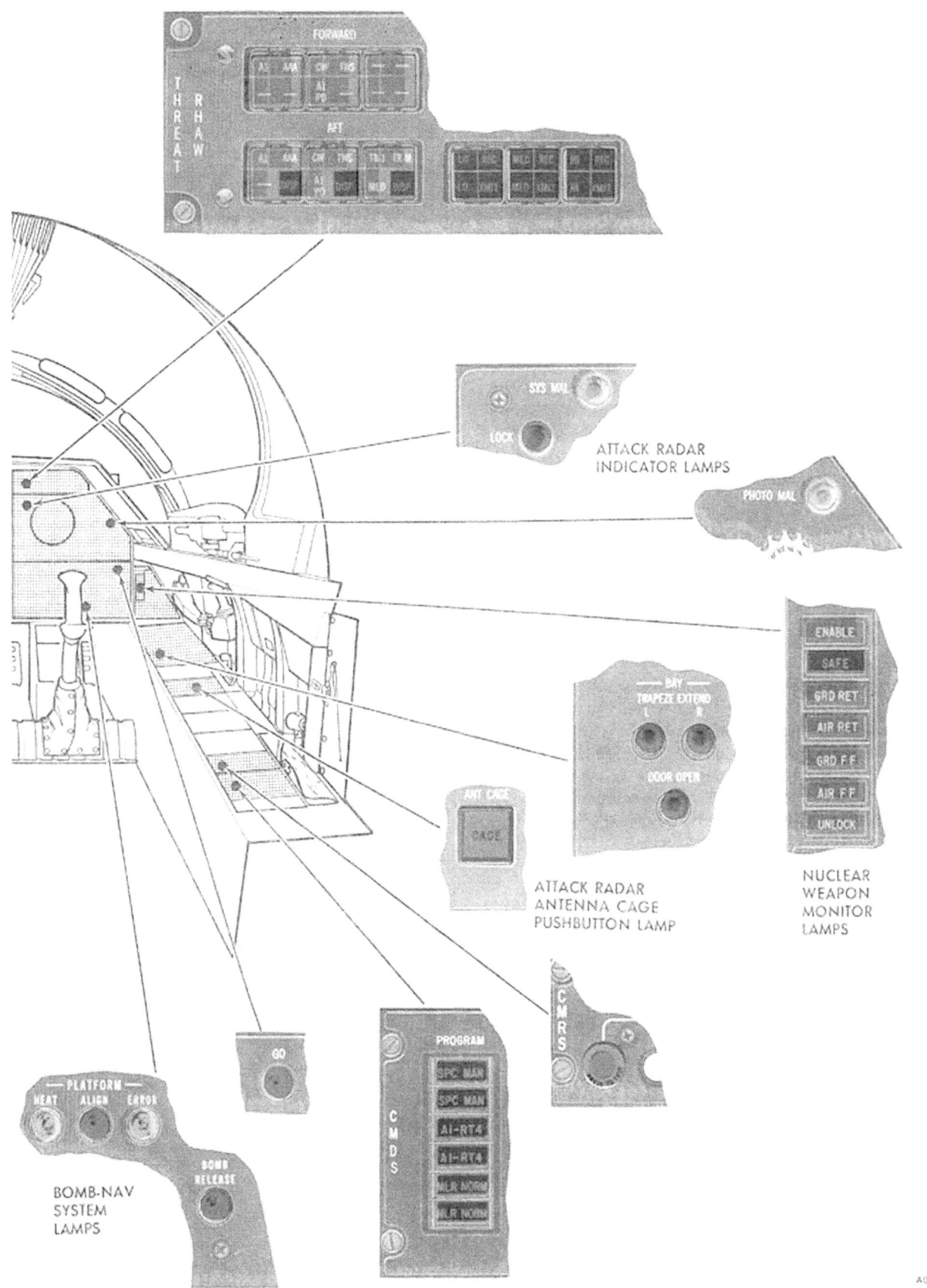

Figure 1-29A. (Sheet 2)

Changed 7 April 1967

1-70C

Section I
Description & Operation

selector window. The selected course is compared with actual course by the bomb nav system and an error signal is provided to display course steering commands on the bank steering bars on the ADI and LCOS and course deviation information on the course deviation indicator on the HSI.

● The MAN HDG (manual heading) position provides the capability of flying any desired heading when use of the bomb nav system is impractical or inefficient or when the system is inoperative. The heading marker on the HSI is set to the desired heading on the compass card by using the heading set knob. Turn the airplane to center the bank steering bars on the ADI and LCOS. Any deviation from this heading will generate a steering command on the bank steering bars on the ADI and LCOS. If the bomb nav system is inoperative the course set knob should be used to set the desired heading in the course selector window. This will provide a digital readout of the heading and align the course arrow with the heading marker to reduce the possibility of heading confusion.

Note

With the instrument system coupler mode selector knob in the OFF, TACAN, CRS SEL NAV, NAV, MAN CRS or MAN HDG positions and with the instrument system coupler pitch steering mode switch at OFF, a fly-up command will be displayed on the pitch steering bars on the ADI and LCOS and the radar altitude low warning lamp will light when the airplane descends below the altitude index setting of the radar altimeter. The fly-up command will be terminated and the radar altitude low warning lamp will go out when the airplane climbs back through the altitude index setting. If a descent is begun from above 5000 feet above the ground with the instrument system coupler mode selector knob and pitch steering mode switch in the above positions the radar altitude low warning lamp will momentarily light and the pitch steering bars on the ADI and LCOS will momentarily indicate a fly-up command when the airplane descends through 5000 feet.

● The AIR/AIR position provides the steering capability to a target being tracked by the attack radar system. In this mode the HSI heading marker is driven by a bearing signal from the attack radar and provides a signal to indicate the necessary steering commands on the bank steering bars on the ADI and LCOS to steer the airplane to the target. The pitch steering bars on the ADI and LCOS will be activated and indicate the necessary pitch steering correction (airplane angle of attack plus radar antenna tilt angle) to be on target.

● The SHRIKE position provides the steering capability for making attacks on ground radar transmitters. In this mode the shrike receiver furnishes direction finding and pitch deviation information to provide target deviation indications on the ADI and LCOS. The pitch steering bars will display "g" command steering signals when a pull-up condition is desired.

Instrument Test Button.

The instrument test button (6, figure 1-25), located on the ground check panel, is provided for ground checking and trouble shooting of the integrated flight instruments, the instrument system coupler, and the total temperature indicator. The button must be used in conjunction with the central air data computer (CADC) power switch when checking the airspeed-mach indicator (AMI), altitude-vertical velocity (AVVI), or the total temperature indicator (TTI). Depressing and holding the button will provide a set of predetermined indications on the above instruments. (Refer to "CADC Test Switch," this section, for AMI, AVVI and TTI test indications.) Test indications on the ADI and HSI will be compatible with the normal indications expected for each mode selected by the instrument system coupler mode selector knob.

WARNING, CAUTION AND INDICATOR LAMPS.

In order to keep instrument surveillance to a minimum, warning, caution, and indicator lamps are located throughout the cockpit. All of these lamps except the master caution lamp are described under their respective systems. For location of the lamps throughout the cockpit see figures 1-29 or 1-29A.

MASTER CAUTION LAMP.

The master caution lamp (19, figure 1-6 or 22, figure 1-6A), located on the left main instrument panel, will light to alert the crew that a malfunction exists when any of the individual caution lamps on the caution lamp panel light to indicate a malfunction. The lamp will remain lighted as long as an individual caution lamp is on; however, it should be reset as soon as possible by depressing the face of the lamp so that other caution lamps can be monitored should additional malfunctions occur. The intensity of the lamp can be adjusted with the malfunction and indicator lamp dimming switch. The lamp can be checked by depressing the malfunction and indicator lamp test button.

Malfunction and Indicator Lamp Dimming Switch.

The malfunction and indicator lamp dimming switch (5, figure 1-51), located on the lighting control panel, is a three position switch marked BRT (bright) and DIM and is spring-loaded to an unmarked center position. The switch controls the light intensity, either bright or dim, of all the warning, caution and indicator lamps in the cockpit.

Note

All lamps are automatically set to bright when:

- The internal lighting control knob (FLT INST) is off.
- The lighing control knob (WHITE FLOOD FLT & ENG., INST) is on.
- When aircraft power is turned off.

Malfunction and Indicator Lamp Test Button.

The malfunction and indicator lamp test button (6, figure 1-51), located on the lighting control panel, is provided to check all warning, caution and indicator lamps in the cockpit for burned out bulbs and the landing gear warning horn.

BOMBING-NAVIGATION SYSTEM (AN/AJQ-20).

The bombing-navigation (bomb nav) system is a self-contained dead reckoning analogue inertial system. The system consists of a stabilized platform (SP), a navigational computer (NC), a remotely located flux valve and a remotely located bomb nav distance time indicator. The system provides the following functions:

- Computed aircraft position in latitude and longitude.
- Range and bearing to target or destination for navigation steering and/or bombing.
- Continuously computed and displayed values of ground speed, ground track, true heading, wind speed, and wind direction.
- Aircraft pitch and roll attitude.
- A stabilized magnetic heading to the pilot's flight instruments.
- Automatic steering signals to the autopilot, attitude director indicator, the horizontal situation indicator, and the lead computing optical sight for navigation and homing.
- Constant ground track steering signals to autopilot.
- Drift Angle.
- Slant range and bearing to a fixpoint for attack radar crosshair laying.
- Provisions for attacking no-show radar targets by off-set radar sighting.

- Position correction via radar fix-taking.
- Determination of the coordinates of unknown radar locations detected by the homing and warning radar.
- Pushbutton fly over fix-taking capability for present position correction.
- Altitude calibration by use of attack radar or radar altimeter.
- Up to three alternate or intermediate destination storages. New destinations may be inserted into storages at any time by the operator.
- Glide path or dive angle deviation steering signals for use in making airborne instrument landing approaches or dive bomb runs.
- A backup capability in case of stabilization platform failure.
- Simple self-test features to isolate system troubles to the stabilized platform or navigational computer while the system is still installed in the airplane.

STABILIZED PLATFORM.

The stabilized platform (SP), located in the forward electronics bay, consists of a four-gimbal, all attitude inertially stabilized platform, and its associated electronics. The SP supplies outputs of pitch, roll, true heading, and north and east components of ground speed. Additionally, signals are provided to indicate (1) progress of initial alignment, (2) proper range of SP gyroscope temperatures, and (3) reliability of SP output data. Prior to flight, the SP is initially aligned by one of three methods: (1) Gyrocompass alignment (the normal method), (2) Alignment to stored magnetic variations, (3) Rapid alignment to stored gyrocompass heading. In normal gyrocompass alignment, the output signals of the inertial sensors (two gyroscopes with two degrees of freedom and two linear accelerometers) are utilized to drive the platform to a true north and plumb-bob level orientation. The orientation is such that the "East" gyroscope senses no angular rotation input (earth-rate) resulting from the earth's rotation and neither accelerometer senses any acceleration effects of the earth's gravity. Both of the other two methods of alignment are rapid alignment modes. Either of these two modes may be used when the correct aircraft true heading has been stored in the navigational computer (NC) from a previous operation or when the correct magnetic variation is known. These two modes bypass the relatively slow gyrocompass process to determine true north, and brings the SP to a ready condition in approximately 90 seconds. After alignment, the SP is placed in the appropriate navigation mode. In navigational modes, the platform is maintained in a north-stabilized plumb-bob level orientation by signals from the gyroscopes, which are precessed by precisely computed signals to compensate for the earth's spin rate and aircraft movement relative to the earth. Accelerometers, mounted in the horizontal plane on the platform, are aligned so that one senses only north-south accelerations and the other senses only east-west accelerations. Their outputs, after correction for Coriolis and centripetal effects, are then integrated to obtain signals proportional to instantaneous north and east velocities. These signals are used to develop gyroscope precession signals in the SP and also to generate ground track data, ground speed data and update computed aircraft position information. All the critical signal loops within the SP are constantly monitored by a go-no-go circuit which, in event of SP failure, turns the SP off and signals the operator by lighting the platform error lamp on the bomb nav control panel. In addition, automatic temperature controls signal the operator when temperatures in the SP are below the required level. When this condition exists, the SP is not required to perform to full accuracy. The SP requires inputs of 115 volt 3 phase ac power from the right main AC bus, 28 volt dc mode control signals from the NC, and synchro analogue data from the NC corresponding to aircraft latitude.

NAVIGATIONAL COMPUTER.

The navigational computer (NC), located in the right main instrument panel, is a self-contained navigation steering, radar sighting and bombing computer. The primary inputs to the NC are north and east components of ground speed, true heading and pitch angle from the stabilized platform (SP), true air speed and pressure altitude from the central air data computer (CADC) and magnetic heading from the system flux valve. The NC provides all the computing, control, and display functions for the bomb nav system. In event of SP failure the NC will continue to operate using computed or handset wind combined with true airspeed from the CADC and magnetic heading from the auxiliary flight reference system (AFRS) to substitute for SP data.

CONTROLS AND INDICATORS.

Bomb Nav Mode Selector Knob.

The eleven position bomb nav mode selector knob (13, figure 1-30), located on the bomb nav control panel is labeled MODE SEL. The knob controls warmup, power turn on, and system operating modes. By rotating the knob clockwise, the 7 and 8 o'clock positions set the system up for operation. The 9 through 12 o'clock positions provide normal navigation modes and the 1 through 4 o'clock positions provide auxiliary navigation modes. The knob must be rotated counterclockwise to turn the system off. This knob has detents at all positions and requires a pullout to rotate from ALIGN to any normal navigation position and from the normal navigation range to any auxiliary navigation position. The knob markings and functions are as follows:

1. OFF—All power off.

2. HEAT—All power off except for inertial platform heater power — provided the platform alignment control knob is in any position except PLATFORM OFF.

3. ALIGN — All power on and stabilized platform sequenced through alignment cycle — provided the platform alignment control knob is in any position except PLATFORM OFF. Computer is operative.

4. GREAT CIRCLE — Normal navigation operating mode, used for ranges in excess of 200 nautical miles, in which the range and course computers solve for the Great Circle route from the geographic position indicated by the present position counters to the geographic position indicated by the destination position counters. In this mode, the radar sighting computer is inoperative.

5. SHORT RANGE—Normal navigation operating mode, used only within 200 nautical miles of the target, in which the computer assumes a flat-earth condition to compute range and course from the geographic positions indicated by the present position counters to the geographic position indicated by the destination position counters. In this mode, the radar sighting computer is operative.

6. TRAIL BOMB—This attack mode is primarily a high altitude weapon delivery mode which utilizes the computer in the short range configuration to develop the bombing equation. In this mode, the radar sighting computer is also operative. Trail and time-of-fall parameters are handset and the bomb release lamp automatically lights when the computed time to release is zero. Time to release is continuously displayed on both the destination distance/time counter and the bomb nav distance/time indicator.

7. RANGE BOMB—This attack mode is a tactical mode used primarily for low-altitude weapon delivery. The computer operates in the basic short range mode and continuously displays the range to the release point, which is the intersection of the course to target line with the release circle, which is a circle centered on the target with the radius selected by the operator for the particular weapons. The bomb release lamp lights when the preselected release range is reached. In this mode, the radar sighting computer is operative.

8. AUX-NAV—During the auxiliary navigation modes, the computer display unit is used as a dead reckoning computer and performs essentially the same functions as during the corresponding normal navigation modes except the inputs from the stabilized platform are replaced by flux valve compass heading from the auxiliary flight reference system (AFRS), true airspeed input from the air-data computer, and handset magnetic variation and wind information. Also, during auxiliary navigation modes, the bomb nav system attitude ready signal is removed, causing other systems to be switched to the AFRS for attitude/heading reference data, and the primary attitude/heading caution lamp is lighted.

Bomb Nav Fix Mode Selector Buttons.

Nine bomb nav fix mode selector pushbuttons (20, figure 1-30) are located on the bomb nav control panel. Only one button can be depressed at a time. With each new mode selection, the preceding mode will disengage. In addition, a bar on the panel below the engaged button will become visible, indicating that the button has been depressed and the indicated mode selected. To disengage an operating mode without engaging another mode, lightly depress any other button. The buttons are labeled and function as follows:

1. PRES POS—Slaves the destination position counters to present position, removes attack radar cursors from display, and de-activates the target bearing, slant range, course angle, and distance to destination servos.

2. TARGET—Selects target set in the destination position counters as the radar sighting point. The present position counters may be corrected by the attack radar tracking handle or hand setting.

3. OFFSET—Selects offset aimpoint as the sighting point. The present position counters may be corrected by the attack radar tracking handle or hand setting.

4. MAN FIX—Applies energizing voltages to the present position hold and present position correction buttons. Removes attack radar cursors from display and de-activates the target bearing, slant range, course angle, and distance to destination servos.

5. DEST STORAGE 1, 2, and 3—Slaves destination shafts to the stored 1, 2, or 3 destination. Removes attack radar cursors from display and de-activates the target bearing, slant range, course angle, and distance to destination servos. Stored information may be changed by hand-setting as desired.

Note

The destination position counters will not slew more than ±18 degrees of latitude or longitude from the latitude and longitude indicated at the time the fix mode DEST STORAGE selector button is depressed. The counter(s) will drive to an erroneous position should this range limitation not be observed during operation. However, even though the limitations are exceeded the stored information will not be lost, unless changed by handsetting, and will drive the counters to the correct stored position when the range limitation is observed.

6. HOMER SET—Causes position of computer destination position relative to present position to be displayed on the radar homing and warning scope. This allows the coordinates of an interrogating radar to be determined by correcting the destination position counters with the attack radar tracking handle until the bomb nav system computer cursor on the radar homing and warning scope is in coincidence with the interrogating radar's indicated position.

7. HOMER TRACK—Selected to obtain second fix on interrogating radar set making use of triangulation to improve accuracy of fixing the interrogating radar coordinates. The computer cursor on the radar homing and warning scope will respond only to cross-track correction commands from the attack radar tracking handle.

Present Position Correction Button.

The present position correction button (3, figure 1-30), located on the bomb nav control panel, is labeled CORRECT PRES POSITION. This button is used, in conjunction with other controls, as a mode of up-dating the present position counters at the time of overflying a fixpoint. The mode cannot be activated until after the fix mode MAN FIX selector button has been depressed. Also, the destination position counters must first be set to the latitude and longitude of the fixpoint to be overflown. With the two preceding requirements satisfied, momentarily depressing the present position correction button at the instant of overflying the fixpoint, will slave the present position counters to the destination position counters. During this time the destination position counters will be tracking actual aircraft position while the present position counters are catching up. The present position up-dating is complete when the readings of the two counters agree, at which time, the mode may be deactivated (deenergized) by depressing any other fix mode selector button.

Changed 18 August 1967

Section I
Description & Operation

T.O. 1F-111A-1

Bomb Nav Control Panel

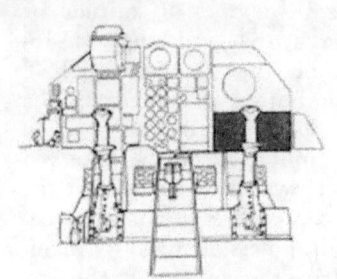

1. Present Position Hold Button.
2. Present Position Counters (2).
3. Present Position Correction Button.
4. Magnetic Heading Synchronization Indicator.
5. Fixpoint Elevation Counter.
6. True Heading Counter.
7. Magnetic Variation Counter.
8. Time-of-Fall Counter.
9. Ground Track and Groundspeed Counters (2).
10. Go Lamp.
11. Altitude/Test Selector Knob.
12. Trail/Range Counter.
13. Bomb Nav. Mode Selector Knob.
14. Destination Distance/Time Counter.
15. Platform Alignment Control Knob.
16. Bomb Release Lamp.
17. Glide/Dive Angle Counter.
18. Platform Indicator Lamps (3).
19. Wind Speed and Wind From Counters (2).
20. Bomb Nav Fix Mode Selector Buttons.
21. Offset Range and Offset Bearing Counters (2).
22. Destination Position Counters.

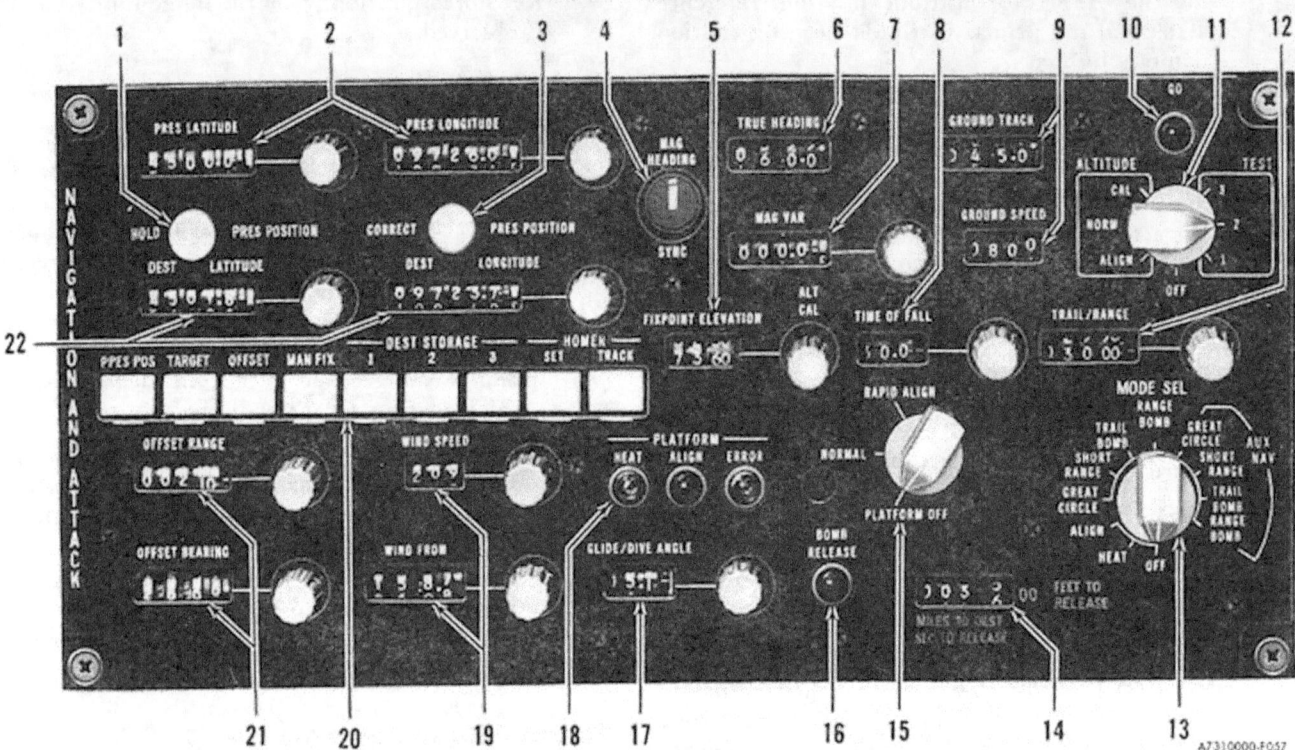

Figure 1-30.

Present Position Hold Button.

The present position hold button (1, figure 1-30), located on the bomb nav control panel, is labeled HOLD PRES POSITION. This button is used, in conjunction with other controls, as a mode of up-dating present position when it is not desired to reset the destination position counters from a distant destination to local fixpoint. The mode cannot be activated until after the fix mode MAN FIX selector button has been depressed. With the above requirement satisfied, depressing and holding the present position hold button while re-setting the present position counters to the latitude and longitude of the fixpoint, and then releasing the button at the instant of overflying the fixpoint will cause the present position counters to start tracking the corrected aircraft position. To deactivate the mode some other fix mode selector button must be depressed.

Platform Alignment Control Knob.

The platform alignment control knob (15, figure 1-30) located on the bomb nav control panel is a three-position rotary knob marked RAPID ALIGN, NORMAL and PLATFORM OFF. The knob must be pulled out before it can be rotated from any position. The knob controls the alignment modes of the stabilized platform when the bomb nav mode selector knob is positioned to ALIGN. In the PLATFORM OFF position, the stabilized platform is completely de-energized. In the NORMAL position, the platform may be aligned in either of two ways, (1) gyrocompass or (2) alignment to stored magnetic variation. The gyrocompass alignment is the slower alignment, but is the more precise and may be used irrespective of the accuracy to which local magnetic variation is known. Alignment to stored magnetic variation may be used when local

Changed 18 August 1967

magnetic variation is accurately known and a rapid alignment is desired. In the gyrocompass alignment, the stabilized platform goes through two modes of azimuth alignment: (1) Alignment to true north as defined by the flux valve magnetic heading plus handset magnetic variation, and (2) Refinement of alignment or gyrocompassing to true north as precisely defined by the direction where the "East" gyroscope senses none of the earth's rotation. In the alignment to stored magnetic variation, the operator manually places the bomb nav mode selector knob to a navigate mode after the stabilized platform has positioned to computed true heading and before the gyrocompass phase of alignment has begun. The decision to use this method is based on three considerations: (1) Urgency of accomplishing alignment rapidly, (2) Accuracy to which local magnetic variation is known, and (3) Whether or not gyrocompass heading information has previously been stored in the system for the rapid align to stored heading mode.

Note

If gyrocompass heading information has previously been stored in the system and the airplane heading has not been changed since the information was stored, the RAPID ALIGN mode should be used. In this mode, the platform will align to the stored heading and will be ready for operation in approximately 90 seconds.

Altitude/Test Selector Knob.

The altitude/test selector knob (11, figure 1-30), located on the bomb nav control panel, is labeled ALTITUDE TEST. The knob has three positions for computer self-testing marked 1, 2 and 3; three positions for altitude calibration marked CAL, NORM and ALIGN; and an OFF position. The knob must be pulled out to go into or out of the Test Sector. The altitude positions control a clutch that connects or disconnects the altitude calibration (ALT CAL) knob to the fixpoint elevation counter and either activates the GO lamp circuitry (in ALIGN) or commands the attack radar system to the altitude calibration mode (in CAL). The CAL position provides for manual calibration of pressure altitude above terrain when over terrain of known elevation with the attack radar system in operation. The ALIGN position works in conjunction with the GO lamp and provides for setting the pressure altitude correction term to zero for test purposes. When set to the NORM position, the signals applied in CAL or ALIGN positions are removed and the system is in the normal mode. Test 1, 2, and 3 positions are used in conjunction with the GO lamp for system operational ground checkout only.

Note

Do not set the switch to any of these test positions in flight.

Platform Indicator Lamps.

Three platform indicator lamps (18, figure 1-30), located on the bomb nav control panel, are labeled HEAT, ALIGN and ERROR. The amber HEAT indicator lamp provides a monitor of the platform heat signal from the stabilized platform (SP). When the system is activated, the lamp will light until the gyroscope temperature reaches the factory-set level. When the lamp is lighted, the SP will not enter the gyrocompass cycle. When the lamp goes out, it will remain out until the system is recycled. The green ALIGN indicator lamp provides for monitoring platform alignment status during the alignment mode (mode selector knob in ALIGN). With the platform alignment control knob in NORMAL, the lamp will light when the SP switches into the gyrocompass phase of alignment. It will remain lighted continuously until the gyrocompass process has attained the required alignment accuracy, at which time it will begin flashing, signaling the operator that the gyrocompass process is complete to required accuracies. The mode selector knob may then be left in ALIGN to allow alignment quality to improve. The knob must be advanced to a navigation mode for taxi. With the platform alignment control knob in RAPID ALIGN, the ALIGN indicator lamp will remain out until alignment is complete at which time (within approximately 90 seconds of turn-on), the lamp will begin flashing. The amber ERROR indicator lamp provides a monitor of the platform reliability signal from the stabilized platform when the mode selector knob is in ALIGN or any of the normal navigation positions. The lamp will light when the SP is off, unless the platform alignment control knob is in PLATFORM OFF and the altitude test selector knob is in any one of the three test positions. The lamp will light, should the platform turn itself off, when the bomb nav mode selector knob is in any of the normal navigation modes and will go out when an auxiliary navigation mode is selected.

Primary Attitude/Heading Caution Lamp.

The primary attitude/heading caution lamp, located on the main caution lamp panel (figure 1-29 or 1-29A), will light when either attitude or heading information from the stabilized platform is interrupted or becomes unreliable due to a platform malfunction. Placing the bomb nav mode selector switch to an auxiliary navigation position or placing the flight instrument reference select switch to AUX will also cause the lamp to light. When the lamp lights the letters PRI

Section I
Description & Operation

ATT/HDG will be visible. Should the lamp light when operating with the flight instrument reference select switch in the PRI position the attitude director indicator and horizontal situation indicator will be automatically switched to the AFRS, however, the AUX position on the flight instrument reference select switch should be selected so that the proper source of signals will be indicated.

Go Lamp.

The green GO lamp (10, figure 1-30), located on the bomb nav control panel, is labeled GO and provides for monitoring the navigational computer self-test circuits and fixpoint elevation counter alignment. The lamp will light when the altitude/test selector knob is placed in ALIGN or Test positions 1, 2, or 3, provided the proper settings have been set on the panel, and the bomb nav system is operational. Align or test positions are not used for inflight operation; therefore, the lamp should remain off during flight.

Present Position Counters.

Two present position counters (2, figure 1-30), located on the bomb nav control panel, are labeled PRES LATITUDE and PRES LONGITUDE. The counters display the geodetic latitude and longitude utilized as the airplane position coordinates. The counters are continuously and automatically up-dated by inputs of true north and east velocity components from the stabilized platform during all normal navigational modes. During all auxiliary navigational modes, the counters are similarly up-dated by north and east velocities as derived from airspeed, handset or last computed wind data, and auxiliary flight reference system heading plus hand-set magnetic variation. Control knobs are provided for electrically slewing the counters to set in initial position or to insert corrections. The speed at which the counter is driven is proportional to the degree the control knob is turned. The counters may also be automatically driven with the attack radar tracking handle.

Fixpoint Elevation Counter.

The fixpoint elevation counter (5, figure 1-30), located on the bomb nav control panel is labeled FIXPOINT ELEVATION. An adjacent altitude calibration knob, labeled ALT CAL, provides control of the counter. The counter is handset to the elevation of the radar aiming point in use; either (1) the position indicated by the destination counters, or (2) the offset aimpoint when using offset sighting, or (3) elevation of terrain below the airplane when calibrating altitude.

Note

The fixpoint elevation counter contains mechanical stops at both the lower and upper limits. Due to the mechanical stops, the counter reading will not change when the ALT CAL knob is rotated either: (1) CCW when the counter is at its lower limit; or (2) CW when the counter is at its upper limit. A slip clutch located in the mechanical linkage between the knob and the counter, however, will slip and result in a change to the setting of the calibration potentiometer. This does not damage the equipment, but does destroy any previously established alignment between the counter and the potentiometer. Alignment can be recovered by performing an altitude calibration procedure.

Destination Position Counters.

The latitude and longitude coordinates of airplane destination, radar fixpoints or targets must be set into the destination latitude and longitude counter in order to use the course computation, radar cursor laying, or automatic bombing functions. Two destination position counters (22, figure 1-30), located on the bomb nav control panel, are labeled DEST LATITUDE and DEST LONGITUDE. The counters, which display destination position in geodetic latitude and longitude, may be handset or automatically slaved to track the present position counters. The counters may also be automatically slaved to positions stored in any of three storage channels or automatically driven with the attack radar system tracking handle. Control knobs are provided for electrically slewing the counters to set in destination position. The speed at which the counter is driven is proportional to the degree the control knob is rotated. The last drum of the destination counters is numbered in tenths of minutes and has intermediate markings at 0.05 minute intervals. These counters can be set to one-half of the half tenths divisions or 0.025 minutes. For accurate radar fixtaking or bombing of targets by techniques other than direct radar sighting, these counters should be set to the nearest 0.025 minutes.

True Heading Counter.

The true heading counter (6, figure 1-30), located on the bomb nav control panel, is labeled TRUE HEADING. The counter continuously displays the computed airplane heading relative to true north as derived from (1) inputs of true heading from the stabilized platform during all normal navigation modes, and (2) magnetic heading input from the auxiliary flight reference system and hand-set magnetic variation during all auxiliary navigation modes.

Magnetic Variation Counter.

The magnetic variation counter (7, figure 1-30), located on the bomb nav control panel, is labeled MAG VAR. The counter displays manually inserted magnetic variation. The counter is varied by manually turning its control knob. In normal navigation modes, the counter is adjusted until the magnetic heading synchronization indicator indicates a null. At this time, the counter will indicate the local variation. In auxiliary navigation modes, the counter must be up-dated to settings specified from map data. This up-dating procedure has no effect on the synchronization meter but will simultaneously up-date the navigational computer true heading.

Magnetic Heading Synchronization Indicator.

The magnetic heading synchronization indicator (4, figure 1-30), located on the bomb nav control panel, is marked MAG HEADING SYNC. In normal navigation modes, the indicator provides an indication of agreement (or disagreement) between computed magnetic heading (which is also being transmitted to the flight instruments) and magnetic heading from a flux valve input. During the normal navigation modes, the indicator is maintained at null by periodic manual correction of handset magnetic variation to correct computed magnetic heading to agree with flux valve data. The indicator should be disregarded when operating in any of the auxiliary navigation modes. In platform align modes, the indicator automatically provides a status of azimuth alignment independent of other parameters.

This page intentionally left blank.

Groundtrack and Groundspeed Counters.

The groundtrack and groundspeed counters (9, figure 1-30), located on the bomb nav control panel, are labeled GROUNDTRACK and GROUNDSPEED. The counters continuously display the computed true groundtrack and groundspeed as derived from (1) inputs of true north and east velocity from the stabilized platform during all normal navigation modes, and (2) airspeed input from the central air data computer, magnetic heading input from auxiliary compass set, handset magnetic variation, and either stored or handset wind information during all auxiliary navigation modes.

Wind Speed and Wind From Counters.

The wind speed and wind from counters (19, figure 1-30), located on the bomb nav control panel, are labeled WIND SPEED and WIND FROM. During all normal navigational modes, the counters continuously and automatically display the computed value of wind direction and magnitude as derived from inputs of true velocity and true heading from the stabilized platform and airspeed from the central air data computer. During auxiliary navigational modes, the counter readings are controlled by adjacent control knobs for manual up-dating wind information as corrected wind information becomes available to the operator. WIND SPEED limits are from 0 to 250 knots. WIND FROM range is 0 to 360 degrees.

Glide/Dive Angle Counter.

The glide/dive angle counter (17, figure 1-30), located on the bomb nav control panel, is labeled GLIDE/DIVE ANGLE. The counter displays the preselected glide or dive angle set into the computer in the vertical steering mode. The glide/dive angle is used to derive information proportional to the difference between the hand-set desired value and the computed value of either aircraft dive angle (in dive mode) or glide slope (in airborne instrument landing approach mode). The resultant steering information is displayed on the attitude director indicator (ADI) and lead computing optical sight (LCOS). The glide/dive angle counter limits are from 00.0 to 99.9 degrees.

Offset Range and Offset Bearing Counters.

The offset range and offset bearing counters (21, figure 1-30), located on the bomb nav control panel, are labeled OFFSET RANGE and OFFSET BEARING. The counters are hand-set by the operator to values derived from map data. They represent the range and bearing from the position represented by the destination counters to the position of a preselected radar sighting point. The information entered into these counters is provided to the computer only when the fix mode OFFSET selector button is depressed. The computer utilizes this information to derive radar sighting parameters for the selected offset sighting point. Derivation of these parameters will allow the offset point to be used as a radar position fix reference while the bombing computer is solving equations for attack of the position indicated by the destination counters. This mode is used when the target is a poor or no-show radar target with a good radar target in the near vicinity. OFFSET RANGE limits are from 0 to 99,990 feet.

Destination Distance/Time Counter.

The destination distance/time counter (14, figure 1-30), is located on the bomb nav control panel. The counter is marked MILES TO DEST, SEC TO REL and FEET TO REL. Each function of the counter is separately lighted so that only the correct marking for the quantity being displayed is visible to the operator. When the mode selector knob is positioned to GREAT CIRCLE or SHORT RANGE, MILES TO DEST will light and display continuous computation of the distance in nautical miles from present position to any destination set into the destination counters (provided the destination is within 4000 nautical miles of the present position). When the mode selector knob is placed to RANGE BOMB, the words, FEET TO REL and two zeroes (00) will light, and display continuous computation of the range to the bomb release point in feet from zero to 400,000 feet. When the mode selector knob is placed to TRAIL BOMB, SEC TO REL will light, and display continuous computation of the seconds remaining before bomb release ranging from zero to 400 seconds.

Trail/Range Counter.

The trail/range counter (12, figure 1-30), located on the bomb nav control panel, is labeled TRAIL/RANGE. The counter displays trail or range bombing parameter information manually set into the computer for trail bomb or range bomb mode. The trail/range knob is mechanically connected to the counter and a potentiometer. The output of the potentiometer is a voltage representing the trail or range value set into the counter for use by the computer during bombing. The counter setting has no effect on the great circle or short range modes. TRAIL RANGE setting limits are from 0 to 99,990 feet.

Time-of-Fall Counter.

The time-of-fall counter (8, figure 1-30), located on the bomb nav control panel, is labeled TIME OF FALL. The counter displays time-of-fall bombing parameter information hand-set into the counter for use during the trail bomb mode. The time-of-fall control knob is mechanically connected to the time-of-fall counter to provide a hand-setting method. Information displayed is entered into the computer only when the system is operating in the trail bomb mode. TIME OF FALL setting limits are from 0 to 99.9 seconds.

Bomb Release Lamp.

The green bomb-release lamp (16, figure 1-30), located on the bomb nav control panel is labeled BOMB RELEASE. The lamp provides monitoring for the automatic release signal that is computed and provided by the navigational computer to other equipment for weapons release. The lamp will light when the computer is in the trail or range bomb configuration and the seconds or feet to release has driven to zero.

Radar Bomb Scoring (RBS) Tone Switch.

The RBS tone switch (5A, figure 1-31), located on the armament select panel, is provided to control a 1020 cps tone transmitted by the UHF radio for scoring practice bomb runs. The switch is a lever lock type with two positions marked RBS TONE (in the ON position) and OFF. The switch is spring loaded to the OFF position and is locked in the OFF position. The switch toggle must be pulled out to move the switch from OFF to ON. Placing the switch to the ON position turns on the tone and energizes a switch solenoid to hold the switch in the ON position. A release signal from the bomb nav system, LCOS, dual bombing timer, or either weapon release button is necessary to break the circuit to the switch solenoid to turn off the tone. The tone can be manually turned off by placing the switch to the OFF position.

Bomb/Nav Distance-Time Indicator.

The bomb/nav distance-time indicator (BNDTI) (23, figure 1-6 or 24, figure 1-6A), located on the left main instrument panel, is a remote indicating type instrument. The indicator displays digital time and distance to target or destination. The display elements are (1) a four-digit counter display and (2) a legend-type tape display. The digital display consists of three synchro drum counters which receive signals from the navigational computer (NC). The fourth digit is fixed at zero and is covered by a shutter except when operating in the great circle navigation mode. The operating modes of the NC are identified on a servo driven tape, containing legends positioned in a window, and functioning in synchronization with the digital display. When operating in great circle mode, the tape will display great circle/miles and the digital display will indicate distance in nautical miles to destination. When operating in short range mode, the tape will display short range/miles and the digital display will indicate distance in nautical miles to destination. When operating in trail bomb mode, the tape will display bomb trail/seconds and the digital display will indicate the time, in seconds, remaining before bomb release. When operating in range bomb mode, the tape will display bomb range/thousands of feet, and the digital display will indicate, in feet, the distance to the bomb release point.

When the bomb nav system is off, or when the operator is changing system modes, the digital display is covered by a shutter.

BOMB NAV SYSTEM OPERATION.

Normal Mode Operation.

During normal operation, the bomb nav mode selector knob is set to either the GREAT CIRCLE, SHORT RANGE, TRAIL BOMB, or RANGE BOMB positions as appropriate to phase of mission. The heading groundtrack, and ground speed counters are controlled by outputs from the stabilized platform. Wind speed and wind direction are computed and displayed on the wind speed and wind from counters. Present position is continuously and automatically updated by input velocity signals from the SP, and may be corrected, as required, by radar sighting and/or manual fix modes. Range and course to target or destination are continuously computed and transmitted to the flight instruments, with range or time to target or destination displayed on the destination distance/time counter. All other counters and controls are hand set, as required, by the operator. If the mode selector knob is in a normal navigation mode, the platform ERROR indicator lamp will light if the SP fails, at which time the NC will automatically switch into auxiliary navigation.

Destination Set Procedure.

Note

- If destination is to be set prior to system operation or preflight alignment, place the platform alignment control knob to PLATFORM OFF before moving the bomb nav mode selector knob from OFF.

- Do not move the mode selector knob from OFF on a system that has been preset for stored heading rapid alignment until ready for alignment.

1. Bomb nav mode selector knob—ALIGN position or above.
2. Fix mode PRES POS selector button—Depress.

Note

Depress to slew destination counters to present position if desired destination is near indicated present position and a distant destination is indicated in the counters. Wait for destination counters to stop slewing.

3. Fix mode TARGET selector button—Depress.
4. Destination counters—Set.
   Set the destination counters to the desired coordinates.

Destination Storage.

Note

Destinations may be stored, without activation of the stabilized platform, by placing the platform alignment control knob to PLATFORM OFF prior to operation of the bomb nav mode selector knob. Exercise of this option, however, will invalidate any previously stored true heading data, thereby precluding use of the rapid alignment to stored gyrocompass heading stabilized platform alignment mode without first repeating the presetting procedure for "Rapid Alignment to Stored Gyrocompass Heading."

1. Bomb nav mode selector knob—ALIGN position or above.
2. Fix mode DEST STORAGE 1, 2, or 3 selector button—Depress.

Note

Computed course and miles to destination will remain at the computed values existing when the button is depressed. The attack radar cursors will be absent in the GND VEL and GND AUTO modes.

3. Destination counters—Set.
   Set the destination counters to the coordinates desired for storage.
4. Repeat steps 2 and 3 for each destination storage desired.
5. Fix mode TARGET selector button—Depress.

Note

If the platform alignment control knob was placed to PLATFORM OFF, set the bomb nav mode selector knob to OFF or HEAT, and then set the platform alignment control knob to NORMAL. Repeat the pre-setting procedure if the stabilized platform is to be subsequently aligned in the "Rapid Alignment to Stored Gyrocompass Heading" mode.

Stored Destination Recall Procedure.

Note

The destination position counters will not slew more than 18 degrees from the destination latitude and longitude indicated at the time the fix mode DEST STORAGE selector button is depressed. The counter(s) will drive to an erroneous position should this range limitation not be observed during operation. However, even though the limitations are exceeded the stored information will not be lost, unless changed by handsetting, and will drive the counters to the correct stored position when the range limitation is observed.

1. Fix mode DEST STORAGE 1, 2, or 3 selector button—Depress.
   Computed course and miles to destination will remain at the computed values existing when the button is depressed. The attack radar cursors will be absent in the GND VEL and GND AUTO modes.
2. Destination counters—Stop driving.
3. Fix mode TARGET selector button—Depress.
   Computed course and miles to destination will resume to new destination. The attack radar GND VEL and GND AUTO mode cursors will appear on the new destination if it is in range and the bomb nav mode selector knob is in any position other than GREAT CIRCLE, HEAT or OFF.
4. Destination counters—Check and refine as desired.

Altitude Calibration. Altitude calibration is necessary prior to position updating, radar bombing and AILA letdown. Altitude calibration is not affected by operations in the auxiliary navigation modes.

Ground Calibration

A. Altitude calibration may be accomplished on the ground in accordance with this procedure.
   1. Fixpoint elevation counter—Set.
      Set the fixpoint elevation counter to runway elevation.
   2. Bomb nav mode selector knob—SHORT RANGE.
   3. Fix mode TARGET selector button—Depress.
   4. Attack radar mode selector knob—GND AUTO.
   5. Altitude/test selector knob—CAL.
   6. Deleted.
   7. Altitude calibration knob—Adjust.
      Turn altitude calibration knob until radar cursor range counter reads zero.

8. Altitude/test selector knob—NORM.
   Calibration is complete.

Normal Airborne Calibration

B. Altitude calibration should be accomplished in accordance with this procedure when flying over level terrain of known elevation at altitudes normally above 1000 feet.

1. Fixpoint elevation counter—Set.
   Set the fixpoint elevation counter to the known elevation of the terrain where the calibration is to be accomplished.
2. Bomb nav mode selector knob—SHORT RANGE.
3. Fix mode TARGET selector button—Depress.
4. Attack radar mode selector knob—GND AUTO or GND VEL.
4A. Attack radar beta switch—MAN.
4B. Antenna tilt—Full down.
5. Altitude/test selector knob—CAL.
6. Altitude calibration knob—Adjust.
   Turn altitude calibration knob until the range cursor is coincident with the first ground return.
7. Altitude/test selector knob—NORM.
   Calibration is complete.

Low Altitude Calibration

Altitude calibration should be accomplished in accordance with this procedure when flying over level terrain of known elevation at altitudes normally below 1000 feet.

1. Fixpoint elevation counter—Set.
   Set the fixpoint elevation counter to the known elevation of the terrain where the calibration is to be accomplished.
2. Bomb nav mode selector knob—SHORT RANGE.
3. Fix mode TARGET selector button—Depress.
4. Attack radar mode selector knob—GND AUTO or GND VEL.
4A. Attack radar beta switch—NORM.
5. Altitude/test selector knob—CAL.
6. Altitude calibration knob—Adjust.
   Turn altitude calibration knob until the radar cursor range counter reading agrees with the radar altimeter reading.
7. Antenna tilt indicator—Minus 30.
   To assure that a positive altitude value was set, check that the antenna tilt indicator reads —30.
8. Altitude/test selector knob—NORM.
   Calibration is complete.

Magnetic Variation Updating. In normal navigation modes, the need for magnetic variation updating is indicated by off-null condition on the magnetic heading synchronization indicator.

1. Magnetic variation counter control knob — Adjust.
   Adjust the knob until the magnetic heading synchronization indicator pointer is centered.

Note

- When in auxiliary navigation modes, magnetic variation control knob adjustments update true heading and do not affect the magnetic heading synchronization indicator.
- When in the ALIGN mode, the MAG HEADING SYNC indicates align status, and cannot be used for magnetic variation updating.

2. Magnetic Variation Counter — Check.
   Check that the magnetic variation counter indicates magnetic variation of the present airplane position.

Auxiliary Mode Operation.

Note

Arbitrary selection of AUX NAV in flight, when the SP is good, should be kept to a minimum. The alignment of the platform will be unnecessarily subjected to possibly incorrect earth rate torquing signals due to degraded accuracy of present latitude updating in auxiliary navigation (AUX NAV) modes.

The auxiliary navigation (AUX NAV) modes are identical to the normal modes with the exception that the wind computation is stopped and the airspeed and stored winds are substituted for the stabilized platform outputs. Navigational computer true heading is derived from the back-up compass system and hand set magnetic variations. Magnetic heading for the horizontal situation indicator (HSI) and the attitude director indicator (ADI) is supplied directly from auxiliary flight reference system (AFRS). The magnetic heading synchronization indicator is not operative. The platform ERROR indicator lamp will be out at all times when the mode selector knob is in an auxiliary navigation mode.

Airplane Position Updating.

The need for airplane position updating is indicated primarily by inaccuracies in attack radar crosshair laying. In addition it is indicated by other reference navigational accuracy information available from other systems. If the attack radar system is not operating, manual position updating should be accomplished periodically. Airplane position updating will be required more often when operating in an auxiliary navigation mode since nav system accuracy will be degraded.

Radar Fix. The following radar fix is applicable only if the attack radar is operating.

1. Altitude calibration — Completed.
2. Fix mode TARGET selector button — Depress.
2A. Destination position counters — Set.
3. Fixpoint elevation counter — Set to fixpoint elevation.
4. Bomb nav mode selector knob — SHORT RANGE.
5. Attack radar mode selector knob — GND AUTO or GND VEL.
6. Destination/present position selector switch — PP.
7. Attack radar range selector knob — Use lowest range setting possible.
8. Radar cursors — Synchronize on target.

Radar Target Position Determination Procedure.

1. Altitude calibration — Complete.
2. Fix mode PRES POS selector button — Depress.
3. Destination counters — Set.
   Set destination to best known coordinates.
4. Fixpoint elevation counter — Set to best known elevation.
5. Attack radar mode selector knob — GND VEL or GND AUTO.
6. Destination/present position selector switch — DEST.
7. Bomb nav mode selector knob — SHORT RANGE.
8. Attack radar range selector knob — Use lowest range setting possible.
9. Radar cursors — Synchronize on target.
10. Destination counters — Record values, then set as desired.

Manual Present Position Fix (Correct Present Position). Fly toward the fixpoint.

1. Destination position counters — Set fixpoint coordinates.
2. Fix mode MAN FIX selector button — Depress.
   Depress the fix mode MAN FIX selector button when approaching the fixpoint. Computed course and miles to destination will remain at the computed values existing when the MAN FIX selector button is depressed. The attack radar cursors will disappear from the scope.
3. Present position correction button — Depress.
   Depress the present position correction button at the instant of overflying the fixpoint as determined visually, or with the attack radar or TFR ground map scope displays. The fix is complete when the present position counters stop slewing and agree with the destination position counters. Both sets of counters will drive at the same rate.
4. Present position and destination position counters — Checked.
5. Fix mode TARGET selector button — Depress.
6. Destination position counters — Reset.
   Course and distance computations will resume to the new destination and the attack radar cursors will fall on the new destination if in range.

Manual Present Position Fix (Hold Present Position). Fly toward the fixpoint.

1. Fix mode MAN FIX selector button — Depress.
   Depress the fix mode MAN FIX selector button when approaching the fixpoint. Computed course and miles to destination will remain at the computed values when the MAN FIX selector button is depressed. The attack radar cursors will disappear from the scope.
2. Present position hold button. Depress, and hold.
3. Present position counters — Set.
   Set the coordinates of the fixpoint in the present position counters.
4. Present position hold button — Release, over fixpoint.
   Release the present position hold button at the instant of overflying the fixpoint as determined visually, or with the attack radar or TFR ground map scope displays.

Note

The fix is complete. The present position counters will start to drive to track the aircraft position.

5. Fix mode TARGET selector button — Depress.
6. Destination position counters — Reset.
   Course and distance computations will resume to the new destination and the attack radar cursors will fall on the new destination if in range.

Normal turn on, gyrocompassing platform alignment procedures are contained within this section as well as within the appropriate portions of Section II. Alignment to stored magnetic variation and rapid alignment to stored gyrocompass heading are covered as alternate procedures in this section.

Gyrocompass Alignment Procedure.

1. Bomb nav mode selector knob — HEAT.
2. Platform heat indicator lamp — On.
3. Altitude/test selector knob — NORM.

4. Magnetic variation counter—Check and set to local variation.

Note

If local magnetic disturbances create excessive deviation they should be applied to the variation.

5. Present position latitude—Checked.
   If latitude is incorrect proceed as follows:
   a. Platform alignment control knob — PLATFORM OFF.
   b. Bomb nav mode selector knob — ALIGN.
   c. Present position latitude counter — Set.
   d. Deleted.
   e. Platform alignment control knob — NORMAL.
6. Platform heat indicator lamp — Out.
7. Bomb nav mode selector knob — ALIGN.
8. Present position longitude counter — Check and set if necessary.
9. Deleted.
10. Platform align indicator lamp — On steady after 1 minute, flashing after additional 4 to 5 minutes.

    The platform align indicator lamp should light within approximately one minute, then commence flashing within an additional 4 minutes. However, if the airplane is parked in an area where the normal earth's magnetic variation is significantly distorted (i.e. magnetic variation is not accurately known) more time may be required. A flashing platform align indicator lamp indicates the platform is sufficiently aligned to meet specification performance.
11. Magnetic heading synchronization indicator — Nulled and steady. (If time permits)

    If the indicator is not nulled, and time permits, the best possible alignment of the platform can be obtained by allowing the magnetic heading synchronization indicator to null. If the airplane is not to be moved immediately, the mode selector knob may be left in the ALIGN position until just before airplane movement. This will prevent any system error buildup during the waiting period.

Alternate Platform Alignment Procedures.
Alignment to Stored Magnetic Variation.
Pre-alignment Procedure

Position the airplane at the approximate location and heading where alignment to stored magnetic variation is anticipated.

1. Gyrocompass alignment — Completed.
2. Bomb nav mode selector knob — GREAT CIRCLE.
3. Magnetic heading synchronization indicator — Nulled.
4. Magnetic variation — Record for future reference.

Note

Pre-alignment is complete. The bomb nav system may be turned off.

Alignment Procedure

1. Altitude/test selector knob — NORM.
2. Platform alignment control knob — NORMAL.
3. Magnetic variation counter — Check and set pre-recorded value.
4. Bomb nav mode selector knob — ALIGN, and note time.
5. Present position counters — Checked. Check and set the present position latitude and longitude if necessary.

After approximately 110 seconds.

6. Bomb nav mode selector knob — GREAT CIRCLE or SHORT RANGE.

   At approximately 110 seconds after step 4 and before moving the airplane place the bomb nav mode selector knob to GREAT CIRCLE or SHORT RANGE.

Note

Any movement of the airplane such as that caused by operation of the flight controls may induce a heading error in the system when switching from ALIGN to GREAT CIRCLE or SHORT RANGE.

Rapid Alignment to Stored Gyrocompass Heading.
Pre-setting Procedure

1. Gyrocompass alignment — Completed.
2. Platform alignment control knob — RAPID ALIGN.
3. Bomb nav mode selector knob — OFF.

Note

Once pre-setting is complete the airplane must not be moved.

Alignment Procedure

1. Altitude/test selector knob — NORM.
1A. Bomb nav mode selector knob — ALIGN.
2. Present position counters — Checked.
3. Platform align indicator lamp — Flashing, within approximately 1 to 2 minutes.
4. Bomb nav mode selector knob — GREAT CIRCLE or SHORT RANGE.
   Place the bomb nav mode selector knob to GREAT CIRCLE or SHORT RANGE after the platform align indicator lamp starts flashing and before moving the airplane.
5. Rapid alignment control knob — NORMAL.

Bombing Procedures.

Range Bomb (Direct Sighting) Procedure.

1. Altitude calibration — Completed.
2. Trail/range counter — Set.
3. Fixpoint elevation counter — Set target elevation.
4. Fix mode TARGET selector button — Depress.
5. Destination counters — Set target coordinates.
6. Bomb nav mode selector knob — RANGE BOMB.
7. LCOS mode selector knob — COM.
8. Instrument system coupler mode selector knob — NAV.
9. Deleted.
10. Weapon release check list — Complete.
11. Attack radar mode selector knob — GND VEL or GND AUTO.
12. Destination present position selector switch — PP.
    DEST position should be used if target coordinates are not known to sufficient accuracy for present position fix use.
13. Attack radar range selector knob — Use lowest range setting possible.
14. Radar cursors — Synchronize on target until bomb release.
15. Airplane Commander — Center bank steering bars, and maintain desired airspeed and altitude.

Trail Bombing (Direct Sighting) Procedure.

1. Altitude calibration — Completed.
2. Trail/range counter — Set.
3. Time of fall counter — Set.
4. Fixpoint elevation counter — Set Target elevation.
5. Fix mode TARGET selector button — Depress.
6. Destination counters — Set to target coordinates.
7. Bomb nav mode selector knob — TRAIL BOMB.
8. LCOS mode selector knob — COM.
9. Instrument system coupler mode selector knob — NAV.
10. Delivery mode selector knob — NAV.
11. Weapon release checklist — Completed.
12. Attack radar mode selector knob — GND VEL or GND AUTO.
13. Destination/present position selector switch — PP.
    DEST position should be used if target coordinates are not known to sufficient accuracy for present position fix use.
14. Attack radar range selector knob — Use lowest range setting possible.
15. Radar cursors — Synchronize on target until bomb release.
16. Airplane Commander — Center bank steering bars and maintain desired airspeed and altitude.

ARMAMENT SYSTEM.

The armament capability of the airplane includes the delivery of conventional and nuclear weapons in various configurations and air-to-ground and air-to-air gunnery. The stores are carried in the weapons bay and on eight wing pylons. Four of the wing pylons pivot to remain streamlined with different positions of the wing. The pivoting pylons are utilized for both stores and gunnery equipment in various configurations. Other gunnery equipment includes a weapons bay gun. Bombing and launching equipment (pylons, stores release system, and missile trapeze), weapons bay doors, the weapons themselves, and the gunnery equipment are herein, considered as the Armament System.

BOMBING AND LAUNCHING EQUIPMENT.

Bombing and launching equipment consists of the various bomb racks, missile trapeze, missile launchers, stationary and pivoting wing pylons, and the release systems. Where applicable, the controls and indicators and operating procedures for the bombing and launching equipment are covered in the following paragraphs, under the associated equipment headings. For bombing system controls and indicators and bombing procedures, refer to "Bombing — Navigation System," this section.

Armament Select Panel (Typical)

Master Power Switch.

The master power switch (11, figure 1-31), located on the armament select panel, is a two position switch marked ON and OFF. When the switch is placed to the ON position electrical power is applied to the armament system.

Weapon Mode Selector Knob.

The weapon mode selector knob (3, figure 1-31), located on the armament select panel, is used to select the type of store to be released or type of release to be accomplished. The knob has 18 positions marked clockwise as follows:

OFF
DISP STEP — dispenser step.
DISP TRAIN — dispenser train.
BOMB STEP S — bomb step singles.
BOMB STEP P — bomb step pairs.
BOMB TRAIN S — bomb train singles.
BOMB TRAIN P — bomb train pairs.
RKT — rockets.
B/C — biological/chemical.
NUC WPN — nuclear weapons.
GAM 83 — GAM-83 (AGM-12B) missiles. (inoperative)
SHRIKE S — shrike missile single. } (inoperative)
SHRIKE P — shrike missile pairs.
GAR 8 LNCH — GAR-8 (AIM-9B) missile launch.
GAR 8 JETT — GAR-8 (AIM-9B) missile jettison.
JETT PYLON 1 & 8 — jettison pylons 1 and 8.
JETT PYLON 2 & 7 — jettison pylons 2 and 7
JETT SEL STORES — jettison selected stores.

For additional information on the weapon mode selector knob positions related to missiles and pylons, refer to the associated paragraphs under "Armament System", this section.

Delivery Mode Selector Knob.

The delivery mode selector knob (14, figure 1-31), located on the armament select panel, provides a means of selecting the source of signal for weapon release. The knob has five positions marked OFF, MAN, NAV, ANGLE and TIMER to provide the following weapon delivery capabilities:

Note

The weapon release button on either control stick must be depressed to complete a release circuit in any of the following knob positions.

OFF — prevents all weapon release capability except jettison.
MAN — provides manual release using the weapon release buttons mounted on the aircraft commander's and pilot's control stick grips.
NAV — provides automatic weapon delivery by utilizing release signals generated by the bomb nav system.

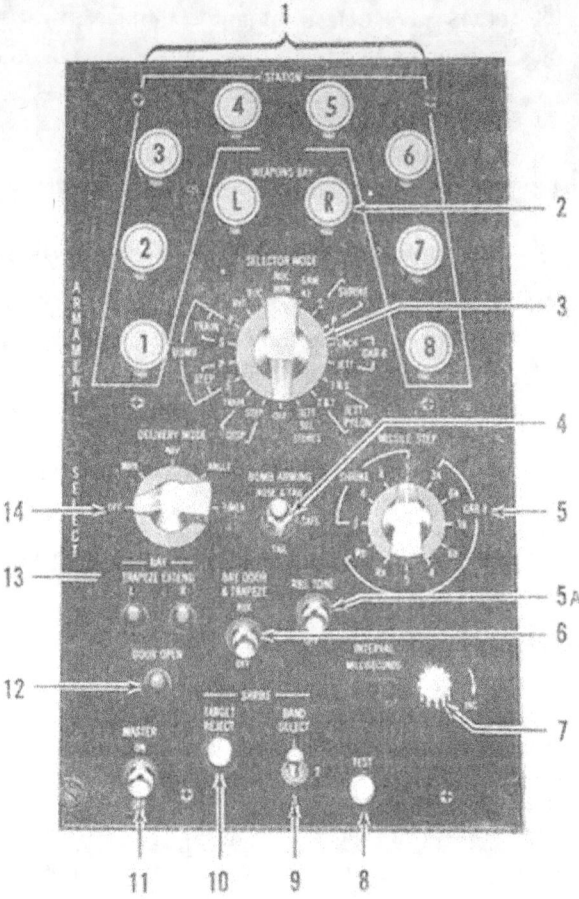

1. Pylon Weapon Selector Button (8).
2. Weapons Bay Control Button (2).
3. Weapon Mode Selector Knob.
4. Bomb Arming Selector Switch.
5. Missile Step Selector Switch.
5A. RBS Tone Switch.
6. Weapons Bay Auxiliary Control Switch.
7. Intervalometer Set Knob.
8. Release System Test Button.
9. Shrike Band Selector Switch.
10. Shrike Target Reject Button.
11. Master Power Switch.
12. Weapons Bay Door Open Lamp.
13. Trapeze Extend Lamps.
14. Delivery Mode Selector Knob.

Figure 1-31.

ANGLE — provides loft type weapon delivery capability at various predetermined angles by utilizing release signals generated by the lead computing optical sight.

TIMER — provides loft and straight fly-over timed weapon delivery capability by utilizing pull-up and release signals generated by the dual bombing timer.

Pylon Weapon Selector Buttons.

Eight push-pull type buttons (1, figure 1-31), located on the armament select panel, provide for the selection of the external pylon stations. The buttons are numbered from 1 to 8. Buttons 1, 2, 7 and 8 are for the fixed pylon stations. Buttons 3, 4, 5 and 6 are for the pivot pylon stations. Depressing a button selects that station for release and a lamp in the button will light to indicate the presence of a store at that station. Pulling the button out will dearm the station and the lamp will go out.

Bomb Arming Selector Switch.

The bomb arming selector switch (4, figure 1-31), located on the armament select panel has three positions marked NOSE & TAIL, SAFE, and TAIL. The switch controls 28 volt dc power from the main dc bus to arm or safe the fusing systems of conventional bombs released from the weapons bay or pylons. The NOSE & TAIL position is used to arm bombs which utilize both a nose and tail fuse. The TAIL position is used to arm bombs which utilize only a tail fuse. Placing the switch to the NOSE & TAIL or TAIL positions will cause the arming solenoids in the bomb racks to retain the arming wires from each bomb fuze thereby arming the bomb fuzes as the bombs are released. Placing the switch to SAFE will allow the arming wires to pull out of the arming solenoids and stay in the fuzes as the bombs are released thereby rendering the weapons safe.

Release System Test Button.

The release system test button (8, figure 1-31), located on the armament select panel, provides a means of monitoring the presence of stores on the pylon and weapon bay stations. Placing the weapon mode selector knob to a position corresponding to the type of weapons being carried and depressing the test button will cause a lamp to light in each pylon weapon selector and weapon bay control button for stations that have weapons loaded.

Intervalometer Counter and Set Knob.

An intervalometer counter and set knob (7, figure 1-31), located on the armament select panel, are provided to set weapon release intervals when releasing more than one weapon. The counter is set by turning the knob clockwise to increase the time interval and vice-versa. The counter has three digits and can be set for weapon release intervals from 0.010 second to .999 second in increments of 1 millisecond.

Nuclear Consent Switch.

The nuclear consent switch (3, figure 1-36), located on the miscellaneous switch panel has three positions marked ARM & REL, OFF and REL ONLY. Placing the switch to the ARM & REL position enables nuclear weapon arming and unlocking of the bomb racks at all stations. Placing the switch to the REL ONLY position enables unlocking of the bomb racks at all selected stations. With the switch in the OFF position all power is removed from the bomb rack and nuclear weapon arming circuits. A red guard must be raised to gain access to the switch. When nuclear weapons are carried the guard is safetied and sealed in the closed position.

Nuclear Weapons Monitor and Release Knob.

The nuclear weapons monitor and release knob (3, figure 1-32), located on the nuclear weapons control panel has seven positions marked OFF, 3, 4, L, R, 5, and 6. Placing the knob to OFF opens the monitoring and release circuits to all stations. Positions 3, 4, L, R, 5, and 6 are for the pivoting pylon and weapon bay stations. Selecting one of these positions completes the monitoring and release circuits to the station selected.

Nuclear Weapons Arm Knob.

The nuclear weapons arm knob (5, figure 1-32), located on the nuclear weapons control panel, has seven positions marked OFF, MON (monitor), SAFE, GRD RET (ground retard), AIR RET, GRD FF (ground freefall), and AIR FF. When the knob is in the OFF, all power is removed from all nuclear weapon arming and monitoring circuits. Placing the knob to the MON position allows monitoring of the condition (safe or armed) of the nuclear weapon selected by the nuclear weapons monitor and release knob. Placing the knob to SAFE provides power to safe all nuclear weapons simultaneously. The SAFE position also allows the knob lock lever to be moved from the OMS position to the S ARM position and return. The GRD RET, AIR RET, GRD FF, and AIR FF positions function in conjunction with the nuclear consent switch and station select buttons to arm the nuclear weapon selected for release to the option desired. The knob controls 28 vdc power from the essential dc bus.

Nuclear Weapons Arm Knob Lock Lever.

The nuclear weapons arm knob lock lever (4, figure 1-32), located on the nuclear weapons control panel, has two positions marked OMS (off, monitor, safe) and S ARM (safe, arm). The lever is safetied and sealed to the OMS position when nuclear weapons are carried. With the lever in the OMS position, the nuclear

Nuclear Weapons Control Panel

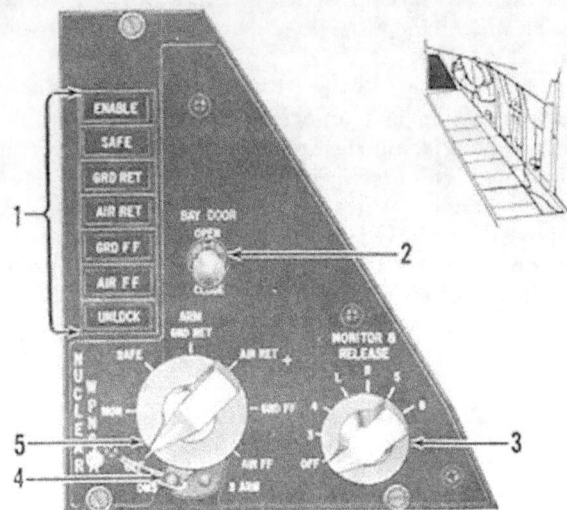

1. Nuclear Weapons Monitor Lamps (7).
2. Weapon Bay Door Switch.
3. Nuclear Weapons Monitor and Release Knob.
4. Nuclear Weapons Arm Knob Lock Lever.
5. Nuclear Weapons Arm Knob.

Figure 1-32.

weapons arm knob can be moved to the OFF, MON, and SAFE positions. Placing the nuclear weapons arm knob to SAFE allows movement of the lever to the S ARM position. The arm knob can then be moved from SAFE to one of the four fuzing option positions and returned.

Nuclear Weapons Monitor Lamps.

Seven nuclear weapons monitor lamps (1, figure 1-32), located on the nuclear weapons control panel, provide monitoring of the bomb racks and nuclear weapons being carried. When lighted the lamps indicate the following condition exists at the station selected by the nuclear weapons monitor and release knob:

ENABLE — This lamp inoperative.

SAFE — Indicates the nuclear weapons are safe.

GRD RET (ground retard)
AIR RET (air retard)
GRD FF (ground freefall)
AIR FF (air freefall)
} Indicate the fusing option setting of the nuclear weapon selected.

UNLOCK — Indicates the bomb rack is unlocked and a nuclear weapon is present at that station.

Nuclear Caution Lamp.

The nuclear caution lamp, located on the main caution lamp panel, (figure 1-29 or 1-29A) will light when one or more of the following conditions exists:

- A nuclear weapon rack is unlocked when not commanded.
- Loss of the monitoring circuit continuity to any nuclear weapon being monitored.
- The bomb arming device remains in an intermediate (not armed, not safe) condition.
- If the weapon is armed when not commanded.

When lighted the word NUCLEAR will appear in the face of the lamp.

Weapon Release Buttons.

Two weapon release buttons (1, figure 1-21), one on each control stick grip, initiate or enable normal weapon release from the pylon or weapon bay stations. The buttons are labeled WPN REL. The function of the button is described under each type of store release capability of the airplane.

External Stores Jettison Button.

The external stores jettison button (9, figure 1-6), located on the left main instrument panel, is a flush mounted push button labeled EXT STORES JETTISON. Depressing the button, when the airplane is on the ground or in flight, will jettison all external stores. Nuclear weapons, if installed, will jettison only if their racks are unlocked.

Pylons.

The airplane can be equipped with eight detachable pylons mounted along the lower surface of the wing. The pylons are designed to accommodate the MAU-12B/A bomb rack or the AERO-3B missile launcher. The pylons are numbered as stations 1 through 8, from left to right. Stations 1, 2, 7 and 8 are fixed pylon stations. The fixed pylons are streamlined at 26 degrees wing sweep angle only. A fixed stores lockout in the wing sweep handle prevents sweeping the wings more than 26 degrees with fixed pylons installed. After the weapons carried on these pylons positions are expended, the fixed pylons can be jettisoned to allow sweeping the wings more than 26 degrees. Stations 3, 4, 5 and 6 are pivoting pylon stations. These pylons are mechanically linked to keep the pylons streamlined as the wings are swept forward or aft. A weapons lockout in the wing sweep handle prevents sweeping the wings more than 55 degrees with certain weapons loaded on the inboard pivoting pylons to prevent damage to the fuselage. Pylon weapon selector buttons, located on the armament select panel, are provided to select individual pylons stations for release or launch. Each button is numbered corresponding to the station it controls.

Fixed Pylon Jettison Procedure. The following procedure will jettison the fixed pylons (stations 1 and 8 or 2 and 7) as selected on the armament select panel. The airplane must be airborne and the landing gear handle must be in the UP position to effect jettison. The pylons can be jettisoned with or without stores installed.

CAUTION

Jettisoning the pylons with stores installed may result in damage to the airplane.

1. Master power switch — ON.
2. Delivery mode selector knob — MAN.
3. Weapon mode selector knob — JETT PYLON 1 & 8 or 2 & 7. (as applicable)
4. Pylon weapon selector buttons 1 and 8 or 2 and 7 — Depressed. (as applicable)

Note

The pylon weapon selector buttons must be selected in pairs, 1 and 8 or 2 and 7, to effect jettison of the respective pair.

5. Left or right weapon release button — Momentarily depress.
6. Repeat steps 3, 4 and 5 to jettison the pair of fixed pylons remaining.

Stores Release System.

The various stores carried on the airplane are released by electrical signals generated by the bomb nav system, lead computing optical sight, dual bombing timer or by manually depressing the weapons release button. To accomplish a release, except jettison, the weapon mode selector knob must be positioned to the appropriate store or type release desired, the station to be released must be selected by depressing the appropriate pylon weapon selector button or weapon bay control button and either weapon release button on the control stick grips must be held depressed to initiate or enable the release. Refer to "Bombing-Navigation System" this section, for the type of release that can be made for the various stores carried.

Dual Bombing Timer.
The dual bombing timer (figure 1-33), mounted on the left main instrument panel, provides a manual method of accurately timed weapon release for back-up weapon delivery. The timer has two counters marked PULL UP and RELEASE. Each may be set by means of knobs on each side of the timer

Dual Bombing Timer

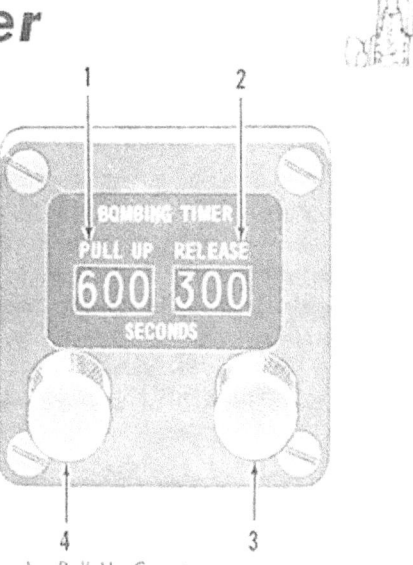

1. Pull Up Counter.
2. Release Counter.
3. Release Counter Set Knob.
4. Pull Up Counter Set Knob.

Figure 1-33.

to an accuracy of one-tenth of a second. The pull up counter can be set from 0.2 to 60.0 seconds and the release counter from 0.2 to 30.0 seconds. The timer is used with the delivery mode selector knob (14, figure 1-31) in either the TIMER or ANGLE mode positions when employing loft bombing delivery tactics. For a loft bombing delivery in the TIMER mode, precomputed values of time from initial point (IP) to pull up point and from pull up point to weapon release point are set in the PULL UP and RELEASE counters and the weapon is released at the expiration of these two times. For a loft bombing delivery in the ANGLE mode, a precomputed value of time from IP to pull up point is set in the pull up counter, and the weapon is released at a predetermined pitch angle during the pull up maneuver. A fly over release is made with the delivery mode selector knob in the TIMER mode position only. For a fly over release the precomputed time from IP to target is divided and set in both counters in any manner so that the time set in the release counter is more than 0.2 seconds and the total of the two is equal to the time from IP to target. This is necessary since a release signal will not be generated with the release counter set at zero. When making a bomb run, either weapon release button (1, figure 1-21), located on either the left or right control stick, must be depressed when over the IP to start the timer, and held until after weapon release. Altitude, heading and airspeed must then be maintained at the predetermined values used for computing the times set into the timer. At the expiration of the time set in the PULL UP counter a lamp (11, figure 1-6 or 16, figure 1-6A) on the left main instrument panel will light displaying the words PULL UP to indicate the point at which the pull up maneuver should commence if a loft bombing delivery is being made. At this time the pilot will initiate a manual constant 4g pull up using the airspeed-mach indicator accelerometer for "g" reference and the attitude director indicator and lead computing optical sight pitch steering bars for pitch steering commands. If the delivery mode selector switch is set to the TIMER position the weapon will be released at the expiration of realease time and a green release lamp (11, figure 1-6 or 16, figure 1-6A), located on the left main instrument panel, will light displaying the words BOMB RELEASE. If the ANGLE position is used, the release portion of the timer is not used and the weapon will be released by a signal from the lead computing optical sight when a predetermined pitch angle is reached. If a straight fly over laydown delivery is being accomplished, disregard the pull up lamp and continue to hold altitude, heading, and airspeed through the expiration of release time to obtain weapon release. The timer receives 28 volt dc power from the 28 volt dc essential bus through the master power switch on the armament select panel.

Missile Trapeze.

A missile trapeze can be mounted in either side of the weapons bay to carry missiles internally. The trapeze functions in conjunction with the weapon bay doors. To launch a missile the weapons bay doors are opened and the trapeze is extended to fire the missile from below the airplane. Normal operation of the system is accomplished with hydraulic power from the utility hydraulic system. Alternate operation, in the event of failure of the utility hydraulic system, is accomplished by operating the weapons bay doors electrically and operating the trapeze with a self contained pneumatic system. Two weapon bay control buttons, located on the armament select panel, marked L and R are provided to open the doors and extend the respective trapeze. An auxiliary bay door and trapeze switch provides for alternate operation of the doors and trapeze in conjunction with the weapon bay control buttons. Electrical interconnects prevent: (1) The trapeze from extending if both weapon bay control buttons are depressed, (2) Trapeze extension when the weapon bay doors are not fully open, (3) Closing the weapon bay doors when the trapeze is not fully retracted and (4) Launching a missile when the trapeze is not fully extended.

Missile Trapeze Controls. The missile trapeze is controlled by the weapons bay door controls; refer to "Weapons Bay Doors" this section.

Trapeze Extend Lamps. Two trapeze extend lamps (13, figure 1-31), located on the armament select panel, are marked L and R for the left or right trapeze. When lighted they indicate the respective trapeze is fully extended.

Missile Trapeze Operation. The missile trapeze operates in conjunction with the weapons bay doors. Refer to "Weapons Bay Doors" this section.

WEAPONS BAY DOORS.

The weapons bay doors enclose the weapons bay area located between the nose and main landing gear. The doors are constructed in left and right clam shell halves which fold outward as they are opened. Normal and alternate systems are provided to operate the doors. The normal system utilizes hydraulic power from the utility hydraulic system to drive a hydraulic motor. The alternate system uses 115 volt ac power from the right main a-c bus to power an electric motor. Either motor drives a gear reduction mechanism, which through a series of drive shafts interconnected to hinges on the inside of the weapons bay, to open and close the doors. Normal time to open or close is 2½ seconds. The alternate system takes approximately 30 seconds to open or close the doors. The weapon bay doors are controlled by either of two weapon bay control buttons which also control the trapeze and weapon stations in the weapons bay and by a weapons bay door switch.

Weapons Bay Control Buttons.

Two weapons bay control buttons (2, figure 1-31), located on the armament select panel, marked L and R are provided to open the weapon bay doors and extend the respective trapeze if installed. Each button will open both weapon bay doors but will extend only its respective trapeze. If both buttons are depressed, an electrical interconnect prevents the trapeze from extending. A lamp in each button indicates the presence of a store on that trapeze station. A door open lamp and the respective trapeze lamp will light when the weapon doors are open and the trapeze is extended.

WARNING

If the position of the weapons bay doors does not agree with the positions of either of the weapons bay control buttons or the weapons bay door switch the doors may actuate (open or close) when power is applied to the system from either an external source or by placing the master power switch to ON.

Weapons Bay Auxiliary Control Switch.

The weapons bay auxiliary control switch (6, figure 1-31), located on the armament select panel, is labeled BAY DOOR & TRAPEZE. The switch has two positions marked AUX and OFF. With the switch in the OFF position the weapons bay doors and trapeze operate on hydraulic pressure from the utility hydraulic system. Placing the switch to AUX provides electrical power to operate the weapons bay doors and pneumatic pressure from self contained pneumatic reservoirs in the weapons bay to extend and retract the trapeze. Refer to "Pneumatic Power Supply Systems" this section.

Weapons Bay Door Switch.

The weapons bay door switch (2, figure 1-32), located on the nuclear weapons control panel, has two positions marked OPEN and CLOSE. The switch is used to open or close the weapons bay doors only when the weapon mode selector knob is in the NUC WPN (nuclear weapons) position.

WARNING

If the position of the weapons bay doors does not agree with the positions of either of the weapons bay control buttons or the weapons bay door switch the doors may actuate (open or close) when power is applied to the system from either an external source or by placing the master power switch to ON.

Weapons Bay Door Open Lamp.

The weapons bay door open lamp (12, figure 1-31), located on the armament select panel, will light when the weapons bay doors are fully open.

Normal Operation of Weapons Bay Doors and Trapeze.

For normal operation of the weapons bay doors and trapeze the utility hydraulic system must be functioning and electrical power must be on.

WARNING

If the position of the weapons bay doors does not agree with the positions of either of the weapons bay control buttons or the weapons bay door switch the doors may actuate (open or close) when power is applied to the system from either an external source or by placing the master power switch to ON.

To open doors and extend trapeze with weapons bay control buttons:

1. Master power switch—ON.
2. L or R weapon bay control button—Depressed.
3. Weapon bay door open lamp—On, after $2\frac{1}{2}$ seconds.
4. L or R trapeze extend lamp—On.
5. Master power switch—OFF.

To retract trapeze and close doors with weapons bay control buttons:

1. Master power switch—ON.
2. L or R weapon bay control button—Pulled.
3. L or R trapeze extend lamp—Out.
4. Weapon bay door open lamp—Out.
5. Master power switch—OFF.

Alternate Operation of Weapon Bay Doors and Trapeze.

For alternate operation of the weapons bay doors and trapeze electrical power must be on.

To open doors and extend trapeze with weapons bay control buttons:

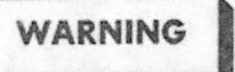

WARNING

Do not extend the trapeze, under any circumstances, after it has been retracted pneumatically. To do so will result in structural damage to the lower surface of the forward fuel tank at the trapeze actuator attachment, since there will be insufficient hydraulic fluid left in the actuator to dampen the downward motion of the trapeze.

1. Master power switch—ON.
2. Weapons bay auxiliary control switch—AUX.
3. L or R weapons bay control button—Depressed.
4. Weapons bay door open lamp—On, after 30 seconds.
5. L or R trapeze extend lamp—On.
6. Master power switch—OFF.

To retract trapeze and close doors with weapons bay control buttons:

1. Master power switch—ON.
2. L or R weapon bay control button—Pulled.
3. L or R trapeze extend lamp—Out.
4. Weapon bay door open lamp—Out.
5. Master power switch—OFF.

MISSILES.

The airplane is equipped to carry AIM-9B (GAR-8) missiles.

AIM-9B (GAR-8) Missile.

The AIM-9B missile is a passive infrared-homing air-to-air supersonic guided missile. Since the missile homes on infrared energy radiated by heated parts of the target, it does not need to transmit a signal for guidance and is therefore relatively impervious to jamming. The missile is composed of four sections; guidance and control section, warhead, influence fuse, and rocket motor. The guidance and control section contains the optical tracking system, a gas operated control servo with four movable control fins to control the flight of the missile to the target, electronic components to convert target signals into missile control signals, a gas driven generator to supply electrical power during missile flight and the contact fuse. When the missile control system has acquired a target, an audio tone is transmitted on the interphone to the crew. The warhead, a 25 pound fragmentation type, is detonated by either the contact or influence fuse. The influence fuse will detonate the warhead if the missile passes within 30 feet of the target. The rocket motor is a standard 5 inch HVAR rocket motor. It will accelerate the missile to mach 1.7 above the speed of the launching aircraft. Four fixed stabilizer fins are mounted around the rocket motor section. The missile is carried on and launched from the AERO-3B launcher. The airplane is equipped to carry eight AIM-9B missiles as follows: Two on each outboard pivot pylon, one on each inboard pivot pylon and two on the right weapons bay trapeze station. When the weapon bay gun is installed in the right side of the weapons bay, a single AIM-9B may be carried on the left trapeze for a total of seven missiles. The missiles are launched individually by selecting the desired missile to be fired and depressing the weapon release button on either control stick. All missiles can be jettisoned simultaneously by depressing the external stores jettison button.

Weapon Mode Selector Knob. The weapon mode selector knob (3, figure 1-31), has 18 positions, two of which are used in conjunction with AIM-9B missile. These knob positions are labeled GAR-8 and are individually marked LNCH (launch) and JETT (jettison). Placing the knob to LNCH will allow the missile selected by the missile step selector knob to be launched when either weapon release button is depressed. Placing the knob to JETT will allow all missiles to be jettisoned when the external stores jettison button is depressed. Other positions of the weapon mode selector knob are described under their associated equipment paragraphs.

Missile Step Selector Knob. The missile step selector knob (5, figure 1-31), located on the armament select panel, controls the launching sequence of GAR-8 missiles. The knob has twelve positions. Four positions are labeled SHRIKE. These positions are inoperative. Eight positions of the knob are labeled GAR-8 and are marked 3A, 6A, 3B, 6B, 4, 5, RA and RB for the respective stations equipped to carry GAR-8 missiles. Pylon weapon station 3 and 6 and the right weapon bay station have the capability of carrying two GAR-8 missiles each therefore the A and B designates individual missiles at these stations. When a GAR-8 is carried in the left weapon bay, the RB position of the knob will control launching the missile on that station. Each time a missile is launched and the weapon release button is released, the knob will step one position clockwise to sequence missile launchings from the left station to right station then back to left until all missiles are expended.

Missile Step Selector Knob. The missile step selector knob (5, figure 1-31), controls the launching sequence of GAR-8 missiles. For description of this knob, refer to "AIM-9B (GAR-8) Missile", this section.

GUNNERY EQUIPMENT.

The airplane is equipped to carry a weapons bay gun in the right side of the weapons bay.

Weapon Bay Gun Module.

The weapon bay gun module provides both air-to-air and air-to-ground gunnery capability. The module is packaged to facilitate installation and removal of components. When installed it supplants all other stores carrying capability in the right side of the weapons bay but does not alter the stores carrying capability in the left side of the bay. The module contains the M61A1 gun, a linkless ammunition feed system and an expended ammunition storage bin. The M61A1 is a 20 MM gun which has a rotating cluster of six barrels. The gun fires electrically primed ammunition at a nominal rate of 6,000 rounds per minute. Hydraulic power from the utility hydraulic system is used to operate the feed mechanism and the gun. The ammunition drum holds 2,050 rounds of which approximately 2000 rounds can be expended. Expended ammunition cases are retained in the storage bin which must be emptied on the ground. A switch is provided for selecting the weapon bay gun for firing. Depressing either gun trigger switch will fire the gun or guns as selected. A safety switch on the main landing gear prevents firing the gun on the ground. In flight, the gun will not fire unless the weapons bay area is vented. The guns are fired by 28 volt dc power from the main dc power panel. A rounds counter provides an indication of remaining ammunition.

Gun Selector Switch.

The gun selector switch (4, figure 1-6 or 9, figure 1-6A), located on the left main instrument panel, is labeled GUNS and has three positions marked PYLONS, BAY, and OFF. With the switch in the OFF position the weapon bay gun and gun pods cannot be fired. Placing the switch to BAY enables firing the weapons bay gun. The PYLONS position of the switch is inoperative.

Rounds Counter.

The rounds counter (7, figure 1-6 or 10, figure 1-6A), located on the left main instrument panel, provides an indication of the amount of ammunition remaining in the weapon bay gun. The counter is graduated from 0 to 20, times 100, in increments of 100.

Gun Trigger Switch.

Two gun trigger switches (5, figure 1-21), one located on each control stick grip, are provided to fire the guns. Depressing either switch will fire the weapon bay gun depending on the position of the gun selector switch.

Operation of the Weapon Bay Gun

Except under actual combat conditions the guns will not be fired unless over a cleared gunnery range.

1. Master power switch—ON.
2. Gun selector switch—BAY.
3. LCOS mode selector knob—GUN-AA or GUN-AG. (as applicable)
4. LCOS range set knob—Set range.
5. LCOS true airspeed knob—Set TAS.
6. LCOS aiming reticle brightness knob—Set as desired.
7. Center pipper on the target.
8. Gun trigger switch—Depress when in range.

TACTICAL AIR NAVIGATION SYSTEM (AN/ARN-52).

The tactical air navigation system (TACAN) enables the airplane to receive continuous indications of its distance and bearing from any selected TACAN station located within a line-of-sight distance of approximately 300 nautical miles. There are 126 channels available for selection. The equipment consists of the TACAN receiver-transmitter and its control panel. Two antennas, one on top of the fuselage and the other beneath the fuselage (figure 1-41), function to keep the TACAN receiver locked on to the antenna receiving a usable signal. The TACAN equipment also has an air-to-air mode and can be used between two aircraft having TACAN with air-to-air capability for range information only. The TACAN works in conjunction with the instrument system coupler, the bearing distance heading indicator, the lead computing optical sight, the horizontal situation indicator, the attitude director indicator, and through the interphone control panel for audio output. The system operates on 28 volt dc from the main dc bus and 115 volt ac from the left main ac bus. The TACAN control panel is located on the right main instrument panel.

TACAN FUNCTION SELECTOR KNOB.

The function selector knob (2, figure 1-34), located on the TACAN control panel, has four positions marked OFF, REC, T/R, and A/A. In the OFF position, electrical power to the TACAN system is off. In any of the other three positions, electrical power is supplied and the TACAN set is on. In the REC position, the set will receive bearing and audio identity signals only. In REC position, range information will not be displayed because the TACAN transmitter is not on. In the T/R position, both the receiver and the transmitter are operative, the system will receive and display both range and bearing of the station being interrogated, and audio identity signals are fed into the interphone system. In the A/A (air-to-air) position, the set will transmit and receive to and from another aircraft having air-to-air capability. To operate in this mode, the air-to-air mode in both aircraft must be selected and the channels selected must be 63 channels apart. As an example, if the TACAN in one aircraft is on channel 10, the TACAN in the other aircraft must be selected to channel 73. In the A/A mode, the TACAN will provide range between aircraft information only (no identity or bearing).

TACAN CHANNEL SELECTOR.

The channel selector (1, figure 1-34), located on the TACAN control panel, consists of inner and outer adjustment controls for selecting any one of the available 126 TACAN channels. The selected channel is digitally displayed on the selector. The outer control is used to select the first two digits of the desired channel and the inner control to select the last digit.

TACAN VOLUME CONTROL KNOB.

A volume control knob (3, figure 1-34), located on the TACAN control panel, provides a means for controlling the volume of the audio identity code.

TACAN ANTENNA SELECTOR SWITCH.

The three position TACAN antenna selector switch (2, figure 1-40), located on the antenna select panel, controls the selection of the upper and lower TACAN antennas. The switch is marked UPPER, AUTO and LOWER. Placing the switch to AUTO causes the antenna selector to control the antenna switching relay to select the correct antenna. Placing the switch to UPPER or LOWER controls the antenna relay directly to allow manual selection of either the upper or lower antenna.

TACAN OPERATION.

1. Function selector knob—As required (REC, T/R, or A/A).
2. Antenna selector switch—AUTO.
3. Channel selector—As required.
4. Volume control knob—Adjust for desired volume level.
5. Instrument system coupler mode selector knob.—TACAN.
6. Horizontal situation indicator (HSI) course selector window—Set.
   Set the desired TACAN course in the HSI course selector window.
7. Monitor ADI, LCOS and HSI for proper indications.

Note

It is possible that improperly adjusted or malfunctioning ground or airborne TACAN equipment may lock on to a false bearing. This error will probably be plus or minus 40° or multiples of 40°. This is an inherent error in the TACAN system, consequently, bearing information should be cross-checked against other navigation aids whenever possible. When false lock on occurs, it is possible to correct the malfunction by switching to another channel and back to the desired channel or turning the set off and back on again. This deficiency does not affect the range display.

INSTRUMENT LANDING SYSTEM.

The instrument landing system (ILS) provides the capability of making instrument approaches to runways equipped with localizer, glide slope and marker beacon equipment. The system consists of three receivers, one each for localizer, glide slope and marker beacon; four antennas, two for localizer and one each

Tacan Control Panel

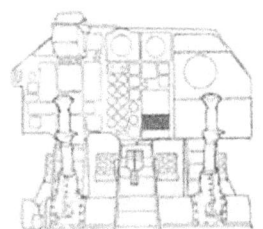

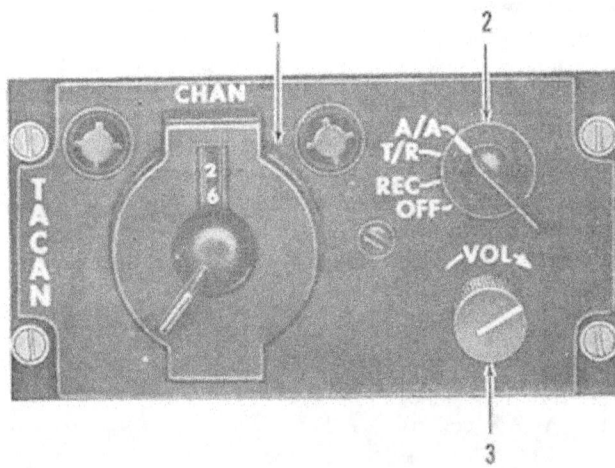

1. Channel Selector.
2. Function Selector Knob.
3. Volume Control Knob.

Figure 1-34.

for glide slope and marker beacon, a control panel and a marker beacon light. The localizer and glide slope receivers operate on 20 fixed frequency channels which may be selected on the control panel. Glide slope frequencies are paired with localizer frequencies so that selection of a localizer channel automatically provides for glide slope reception. Localizer identification signals are supplied to the headset for station identification. Localizer and glide slope steering and deviation signals are provided to the instrument system coupler for display on the attitude director indicator (ADI), horizontal situation indicator (HSI) and lead computing optical sight (LCOS). Warning flags on the ADI become visible whenever the signal level on the selected frequency is too weak to be usable or is unreliable. Refer to "Instruments," this section, for the tie-in of the ILS and Integrated Flight Instruments. The marker beacon receiver operates on a fixed frequency of 75 megacycles and when over a beacon facility will provide a coded station signal to the headset and to the marker beacon lamp. Power is applied to the marker beacon receiver whenever power is on the airplane. The ILS operates on 28 volt dc power from the 28 volt dc main bus. Refer to Instrument Procedures, Section VII for instrument landing system operating procedures.

ILS FREQUENCY SELECTOR KNOB.

The frequency selector knob (2, figure 1-35), located on the ILS control panel, allows individual selection of 20 ILS channels ranging in localizer frequencies from 108.1 to 111.9 mc in 0.2 mc increments. There is a detent position of the knob for each channel. One complete rotation of the knob covers the full range of frequencies. Each localizer frequency selected is paired with a glide slope frequency between 329.3 and 335.0 mc. The frequency of each channel selected is displayed in a digital window to the left of the knob.

ILS POWER SWITCH.

The power switch (3, figure 1-35), located on the ILS control panel, is a two position switch marked POWER and OFF. In the OFF position power is removed from the localizer and glide slope receivers. When the switch is placed to POWER 28 volt dc power is applied to the localizer and glide slope receivers.

ILS VOLUME CONTROL KNOB.

The volume control knob (4, figure 1-35), located on the ILS control panel, adjusts the volume of the localizer station identification signal. Clockwise rotation increases volume.

MARKER BEACON LAMP.

The marker beacon lamp (13, figure 1-6 or 16, figure 1-6A), located on the left main instrument panel, provides a visual coded station signal when the airplane is over a marker beacon facility. When lighted the words MARKER BEACON are displayed in green.

ILS Control Panel

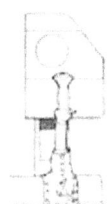

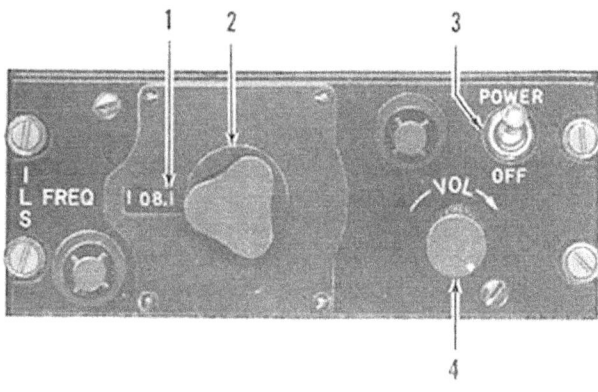

1. Frequency Window.
2. Frequency Selector Knob.
3. Power Switch.
4. Volume Control Knob.

Figure 1-35.

RADAR ALTIMETER SYSTEM (AN/APN-167).

The radar altimeter system is a dual channel low altitude radar system which provides precise absolute altitude, rate of altitude change and minimum altitude penetration information. Absolute altitude from 0 to 5000 feet is read on the radar altimeter. Rate of altitude change from 0 to 500 feet per second is furnished to the terrain following radar. Minimum altitude penetration fly-up signals are provided to the integrated flight instruments. The system is composed of two receiver-transmitter (RT) units; two antennas, one for transmitting and one for receiving; a distribution box; a radar altimeter and the necessary controls. The RT units are located in the forward electronic equipment bay. When the system is placed in operation, one RT unit is activated and the other is in standby for use in event the operating unit malfunctions. In the event of a malfunction the standby RT unit must be manually selected. The RT unit in operation is connected to the antennas and its outputs are distributed to other airplane systems by circuits in the distribution box. A pressure operated switch in each RT unit will place the operating unit to standby when above approximately 38,000 feet pressure altitude. The radar altimeter will break lock if the bank angle exceeds 45 degrees or if pitch angle exceeds ±25 degrees. The system incorporates a self-test feature for checking reliability. The system operates on 115 volt ac power

Section I
Description & Operation

Miscellaneous Switch Panel

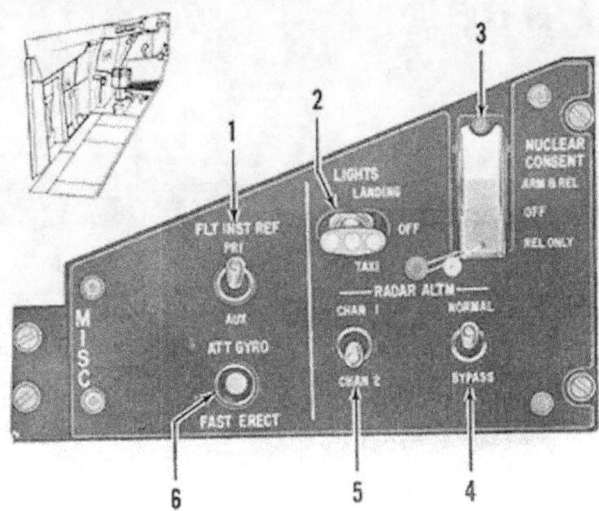

1. Flight Instrument Reference Select Switch.
2. Landing and Taxi Lights Switch.
3. Nuclear Consent Switch.
4. Radar Altimeter Bypass Switch.
5. Radar Altimeter Channel Selector Switch.
6. AFRS Gyro Fast Erect Button.

Figure 1-36.

from the main ac bus and 28 volt dc power from the main dc bus. Refer to figure 1-41 for antenna location.

RADAR ALTIMETER CHANNEL SELECTOR SWITCH.

The radar altimeter channel selector switch (5, figure 1-36), located on the miscellaneous switch panel, is labeled RADAR ALTM and has two positions marked CHAN 1 and CHAN 2. Placing the switch in either position will allow the RT unit in the respective channel to transmit and receive.

RADAR ALTIMETER BYPASS SWITCH.

The radar altimeter bypass switch (4, figure 1-36), located on the miscellaneous switch panel, is a two position switch marked NORMAL and BYPASS. Placing the switch to BYPASS when above 5000 feet over the terrain provides a signal to the TFR to permit automatic blind letdowns. As 5000 feet is passed during descent, the switch will go to NORMAL. When the switch is in the NORMAL position, automatic blind letdowns from below 5000 feet above terrain only, may be accomplished.

RADAR ALTIMETER.

The radar altimeter indicator (17, figure 1-6 or 20, figure 1-6A), located on the left main instrument panel, provides absolute altitude indications from 0 to 5000 feet. Indications are provided by a pointer on a dial graduated in increments of 10 feet from 0 to 500, 50 feet from 500 to 1000, and 500 feet from 1000 to 5000. An OFF warning flag in a window on the right side of the dial will appear when power is removed from the system or when the altitude of the airplane is over 5000 feet above the terrain. The radar altimeter control knob on the lower right of the altimeter serves three functions; as an on-off control, to set a minimum altitude index pointer on the dial and as a test button to check the system. Initially turning the knob clockwise applies power to the system, further rotation of the knob rotates the index pointer from zero to any desired minimum altitude setting. Depressing and holding the knob activates the self-test feature of the system and provides an indication of 100 ±12 feet if the RT unit is operating properly. The self-test feature may be used at any time and at any altitude below approximately 38,000 feet.

RADAR ALTITUDE LOW WARNING LAMP.

The radar altitude low warning lamp (18, figure 1-6 or 21, figure 1-6A), located on the left main instrument panel, will light when the absolute altitude of the airplane is at or below the minimum altitude set into the radar altimeter. When lighted the letters RADAR ALT LOW are displayed on the face of the lamp in red.

TERRAIN FOLLOWING RADAR (AN/APQ-110).

The terrain following radar (TFR) provides low altitude terrain following, obstacle avoidance and blind letdown capability. The TFR consists of left and right antenna receivers, synchronizer transmitters, power supplies and computers in a dual channel configuration; a radar scope panel and a control panel. Each channel may be operated independently of the other in any one of three modes; terrain following (TF), situation display (SIT), or ground mapping (GM). The TFR receives inputs from the radar altimeter, attack radar, bomb-nav system or auxiliary flight reference system, central air data computer and LCOSS. The TFR operates on 115 volt ac power from the main ac bus and 28 volt dc power from the main dc bus. For TFR operating procedures, refer to TFR Operation, Section II.

TERRAIN FOLLOWING (TF) MODE.

The TF mode allows the airplane to be flown manually or automatically at a preselected terrain clearance. Climb and dive signals generated in this mode are furnished to the attitude director indicator (ADI), lead computing optical sight (LCOS) and to the flight control system. The set terrain clearance can be manually maintained by flying pitch steering commands on the ADI and LCOS. In auto TF operation the set terrain clearance will be automatically held. Should the airplane descend to below 68 percent of the selected terrain clearance altitude setting, the ADI and LCOS will indicate a fly-up command and a "2g" (incremental) pull-up will be initiated, if the airplane is being flown with the auto TF switch in either the AUTO TF or OFF positions. The TF mode can also be used to make blind letdowns to a preselected terrain clearance. When using this capability, descent can be made manually using the pitch steering commands on the ADI and LCOS, or automatically by placing the auto TF switch to the AUTO TF position. The descent is limited to a 12 degree dive. Only one channel at a time can be operated in TF mode. If both channels are placed to TF the second channel placed to TF will go to a standby condition as a backup and will automatically take over should the operating channel fail. A failure in the operating TFR channel will provide a 2g (incremental) fly-up signal to the pitch damper with the auto TF switch in either AUTO TF or OFF and a fly-up steering command will be displayed on the ADI and LCOS pitch steering bars if the instrument system coupler pitch steering mode switch is in the TF position.

Note

- The fly-up command can be interrupted by holding the autopilot release lever depressed. To get rid of the fly-up signal the TFR channel controlling the airplane must be turned off. If the auto TF switch is in the AUTO TF position it must be positioned to OFF prior to turning off the TFR. Placing the autopilot emergency override switch (flight control disconnect switch on airplanes ③①♦) to OVRD will also remove the fly-up signal.

- The fly-up signal is locked out to prevent automatic fly-up when the landing gear is in the down position, when the flight control system switch is in the T.O. & LAND position and on airplanes ③①♦ when the control system switch is in the NORMAL position and the slats are extended.

Refer to "Flight Control System" this section, for information pertaining to operation of the TFR with the flight control system. In the TF mode, antenna scan is vertical and the scope display is in the form of a non-linear E type presentation. A cursor, displayed on the scope, provides a terrain clearance reference. The slope of the cursor will vary with the speed of the airplane, terrain clearance setting, the type of ride selected, pitch and angle of attack. Range displays on the scope are from left to right on a nonlinear scale so that ranges up to two miles are displayed over three-fourths of the scope and the remaining one-fourth of the scope displays returns up to ten miles. Elevation of returns along the ground track are displayed vertically on the scope. In this manner the close returns are displayed in clearer definition than those at greater range.

WARNING

The TFR does not provide terrain avoidance information on either side of the flight path when operating in the TF mode. If coordinated turns are made while flying TF mode, do not exceed 10 degree of bank angle.

SITUATION (SIT) MODE.

This mode of operation is used in conjunction with TF mode for obstacle avoidance. Antenna scan is in azimuth, 30 degrees either side of ground track. Antenna tilt cannot be adjusted. Returns of the terrain that is higher than the airplane altitude are displayed on the radar scope in a one radius offset PPI presentation. Ground track is stabilized vertically along the center of the scope. Range graduations in this mode are linear.

GROUND MAPPING (GM) MODE.

The GM mode provides a scope presentation of the terrain that is ahead of the airplane below the altitude being flown. Antenna tilt can be adjusted for best picture. This mode is used primarily for navigation. The antenna scan and the type of scope display are the same as when operating in SIT mode.

TFR CONTROL AND INDICATORS.

TFR Channel Mode Selector Knobs.

Two, five position rotary channel mode selector knobs, (2, figure 1-37), located on the TFR control panel, permit selection of the desired operating mode in each of the two channels. The knobs are labeled L and R for the respective channel and are individually marked OFF, STBY, TF, SIT and GM. In the OFF position, power is removed from the channel. In the STBY position, power is applied to the channel for warm-up. The TF, SIT and GM positions provide terrain following, situation display or ground mapping modes of operation respectively. Each channel may be operated in a different mode; however, unless one channel is in TF mode the reference not engaged lamp will light when AUTO TF is selected. If both knobs are positioned to TF the second channel will automatically go to a standby condition, then, should the operating channel fail the one in standby will automatically take over.

Auto Terrain Following Switch.

The auto terrain following (auto TF) switch (3, figure 1-24), located on the autopilot/damper panel, is a two position lever lock switch marked AUTO TF and OFF. The switch is locked in the OFF position and must be pulled out to move from OFF to AUTO TF. When the switch is in the OFF position and either TFR channel mode selector knob is in the TF position,

TFR Control Panel

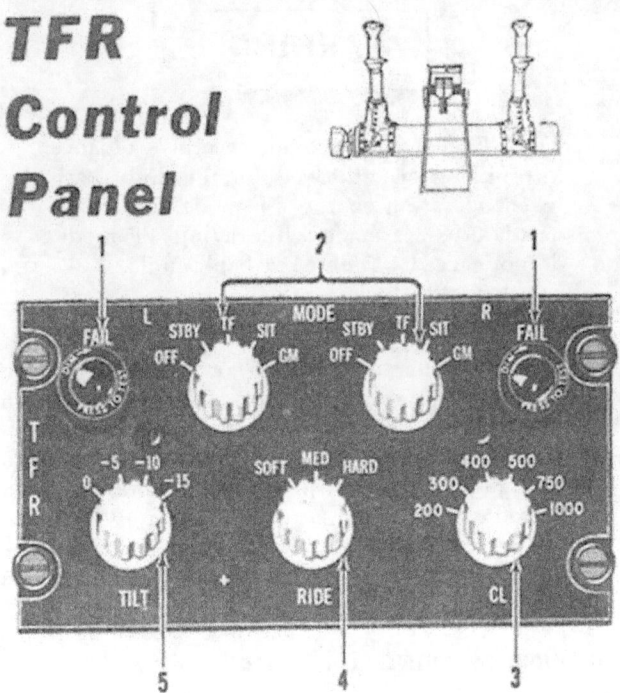

1. TFR Channel Failure Caution Lamps (2).
2. TFR Channel Mode Selector Knobs (2).
3. Terrain Clearance Knob.
4. Ride Control Knob.
5. Antenna Tilt Control Knob.

Figure 1-37.

the airplane must be flown manually using the pitch steering commands on the ADI and LCOS to hold the terrain clearance selected on the TFR terrain clearance knob. With the switch in the OFF position the reference not engaged lamp will remain on. When the switch is placed to the AUTO TF position and either TFR channel mode selector knob is in the TF position signals from the TFR will control the pitch damper to automatically hold the airplane on the terrain clearance setting selected by the TFR terrain clearance knob. With the switch in AUTO TF the reference not engaged lamp will go out.

Note

When auto TF is selected at least one TFR channel must be in the TF mode or the fly-up off caution lamp and the reference not engaged lamp will light.

Should the TFR fail with the switch in either the OFF or AUTO TF position, the TF failure warning lamp will light, a 2g (incremental) fly-up signal will be sent to the pitch damper and the pitch steering bars on the ADI and LCOS will indicate a fly-up command. The fly-up signal can be interrupted by depressing and holding the autopilot release lever. The malfunctioning TFR channel must be turned off to get rid of the fly-up signal when operating with the auto TF switch in the OFF position. If the auto TF switch is in the AUTO TF position it must be placed to OFF before turning off the malfunctioning TFR channel to get rid of the fly-up signal. Placing the autopilot emergency override switch (flight control disconnect switch on airplanes ㉛ ◆) to OVRD will also remove the fly-up signal.

Terrain Clearance Knob.

The terrain clearance knob (3, figure 1-37), located on the TFR control panel, has six positions marked 200, 300, 400, 500, 750 and 1000. Rotating the knob clockwise increases the altitude clearance setting corresponding to the position selected and vice versa.

Note

When flying at one clearance setting and the knob is positioned to a higher setting, a TF failure and fly-up may be generated until the aircraft is maneuvered outside the radar altimeter fly-up range.

Ride Control Knob.

The ride control knob (4, figure 1-37), located on the TFR control panel is a three position rotary knob marked SOFT, MED and HARD. The knob controls the magnitude of the negative "g" forces imposed on the airplane by the flight control system as it maintains a set altitude clearance above the terrain. Negative "g"

TFR Scope Panel

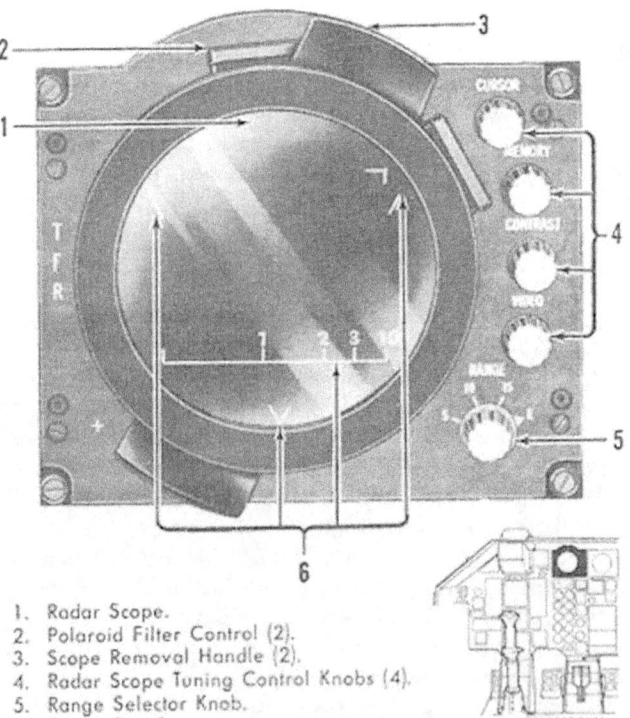

1. Radar Scope.
2. Polaroid Filter Control (2).
3. Scope Removal Handle (2).
4. Radar Scope Tuning Control Knobs (4).
5. Range Selector Knob.
6. Scope Overlay.

Figure 1-38.

(incremental) forces of —1.0, —0.5, and —0.25 will be experienced in the HARD, MED, and SOFT positions respectively. The system will automatically provide a "2g" (incremental) pull up if necessary to avoid an obstacle regardless of the ride selected.

Antenna Tilt Control Knob.

The antenna tilt control knob (5, figure 1-37), located on the TFR control panel is used to position antenna tilt between zero and —15 degrees for the best ground return when operating in the GM mode. The knob will continuously vary the antenna position between zero and —15 degrees. The knob has antenna tilt angles of 0, —5, —10 and —15 marked for reference.

Range Selector Knob.

The range selector knob (5, figure 1-38), located on the TFR scope panel, has four positions marked 5, 10, 15 and E. The first three positions change range of the scope presentation when using SIT or GM modes. The E position is used with the TF mode only.

Radar Scope Control Knobs.

Four radar scope control knobs (4, figure 1-38), located on the TFR scope panel provide a means of adjusting the scope to obtain the best display. The knobs are labeled CURSOR, MEMORY, CONTRAST and VIDEO from top to bottom. The cursor knob adjusts the brilliance of the range cursors. The memory knob increases or decreases scope storage retention time. The contrast knob adjusts scope contrast for optimum viewing. The video control adjusts the video return brightness to desired level.

Radar Scope.

The radar scope (1, figure 1-38), located on the TFR scope panel, provides a direct viewing presentation of either an E (vertical scan) display when in TF mode or a sector PPI (azimuth scan) display when operating in SIT or GM modes. The scope overlays provide a rectangular grid with a 0 to 10 nautical mile scale at the bottom of the scope for TF mode and a "V" shaped grid for sector PPI presentations in SIT or GM modes. The polaroid filter controls around the face of the scope can be rotated to adjust polarization of light for the best display under various degrees of light. A red scope presentation for night vision adaptation can be obtained with the filter controls. The ear type handles on each side of the scope are provided to facilitate removal or installation of the unit.

Note

When the LCOS mode select knob is placed to the DIV BOMB, RKT AG or GUN AG position, the attack radar and TFR are used in conjunction with the LCOS for air-to-ground ranging. Under this condition the attack radar and TFR ground mapping or situation scope presentations will be unusable and should be ignored. If one channel is in TF mode, the E scope presentation will be normal.

TFR Channel Fail Caution Lamps.

Two amber channel failure caution lamps (1, figure 1-37), located on the TFR control panel, are individually marked FAIL and are labeled L and R for the respective left and right channels. When the channel mode selector knob is placed from OFF to STBY the fail lamp will light to indicate that channel is not yet ready to operate. The lamp will go out after approximately 3 minutes indicating the channel is ready. After the channel is ready, a fail light with the mode selector switch in TF, SIT or GM position, indicates a malfunction in that channel. The lamps will also light when the airplane is above 5000 feet absolute altitude and the radar altimeter bypass switch is in the NORMAL position. A press-to-test feature allows each lamp to be checked.

Note

The lamps will momentarily blink when changing the TFR terrain clearance knob from low to higher clearance settings. This is a normal indication.

TF Fly-Up Off Caution Lamp.

The TF fly-up caution lamp, located on the main caution lamp panel (figure 1-29 or 1-29A) provides an indication that fly-up protection is not available. The lamp will light when the flight control system is in a takeoff or landing configuration and either TFR mode selector knob is in TF or the auto TF switch is in the AUTO TF position. The letters TF FLY-UP OFF are visible on the face of the lamp when it is lighted.

TFR Failure Warning Lamp.

A TFR failure warning lamp (13, figure 1-6 or 16, figure 1-6A), located on the left main instrument panel, provides a more apparent indication of TFR channel malfunctions. If each channel is being operated in a different mode the lamp will light when the channel in TF mode malfunctions. If both channels are in TF mode, the lamp will momentarily light when the channel in operation fails and the backup channel take over. Should the backup channel in turn fail, the lamp will light and remain on.

TERRAIN FOLLOWING RADAR OPERATION.

1. Left and right channel mode selector knobs— STBY.
2. Radar altimeter control knob—ON and set. Rotate the altimeter control knob clockwise to turn the altimeter on and to set altitude index pointer to minimum desired altitude.

2A. Radar altimeter bypass switch—Bypass (if above 5000').

2B. Channel fail caution lamps—Out.

3. Drift angle accuracy—Check. (AC-P)

The following checks should be made prior to and during terrain following operation to determine if drift angle information is accurate.

WARNING

Before beginning terrain following and during terrain following operation it is essential that the TFR receive accurate drift angle information. Inaccurate drift angle information to the TFR could result in the airplane flying into the ground since the antenna search pattern will not be along the ground track being flown.

a. HSI—Check.

Check that course arrow indicates a realistic drift angle as compared with the lubber line.

b. Attack radar scope display—Check. (P)

Check the display with the attack radar mode selector knob in one of the following positions:

(1) GND MAN—With the antenna uncaged, check that the radar return moves straight down the scope with no apparent drift to either side.

(2) GND VEL—Check that rate of cursor drift is not excessive.

(3) GND AUTO—Check that radar return moves straight down the scope with no apparent drift to either side and that rate of cursor drift is not excessive.

c. Bomb nav system—Check. (P)

(1) Check for realistic computed drift angle by comparing groundtrack and true heading.

(2) Check wind speed counter for realistic value.

(3) Compare groundspeed counter with true airspeed for reasonable difference.

(4) Check for absence of gross error in present position by observing the position counters or the attack radar scope display.

4. Drift angle accuracy check—Complete. (AC-P)

5. Right channel mode selector knob—As desired.

6. Terrain clearance knob—Desired altitude.

7. Ride control knob—As desired.

8. Antenna tilt control knob—Adjust as required. (For ground map mode only)

9. Range selector knob—As desired.

For a scope presentation in TF mode, rotate the knob to the E position.

10. Radar scope tuning control knobs—Adjust for best scope presentation.

11. Polaroid filter—Adjust as required.

12. ISC pitch steering mode switch—TF.

13. Auto TF switch—As desired.

Place the auto TF switch to AUTO TF for automatic TFR operation or to OFF if the airplane is to be flown manually.

14. Deleted.

WARNING

- The TFR does not provide terrain avoidance information on either side of the flight path when operating in the TF mode. If coordinated turns are made while flying TF mode, do not exceed 10 degrees of bank angle.

- Over calm water or flat terrain such as dry lake beds, dry wheat fields, or smooth sand, there will be little energy returned back to the radar. When forward video is lost while flying over smooth water or certain terrain, terrain following will be commanded by the radar altimeter. The radar altimeter looks only below the airplane and has no forward looking capability; therefore, it will provide safe flight only if the ground does not rise rapidly. Thus if forward video is lost on the scope from inadequate returns over certain terrain, the terrain following radar cannot be expected to provide safe flight.

> **CAUTION**
>
> The back scatter from drizzle or rain and other forms of precipitation will often be visible on the scope. The operator should recognize that if the precipitation is so heavy that he cannot determine visually where the terrain ends and the precipitation begins, the automatic signal detection circuitry will also be incapable of the discrimination and a climb command will result.

IFF SYSTEM (AN/APX-64).

The air-to-ground IFF system provides the airplane with an automatic means of selective identification to ground recognition installations operating in the L-band frequency range. The system replies to proper interrogation from Mark X IFF systems and SIF (selective identification feature) stations. Operation is possible in any one of five modes, with the capabilities of I/P (identification of position) and emergency identification. The modes of operation have the following significance: Mode 1—Security Identity, Mode 2—Personal Identity, Mode 3—Traffic Identity, Mode 4—Classified and Mode C—Altitude Interrogation. The equipment consists of an IFF control panel, a transmitter-receiver, an inflight test set, a mode 4 computer, an antenna lobing switch, and two radiator-type antenna. The equipment does not perform interrogation but only transmits coded replies to correctly coded interrogations. Two blade type antennas, an upper and lower, are provided. See figure 1-41 for antenna locations. The lobing switch rapidly transfers contact of the transmitter-receiver from one antenna to the other. This constant alternation eliminates blank spots in the antenna pattern caused by airplane structure. The receiver is sensitive to all signals within its frequency range; however, only those signals meeting the complete predetermined requirements of the code being used will be recognized and answered. Mode 2 code settings are set into the receiver-transmitter on the ground and thus are fixed for any one flight. All other codes are set up at the control panel. All other modes can be turned on or off at the control panel. Replies to modes 1, 2, 3, 4 and C interrogations, as well as to I/P and emergency replies, are shown on the ground station equipment. In the case of the more complicated SIF codes, ground stations will use a plan position indicator (PPI) and letter symbol indicator to decode and indicate supplementary information, such as specific identification and location, and flight or airplane conditions. Modes 4 and C will be operable as soon as airborne and ground portions of these functions are available. The Mode C airborne portion will be operational when the central air data computer is modified to provide altitude encoding. An optional low-power setting provision restricts sensitivity so that replies are made only

IFF Control Panel

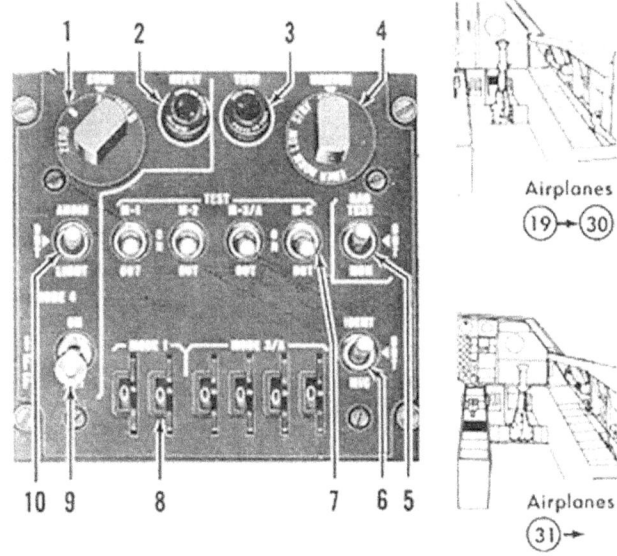

1. Mode 4 Code Control Knob.
2. Reply Lamp.
3. Test Lamp.
4. Master Control Switch.
5. Rad Test/Monitor Switch.
6. Identification-of-Position Switch.
7. Mode Select/Test Switches (4).
8. Code Selector Knobs.
9. Mode 4 Control Switch.
10. Mode 4 Monitor Control Switch.

Figure 1-39.

to local interrogations. Airplane electrical power is supplied to the IFF system from the 115 volt ac essential bus and the 28 volt dc essential bus. See figure 1-48 for a listing of communications and avionics equipment.

IFF MASTER CONTROL KNOB.

The five-position IFF master control knob (4, figure 1-39), is located on the IFF control panel. The knob positions are marked OFF, STBY, LOW, NORM and EMER. When positioned to STBY, the equipment is turned on and warmed up but will not transmit. When positioned to LOW, only local (strong) interrogations are recognized and answered. When positioned to NORM, full range recognition and reply occurs. Transmitted power from the IFF system is the same for both the LOW and NORM positions. The knob must be pulled outward to position it to EMER. When the knob is positioned to EMER, an emergency-indicating pulse group is transmitted each time a mode 1 or mode 3 interrogation is recognized.

IDENTIFICATION-OF-POSITION SWITCH.

The identification-of-position (I/P) switch (7, figure 1-39), located on the IFF control panel, is used to control transmission of I/P pulse groups. The switch has

Antenna Select Panel

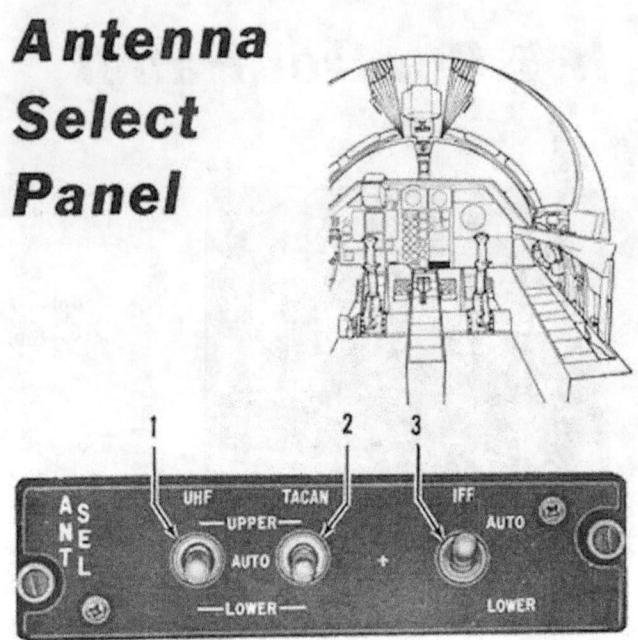

1. UHF Antenna Selector Switch.
2. TACAN Antenna Selector Switch.
3. IFF Antenna Selector Switch.

Figure 1-40.

three positions marked MIC, OUT, and IDENT. When the switch is momentarily held in the spring loaded IDENT position, the I/P timer is energized for 30 seconds. If a mode 1 or mode 3 interrogation is recognized within this 30 second period, I/P replies will be made. When the switch is placed in the MIC position, the I/P pulse group will be transmitted in reply to a mode 1 or 3 interrogation as long as the microphone switch on either throttle is held to the TRANS position and for 30 seconds after the microphone switch is released. The transmitter selector knob, at the crew station being used, must be in the UHF position to allow transmission of I/P groups with the microphone switch. When the microphone switch is open, transmission of the I/P pulse groups will be withheld. Placing the switch to the OUT position prevents transmission of I/P groups.

IFF ANTENNA SELECTOR SWITCH.

The two-position antenna selector switch (3, figure 1-40), located on the antenna select panel, is marked AUTO and LOWER. When the switch is placed to AUTO, the antenna lobing switch rapidly cycles contact of the receiver-transmitter between the upper and lower antenna to provide thorough antenna pattern coverage. When the antenna selector switch is placed to LOWER only, the lower antenna will be used to receive and reply to interrogation signals.

MODE SELECT/TEST SWITCHES.

Four mode select/test switches, (5, figure 1-39) located on the IFF control panel, are marked TEST, ON and OUT. The switches are labeled M-1, M-2, M-3/A and M-C from left to right to correspond to mode 1, mode 2, mode 3/A and mode C. The mode C switch is temporarily inoperative pending modification of the central air data computer. The OUT position for each switch disables the transmitter-receiver for the mode selected. The ON position for each switch enables the transmitter-receiver to reply to interrogations for the mode selected. If more than one switch is placed to ON the transmitter-receiver will reply to interrogations for all modes selected. The switches are spring-loaded to the ON position from the TEST position. The TEST positions are used for functional testing and trouble shooting and are temporarily inoperative pending installation of the inflight test set.

CODE SELECTOR KNOBS.

Two sets of thumb actuated code selector knobs (8, figure 1-39), located on the IFF control panel, are provided to set mode 1 and mode 3 codes. The set of knobs labeled mode 1, consists of two knobs which allow selection of 32 different codes. The set of knobs labeled mode 3, consists of four knobs which provide the capability of setting 4096 codes. Code digits on each knob are read in windows recessed in the face of the panel.

TEST LAMP.

The test lamp (3, figure 1-39), located on the IFF control panel, is used for functional testing and trouble shooting of the IFF equipment.

MODE 4 CODE CONTROL KNOB.

MODE 4 CONTROL SWITCH.

MODE 4 MONITOR CONTROL SWITCH.

RAD TEST/MONITOR SWITCH.

REPLY LAMP.

The above control and indicators are temporarily inoperative.

ATTACK RADAR (AN/APQ-113).

The attack radar provides all weather navigation, air-to-ground and air-to-air attack capability. Basic components of the system consist of an antenna, an antenna roll unit and antenna control, located in the radome and a modulator-receiver-transmitter (MRT) and synchronizer, located in the forward electronic bay. The radar scope and the controls, including the tracking control handle, are located at the pilot's station. A recording camera is provided to take radar scope photographs. The antenna is stabilized in pitch by signals from the bomb nav system and in roll by signals from the bomb nav system or AFRS. Should the attitude signal fail the antenna can be caged in alignment with the airplane longitudinal and lateral axes. For location of the antenna, see figure 1-41. The MRT operates in the KU frequency band and has the capability of automatic frequency control (AFC) for normal operation and manual frequency control (MFC) for backup. When operating in AFC-1 the transmitter is swept through the frequency band with random reversal. This provides a measure of immunity to many types of jamming and improves stability and legibility of returns. The synchronizer provides system timing, target declaration and range tracking. The radar scope panel contains the radar scope, recording camera and the necessary operating and tuning controls for the scope and camera. The recording camera is mounted behind the radar scope. A small window in the side of the cathode ray tube allows the camera to take exposures of the back of the radar scope. The image on the scope is reversed by optics so that the film exposure will represent the scope presentation as seen by the operator. A film exposure is taken automatically at weapon release on a signal from the bomb nav system or manually when desired. A lamp on the radar scope panel will blink each time an exposure is taken. A film magazine in the face of the radar scope panel provides a minimum of 500 exposures of 35 millimeter film. A readout window on the magazine shows film remaining. The magazine is installed or removed by means of a handle recessed in the front of the magazine. Simultaneous film exposure of a clock, data slate and 12 code lamps is made with each scope exposure to identify each frame of the film as shown in figure 1-40A. The clock and slate provide time of exposure and operator's name, date, mission etc. The code lamps are identified on the film and indicate the following:

1—weapon release
2—spare
3—ground velocity mode
4—ground auto mode
5—ground manual mode
6—air mode
7—spare
8—160/160 miles diameter
9—80/160 miles diameter/range
10—30/90 miles diameter/range
11—10/30 miles diameter/range
12—5/15 miles diameter/range

Photo Data Recording

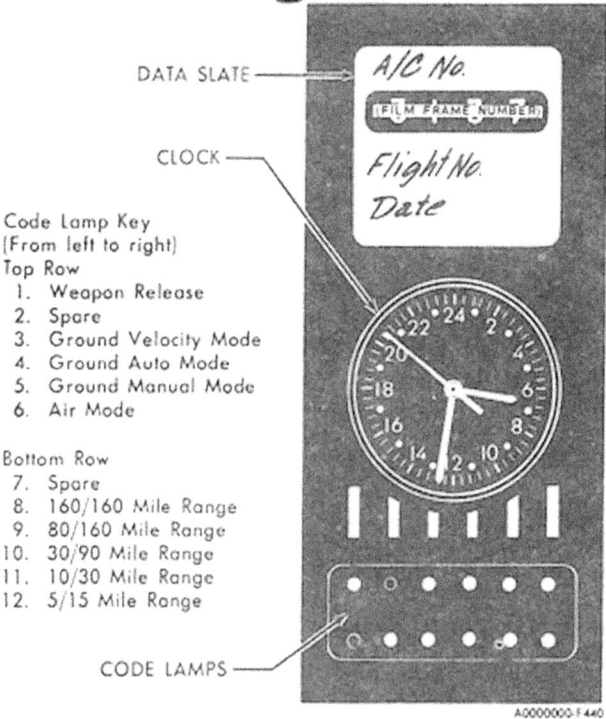

Figure 1-40A.

The tracking control handle is used to position the azimuth and range cursors for fix taking, bombing and target tracking. Self test features incorporated into the system are used for preflight and maintenance malfunction analysis and trouble shooting. The system operates on 115 volt ac power from the left main ac bus and 28 volt dc power from the main dc bus. The system operates in two basic modes, air and ground.

ATTACK RADAR AIR MODE.

The air mode is used for the detection, selection and tracking of airborne targets. At the time the tracking operation begins, the target will be tracked in range, azimuth and elevation. The detection and selection of a target to be tracked occurs during the wide scan operation of the air mode. Wide scan is selected by placing the sector switch in the aft position. The selection of wide scan will result in the antenna scanning an azimuth area of 45 degrees on both sides of the aircraft longitudinal axis. The pointing elevation of the antenna, with respect to the longitudinal plane of the aircraft, is controlled by the fore-and-aft movement of the tracking handle with the enable switch actuated. The elevation of the antenna can be varied ±30 degrees from the aircraft longitudinal axis. To increase the elevation area scanned during wide azimuth scan, a box scan is utilized during air mode.

Section I
Description & Operation

T.O. 1F-111A-1

The box scan is formed by increasing or decreasing the antenna tilt at the azimuth limits. Selection of a target to be tracked can be accomplished by placing the azimuth cursor to within 10 degrees of the desired target and the range cursor to a lesser range than the range to the target.

The command for the radar to begin tracking a target is initiated by placing the sector switch in the forward position (selection of narrow scan). By selecting narrow scan, the area scanned in azimuth is reduced to 20 degrees centered about the azimuth cursor position. In narrow scan the range cursor begins to step out in range at each azimuth turn-around point. Situated about the range cursor is a range gate which is not visible on the presentation. As the range cursor steps out in range, the range gate samples the area scanned for a target. Once the target falls within the range gate, the range cursor will cease to step in range and will disappear from the scope presentation. A portion of the azimuth cursor will be blanked, at the range of the target, and the cursor will be automatically repositioned to a point directly over the target. The operation of the box scan during the tracking operation is such that it keeps the elevation of the antenna pointed in a direction to keep the target in the vertical center of the azimuth scan. After the target being tracked is detected seven times, the range lock indicator lamp will light. The information supplied to the Lead Computing Optical Sight during the tracking operation is a signal indicating that a target is being tracked, the range to the target, and the range rate of the target. The range to the target is also displayed on the range readout on the radar scope. Range lock will be broken if: wide scan is selected, the range cursor position is moved off target,

Antenna Locations

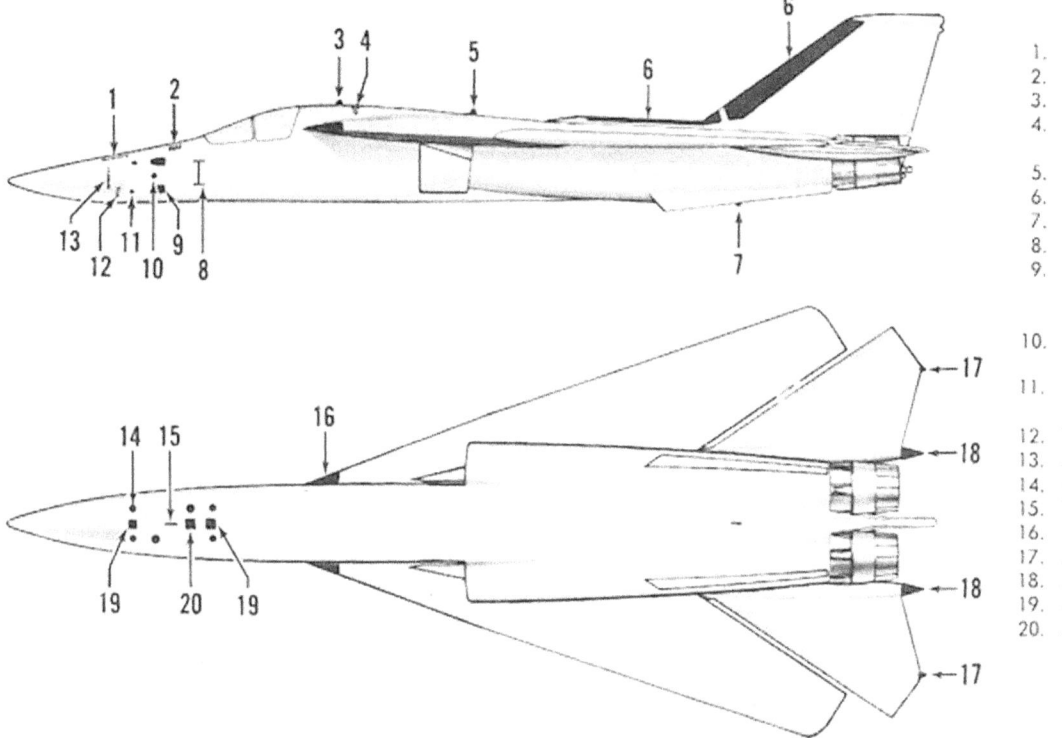

1. Glide Slope.
2. ADF
3. IFF Upper.
4. Radio Beacon Set (AN/URT-21).
5. TACAN and UHF Upper.
6. HF.
7. IFF Lower.
8. Localizer. (2)
9. Low and Medium Frequency Radar Homing. (4)
10. Forward Radar Warning. (2)
11. High Frequency Radar Homing. (4)
12. TFR. (2)
13. Attack Radar.
14. Lower Trackbreaker. (6)
15. TACAN and UHF Lower.
16. Forward Trackbreaker. (2)
17. Aft Radar Warning. (2)
18. Aft Trackbreaker. (2)
19. Radar Altimeter. (2)
20. Marker Beacon.

Figure 1-41.

loss of detection during a four second interval or a mode other than the air mode is selected. If range lock is broken because of loss of detection in the air mode and narrow scan or because the range cursor position is changed, the range cursor will begin to step out in range in search of a target.

ATTACK RADAR GROUND MODES.

Three ground modes of operation are provided for radar navigation, fix-taking and fixed angle or automatic bombing. The ground modes are: ground manual (GND MAN), ground auto (GND AUTO) and ground velocity (GND VEL). In all three ground modes the antenna scans with a fan beam 45 degrees either side of the longitudinal axis. A drift stabilized map of the terrain is displayed on the scope at the range selected. Drift signals are provided from the bomb nav system. The ground manual mode operates independently of the bomb nav system and is used as the primary mode for radar navigation and as a back up method for fixed angle bombing in the event of a failure of the bomb nav system. Antenna tilt adjustment and azimuth and range cursor positioning is accomplished manually for navigation and fix-taking. If the antenna is caged, the scope display is not ground track stabilized in the ground manual mode. In the ground manual mode with the antenna caged, zero degrees on the radar scope represents aircraft heading. In the ground automatic or ground velocity modes, zero degrees on the radar scope represents the ground track of the aircraft even if the antenna is caged. The operation of the system is similar in the ground automatic and ground velocity modes. During both modes of operation, the navigation computer is supplied with information to update the navigational fix bearing or range or to update the target bearing and range. The navigation fix bearing and range is corrected when the destination/present position selector switch is in the present position. The navigational computer target range and bearing is updated when the destination/present position selector switch is in the destination position. In the ground velocity mode, the display is ground stabilized; however, in ground automatic, the display is not ground stabilized. Movement of the tracking handle in the ground automatic mode will position the azimuth and range cursors. Movement of the tracking handle in the ground velocity mode will move the display in azimuth or range with the azimuth and range cursors remaining fixed in the center of the scope. Antenna tilt is automatically adjusted by inputs from the bomb nav system, however corrections for scope display refinement can be made with the antenna tilt knob. The tracking control handle is used to drive the destination or present position counters in the bomb nav system for positioning the azimuth and range cursors.

ATTACK RADAR FUNCTION SELECTOR KNOB.

The attack radar function selector knob (3, figure 1-42), located on the attack radar control panel, has five positions marked OFF, STBY, ON, XMIT and TEST. In the OFF position the entire system is de-energized. Placing the switch to STBY supplies power to all system filaments for warm-up and energizes a 40 second warmup delay and a 5 minute transmitter high voltage delay. Also the antenna is caged in pitch and stowed full up in tilt and full left in azimuth. Placing the switch to ON energizes the entire system, except for the transmitter, after the 40 second warm-up delay has expired. The XMIT position places the system in operation after the 5 minute high voltage delay has expired. The TEST position allows self test of the system for malfunction trouble shooting and ground maintenance.

ATTACK RADAR MODE SELECTOR KNOB.

The attack radar mode selector knob (1, figure 1-42), located on the attack radar control panel, has four positions marked GND MAN (ground manual), GND AUTO (ground auto), GND VEL (ground velocity) and AIR. In the GND MAN position the range and azimuth cursors are positioned with the tracking control handle independently of the navigational computer. In the GND AUTO position the cursors are automatically positioned by the navigational computer. The tracking control handle is used to correct the bomb nav system destination and present position counters. Operation in the GND VEL position is the same as in the GND AUTO position except the scope display is a ground velocity stabilized magnified picture and the intersection of the cursors remains in the center of the scope.

ATTACK RADAR FREQUENCY CONTROL KNOB.

The frequency control knob (2, figure 1-42), located on the attack radar control panel, has three positions marked AFC 1 (automatic frequency control), AFC 2, and MFC (manual frequency control). In the AFC 1 position the receiver operates in automatic frequency control and the transmitter operates in a frequency agility mode in which the transmitter sweeps through the frequency band with random reversal. The changing frequency and rapid scanning rate provided in this position provides immunity to many types of jamming and improves stability and legibility of the PPI display. In the AFC 2 position the receiver operates in automatic frequency control and the transmitter is manually tuned using the transmitter tune control knob. The MFC position of the knob is variable over a range between the 12 and 6 o'clock positions. In this position the transmitter operates in a mid-band fixed frequency and receiver is manually tunable by adjusting the knob over the MFC range.

ATTACK RADAR FAST TIME CONSTANT SWITCH.

The fast time constant switch (4, figure 1-42), located on the attack radar control panel, has two positions marked FTC (fast time constant) and NORM. The switch provides a means of selecting the desired receiver time response characteristics. The FTC position is used to minimize the effects of jamming in any mode of operation. In the NORM position anti-jamming capabilities are inoperative.

Note

FTC should be used in air mode of operation only when obvious jamming signals are present on the attack radar scope display.

ATTACK RADAR SIDE LOBE CANCELLATION SWITCH.

The side lobe cancellation (SLC) switch (5, figure 1-42), located on the attack radar control panel, is a two position switch marked SLC and OFF. Placing the switch to the SLC position will cancel the energy received from the side lobes of the radar beam to reduce ground clutter. The SLC position may be selected in any mode of operation, however, it is most effective when operating in the AIR mode at low altitudes.

ANTENNA POLARIZATION SWITCH.

The antenna polarization switch (7, figure 1-42), located on the attack radar control panel is a two position switch marked CIR (circular) and NORM. With the switch in the NORM position antenna polarization is horizontal when operating in the ground modes and vertical when operating in the air mode. Placing the switch to CIR changes antenna polarization to circular when operating in either ground or air modes. The CIR position may be used to reduce rain clutter interference on the scope.

DESTINATION/PRESENT POSITION SELECTOR SWITCH.

The destination/present position selector switch (8, figure 1-42), located on the attack radar control panel, is a two position switch marked DEST (destination) and PP (present position). The switch is used in the ground auto and ground velocity modes of operation when correcting the bomb nav system destination or present position counters.

ATTACK RADAR TRACKING CONTROL HANDLE.

The tracking control handle (figure 1-43) is mounted on a pivot pedestal on the right side of the pilot's station. The pedestal is stowed out of the way under the right canopy sill when not in use. To gain access to the tracking handle the pedestal is rotated outward. A blade type enable switch (3, figure 1-43), recessed

Attack Radar Control Panel

1. Mode Selector Knob.
2. Frequency Control Knob.
3. Function Selector Knob.
4. Fast Time Constant Switch.
5. Side Lobe Cancellation Switch.
6. Antenna Cage Pushbutton Indicator Lamp.
7. Antenna Polarization Switch.
8. Destination/Present Position Selector Switch.

Figure 1-42.

in the front of handle must be depressed and held to activate the handle. When operating in the air mode with the range search button depressed or any of the three ground modes, fore and aft movement of the handle will slew the range cursor out or in respectively. Moving the handle fore and aft in the air mode without depressing the range search button will adjust antenna elevation down and up respectively. When operating in any mode left or right movement of the handle will slew the azimuth cursor left or right. Slewing speed is proportional to the amount of handle deflection.

ATTACK RADAR RANGE SEARCH BUTTON.

The range search button (2, figure 1-43), located on the right top of the tracking control handle, is used in the air mode of operation only. The button is labeled R_S AIR and must be depressed and held to break lock then the tracking control handle will override automatic range search when the range cursor is slewed fore and aft. When operating with the sector switch in the narrow sector position, range searching will resume from the point at which the range cursor was positioned by slewing. When operating with the sector switch in the wide sector position the range cursor will remain stationary after slewing.

ATTACK RADAR SECTOR SWITCH.

The sector switch (1, figure 1-43), located on the left top of the tracking control handle, is labeled SECTOR and is a two position, thumb actuated, sliding switch. The switch is used in either the ground or air modes of operation to change the sector of antenna sweep. In the aft position (wide scan) antenna sweep is 45 degrees either side of the longitudinal axis of the airplane. In the forward position (narrow scan) antenna sweep is 10 degrees either side of the azimuth cursor. When operating in the air mode and in narrow scan, automatic range searching is automatically initiated after the target being tracked is detected seven times; then the range lock indicator lamp will light.

ATTACK RADAR MANUAL PHOTO BUTTON.

The manual photo button (7, figure 1-44), located on the attack radar scope panel, provides a manual means of taking a film exposure of the radar scope display whenever desired. The button must be depressed each time a photo is desired.

INTERMEDIATE FREQUENCY GAIN KNOB.

The intermediate frequency gain knob (9, figure 1-44), located on the attack radar scope panel, is labeled IF GAIN and permits adjustment of receiver gain when operating in the ground modes.

Attack Radar Tracking Control Handle

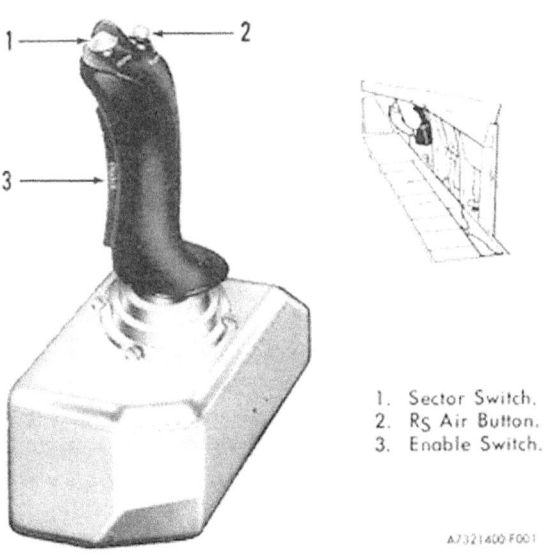

1. Sector Switch.
2. R_S Air Button.
3. Enable Switch.

Figure 1-43.

ANTENNA TILT CONTROL KNOB.

The antenna tilt control knob (9, figure 1-44), located on the attack radar scope panel, provides a means of manually adjusting antenna tilt position when operating in the ground modes. The knob is labeled ANT TILT. In the ground manual mode the knob is the only means of adjusting antenna tilt. In the ground auto and ground velocity modes antenna tilt is automatically positioned by signals from the bomb nav system and the knob is used to refine this position. The knob has a detent corresponding to zero antenna tilt position for reference. Rotating the knob clockwise adjusts the tilt up to 30 degrees and vice versa. However, with the terrain following radar (TFR) operating the antenna can only be physically adjusted to -10 degrees (pitch plus tilt) to prevent interference with the TFR. Antenna position is indicated on the antenna tilt indicator (17, figure 1-44), located on the attack radar scope panel. The indicator is graduated in 5 degree increments from zero to ±30 degrees. The knob has no control over antenna tilt when operating in the AIR mode.

ATTACK RADAR SCOPE INTENSITY CONTROL KNOB.

The attack radar scope intensity control knob (14, figure 1-44), located on the attack radar scope panel, provides an adjustment of scope baseline intensity from zero to full brightness. Turning the knob clockwise increases brightness and vice versa. The knob is labeled CRT INT.

BEZEL/RANGE MARKS INTENSITY CONTROL KNOBS.

Two coaxial knobs (15, figure 1-44), located on the attack radar scope panel, provide an adjustment of bezel and range marks intensity. The knobs are labeled INT. The outer knob is marked BEZEL, and the inner knob is marked RANGE MK. Turning either knob clockwise increases intensity from zero to full brightness.

RANGE AND AZIMUTH CURSOR INTENSITY CONTROL KNOBS.

Two cursor intensity control knobs (16, figure 1-44), located on the attack radar scope panel, provided an adjustment of range and azimuth cursor intensity. The knobs are labeled CURSOR INT and are individually marked RANGE and AZIMUTH. Turning either knob clockwise increases intensity of the respective cursor from zero to full brightness.

ATTACK RADAR TEST SWITCH.

The test switch (18, figure 1-44), located on the attack radar scope panel, is a three position switch marked LAMP, CKT (circuit) and OFF. The switch is used when performing preflight confidence and ground maintenance checks and is normally left in the OFF position.

ATTACK RADAR SWEEP CONTROL SWITCH.

The sweep control switch (19, figure 1-44), located on the attack radar scope panel, is a two position switch marked SLANT and NORM. The switch is used in the ground modes of operation to provide ground range in the NORM position and slant range in the SLANT position. The switch is inoperative in the air mode.

ATTACK RADAR BETA SWITCH.

The beta switch (20, figure 1-44), located on the attack radar scope panel, is a two position switch marked MAN (manual) and NORM. The switch functions in the ground auto and ground velocity modes to select automatic sighting angle in the NORM position and manual sighting angle in the MAN position. In the normal position sighting angle is automatically adjusted by signals from the bomb nav system. In the manual position sighting angle is adjusted with the antenna tilt knob. The switch is inoperative in the ground manual and air modes of operation.

SENSITIVITY TIME CONTROL KNOBS.

Two coaxial rotary sensitivity time control (STC) knobs (11, figure 1-44), located on the attack radar scope panel, provide a means of equalizing radar intensity over the entire scope display when operating in the ground modes at low altitude. The outer knob labeled AMPL/OFF, has an OFF position at nine o'clock, and is used to obtain an initial adjustment of display intensity or to turn the STC function OFF in the event of a malfunction in the STC circuit. The inner knob, labeled SLOPE, is used to balance the display intensity throughout the sweep. The STC slope function is inoperative in the AIR mode.

VIDEO/TRANSMITTER TUNING CONTROL KNOBS.

Two coaxial rotary control knobs (12, figure 1-44), located on the attack radar scope panel, provide a means of adjusting video and tuning the transmitter. The outer knob, labeled VIDEO, is used to increase the amplitude of the video signal supplied to the attack radar scope when it is turned clockwise. The inner knob, labeled XMTR TUNE, allows continuous tuning of the transmitter over its entire frequency range when

Attack Radar Scope Panel

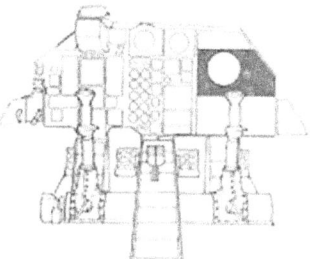

1. System Malfunction Lamp.
2. Azimuth Bezel.
3. Radar Scope.
4. Ground Adjustment Access Door.
5. Film Magazine Removal Handle.
6. Unused Film Indicator.
7. Manual Photo Button.
8. Photo Malfunction Indicator Lamp.
9. Intermediate Frequency Gain/Antenna Tilt Control Knobs.
10. Cursor Range Counter.
11. Sensitivity Time Control Knobs.
12. Video Adjustment/Transmitter Tuning Control Knobs.
13. Range Selector Knob.
14. Scope Intensity Control Knob.
15. Bezel/Range Marks Intensity Control Knobs.
16. Range/Azimuth Cursor Intensity Control Knobs.
17. Antenna Tilt Indicator.
18. Test Switch.
19. Sweep Control Switch.
20. Beta Switch.
21. Range Lock Indicator Lamp.

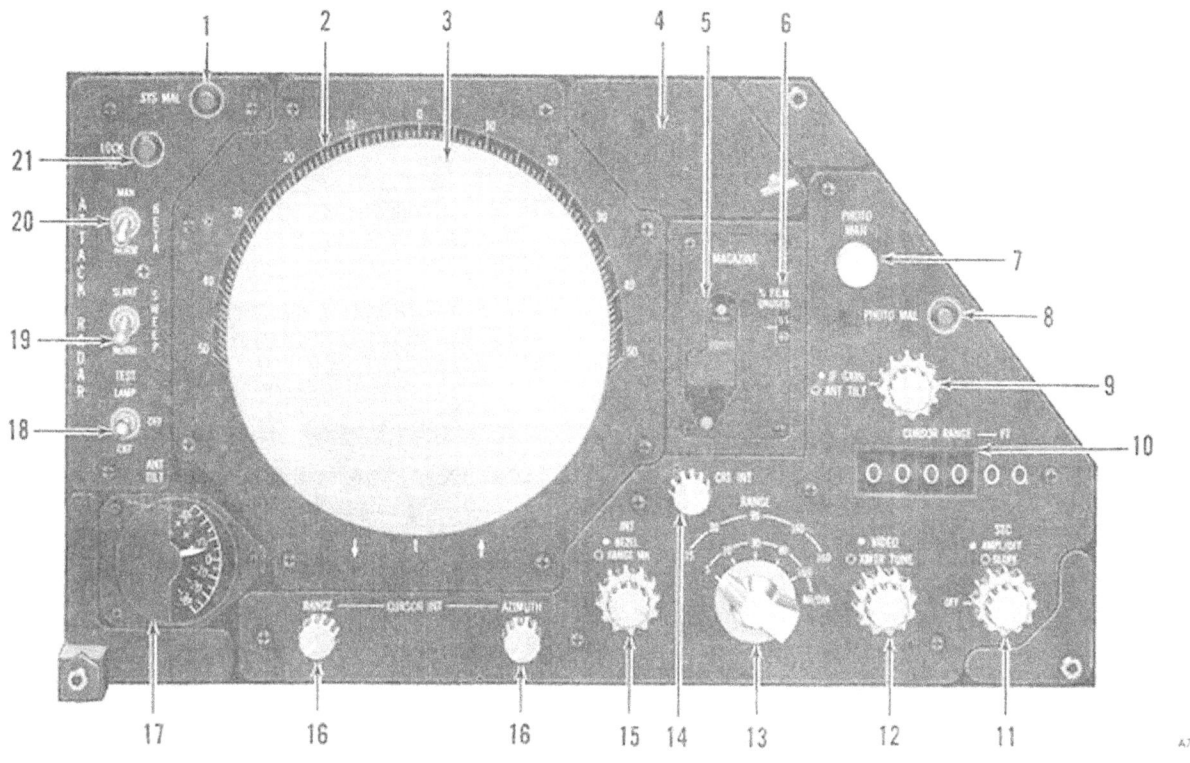

Figure 1-44.

operating with the frequency control knob in the AFC-2 position.

ATTACK RADAR RANGE SELECTOR KNOB.

The range selector knob (13, figure 1-44), located on the attack radar scope panel, allows selection of various scope display ranges. The knob is marked RANGE with 15, 30, 90, 160, and 160 miles positions on an outer scale and miles/diameter (MI/DIA) with 5, 10, 30, 80 and 160 mile positions on an inner scale. The inner scale numbers and range are lighted when operating in air, ground manual and ground auto modes. When operating in the ground velocity mode both inner and outer scales and MI/DIA are lighted. This indicates that the scope is displaying a fractional part of a range. For example, when the switch is set to the 5/15 mile position, the scope is displaying 5 miles of the 15 mile range.

ATTACK RADAR SCOPE.

The radar scope (3, figure 1-44) provides a sector scan plan position indicator (PPI) display with a fixed one radius offset sweep in all modes of operation except ground velocity mode. In ground velocity mode the sweep is a variable offset with a maximum displacement of six radii. The airplane position on the scope is at the bottom in vertical alignment with the center of the scope. The scope is 6 inches in diameter. The sector displayed is a 90 degree area ahead of the airplane when in wide scan and a 20 degree area centered on the azimuth cursor when in narrow scan. An azimuth bezel (2, figure 1-44), around the top of the scope, is graduated in one degree increments with each 10 degrees marked to show azimuth displacement up to 50 degrees either side of the airplane heading or ground track. When operating in the air mode, or when the antenna is caged in the ground manual mode, zero degrees on the scale represents aircraft heading. In any of the ground modes the scan is displaced in azimuth to compensate for drift, and zero degrees represents ground track. In the air mode of operation two arrows in the bottom of the bezel indicate target position relative to antenna scan. When both arrows are lighted the target is in the center of the scan. Range and azimuth cursors are displayed on the scope for fix taking and target tracking. The cursors are positioned with the tracking control handle. Fixed range markers are provided for various ranges of operations. For 5, 10, 30, 80 and 160 ranges each range mark represents 1, 2, 5, 20 and 40 mile range increments respectively, except there are no range marks displayed in ground auto or ground velocity modes when in the 5 or 10 mile range. Scope brilliancy and intensity of the bezel, cursors and range marks are controlled by knobs on the scope panel.

Note

When the LCOS mode select knob is placed to the DIV BOMB, RKT AG or GUN AG position, the attack radar and TFR are used in conjunction with the LCOS for air-to-ground ranging. During the air to ground ranging, the attack radar provides the TFR system with its computer function to compute the slant range to a ground point for use in the LCOS. For the attack radar computer to accurately compute the air to ground range, it is necessary that the attack radar computer be synchronized with the TFR transmitter. The TFR, therefore, supplies the attack radar computer with a pulse indicating the fixing time of the TFR transmitter and a sample of the video to which the range is desired. The pulse from the TFR, indicating fixing time, will determine when the sweep on the attack radar begins. However, the video display on the attack radar scope is provided by the attack radar receiver. Since the video and the sweep on the attack radar scope are not synchronized, a range error exists for any arbitrary returns displayed making the video presentation unsuitable for data extraction. The range readout on the attack radar will indicate the slant range to the video pulse supplied by the TFR. The tracking handle for the attack radar is rendered inoperative and the plan position indicator presentation on the TFR is blanked during air to ground ranging. Therefore the attack radar and TFR ground mapping or situation scope presentations will be unusable and should be ignored.

ATTACK RADAR CURSOR RANGE COUNTER.

The cursor range counter (10, figure 1-44), located on the attack radar scope panel automatically indicates slant range in all modes of operation. The counter has four digital readout windows capable of indicating distances up to 799,900 feet in increments of 100 feet.

ATTACK RADAR SYSTEM MALFUNCTION LAMP.

An amber system malfunction lamp (1, figure 1-44), located on the attack radar scope panel, provides the operator with an indication of a failure in the system. When lighted, SYS MAL is displayed on the face of the lamp. The lamp will not light when the function selector knob is in any position other than TRANSMIT or TEST. The lamp will light indicating any of the following: (1) function selector knob inadvertently left in the TEST position; (2) failure in the antenna system, or input to the antenna system; (3) failure in the transmitter system.

Note

- The attack radar system malfunction lamp will light anytime the combined antenna pitch plus tilt angle exceeds the vertical limits. Limits with TFR on are —10 to +30 degrees longitudinally. It will be normal for the attack radar system malfunction lamp to light intermittently during TFR operation.
- If the system is not useable the function selector knob should be placed to STBY to stow the antenna.

ATTACK RADAR RANGE LOCK INDICATOR LAMP.

An amber range lock indicator lamp (21, figure 1-44), located on the attack radar scope panel, will light when a range lock is acquired on a target when operating in the air mode. When lighted, the word LOCK is visible on the face of the lamp.

PHOTO MALFUNCTION INDICATOR LAMP.

The photo malfunction indicator lamp (8, figure 1-44), located on the attack radar scope panel, provides an indication of camera operation or malfunctions. The lamp will blink each time a film exposure is made. The lack of a light indicates a camera shutter malfunction. A steady light indicates film breakage or failure of the film feed mechanism.

UNUSED FILM INDICATOR.

The unused film indicator (6, figure 1-44), located on the attack radar scope panel, is a digital readout indicator that displays the percent of film remaining in the magazine.

ANTENNA CAGE PUSHBUTTON INDICATOR LAMP.

The antenna cage pushbutton indicator lamp (6, figure 1-42), located on the attack radar control panel, provides a means of caging the antenna in the event of a failure in pitch or roll stabilization. The button is labeled ANT-CAGE. Depressing the button will cage the antenna pitch and roll axes and align the antenna with the longitudinal and lateral axes of the airplane, however, the antenna will continue to sector in azimuth, and tilt can be adjusted. When operating in the ground manual mode with the antenna caged the radar scope will display airplane heading at zero degrees azimuth and range sweep will be slant range instead of ground range. When the antenna is caged a lamp in the button will light displaying the word CAGE. Depressing the button again after the antenna has been caged will uncage the antenna and the lamp will go out. Should the bomb nav system stabilization platform fail the lamp will light and remain on until the flight instrument reference select switch is placed to AUX position.

LEAD COMPUTING OPTICAL SIGHT SYSTEM (AN/ASG-23).

The lead computing optical sight system (LCOS) provides the aircraft commander with information required to accurately deliver gun fire or missiles against aerial or ground targets and to deliver bombs or rockets against ground targets. The LCOS also provides homing, navigation, and landing information. The LCOS consists of a lead and launch computing amplifier, a lead computing gyro, and an optical sight and control panel. Information is displayed on the optical sight in the form of two presentations: an aiming reticle presentation and a command steering bar presentation. The LCOS utilizes 28 volt dc power from the main dc bus and 115 volt, three-phase, 400 cycle, ac power from the left main ac bus.

LCOS AIMING RETICLE.

The aiming reticle, (figure 1-45), which is a lighted image projected on the optical sight, consists of a 2 milliradian center pipper, a 30 milliradian circle, roll reference tabs, a 50 milliradian circle, fixed index reference tabs and range scale, an analog bar presentation, and two deviation indicators. All elements of the aiming reticle are lighted red and are fixed with respect to one another as the aiming reticle display moves about on the optical sight. Pitch limits of the aiming reticle are +2° to -11°. Azimuth limits are ±5.5°. The analog bar appears as a bar of light on the lower half of the 50 milliradian circle. The bar represents radar range deviation in gun, rocket, dive bomb, and GAR-8 modes and pitch angle deviation in loft bomb mode. When a target has been acquired by the attack radar system, the analog bar will appear. In the gun, rocket, and dive bomb modes, the 3 o'clock position of the analog bar represents the maximum range in feet as set on the control panel plus 3000 feet. The 6 o'clock position represents maximum range, and the 9 o'clock position represents maximum range minus 3000 feet. In the GAR-8 mode, the analog bar represents the range envelope of the GAR-8 missile. The 3 o'clock position represents the maximum missile firing range plus a fixed value. The 6 o'clock position represents

Aiming Reticle & Steering Bar Presentations

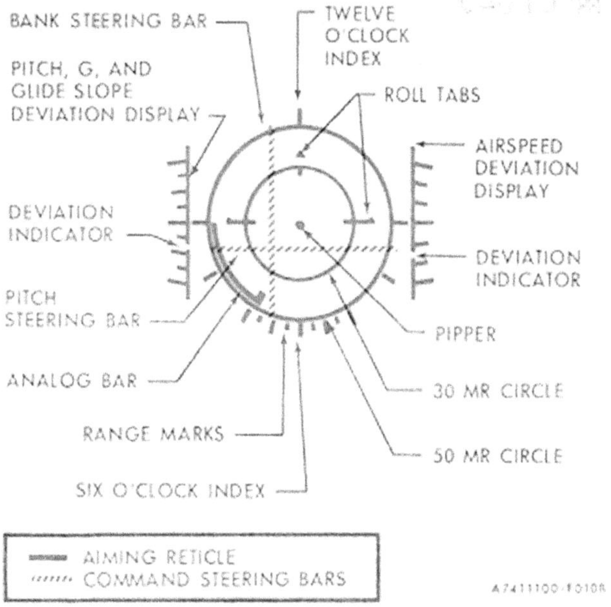

Figure 1-45.

the maximum range, and the 9 o'clock position represents minimum launch and breakaway range. In loft bomb mode, the analog bar represents deviation from a pitch angle preset into the glide/dive angle counter on the bomb nav control panel. During pull-up for a loft bomb delivery, the analog bar will recede from the 3 o'clock position (set angle minus 15°) toward the 9 o'clock position (set angle plus 15°). When the analog bar passes through the 6 o'clock position, the airplane pitch angle equals the preset angle and the LCOS will generate a weapon release signal. The three movable indices of the reticle display are the roll tabs. The roll tabs indicate airplane roll attitude. Roll tab reference indices are located at nine, twelve, and three o'clock positions on the 30 milliradian circle. The deviation indicators to the left and right of the reticle rings indicate aircraft performance and attitude deviations from preset conditions. The left hand deviation indicator displays deviation from G, pitch, or glide slope, depending on selected mode of operation. In the COM, GUN-AG, RKT-AG, DIVE BOMB, and HOM modes, the indicator displays deviation from the pitch angle set into the glide/dive angle counter on the bomb nav control panel. In the LOF BOMB mode, the indicator displays deviation from a fixed value of 4 G's. In the GAR-8, GUN-AA, and LEV BOMB modes, the indica-

Section I
Description & Operation

tor is zeroed. When the instrument system coupler mode selector switch is in ILS or AILA; the left deviation indicator will always present glide slope deviation regardless of the position of the LCOS mode select switch. The right hand indicator displays deviation from the airspeed preset into the true airspeed indicator on the LCOS control panel. In the GAR-8 and GUN-AA modes, the indicator is zeroed. In GAR-8 mode, a G limit indication is provided. The 6 o'clock index area of the 50 milliradian circle will be blanked out when the G limit of the GAR-8 missile is exceeded.

COMMAND STEERING BARS.

The command steering bars (figure 1-45) are presented as a vertical bank steering bar and a horizontal pitch steering bar. The steering bars are lighted green and are in parallel with the ADI steering bars. The aiming reticle pipper is used as the zero reference point for the steering bars. During a loft bomb delivery, at point of pull-up, the pitch steering bar will command a fly-up signal. The pitch steering bar indicates a deviation from 4 g's. Full deflection of the bar indicates a 3g deviation from the fixed 4g value. When operating the attack radar in the air mode, placing the instrument system coupler mode selector knob to the AIR/AIR position will provide both bank and pitch steering

commands to the target. The command steering bars function independently of the LCOS mode select knob. The operator has the option of having the bars displayed by use of the command bar brightness knob.

LCOS RANGE SET KNOB.

The range set knob (11, figure 1-46), located on the optical sight and control panel, is used to set in the six o'clock range index. A preset range indicator (12, figure 1-46), located directly above the knob will display the range in feet set in by the range set knob.

LCOS RETICLE DEPRESSION SET KNOB.

The reticle depression set knob (5, figure 1-46), located on the optical sight and control panel, is used to set in desired depression angles of the aiming reticle. A reticle depression indicator (4, figure 1-46), located directly above the set knob, indicates in milliradians the reticle depression set by the depression set knob.

TRUE AIRSPEED SET KNOB.

A true airspeed set knob (3, figure 1-46), located on the optical sight and control panel, is used to set in a

Lead Computing Optical Sight and Control Panel

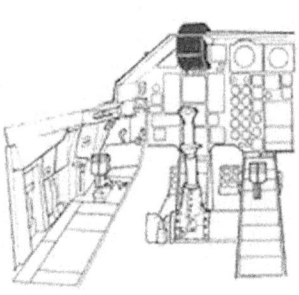
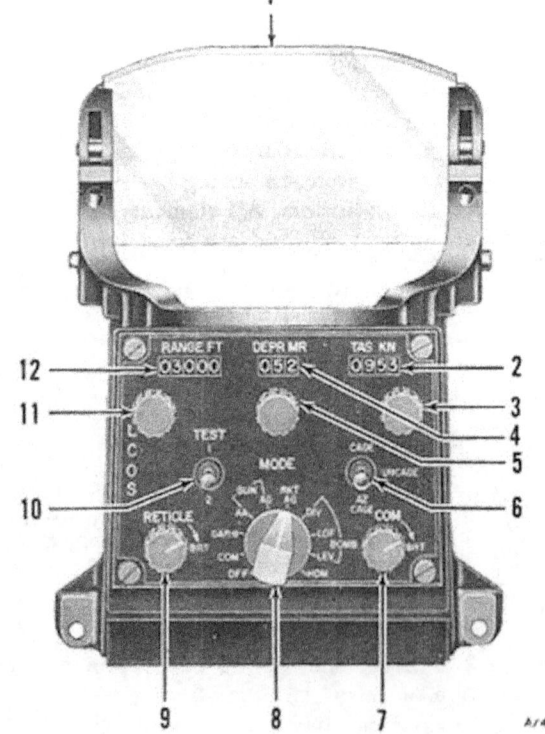

1. Optical Sight.
2. Preset True Airspeed Indicator.
3. True Airspeed Set Knob.
4. Reticle Depression Indicator.
5. Reticle Depression Set Knob.
6. Aiming Reticle Cage Switch.
7. Command Bar Brightness Knob.
8. Mode Select Knob.
9. Aiming Reticle Brightness Knob.
10. Test Switch.
11. Range Set Knob.
12. Preset Range Indicator.

Figure 1-46.

desired true airspeed. A preset true airspeed indicator (2, figure 1-46), located directly above the set knob, indicates true airspeed in knots set in by the true airspeed set knob.

LCOS TEST SWITCH.

The LCOS test switch (10, figure 1-46), located on the optical sight and control panel, is provided to allow an operational check and a fault isolation check to be performed on the LCOS while installed in the airplane without the aid of test equipment. The switch has positions 1 and 2 and is spring-loaded to the center OFF position. Position 1 is used for performing in-flight and ground self tests. Position 2 is used for performing ground fault isolation tests.

AIMING RETICLE CAGE LEVER.

The aiming reticle cage lever (6, figure 1-46), located on the optical sight and control panel, has positions AZ CAGE, CAGE, and UNCAGE. In the AZ CAGE position, the aiming reticle is mechanically caged in azimuth only. In the CAGE position the aiming reticle is mechanically caged to the armament datum line. In the UNCAGE position, the aiming reticle is free to move in azimuth and in elevation.

AIMING RETICLE CAGE BUTTON.

The aiming reticle cage button (1, figure 1-5), located under the forward contour of the aircraft commander's left throttle, is a push button marked CAGE. Depressing and holding the button will cage the aiming reticle to the armament datum line.

AIMING RETICLE BRIGHTNESS KNOB.

The aiming reticle brightness knob (9, figure 1-46), located on the optical sight and control panel, is provided to adjust the brilliance of the aiming reticle. Rotating the knob full clockwise will provide full brilliancy. Rotating the knob full counterclockwise will turn off the aiming reticle.

COMMAND BAR BRIGHTNESS KNOB.

The command bar brightness knob (7, figure 1-46), located on the optical sight and control panel, is provided to adjust brilliance of the command steering bars. Rotating the knob full clockwise will provide full brilliancy. Rotating the knob full counterclockwise will turn off the command steering bars.

LCOS MODE SELECT KNOB.

The LCOS mode select knob (8, figure 1-46), located on the optical sight and control panel, is used to select the various modes of LCOS operation.

Note

When the LCOS mode select knob is placed to the DIV BOMB, RKT AG or GUN AG positions, the attack radar and TFR are used in conjunction with the LCOS for air-to-ground ranging. Under this condition the attack radar and TFR ground mapping or situation scope presentations will be unusable and should be ignored.

Refer to figure 1-47 for LCOS indications in the various knob positions.

Refer to classified Supplement, 1F-111A-1B, for information pertaining to the following systems:

PENETRATION AIDS.

COMMUNICATION EQUIPMENT.

For a listing and function of communications equipment see figure 1-48.

UHF COMMAND RADIO (AN/ARC-109).

The UHF command radio provides air-to-air and air-to-ground communications and automatic direction finding (ADF) in conjunction with the AN/ARA-50. The radio equipment consists of a receiver-transmitter (RT) unit, a control panel, an antenna selector, blade type upper and lower antenna, and a loop ADF antenna. See figure 1-41 antenna locations. There are 3500 channels available in 50 kilocycle increments in the frequency range from 225.00 to 399.95 mc (megacycles). The RT unit and guard receiver are located in the right forward equipment bay. The receiver section of the RT unit provides ADF bearing signals to the number two pointer of the bearing distance heading indicator (BDHI) and audio to the interphone when the ADF function is selected. The guard receiver monitors the guard frequency of 243.0 mc when guard function is selected. The control panel allows selection of 20 preset channel and manual selection of any frequency in the frequency range of the radio. The upper and lower antenna compliment each other to provide omni-directional antenna coverage. An automatic feature allows the receiver to select the antenna which receives the first usable signal; however, either the upper or lower antenna may be manually selected.

Changed 18 August 1967

LCOS Mode Select Knob Positions Versus Indications

Mode Select Knob Positions	Aiming Reticle	Analog Bar	Pitch, G, and Glide Slope Deviation Indicator	Airspeed Deviation Indicator
OFF	LCOS deenergized			
COM	Positioned to preset depression angle. Caged in azimuth	Not displayed	Deviation from preset pitch angle	Deviation from preset airspeed
GAR-8	Caged, with pipper on armament datum line	Range envelope of GAR-8 missile	Zero (Inoperative)	Zero (Inoperative)
GUN-AA	Positioned to computed lead angle	Deviation from preset maximum gun range	Zero (Inoperative)	Zero (Inoperative)
GUN-AG	Positioned to preset depression angle. Caged in azimuth	Deviation from preset range	Deviation from preset pitch angle	Deviation from preset airspeed
RKT-AG	Positioned to preset depression angle. Caged in azimuth	Deviation from preset range	Deviation from preset pitch angle	Deviation from preset airspeed
DIV BOMB	Positioned in elevation by manual depression and in azimuth by drift angle	Deviation from preset range	Deviation from preset pitch angle	Deviation from preset airspeed
LOF-BOMB	Positioned in elevation by manual depression and in azimuth by drift angle	Deviation from preset pitch angle	Deviation from 4G	Deviation from preset airspeed
LEV-BOMB	Positioned in elevation by manual depression and in azimuth by drift angle	Not displayed	Zero (Inoperative)	Deviation from preset airspeed
HOM	Positioned by radar homing and warning signals	Not displayed	Deviation from preset pitch angle	Deviation from preset airspeed

Figure 1-47.

Note

When operating the UHF in the automatic antenna selection mode, the antenna selector has a transmission memory circuit which automatically connects the transmitter to the antenna last used for transmission. If the channel or frequency is changed to another station or the airplane position has changed relative to the station, this may be the wrong antenna for the next transmission and difficulty will be encountered in gaining contact. Should this occur, manually select the upper or lower antenna and repeat the transmission to gain contact.

The antenna also serve the TACAN. When the ADF function is selected the receiver is connected to the ADF loop antenna. The UHF radio operates on 115 volt ac power from the ac essential bus and 28 volt dc power from the main dc bus.

UHF Radio Function Selector Knob.

The UHF radio function selector knob (4, figure 1-49), located on the UHF radio control panel, has four positions marked OFF, MAIN, BOTH, and ADF. Rotating the knob to the MAIN position activates the RT unit for normal transmission and reception on the channel selected; the guard receiver is inoperative. Rotating the

Communications and Avionics Equipment

Type	Designation	Function	Operator	Range	Control Location
UHF COMMAND RADIO	AN/ARC-109	Air-to-air and air-to-ground voice communication	AC Pilot	Line-of-Sight	Right Main Instrument Panel
UHF ADF	AN/ARA-50	Provides bearing information to selected UHF stations	AC Pilot	Line-of-Sight	Right Main Instrument Panel
HF RADIO	AN/ARC-123	Air-to-air and air-to-ground long range voice communications	AC Pilot	5000 miles	Right Console
INTERPHONE	AN/AIC-25	Interphone between crew members and monitoring of all communications facilities	AC Pilot		Left & Right Console
IDENTIFICATION RADAR (IFF-SIF)	APX 64 A/G	Provides coded IFF replies to an interrogating ground radar station	Pilot	Line-of-Sight	Right Pedestal or Center Console
TACAN	AN/ARN-52	Provides bearing and distance information to TACAN stations	AC Pilot	Line-of-Sight up to 300 NM	Right Main Instrument Panel
ILS	AN/ARN-58	Provides visual indications for ILS approaches	Pilot	Localizer 45 NM Glide Slope 25 NM	Right Pedestal
RADAR ALTIMETER	AN/APN-67	Provides precise altitude measurements from 0 to 5,000 feet	AC	0-5000 feet	Left Main Instrument Panel
TERRAIN FOLLOWING RADAR	AN/APQ-110	Provides all weather, low altitude terrain following, obstacle avoidance and blind letdown capability	Pilot	Line-of-Sight up to 15 miles	Right Main Instrument Panel
ATTACK RADAR	AN/APQ-113	All weather navigation, fix-taking, bombing, and air-to-air attack	Pilot	Line-of-Sight up to 160 miles	Right Main Instrument Panel and Right Console
LEAD COMPUTING OPTICAL SIGHT	AN/ASG-23	Provides air-to-air and air-to-ground attack capability and duplicate information as displayed on ADI for instrument flying	AC	Line-of-Sight	Left Main Instrument Panel

Figure 1-48.

UHF Radio Control Panel

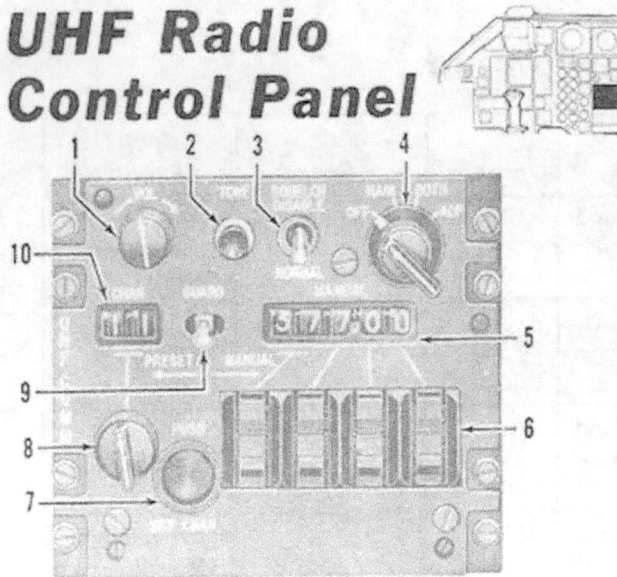

1. Volume Control Knob.
2. Tone Button.
3. Squelch Switch.
4. Function Selector Knob.
5. Frequency Indicator Window.
6. Manual Frequency Selector Knobs (4).
7. Channel Set Pushbutton.
8. Preset Channel Selector Knob.
9. Mode Selector Switch.
10. Preset Channel Indicator Window.

Figure 1-49.

knob to the BOTH position also activates the RT unit for normal use and in addition activates the guard receiver to allow monitoring guard frequency. In the ADF position the receiver is switched to the ADF loop antenna and bearing information and audio are supplied to the BDHI and interphone respectively. Audio range is reduced considerably when operating on the ADF antenna and it may be necessary to return the knob to MAIN or BOTH for better reception. If the microphone switch is held to TRANS while in the ADF position the UHF antennas are switched back into the circuit and the ADF antenna is disabled until the microphone switch is released. The ADF position of the switch is inoperative when operating on emergency electrical power.

UHF Radio Mode Selector Switch.

The three position UHF radio mode selector switch (9, figure 1-49), located on the UHF radio control panel, permits selection of the desired operating mode. The switch is marked PRESET, MANUAL, and GUARD. The PRESET position is used when selecting one of the 20 preset frequencies. The MANUAL position is used when utilizing frequencies that are selected by the manual frequency selector knobs. The GUARD position tunes the main RT unit to the guard frequency of 243.0 megacycles.

UHF Radio Preset Channel Selector Knob.

The preset channel selector knob (8, figure 1-49), located on the UHF radio control panel, permits selection of one of twenty preset frequencies. With the mode selector switch at PRESET, movement of the preset channel selector knob changes the frequency to that of the channel selected. There are 20 channels, numbered 1 through 20, that may be individually selected. The number of the channel selected is displayed in a window above the knob. Frequencies for each channel are written on a channel frequency log located under the aircraft commander's shield. Frequencies of the preset channels can be changed during flight.

UHF Radio Manual Frequency Selector Knobs.

Four thumb actuated UHF radio manual frequency selector knobs (6, figure 1-49), located on the UHF radio control panel, are provided for manually selecting frequencies. Manual frequency selection can be made in steps of 50 kilocycles from 225 through 399.95 megacycles. The first selector knob will select the first two digits of the desired frequency. The second, third and fourth knobs select the third, fourth and fifth frequency digits respectively. The selected frequency is displayed in a window on the face of the UHF radio control panel.

UHF Radio Volume Control Knob.

The volume control knob (1, figure 1-49), located on the UHF radio control panel, increases the volume of the receiver when turned clockwise and decreases it when turned counterclockwise.

Squelch Switch.

The squelch switch (3, figure 1-49), located on the UHF radio control panel, is a two-position switch marked DISABLE and NORMAL. The switch is provided so that the squelch can be selected for compatibility with the strength of the signal being received. Placing the switch to DISABLE turns off the squelch. Placing the switch to NORMAL turns the squelch on.

Tone Button.

The tone button (2, figure 1-49), is located on the UHF radio control panel. With the UHF radio in operation, depressing the button will interrupt reception and transmit a continuous wave (CW) 1000 cps tone signal on the selected frequency.

Channel Set Pushbutton.

The channel set pushbutton (7, figure 1-49) located on the UHF radio control panel, is used to set or change preset channel frequencies. The button is only effective when the mode selector switch is in the PRESET position. With the mode selector switch in the PRESET position and with the preset channel selector knob set to the desired channel, depressing the button will set the frequency selected in the manual frequency window into the desired channel. The button is recessed in a guard to prevent inadvertent actuation.

Transmitter Selector Knobs.

Two transmitter selector knobs (3, figure 1-50), labeled HF, UHF, and INT, are located on the left and right interphone control panels to select either the HF or UHF radio or interphone as desired for transmission.

Microphone Switches.

A three position spring loaded, pivot type microphone switch, marked TRANS and INPH with an unmarked off center position, is located on each right throttle (5, figure 1-5). The switch is moved forward to the TRANS position for radio transmission or back to INPH for interphone operation. It is spring loaded to the center OFF position.

UHF Radio Antenna Selector Switch.

The three position UHF radio antenna selector switch (1, figure 1-40), located on the antenna select panel, controls the selection of the upper and lower UHF antennas. The switch is marked UPPER, AUTO, and LOWER. Placing the switch to AUTO causes the antenna selector to control the antenna switching relay to select the correct antenna. Placing the switch in the LOWER or UPPER position controls the antenna relay directly to allow manual selection of either the upper or lower antenna.

UHF Radio Frequency Indicator Window.

The UHF radio frequency indicator window (5, figure 1-49), located on the UHF radio control panel, indicates the frequency selected for transmission or receiving. The window has five digits, which are set by frequency selector knobs below the window.

AUTOMATIC DIRECTION FINDER OPERATION.

1. UHF function selector knob—ADF.
2. UHF mode selector knob—PRESET or MAN. Select the desired frequency with the preset channel selector knob or with the manual frequency selector knobs.
3. Observe bearing under the ADF bearing pointer and turn the airplane as required.
4. To turn off, move the UHF function selector knob from the ADF position.

HF RADIO (AN/ARC-123).

Information on the HF radio will be included when available.

INTERPHONE (AN/AIC-25).

The interphone provides the following functions: Communications between crew members and between crew members and ground crew; monitoring and volume control UHF radio, HF radio, TACAN, ILS, marker beacon, RHAW and missile tone reception; and hot mic and call capability. Two identical interphone control panels (figure 1-50) located on the left and right consoles are provided for the aircraft commander and pilot. Interphone stations for ground crew operation are located in the nose wheel well and main landing gear well. The interphone operates on 28 volt dc power from the essential dc bus. Power is applied to the interphone whenever power is on the airplane.

Communications Monitor Knobs.

Eight push-pull communications monitor knobs (1, figure 1-50), located on each interphone control panel, are marked and monitor the functions as follows:

```
INT      — Interphone
UHF      — UHF Command Radio
HF       — HF Radio
ILS      — ILS and Localizer
MB       — Marker Beacon 19 ♦ 23
TACAN    — TACAN Identification
RHAWS    — Radar Homing and Warning System
MISSILE  — Missile Tones
HOT MIC
   LISTEN — Hot Mic Transmissions 26 ♦
```

Other signals fed to the interphone panel are a landing gear warning tone and a reduce speed warning tone. The monitor knobs are pulled out to turn on and pushed in to turn off. When pulled out, each knob may be rotated for volume control. On airplanes 26 ♦ and those modified by T.O. 1F-111A-550 the marker beacon monitor knob is replaced by a hot mike listen monitor knob. The knob is marked LISTEN.

Master Volume Control Knob.

A master volume control knob (4, figure 1-50), located on each interphone control panel, controls the volume of all of inputs to the panel. If a change to an individual input volume is desired, it can be accomplished by rotating the appropriate monitor knob.

Hot Microphone Talk Buttons.

A push-pull (HOT MIC) hot microphone talk button (5, figure 1-50), located on each interphone control panel, provides a continually operating mirophone when it is pulled. When this switch is pulled, the crew member can transmit without using the microphone switch,

Interphone Control Panel

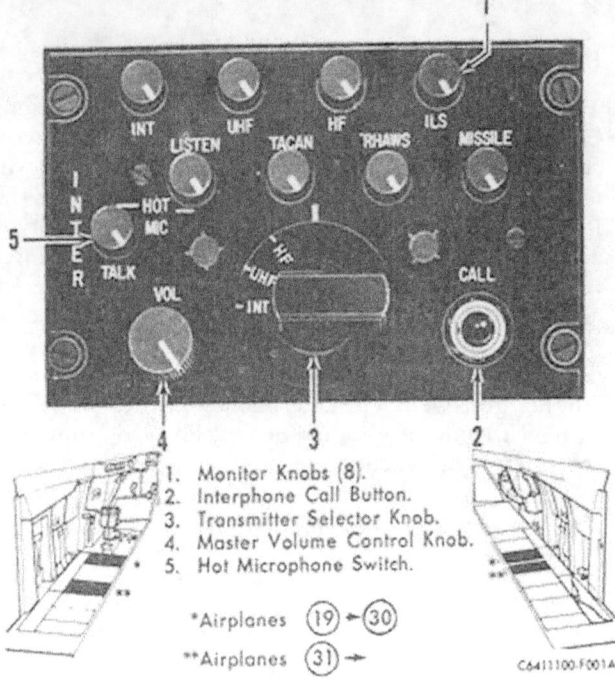

1. Monitor Knobs (8).
2. Interphone Call Button.
3. Transmitter Selector Knob.
4. Master Volume Control Knob.
5. Hot Microphone Switch.

*Airplanes (19) — (30)
**Airplanes (31) →

Figure 1-50.

however, the crew member at each station must have his hot mic listen monitor buttons pulled to receive the transmission.

Note

The use of HOT MIC TALK when there is a high background noise level in the cockpit will interfere with UHF communications. Under these conditions, use of the INPH push-to-talk mode rather than HOT MIC TALK is recommended.

Interphone Call Button.

The interphone call button (2, figure 1-50), located on the interphone control panel, permits either crew member to call the other crew member or the ground crew. To use the call button both cockpit stations must have their interphone monitor knobs pulled out or their transmitter selector knobs positioned to INT. Depressing either call button boosts the interphone volume of the other stations and reduces the operator's side tone level, allowing the call signal to override the other stations reception. On airplanes (26) ♦ plus T.O. 1F-111A-550, the call signal will override the reception at the other station regardless of the position of the communications monitor knob or transmitter selector knobs at either station.

Transmitter Selector Knobs.

Two three position transmitter selector knobs (3, figure 1-50), located on each interphone control panel, are provided to select either UHF or HF radio. The knobs are marked UHF, HF and INT. In either the HF or UHF positions only the radio transmitter selected will be keyed when the microphone switch is moved to the TRANS position. In addition, the UHF or HF position will allow continuous monitoring of the respective receiver (UHF or HF) regardless of the position of the communications monitor knobs. Regardless of the position of the transmitter selector switch, the interphone may be used by moving the microphone switch on the throttle to the INPH position. The INT position of the transmitter selector switch has no operational function.

Microphone Switch.

A three position pivot type microphone switch, marked TRANS and INPH with an unmarked OFF position, is located on each right throttle (5, figure 1-5). The switch is moved forward to TRANS position for radio transmissions or back to INPH position for interphone transmission without having to change the position of the transmitter selector knobs. The switch is spring loaded to the center OFF position. When the transmitter selector switch is in the INT position, moving the switch to either position allows interphone use.

Exterior Interphone Stations.

Exterior interphone stations in the nose wheel well and the main landing gear wheel well have a volume control knob, a call pushbutton, and a receptacle for ground cord plug in. The call pushbutton and volume control knob function the same as these controls on the interphone control panel.

LIGHTING SYSTEM.

The lighting system is divided into external and internal lights.

EXTERIOR LIGHTING.

The exterior lights include; position lights, formation lights, anti-collision/fuselage lights, air refueling lights, landing lights and a taxi light. The position lights consist of green lights in the right glove and wing tip, red lights in the left glove and wing tip and a white tail light. The wing tip position lights will light when the wing sweep angle is between 16 and 30 degrees. When the wings are swept aft of 30 degrees the wing tip light will go out and the glove light will light. The reverse will occur as the wings are swept forward. The formation lights consist of a set of three yellow lights, located on the upper and lower surfaces of each wing tip, and four lights located forward and aft of each side of the fuselage. Two anti-collision/fuselage lights, one located on top and one located on the bottom of the fuselage, serve as white fuselage lights when retracted and flashing red anti-collision lights when extended. Two air refueling lights mounted in the air refueling receptacle are provided for night refueling operations. A limit switch on the air refueling receptacle door provides power to the receptacle light control knob when the door is open. Two landing lights and a taxi light are located on the nose landing gear. A limit switch on the nose gear doors will turn the lights off if they are on when the gear is retracted.

This page intentionally left blank.

Position Light Switches.

Three position light switches (7, figure 1-51), are located on the lighting control panel. Two switches, labeled WING and TAIL, have three positions, marked BRT (bright), OFF and DIM, for selecting the desired intensity of the position lights. The third switch is a two position switch marked FLASH and STEADY to control the operation of the position lights. Placing the switch to FLASH causes the position lights to flash at a rate of 80 cycles per minute. The switches control 28 volt dc power from the engine start bus.

Position Lights/Stores Refuel Battery Power Switch.

The position lights/stores refuel battery power switch (5, figure 1-25), located on the ground check panel, has three positions marked POS LIGHTS, NORM and STORES REFUEL. Placing the switch to the POS LIGHTS position will supply battery power to the position lights for added safety during ground handling. Placing the switch to NORM deenergizes the circuit. The switch is held in the NORM position when the ground check panel door is closed. For a description of the STORES REFUEL position of the switch refer to the Fuel Supply System this section.

Formation Lights Switch.

The formation lights switch (1, figure 1-51), located on the lighting control panel, provides selection of the desired intensity of the lights. The switch is marked BRT (bright), OFF and DIM and controls 28 volt dc power from the main dc bus.

Anti-Collision Lights Switch.

The anti-collision lights switch (3, figure 1-51), is located on the lighting control panel. The switch is labeled ANTI-COLLISION and has one position marked OFF and an unmarked ON position. Placing the switch to ON causes the anti-collision lights to light, extend and rotate. Placing the switch to OFF causes the lights to retract, go out and stop rotating. The switch controls 115 volt ac power from the main ac bus.

Fuselage Lights Switch.

The fuselage lights switch (2, figure 1-51), is located on the lighting control panel. The switch is labeled FUSELAGE and has a position marked OFF and an unmarked ON position. Placing the switch to ON, lights a white light in the top and bottom of the fuselage.

Air Refueling Receptacle Lights Control Knob.

The air refueling receptacle lights control knob (36, figure 1-21), is located on the right main instrument panel. The knob is labeled A/R RECP LT. The full

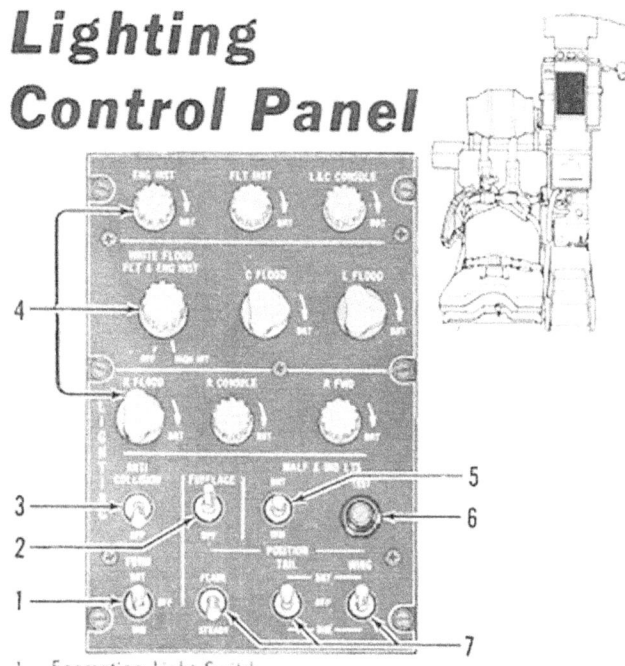

1. Formation Light Switch.
2. Fuselage Light Switch.
3. Anti-Collision Light Switch.
4. Internal Lighting Control Knobs (9).
5. Malfunction Indicator Lamp Dimming Switch.
6. Malfunction Indicator Lamp Test Button.
7. Position Light Switches.

Figure 1-51.

counterclockwise position of the knob turns the lights off. As the knob is turned clockwise detent positions at spaced intervals vary the intensity of the lights from off to full brightness. The knob controls 28 volt ac power from the main ac bus.

Landing and Taxi Lights Switch.

The landing and taxi lights switch (2, figure 1-51) is located on the miscellaneous control panel. The switch is marked LANDING, OFF and TAXI. The switch controls 115 volt ac power from the ac essential bus which in turn controls relays to provide 28 volt dc power to the filaments in the lights.

INTERNAL LIGHTING.

The internal lights include; red instrument panel and console lights, red and white flood lights and utility lights. The instrument panel and console lights consist of five circuits, each with an individual control knob, for the flight instruments, engine instruments, left and center console, right console and right main instrument panel. They are powered by 115 volt ac power from the right main ac bus. The flood lights consist of left, center and right red flood lights and high intensity white flood lights at various locations around the cockpit. The red flood lights provide cockpit lighting in the event the instrument panel and console lights fail. Each red flood light has an individual control knob. The white flood lights provide high intensity lighting to prevent temporary blindness from lightning when flying in weather. One control knob adjusts the intensity of all the white flood lights. Both the red and white flood lights receive 115 volt ac power from the ac essential bus. Two utility lights, (25, figure 1-2 and 8, figure 1-55) one for each side of the cockpit, are provided for individual work lights. They are normally stowed on the left side of the aft console and on the right side wall but can be moved to various locations about the crew station. The front of each utility light can be rotated to change color from white to red and vice versa. A rheostat on the aft end of each light must be turned clockwise to turn the light on and set the desired intensity. The utility lights are powered by 28 volt dc from the engine start bus.

Internal Lighting Control Knobs.

Nine internal lighting control nobs (4, figure 1-51), located on the lighting control panel, control the various internal lighting circuits. The full counterclockwise position of each nob turns the lights off. As the knobs are turned clockwise, detent positions at spaced intervals vary the intensity of the lights from off to full brightness. Five of the knobs control the red instrument panel and console lighting. Knobs are labeled and control the respective circuits as follows:

FLT INST—Left main instrument panel.

ENG INST—Engine instruments.

L&C CONSOLE—Left and center consoles.

R CONSOLE—Right console.

R FWD—Right main instrument panel.

The red flood lights are controlled by individual knobs marked R FLOOD, C FLOOD and L FLOOD for the right, center and left flood lights respectively. A single knob marked WHITE FLOOD FLT & ENG INST controls all the white flood lights. This knob is similar to the other knobs except it is marked OFF at the full counterclockwise position and HIGH INT (high intensity) near the full clockwise position. Turning the knob past HIGH INT turns all the white flood lights to maximum intensity.

CANOPY.

The canopy consists of left and right clam shell hatches hinged to a center beam assembly. The hatches open to a maximum of 65°. Each hatch has an external and internal canopy latch handle for opening or closing. When the hatches are closed and latched, the internal handle locks in place to prevent inadvertent unlatching of the hatch inflight. Each hatch is manually raised or lowered with the aid of an air/oil counterpoise. The counterpoise will also hold the hatch in any position selected. An external emergency canopy release handle, located outside on the right side of the fuselage, provides a means of explosively releasing the canopy hatches for emergency entrance to the crew module. The left canopy hatch can be explosively detached along the canopy center beam to allow crew rescue from above by helicopter.

INTERNAL CANOPY LATCH HANDLES.

Two canopy latch handles are located on the inside lower horizontal frame member of each canopy hatch (4, figure 1-2). An over-center spring-loaded canopy latch handle lock tab, in the face of each canopy latch handle, locks the handle in the latched position to prevent inadvertent opening inflight. When the lock tab is flush the canopy latch handle is locked. Pressing in on the forward part of the lock tab will cause the rear part of the tab to snap out, unlocking the canopy latch handle. The handle must then be pulled out and aft to a detent position to unlatch the hatch. Once the hatch is unlatched, pulling the handle further aft past detent engages the counterpoise to aid in opening. When the desired hatch position is attained, the handle will return to detent when released and lock the counterpoise to hold the hatch. Each handle is mechanically linked to a flush external canopy latch handle located outside of each hatch. Inflation of the canopy pressurization seal is automatically operated by closure of the canopy hatch. The actuator mounted on the hatch lower surface depresses a plunger in the canopy sill to inflate the seals and turn off the canopy unlock warning lamp.

CANOPY EXTERNAL LATCH HANDLES.

Two flush mounted canopy external latch handles are located on the lower horizontal frame member of each canopy hatch. Each handle is mechanically linked to its respective internal handle. Pressing in on the forward part of the handle will extend the rear portion of the handle so that it may be grasped to unlatch and raise the hatch. If the internal handle is locked in the closed position the hatch cannot be opened from the outside except by actuation of the canopy external emergency release handle.

LEFT CANOPY DETACH HANDLE.

The left canopy hatch can be detached along the center canopy beam by pulling the left canopy detach handle (19, figure 1-59), located on the aft bulkhead above the aircraft commander's seat. Pulling the handle fires an initiator which in turn fires an explosive charge to separate the left canopy hatch along the center beam. The handle is marked CANOPY DETACH. A safety pin is inserted in the handle to prevent inadvertent actuation.

CANOPY EXTERNAL EMERGENCY RELEASE HANDLE.

A flush mounted round spring-loaded external emergency canopy release handle on the right side of the fuselage provides a means of gaining access to the crew module in event of an emergency on the ground when the latches are locked from the inside. Pressing in on the center of the handle will release a latch and allow the handle to spring out. This will expose enough of the handle so that it can be grasped. Pulling the handle after approximately six feet of cable uncoils, will fire the external canopy release initiator which in turn fires an explosive strip along the canopy sills. Detonation of the explosive strip will remove the canopy latch hooks to release the hatches. The canopy hatches must then be manually raised to gain access to the cockpit.

WARNING

Do not pull the canopy external emergency release handle unless both hatches are closed and latched. To do so could result in fatal injury to the occupants from flying debris from the canopy sill.

CANOPY INTERNAL EMERGENCY RELEASE HANDLE.

The T-shaped canopy internal emergency release handle (6, figure 1-59), located on the canopy center beam assembly, is provided to release the canopy hatches in the event that the normal canopy latch handles fail. Depressing a release button on either side of the handle and pulling the handle out, will fire an initiator which in turns fires an explosive strip along the canopy sills. Detonation of the explosive strip will remove the canopy latch hooks to release the hatches. The canopy hatches may then be raised manually.

WARNING

Do not pull the canopy internal emergency release handle unless both hatches are closed and latched. To do so could result in fatal injury to the occupants from debris from the canopy sill.

CANOPY UNLOCK WARNING LAMP.

A red canopy unlock warning lamp located on the left warning and caution lamp panel (figure 1-29 or figure 1-29A), will light when either hatch is not locked. When lighted the word CANOPY is visible on the face of the lamp.

AIR CONDITIONING AND PRESSURIZATION SYSTEMS.

The air conditioning and pressurization systems (figure 1-52), combine to provide temperature-controlled, pressure-regulated air for heating, ventilating, pressurizing the cockpit and inflating the canopy seals. The system also provides air to the forward and aft electronic equipment bays, anti-icing and defog systems, windshield rain removal system and anti-G and pressure suits.

AIR CONDITIONING SYSTEM.

The air conditioning system provides temperature controlled air for the cockpit. The system also provides a temperature controlled flow of cooling air to the electronic equipment that requires a controlled environment for efficient operation. See figure 1-52. High pressure hot air is bled from the sixteenth stage compressor of each engine. This bleed air is directed through a tee fitting to a common duct and is routed through an air-to-air heat exchanger, where it is cooled by ram air that is circulated through the heat exchanger. The air is then routed through an air-to-water heat exchanger where it is further cooled and then enters the cooling turbine. The cooling turbine further cools the air to a temperature suitable for cooling the cockpit and electronic equipment bays. The cold air leaving the turbine passes through a water separator to remove most of the free moisture. A cabin temperature controller is fed signals from temperature sensors and from a pilot operated control panel. The temperature controller controls the setting of the cold air modulating valves. It also controls the setting of the cockpit hot air modulating and shutoff valve which allows hot air to mix with the refrigerated air stream, obtaining air at the selected temperature. This air then enters the cockpit through diffusers. An air connection is located on the lower right side of the fuselage aft of the cockpit and can be connected to a ground cooling cart to provide cooling air to the cockpit and all equipment. In the event the air conditioning system malfunctions, emergency ram air operation is available for ventilation and cooling.

Cabin Air Distribution Control Lever.

A cabin air distribution control lever (9, figure 1-55), located on the right side wall, controls distribution of air flow in the cockpit. The lever is labeled CABIN AIR DISTR and has two positions marked FWD DEFOG and AFT. The normal position of the lever is the AFT position. In this position air-flow into the cockpit is separated between the rear bulkhead diffusers and the windshield defog system with approximately 85% directed to the diffusers. Moving the lever towards the FWD DEFOG position will decrease air-

Section I
Description & Operation

T.O. 1F-111A-1

Air Conditioning and Pressurization System

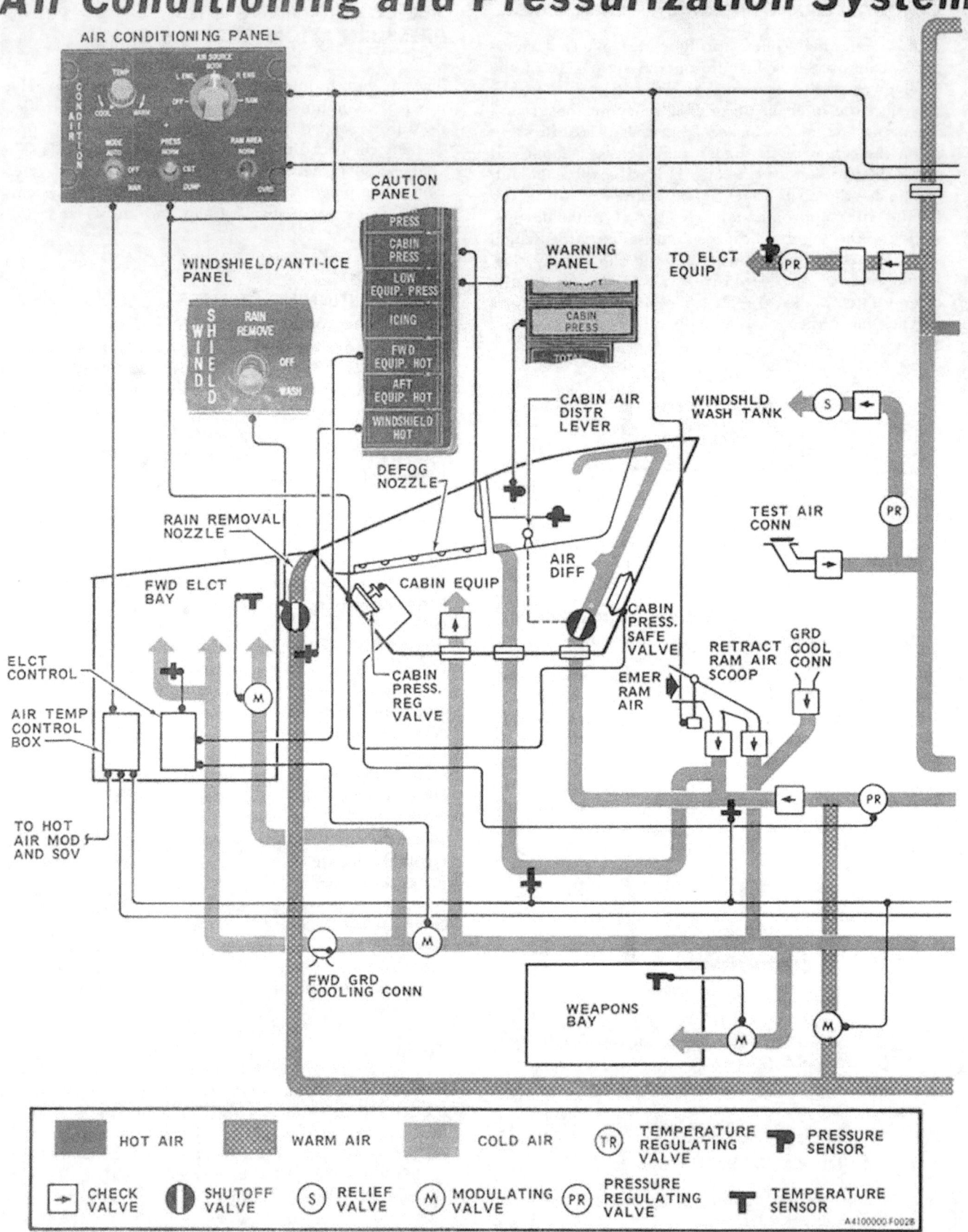

Figure 1-52. (Sheet 1)

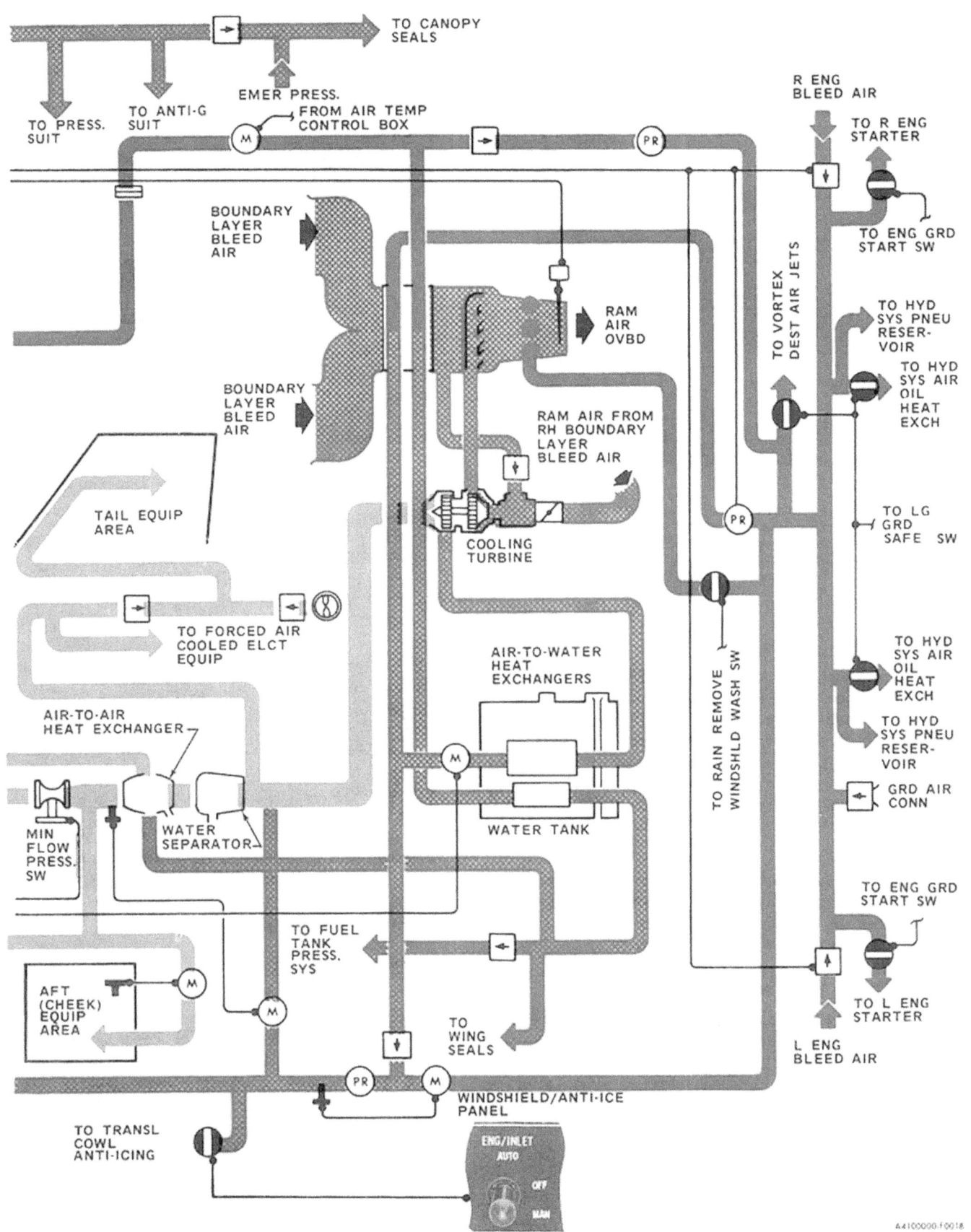

Figure 1-52. (Sheet 2)

Section I
Description & Operation

T.O. 1F-111A-1

Air Conditioning Control Panel

1. Temperature Control Knob.
2. Air Source Selector Knob.
3. Ram Area Control Switch.
4. Pressurization Selector Switch.
5. Mode Selector Switch.

Figure 1-53.

flow through the air diffusers and increase airflow through the defog system. When the lever is in the full forward position all the airflow will be directed through the defog system. Although the AFT position is considered normal to obtain maximum airflow, desired crew comfort is accomplished by selecting any intermediate position between FWD DEFOG and AFT.

Note

High airflow through the windshield defog nozzles may cause an excessively high noise level in the cabin. Should this happen, position the cabin air distribution lever to full aft.

Air Source Selector Knob.

The air source selector knob (2, figure 1-53), located on the air conditioning control panel, has five positions marked OFF, L ENG, BOTH, R ENG, and RAM. The knob controls bleed air source or allows selection of emergency ram air operation when the normal system is not operating. In the OFF position, both the left and right bleed air check and shutoff valves are closed. In the L ENG position, the left engine is the source of bleed air and the right bleed air check and shutoff valve is closed. In the BOTH position, both the left and the right bleed air check and shutoff valves are open and supplying bleed air to the air conditioning system. In the R ENG position, the right engine is

the source of the bleed air and the left bleed air check and shutoff valve is closed. In the RAM position, the normal pressurization system pressure regulating and shut off valve is closed, the ram air door is open, and the cockpit pressure regulating and relief valves are open. This will dump cabin pressure and allow combined ram air flow and regulated engine bleed air to ventilate the cabin. Temperature control of this air is available by using the temperature control knob to control the amount of engine bleed air mixed with ram air.

WARNING

To prevent excessive temperatures when pressure suits are being worn, the air conditioning system mode selector switch must not be placed to the OFF position prior to or while operating in the RAM position.

Air Conditioning System Mode Selector Switch.

The mode selector switch (5, figure 1-53), located on the air conditioning control panel, is a three position switch marked AUTO, OFF, and MAN. In the AUTO position, the cockpit temperature is automatically controlled at the temperature selected by the temperature control knob. A signal goes to the controller which opens or closes the modulating valves to maintain the selected temperature. In the MAN position, the cockpit temperature controller is bypassed and control of the modulating temperature control valves is directly from the temperature control knob. In the OFF position all power is removed from the system and the valves in the system, which control cabin temperature, will declutch and go to the full cool position. The valve controlling pressure suit ventilation temperature will remain in the position it was in when power was removed. On airplanes ㉛ ♦ and those modified by T.O. 1F-111A-515, the air conditioning system mode selector switch is a lock lever type switch which must be pulled out to change positions.

Temperature Control Knob.

The temperature control knob (1, figure 1-53), located on the air conditioning control panel, is provided to select cockpit temperature. The knob can be rotated through a 300° arc and has mechanical stops at each end. The extreme counterclockwise end is marked COOL and the clockwise end is marked WARM. With the mode selector switch in AUTO, rotating the knob in either direction sends a signal to the cockpit temperature controller which constantly positions the modulating temperature control valves to maintain the selected temperature. When the temperature control knob is positioned at the mid-point between COOL and WARM, the cockpit temperature is maintained at approximately 19°C (67°F).

Note

Operation with the temperature control knob at full COOL in warm weather or full WARM in cool weather with the mode selector knob in AUTO may result in an objectionable noise with the high flow in the cockpit. The amount of airflow can be reduced by backing the knob off the full COOL or WARM position.

With the mode selector switch in MANUAL, the signal goes directly to the modulating temperature control valves, opening or closing them as directed by the signal generated from the temperature control knob. During manual operation the valves will respond only when the knob is held against one of the extreme positions, COOL or WARM. Maximum valve travel time from maximum cold to maximum warm is approximately 45 seconds.

Ram Area Control Switch.

The ram area control switch (3, figure 1-53), located on the air conditioning control panel, is a two position switch marked NORM and OVRD. The switch provides a means of controlling the amount of ram airflow through the air-to-air heat exchanger by opening or closing an exit door in the ram air discharge exit. In the NORM position, the central air data computer automatically controls the position of the door. When the outside air temperature is below 75°F and airspeed is above 225 knots the door will be closed to reduce drag. All other combinations of outside temperature and airspeed will result in automatic door opening. Placing the switch to OVRD will override the automatic functions of the central air data computer and open the door to its full travel. On some airplanes the ram air discharge exit door has been removed, therefore the switch is inoperative.

Equipment Hot Caution Lamp.

The amber equipment hot caution lamp, marked FWD EQUIP HOT, is located on the main caution light panel (figure 1-29 or 1-29A). The lamp will light if the cooling air flow is insufficient.

Air Conditioning System Alternate Operation.

Manual Mode.

In the event of a malfunction of the cabin temperature controller, cabin temperature may be manually controlled as follows:

1. Air source selector knob — BOTH.
2. Mode selector switch — MAN.
3. Temperature control knob — Set for desired temperature.

The temperature control knob must be held to either full COOL or full WARM position to adjust for desired temperature.

Ram Air Mode.

In the event the air conditioning system fails, ram air mode can be used for cockpit and equipment cooling. Refer to "Ram Air Mode Limit Speed," Section V. During ram air mode operation, cockpit temperature can be controlled as follows:

1. Air source selector knob — RAM.

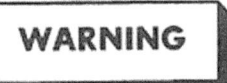

To prevent excessive temperatures when pressure suits are being worn, the air conditioning system mode selector switch must not be placed to the OFF position prior to or while operating in the RAM position.

2. Mode selector switch — AUTO or MAN.
3. Temperature control knob — Set for desired temperature.

If the mode selector switch is positioned to MAN, the temperature control knob must be held to either full COOL or WARM position to adjust for desired temperature.

PRESSURIZATION SYSTEM.

Pressurization of the cockpit, canopy seals, anti-g suits, pressure suits, attack radar, terrain following radar and track breaker is provided by the pressurization system. Pressure in the cockpit is controlled by a pressure regulating valve located in the front of the cockpit. When the airplane is below 8000 feet, the pressure regulating valve automatically maintains an unpressurized condition in the cockpit regardless of the schedule selected. Cockpit ventilation is provided by the regulating valve continually modulating, depending on the volume of input air. A cabin pressure safety valve located at the rear of the cockpit will relieve pressure any time the cockpit pressure exceeds outside pressure by 11.2 psi. An emergency ram air scoop, which can be opened into the airstream, will admit air into the crew and electronic equipment compartments in the event of loss of cooling and pressurization air from the cooling turbine. When combat cabin pressure schedule is selected, the system maintains a maximum pressure differential of 5 psi above ambient pressure at altitudes above 23,000 feet. See figure 1-54 for cockpit pressure schedule for normal and combat conditions.

Cabin Pressure Schedule

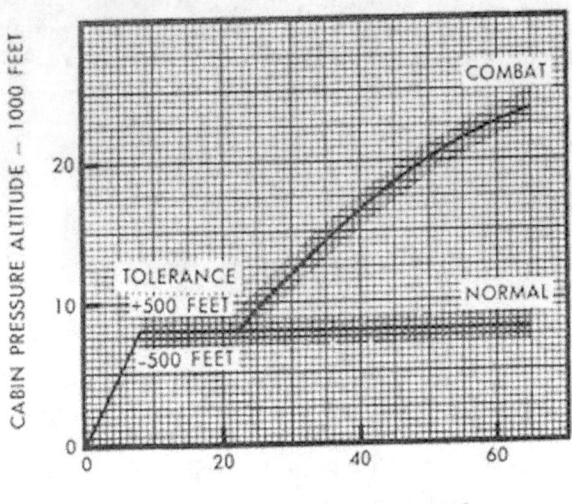

Figure 1-54.

Pressurization Selector Switch.

The pressurization selector switch (4, figure 1-53), located on the air conditioning control panel, is a three position lever lock switch with positions NORM, CBT, and DUMP. In the NORM position, the cockpit pressure is selected to a schedule that will maintain an 8000 foot cabin altitude from 8000 feet up to the operational ceiling of the airplane. In the CBT (combat) position, the cockpit maintains an 8000 foot cabin altitude from 8000 feet up to 22,500 foot altitude and then maintains a constant 5 psi differential above 8000 feet up to the operational ceiling of the airplane. In DUMP position, the cabin pressure regulator and the cabin pressure safety valve are open and the cockpit is not pressurized.

Cabin Altitude Indicator.

A cabin altitude indicator (1, figure 1-15), located on the auxiliary gage panel, is provided to monitor cabin altitude.

Pressurization Caution Lamp.

An amber pressurization caution lamp marked CABIN PRESS is located on the main caution light panel (figure 1-29 or 1-29A). The lamp will light when the cabin altitude is above 10,000 feet.

Pressurization Warning Lamp.

A red pressurization warning lamp (1, figure 1-6 or 6, figure 1-6A) marked CABIN PRESS is located on the left main instrument panel. The lamp will light when the cabin pressure is above 38,000 feet.

Equipment Low Pressure Caution Lamp.

An amber low equipment pressure caution lamp marked LOW EQUIP PRESS is located on the main caution light panel (figure 1-29 or 1-29A). The lamp will light when the supply pressure to the pressurized electronic equipment requiring one atmosphere pressure drops below 12.5 ($\pm$0.5) psia.

Emergency Pressurization System.

The crew module escape system incorporates an emergency pressurization system. The system operates automatically during ejection to maintain pressurization of the module and canopy hatch seals, or in event of failure of the automatic feature, the system is manually activated with a ring-shaped handle. Also, during other phases of flight, this system provides an alternate pneumatic supply source for pressurization of the crew module and canopy hatch seals in event of failure of the normal pressurization system. Pressure for the system is contained in a 650 cubic inch storage bottle located behind the seat bulkhead. When activated, an aneroid-operated absolute pressure regulator which senses cabin altitude, will open if cabin altitude is above 24,000 feet. Volume of the storage bottle is sufficient to maintain this cabin altitude for approximately 4 minutes at maximum ejection altitude even with high leakage.

Emergency Pressurization Handle.
The emergency pressurization handle (52, figure 1-2), located on the aft console, is provided to manually activate the emergency pressurization system. Pulling the handle out will open the aneroid-operated absolute pressure regulator.

Emergency Pressurization System Gage.
An emergency pressurization system gage, located on the cockpit aft bulkhead, is provided to indicate the pressure within the emergency pressurization system storage bottle. The gage is calibrated from 0 to 4000 psi in 500 psi increments.

ANTI-ICING AND DEFOG SYSTEMS.

Probe Anti-Icing.

Heating elements powered by 115 volt ac are provided on the pitot-static, total temperature and angle-of-attack probes for anti-icing. Power to the probes is controlled by the pitot heater switch located on the windshield wash/anti-icing control panel. In addition on airplanes ㉛ ◆ the side slip angle probe is equipped with a probe heater. On these airplanes power to all of the above probes is controlled by a pitot/probe heater switch. Also an alpha/beta probe caution lamp is provided to monitor the function of the heaters in the angle-of-attack and side slip angle probes.

Pitot Heater Switch. ㉙ ◆ ㉚ The pitot heater switch (4, figure 1-56), labeled PITOT HEATERS, is a two position switch marked OFF with an unmarked ON position and is located on the windshield wash anti-icing control panel. When the switch is placed to ON, 115 volt ac power is furnished to heating elements in the pitot-static tube, the angle of attack and, when the landing gear is retracted, to the total temperature probe. To ground check the heater in the total temperature probe, the CADC test switch must be held to the HIGH position in addition to placing the pitot heater switch to ON. When the switch is OFF, the heaters are deenergized. The switch controls 28 volt dc power from the main and essential buses.

Pitot/Probe Heater Switch. ㉛ ◆

The pitot/probe heater switch, located on the windshield wash/anti-icing control panel, has two positions marked HEAT and OFF/SEC (secondary). The switch controls 115 volt ac power to the heating elements in the pitot-static probe and total temperature probe, when the landing gear is retracted, and to the primary or secondary heating elements in the angle-of-attack (alpha) probe and side slip angle (beta) probes. An alpha/beta probe heater caution lamp monitors the function of the heaters in the angle-of-attack and side slip angle probes. Placing the switch to the HEAT position, while either on the ground or inflight, supplies power to the pitot-static probe and to the primary elements in the angle-of-attack and side slip probes. When the landing gear is retracted the total temperature probe heater also receives power with the switch in the HEAT position. The HEAT position is used to ground check the heater in the pitot-static probe and the primary heaters in the angle-of-attack and side-slip angle probes. To ground check the heater in the total temperature probe the CADC test switch must be held to the HIGH position in addition to placing the switch to the HEAT position. Placing the switch to OFF/SEC while on the ground deenergizes the circuits to all the probes. On take off a safety switch on the landing gear actuates to arm the secondary heater circuits to the angle-of-attack and side slip angle probe heaters. During flight if the primary heaters in either the angle-of-attack or side slip angle probe malfunction the alpha/beta probe heat caution lamp will light and the secondary heaters in these probes will be automatically energized. Placing the switch to OFF/SEC will check the secondary heaters for proper operation and the caution lamp should go out. The pitot-static and total temperature probes also receive power with the switch in the OFF/SEC position while inflight.

> **CAUTION**
>
> To prevent overheating the probes during ground operation the switch should not be positioned to HEAT until just prior to takeoff.

Alpha/Beta Probe Heat Caution Lamp. ㉛ ◆

The alpha/beta probe heat caution lamp, located on the main caution lamp panel (figure 1-29A), provides indications that the angle-of-attack and/or side slip angle probe heaters are not functioning properly as follows:

This page intentionally left blank.

Right Sidewall

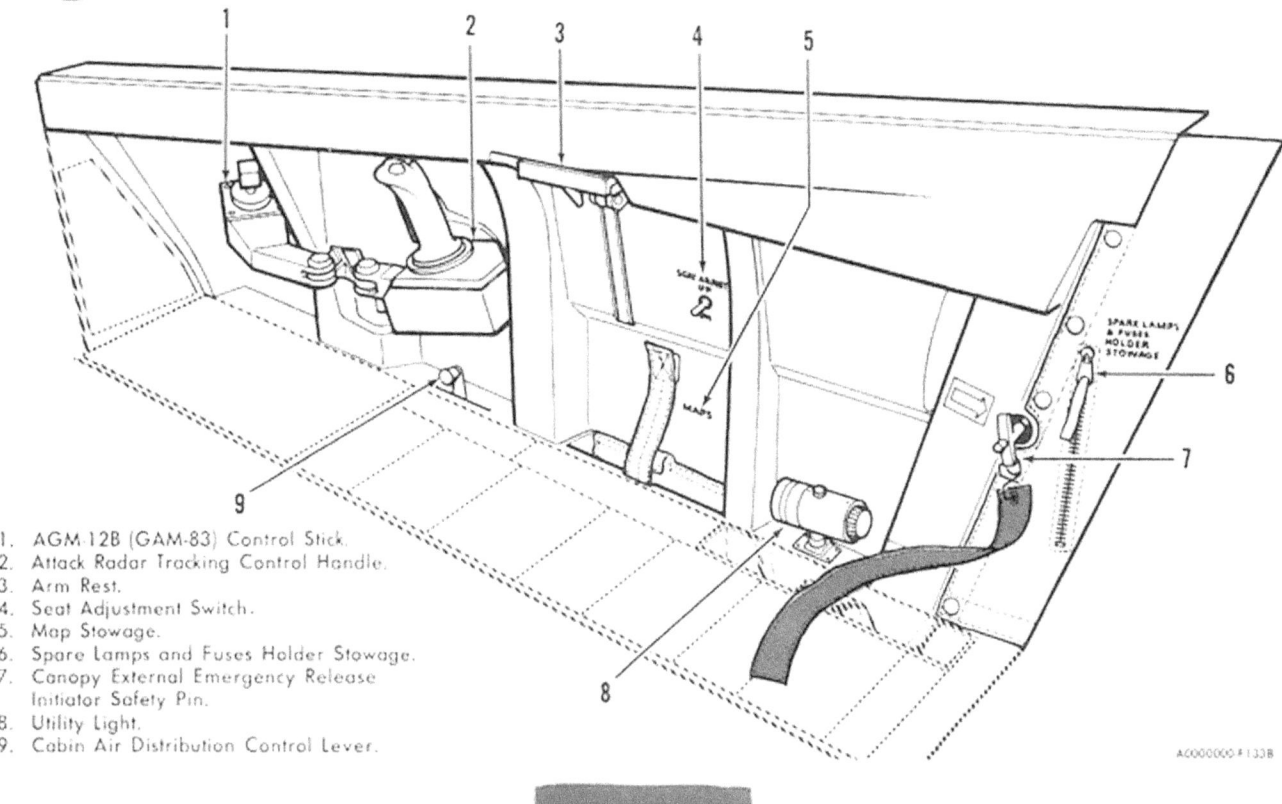

1. AGM-12B (GAM-83) Control Stick.
2. Attack Radar Tracking Control Handle.
3. Arm Rest.
4. Seat Adjustment Switch.
5. Map Stowage.
6. Spare Lamps and Fuses Holder Stowage.
7. Canopy External Emergency Release Initiator Safety Pin.
8. Utility Light.
9. Cabin Air Distribution Control Lever.

Figure 1-55.

On the ground.

- Indicates the pitot/probe heater switch is in the OFF/SEC position.
- With the pitot/probe heater switch in the HEAT position, indicates the primary heater element(s) in either or both probes are overheated.

Inflight.

- With the pitot/probe heater switch in the HEAT position, indicates the primary heater element(s) in either or both probes are not functioning.
- With the pitot/probe heater switch in the OFF/SEC position, indicates the secondary heater element in either or both probes are not functioning.

Engine Anti-Icing Systems.

The engine anti-icing system prevents formation of ice on the engine inlet guide vanes, and the engine nose cone. The engine anti-icing system uses regulated compressor bleed air. The engine inlet anti-icing system prevents formation of ice on the spike tip, the leading edge of the auxiliary cowl and inside the main engine air duct of the auxiliary cowl. The engine inlet anti-icing system uses air from the air conditioning system hot air manifold in the main landing gear wheel well. Idle rpm will provide sufficient hot air for anti-icing. The spike sensing probe anti-icing system prevents formation of ice on the spike local mach probe and spike lip shock probe. The probes are heated by 115 volt ac electrical heaters. Although the engine anti-icing, engine inlet anti-icing, and spike sensing probe anti-icing are three separate systems, they are controlled by a single, three position switch. Both automatic and manual modes of operation are provided. An electronic ice detector is located in the left engine air inlet. When icing conditions exist, a signal is transmitted to the icing caution lamp regardless of the position of the engine/inlet anti-icing switch.

Engine/Inlet Anti-Icing Switch. The engine/inlet anti-icing switch (3, figure 1-56), located on the windshield wash/anti-icing control panel, is a three position switch marked AUTO, MAN and OFF. The lever lock-type switch locks in all three positions. In the AUTO position, the anti-icing circuitry is armed, and when the electronic ice detector senses an icing condition a signal is transmitted to the icing caution lamp. The signal also energizes a relay which turns on the elements in the spike sensing probe heaters and opens the engine anti-icing and engine inlet anti-icing con-

Changed 18 August 1967

1-121

Section I
Description & Operation

T.O. 1F-111A-1

Windshield Wash / Anti-Icing Control Panel

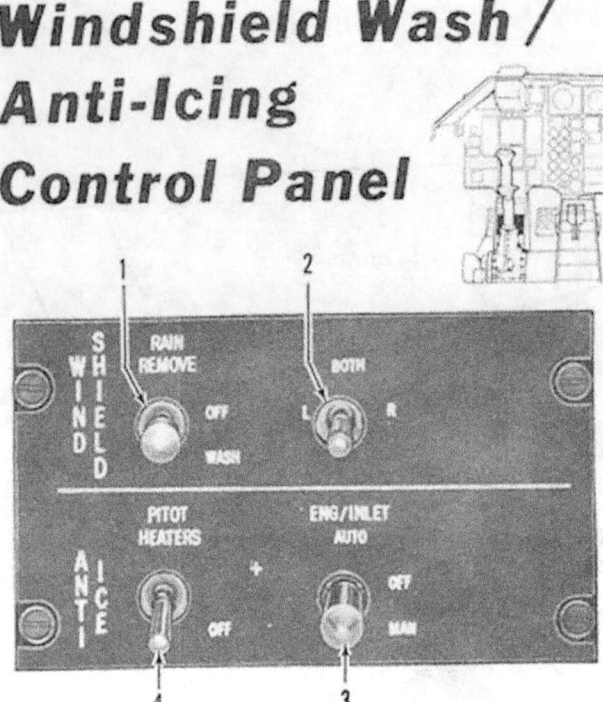

1. Windshield Wash/Rain Removal Selector Switch.
2. Windshield Wash Selector Switch.
3. Engine/Inlet Anti-Icing Switch.
4. Pitot Heaters Switch.

Figure 1-56.

trol valves allowing the circulation of hot air through the anti-iced components. Approximately 60 seconds after the icing condition ceases, the hot air valves will close, the spike probe heating elements will be deenergized and the engine icing caution lamp will go out. When the switch is placed to MAN, the engine anti-icing and engine inlet anti-icing valves open and the spike probe heating elements are energized whether or not the ice detector senses an icing condition. Placing the switch to OFF shuts off air to the engine anti-icing and engine inlet anti-icing systems, and turns off the spike probe heating elements; however, the icing caution lamp will still be operational.

Engine Icing Caution Lamp. The engine icing caution lamp, located on the main caution lamp panel (figure 1-29 or 1-29A), will light when the electronic ice detector senses an icing condition. While the icing condition exists, the caution lamp will remain lighted regardless of the position of the engine/inlet anti-icing switch. The lamp will go out 60 seconds after the icing condition ceases.

Inlet Hot Caution Lamp. The inlet hot caution lamp, located on the main caution lamp panel (figure 1-29 or 1-29A), provides an indication that the temperature of anti-icing bleed air to the translating cowls has exceeded 450 ($\pm$10) degrees fahrenheit. When the lamp lights the words INLET HOT are visible and anti-icing air to the translating cowls is automatically shut off, then the lamp will go out.

Windshield Defog System.

Air for windshield defogging and cabin air distribution share the same control lever. For description, refer to "Cabin Air Distribution Control Lever", this section.

WINDSHIELD WASH AND RAIN REMOVAL SYSTEM.

The windshield wash and rain removal system is provided to keep both the windshields clear of impinging rain and insects. Compressor bleed air at a temperature of 390°F and a pressure of 45 psi is directed over the outside of the windshields by a fixed area nozzle. This hot air blast will evaporate impinging rain and prevent further accumulation of rain on the windshield. Windshield wash is accomplished by injecting a liquid wash solution into the rain removal nozzle. This serves as a wetting and scrubbing action to remove insects from the windshields. The windshield wash solution is contained in a one gallon tank located on the right side of the nose wheel well. The tank is pressurized to 15 psi by compressor bleed air.

Windshield Wash/Rain Removal Selector Switch.

The windshield wash/rain removal selector switch (1, figure 1-56), located on windshield wash/anti-icing control panel, has three positions marked RAIN REMOVE, WASH, and OFF. The switch is spring loaded from the WASH to the OFF position, and is locked out of the RAIN REMOVE position. The switch must be pulled out to move from OFF to RAIN REMOVE. Placing the switch to RAIN REMOVE will open the rain remove shutoff valves, allowing temperature and pressure regulated compressor bleed air to be directed to the windshield(s) selected by the windshield selector switch. When the switch is placed to WASH a time delay relay is energized to open the rain remove shutoff valve and the windshield wash shutoff valve selected by the windshield wash selector switch. While these valves are open, compressor bleed air and liquid windshield wash solution will be directed to the selected windshield(s). Allowing the switch to return from WASH to OFF will close the valves after a 5-second delay, shutting off the air and windshield wash solution. When the switch is in the OFF position the windshield wash and rain removal system is deenergized.

Windshield Selector Switch.

The windshield selector switch (2, figure 1-56), located on the windshield wash/anti-icing control panel, has three positions marked L (left), R (right), and BOTH. Selection of any of the positions will determine

1-122

Changed 18 August 1967

the windshield(s) to be washed or receive rain removal air as a function of the position of the windshield wash/rain removal selector switch.

Windshield Hot Caution Lamp.

The windshield hot caution lamp, located on the main caution lamp panel (figure 1-29 or 1-29A) indicates windshield high temperature. An overheat switch, installed in the rain removal air supply duct upstream of the shutoff valve, will close when the air temperature is above 450°F. When the overheat switch closes, a circuit is completed to close the rain remove shutoff valves and light the windshield hot caution lamp. After the switch closes the caution lamp will normally go out within 15 seconds.

OXYGEN SYSTEM.

The oxygen system consists of a normal (liquid) system located in the forward fuselage and cockpit and an emergency (gaseous) system located behind the cockpit aft bulkhead.

NORMAL OXYGEN SYSTEM.

The normal oxygen system is designed for use with a pressure demand type oxygen regulator and mask to provide pressure regulated 100 percent oxygen to the crew members. See figure 1-57 for oxygen duration. A converter, located in right side of the forward equipment bay changes the liquid oxygen to gaseous oxygen that is pressure regulated at 70 to 80 psi during normal usage. From the converter, the gaseous oxygen passes through a heat exchanger that warms it for breathing. The oxygen is then directed through a manually operated control valve, a regulator, and into the face mask. Oxygen regulation is accomplished by a demand type mini-regulator mounted on the right side of the torso harness. Maximum duration of the normal oxygen supply is 31.2 hours when both crew members are on oxygen at a cabin altitude greater than 35,000 feet. Maximum normal oxygen duration for two crew members at a cabin altitude of 8000 feet is 7.8 hours. Evaporation loss will completely empty the fully serviced system in approximately 10 days. The system has a ten liter capacity and is serviced through a single point filler valve located within an access door on the left side of the fuselage (figure 1-62).

Oxygen Duration

*2 crew members (double duration for 1 crew member)

CABIN ALTITUDE	CONSUMPTION cu. ft./hr.	DURATION — HOURS*									
35,000	9.8	31.2	28.1	25.0	21.8	18.7	15.6	12.5	9.4	6.2	3.1	DESCEND TO BELOW 10,000' MSL.
30,000	13.4	22.8	20.5	18.3	16.0	13.7	11.4	9.1	6.8	4.6	2.3	
28,000	15.0	20.4	18.4	16.3	14.3	12.2	10.2	8.2	6.1	4.1	2.0	
26,000	16.0	19.1	17.2	15.3	13.4	11.5	9.6	7.6	5.7	3.8	1.9	
24,000	18.52	16.5	14.9	13.2	11.6	9.9	8.3	6.6	5.0	3.3	1.6	
22,000	20.76	14.7	13.3	11.8	10.3	8.8	7.4	5.9	4.4	2.9	1.5	
20,000	23.0	13.3	12.0	10.6	9.3	8.0	6.6	5.3	4.0	2.7	1.3	
18,000	25.24	12.1	10.9	9.7	8.5	7.3	6.1	4.8	3.6	2.4	1.2	
16,000	27.48	11.1	10.0	8.9	7.8	6.7	5.6	4.4	3.3	2.2	1.1	
14,000	30.0	10.2	9.2	8.2	7.1	6.1	5.1	4.1	3.1	2.0	1.0	
12,000	32.8	9.3	8.4	7.5	6.5	5.6	4.7	3.7	2.8	1.9	0.9	
10,000	35.6	8.6	7.7	6.9	6.0	5.1	4.3	3.4	2.6	1.7	0.8	
8,000	39.4	7.8	7.0	6.2	5.4	4.7	3.9	3.1	2.3	1.5	0.7	
0	55.6	5.5	4.9	4.4	3.8	3.3	2.7	2.2	1.6	1.1	0.5	
AVAILABLE OXYGEN	LITERS	10	9	8	7	6	5	4	3	2	1	LESS THAN 1
	Cu Ft GAS	306.0	275.4	244.8	214.2	183.6	153.0	122.4	91.8	61.2	30.6	

Figure 1-57.

Section I
Description & Operation

T.O. 1F-111A-1

Oxygen-Suit Control Panel

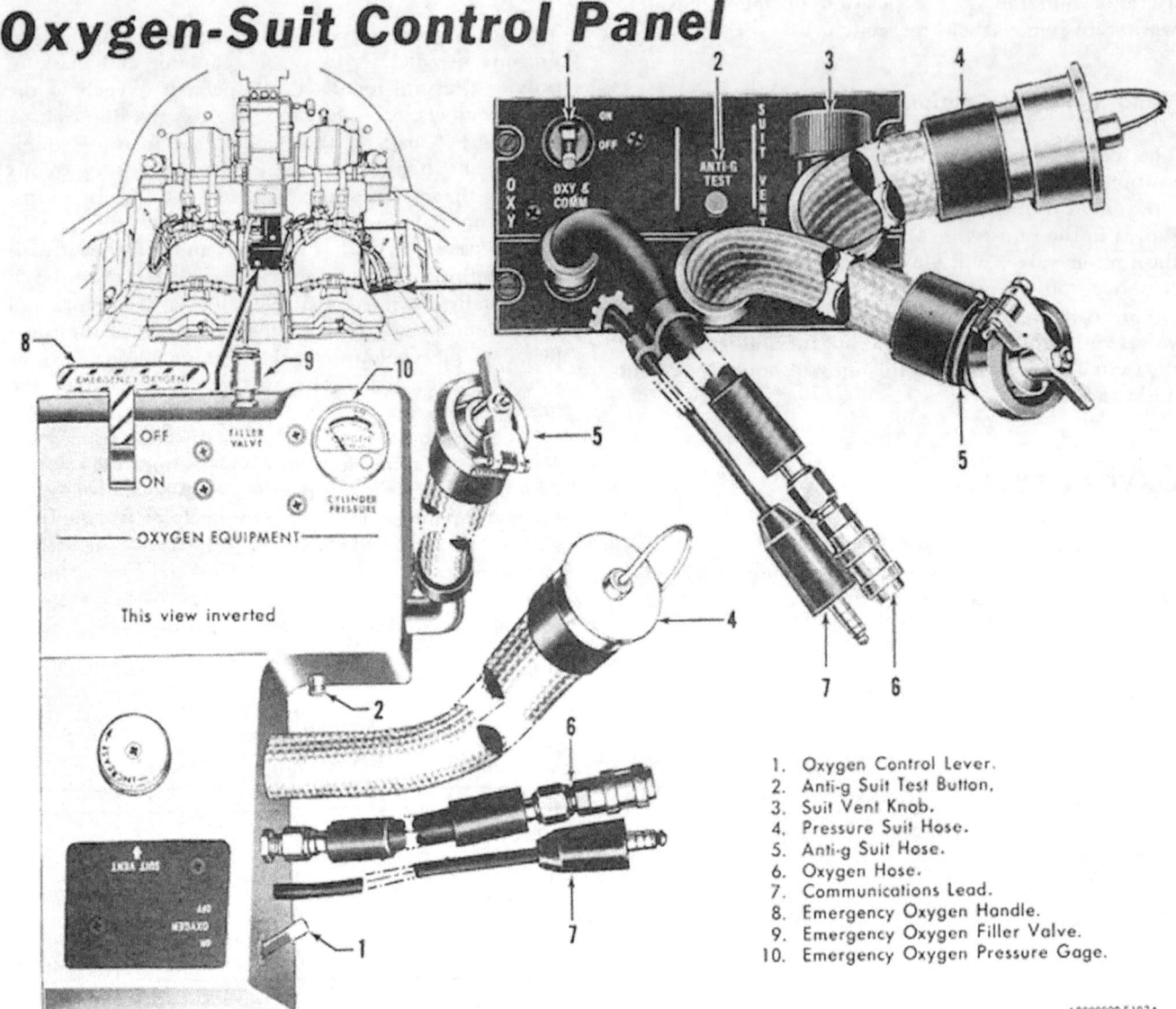

1. Oxygen Control Lever.
2. Anti-g Suit Test Button.
3. Suit Vent Knob.
4. Pressure Suit Hose.
5. Anti-g Suit Hose.
6. Oxygen Hose.
7. Communications Lead.
8. Emergency Oxygen Handle.
9. Emergency Oxygen Filler Valve.
10. Emergency Oxygen Pressure Gage.

Figure 1-58.

Oxygen Control Levers.

Two oxygen control levers are provided to control flow of oxygen from the supply system to the oxygen regulator. Each lever has positions ON and OFF. When in the ON position, oxygen is supplied from the converter to the regulator; when in OFF, oxygen flow is shut off at the control valve in the oxygen-suit control panel. The levers are located on the aircraft commander's and pilot's oxygen-suit control panel (1, figure 1-58).

Oxygen Quantity Indicator.

An oxygen quantity indicator is located on the auxiliary gage panel (2, figure 1-15). The indicator indicates the total quantity of liquid oxygen in the converter. The indicator dial is graduated from zero to 20 liters in increments of one liter. The indicator operates on 115 volt ac power from the essential bus. In the event of power failure, the indicator pointer will drive below zero, a fail safe indication.

Oxygen Quantity Indicator Test Button.

A test button used for checking the oxygen quantity indicator is located on the left console (3, figure 1-15). When the button is held depressed, the indicator pointer will move to the zero liter indication if the indicating system is operating properly. When the button is released, the pointer will move back to the original reading. The oxygen caution lamp will light during an indicator check when the pointer indicates a quantity of 2 liters or less.

Changed 18 August 1967

Oxygen Caution Lamp.

An amber caution lamp on the main caution lamp panel (figure 1-29 or 1-29A) will light when oxygen quantity indicator indicates 2 liters or less or when oxygen system pressure is less than 42 ($\pm$2) psi. When the caution lamp lights, inspection of the oxygen quantity gauge will determine whether the lamp came on because of low quantity or low pressure. When the lamp is lighted, the letters OXY will be visible on the caution lamp panel, and the master caution lamp will light. The oxygen caution lamp operates on 28 volt dc power from the 28 volt dc essential bus.

EMERGENCY OXYGEN SYSTEM.

The crew module is equipped with an emergency oxygen system consisting of two oxygen bottles, a pressure reducer, a pressure gage, and a manual handle. The system is activated automatically during ejection or in event of failure of the automatic feature, it is manually activated by a handle. Also, during other phases of flight, this system provides an emergency oxygen supply in event of failure of the normal oxygen system. When activated either manually or automatically, gaseous oxygen at 1800 to 2100 psi flows to a pressure reducer where it is reduced to 50 to 90 psi. It is then routed into the normal oxygen system upstream of the oxygen control valves. Sufficient emergency oxygen is available for 10 minutes duration at 27,000 feet.

Emergency Oxygen Handle.

The green emergency oxygen handle (8, figure 1-58), is located on the pilot's oxygen-suit panel. During ejection, this handle is used to manually activate the emergency oxygen system in the event automatic activation fails. Also, in event of failure of the normal oxygen system during other phases of flight this handle is used to provide an emergency oxygen supply. Raising the handle will open the emergency oxygen pressure reducer allowing oxygen to flow to each oxygen control valve.

Emergency Oxygen Pressure Gage.

The emergency oxygen pressure gage (10, figure 1-58), located on the pilot's oxygen-suit control panel, indicates the pressure in the emergency oxygen bottles. The gage is marked REFILL in the red region and FULL in the black region with index marks at 1800 and 2500 psi.

OXYGEN SYSTEM ALTERNATE OPERATION.

If the normal oxygen system fails or is depleted, proceed as follows:

1. Emergency oxygen handle — Pulled.

Note

The emergency oxygen system will provide oxygen for approximately 10 minutes.

CREW MODULE ESCAPE SYSTEM.

The crew module (figure 1-59), forms an integral portion of the forward fuselage and encompasses the pressurized cabin and forward portion of the wing glove. Crew entrance to the module is provided through left and right canopy hatches. Refer to canopies this section. The system protects the occupants from environmental hazards on either land or water and provides underwater escape capabilities. Also provided, are an emergency oxygen supply system and a self-contained emergency pressurization system. Both of these systems are provided, primarily, for use during ejection. However, either system can be manually activated during normal phases of flight, as a backup to the associated normal system.

WARNING

The removal or addition of components in the crew module or the absence of a crew member will change the center of gravity of the module and adversely affect its stability on ejection.

For additional information, refer to "Oxygen System", and "Air Conditioning and Pressurization System", this section.

CREW MODULE SEATS.

The crew module seats (figure 1-60), are electrically adjustable vertically and manually adjustable forward and aft. The seat headrest structure, which is attached to the aft bulkhead, and the seat pan are manually adjustable forward and aft. The forward adjustment of the headrest requires the inertial reel to be unlocked. The seat back is attached by pivot pins to the back of the seat pan and is attached through telescopic structures to pivot pins on the headrest. Each seat is equipped with an upper and a lower torso harness. The upper torso harness consists of adjustable shoulder straps, chest straps, and trunk straps. These straps attach at the center of the crewmember's chest by means of a quick-release buckle. The chest straps and trunk straps are attached to the seat structure and the shoulder straps are attached to the inertia reel. Wedge shaped plastic blocks are attached on the right chest

Section I
Description & Operation

T.O. 1F-111A-1

Crew Module General Arrangement

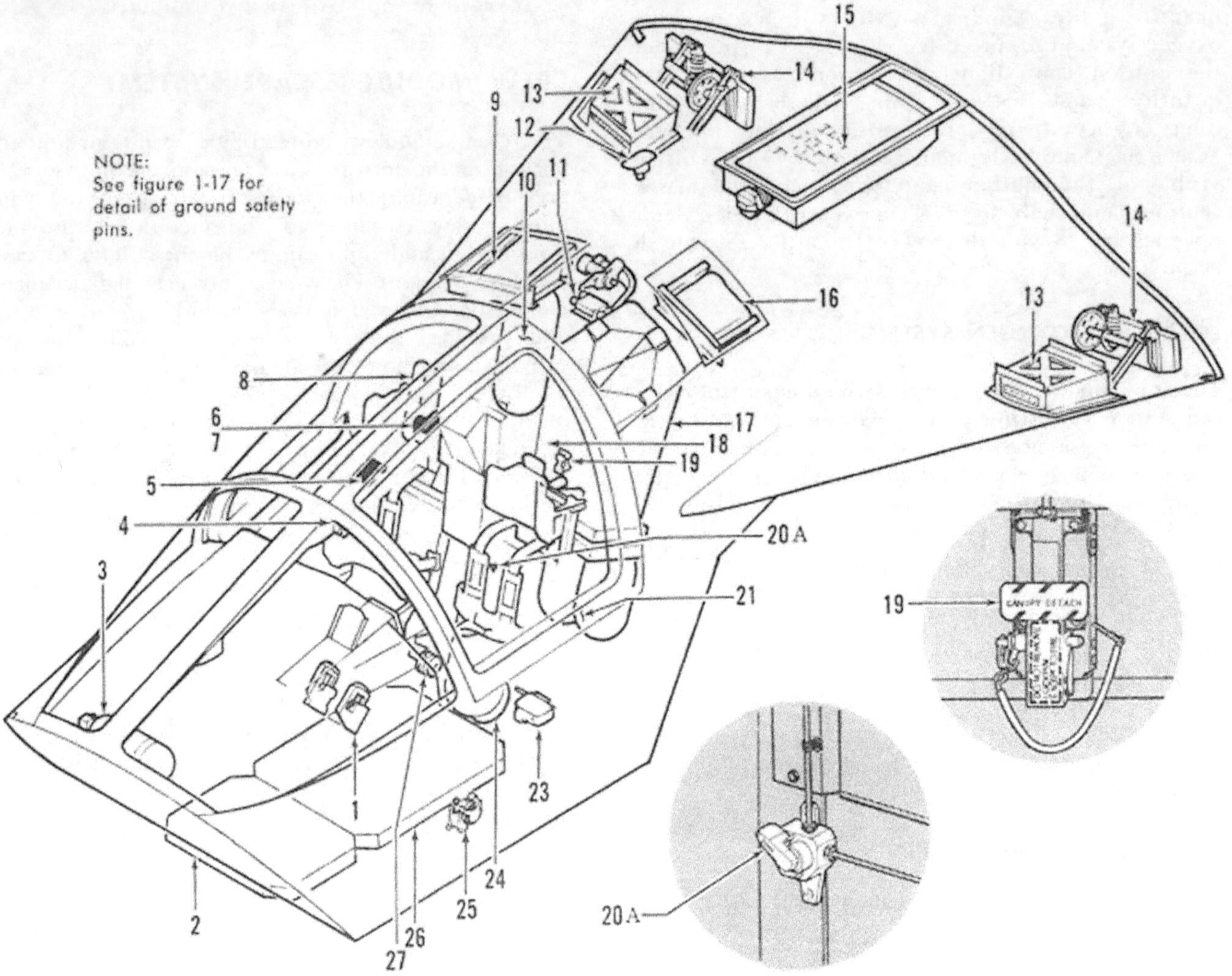

NOTE:
See figure 1-17 for detail of ground safety pins.

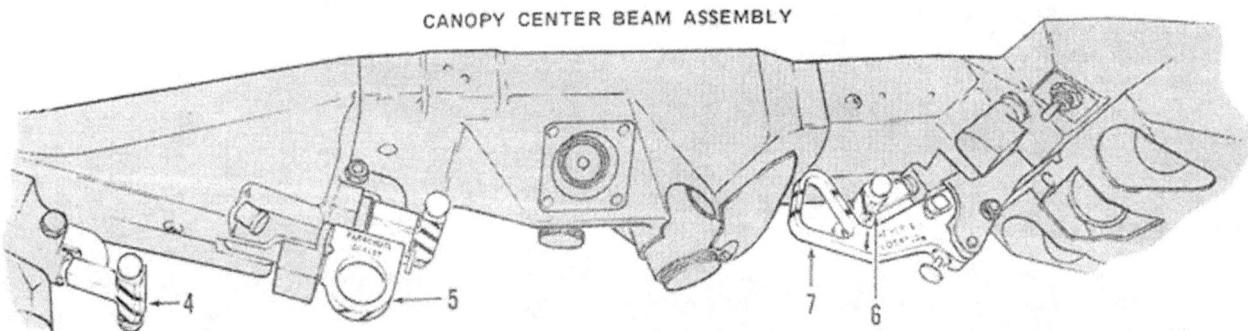

CANOPY CENTER BEAM ASSEMBLY

1. Ejection Handles (2).
2. Auxiliary Flotation Bag.
3. Auxiliary Flotation Bag Pressure Bottle.
4. Canopy Internal Emergency Release Handle.
5. Auxiliary Flotation and Recovery Parachute Deploy Handle.
6. Recovery Parachute Release Handle.
7. Severance and Flotation Handle.
8. Emergency Oxygen Bottles.
9. Right Self-Righting Bag.
10. Emergency Pressurization Bottle.
11. Barastat Lock Initiator.
12. Emergency UHF Antenna.
13. Aft Flotation Bag.
14. Pitch Flap.
15. Stabilization-Brake Parachute.
16. Left Self-Righting Bag.
17. Recovery Parachute.
18. Survival Gear.
19. Left Canopy Detach Handle.
20. (Deleted)
20A. Chaff Dispenser Control Lever.
21. Impact Attenuation Bag Pressure Bottles.
22. (Deleted)
23. Chaff Dispenser.
24. Rocket Motor.
25. Bilge Pump.
26. Impact Attenuation Bag.
27. Automatic Underwater Severance Initiator.

Figure 1-59.

1-126　　　　Changed 18 August 1967

Crew Module Seats

strap and right trunk strap on each seat harness, to attach the oxygen regulator in either position as convenient to the crew member. The lower torso harness consists of an adjustable lap belt which is attached to each side of the aft seat pan structure. The lower torso harness attaches on both sides by means of quick release buckles. Each seat is equipped with an inertia reel located behind the head rest. When unlocked, the inertia reel will allow the shoulder straps to extend or retract automatically to allow freedom of movement of the crew member. When an excessive g-force is encountered or when manually locked, the inertia reel will prevent further shoulder strap extension and will take up shoulder strap slack as the crew member returns to a normal position. The inertia reel is also equipped with an explosive cartridge in a power retraction device which, during ejection, will retract the shoulder straps and lock the reel. The right seat must be removed to gain access to the survival equipment compartment. Instructions for removing the seat are located on the back of the seat under the back cushion.

EJECTION EQUIPMENT.

The ejection equipment consists of the necessary initiators, severance components and the rocket motor. Actuation of either ejection handle initiator provides an explosive impulse sequenced to lock the shoulder harness inertia reels in the retracted position, activate the emergency oxygen and cockpit pressurization system, release the chaff dispenser, activate guillotine cutters, and to ignite the rocket motor. Two pressure initiators which are activated by rocket motor pressure build-up after ignition are provided to activate the severance components and to deploy the stabilization-brake and recovery parachutes and impact attenuation bag. The severance components consist of the flexible liner shaped charges (FLSC) and explosive guillotine cutters. The FLSC is located around the crew module so that detonation will cut the splice plate joining the crew module to the airplane. FLSC is also used to remove the covers over the parachutes and flotation, self righting, and impact attenuation bags. The explosive guillotine cutters are provided to sever antenna leads, secondary control cables, and an oxygen line. Quick disconnects located in the crew module floor are used for separation of the normal air conditioning and pressurization system ducts, the flight controls, and the electrical wiring. The rocket motor, located between the crew members and behind the seat bulkhead, provides the thrust to propel the crew module up and away from the aircraft.

RECOVERY AND LANDING EQUIPMENT.

The recovery and landing equipment consists of stabilization components, the recovery parachute, landing and flotation components, and underwater escape components. The stabilization components consist of the stabilization glove, stabilization-brake parachute, and

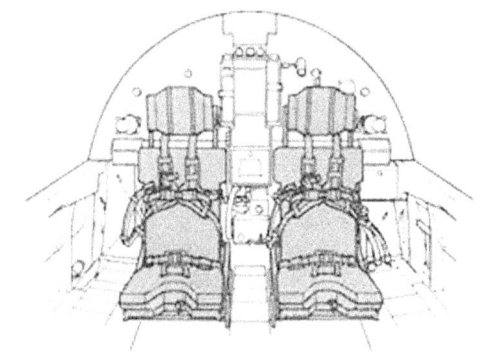

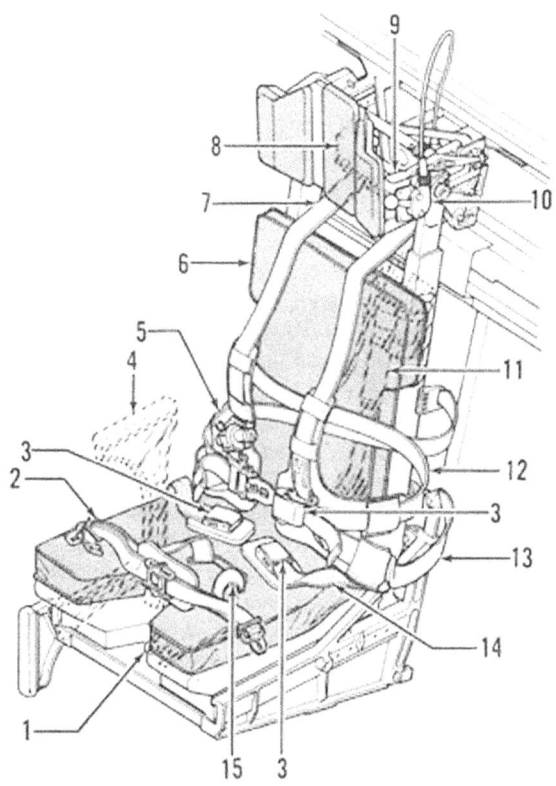

1. Seat Fore and Aft Adjustment Lever.
2. Lower Torso Restraint Harness.
3. Quick Release Buckle (3).
4. Inboard Arm Rest.
5. Upper Torso Restraint Harness.
6. Seat Back Cushion.
7. Shoulder Strap.
8. Inertia Reel.
9. Headrest Adjustment Lever (2).
10. Inertia Reel Control Handle.
11. Seat Adjustment Actuator.
12. Chest Strap.
13. Trunk Strap.
14. Lap Belt.
15. Crotch Straps.

Figure 1-60.

the pitch flaps. The stabilization glove which forms the forward portion of the wing glove is an integral part of the crew module. This glove section serves to stabilize the flight of the crew module until deployment of the recovery parachute. The pitch flaps, in the under surface of the glove section, assist in maintaining crew module horizontal stability. The stabilization-brake parachute, which is contained in a compartment in the center of the top aft section of the glove, is used to decelerate the crew module and assist in maintaining stable flight prior to recovery parachute deployment. The stabilization-brake parachute is a six foot diameter ribbon type parachute attached by two bridles to the outboard aft sections of the glove section. The recovery parachute has a ringsail canopy with a 49 foot deployed diameter. The parachute is attached by two bridles to the crew module so that the module will maintain an upright and level attitude during descent. The parachute is housed in a container located between the seat bulkhead and the aft pressure bulkhead. This container rests on the parachute catapult pan. The catapult forcibly deploys the parachute at a velocity sufficient to ensure proper bag strip-off. A q operated selector monitors airplane speed to select one of three possible time delays in unlocking a barostat initiator. When below 15,000 feet, the barostat initiator, if unlocked will fire and in turn fire the catapult to deploy the recovery parachute. The parachute is initially deployed in a reefed configuration. The parachute is disreefed by three cutters which sever the reefing line shortly after line stretch is reached. The landing and flotation components consist of an inflatable landing impact attenuation bag, flotation bags and self-righting bags. The impact attenuation bag, located in the crew module floor, inflates automatically during descent and serves to cushion the landing impact. Regulated pneumatic pressure for inflation of the bag is contained in two storage bottles in the crew module. Pressure within the bag is maintained at 2 psi. Although the crew module is watertight and will float, additional buoyancy is provided by a flotation bag at each aft corner of the glove section and by an auxiliary flotation bag at the front of the crew module. Inflation of the aft flotation bags is accomplished either manually by use of a T-handle initiator in the cockpit or automatically by action of the underwater severance initiator. Inflation of the auxiliary flotation bag is accomplished manually by a T-handle initiator in the cockpit. The pressure source for inflation of the flotation bags is contained in two storage bottles located in the crew module. The underwater escape components provide either manual or automatic crew module severance, inflation of the aft flotation and self-righting bags, and actuation of the emergency oxygen system. This system is used in the event that an airplane has ditched with the crew module still attached. Manual actuation is accomplished by pulling a T-handle initiator in the cockpit. Automatic actuation is accomplished by an underwater severance initiator. This initiator when submerged in water and sensing a depth of between 10 and 20 feet will actuate to perform the same functions as the T-handle initiator.

SURVIVAL EQUIPMENT.

The survival equipment consists of locating aids, special equipment, and standard survival equipment. The locating aids consist of a chaff dispenser, an AN/URT-21 radio beacon set, an AN/URC-10 radio set, and a portable distress beacon light. The chaff dispenser, when armed, will activate to dispense chaff automatically during the ejection sequence. A control lever in the cockpit is provided to either arm or disarm the dispenser prior to ejection. The AN/URT-21 radio beacon set, located in the right console, will emit an intermittent, modulated tone to aid in rescue operations. The manually operated set is connected to the crew module mounted emergency UHF antenna which erects upon ejection. The set may also be used with its own retractable antenna. The AN-URC-10 radio, located in the survival equipment stowage compartment, provides a means of voice communication. The portable distress beacon light, also located in the survival equipment stowage compartment, produces a powerful flashing light to aid in night rescue operations. The special survival equipment consists of two air ventilation masks and a combination bilge/flotation bag inflation pump. The air ventilation masks located in the survival equipment stowage compartment, are provided for use when the canopy hatches must remain closed because of rough seas or inclement weather. The mask hoses may be connected to air mask connector valves located adjacent to the crew seats. An air supply tube leads from each connector valve to an outside opening well above the water line. The combination bilge/flotation bag inflation pump is operated by fore and aft motion of the control stick. This will cause simultaneous pumping of water overboard and inflation of the flotation bags. Over-inflation of the bags is prevented by relief valves. Standard survival equipment is provided for all climatic conditions. This equipment is stored in the survival equipment stowage compartment behind the pilot's seat. Instructions on how to gain access to the survival equipment compartment are contained on a detachable instruction plate mounted on the back of the pilot's seat behind the back seat cushion. The contents of the survival equipment stowage compartment will be determined by the applicable using command.

CREW MODULE EJECTION SEQUENCE.

When either ejection handle is pulled, the following ejection sequence (figure 1-61) occurs automatically. Pulling either handle fires an initiator that simultaneously retracts both inertia lock reels, actuates the emergency oxygen and cabin pressurization systems, actuates

T.O. 1F-111A-1

Section I
Description & Operation

Crew Module Ejection Sequence

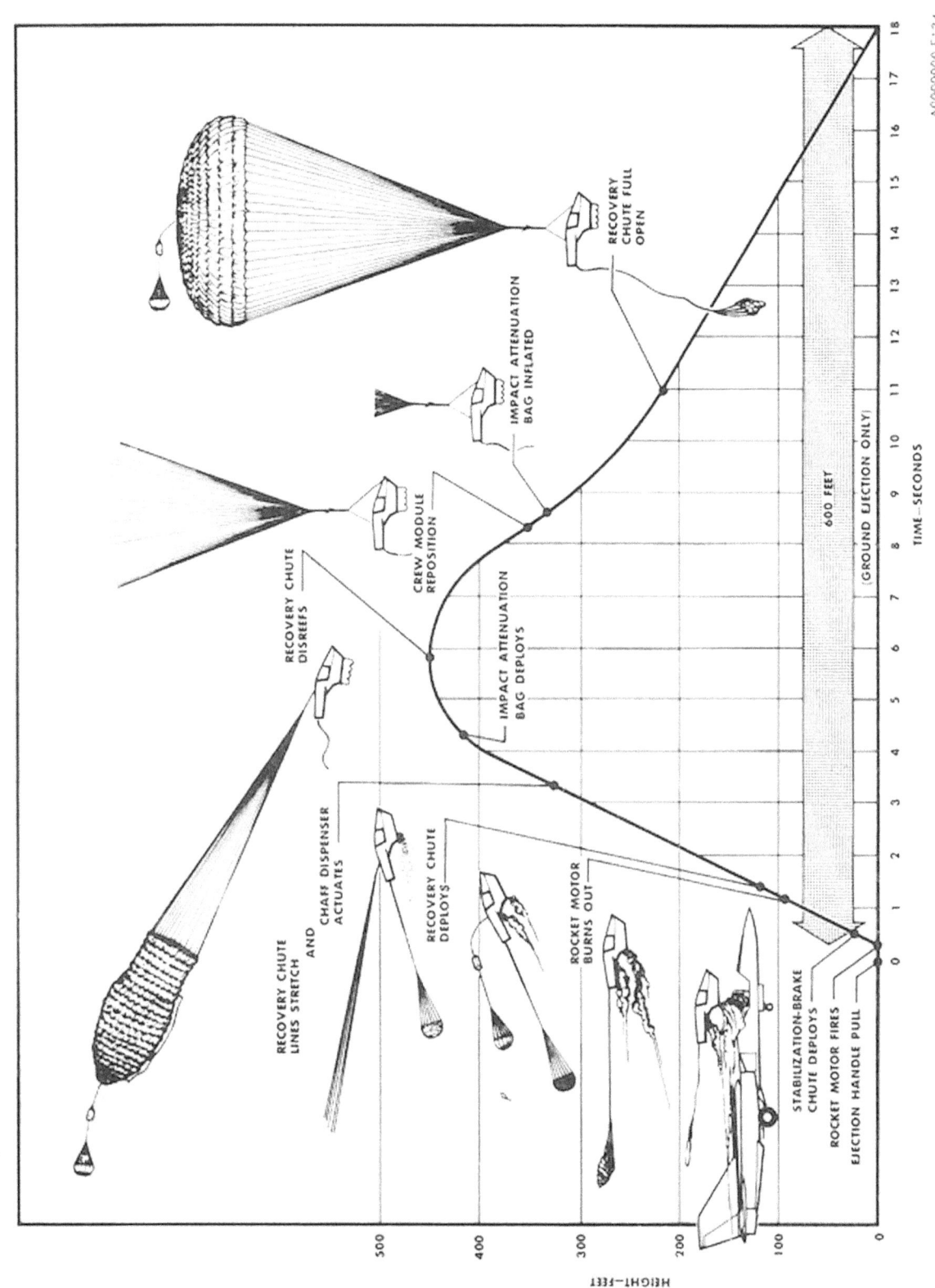

Figure 1-61.

1-129

Section I
Description & Operation

T.O. 1F-111A-1

the chaff dispenser, if armed, fires the explosive guillotines, ignites the rocket motor, and unlocks the manual recovery chute deployment handle. Pressure build-up of the rocket motor fires two additional initiators. The first initiator acts as a backup to actuate the emergency oxygen and cabin pressurization system, the chaff dispenser, and guillotines, and also activates the crew module severance system. The FLSC detonates and severs the crew module from the airplane. The second initiator actuates the stabilization-brake parachute, the thrust reducer, and unlocks the barostat initiator. When the barostat initiator is unlocked and senses an altitude below 15,000 feet, it will fire and ignite the SMDC train to remove the recovery parachute severable cover and fire the parachute catapult. This barostat initiator, will also remove the impact attenuation bag severable cover and fire the explosive valves in the impact attenuation bag air bottles causing the bag to inflate. A third function of the barostat initiator is, to erect the emergency UHF antenna and to fire the explosive pin retractor, releasing the repositioning bridle cable which allows the crew module to assume the correct touchdown attitude.

DITCHING ESCAPE SEQUENCE.

If the airplane is ditched, crew module severance and flotation bag deployment may be initiated either manually or automatically. If the severance and flotation handle is pulled or the automatic underwater severance initiator is actuated, the following sequence of events occurs: An initiator is fired to (1) fire the FLSC to separate the crew module from the airplane, (2) remove the severable covers over the aft flotation bags and the self-righting bags, (3) fire the explosive valve in an air storage bottle to inflate the aft flotation bags and the left self-righting bag and (4) fire the explosive valve in an air storage bottle to inflate the right self-righting bag.

Seat Forward and Aft Adjustment Lever.

The seat forward and aft adjustment lever (1, figure 1-60), located in front of the seat pan between the crewmember's legs, is provided to unlock the seat from the carriage to allow forward and aft adjustment. When the handle is pulled up, the seat will unlock to allow a maximum of 3 inches travel from full aft to full forward. Since this lever does not provide headrest adjustment, forward and aft adjustment of the seat will result in a tilting of the seat back.

Seat Adjustment Switches.

Vertical adjustment of each seat is provided by a switch located on each left and right sidewall (2, figure 1-19 and 4, figure 1-55) adjacent to the seat. Each switch has positions marked UP and DOWN and is spring-loaded to the center unmarked OFF position. Positioning a switch to either UP or DOWN energizes an electrical actuator to raise or lower the seat as selected. The seat has a maximum vertical travel of 5 inches.

Headrest Adjustment Lever.

A headrest adjustment lever (9, figure 1-60), located on either side of each seat headrest is provided for fore and aft adjustment of the headrest. Depressing either lever will unlock the headrest allowing it to be moved either forward or aft. Releasing the lever will lock the headrest in place. Since the seat back is attached to the headrest, fore and aft movement of the headrest will cause the seat back to tilt.

Inertia Reel Control Handle.

The inertia reel control handle (10, figure 1-60), located on the left side of each seat headrest is provided to lock or unlock the inertia reel.

Ejection Handles.

Two ejection handles (1, figure 1-59), one located on either side of the center console adjacent to the crewmember's seat, are provided to initiate the ejection cycle. When the lock release on the top of handle is depressed the handle is released and may be pulled out. Pulling the handle out approximately ½ inch will fire the initiator to start the ejection sequence.

Recovery Parachute Deploy Handle.

The ring-shaped recovery parachute deploy handle (5, figure 1-59), located on canopy center beam assembly, is provided as an emergency means of deploying the recovery parachute should the normal method fail. Pulling the handle will fire an initiator to unlock the barostat and will also fire the stabilization brake parachute catapult. The chute deploy handle cannot be pulled until an ejection initiator has been fired.

Recovery Parachute Release Handle.

The ring-shaped recovery parachute release handle (6, figure 1-59), located on the canopy center beam assembly, is provided to release the recovery parachute from the crew module after landing. Pulling the handle fires the parachute release retractors at the bridle attaching points releasing the bridles from the crew module. The recovery parachute release handle cannot be pulled until the severance and flotation handle has been pulled.

Auxiliary Flotation Handle.

The T-shaped auxiliary flotation handle (5, figure 1-59), located on the canopy center beam assembly, is provided to inflate the auxiliary flotation bag on the front of the crew module. Pressing a release button on either side of the handle and pulling the handle out fires an initiator which in turn removes the severable cover over the auxiliary flotation bag and fires an explosive valve in an air storage bottle to inflate the bag.

Severance and Flotation Handle.

The severance and flotation handle (7, figure 1-59), located on the canopy center beam assembly, is provided for escape in the event the airplane has ditched. Pressing a release button on either side of the handle and pulling the handle out will fire the FLSC and guillotines, separating the crew module from the airplane, and will inflate the aft flotation bags and the self righting bags. Pulling the handle will also activate the emergency oxygen system.

Control Sticks.

The control sticks are used after a water landing as a combination bilge/flotation bag inflation pump. After landing, the bilge pump drive connector pin is removed from the pin stowage hole and inserted in the operating hole. This connects the pump to the control stick. A plunger, adjacent to the pin stowage hole, must be pushed in to open the pump air and water outlet valves. Fore and aft motion of the stick will then operate the pump. For description of the control sticks, refer to "Flight Control System," this section.

Chaff Dispenser Control Lever.

The chaff dispenser control lever (20A, figure 1-59) located on the aft bulkhead, is used to arm or disarm the crew module chaff dispenser. The lever is labeled CHAFF and has two positions marked ON and OFF. Placing the lever to the ON position opens a mechanical interrupt to allow explosive train propagation to the chaff dispenser release mechanism. When the crew module is ejected, the explosive train releases the chaff dispenser and the slip stream dispenses the chaff. Placing the lever to the OFF position closes the mechanical interrupt, thereby disarming the dispenser.

Note

The lever should be ON over friendly territory and placed to OFF as directed by tactical requirements.

MISCELLANEOUS EQUIPMENT.

THERMAL RADIATION PROTECTION.

Thermal radiation protection for the crew is provided by side curtains on the canopy hatches and a hinged forward panel located between the glare shield and windshield.

Side Curtains.

The side curtains (18, figure 1-2) are mounted along the upper edge of each canopy hatch on either side of the center canopy beam. When stowed the curtains are folded as an accordion in the shape of a fan with the hinge forward. As each curtain is extended it unfolds to form an arc from the top rear to the bottom forward edge of the hatch. The rim of the arc rides in a track to form a light seal. When fully extended the forward edge of the curtain forms a light seal against the forward hatch structure, thus completely covering the canopy hatch glass. The curtain is retained in the stowed position by a spring tension latch. A handle labeled RADIATION CURTAIN is provided on the forward edge of the curtain to extend or retract the curtain. A positive latch on the forward seal locks the curtain in the extended position. A push button labeled CURTAIN RELEASE must be depressed to release the curtain for retraction. A decal located adjacent to the curtain release button contains instructions for extending or stowing the curtain.

Forward Panel.

The forward panel is constructed in two sections to form a thermal radiation shield across the front of the cockpit between the top of the glare shield and the windshield. The panel is hinged along the aft edge of the glare shield and folds forward to lie on top of the glare shield when not needed. A slide catch on each section secures the panel against the glare shield. A cable lanyard attached to the slide catch is provided to unlatch the catch and erect each section. The right section must be raised first. When erected a friction catch retains the upper edge of each section against the windshield arch to provide a light seal. To stow the panel each crew member disengages the friction catch by pushing forward on his section adjacent to the catch. When disengaged the panel will fall forward on the glare shield. The slide catches on each section should be engaged to retain the panel in the stowed position. A decal located on the forward canopy hatch structure contains instructions for erecting and stowing the panel.

CREW ENTRANCE LADDERS AND STEPS.

Crew entrance ladders and steps, located on each side of the fuselage, provide crew access to the cockpit without the aid of ground support equipment. When not in use both sets of ladders and steps are retracted into the sides of the fuselage. Each left or right ladder and step can be electrically extended from inside the cockpit. Push-button releases are provided on the outside of the fuselage to manually extend the ladders and steps from the ground. The ladders and steps must be manually stowed from the ground. The crew entrance ladder is temporarily deactivated by T.O. 1F-111A-795.

Section I
Description & Operation

T.O. 1F-111A-1

Servicing Diagram

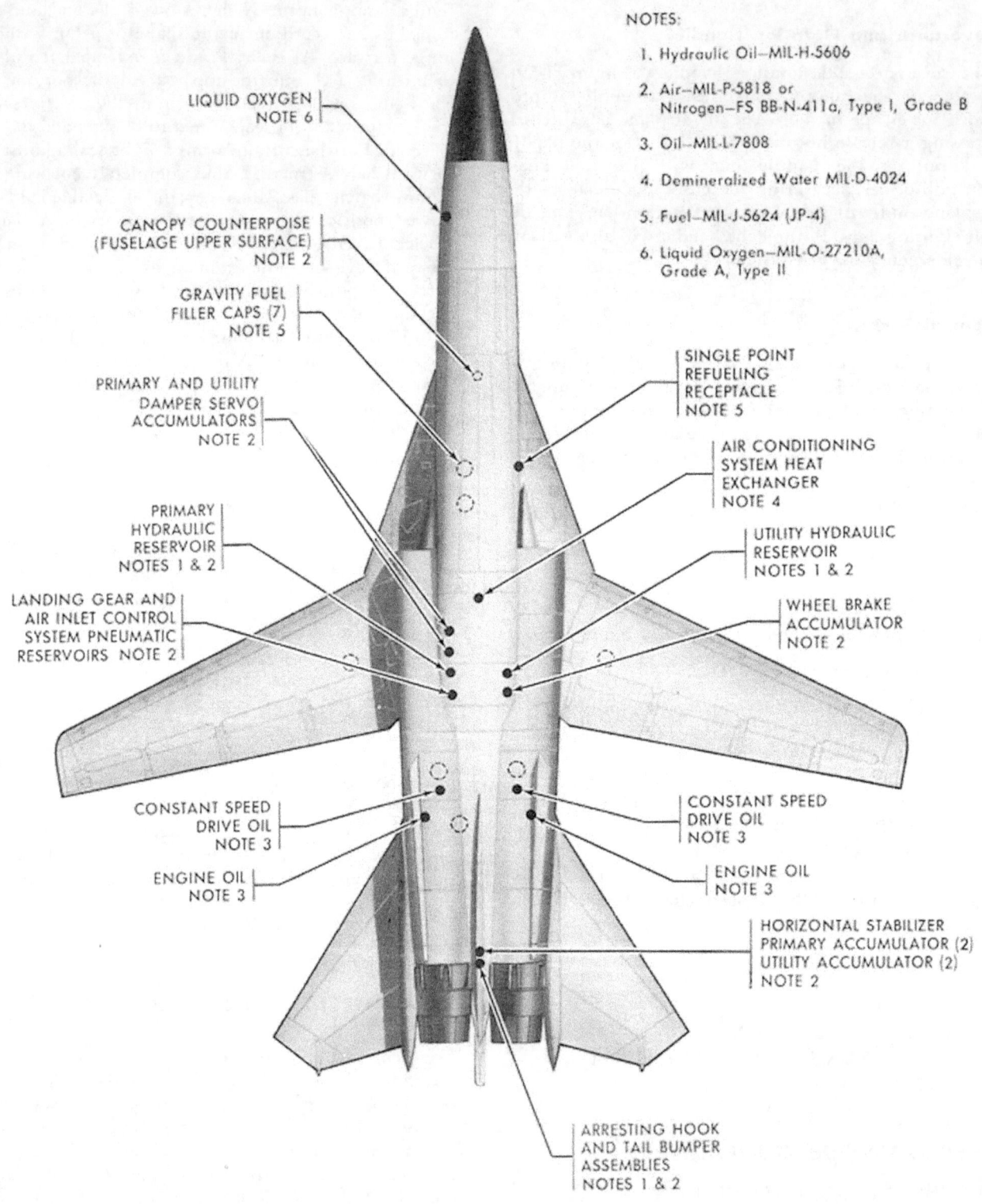

Figure 1-62.

1-132

Changed 18 August 1967

Entrance Ladder Switch.

The entrance ladder switch (4, figure 1-25), located on the ground check panel, has three positions marked L (left), R (right) and OFF. Placing the switch to L or R will provide 28 volt d-c power to a solenoid in the respective ladder and step to release the ladder and step for extension. The switch is spring-loaded to the center OFF position. The switch is temporarily deactivated by T.O. 1F-111A-795.

ANTI-G SUIT.

Each anti-G suit is connected to the airplane pressure source by an anti-G suit hose (5, figure 1-58), located on the aircraft commander's and pilot's oxygen-suit control panels. Pressure for the anti-G suit is supplied from the engine compressor section. A test button (2, figure 1-58) marked ANTI-G PUSH-TO-TEST, is provided to check operation of the anti-G suit valve. When the button is depressed, the anti-G suit bladders will inflate. When the button is released, the bladders will deflate.

MIRRORS.

Four rear view mirrors, two on each side of the cockpit canopy frame (15, figure 1-2) are installed to permit the crew rearward vision without moving from their normal sitting position. The mirrors are adjustable in tilt only.

MAP STOWAGE.

The cockpit is furnished with two map cases, located on the left and right sidewalls (9, figure 1-19) and (5, figure 1-55). A nylon retaining strap, attached to each map case, extends upward, and attaches to the cockpit sidewall fairing.

DATA STOWAGE CASE.

The cockpit contains a black nylon vinyl coated data case located in the outboard aft end of the right console. The data case consists of the case and a flap with a metal snap fastener to prevent data from inadvertently falling from the case. The case is labeled DATA STOWAGE.

CHART STOWAGE.

Two chart stowage compartments are located on each side of the lighting control panel (52 and 58, figure 1-2). The right compartment is labeled LETDOWN CHART HOLDER, the left compartment is labeled LETDOWN CHARTS. Each compartment is provided with a strap and fastener to secure the charts and holder.

EJECTION SYSTEM SAFETY PIN STOWAGE.

A stowage compartment (10, figure 1-19), located at the aft end of the left sidewall, is provided for stowing the ejection system safety pins.

SPARE LAMP AND FUSE HOLDER STOWAGE.

A stowage compartment (6, figure 1-55), located at the aft end of the right sidewall, is provided for stowing spare light bulbs and fuses.

CHECKLIST STOWAGE.

A space for stowing the checklist is provided on the left sidewall (1, figure 1-19). A nylon strap retains the checklist in place.

FOOD STOWAGE COMPARTMENT.

A food stowage compartment (60, figure 1-2) is provided for the crew on the aft bulkhead at the left of the aircraft commander's seat. The door of the compartment is held closed by a spring-loaded latch.

CHART BOARD STOWAGE.

Space is provided for stowage of a chart board on the right side of the pilot's seat. A fabric strap snaps over the chart board when it is stowed to hold it securely in place.

RELIEF CONTAINER STOWAGE.

Relief containers for each crew member are located in small compartments (47, figure 1-2) on the aft bulkhead, outboard of each seat. Each compartment is enclosed by a fabric cover with a zipper opening. The relief containers are plastic bottles with screw caps to prevent leakage. Each bottle holds approximately 3 pints.

HOOD STOWAGE COMPARTMENT.

A hood stowage compartment (48, figure 1-2), located on the right side of the aft bulkhead just above the pilot's relief container, is provided to store the attack radar scope hood.

CORRECTION CARD HOLDERS.

The cockpit is provided with three correction card holders. One four inch holder is attached underneath the left-aft section of the glare shield. The card holder is labeled EPR SETTING. One four inch and one two inch card holders are attached underneath the right-aft section of the glare shield on the approximate centerline of the airplane. The four inch holder is labeled UHF FREQUENCY CARD. The two inch holder is labeled COMPASS CORRECTION CARD and is to the right of the four inch holder. Each card holder is attached by spring tensioned hinges riveted to the glare shield. The card holders are pulled out into position for reading purposes and spring back against the lower side of glare shield when released.

CHART HOLDER.

A chart holder is provided to clearly display approach charts where they can be easily followed during instrument letdowns. The holder is a rectangular transparent pane the size of an approach chart and is attached in a swivel socket on the canopy center beam. It can be swivelled to the left or right and latched in place for use by either crew member. The holder has both red and white lighting which can be mixed as desired by control knobs located on the top of the holder. The holder is stowed in a receptacle (58, figure 1-2), located in the aft console, when not in use.

ARM RESTS.

Arm rests (3, figure 1-19 and figure 1-55) are provided on each sidewall. When not in use they are folded upwards under the canopy sill.

LIQUID CONTAINERS.

Two insulated liquid containers (50, figure 1-2) provide the crew with hot or cold liquids during flight. The containers are stowed in recessed receptacles in the aft bulkhead, outboard of each head rest. A spring-loaded latch on the front of each receptacle holds the respective containers firmly in place against a coil spring in the bottom of the receptacle when the container is stowed. Each container holds approximately 1 quart.

STARTER CARTRIDGE STOWAGE CONTAINER.

A starter cartridge stowage container, located on the left forward side of the main landing gear wheel well, is provided to carry two spare starter cartridges. The container is made of plastic and has a detachable cover to allow servicing or access to the spare cartridges when needed.

This is the last page of Section I.

SECTION II
NORMAL PROCEDURES

TABLE OF CONTENTS.

Preparation For Flight	2-1
Preflight Check	2-2
Before Starting Engines	2-7
Starting Engines	2-7
Before Taxiing	2-10
Taxiing	2-12
Before Takeoff	2-13
Takeoff	2-13
After Takeoff	2-13
Climb	2-15
Cruise	2-15
Air Refueling	2-15
Flight Characteristics	2-15
Descent	2-15
Before Landing	2-15
Landing	2-16
Landing On Slippery Runways	2-16
Touch And Go Landing	2-18
Simulated Single Engine Landing	2-18
Go-Around	2-18
After Landing	2-18
Engine Shutdown	2-18
Before Leaving Airplane	2-18
Strange Field	2-20

Note

- Items coded (AC-P) are applicable to both the aircraft commander and the pilot. Items coded (P) are applicable to the pilot only, and items not coded are applicable to the aircraft commander only. Items coded (GO) require action by the ground observer. (A ground observers' checklist is included at the end of this section.)

- Differences between airplanes are designated by number symbols such as , etc. For an explanation of airplane code numbers, refer to "Airplane Designation Codes," in the front of the manual.

- The airspeed indicated on the airspeed mach indicator has been calibrated for pitot-static system errors by the CADC and therefore is actually KCAS (knots calibrated airspeed). However, this air speed is referred to as KIAS (knots indicated airspeed) throughout this manual since it is read directly from the instrument.

PREPARATION FOR FLIGHT.

FLIGHT RESTRICTIONS.

Refer to Section V for the operating limitations imposed on the airplane.

FLIGHT PLANNING.

Refer to Appendix I to determine takeoff, cruise control, fuel planning and management, and landing data necessary to complete the mission.

TAKEOFF AND LANDING DATA CARDS.

Refer to Appendix I for information necessary to complete the Takeoff and Landing Data Card in the Flight Crew Checklist, T.O. 1F-111A-1CL-1. Recheck data just prior to flight to determine the effect of atmospheric, runway, or airplane configuration changes. If required, revise Takeoff and Landing Data Card to reflect latest information.

WEIGHT AND BALANCE.

Refer to Section V for weight limitations and to the Manual of Weight and Balance Data, T.O. 1-1B-40, for airplane and crew module loading information.

WARNING

The crew module shall not be considered flyable without its full crew and complement of survival equipment, or the equivalent ballast to maintain center of gravity. Personal belongings or additional heavy equipment shall not be carried in the cockpit without compensation for cg effect. To assure stability of the module in event of ejection, it must be loaded in accordance with T.O. 1-1B-40.

CHECKLISTS.

This Flight Manual contains only amplified procedures. Flight Crew Checklist T.O. 1F-111A-1CL-1 is issued as a separate document.

Section II
Normal Procedures

ENTRANCE.

To extend either entrance ladder, proceed as follows:

1. Entrance step—Extend. (AC-P)
   Rotate screw in center of step until step extends.
2. Entrance ladder—Extend. (AC-P)
   Support the entrance ladder door by hand and depress the unlock button on the door. Allow the door to extend.

Note

After entering the airplane, the entrance ladder and step must be manually stowed by the ground crew.

PREFLIGHT CHECK.

BEFORE EXTERIOR INSPECTION.

1. Form 781—Check for aircraft status and release. (AC-P)
2. Aircraft and crew module weight and balance chart C—Checked for correct limits.

EXTERIOR INSPECTION.

The exterior inspection is based upon the fact that maintenance personnel have completed all of the requirements of the Scheduled Inspection and Maintenance Requirements Manual for preflight and post flight; therefore, duplicate inspections and operational checks of systems have been eliminated except for those needed in the interest of flight safety: Following the route shown in figure 2-1, check all surfaces for any type of damage; signs of fuel, oil, hydraulic or other fluid leaks that may have developed since the preflight inspection. Check all access doors and covers for security.

Note

With the airplane parked at a certain angle to the prevailing wind, it is not unusual for the engine fan and compressor to windmill. This rotation will cause no damage.

BEFORE ENTERING COCKPIT.

1. Windshield and canopy glass—Check. (AC-P)
   Check all enclosure glass for condition and cleanliness.
2. Canopy hatches—Check. (AC-P)
   Check the hatch for proper operation, condition and condition of seal.

3. Canopy external emergency release handle—Check. (P)
   Check that plunger of the release handle is sealed and flush with fuselage surface.
4. Ejection handle safety pins (2)—Installed.
   Before entering the cockpit, check that a safety pin is installed in each ejection handle.
5. Severance and flotation, recovery parachute release, auxiliary flotation and canopy internal emergency release handle safety pins (3)—Removed.
   Upon entering the cockpit, check that the above safety pins are removed.
6. Emergency pressurization bottle pressure—3000 psi minimum at 70°F.
7. Emergency oxygen bottle pressure — 1800 psi minimum at 70°F.
8. Survival equipment compartment—Checked.
   Check the survival equipment compartment for security, seals intact.
9. Canopy external emergency release initiator safety pin (1)—Check removed. (P)
10. Left canopy detach handle safety pin—Check installed.
11. Aft console—Checked.

INTERIOR INSPECTION.

Power Off.

1. Enter cockpit, adjust rudder pedals and attach and secure all personal equipment.
   a. Torso restraint harness and inertia reel—Checked. (AC-P)
      Check the condition of the restraint harness. Check operation of the inertia reel in the locked and unlocked position.
   b. Oxygen regulator—Inserted in torso harness receptacle. (AC-P)
   c. Oxygen mask and communication cord—Connected. (AC-P)
   d. Oxygen lever—ON, flow check. (AC-P)
      Check that there is a normal flow of oxygen.
   e. Anti-G suit hose—Connect and check. (AC-P)
      Check for proper routing and make sure that the hose is not restricted by personal harnesses.
   f. **19** ♦ **30** Pressure suit vent knob — Full CCW. (AC-P)
2. Throttles—OFF.
3. Landing gear handle—DN.

T.O. 1F-111A-1

Section II
Normal Procedures

Exterior Inspection

A. Nose Wheel Area.
B. Right Side.
C. Right Engine.
D. Weapons Bay Area.
E. Wheel Well Area.
F. Right Wing
G. Tail Area.
H. Left Wing.
I. Left Engine.
J. Left Side.

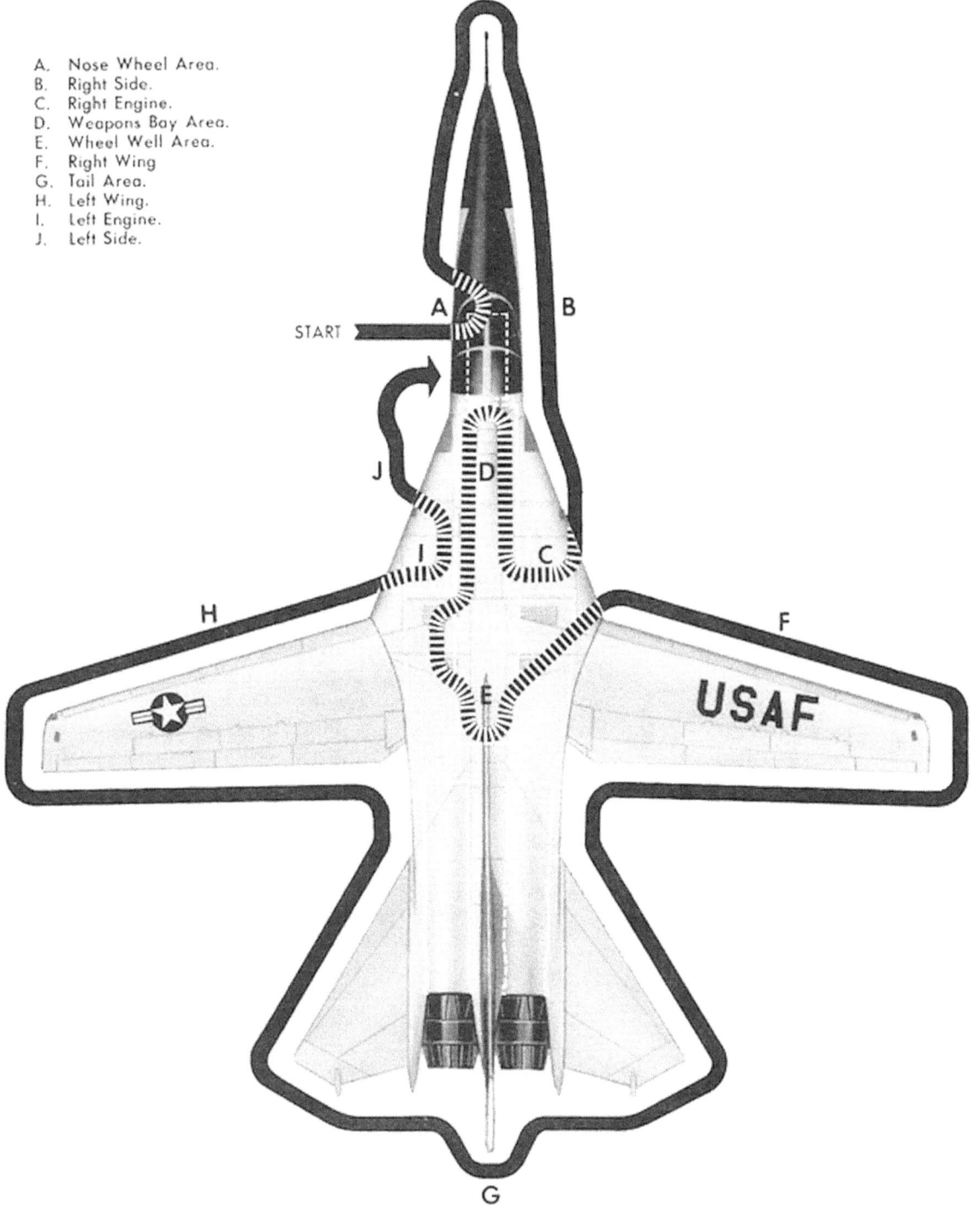

Figure 2-1.

Section II
Normal Procedures

4. Auxiliary brake handle—Pulled.

> **CAUTION**
>
> If the previous landing was made within the past three hours, do not perform this step. To do so could damage the brakes from over heating.

5. Arresting hook handle—In.
6. Landing gear emergency release handle—In.
7. Fuel dump switch—OFF.
8. Spike control switches—NORM.
9. Engine ground start switch—OFF.
10. ⓳ ⧫ ㉚ Translating cowl switches—OPEN.
11. ㉛ ⧫ Translating cowl switches—AUTO.
12. CMDS arming switch—SAFE. (P)
13. Attack radar function selector knob—OFF. (P)
14. Armament system master power switch—OFF. (P)
15. Weapon mode selector knob—OFF. (P)
16. Pylon weapon selector and weapon bay control buttons (8)—Pulled. (P)
17. Weapon bay door switch—Checked. (P-GO)
    Check that the position of the weapon bay door switch, located on nuclear weapons control panel, is in agreement with the position of the weapon bay doors.

> **WARNING**
>
> If the position of the weapon bay doors is not in agreement with the weapon bay door switch, the doors will actuate (open or close) when hydraulic and electrical power are applied to the airplane.

18. Bomb nav mode selector knob—OFF. (P)
19. RHAWS power audio control knob—CCW. (P)
20. ILS power switch—OFF. (P)
21. Publications and flight data—Checked. (AC-P)
    Check that all applicable current flight information publications are aboard.
22. Pilot—Ready for electrical power.

Power On. (Aircraft Commander)

1. Battery switch—ON.
   Check the engine turbine inlet temperature indicators. The power-off flag in the indicators will go out of view when the battery is on.

Note

If the engines are to be started using battery power, the following "Power On" checks must be delayed until the engines are running.

2. External power switch—ON. (If applicable)
   If external power is to be used, place the external power switch ON and check that the electrical power flow indicator displays TIE.

Note

With power on the airplane but without engines running the following lamps will normally be lighted:

CANOPY
RADAR ALT LOW
L and R PRI HYD
L and R UTIL HYD
L and R FUEL PRESS
L and R ENG OVERSPEED
PRI ATT/HDG
α/β PROBE HEAT (㉛ ⧫).

3. Lighting control panel—Checked. (AC-P)
   Check operation of the interior light rheostats and set for desired intensity. Check operation of bright and dim switch and select desired intensity. Check external lights if night flight is anticipated.
4. Malfunction and indicator lamps—Checked. (AC-P)
   Pilot depresses the malfunction and indicator lamps test button, and aircraft commander and pilot check that all malfunction and indicator lamps light. If the damper channel caution lamps are lighted, depress damper reset button. If lamps remain lighted, a malfunction is indicated.
5. Air conditioning—Check.
   Check that air conditioning is connected and functioning properly to provide equipment cooling.
6. Seats—Adjusted. (AC-P)
   Check operation of the seats and adjust as desired.
7. Interphone panel—Set and checked. (AC-P)
   Pull mixer knobs to ON and adjust volume on those functions that are to be used.
8. ⓳ ⧫ ㉚ Compressor bleed valve switches—CLOSED.
9. Auxiliary pitch trim switch—STICK.
10. Slat/flap switch—NORM.
11. Rudder authority switch—AUTO.
12. ⓳ ⧫ ㉚ Autopilot emergency override switch—NORM.

13. 🟦 Flight control disconnect switch—NORM.
14. Wing sweep handle—Corresponds with wing position.
    Check that the wing sweep handle corresponds with the position of the wing prior to applying hydraulic pressure to the system.
15. Flap and slat handle—Corresponds with surface position.
16. 🟦 Compressor bleed valve switches—AUTO.
17. Anti-skid switch—ON.
18. Flight instrument reference select switch—PRI.
19. Oxygen quantity—Checked.
    Check that oxygen quantity is adequate for mission. Depress oxygen quantity test button; oxygen quantity indicator should decrease to zero. Note that the oxygen quantity caution lamp lights when indication is 2 liters. Release the test button and note that the caution lamp goes out and that the quantity indication returns to original value.
20. Utility hydraulic system isolation switch—NORM.
21. Flight control system switch—NORM.
22. Fire detect circuit—Checked.
    Check that both fire warning lamps light while holding the agent discharge/fire detect test switch to the FIRE DETECT TEST position.
23. Instrument system coupler mode selector knob—NAV.
    Check that the ADI bank and pitch steering bars come into view.
24. LCOS mode select knob—OFF.
25. Radar altimeter—Checked and set.

Note

This check cannot be accurately performed in an enclosure such as a maintenance dock or hangar.

   a. Minimum altitude index pointer—50 feet.
   b. Channel selector switch—CHAN 1.
   c. Power-off warning flag—Out of view.
      After approximately 120 seconds warmup time, the power-off warning flag should disappear from view. The altitude pointer should read zero and the radar altitude low warning lamp should light.
   d. Radar altimeter control knob—Depressed.
      Observe that the altitude pointer drives to 100 (±12) feet and the radar altitude low warning lamp goes out.
   e. Radar altimeter control knob—Release.
      Observe the altitude pointer returns to zero and the radar altitude low warning lamp lights.
   f. Channel selector switch—CHAN 2.
   g. Repeat steps d and e.
   h. Set the minimum altitude index pointer compatible with mission to be flown.

26. AFRS compass and latitude knobs—SLAVED and set.
27. AFRS synchronization indicator—Nulled.
28. Windshield wash/rain removal selector switch—OFF.
29. Pitot heater (pitot/probe heater 🟦) and engine/inlet anti-icing switches—OFF.
30. UHF radio—ON and set.
31. TACAN—T/R and set.
32. Oil quantity indicators—Checked.
    Check that indicators show 8 to 16 quarts, depress the oil quantity indicator test button, and check that indicators show decrease. Then release test button and check that indicators return to original readings.
33. Fuel quantity indicators—Checked.
    Check fuel quantity, momentarily depress the fuel quantity indicator test button and check that the indicators show decrease. Release test button and check that indicators return to original readings.
34. Engine feed selector knob—AUTO.
    Place the engine feed selector knob to AUTO and check that fuel pump low pressure indicator lamps number 1 through 6 blink.
35. Engine feed selector knob—AUTO, or BOTH.
    AUTO if forward and aft tanks are within normal 8200 (±300) pound differential. BOTH if tanks are not within this differential.
36. Fuel transfer knob—AUTO.
    Fuel pump low pressure indicator lamps 7, 8, 9, and 10 should blink.
37. Fuel transfer knob—OFF.
38. Air refueling switch—CLOSE.
39. Fuel tank pressurization selector switch—AUTO.
40. TFR L and R channel mode selector knobs—STBY.
41. Generator switches—ON.
42. Emergency generator switch—AUTO.
43. 🟦 Emergency generator indicated cutoff pushbutton—OPR, pushed in.
44. Air source selector knob—BOTH.
45. Temperature control knob—Full cool.
46. Pressurization selector switch—NORM.
47. Air conditioning mode selector switch—AUTO.
48. Temperature control knob—As desired.
49. Ram area control switch—NORM.

Section II
Normal Procedures

Power On. (Pilot)

1. IFF—STBY and set.
2. Bomb nav mode selector knob—HEAT.
3. Platform alignment control knob—NORMAL.
4. Platform heat indicator lamp—Lighted.

Note

The platform heat indicator lamp may not light if the stabilization platform has been operating within 30 minutes preceding this alignment.

5. Altitude/test selector knob—NORM.
6. Magnetic variation counter—Set to local variation.
7. Present position latitude counter—Checked.
   If latitude is incorrect proceed as follows:
   a. Platform alignment control knob—PLATFORM OFF.
   b. Bomb nav mode selector knob—ALIGN.
   c. Present position latitude counter—Set.
   d. Platform alignment control knob—NORMAL.
8. Bomb nav mode selector knob—ALIGN. (If steps 7a thru d were not performed)
9. Attack radar function selector knob—STBY.
   Check that the antenna cage pushbutton indicator lamp is lighted and that the antenna tilt indicator indicates + 30 degrees.
10. Attack radar function selector knob—ON.
    The function selector knob should remain in the ON position for a minimum of 5 minutes.
11. Present position longitude counter—Check and set if necessary.
12. RHAW power/audio control knob—CW to mid range.

Note

The RHAW system requires approximately 5 minutes for warmup.

13. Countermeasures receiver function selector knob—As required.
14. UHF radio—Checked.
    a. Check for side-tone.
    b. Check for tone when tone button is depressed.
15. HF radio—On and checked. (If applicable)
16. Bomb nav destination storage—Set.

a. Fix mode DEST STORAGE 1 button—Depress.
   When counters stop driving, enter number one destination storage coordinates into the destination position counters.
b. Fix mode DEST STORAGE 2 button—Depress.
   When counters stop driving, enter number two destination storage coordinates into the destination position counters.
c. Fix mode DEST STORAGE 3 button—Depress.
   When counters stop driving, enter number three destination storage coordinates into the destination position counters.
d. Fix mode TARGET selector button—Depress.

17. Destination counters—Set to coordinates of destination or first steering point.
18. Radar homing and warning system—Checked.
    a. Turn on:
       (1) View control—Full CCW.
       (2) Gate control—N position.
       (3) BRT knob—Adjust.
       (4) RTL knob—Adjust.
       (5) Sensitivity knob—Full CW.
       (6) Memory control knob—Full CCW.
    b. Lamp Test:
       (1) Test knob—LAMP.
       (2) All indicator lamps—Lighted.
    c. Display Test:
       (1) Test knob—DISPLAY.
       (2) Mode selector knob—IRT.
          Check that target display is in center of scope.
    d. CMDS arming switch—TEST.
    e. System Test:
       (1) Test knob—SYSTEM.
       (2) Mode selector switch—Rotate through H1, H2, and H3.
          In each position check the following:
          (a) Indicator lamps—Lighted.
             All forward and aft indicator lamps will light.
          (b) Target—Adjusted.
             Rotate the azimuth and elevation controls to position the target at the center of the scope.
       (3) Test knob—OFF.
    f. CMDS arming switch—SAFE.
19. Attack radar—Set. (P-GO)
    a. Mode selector knob—GND MAN.
    b. CRT intensity control knob—As desired.

Pages 2-6A thru 2-6B deleted.

c. Bezel/range marks—Checked and set.
d. Range azimuth cursors—Checked and set.
e. Function selector knob—XMIT.

WARNING

Clear the area to insure that personnel and equipment are not exposed to dangerous radiation. Refer to figure 2-2, for radar emission danger area.

f. IF gain knob—Tune for best picture.
g. Video adjustment knob—Tune for best picture.
h. Antenna tilt control knob—Detent.
i. Range selector knob—Desired range.
20. Platform align indicator lamp—Flashing.
21. Magnetic heading synchronization indicator—Nulled and steady. (If time permits)
The best possible alignment of the platform can be obtained by allowing the magnetic hearing synchronization indicator to null.

BEFORE STARTING ENGINES.

Refer to figure 2-2, Danger Areas for the extent of engine intake and exhaust hazard areas, and the engine turbine and starter turbine planes of rotation.

1. Ground crew report—Ready for engine start. (GO)
Fire guard posted, engine and run area clear, chocks in place, translating cowls open, external starter air available, ready for engine start.

DEFINITIONS.

Hot Start—TIT indicates engine ignition but exceeds the limit specified in Section V. If at any time during start the TIT increases at an abnormally rapid rate or approaches within 50°C of the limit and is still climbing, a hot start can be anticipated.

False or Hung Start—TIT indicates engine ignition but RPM will not increase to IDLE within 2 minutes.

Failure to Start—TIT indicates ignition did not occur. RPM will stabilize at the maximum for starter output.

Cartridge Start Misfire—Cartridge fails to ignite as indicated by lack of smoke at the starter exhaust port. There will be no engine RPM indication.

Cartridge Start Hangfire—Cartridge ignites as indicated by smoke at the starter exhaust port, however there will be little or no RPM indication.

If any of the above conditions occurs return the throttle to OFF and investigate. The engine should be inspected for residual fuel before a second start is attempted. If no fuel is visible a second start may be attempted. The engine should be motored until TIT is approximately 100°C before advancing the throttle to minimize the possibility of a hot start. If visible fuel or vapors are found the engine must be cleared using the pneumatic starter as follows:

Engine Clearing.

1. Engine ground start switch—PNEU.
2. Affected engine throttle—Lift.
Lift the throttle of the affected engine out of the OFF detent to motor the engine.

CAUTION

- Do not lift the throttle until engine rotation has stopped. To do so will damage the starter.
- To avoid a possible hot start do not advance the throttle.

3. Affected engine throttle—Release.
Release the throttle to OFF prior to the time limit specified for starter operation in Section V.

STARTING ENGINES.

Engine starts can be accomplished by using air pressure from a ground source or by a pyrotechnic cartridge. Only the left engine has cartridge starting capability. Either engine may be started by the use of external air when supplied by an adequate source; however, when using the MA-1A starter cart, left engine starting capability is marginal. For normal flight operations it is recommended that the right engine be started first with external air due to the higher starter torque available. With either engine operating, the remaining engine may then be started by pneumatic crossbleed. Electrical power required for engine starting may be supplied either by the airplane battery or by an external source.

WARNING

If battery power only is used during start, a check of the fire detection system cannot be made until one engine driven generator is supplying power to the ac buses.

Section II
Normal Procedures

T.O. 1F-111A-1

Danger Areas

MAXIMUM THRUST				MILITARY THRUST			TAXI THRUST		
DISTANCE FROM JET NOZZLE (FEET)	TEMPERATURE (FAHRENHEIT)	VELOCITY (MPH)		TEMPERATURE (FAHRENHEIT)	VELOCITY (MPH)	DISTANCE FROM JET NOZZLE (FEET)	TEMPERATURE (FAHRENHEIT)	VELOCITY (MPH)	
			25 FT				350°	200	
20	2000°	1750		500°	1100	20	250°	140	
	1000°	1160		300°	455		150°	70	
40						40	125°	40	
60	600°	410		200°	210				
80						JET WAKE RADIUS (FEET)		20 0 20	
100	400°	200		150°	105				
120				125°	70				
140	300°	125							
160				110°	50				
180									
200									
220									
240	200°	55							
260									
280									
300									
320									
340									
	150°	30							
JET WAKE RADIUS (FEET)			20 0 20 40						

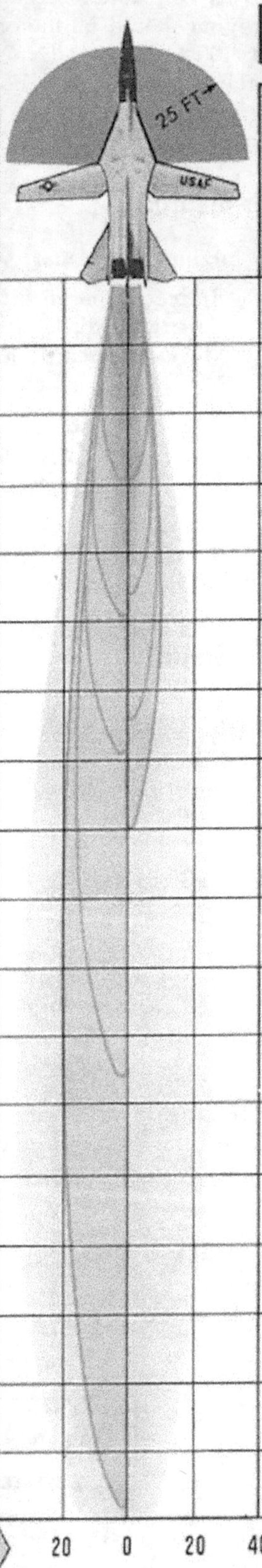

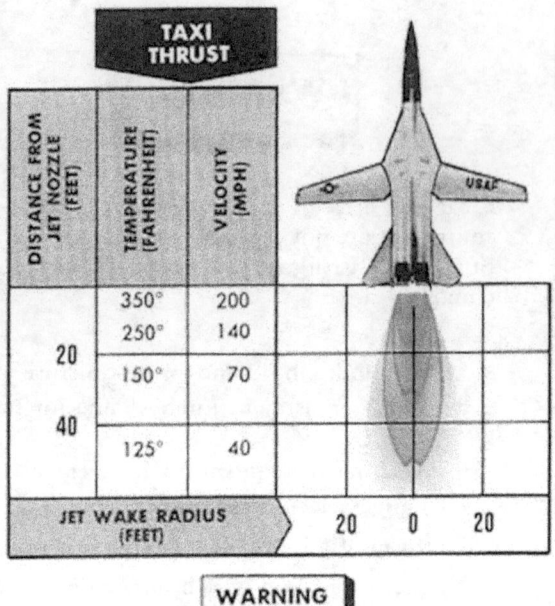

WARNING

At high thrust settings, the danger area around the intake ducts may extend as far as four feet aft of the duct lip.

With engines operating above idle RPM ear protection should be worn due to high engine noise levels. At idle RPM do not expose unprotected ears to engine noise for periods greater than 5 minutes.

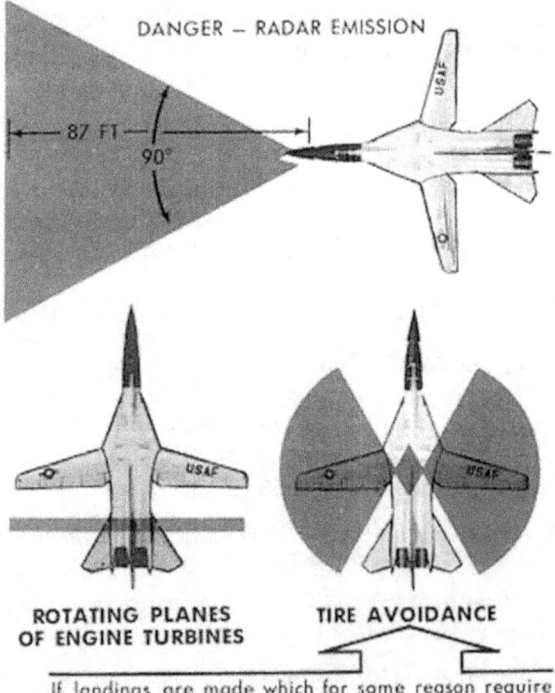

DANGER — RADAR EMISSION
87 FT 90°

ROTATING PLANES OF ENGINE TURBINES

TIRE AVOIDANCE

If landings are made which for some reason require maximum braking to stop the airplane, avoid tire area for 45 to 60 minutes after airplane has stopped. If necessary, approach from the front or rear only.

Figure 2-2.

Changed 18 August 1967

WARNING

- Do not attempt a pneumatic start or fly the airplane with an unfired cartridge in the breech. To do so could result in damage to the cartridge causing it to explode if used for subsequent starts.
- Do not initiate a cartridge start with any nacelle door open on the engine being started. To do so could result in possible overheating of adjacent structure and/or ignition of accumulated fuel and oil.

1. Engine ground start switch — PNEU or CARTRIDGE. (As applicable)

   Place the engine ground start switch to PNEU when starting the engines with external starter air or to CARTRIDGE for a cartridge start.

2. Applicable engine throttle—Start position.
   a. On a cartridge start advance the throttle to IDLE after the first indication of rpm.
   b. Hydraulic low pressure caution lamps—Out.

   Check that hydraulic low pressure caution lamps go out below 16.5 percent and before 1100 psi.

WARNING

In the event of aborted start during a cartridge start due to misfire, hangfire or slow burning cartridge, a mandatory 30 minute waiting period must be observed before opening the breech for cartridge removal.

3. Engine throttle—IDLE.

   On a pneumatic start advance the throttle to IDLE after the engine rpm reaches 17 percent. (16.5 percent on P-1 engines)

4. Engine instruments—Check.
   a. Fuel flow—1100 pph max.
   b. TIT indicator—705°C max.
   c. Engine oil pressure—Check for indication.
   d. Idle rpm—54.0 to 62.0 percent.
   e. Idle oil pressure—30 to 50 psi.
   f. Nozzle position—Open.

5. Generator caution lamp—Out.

   The operating generator caution lamp will go out before the engine reaches idle rpm.

6. Power flow indicator—TIE or NORM. (As applicable)

   The power flow indicator will read NORM if a ground power unit is plugged in or TIE if battery was used or if number one engine was started first.

7. Engine overspeed caution lamp—Out.
8. Hydraulic pressure indicators—2950 to 3250 psi.
9. External air conditioning—Disconnected.

CAUTION

If a period of 3 minutes or more will lapse prior to starting the other engine, the engine ground start switch must be positioned to OFF. This will allow the air conditioning system to provide cooling air for the equipment bays and hydraulic fluid thus preventing equipment damage due to overheating. This procedure will also provide cooling air to the crew compartment.

10. Engine starter air—Disconnected. (If applicable)

    If a pneumatic start is being made, disconnect the engine start air source.

11. External power switch—OFF, power unit removed. (If applicable)

    If external power was used for engine start turn the external power switch OFF and remove the ground power unit from the airplane.

12. Remaining engine—Started.

    Repeat steps 1 thru 8. If crossbleed is being used for starting second engine, advance the throttle to 85 percent on the operating engine, until second engine reaches 50 percent, then retard throttle to IDLE.

13. Engine ground start switch—OFF.
    a. After a pneumatic start check that the engine ground start switch returns to OFF.

14. Generator caution lamp—Out, power flow indicator NORM.

    The second generator caution lamp will go out and the power flow indicator will go from TIE to NORM before the engine reaches idle rpm.

15. Oil quantity indicators—16 quarts.
16. Emergency generator switch — TEST, then AUTO.

    Place the emergency generator switch to TEST. The emergency generator indicator lamp will light after 3 seconds indicating that the emergency generator is operating within limits. The power flow indicator should display a crosshatch. Check voltages at 115 (±5) volts and frequency at 400 (±8) cps. Place the emergency generator switch to AUTO. Check that indicator lamp goes out and that the power flow indicator displays NORM.

17. Air source selector knob—L ENG, R ENG then BOTH.

    Increase engine RPM to approximately 75 percent for 30 seconds to 1 minute and check for air conditioning air flow in L ENG and R ENG positions, then place the knob to BOTH.

Note

If battery power was utilized for engine start complete the "power on" checks prior to proceeding to the next checklist.

BEFORE TAXIING.

1. Flight controls—Clear. (AC-GO)
2. Flight control system—Checked. (AC-GO)

Note

During the following checks, the flight control surface position can be verified by the ground observer (GO) or with the control surface position indicator (if installed).

   a. Pitch and roll autopilot/damper and yaw damper switches—OFF.
      Place the pitch and roll autopilot/damper and yaw damper switches to OFF and check that the pitch, roll and yaw damper caution lamps light.
   b. Flight controls—Check for freedom of movement.
   c. Auto TF switch—OFF.
   d. Pitch and roll autopilot/damper and yaw damper switches—DAMPER.
   e. Damper reset button—Momentarily depressed.
      Check that the pitch, roll and yaw damper caution lamps go out.
   f. Cycle the control stick full forward, full aft, then return to neutral and check that the pitch damper and channel caution lamps do not light.
   g. Auxiliary pitch trim switch—Checked and STICK:
      Move the auxiliary pitch trim switch to NOSE DN, NOSE UP, and then to the STICK position. Control surface travel should correspond to switch position.
   h. Control system switch—NORM.

Note

On airplanes ③ ♦ the slats must be retracted to complete steps i through o.

   i. Take off trim—Set, then trim nose down for one second.
   j. Check horizontal stabilizers drive trailing edge down below zero (neutral) position. (GO)
   k. Stability augmentation test switch—SURFACE MOTION and hold until next step is completed.
   l. Flight control master test button—Depress and hold for the following checks:
      (1) Rudder moves to right and then to the left. (GO)
      (2) Left horizontal stabilizer trailing edge moves slightly down. (GO)
      (3) Right horizontal stabilizer trailing edge moves full down. (GO)
      (4) Control system caution lamps do not light.
   m. Stability augmentation test switch—SURFACE MOTION & LIGHTS and hold until next step is completed.
   n. Flight control master test button—Depress and hold for the following checks:
      (1) Rudder initially drives right then returns to neutral. (GO)
      (2) Left horizontal stabilizer trailing edge moves slightly down. (GO)
      (3) Right horizontal stabilizer trailing edge moves full down. (GO)
      (4) Check pitch, roll and yaw damper and channel caution lamps and pitch and roll gain changer caution lamps light (8).
   o. Control system switch—T.O. & LAND.
   p. Damper reset button—Depress momentarily.
   q. All caution lamps (8)—Out.

3. ③ ♦ Translating cowls—Checked. (AC-GO)

Note

During the following check the position of the translating cowls can be verified by the cowl position indicators and by the ground observer if available.

   a. Flight control master test button—Hold depressed and check:
      (1) Cowl caution lamp—On.

b. CADC test switch—Hold to HIGH and check:
   (1) Cowl position indicators—Momentarily crosshatched, then CLOSED.
   (2) Cowl caution lamp—Out, momentarily, then on as airspeed mach indicator reaches mach 1.1.
c. Flight control master test button and CADC test switch—Release.
   (1) Cowl position indicators—Momentarily crosshatched, then OPEN.
   (2) Cowl caution lamp—On, until altitude stabilizes, then out.
d. L and R cowl test switches—HI MACH.
   (1) Cowl warning lamp—On.
   (2) Cowl position indicators—Momentarily, crosshatched, then CLOSED.
e. R cowl test switch—NORM.
   (1) R cowl indicator—Momentarily crosshatched, then OPEN.
   (2) Cowl caution lamp—On.
f. L cowl test switch—NORM.
   (1) L cowl indicator — Momentarily crosshatched, then OPEN.
   (2) Cowl caution lamp—Out.
   (3) Cowl warning lamp—Out.
g. Ground check panel access panel door—Closed

4. Takeoff trim button—Depress and hold until the takeoff trim lamp lights.
5. Wing sweep handle—Set for takeoff. (16 or 26 degrees)
6. Wing sweep handle fixed stores and weapons lockout controls—ON (If applicable)
   If fixed stores or multiple weapon racks are being carried, place the respective lockout control to ON.
7. Flap and slat handle—Set for takeoff.
8. ㉛ ♦ Flight control spoiler monitor test — Checked.
   a. Flight control master test button—Depress and hold.
   b. Spoiler test switch—OUTBD and release. Check:
      (1) Outboard spoilers momentarily extend, then retract. (GO)
      (2) Spoiler caution lamp will light.
   c. Spoiler reset button—Depress.
      Check spoiler lamp out.
   d. Spoiler test switch—INBD and release. Check:
      (1) Inboard spoilers momentarily extend, then retract. (GO)
      (2) Spoiler caution lamp will light.

e. Flight control master test button—Release.
f. Spoiler reset button—Depress.
   Check spoiler caution lamp out.
9. Ground roll spoilers — Checked.
   a. Ground roller spoiler switch—Brake.
      Check all spoilers extend.
   b. Left throttle—3 degrees, then IDLE.
      Check all spoilers retract, then extend.
   c. Right throttle—3 degrees, then IDLE.
      Check all spoiler retract, then extend.
   d. Ground roll spoiler switch—OFF.
      Check all spoilers retract.
10. Heading indicators—Crosschecked. (AC-P)
    All heading information should agree within 3 degrees.
11. TACAN—Checked. (P)
12. Altimeters—Set. (AC-P)
13. EPR—Set.
    Set the EPR indicators using the EPR data cards located in the cockpit.
14. ㉔ ㉖ ♦ ㉚ EPR—Check.
    a. Obtain correct runway temperature.
    b. EPR indicator—Set, to computed value.
       Using the correct runway temperature compute the minimum EPR setting from figure 2-2A.

EPR Check Values

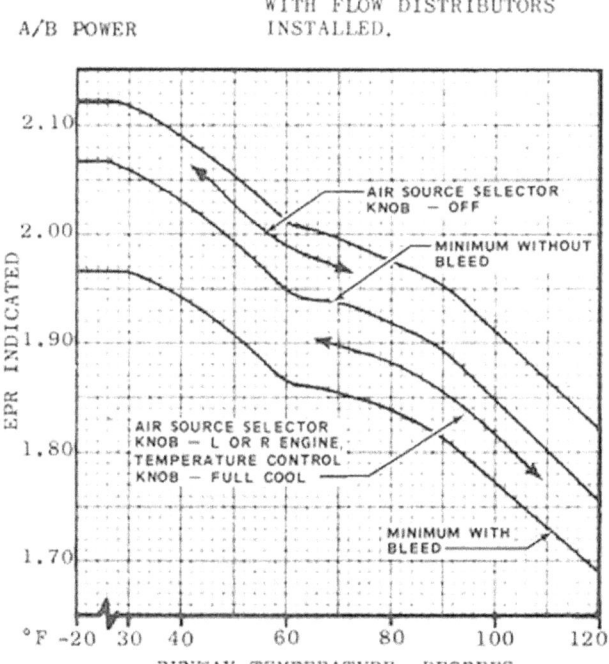

Figure 2-2A.

Section II
Normal Procedures

T.O. 1F-111A-1

    c. Throttles—MAX A/B.
    d. Nozzle position indicators—Full open (position 10).
    e. Air source selector knob—R ENG.
    f. Left engine EPR indicator — Minimum or above.
    g. Air source selector knob—L ENG.
    h. Right engine EPR indicator—Minimum or above.
    i. Air source selector knob—BOTH.
15. Clock—Set. (P)
16. Bomb nav mode selector knob—As required. (P)
17. Magnetic heading synchronization indicator — Nulled. (P)
    Rotate the magnetic variation counter control knob until a null is obtained on the indicator.
18. Attack radar antenna—Uncaged. (P)
19. Weapon bay doors—Closed. (P-GO)
    a. Weapon bay door lockpin—Removed. (GO)
    b. Weapon bay door safety switch—NORMAL. (GO)
    c. Weapon bay door safety panel cover—Closed. (GO)
    d. Weapon bay doors—Clear. (GO)
    e. Weapon bay door switch—CLOSE. (P)
    f. Report weapon bay doors closed. (GO)
20. Autopilot—Checked. (Optional)
    a. Pitch and roll autopilot/damper switches—AUTOPILOT.
    b. Autopilot release lever—Depressed.
        Check that pitch and roll autopilot/damper switches go to the DAMPER position.
    c. Pitch and roll autopilot/damper switches—AUTOPILOT.
    d. Control stick steering—Checked.
        Move control stick and check that reference not engaged caution lamp lights. Lamp will go out when stick is returned to neutral.
    e. Altitude hold and constant track switches—Engaged.
        Reference not engaged caution lamp lights.
    f. Reference engage button—Depressed.
        Reference not engaged caution lamp goes out.
    g. Move stick, then release.
        Reference not engaged caution lamp lights.
    h. Reference engage button—Depressed.
        Reference not engaged caution lamp goes out.
    i. Autopilot release lever—Depressed.
        Check that the roll and pitch autopilot/damper switches go to DAMPER and that the altitude/mach hold and constant track/heading nav selector switches go to OFF.
21. Crew module ejection handle safety pins (2)—Removed and stowed.
22. Crew module chaff dispenser control lever—As required.
23. Air refueling receptacle—Checked. (If required)

Note

If receptacle is open no nose wheel steering is available.

24. Ground crew and pilot report—Ready to taxi. (AC-P-GO)
    The ground crew will report all ground service disconnected and removed from the airplane, slats and flaps configuration, all ground locks removed and in sight, disconnect ground interphone and remove chocks.

TAXIING.

Note

During hot weather, when long taxi distances are required, an appreciable increase in cooling can be achieved, if needed, by advancing one throttle to just below the point of nozzle closure. This can be done without greatly increasing braking requirements.

1. Canopy hatches—As desired. (AC-P)
2. Auxiliary brake handle—In.
3. Nose wheel steering—Engaged.
    Check that the nose wheel steering indicator lamp is on. Check engagement of nose wheel steering by slight movement of rudder pedals.
4. Brakes—Checked.
    At normal taxi speed depress brake pedals and check for proper braking and anti-skid action.

Note

Anti-skid cycling below 20 knots taxi speed denotes a malfunction.

5. Flight instruments—Checked. (AC-P)
    Check the flight instruments for proper operation during taxi.
6. Hydraulic pressure—Checked.
    Check for 2950 to 3250 psi indication.

Changed 18 August 1967

Turning Radius and Ground Clearance

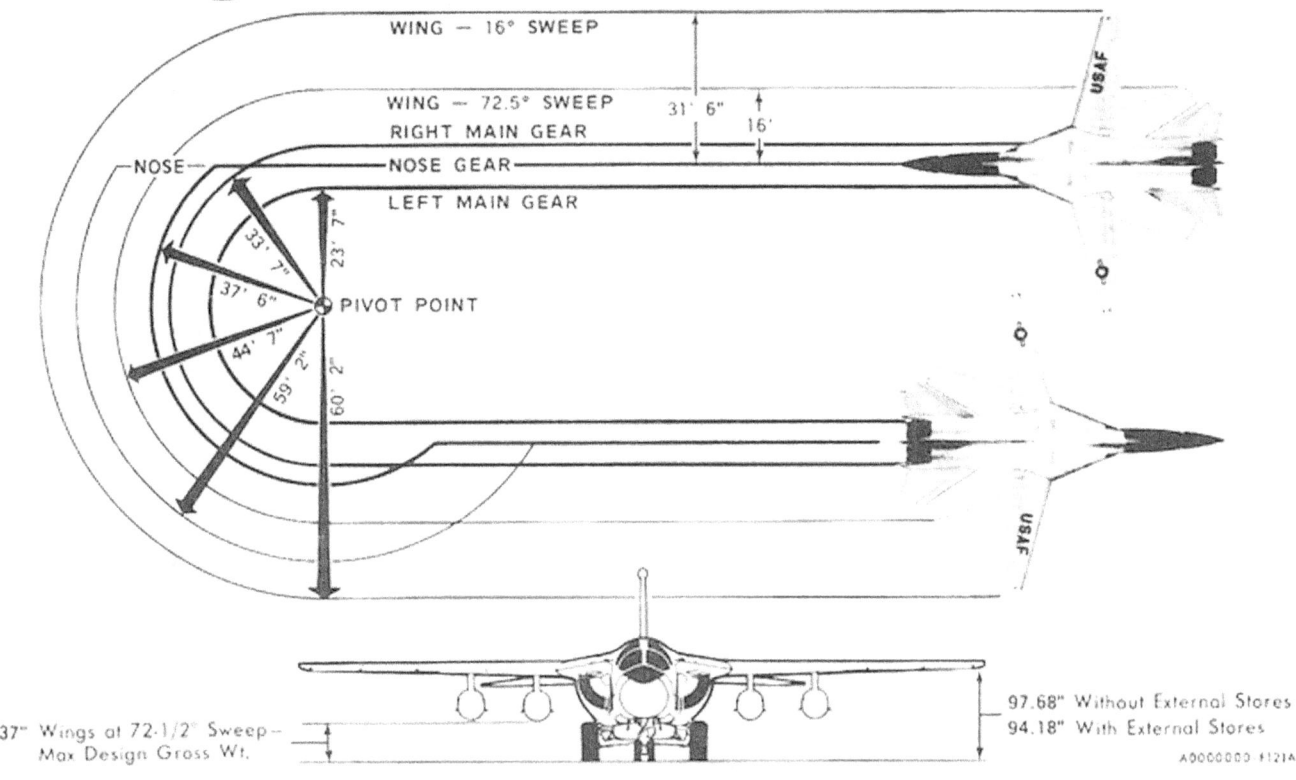

Figure 2-3.

BEFORE TAKEOFF.

1. Canopy hatches—Closed and latched, unlocked warning lamp out. (AC-P)
2. Canopy latch handle lock tab—Flush. (AC-P)
   Snap the spring-loaded latch handle lock tab into the locked (flush) position and pull on the latch handle to check that it is locked.
3. Anti-collision light—ON.
4. Wings, flaps, and slats—Set for takeoff.
   Check the surface position indicator for selected wing, flap, and slat settings.
5. Ground roll spoiler brake switch—BRAKE.
6. Speed brake switch—IN.
7. ⑲ ♦ ㉚ Control system switch—T.O. & LAND.
8. ㉛ ♦ Control system switch—NORM.
9. Takeoff trim—Checked.
   Depress the takeoff trim button and hold until the takeoff trim indicator lamp lights. Release the button and the lamp should go out.
10. Warning and caution lamps—Checked. (AC-P)
    Check that all warning lamps are out and that caution lamps are compatible with mission.
11. Pitot heater (pitot/probe heater ㉛ ♦) and engine/inlet anti-icing switches—Climatic.
12. Fuel quantity and fuel distribution—Checked.
13. ⑲ ♦ ㉚ Translating cowl switches—OPEN.
14. ㉛ ♦ Translating cowl switches—AUTO.
15. IFF master control knob—As required. (P)
16. Takeoff data—Checked. (AC-P)

TAKEOFF.

1. Brakes—Set.
   Do not set the parking brakes with the airplane in motion.
2. Engines—Checked and set for takeoff.
3. Flight instruments—Checked and set for takeoff.
4. Brakes—Release.
5. Go-no-go speed—Checked.

AFTER TAKEOFF.

1. Landing gear handle—UP.
   When the airplane is definitely airborne, retract the landing gear. Check that the landing gear position indicator lights and the warning light in the landing gear handle go out. The landing gear and landing gear doors should be up and locked before reaching 295 KIAS.

Section II
Normal Procedures

Takeoff (Typical)

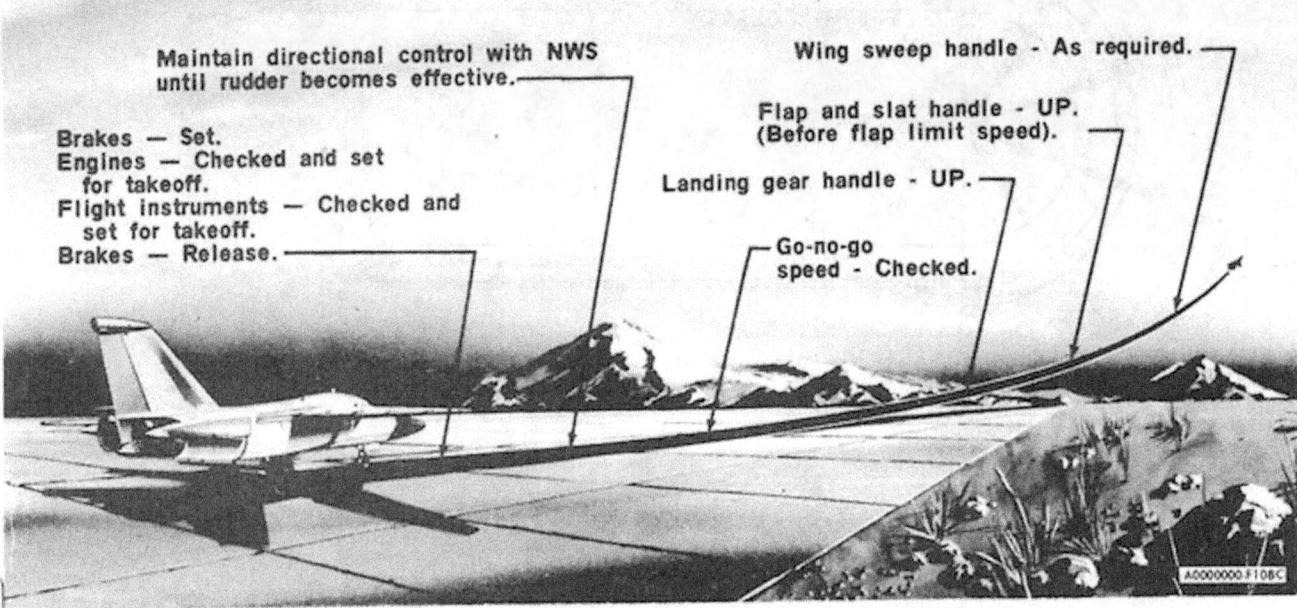

Figure 2-4.

WARNING

If it is necessary to depress the landing gear handle lock release button to move the handle to the UP position, the crew member should suspect a malfunction of the landing gear ground safety switch. In this event the spoilers will remain armed even with the landing gear retracted and the ground roll spoiler switch should be placed to OFF.

Note

The fuel tank pressurization caution lamp will momentarily light when the landing gear handle is moved to the UP position.

2. Flap and slat handle—UP.
   Raise the flaps prior to reaching flap limit speed. Normally the flaps should be raised in two increments.

Note

- On airplanes ❸❶ ♦ a detent position at 15 degrees flaps is provided for selecting this position.

- On airplanes ❸❶ ♦ the rudder authority caution lamp will light momentarily as the slats are retracted.

3. Wing sweep handle—As required.
4. ❶❾ ♦ ❸⓿ Control system switch—NORM.

Note

The rudder authority caution lamp will light momentarily when the control system switch is placed to NORM.

5. Engine instruments—Checked.
6. Fuel quantity indicators—Checked.
   Check the fuel quantity indicators for normal fuel usage.

7. ⑲ ♦ ㉚ Translating cowl switches—CLOSE, at mach 0.45.
   Check cowl caution lamp out above mach 0.50 and indicators show CLOSED.
8. ㉛ ♦ Translating cowls—Check closed at mach 0.50.
9. Altimeters—Reset. (AC-P)

CLIMB.

The recommended climb speed, as shown in Appendix I, should be followed.

CRUISE.

Refer to Appendix I for cruise operating data. Refer to Section I for fuel system operation.

AIR REFUELING.

NORMAL OPERATION.

1. Engine feed selector knob—AUTO or BOTH.
2. Air refueling switch—OPEN.

CAUTION

The air refueling receptacle door will not open if the engine feed selector knob is in any position other than AUTO or BOTH.

3. Air refueling receptacle light control knob—Bright.
4. Nose wheel steering/air refueling indicator lamp—Checked.
   Check that the nose wheel steering/air refueling indicator lamp lights indicating that the refueling receptacle is extended.
5. Tanker aircraft boom—Engaged.
   Check that the nose wheel steering/air refueling indicator lamp goes out indicating that the boom is latched in place.
6. Fuel quantity indicators—Checked.
   Check the fuel quantity indicators to insure that fuel is being transferred.
7. Refueling—Completed.
   Check that the nose wheel steering/air refueling indicator lamp lights when all tanks are full, indicating that the boom has disconnected.
8. Air refueling switch—CLOSE.
   Check that the nose wheel steering/air refueling indicator lamp goes out.
9. Engine feed selector knob—As required.

ALTERNATE OPERATION.

If the automatic latching mechanism fails to latch the boom in place, as indicated by the nose wheel steering/air refueling indicator lamp remaining on after boom engagement, proceed as follows:

1. Air refueling switch — EBL.
2. Tanker aircraft boom — Engaged.
   Check that the nose wheel steering/air refueling indicator lamp goes out indicating that the boom is latched in place.
3. Fuel quantity indicators — Checked.
   Check the fuel quantity indicators to insure that fuel is being transferred.
4. Nose wheel steering/air refueling button — Depressed (at completion of refueling).
   When the tanks are full, depress the nose wheel steering/air refueling button to disengage the refueling boom. Check that the nose wheel steering/air refueling indicator lamp lights indicating boom disconnection.
5. Air refueling switch — CLOSE.
   Check that the nose wheel steering/air refueling indicator lamp goes out.
6. Engine feed selector knob—As required.

FLIGHT CHARACTERISTICS.

Refer to Section VI for flight characteristics.

DESCENT.

1. Pitot heater (pitot/probe heater ㉛ ♦) and engine/inlet anti-icing switches—Climatic.
2. Cabin air distribution control lever — DEFOG. (P)
3. Fuel quantity and fuel panel — Checked.
4. Hydraulic pressure — Checked.
   Check for 2950 to 3250 psi indication.
5. Wing sweep handle — As required.
6. Translating cowls—As required.
   On airplanes ⑲ ♦ ㉚ open the translating cowls for slow speed descents. On airplanes ㉛ ♦ check that the cowls open below mach 0.44.
7. Altimeter—Set. (AC-P)

BEFORE LANDING.

WARNING

To prevent engine compressor stall and subsequent loss of power during the critical phases of landing, or in event of a go-around, the translating cowls must be open.

1. ⑲ ⬥ ㉚ Translating cowl switches—OPEN.
   Position both cowl switches to OPEN at mach 0.44 and check that indicators show OPEN.
2. ㉛ ⬥ Translating cowls—Check open.
   Check that the translating cowls open below mach 0.44.
3. Wing sweep handle—Set for landing. (16 or 26 degrees)
4. Antiskid switch—ON.
5. Hydraulic pressure—Checked.
   Check for 2950 to 3250 psi indication.
6. ⑲ ⬥ ㉚ Control system switch—T.O. & LAND.
   When below 300 KIAS, place the control system switch to T.O. & LAND. The rudder authority caution lamp will light momentarily when this switch position is selected.
7. Fuel quantity and feed—Checked.
8. Landing data—Checked. (AC-P)
9. Speed brake switch—As required.
10. Flap and slat handle—Set 15 degrees.
    When below 297 KIAS, extend flaps to 15 degrees.

Note

On airplanes ㉛ ⬥ the rudder authority caution lamp may light momentarily while slats are in transit.

11. Landing gear handle—DN.
    Extend the landing gear after airspeed is below 295 KIAS. Check that warning light in landing gear handle is out and landing gear position indicators lights are lighted. The pitch and roll gain changer lamps will light until the slats are extended.

CAUTION

At speeds above 250 KIAS the nose gear may not lock in the down position. Should this occur, decelerate to below 250 KIAS and check for nose gear down and locked indication. If a down and locked indication is not obtained, recycle the landing gear up and down.

Note

On airplanes ㉛ ⬥ the pitch and roll gain changer caution lamps will light.

12. Flap and slat handle—FLAP DOWN.
    When below 225 KIAS, position handle to FLAP DOWN and check flap and slat position indicator to assure that surfaces have moved to the selected position.
13. Translating cowl caution and warning lamps—Out.

LANDING.

Note

See figure 2-5 for normal landing pattern and airspeeds.

1. Touchdown — As computed.
2. Throttles — IDLE.
3. Nose wheel — Lower to runway.
4. Brakes — As required.
5. Nose wheel steering — Engaged.

LANDING ON SLIPPERY RUNWAYS AND/OR MINIMUM RUN LANDINGS.

Note

Based on preliminary test data, the landing roll on wet runways may be at least 50 percent greater than for dry runways.

The technique for a wet runway landing is essentially the same as for a normal landing. Particular attention should be paid to maintaining final approach speed and touching down as close to the end of the runway as safety permits. The ground roll spoiler switch should be positioned to BRAKE prior to landing. As with the normal landing technique, power should be reduced to IDLE immediately upon touchdown. If maximum deceleration is desired, maximum antiskid braking should be initiated immediately upon touchdown and held throughout the ground roll. For this purpose, any amount of excess pedal displacement is satisfactory, up to and including full deflection. Full aft stick should

Landing Pattern (Typical)

BASED ON LANDING GROSS WEIGHT OF 50,000 POUNDS.

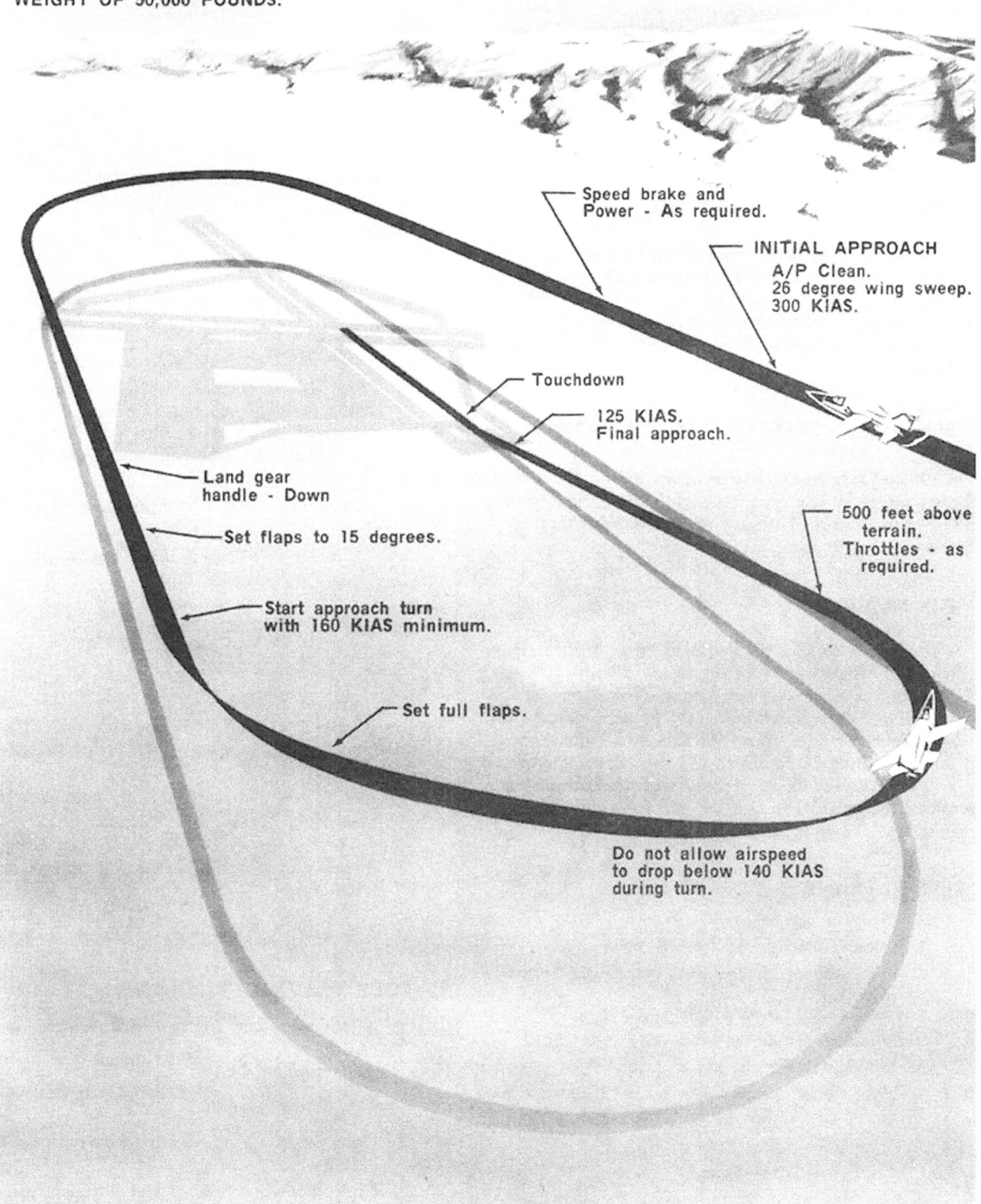

Figure 2-5.

Section II
Normal Procedures

be applied at approximately 90 KIAS and held throughout the remainder of the ground roll. Full aft stick at this speed should not lift the nose gear from the runway, under normal landing gross weight and cg configurations. Full aft stick provides additional aerodynamic drag and transfers aircraft weight to the main gear to provide maximum wheel braking potential. Be prepared to lower the arresting hook to engage the runway barrier if the airplane cannot be stopped prior to reaching the end of the runway. Refer to Appendix I for landing data.

TOUCH AND GO LANDING.

Prior to accomplishing a touch and go landing, perform the normal before landing cockpit check. After touchdown, smoothly advance the throttles to MIL or A/B power as required and check engine instruments for normal indication. When airborne, proceed with the normal after takeoff-climb checklist if required.

SIMULATED SINGLE ENGINE LANDING.

Simulated single engine landing should be flown with one engine at idle rpm, following the "Landing and Go-around with One Engine Out" procedure, Section III.

GO-AROUND.

The decision to go around should be made as early as possible. When the decision to go around is made, smoothly advance the throttles and continue the approach because a touchdown may be necessary. As the airplane accelerates, rotate the nose to a climbing attitude and when the altimeter and vertical velocity show a definite rate-of-climb proceed with the normal after takeoff checklist. Fly clear of the runway as soon as practicable. (See figure 2-6.)

AFTER LANDING.

1. Ground roll spoiler switch—OFF.
2. Flap and slat handle—As required (Normally extended).
   On airplanes ③①, if slats are retracted, place control system switch to T.O. & LAND.
3. IFF master control knob—OFF. (P)
4. Pitot heater (pitot/probe heater ③①) and engine/inlet anti-icing switches—OFF.

Note

If the aircraft is taxied with wings swept full aft at light gross weights, excessive nose strut bottoming will occur.

ENGINE SHUTDOWN.

CAUTION

To prevent possible damage to the brakes from overheating, do not pull the auxiliary brake handle.

1. Wheels—Chocked.
2. Wing sweep handle—As required.
3. Flap and slat handle—As required.
4. Weapon bay doors—Clear. (GO)
5. Weapon bay door switch—OPEN. (As required) (P)
6. Report weapon bay doors—Open. (GO)
7. Bomb nav mode selector knob—OFF. (P)
8. Attack radar function selector knob—OFF. (P)
9. Throttles—75 percent, for 15 to 20 seconds.
   Run the engines up to 75 percent for 15 to 20 seconds prior to shutdown to scavenge oil accumulated in the bearing compartments.
10. Applicable throttle—OFF.
    Place throttle of first engine started to OFF.
11. Hydraulic pressure—Checked.
    Check for 2950 to 3250 psi indication.
12. Remaining throttle—OFF.

CAUTION

To prevent possible engine damage due to overtemperature, do not attempt to restart the engine for at least five minutes after shutdown.

13. Emergency generator—Checked.
    The emergency generator indicator lamp will light momentarily as the last engine driven generator disconnects from the ac buses. The lamp will go out when hydraulic pressure driving the emergency generator is depleted.

BEFORE LEAVING AIRPLANE.

1. All switches and controls—Off, normal or safe. (AC-P)
   Starting on the left side of the crew compartment, position all switches and controls off, normal or safe.
2. Crew module ejection handle safety pins (2)—Installed.
3. Crew module severance and flotation, recovery parachute release, auxiliary flotation and canopy internal emergency release handle safety pins (3)—Installed.

Go-Around (Typical)

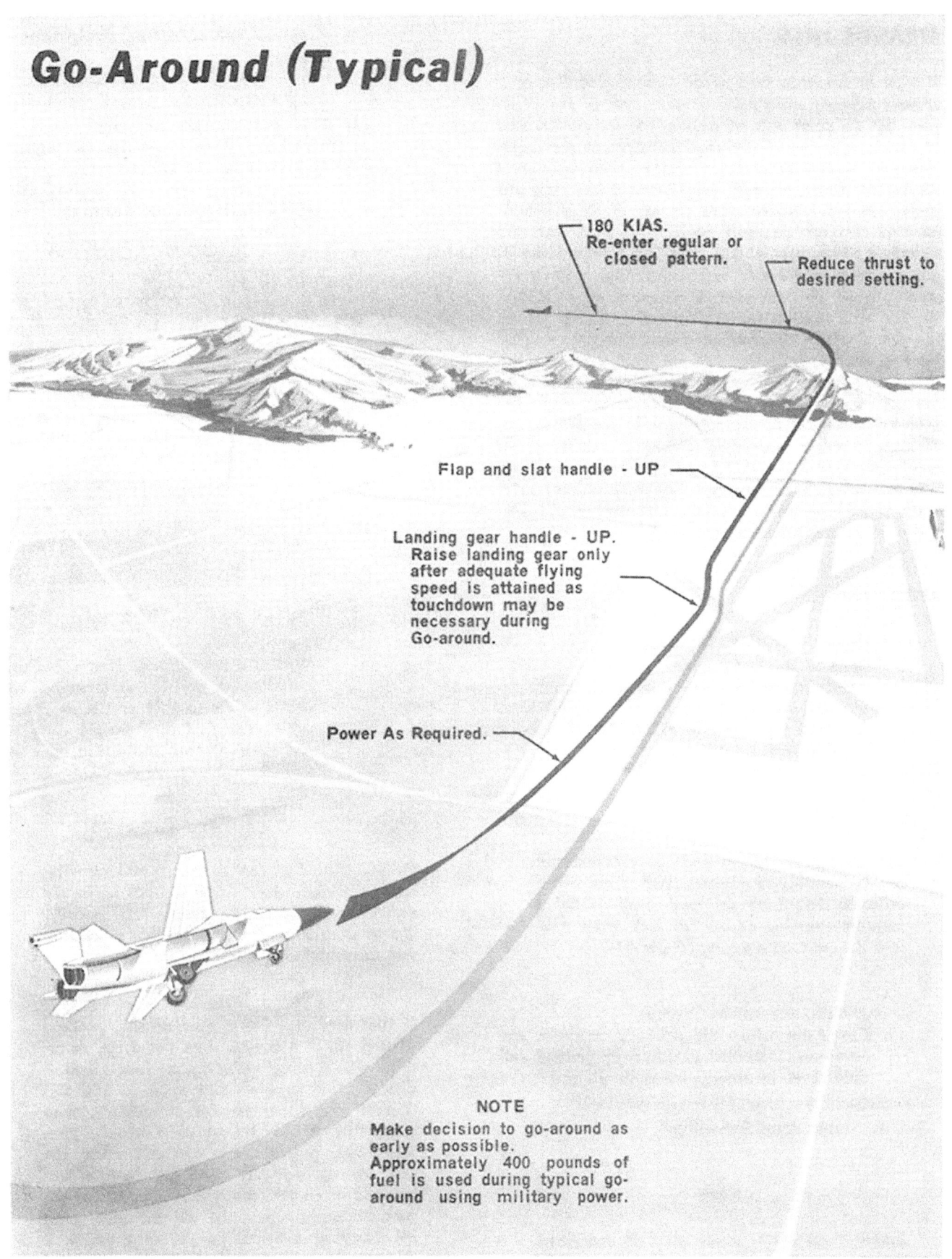

Figure 2-6.

Section II
Normal Procedures

T.O. 1F-111A-1

STRANGE FIELD.

If it is necessary to land at an airfield where normal ground support equipment or personnel is not available, the air crew will be responsible for performing or closely supervising the required airplane servicing. There are several items which must be performed after engine shutdown, and additional items of servicing and inspection are required prior to takeoff. It is recommended that the air crew become familiar with the servicing procedures for all items listed on the Servicing Diagram, Section I. Engine starting is normally accomplished with gas turbine generator set A/M32A-60. The unit supplies engine starting air and ac power for the airplane electrical systems. Alternate engine starting equipment consists of an MA-1A gas turbine as a source of air pressure with MD-3A, or MD-4, or the airplane battery as a source of electrical power for ignition. Electrical power requirement for ground refueling, if power is deemed necessary consists of an A/M32A-60, or either MD-3A or MD-4 as a substitute. The following check list supplements the normal operating procedures and includes items that would normally be accomplished by the ground crew.

AFTER LANDING.

1. Ground safety pins—Installed.
2. Engine oil level—Checked.
   Check oil level indication on dipstick and determine quantity required to bring oil level to the 20 quart level or FULL MARK. Service with oil MIL-L-7808.

Note

The engine oil system must be checked and serviced within 15 minutes after shutdown in order to determine accurate consumption as variable amounts of oil can leak from tank into the gearbox over longer periods.

3. Hydraulic reservoirs—Checked.
   Check the utility and primary hydraulic reservoirs for specified accumulator preload and fluid level in accordance with placard.
4. Refueling—Accomplish. (As required)
   a. Single Point Refueling.

Note

External electrical power may be connected during refueling if desired for monitoring instruments; otherwise, external power is not necessary.

(1) Airplane and refueling equipment—Grounded.
   Insure that the airplane and all refueling equipment are statically grounded.
(2) Nose gear chocks—Removed.
   Remove all work stands and equipment under the aircraft which might cause damage when the landing gear shock struts compress due to increased fuel load.
(3) Precheck selector valves—REFUEL.
(4) Position lights/stores refuel battery power switch—STORES REFUEL.
   If external tanks are installed, place the position lights/stores refuel battery power switch to STORES REFUEL.
(5) Fueling hose ground cable—Connected.
   Connect the grounding cable from the fueling hose to the airplane.
(6) Ground refueling receptacle cap—Removed.
(7) Fuel nozzle—Connected to refueling receptacle.
(8) Start fuel servicing unit and open fuel nozzle.
(9) Precheck selector valves—PRI or CK. (As applicable)
   Within a few seconds after fuel flow is indicated, position all precheck selector valves to PRI or CK as applicable. The fuel flow should drop to less than 10 gpm indicating that all primary valves have closed.

CAUTION

Do not allow fuel flow to the aft tank or wing tanks for more than a few seconds when the forward tank quantity is below 7500 pounds. To do so may cause a longitudinal unbalance and cause the airplane to tip up.

Note

If fuel flow drops to 5 gpm or less, proceed to step 10. If fuel flow does not drop, determine which refuel valve has malfunctioned as follows. Select the aft tank valve to SEC and observe the flowmeter for 30 seconds, then select PRI. If flow did not drop below 5 gpm when SEC position was selected, repeat the test for the forward tank. If flow is not stopped when SEC position is selected for the forward tank, repeat the test for each wing by changing positions for the wing precheck selector valve located on the lower surface of each wing. The defective valve will be indicated by a drop of flow.

Changed 18 August 1967

(10) Fuselage tank precheck selector valves—REFUEL then SEC.

Individually rotate the fuselage tank precheck selector valves to REFUEL and then to SEC while observing the flowmeter. Flow should rise at least 100 gpm while in the REFUEL position, indicating that the selected refuel valve has opened. The valve should then close when the SEC position is selected.

(11) Precheck selector valves—REFUEL. Continue refueling operations.

(12) Tank pressure gage—Monitor.

If pressure exceeds 3 psi, discontinue refueling operation and determine the cause. The tanks should be depressurized and air should flow from the vent during fueling.

Note

Fuel tanks are full and valves are closed when the flowmeter on the fuel truck falls to zero.

(13) Fuel nozzle—Closed.

At completion of refueling, close the fuel nozzle and stop the refueling truck pump.

(14) Fuel nozzle and grounding cable—Disconnected.

(15) Refueling receptacle cap—Installed.

(16) Single point refueling control access doors—Closed and latched.

(17) Position lights/stores refuel battery power switch—NORM (If external tanks were fueled).

Note

Failure to return position lights/stores refuel battery power switch to NORM will produce drain on the battery when external electrical power is not connected.

b. Gravity Refueling.
   (1) Connect external power.

Note

External power is not required; however, a full reservoir tank will not be assured until after engine start unless engine feed is selected and fuel pumps operated for approximately 2 minutes with the forward tank at 4000 pounds or more.

(2) Airplane and refueling equipment—Grounded.

Insure that the airplane and all refueling equipment are statically grounded.

(3) Nose gear chocks—Removed.

Remove all work stands and equipment under the aircraft which might cause damage when the landing gear shock struts compress due to the increased fuel load.

(4) Fuel Tank Pressurization.

If tanks are pressurized, place the tank pressurization switch to AUTO to relieve pressure.

CAUTION

The vent tank is within the vertical stabilizer and extends near the top; therefore, if fuel has entered the vent tank a head pressure will exist. Extreme care must be exercised when removing the gravity refuel caps from any fuel tank. Loosen the cap slightly watching for signs of fuel flow prior to removing the cap.

(5) If the forward tank quantity is 4000 pounds or greater, place forward tank selection switch to ENG FEED and allow fuel pumps to operate for approximately 2 minutes to assure a full reservoir tank.

(6) Bay F-1 and F-2—Refueled.

Note

● Remove filler cap from bay F-1 and then bay F-2. If fuel seeps out as bay F-2 filler cap is loosened, do not continue removing cap as bay F-2 is full. Fill bay F-1 only. Otherwise, fill bay F-2 and then bay F-1.

● If forward tank initially had less than 4000 pounds, perform step 4 after the forward tank has been filled above 4000 pounds, and then continue filling.

(7) Gravity refuel the remaining tanks in the following order:
   (a) Bay A-1
   (b) Bay A-2
   (c) Wing Tanks

Note

If a partial fuel load is required, the forward tank should contain 8200 pounds more fuel than the aft tank. Any fuel added to the wings shall be distributed equally between the wing tanks.

(8) Fuel Filler Caps—Secure.

POSTFLIGHT.

1. Exterior inspection—Complete.
   Follow route shown in figure 2-1. Make necessary entries in the Form 781.

Note

While performing the strange field postflight, and preflight, exterior inspections check for the following:

- Cuts, scratches, loose rivets and fuel leaks.
- All drain plugs for leakage.
- That all access doors and panels are secure.
- Reservoirs and accumulators for proper servicing. Refer to figure 2-7.
- Ground area around airplane for cleanliness.

Airplane is now ready for relaunch; however, if flight is terminated or takeoff substantially delayed, accomplish the following:

   a. Canopies—Closed.
   b. Ground locks—Installed. (If available)
   c. Pitot cover—Installed. (If available)

DELAYED TAKEOFF.

If takeoff has been delayed for an extended time (over 12 hours), a normal exterior preflight should be accomplished following route shown in figure 2-1. The following systems should be checked and serviced as required. Upon completion, follow normal procedures Section II. Complete required Form 781 entries prior to takeoff.

1. Preflight and Form 781—Completed.
2. Liquid oxygen—Checked.
   Service with liquid oxygen MIL-O-27210, Grade A, Type II.
3. Pneumatic pressure—Checked.
   The following accumulators or reservoir pneumatic pressures should be checked for required pressure range specified for the ambient temperature. Service with Air: MIL-P-5518 or Nitrogen: FS BB-N-411, Type I, Grade B.

Pneumatic Servicing Requirements Table

System or Component	Pressure (PSIG) (At 70°F, 21°C)
Landing gear pneumatic reservoir	3000
Alternate trapeze system (2)	3000
Alternate spike (air inlet) control (2)	3000
Primary/utility hydraulic accumulator	500
Primary and utility damper servos	1400
Wheel brake accumulators (2)	800
Horizontal stabilizer accumulators, utility (2)	1400
Horizontal stabilizer accumulators, primary (2)	1400
Overwing fairing	1800
Canopy Counterpoise (2)	860 (Hatch Open) 1063 (Hatch Closed)

Figure 2-7.

4. Constant speed drive—Checked.
   Check outboard sight gage on both left and right drive units. If oil is in the green band, no servicing is required. If servicing is required, proceed as follows. Service with oil MIL-L-7808.
   a. Refill very slowly until oil level reaches the bottom of the green band. Shut off oil supply to avoid overfilling, and allow oil level to equalize. As much as 5 minutes may be required.
   b. Repeat preceding step until oil level is stabilized in the green band.
5. Utility and primary hydraulic reservoirs—Checked.
   Check the utility and primary hydraulic reservoirs for specified accumulator preload and fluid level in accordance with instruction placard. If servicing is required, proceed as follows. Service with oil: MIL-H-5606.
   a. Check the hydraulic reservoir pneumatic pressurization system for proper service.
   b. Position aircraft hydraulic hand pump selector valve to BRAKE and pump brake accumulators to 3100 psi pressure prior to servicing the utility reservoir.

c. Fill reservoir slowly until quantity gage indicates proper fluid level as shown on reservoir service placard.

d. Open reservoir air bleed valve (lower aft end of reservoir) sufficiently to bleed trapped air from the reservoir fluid chamber.

e. Check the reservoir quantity indicator for proper fluid level.

f. Repeat steps 4 through 5 until the reservoir is fully serviced and free of air.

6. Landing gear shock struts—Checked.

   Check nose landing gear shock strut and main landing gear shock struts inflated in accordance with strut instruction placard. Service with Air: MIL-P-5518 or Nitrogen: FS BB-N-411, Type I, Grade B.

7. Tires—Checked.

   a. Main landing gear tires—140 ±10 psi.

   b. Nose landing gear tire—170 ±10 psi.

This is the last page of Section II.

This page intentionally left blank.

T.O. 1F-111A-1

Section III
Emergency Procedures

SECTION III

EMERGENCY PROCEDURES

TABLE OF CONTENTS.

	Page
GROUND OPERATION EMERGENCIES	3-2
Engine Fire During Start	3-2
Wheel Brake System Emergency Operation	3-2
Emergency Entrance	3-2
Abandoning the Airplane on the Ground	3-2
TAKEOFF EMERGENCIES	3-3
Abort	3-3
Engine Failure During Takeoff	3-3
Engine Fire During Takeoff	3-3
Afterburner Failure During Takeoff	3-3
Tire Failure During Takeoff	3-3
INFLIGHT EMERGENCIES	3-3
Caution Lamp Analysis	3-3
Emergency Wing Sweep Operation	3-3
Engine Failure During Flight	3-4
Airstart	3-4
Compressor Stall	3-5
Engine Fire During Flight	3-5
Smoke and Fume Elimination	3-5
Unlocked Canopy Indication	3-6
Glass Panel Failure	3-6
Ejection	3-6

	Page
Left Canopy Removal	3-8
Hydraulic System Failure	3-8
Flight Control System Malfunctions	3-9
Generator Failures	3-10
Emergency Generator Operation With One Engine Shutdown	3-10
Fuel System Emergency Operations	3-10
Oil System Malfunctions	3-12
Spike System Failure	3-12
Air Conditioning and Pressurization System Failure	3-12
LANDING EMERGENCIES	3-12A
Landing With Primary or Utility Hydraulic System Failure	3-12A
Landing Gear Emergency Operations	3-12A
Landing With Blown Tire	3-14
Emergency Extension of Flaps and Slats	3-14
Landing and Go-Around with One Engine Out	3-14
Translating Cowl Malfunctions	3-14
Landing With Wings at 26 Degrees Sweep or Greater and No Flaps	3-15
Emergency Landing Airspeeds and Ground Roll Distances	3-16
Emergency Entrance	3-21

This section contains procedures to be followed to correct an emergency condition. These procedures will insure maximum safety for the crew and/or aircraft until a safe landing or other appropriate action is accomplished. Multiple emergencies, adverse weather, and other peculiar conditions may require modification of these procedures. The CRITICAL items (ALL CAPITAL BOLD FACE LETTERS) contained in the various emergency procedures are those steps which must be performed immediately without reference to written checklists. These critical steps shall be committed to memory. All other steps, wherein there is time available to consult a checklist, are considered NON-CRITICAL. The nature and severity of the encountered emergency will dictate the necessity for complying with all or part of the steps in a particular procedure. It is essential, therefore, that aircrews determine the correct course of action by use of sound judgment. As soon as possible, the aircraft commander should notify the pilot and flight leader of any existing

Changed 18 August 1967

Section III
Emergency Procedures

emergency and of the intended action. When an emergency occurs, three basic rules are established which apply to airborne emergencies. They should be thoroughly understood by all aircrews.

1. Maintain aircraft control.
2. Analyze the situation and take proper action.
3. Land as soon as practicable.

Note

The canopy hatches should remain closed during all emergencies that could result in a crash or fire such as crash landings, aborted takeoffs, and barrier engagements. The protection the canopies afford the crew during these emergencies far outweighs the isolated risk of entrapment due to a canopy malfunction or overturn.

GROUND OPERATION EMERGENCIES

ENGINE FIRE DURING START.

1. THROTTLE(S)—OFF.
2. Engine start switch—Activate for 20 seconds (if external air is available).

If Fire Persists:

3. Fire push button—Depress.
   Depress the fire pushbutton for affected engine.
4. Agent discharge/fire detect test switch—AGENT DISCH.

WARNING

The fire extinguishing agent is available for one engine only. Selection of the engine to which the agent is to be directed is made by depressing the appropriate fire pushbutton.

5. All switches—OFF.
   If time and conditions permit, turn all switches off.
6. Abandon the airplane.

WHEEL BRAKE SYSTEM EMERGENCY OPERATION.

In the event of utility hydraulic system failure, normal braking technique should be used until no longer effective. If airplane is not stopped, pull the auxiliary brake handle.

CAUTION

With the auxiliary brake handle pulled, the brakes are locked.

EMERGENCY ENTRANCE.

Emergency entrances are shown in Figure 3-6.

WARNING

With the hatches closed and locked from the inside, the hatches can not be opened with the normal exterior canopy latch handle.

ABANDONING THE AIRPLANE ON THE GROUND.

In an emergency requiring ground abandonment, the primary concern should be to leave the immediate area of the aircraft as soon as possible. Salvaging emergency and survival equipment should not be considered. To abandon the aircraft, disconnect personal leads and harness and open canopy hatches by the normal method if possible; if not possible, make sure the canopy latch handle is returned to the closed and latched position, then pull the canopy internal emergency release handle. If time and conditions permit, extend the entrance ladder for use in leaving the aircraft.

WARNING

- Do not actuate the canopy internal emergency release handle unless both canopy hatches are closed and latched. To do so could result in fatal injury from debris flying from the canopy sill.

- The upper and lower restraint harness should remain fastened and the inertia reel locked until the airplane is stopped.

Changed 7 April 1967

TAKEOFF EMERGENCIES

During all takeoff emergencies when takeoff is aborted, the canopy will not be jettisoned.

ABORT.

1. THROTTLE(S)—IDLE (OFF FOR FIRE).
2. EXTERNAL LOAD—JETTISON (IF NECESSARY).
3. ARRESTING HOOK—EXTEND (IF REQUIRED).
4. Shoulder harness—Locked.

ENGINE FAILURE DURING TAKEOFF.

If Decision Is Made To Stop:

1. ABORT.
   Refer to "Abort" procedures, this section.

If Takeoff Is Continued:

1. THROTTLE—MAXIMUM (NORMAL OPERATING ENGINE).
2. EXTERNAL LOAD—JETTISON (IF NECESSARY).
3. Landing gear handle—UP (when airborne).
4. Flap and slat handle—As required.
5. Throttle of failed engine—OFF.
6. Attempt airstart if failure was non-mechanical and engine appears normal.
7. Fuel—Dump. (As required).
8. Land as soon as possible.

ENGINE FIRE DURING TAKEOFF.

If Decision Is Made To Stop:

1. ABORT.
   Refer to "Abort" procedure, this section.

If Takeoff Is Continued:

1. THROTTLE—MAXIMUM (NORMAL OPERATING ENGINE).
2. THROTTLE—OFF (ENGINE INDICATING FIRE).
3. EXTERNAL LOAD—JETTISON (IF NECESSARY).
4. FIRE PUSHBUTTON—DEPRESS.
5. AGENT DISCHARGE/FIRE DETECT TEST SWITCH—AGENT DISCH.
6. IF FIRE CONTINUES—EJECT.
7. Landing gear handle—UP (When airborne).
8. Flap and slat handle—As required.
9. If fire goes out—Land as soon as possible.

AFTERBURNER FAILURE DURING TAKEOFF.

If an afterburner fails during takeoff, the resulting loss of power is significant. Takeoff need not be aborted if takeoff speed and distance are compatible with computed takeoff minimums.

TIRE FAILURE DURING TAKEOFF.

If Decision Is Made To Stop:

1. ABORT.
   Refer to "Abort" procedures, this section.
2. ANTI-SKID—OFF.
3. Brakes—Applied as necessary.

If Takeoff Is Continued:

1. EXTERNAL LOAD—JETTISON (IF NECESSARY).
2. DO NOT RETRACT GEAR.

Note

If it can be determined that the blown tire has been torn from the wheel, the gear may be retracted, depending upon mission urgency.

3. Instruments—Check.
   Monitor hydraulic pressures and fuel quantities.
4. Dump fuel as necessary and land as soon as possible.

INFLIGHT EMERGENCIES

CAUTION LAMP ANALYSIS.

See Figure 3-4 for analysis and suggested corrective action to be taken whenever a caution lamp is lighted.

EMERGENCY WING SWEEP OPERATION.

The necessity for emergency wing sweep operation may arise from either of two conditions; one engine

Section III
Emergency Procedures

T.O. 1F-111A-1

inoperative, or one hydraulic system inoperative. In either condition, normal wing sweep commands can result in a severe drop in available hydraulic pressure thus degrading flight control response. While sweeping the wings under the above conditions, maintain as high an rpm on the engine(s) as practicable, and maintain 1 g straight and level flight. When operating with one engine out, if the operating engine rpm is allowed to drop below 90 percent and the windmilling engine is below 40 percent rpm, it will be necessary to sweep the wings by moving the wing sweep handle at a smooth rate not to exceed 1 degree of sweep per second.

If Supersonic:

1. Wing sweep handle—50 degrees.

    If an engine failure or hydraulic system failure occurs at supersonic speed, sweep the wings to 45 degrees as soon as practicable, while still supersonic. Refer to "Primary or Utility Hydraulic System Failure", this section.

Subsonic:

1. Wing sweep handle—26 degrees.

    When subsonic, sweep the wings to 26 degrees while maintaining straight and level 1 g flight.

ENGINE FAILURE DURING FLIGHT.

SINGLE ENGINE FAILURE.

Nonmechanical Failure.

1. Attempt airstart.

    If the engine failure is attributed to something other than a mechanical failure, an airstart may be attempted. Follow "Airstart" procedures, this section.

Mechanical Failure.

1. Throttle of affected engine—OFF.
2. Translating cowl on good engine—Open.
3. Land as soon as possible.

DOUBLE ENGINE FAILURE.

WARNING

Should a double engine failure occur and an airstart of at least one engine cannot be effected, the flight control system will become inoperative when hydraulic pressure is lost and flight cannot be continued.

1. **EJECT.**

AIRSTART.

See figure 3-1 for Airstart Envelope.

Note

The engine is equipped with auto ignition and will normally restart automatically. If the engine has flamed out because of other problems such as fuel starvation, the following procedure is recommended for airstarting.

1. **FUEL PANEL—CHECKED.**
    Check fuel feed selection and fuel quantities to assure that fuel is available to the engine.
2. Throttle of affected engine—OFF.
3. Airstart ignition button—Depress momentarily.
4. Throttle of affected engine—IDLE.
    Check for relight.
5. Generator switch of affected engine—OFF, then ON. (if necessary)
    If the generator caution lamp remains on place the generator switch to OFF, then ON and check that the lamp goes out and the power flow indicator indicates NORM.

If airstart has not been accomplished by the time engine rpm is below 16 percent:

6. Throttle of affected engine—OFF.
7. Engine ground start switch—PNEU.
8. Throttle of affected engine—Start position.
9. Throttle of affected engine (at 17 percent)—IDLE.
    Check for relight.
10. Generator switch of affected engine—OFF, then ON. (if necessary)
    If the generator caution lamp remains on place the generator switch to OFF, then ON and check that the lamp goes out and the power flow indicator indicates NORM.

Changed 18 August 1967

Airstart Envelope

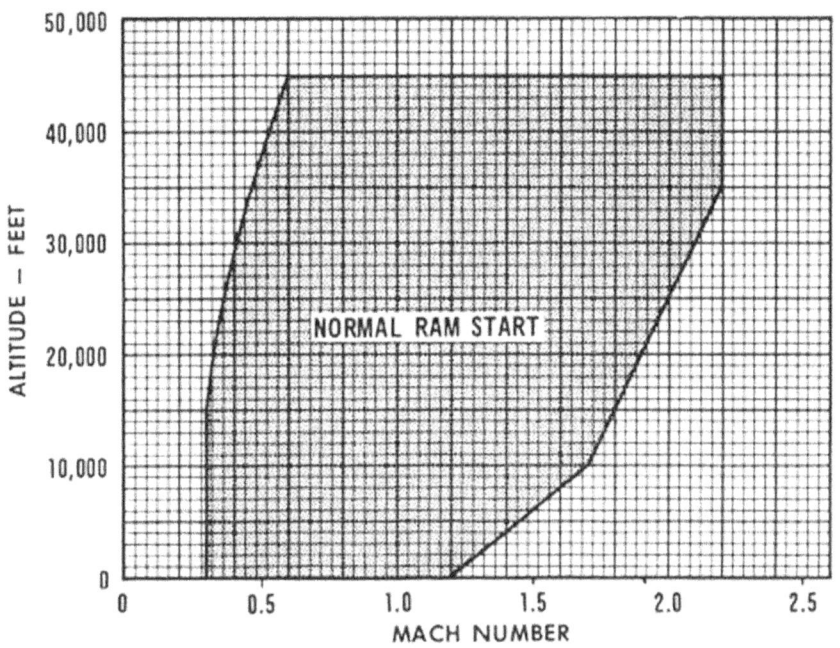

Figure 3-1.

This page intentionally left blank.

COMPRESSOR STALL.

A compressor stall is an aerodynamic disruption of the airflow through the compressor and is caused by subjecting the compressor to a pressure ratio above its capabilities at the existing conditions. Compressor stalls may be induced by engine or inlet control malfunction, excessive angle of attack or yaw causing poor inlet air distribution, or rapid throttle reversal (high power to low power and return). Compressor stalls may be self clearing, may cause flameout, or may result in a steady state fully developed stall. In the first case no immediate action is required. In some cases the engine will stall and immediately recover with only an evidence of a stall being a light to moderate "bang". In the second case the automatic restart circuit in the engine will furnish ignition and the engine may be recovered by moving the throttle to idle to gain a restart and then reapplying power. The third case requires recognition and corrective action to restore power and prevent damage to the engine from over temperature. A compressor stall may be recognized by a pulsation felt through the airframe, an audible noise which may vary from a faint muffled thud to a very loud "bang", a loss of thrust indicated on the engine instruments, no EPR response to throttle movement and as a general rule a rise in turbine inlet temperature. In the event of compressor stall on one or both engines proceed as follows:

1. Throttle of affected engine(s)—IDLE.
   Move the throttle of the affected engine to IDLE and check for recovery. If the engine recovers, attempt gradual application of power. If supersonic, advance throttle to MIL or above.

If Stall Does Not Immediately Clear:

2. Decelerate to below mach 0.9 or 417 KIAS.
   Decelerate to below the translating cowl open limit speed.
3. Translating cowl switch(es)—OPEN.
4. When engine recovers, set power as desired.

Note

In the event that a compressor stall and/or afterburner blowout occurs in afterburner operation, but a fully stalled engine condition does not follow, an afterburner relight from military power may be attempted immediately at any flight condition.

ENGINE FIRE DURING FLIGHT.

1. **THROTTLE—OFF (ENGINE INDICATING FIRE).**
2. **FIRE PUSHBUTTON OF AFFECTED ENGINE—DEPRESS.**
3. **AGENT DISCHARGE—ACTUATE.**
4. **IF FIRE CONTINUES—EJECT.**
5. If fire ceases—Land as soon as possible.

CAUTION

Do not attempt to restart the failed engine. If the fire ceases, and a landing is to be accomplished, make a single engine landing.

SMOKE AND FUME ELIMINATION.

1. Oxygen mask and fittings—Checked.
   Check oxygen mask and oxygen hose fittings for security.
2. Air source selector knob—L. ENG, R. ENG.

Note

Attempt to determine if the engines are the source of smoke by selecting L. ENG and R. ENG positions. If source of smoke cannot be isolated to an engine, proceed as follows:

3. Air source selector knob—OFF.
4. Airspeed and altitude—As required.
   Descend to between 25,000 and 15,000 feet and/or decelerate to between 1.0 and 0.5 mach depending on altitude and airspeed, and refer to "Ram Air Mode Limits," Section V.

Attempt to isolate source of smoke or fumes as follows:

5. Electrical equipment—OFF.
   Turn off all electrical equipment not considered essential for flight.
6. Electrical equipment—ON, as required.
   Turn on electrical equipment, one system at a time, and check for smoke until source is determined.

Section III
Emergency Procedures

7. Air source selector knob—RAM. (if smoke or fumes persist).

WARNING

To prevent excessive temperatures when pressure suits are being worn, the air conditioning system mode selector switch must not be placed to the OFF position prior to or while operating in the Ram position.

Note

- Moving the air source selector knob from OFF to RAM should be accomplished without pausing in the intermediate positions, to prevent the possible introduction of more smoke from one or both of the engines.
- Selecting RAM position will open the ram air scoop, dump cabin pressure, and close the pressure regulating and shutoff valve.

UNLOCKED CANOPY INDICATION.

1. Visors—Down.
2. Oxygen mask and fittings—Checked.
    Check oxygen mask and oxygen hose fittings for security.

WARNING

When the cabin pressure schedule is changed from normal to combat, monitor the cabin pressure altimeter for a rapid increase in cabin altitude. If the cabin altitude does not increase, immediately position the pressurization selector switch to DUMP.

3. Canopy latch handle—Check locked.
4. Pressurization selector switch—COMBAT (when above 30,000 feet), DUMP (when below 30,000 feet).
5. Decelerate and descend.
    Maintain low subsonic airspeeds to minimize possibility of loss of a canopy hatch.
6. Land as soon as possible if caution lamp remains lighted.

GLASS PANEL FAILURE.

In the event of glass panel cracks or failure inflight, proceed as follows:

1. Visors—Down.
2. Oxygen mask and fitting—Checked.
    Check oxygen mask and oxygen hose fittings for security.
3. Pressurization selector switch—COMBAT (when above 30,000 feet), DUMP (when below 30,000 feet).

WARNING

When the cabin pressure schedule is changed from normal to combat, monitor the cabin pressure altimeter for a rapid increase in cabin altitude. If the cabin altitude does not increase, immediately position the pressurization selector switch to DUMP.

4. Decelerate and descend.
5. Pressurization selector switch—DUMP (when subsonic).
6. Land as soon as possible.

EJECTION.

Every emergency in which ejection is considered will have its particular set of circumstances, involving such factors as speed, attitude and control, and altitude. Under level flight conditions, eject at least 2000 feet above the terrain whenever possible.

WARNING

Do not delay ejection below 2000 feet above the terrain in futile attempts to start the engines or for other reasons that may commit you to marginal conditions for safe ejection. Accident statistics emphatically show a progressive decrease in successful ejections as altitude decreases below 2000 feet above the terrain.

Under spin or dive conditions, eject at least 15,000 feet above the terrain whenever possible. If the airplane is controllable, attempt to decelerate as much as practical prior to ejection by zooming the airplane, thus trading airspeed for altitude. If the airplane is not controllable, ejection must be accomplished at whatever

Ejection Procedures

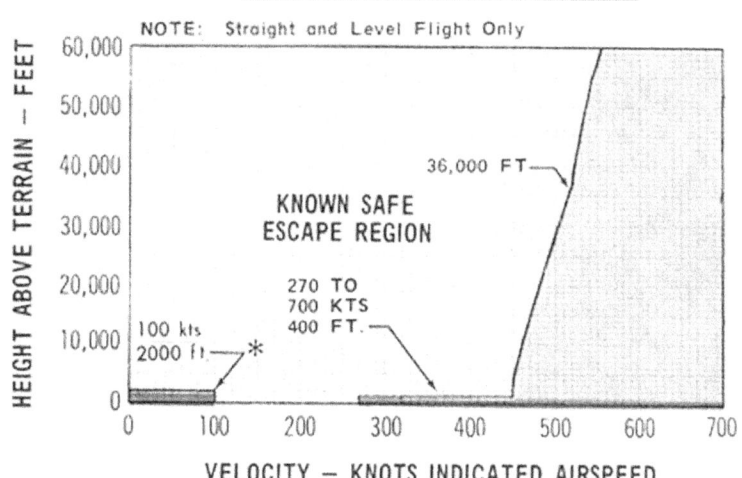

BEFORE EJECTION

NOTE: Straight and Level Flight Only

KNOWN SAFE ESCAPE REGION

36,000 FT
270 TO 700 KTS
400 FT.
100 kts 2000 ft. *

POSSIBLE INJURY
POSSIBLE FATALITY

* This limit does not apply to airplanes (31) which are limited to 50 feet only after cold soak at minus 40°F

HEIGHT ABOVE TERRAIN — FEET
VELOCITY — KNOTS INDICATED AIRSPEED

PREPARATION FOR EJECTION (IF TIME PERMITS)

1. Reduce airspeed (as practicable).
2. Advise crewmember of situation.
3. Transmit MAYDAY (give position).
4. Emergency radio beacon switch — ON (P)
5. Chaff dispenser control lever — ON (OFF for tactical considerations only) (AC).
6. IFF master control knob — EMERGENCY (P).
7. Inertia reel control handle — LOCKED (AC-P).

EJECTION

EJECTION HANDLE — SQUEEZE AND PULL (AC or P)

DURING DESCENT

1. Emergency oxygen handle — Pull (If required).
2. Emergency pressurization ring — Pull (If required).
3. Parachute deploy handle (when below 15,000 feet) — Pull (If required).

WARNING

Minimum safe ejection altitude presented in this chart were determined through sled tests and are based on distance above terrain on initiation of ejection (i.e., time module is fired). These figures do not provide any safety factor for such matters as equipment malfunction, etc. These figures are quoted only to show the minimum altitude you must attain in the event of such low altitude emergencies as fire on takeoff. These minimum altitudes are much higher when the aircraft is losing altitude.

Under spin or dive conditions, ejection should be accomplished above 15,000 feet above the terrain.

AFTER LANDING

1. Severance and flotation handle — Pull.
2. Parachute release handle — Pull.
2A. Canopy hatch(es) — Open.

WARNING

Crew exposure to the unventilated cabin environment is limited to 15 minutes after the oxygen supply is exhausted.

NOTE

Instructions for gaining access to survival equipment are located behind the back cushion of the right seat.

If landing is made in water, proceed as follows:
3. Auxiliary flotation handle — Pull (If required).
4. Bilge pump — Engage and operate (If required).
5. Air ventilation masks — Connect (If required).

NOTE

Refer to "Helicopter Rescue From Crew Module in Water," this section.

If the crew module lands inverted:
6. Inertia reel control handle — Cycle to relieve tension.
7. Use caution in getting out of harness.

Figure 3-2.

speed exists, as this offers the only opportunity for survival. An ejection at low altitudes is facilitated by pulling the nose of the aircraft above the horizon ("zoom-up maneuver"). This maneuver affects the trajectory of the crew module, providing a greater increase in altitude than if ejection is performed in a level flight attitude. Provided a positive rate of climb is maintained, this gain in altitude will increase the time available for complete actuation of the ejection equipment. To ensure survival during extremely low-altitude ejections, the automatic features of the equipment must be used and depended upon. Refer to "Crew Module Escape System", Section I, for sequence of events after ejection. As with all aircraft ejection systems, safe ejection is enhanced by establishing the best conditions possible prior to ejection. The ejection envelope is shown in figure 3-2. The envelope reflects only the best or safest conditions; the decision as to when to eject or not eject in an emergency should not be rigidly determined by the fact that the aircraft is in or out of the "Known Safe" envelope. For example, figure 3-2 shows that the safest low speed/low altitude minimums for ejection are 100 KIAS and 2000 feet respectively. However, this in no way denies the possible need to eject under less desirable conditions. See figure 3-2 for ejection procedures.

LEFT CANOPY REMOVAL.

1. Internal canopy latch handle—Move aft to first detent position.

WARNING

Moving the canopy latch handle to the first detent position locks the counterpoise. If the counterpoise is not locked, the piston may extend rapidly when released in the following step 2 and cause injury.

2. Remove the ball-lock pin from the counterpoise inboard attach fitting.
3. Remove the ball-lock pin from the initiator.

WARNING

Don helmet for noise attenuation.

4. Canopy seal hose—Disconnected (at quick-disconnect).
5. Canopy detach handle—Pull.
6. Push the left canopy hatch overboard.

WARNING

If for some reason the hatch(es) is unlatched but the occupants are unable to complete the above procedures, the rescue crew must observe the "Emergency Entrance" procedures for safety of the occupants.

HYDRAULIC SYSTEM FAILURE.

PRIMARY OR UTILITY HYDRAULIC SYSTEM FAILURE.

Failure of either hydraulic system will cause the pitch, roll, and yaw damper caution lamps and the hydraulic low pressure caution lamps to light. The damper servo-actuators will operate as non-redundant servos. As the hydraulic pressure drops and the damper caution lamps light, forces may be felt in the control stick.

SUPERSONIC.

1. Throttles—Retard.
   Reduce airspeed to subsonic.
2. Depress the damper reset button only if the affected system pressure is more than 2000 psi.
3. Wing sweep handle—50 degrees.
   If wings are aft of 50 degrees, sweep forward slowly to 50 degrees.

CAUTION

Maintain 1 g flight while changing wing position. Change wing sweep position by moving the wing sweep handle at a smooth rate not to exceed 1 degree of sweep per second to avoid depleting hydraulic pressure.

Note

If possible maintain cruise airspeed compatible with 50 degree wing sweep until just prior to landing.

SUBSONIC.

1. Wing sweep handle—Extend.
   Maintain wing sweep position compatible with airspeed and sweep wings to 26 degrees when at appropriate airspeed. Minimize flight control movement during wing sweep and speed brake operation.
2. Maintain airspeed within the damper off operating limits.
3. Depress the damper reset button only if the affected system pressure is more than 2000 psi.
4. Land as soon as possible.
   Refer to "Landing With Primary or Utility Hydraulic System Failure," this section.

COMPLETE HYDRAULIC SYSTEM FAILURE.

If both hydraulic systems fail during flight the flight control system will be inoperative and flight can not be continued.

1. EJECT.

FLIGHT CONTROL SYSTEM MALFUNCTIONS.

Various flight control system malfunctions are indicated by the lighting of an associated caution lamp. All system malfunctions, however, do not constitute a potential emergency, even though the associated caution lamp is lighted. Therefore, only those malfunctions which may develop into an emergency are covered here. Refer to Figure 3-4 for analysis of all caution lamps.

PITCH OR ROLL GAIN CHANGER CAUTION LAMP LIGHTED.

An error in one of the redundant gain changers will cause the pitch or roll gain changer caution lamp to light.

1. Damper reset button—Depress momentarily.
   a. If lamp does reset, continue normal operation.
   b. If lamp does not reset, decrease speed to less than 320 KIAS or mach 0.8.

PITCH, ROLL, OR YAW CHANNEL CAUTION LAMP LIGHTED.

Failure of one of the redundant electrical signal paths causes the appropriate channel caution lamp to light. The failed signal will be electronically rejected and aircraft damping will be unaffected. If failure was a zero command, the appropriate channel lamp will come on during a maneuver. Depressing the damper reset button will cause the caution lamp to reset for this type of failure. Normal operation can be continued as long as the channel lamp can be reset since any subsequent failure will cause either no effect, or zero stability augmentation in the affected channel. If the failure is a hardover signal, the system electrically rejects the failed signal and the channel lamp will immediately light and will not reset. For this condition, normal damping is present, however, a secondary failure could cause either no effect, or a hardover damper servo. For this reason, airspeed should be reduced to the "Stability Augmentation Off Limits," Section V, the affected damper turned off, and the aircraft returned for landing when possible.

1. Damper Reset Button—Depress.
   a. If lamp does reset, continue normal operation.
   b. If lamp does not reset, change speed to a stability augmentation off region and land as soon as possible.

PITCH, ROLL, OR YAW DAMPER CAUTION LAMP LIGHTED.

A lighted damper lamp indicates that the three signals to the damper servo do not agree. If the lamp remains out after the damper reset button is momentarily depressed, one of the three signals has failed to a zero or null command. Any subsequent failure in that axis will result in either normal operation or zero damping. If the damper lamp remains lighted after the damper reset button is momentarily depressed, one of the three signals has failed to a hardover command and has been voted out. A subsequent failure in that axis could cause the damper to go hardover. Certain power failures to the flight control computers have the effect of causing one damper command to fail to a zero or null command. These cases should be treated the same as a damper lamp that will reset. If a damper lamp lights proceed as follows:

1. Reduce speed to the applicable "Stability Augmentation Off Limits," Section V.
2. Damper reset button—Depress momentarily.
   a. If lamp does reset, continue normal operation.
   b. If lamp does not reset, turn off affected damper and land as soon as possible.

RUDDER AUTHORITY CAUTION LAMP LIGHTED.

If rudder authority differs from that programmed by the control system switch, or, on airplanes 31 ♦, differs from that called for by slat position with the control system switch in NORM, the rudder authority caution lamp will light.

1. Rudder authority switch—Check.
   Check that the rudder authority switch is in AUTO. If lamp remains lighted, the rudder authority may be unscheduled.

At high speeds, exercise caution in the use of rudder pedals. For landing, if lamp remains lighted, place the rudder authority switch to FULL. If the lamp still remains on, rudder and nose wheel steering authority may be limited.

Section III
Emergency Procedures

T.O. 1F-111A-1

TF FLY-UP OFF CAUTION LAMP LIGHTED.

The TF fly-up off caution lamp will light, denoting that the automatic TF fly-up signal is not available if either TFR channel is in the TF mode or the auto TF switch is in the AUTO TF position and the flight control system is in the take off and land configuration.

GENERATOR FAILURES.

SINGLE GENERATOR FAILURE.

Failure of one generator will be noted by the lighting of the applicable caution lamp. One generator in normal operation is sufficient to support the entire electrical load or demand. Should generator caution lamp light proceed as follows:

1. Electrical control panel—Check.
    Check electrical control panel for TIE indication in power flow indicator.
2. Generator switch—OFF, then ON.
3. Generator caution lamp—Check.
    If the generator fault has been corrected, the generator will be reconnected to the system and the caution lamp will go out. If the generator caution lamp remains lighted, proceed as follows:
4. Generator switch—OFF then TEST.
    If the caution lamp goes out with the switch in TEST position, it indicates that the generator is operating normally and the malfunction is associated with the contactor circuit or the caution lamp circuit. The generator switch should then be returned to OFF and left there. If the caution lamp remains lighted in TEST, proceed as follows:
5. Generator switch—OFF.
6. Generator decouple button—Depress.

DOUBLE GENERATOR FAILURE WITH BOTH ENGINES OPERATING.

Double generator failure will not result in a total loss of electrical power for more than the maximum of 3 seconds required for the emergency generator to provide power for the essential AC and DC buses. See Section I for list of equipment that is powered by the essential buses.

Note

In the event that the emergency generator does not come on within three seconds, place the emergency generator switch to ON.

1. Electrical control panel—Check.
    Check electrical control panel for EMER indication in power flow indicator.
2. Generator switches—OFF then ON.
3. Reduce electrical load to minimum necessary to sustain safe flight.
4. Maintain 1G Flight.

WARNING

To assure adequate hydraulic pressure for emergency generator operation, do not open speedbrake. Maintain a minimum of 90 percent rpm on both engines while closing speedbrake, if it is open, and for wing sweep and landing gear extension.

5. Fuel Panel—Check.
    With only the emergency generator providing electrical power, only fuel boost pumps 4 & 5 will be operable. Refer to "Fuel System Operation on Emergency Electrical Power", this section.
6. Land as soon as possible.

EMERGENCY GENERATOR OPERATION WITH ONE ENGINE SHUTDOWN.

Note

In the event that the emergency generator does not come on within 3 seconds, place the emergency generator switch to ON.

1. Establish and maintain 1G flight and an airspeed of 350 KIAS. Then, maintain a minimum of 90 percent rpm on the operating engine.
2. Do not open or close speedbrake.
3. Sweep wings forward to 26 degrees by moving the wing sweep handle at a smooth rate not to exceed 1 degree of sweep per second.

Note

Flight control damper transients may be experienced if hydraulic demands cause an interruption of the emergency generator power.

4. Land as soon as practicable.
5. For landing, extend gear using "Landing Gear Emergency Extension" procedures, this section.

FUEL SYSTEM EMERGENCY OPERATIONS.

FUEL SYSTEM OPERATION ON EMERGENCY ELECTRICAL POWER.

When operating on the emergency generator, the electrical power provided will operate only one fuel booster pump at a time (number 4 pump in the forward tank or number 5 pump in the aft tank) or the two outboard wing transfer pumps. The transfer pumps cannot be operated while one of the fuselage booster pumps is operating. When the engine feed selector switch is in FWD, only the number 4 pump in the forward tank will be operating and will supply fuel to both engines. When the engine feed selector switch is in AFT or BOTH, only the number 5 pump in the aft tank will be operating and will supply fuel to both engines. When the engine feed selector switch is in AUTO, either pump 4 or pump 5 will operate depending on fuel distribution. If the fuel differential is greater than 8500 pounds, number 4 pump will supply fuel to the engines. If the fuel differential is less than 7900 pounds, number 5 pump will supply fuel to the engines. If, when the AUTO position is initially selected, the fuel differential is less than 7900 pounds, the number 5 pump will transfer fuel to the forward tank until the proper fuel differential is established. From this point on, either pump 4 or 5 will be automatically selected to supply fuel directly to the engines. During the period that pump 5 is transferring fuel forward, the engines will be operating on suction feed. In order to transfer fuel from the wing tanks, the engine feed selector switch must be turned OFF and the fuel transfer switch placed to WING. This will result in the engines being fed by suction from the forward tank. Fuselage tank fuel quantities must be closely monitored to maintain the proper distribution during wing transfer. If distribution gets out of tolerance, it can be corrected by positioning the engine feed selector switch to AUTO. During suction feed, the fuel manifold low pressure caution lamps may come on. This should cause no concern since sufficient fuel flow should be available to operate in maximum afterburner up to 6000 feet or military power up to 30,000 feet.

Engine Feed.

1. Engine feed selector knob—AUTO.
   Closely monitor fuel quantity in the fuselage tanks to maintain 8200 (±300) pounds fuel differential.
2. Fuel tank pressurization selector switch—PRESSURIZE.

Fuel Transfer.

1. Fuel transfer knob—WING.
2. Engine feed selector knob—OFF.
   Monitor fuel quantity in the fuselage tanks to maintain 8200 (±300) pounds fuel differential.

Note

When the wings are swept aft, a larger amount of fuel will be trapped in the wing tanks. To transfer all available fuel from the wing tanks, the wings must be in the extended positions. Gravity transfer of fuel is not possible.

FUEL PRESSURE CAUTION LAMP INDICATION.

Either Fuel Pressure Caution Lamp.

1. Flowmeter—Checked.
   Check appropriate fuel flowmeter to determine if fuel flow is excessive.
2. If flow is excessive, shut down the affected engine, depress the fire pushbutton, and extend the speed brakes.
3. If fuel flow is normal, check totalizer to determine if there is an excessive loss of fuel.
4. If fuel loss is excessive, shut down the affected engine, depress the fire pushbutton, and extend the speed brakes.
5. If fuel consumption is normal, check the fuel booster pump low pressure indicator lamps.
6. If fuel booster pump low pressure indicator lamps are on, indicating booster pump failure, retard appropriate throttle until manifold low pressure caution lamp goes out.

Note

With all booster pumps inoperative and normal tank pressurization available, the engines will operate in maximum after-burner up to 6000 feet or military power up to 30,000 feet.

7. If fuel booster pump low pressure indicator lamps are normal, descend to 30,000 feet and land as soon as possible.

Both Fuel Pressure Caution Lamps.

1. Engine fuel feed selector knob—Checked.
   Check engine fuel feed selection to insure that fuel is available to the engines.
2. Flowmeters—Checked.
   Check fuel flowmeters to determine if fuel flow to either engine is excessive.
3. If either flowmeter indicates excessive fuel flow, shut down that engine, depress the fire pushbutton and extend the speed brakes.
4. If fuel flow is normal, check the totalizer to determine if there is an excessive loss of fuel.
5. If fuel loss is excessive, retard throttles until one caution lamp goes out. Then shut down the engine with the caution lamp still on. Depress the fire pushbutton and extend the speed brakes.
6. If fuel consumption is normal, check the fuel booster pump low pressure indicator lamps.
7. If fuel booster pump low pressure indicator lamps are on, indicating pump failure, retard throttles until the manifold low pressure caution lamps go out.

Note

With all booster pumps inoperative and normal tank pressurization available, the engines will operate in maximum after-burner up to 6000 feet or military power up to 30,000 feet.

8. If fuel booster pump low pressure lamps are normal, descend to 30,000 feet or below and land as soon as possible.

OIL SYSTEM MALFUNCTIONS.

An oil system malfunction on either engine is recognized by a change in oil pressure, a complete loss of oil pressure, or excessive oil temperature. In general, it is advisable to shut the engine down as soon as possible after a drop in oil pressure is indicated, to minimize the possibility of damage to the engine. However, if thrust is critical, the engine may be utilized as long as it continues to produce power.

OIL PRESSURE BELOW 30 PSI.

1. Throttle of affected engine—OFF. (If flight conditions permit).

> **CAUTION**
>
> If oil pressure goes to below 30 psi and it is necessary to keep the engine operating to sustain flight, engine seizure can be expected.

OIL PRESSURE BETWEEN 30 AND 40 PSI (EXCEPT AT IDLE).

1. Throttle of affected engine—IDLE.
2. Monitor oil pressure.

OIL PRESSURE ABOVE 50 PSI.

1. Throttle of affected engine—Retard.
    Reduce thrust on affected engine. If oil pressure can be maintained below 50 psi continue to operate engine at the reduced power setting. If oil pressure can not be reduced below 50 psi, shut the engine down.

EXCESSIVE OIL TEMPERATURE WITH NORMAL OIL PRESSURE.

An oil hot caution lamp with normal oil pressure usually indicates insufficient oil cooling. It is recommended that the throttle be advanced to a higher thrust setting if possible. This will increase the fuel flow to the cooler and will increase the cooling capacity of the oil cooling unit until the heat rejection from the engine can be accommodated by lower fuel flow through the fuel oil cooler. Retarding the throttle will not normally reduce the oil temperature. If the oil hot caution lamp does not go out within 10 seconds, the engine should be shut down.

SPIKE SYSTEM FAILURE.

Since there is no positive means of determining spike position, a spike system failure or spike mispositioning can be recognized only by a reduction in engine or engine inlet performance. The evidence of a spike system failure will differ according to airspeed at the time of failure. Failure of the spike system at mach numbers above 1.5 will most probably be evidenced by inlet buzz and/or compressor stall. Failure of the spike in the lower speed range may result in an engine compressor stall.

1. Airspeed—Reduce as necessary.
    If above mach 1.5 and inlet buzz and/or compressor stall is present, decelerate to mach 1.5 or until buzz or compressor stall disappear.

LANDING.

1. Engine spike caution lamps—Out.
    When at mach 0.3 (approximately 200 KIAS at sea level or 175 KIAS at 6000 ft), check that engine spike caution lamps are out. If either lamp is lighted, proceed with next step.
2. Applicable spike control switch—Move to OVERRIDE position.

AIR CONDITIONING AND PRESSURIZATION SYSTEM FAILURE.

UNCONTROLLED CABIN OVERHEAT.

If uncontrolled cabin overheat occurs, place the air source selector knob to OFF and turn off all non-essential electronic equipment. Descend to an altitude where cockpit pressurization and/or heating is not required, and land as soon as possible.

LANDING EMERGENCIES

The canopy will be retained during all landing emergencies.

LANDING WITH PRIMARY OR UTILITY HYDRAULIC SYSTEM FAILURE.

Fly an extended downwind leg sufficiently long to provide time for lowering the landing gear and flaps by the alternate method. After touchdown, normal braking and anti-skid will be available until the brake accumulator pressure has been reduced to 1100 ±100 psi (after approximately 10-14 full brake applications). Differential braking must be used to maintain directional control during landing roll. To minimize consumption of brake accumulator hydraulic fluid, braking should be accomplished by as few brake applications as possible. A single moderate and steadily increasing brake application is recommended. If the number of brake applications utilized or the amount of anti-skid cycling is great enough to reduce accumulator pressure to less than 1100 ±100 psi, normal braking will not be available and it will be necessary to pull the auxiliary brake handle to stop the airplane.

1. Control system switch—T.O. & LAND.
2. Do not attempt to reset the damper caution lamps.
3. Landing Gear—Extend.
   Extend the landing gear using the "Landing Gear Emergency Extension" procedures, this section.
4. Spike control switches—As required.
   Prior to landing with either hydraulic system inoperative, decelerate to mach 0.3 (approximately 200 KIAS at sea level or 175 KIAS at 6000 ft), and check that engine spike caution lamps are out. If either lamp is lighted, place the affected spike control switch to OVERRIDE.
5. Flaps and slats—Extend.
   Extend the flaps and slats using the "Emergency Extension of Flaps and Slats" procedures, this section.

Note

Lateral response rates will be reduced due to one pair of spoilers being inoperable.

6. Maintain directional control after touchdown by differential braking.

Note

- If only the utility hydraulic system is operative, only the outboard spoilers will be available. If only the primary hydraulic system is operative, the inboard spoilers only will be available.

LANDING GEAR EMERGENCY OPERATIONS.

MAIN LANDING GEAR FAILURE TO EXTEND AND LOCK AFTER RELEASING FROM UPLOCK.

1. Landing gear handle—Recycle.
   Recycle the landing gear handle from DN to UP then back to DN. Check for gear down indication.
2. Impose a g load on the airplane and check for gear down indication.
3. Follow "Emergency Landing Gear Extension" procedure, this section.

LANDING GEAR EMERGENCY EXTENSION.

If the landing gear can not be lowered using the normal procedures, or if due to some other system failure, emergency gear extension is to be used, proceed as follows:

1. Landing gear handle—UP.

Note

Placing the landing gear handle to UP as the first step in this procedure, is necessary for compatibility with other emergencies such as landing with primary or utility hydraulic system failure or emergency generator operation with one engine shutdown. If hydraulic and electrical systems are normal, emergency gear extension may be made with the landing gear handle positioned to DN.

2. Landing gear emergency (alternate) release handle—Pull (at recommended minimum flying speed).
   After pulling the emergency release handle, allow time, as practicable, for the gear to fully extend.
3. Landing gear handle—DN.
4. Green landing gear position indicator lamps—Lighted.
5. Landing gear handle warning lamp—Out.

Note

After the landing gear emergency release handle is pulled, nose wheel steering will be inoperative and the nose wheel will be cocked to one side. The nose wheel being cocked will present no directional control difficulty on touchdown however since the hydraulic pressure holding it cocked is slight. During landing roll, the nose wheel should be held off the runway as long as possible.

This page intentionally left blank.

T.O. 1F-111A-1

Section III
Emergency Procedures

If the speed brake fails to retract to the trail position, as indicated by the landing gear handle warning lamp remaining on after the gear has extended and locked:

6. Landing gear emergency release handle—IN. (if applicable)

Note

Reduced air loads during landing will allow the speed brake to extend and drag the landing surface.

If landing gear fails to extend or lock down after the landing gear emergency release handle is pulled, follow "Landing With Gear Up or Unlocked and Nose Gear Down or Landing with All Landing Gear Up or Unlocked" procedures, this section.

LANDING WITH UNSAFE GEAR INDICATION.

1. Slow aircraft to appropriate limit speed and extend flaps to 15 degrees.
2. Landing gear circuit breakers—Check.
   Check the landing gear control, landing gear warning circuit breakers.
3. Landing gear handle—Recycle.

If landing gear is still unsafe:

4. Landing gear emergency release handle—Pull.

Note

After the landing gear emergency release handle is pulled nose wheel steering will be inoperative.

If landing gear is still unsafe:

5. Obtain a visual gear check from another airplane and/or the control tower if possible.

If landing gear is still unsafe follow "Landing With Landing Gear Up or Unlocked and Nose Gear Down or Landing with All Landing Gear Up or Unlocked" procedures, this section.

LANDING WITH MAIN GEAR UP OR UNLOCKED AND NOSE GEAR DOWN OR LANDING WITH ALL LANDING GEAR UP OR UNLOCKED.

1. Landing gear handle—DN.
2. Landing gear emergency release handle—Pull.
3. External load—Jettison.
4. Dump or burn excess fuel.
   Lighten the aircraft as much as possible by dumping or burning excess fuel.

Note

If dumping operation is necessary during afterburner operation, the fuel may ignite behind the airplane. This should cause no concern however since the fire will remain behind the airplane. Other aircraft in the immediate vicinity should be advised to stay well clear during dumping operations.

5. External tanks—Retain if empty.
6. Battery switch—OFF.
7. Shoulder harness—LOCKED.
8. Fly a normal landing pattern and make a normal landing.

Note

Attempt to touchdown at normal landing attitude. Do not try to hold the aircraft off the runway by increasing angle of attack. Lower the nose to the runway while elevator control is still available.

9. Throttles—OFF.
   Immediately after touchdown, shut down the engines.
10. Fire pushbuttons—Depress.
11. Abandon the airplane.

LANDING WITH NOSE GEAR UP OR UNLOCKED, MAIN GEAR DOWN.

1. Landing gear handle—DN.
2. External load—Jettison.
3. Dump or burn excess fuel.
   Lighten the aircraft as much as possible by dumping or burning excess fuel.

Note

If dumping operation is necessary during afterburner operation, the fuel may ignite behind the airplane. This should cause no concern however since the fire will remain behind the airplane. Other aircraft in the immediate vicinity should be advised to stay well clear during dumping operations.

4. External tanks—Retain if empty.
5. Battery switch—OFF.
6. Antiskid switch—ON.
7. Shoulder harness—LOCKED.
8. Fly a normal landing pattern and make a normal landing.

Changed 18 August 1967

3-13

Section III
Emergency Procedures

Note

Attempt to touch down at normal landing attitude. Hold the nose off the runway as long as practicable. Aerodynamic braking is very effective in the nose high attitude, however, if braking is required, use light braking so as not to override elevator control. Lower the nose gently to the runway before elevator control is lost. Do not use ground roll spoiler brakes.

9. Throttles—OFF.
   After the nose is on the runway shut down the engines.
10. Fire pushbuttons—Depress.
11. Abandon the airplane.

LANDING WITH A BLOWN TIRE.

MAIN GEAR TIRE.

1. Fly a normal landing pattern.
   Arresting hook—Extend.
2. Antiskid switch—OFF.
   With the antiskid switch OFF, and using differential braking, the wheel with the blown tire can be locked.
3. Touch down on side of runway opposite the blown tire.
4. Ground roll spoiler switch—BRAKE.
5. Lower nose and use nosewheel steering and brakes as required to keep airplane on runway.
6. Brakes—Lock brake with blown tire. Use other brake as required.

NOSE GEAR TIRE.

Use same procedure as with a main tire except land in the center of the runway and hold the nose off the runway as long as possible. Anti-skid should be left on when landing with a blown nose wheel tire. Do not lock either brake on landing.

EMERGENCY EXTENSION OF FLAPS AND SLATS.

1. Flap and slat switch—EMER.
2. Emergency flap and slat switch—EXTEND.
   Hold the emergency flap and slat switch in EXTEND until the slats are down and the flaps are in the desired position. Emergency extension of the flaps to full down requires 60 seconds.

LANDING AND GO-AROUND WITH ONE ENGINE OUT.

During single engine operation, utility and primary hydraulic system flow is reduced by almost 50 percent. Because of this, the landing gear system, speed brake system, and air inlet control system will each absorb total flow of the utility hydraulic system when actuated. Avoid operation of more than one utility hydraulic system function at a time. Since the flight control system utilizes both utility and primary pressure, operation of necessary utility hydraulic system functions should be accomplished while in level flight. Wing sweep changes may require as much as 20 seconds for completion. During wing sweep operation, no other demands should be placed on the utility system such as speed brakes, air inlet control or flaps. Changes in wing sweep should be accomplished in straight and level flight. During the landing approach, keep rpm on the operating engine as high as practicable until touchdown. The possibility of a go-around should be recognized early. If a go-around is necessary, advance the throttle of the operating engine and continue approach until go-around airspeed is reached. Refer to Appendix I for single engine climb speeds. When landing in a gusty crosswind, final approach airspeed should be increased by ten knots.

TRANSLATING COWL MALFUNCTION.

Airplanes **19** ♦ **30**:

No alternate means of opening the cowls is provided should either or both cowls fail in the closed position. If this occurs in flight, follow the procedures for landing with translating cowl(s) closed.

Airplane **31** ♦:

In the event either or both translating cowl fails to open as indicated by the position indicators and warning lamp proceed as follows:

1. Translating cowl switch(es)—OPEN.

If cowl(s) fail to open:

2. Translating cowl emergency override switch—OVERRIDE (OPEN).
3. Translating cowl position indicators—OPEN.

If cowl(s) still do not open, follow the procedures for landing with translating cowl(s) closed.

LANDING WITH ONE TRANSLATING COWL CLOSED.

The following procedure is recommended for the prevention of, or operating with, an engine compressor stall occurring in the lower speed range (below mach

0.35) as a result of a translating cowl failing in the closed position. An imminent engine compressor stall may be evidenced by vibration and/or fluctuating engine instruments. An actual compressor stall is evidenced by an explosive like disturbance which is heard and felt.

1. Burn or dump excess fuel.
2. Accomplish normal pattern and landing procedures.
3. Affected engine power—Set.
   Set power on affected engine to approximately 75-78 percent rpm and use the other engine for all subsequent power requirements.
4. Reduce airspeed with flaps and landing gear as necessary.

WARNING

Inducing a nose high attitude to reduce speed should be avoided to prevent possible excessive sink rate.

LANDING WITH BOTH TRANSLATING COWLS CLOSED.

Follow same procedures as those listed for "Landing With One Translating Cowl Closed" except, establish landing pattern as necessary to avoid power settings that exceed those listed.

LANDING WITH WINGS AT 26 DEGREES SWEEP OR GREATER AND NO FLAPS.

Landing with wings and flaps in other than normal landing configuration will necessitate a long, shallow, straight-in approach. Avoid abrupt maneuvers or flight in excess of 1 g.

1. Burn or dump excess fuel.
   Because of the high approach and touchdown airspeeds involved during landing with wings swept past 26 degrees, burn or dump as much fuel as practicable prior to entering traffic pattern.

Note

If dumping operation is necessary during afterburner operation, the fuel may ignite behind the airplane. This should cause no concern however since the fire will remain behind the airplane. Other aircraft in the immediate vicinity should be advised to stay well clear during dumping operations.

2. Landing cockpit check—Completed.
   Perform normal landing cockpit check.

3. Touchdown airspeed—As required.
   During transition from 50 feet altitude to touchdown, the rate of descent should be approximately 480 FPM. The angle of attack should be approximately 13° for wing sweep or 50° or greater and 10° for wing sweep of 35° or less. Touch down as near to the approach end of the runway as possible.

Note

The following braking technique is based on the assumption that sufficient runway is available. If less than the required runway is available, maximum braking should be initiated as soon as possible.

4. Throttles—IDLE.

Note

Ground roll spoilers will not be available at wing sweep angles of 35° or greater.

5. After touchdown, hold the nose wheel off the runway (approximately 10° angle of attack). At 173 KIAS, apply as much braking pressure as possible while still maintaining a 10° angle of attack.
6. At 135 KIAS, smoothly lower the nose wheel to the runway and apply maximum braking. Hold the control stick full back to utilize the maximum drag of the horizontal tail.

CAUTION

If excessive braking is used to high speeds, the wheel blowout plugs may relieve tire pressure within 3 to 15 minutes after stop. Provisions should be made to cope with wheel fires which may start shortly after the blowout plugs relieve.

7. Arresting hook—As required.

Note

Figure 3-3 provides airspeeds and ground roll distances for specific gross weights. For gross weights in excess of these, refer to Appendix I.

CAUTION

Call the fire department after any emergency landing which results in hot wheels or brakes or tail hook. Do not shut the engines down until after the fire trucks arrive. Fuel venting from the engines after shut down may be ignited by the affected hot part.

Section III
Emergency Procedures

T.O. 1F-111A-1

Emergency Landing Airspeeds and Ground Roll Distances

50,000 POUNDS GROSS WEIGHT				
Wing Sweep (Degrees)	Pattern Speed (Knots)	Final Approach Speed (Knots)	Touchdown Speed (Knots)	Ground Roll Distance (Feet)
26	220	175	165	5000 4100*
50	250	184	174	6000
60	265	193	183	8300
72.5	280	205	195	9800

55,000 POUNDS GROSS WEIGHT				
Wing Sweep (Degrees)	Pattern Speed (Knots)	Final Approach Speed (Knots)	Touchdown Speed (Knots)	Ground Roll Distance (Feet)
26	220	187	177	8700 5600*
50	250	196	186	10,600
60	265	206	196	12,600
72.5	280	218	208	14,000

WARNING

Minimum allowable gross weight at 16 degrees wing sweep is 56,000 pounds.

16 DEGREE WING SWEEP (56,000 POUNDS)				
	Pattern Speed (Knots)	Final Approach Speed (Knots)	Touchdown Speed (Knots)	Ground Roll Distance (Feet)
SLATS AND FLAPS RETRACTED	215	180	170	5000* 6600
SLATS AND FLAPS EXTENDED	140	128	120	1800*

*Ground roll spoilers extended at touchdown.

Figure 3-3.

T.O. 1F-111A-1

Section III
Emergency Procedures

Caution Lamp Analysis

Indicator	Cause	Corrective Action
ROLL OR PITCH GAIN CHANGER	One of the redundant roll or pitch gain changers is in error (all airplanes)	Depress damper reset button momentarily. If lamp resets, continue normal operation. If lamp does not reset, decrease speed to less than 320 knots & .8 Mach
	③① ♦ Gear handle DN but flight control system not in takeoff and land configuration	③① ♦ Extend slats, if lamps stay on place control system switch to T.O. & LAND to override the automatic switching
	③① ♦ Slats retracted and control system still in takeoff and land configuration	③① ♦ Check that control system switch is in NORM. If lamps remain on the automatic switch is in error and only takeoff and landing operation can be performed.
ROLL CHANNEL OR PITCH CHANNEL OR YAW CHANNEL	One of the triple redundant channels is in error	Depress the damper reset button momentarily. If lamp resets, continue normal operation. If lamp does not reset, change speed to a stability augmentation off region, turn the affected damper OFF and land as soon as possible.
ROLL DAMPER OR PITCH DAMPER OR YAW DAMPER	One of the triple redundant commands to a damper servo is in error	Depress reset button momentarily, if lamp does reset, continue normal operation. If lamp does not reset, reduce speed to the applicable stability augmentation off limits, turn affected damper off and land as soon as possible.
L PRI HYD R PRI HYD	Pressure output of the indicated primary hydraulic pump is below 400 to 600 PSI	Monitor primary hydraulic pressure. If normal pressure — continue flight. If abnormal pressure — follow HYDRAULICS SYSTEM FAILURE, this section
L UTIL HYD R UTIL HYD	Pressure output of the indicated utility hydraulic pump is below 400 to 600 PSI	Monitor utility hydraulic pressure. If normal pressure — continue flight. If abnormal pressure — follow HYDRAULICS SYSTEM FAILURE, this section
ROLL, PITCH, AND YAW DAMPER WITH EITHER PRIMARY OR UTILITY HYDRAULIC SYSTEM CAUTION LAMPS.	One hydraulic system pressure is low.	Reduce Speed to Subsonic. Monitor hydraulic pressure. Depress damper reset button only if affected system pressure is greater than 2000 psi. Follow normal operating procedures. Sweep wings forward at reduced rate to prevent hydraulic pressure depletion
L FUEL PRESS R FUEL PRESS	Affected fuel manifold pressure is less than 15.5 PSIA	Check fuel feed selector switch and fuel pump pressure lamps. Check fuel flow. If fuel pressure continues to drop, consult emergency procedures
L ENG SPIKE R ENG SPIKE	Airspeed is 0.3 mach or below and the affected spike has not extended or has not collapsed	Position appropriate spike control switch(es) to OVERRIDE. Do not attempt to return to AUTO position after the spike control switch has been placed to OVERRIDE
L ENG OIL HOT R ENG OIL HOT	Oil temperature of affected engine exceeds 245°F (118°C)	Retard throttle of affected engine to IDLE and monitor oil pressure. If oil pressure drops below 30 PSI, shut down the affected engine Note: Also, refer to "Excessive Oil Temperature Following Thrust Reduction," this section

Figure 3-4. (Sheet 1)

Changed 18 August 1967

Section III
Emergency Procedures

T.O. 1F-111A-1

Caution Lamp Analysis

Indicator	Cause	Corrective Action
L ENG OVERSPEED R ENG OVERSPEED	Excessive N1 RPM	Retard throttle of affected engine. Lamp should go out at reduced power. If lamp remains on, operate engine at reduced power
L GEN R GEN	Indicated generator has malfunctioned and has disconnected from its ac bus	Check power flow indicator displays TIE. The operating generator will automatically connect to the inoperative bus
ANTISKID	Antiskid system has detected a malfunction and has automatically turned itself off	Avoid hard braking if possible to prevent tire skids because antiskid is off. Antiskid automatically turns itself off if a malfunction occurs which results in a skid control valve being continuously energized (brakes released) for 1.35 seconds, or if an electrical open circuit or short circuit occurs within the antiskid system
NUCLEAR	Refer to T.O. 1F-111A-25-2	
SPOILER	One pair of spoilers has been voted out and locked down	Maintain positive control of aircraft attitude and decelerate to safe speed. Attempt to reset spoiler one time only but expect a rapid roll transient if spoiler is still failed. A spoiler that was voted out because of an active failure will not likely reset. The roll rate capability during landing will be reduced by approximately 50 percent
FOD	Not operable ⑲ ♦ ㉚, deleted ㉛ ♦	
CADC (CADS ㉛ ♦)	One of CADC monitors indicates malfunction	Cross check flight instruments to determine if any are inoperative. Use standby instruments in lieu of malfunctioning primary instruments
PRI HOT UTIL HOT	Indicated hydraulic system fluid temperature is above 230°F (110°C)	Reduce speed. Monitor hydraulic pressure. Reduce demand on hydraulic system. At temperatures above 230°F, the hydraulic system may aerate and develop those characteristics associated with air in hydraulic system
FUEL FLOW	Useable fuel in fuselage reservoir tank is 2115 to 2585 pounds or less	Transfer any available fuel into forward fuselage tank. If no other fuel is available, land as soon as possible. Fuel conditions may vary when this lamp comes on. Evaluate the condition and take necessary action
COWL	One or both cowls not fully closed above mach 0.50	⑲ ♦ ㉚ Manually close cowl. ㉛ ♦ Continue to accelerate to mach 0.80. If cowls do not close do not exceed cowl open limit speed
OIL LOW	Oil level in either engine down to 4 quarts	Check oil quantity indicators. Shutdown affected engine if not needed. If engine needed shutdown when oil pressure starts to drop.
INLET HOT	Anti-icing air temperature excessive	Shut off engine inlet anti-icing. Lamp should go out. If not, slow airplane

Figure 3-4. (Sheet 2)

Changed 18 August 1967

T.O. 1F-111A-1

Section III
Emergency Procedures

Caution Lamp Analysis

Indicator	Cause	Corrective Action
OXY	Total liquid oxygen remaining is two liters or less or pressure is 42 psi or less	Descend to a safe altitude. Refer to "Oxygen Duration Table," Section I
HOOK DOWN	Arresting hook is not up and locked	Land past the approach end barrier. Arresting hook cannot be retracted in flight
AUX ATT	AFRS altitude information unreliable	Place flight instrument reference select switch to PRI. The standby attitude indicator will be unreliable.
IFF (temporarily inoperative)	Mode 4 inoperative or improperly comparing code	Take action to obtain IFF identification on other modes
PRI ATT/HDG	Failure of inertial reference unit or computer display unit	Position flight instrument reference select switch to AUX. Autopilot switches will go to DAMPER in the AUX mode. Caution lamp will remain lighted whenever switch is not in PRI position
TF FLY-UP OFF	TF Radar is in TF or auto TF switch is in AUTO TF and the flight control system is in takeoff & land configuration	Turn TF radar out of TF mode, auto TF switch to OFF or place control system switch to NORM. If the lamp remains lighted, the automatic fly-up capability is not available
RUDDER AUTHORITY	Rudder authority differs from that programmed by the control system switch or, on ⑪ ◆, differs from that called for by slat position when control system switch is in NORM	Check rudder authority switch in AUTO. If lamp remains on, the rudder authority may be unscheduled. At high speeds, exercise caution in the use of rudder pedals. For landing, if lamp remains on, place the rudder authority switch to FULL. If the lamp still remains on, rudder and nose wheel steering authority may be limited
FUEL DISTRIB	The automatic fuel distribution has failed. Fuel distribution is out of limits	Select FWD or AFT tank feed until proper fuel distribution is regained. Monitor fuel quantities and fuel distribution
TANK PRESS	Fuel tank pressurization is not compatible with aircraft configuration	Place fuel tank pressurization selector switch to appropriate position to cause the lamp to go out. Monitor fuel quantities and assure that pressure loss has not affected fuel quantity or distribution
CABIN PRESS	Cabin altitude above 10,000 feet	Check oxygen equipment. Assure oxygen is on. Check that pressurization selector switch is in NORM
LOW EQUIP PRESS	Pressure to forward equipment bay pressurized components is less than 12.5 ($\pm$ 0.5) psi	Turn off TFR, Attack Radar, CMRS, and Track-breaker. This equipment requires one-atmosphere pressurization for proper operation
ICING	Icing condition sensed by ice detector	Place pitot heater anti-icing switch to ON. Check engine inlet anti-icing system is operating. If not, go to MANUAL. Lamp will remain on until 60 seconds after icing condition ceases

Figure 3-4. (Sheet 3)

Changed 18 August 1967

Section III
Emergency Procedures

T.O. 1F-111A-1

Caution Lamp Analysis

Indicator	Cause	Corrective Action
FWD EQUIP HOT	Low airflow and/or high temperature airflow supplied for equipment cooling	Switch to manual operation and rotate temperature control knob to COOL, or when practicable, increase engine rpm. If lamp remains on, turn off all nonessential equipment until lamp goes out
AFT EQUIP HOT	Not operable	
WINDSHIELD HOT	Supply air exceeds 450°F	Place rain removal switch to OFF
α/β PROBE HEAT	On the ground: 1. Pitot/probe heater switch OFF/SEC 2. Primary heater in angle-of-attack or side slip angle probe overheated	1. Place pitot/probe heater switch to HEAT 2. Place pitot/probe heater switch to OFF/SEC
	Inflight: 1. Primary heater in angle-of-attack or side slip probe not functioning	1. Place pitot/probe heater switch to OFF/SEC

Figure 3-4. (Sheet 4)

Changed 18 August 1967

Emergency Entrance

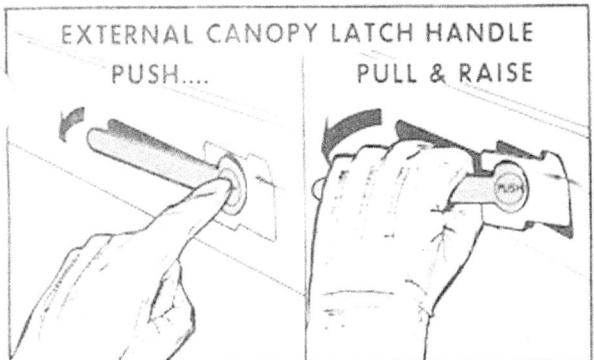

NOTE:
The external canopy latch handle may be used only when the internal canopy latch handle is unlocked.

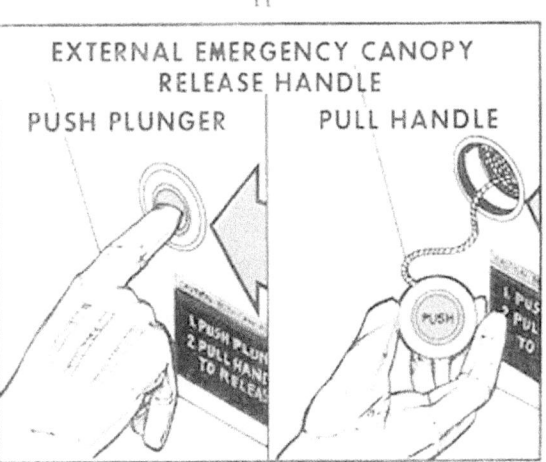

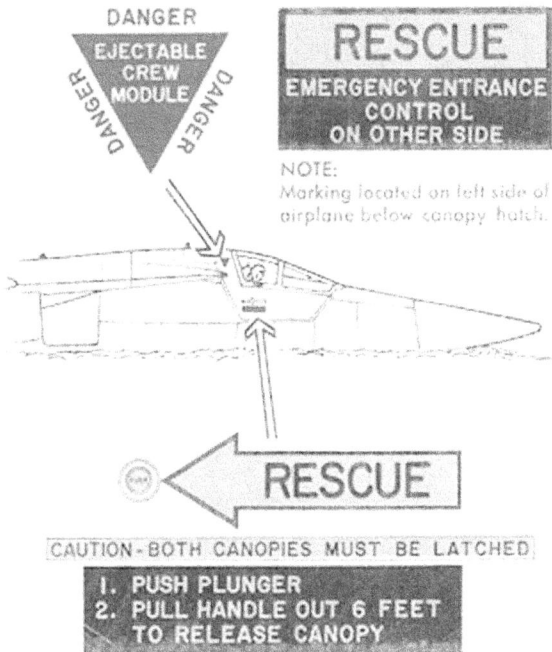

Canopy emergency opening provisions are installed on the right side of the exterior of the airplane below the canopy hatch.

To release both canopy hatch latches:

1. Push plunger to release spring-loaded handle.

2. Grasp handle which is attached to cable and pull out approximately six feet.

Do not pull the canopy external emergency release handle unless both canopy hatches are closed and latched. To do so may result in fatal injury to the occupants from debris flying from the canopy sill.

When latch handle is rotated, sill hook which has been severed from cabin sill may drop off when canopy is raised.

NOTE

Actuating emergency release handle will unlock hatches only. Hatches must then be raised manually.

3. If crew is incapacitated, remove oxygen mask immediately.

Figure 3-5.

This is the last page of Section III.

SECTION IV
CREW DUTIES

This section not applicable.

T.O. 1F-111A-1

Section V
Operating Limitations

SECTION V
OPERATING LIMITATIONS

Note

The airspeed indicated on the airspeed mach indicator has been calibrated for pitot-static system errors by the CADC and therefore is actually KCAS (knots calibrated airspeed). However, this air speed is referred to as KIAS (knots indicated airspeed) throughout this manual since it is read directly from the instrument.

TABLE OF CONTENTS.

	Page
Introduction	5-1
Minimum Crew Requirements	5-1
Engine Limitations	5-1
Starter Limitations	5-3
Airspeed Limitations	5-3
Maneuverability Limitations	5-7
Center-of-Gravity Limitations	5-11
Gross Weight Limitations	5-12A
Flight with Augmentation Off	5-20
Brake Limitations	5-20
Miscellaneous Operational Limitations	5-25

INTRODUCTION.

This section includes limitations that must be observed for safe and efficient operation of the engines and the airplane. Special attention should be given to the instrument marking illustration (figure 5-1), since these limitations are not necessarily repeated under their respective sections. When necessary, an additional explanation of instrument markings is covered under appropriate headings.

Note

The flight crew will make all necessary entries in Form 781 to indicate when any limitations have been exceeded. Entries shall include the time interval, where applicable, as well as the actual instrument reading value for the limitation that was exceeded.

The limitations contained herein, other than those associated with engine ground operation, are applicable for operations within 80 percent of airplane design limits.

MINIMUM CREW REQUIREMENTS.

The minimum crew for normal flight is two. The minimum crew for mission completion is two.

ENGINE LIMITATIONS.

GROUND OPERATION.

Engine idle speed:
  P-1 Engine: 54 to 62 percent.
  P-3 Engine: 56 to 65 percent.

Maximum IDLE time is unlimited.

Maximum time at MIL power—45 minutes.

Maximum time at any A/B power—3 minutes.

CAUTION

After operating in A/B power for 3 minutes, retard the throttle to 70 percent rpm for 3 minutes before advancing to any higher power.

Changed 18 August 1967

5-1

Section V
Operating Limitations

T.O. 1F-111A-1

Instrument Markings

BASED ON JP-4 FUEL

TACHOMETER

	ENGINE	
	TF30-P-1	TF30-P-3
Normal operating range — percent	54 to 95.7	56 to 104.2
Maximum operating speed — percent	95.7	104.2

NOTE:
Tachometer and Turbine inlet Temperature markings are depicted for TF30-P-1 Engine.

TURBINE INLET TEMPERATURE

		ENGINE	
		TF30-P-1	TF30-P-3
▬▬▬	Normal operating range.	300 to 1110°C	300 to 1110°C
▲	Starting (momentary).	705°C	705°C
▬	Maximum Military operation.	1110°C	1110°C
▬	During acceleration (2 minutes) (Engine transients).	1130°C	1130°C
(Unmarked)	Maximum Continuous	930°C	930°C

OIL PRESSURE

▬▬▬ 40 to 50 psi — Normal range.
▬ 30 psi — Minimum during idle.
▬ 50 psi — Maximum.

HYDRAULIC PRESSURE

▬▬▬ 2950 to 3250 psi — Normal range.
▬ 3250 psi — Maximum.

Figure 5-1.

INFLIGHT OPERATION.

The following limits for flight operation must be observed.

- Maximum continuous—Do not exceed 930° C Turbine Inlet Temperature.
- Turbine Inlet Temperature above 930° C — 45 minutes.
- Afterburner operation—45 minutes.

ENGINE ACCELERATION LIMITS.

Refer to figure 5-1.

ENGINE OVERSPEED LIMIT.

Refer to figure 5-1.

ZERO "G" AND NEGATIVE "G" TIME LIMIT — 10 SECONDS AT MAX A/B POWER.

WARNING

Do not initiate a zero or negative "g" maneuver when the fuel level caution lamp is lighted. To do so could result in a flameout of both engines.

Note

The fuel low caution lamp may light during a negative "g" maneuver.

ALTERNATE FUEL.

Refer to figure 5-2 for a listing of approved fuels.

OIL TEMPERATURE LIMITATIONS.

Maximum temperature is 120°C (248°F). ENG OIL HOT caution lamp will light at 121°C (250°F).

Note

Engine oil overheat may occur during supersonic operation with one engine at MIL or below.

STARTER LIMITATIONS.

The starter is limited to 2 cartridge starts in a 15 minute period or 5 consecutive pneumatic starts after which a 1 hour cooling period must be observed. The starter is limited to the following periods of continuous operation after which a 15 minute cooling period must be observed:

Left Starter .... 10 minutes
Right Starter .... 2 minutes

TRANSLATING COWL.

Do not exceed 417 KIAS or mach 0.90, whichever is less, with the translating cowl in any position other than fully closed.

19 ♦ **30** The translating cowl is limited to two complete cycles of operation in a 10 minute period.

19, 20, 23, and **26,** until modified by TCTO 1F-111A-819:

1. Do not exceed 550 KIAS or mach 0.95, whichever is less.
2. Do not exceed 15 degrees angle of attack with cowls closed.
3. Do not initiate afterburner operation at altitudes above 25,000 feet.

21, 22, 24, 25, 27 ♦ **30,** and those modified by TCTO 1F-111A-819, refer to figure 5-3, translating cowl flight limitations.

AIRSPEED LIMITATIONS.

FLUTTER LIMITATIONS.

Refer to T.O. 1F-111A-1A.

AIRSPEED AND ALTITUDE OPERATIONAL LIMIT ENVELOPES.

Refer to T.O. 1F-111A-1A.

SLAT/FLAP LIMIT SPEEDS.

The slat/flap limit speeds are presented in figure 5-4.

LANDING GEAR OPERATION LIMIT.

The maximum speeds at which the landing gear may be operated are:

Retraction .... 295 KIAS
Extension .... 295 KIAS
With landing gear extended .... 295 KIAS
Emergency extension 160 KIAS or minimum flying speed whichever is higher.

Approved Fuels

	PREFERRED FUEL	ALTERNATE FUELS				EMERGENCY FUEL
Fuel Specification	MIL-J-5624 Grade JP-4	MIL-J-5624 Grade JP-5	ASTM D1655 Type A	ASTM D1655 Type A-1	ASTM D1655 Type B	MIL-G-5572 Grade 115/145 Gasoline Blended with 3% MIL-L-6082 Grade 1100 Petroleum Oil
NATO Equivalent		F-44	F-30	F-35	F-40	F-22 Gasoline/O-117 Oil
Freezing Point (Max.)	−76°F −60°C	−40°F −40°C	−40°F −40°C	−58°F −50°C	−60°F −51°C	−76°F
Engine Recommended Fuel Gravity Fuel Control Specific Gravity Adjustment Setting	JP-4 See Note A	JP-5 See Note A	JP-5 See Note A	JP-5 See Note A	JP-4 See Note A	Min Value on Scale (.75) See Note "A"
Contains Anti-Icing Additive	Yes	No	No	No	No	No
Limitations	None	See Note B	See Note B	See Note B	See Note B	See Note "C"
System Refurbishing Requirements After Use	None	None	None	None	None	Defuel A/C to the Unpumpable Quantity and Refuel with Preferred or Alternate Fuel

NOTE A:

It is not mandatory to change the setting of the fuel control specific gravity adjustment pointer. However, if it is not made, the specific fuel consumption may deviate from the normal values.

NOTE B:

Since this fuel does not contain an anti-icing additive and the engines are not equipped with fuel heaters, consideration should be given to blending an anti-icing additive with the fuel if extensive operation is to be performed with fuel at a temperature of 32°F or less. The additive will prevent ice from accumulating in the fuel controls and strainers.

NOTE C:

1. This fuel is approved for a one flight emergency situation only. An alternate fuel should be used if available.
2. Fuel Tank Pressure switch must be selected to PRESS prior to take-off. The TANK PRESS caution lamp will be lighted when the landing gear is down or the refuel receptacle is extended.
3. Throttle movements should be as slow as practical.
4. Altitude should remain as low as practical and must not exceed 35,000 feet.
5. Engine thrust available may be reduced approximately 10 percent.
6. The aircraft should be filled with fuel at a temperature of less than 100°F and maintained as cool as possible thereafter. Supersonic flight should be avoided.
7. It is permissible to mix this fuel with a preferred or alternate fuel in the aircraft. However the above restrictions are still applicable.

Figure 5-2.

Translating Cowl Flight Limitations

DATA BASIS: ESTIMATED
DATE: 18 AUGUST 1967

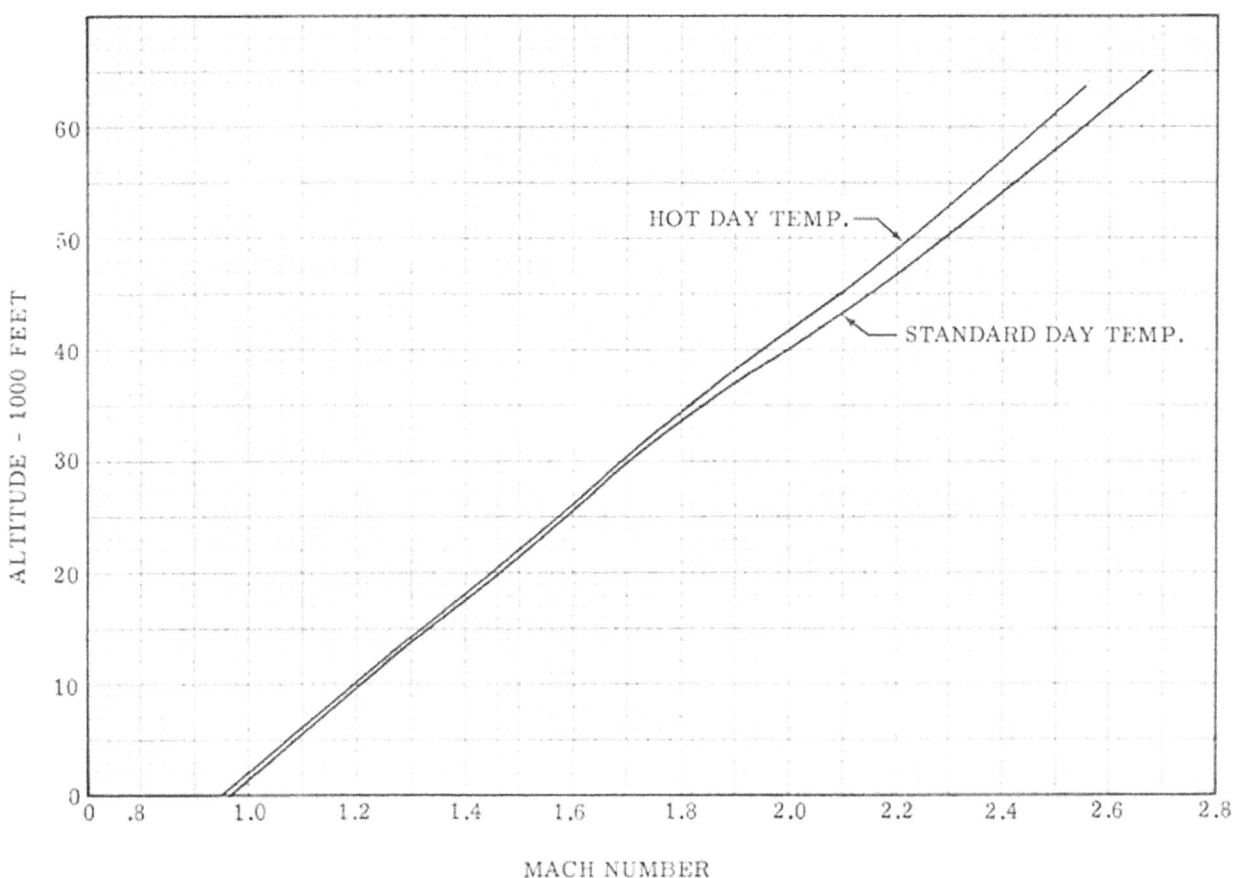

Figure 5-3. ㉑, ㉒, ㉓, ㉗ ∮ ㉚, and those modified by T.C.T.O. 1F-111A-819

Section V
Operating Limitations

T.O. 1F-111A-1

Slat/Flap Limit Speeds

	POSITION		AIRSPEED — KIAS/MACH Whichever is less
SLATS	⑲ ♦ ㉚	Extended	280/0.62
	㉛ ♦	Extended	297/0.62
FLAPS	⑲ ♦ ㉚	0—15 degrees	250/0.62
	㉛ ♦	0—15 degrees	270/0.62
	⑲ ♦ ㉚	15—30 degrees	250/0.62
	㉛ ♦	15—30 degrees	270/0.62
		30—37.5 degrees	225/0.48

Figure 5-4.

Note

On aircraft ⑲ ♦ ㉚, to maintain the required pneumatic pressure, as a function of temperature, for emergency extension of the landing gear, it is recommended that unnecessary operation of the speed brake or landing gear cycling be avoided if ram air temperature is —29 degrees C (—20 degrees F) or less.

TERRAIN FOLLOWING RADAR OPERATION.

- Manual mode using only E scope display must not be flown below 500 feet set clearance.

- ⑲ ♦ ㉚ Auto—Limited to not less than 1000 feet set clearance and/or not greater than mach 0.80.

- ⑲ ♦ ㉚ Manual—Limited to not less than 400 feet set clearance and/or not greater than mach 0.80.

RAM AIR MODE LIMIT SPEED.

WARNING

Aircraft ⑲ ♦ ㉚ are restricted to 330 KIAS when operating in the RAM Air Mode. Airspeed above 330 KIAS may result in structural failure of the ground cooling service air door.

Maximum speeds for ram air operation at various altitudes for aircraft ㉛ ♦ are shown in figure 5-5. Operation outside the continuous envelope is not recommended because there is inadequate air flow for cooling at the lower airspeeds and cabin temperature will be too warm at the higher airspeeds.

Ram Air Mode Limits

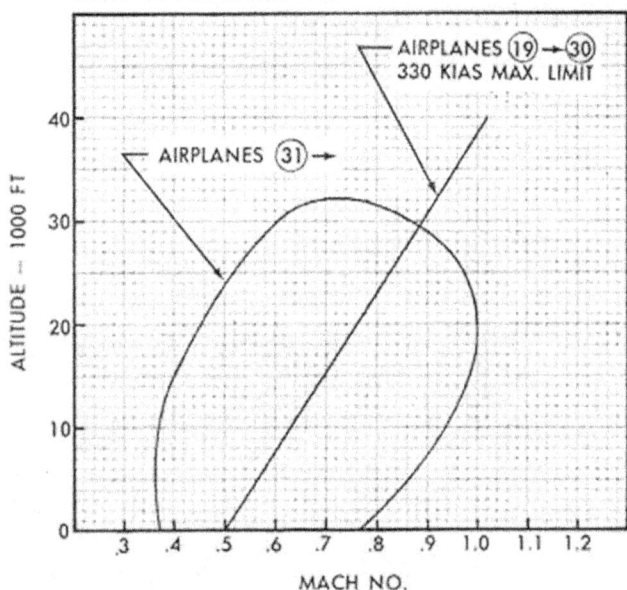

Figure 5-5.

TIRE LIMIT SPEED (ZERO WIND).

Maximum tire takeoff speed .... 157 KIAS
Emergency landing maximum tire speed .... 200 KIAS

Note

Tail wind component must be subtracted from the zero wind tire limit speed. The headwind component must be added to the zero wind tire limit speed.

TAXI SPEED.

Maximum taxi speed .... 25 knots

ARRESTING HOOK ENGAGING SPEED.

For maximum arresting hook engaging speed, refer to figure 5-6.

CAUTION

The maximum barrier cable the arresting hook will accept is 1¼ inches in diameter.

MINIMUM FLYING SPEEDS.

The minimum flying speeds are defined by the maximum angle of attack limits presented in figure 5-8. For a description of minimum flying speeds, refer "Minimum Flying Speeds", Section VI.

MINIMUM FLYING SPEEDS FOR SINGLE GENERATOR CONSTANT SPEED DRIVE OIL COOLING.

Minimum airspeeds/altitudes for constant speed drive oil cooling for continuous single alternator operation are as follows:

- 250 KIAS—20,000 feet and above.
- 200 KIAS—below 20,000 feet.

Note

Flight below minimum speeds is permitted for time not to exceed five minutes to accomplish required maneuvers.

MANEUVERABILITY LIMITATIONS.

LONGITUDINAL LIMITATIONS.

Refer to T.O. 1F-111A-1A.

LIMIT MANEUVER LOAD FACTORS.

Wing Sweep.

- ⑲ ♦ ㉚ Aircraft modified by TCTO 1F-11A-818 are restricted to −1.5g with wing sweep angles of 60 through 72.5 degrees.

- ⑲ ♦ ㉚ Do not exceed + 4.5 "g" with sweep greater than 66 degrees.

Slats.

Do not operate slats during aircraft maneuvers that exceed 2 "g's". Do not exceed 2 "g" maneuver with the slats in any intermediate position.

For other limit maneuver load factors not contained herein, refer to T.O. 1F-111A-1A.

ROLL LIMITATIONS.

The following roll limitations are based on 80 percent limit strength values. It should be noted that full normal lateral stick deflection is indicated by a force detent.

At All Wing Sweep Angles.

Do not exceed the force detent at any mach number at any altitude except under emergency conditions requiring more than normal lateral control.

At Wing Sweep Angles Where Spoilers Are Operational. (Sweep Angles of 45 Degrees or Less).

- Do not exceed ½ normal lateral stick deflection at speeds greater than 450 KIAS at any altitude.
- With fuel in wings, do not exceed ½ normal lateral stick deflection at any mach number at any altitude.
- Limitations with external stores will be incorporated when available.

At Wing Sweep Angles Where Spoilers Are Not Operational. (Sweep Angles Greater Than 45 Degrees).

- ⑲ ♦ ㉚ At altitudes less than 45,000 feet, do not exceed ½ normal lateral stick deflection at speeds greater than 450 KIAS.
- ㉛ ♦ At altitudes less than 25,000 feet, do not exceed ½ normal lateral stick deflection at speeds greater than 525 KIAS.

YAW LIMITATIONS.

The yaw limitations presented in figure 5-7 are based upon 80 percent limit strength values and are presented in terms of rudder pedal deflection.

Section V
Operating Limitations

T.O. 1F-111A-1

Maximum Arresting Hook Engaging Speed

DATA BASIS: ESTIMATED
DATE: 18 AUGUST 1967

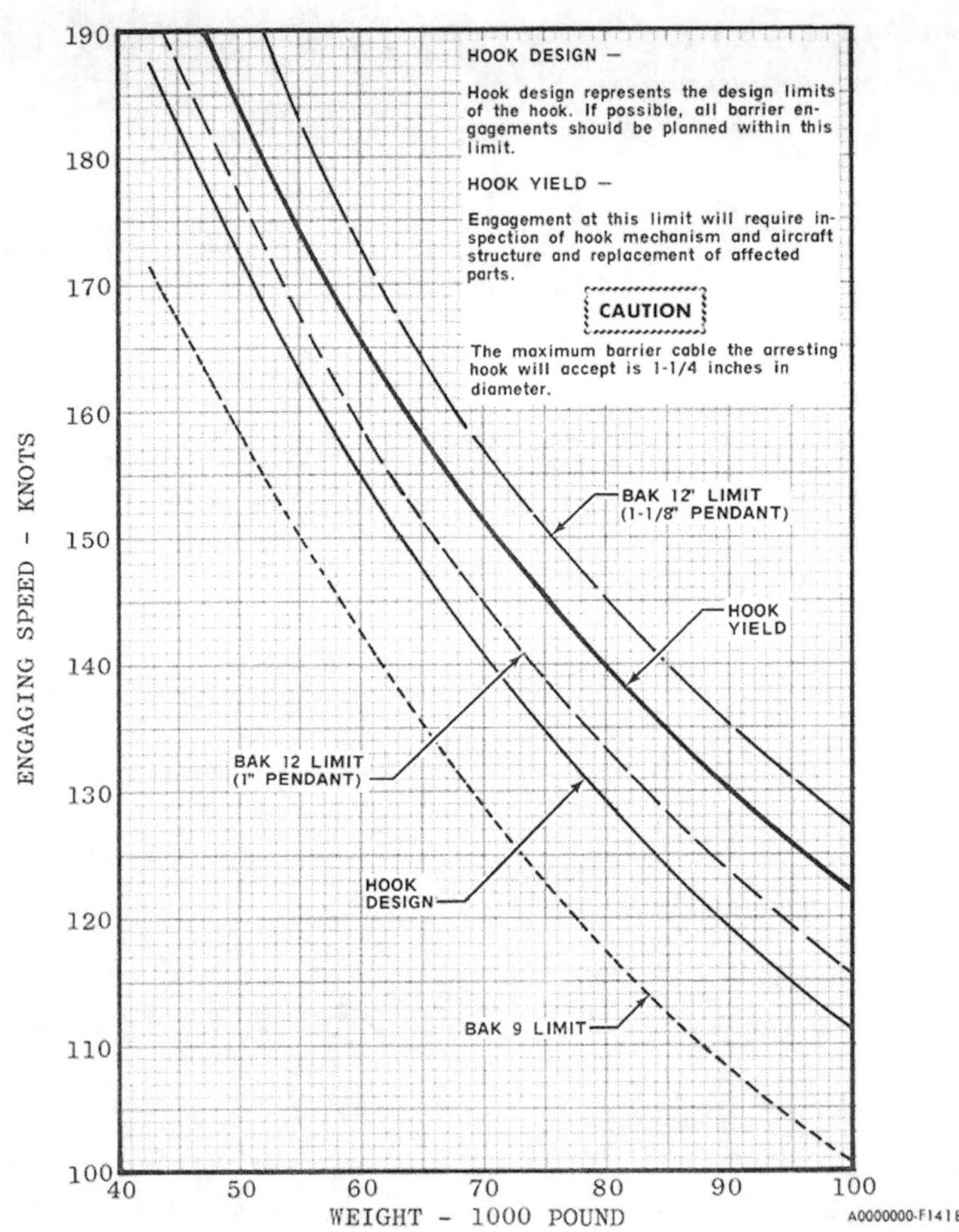

Figure 5-6.

Allowable Rudder Command

DATA BASIS: ESTIMATED
DATE: 18 AUGUST 1967

FUEL GRADE: JP-4
ENGINES: TF30-P-1/P-3

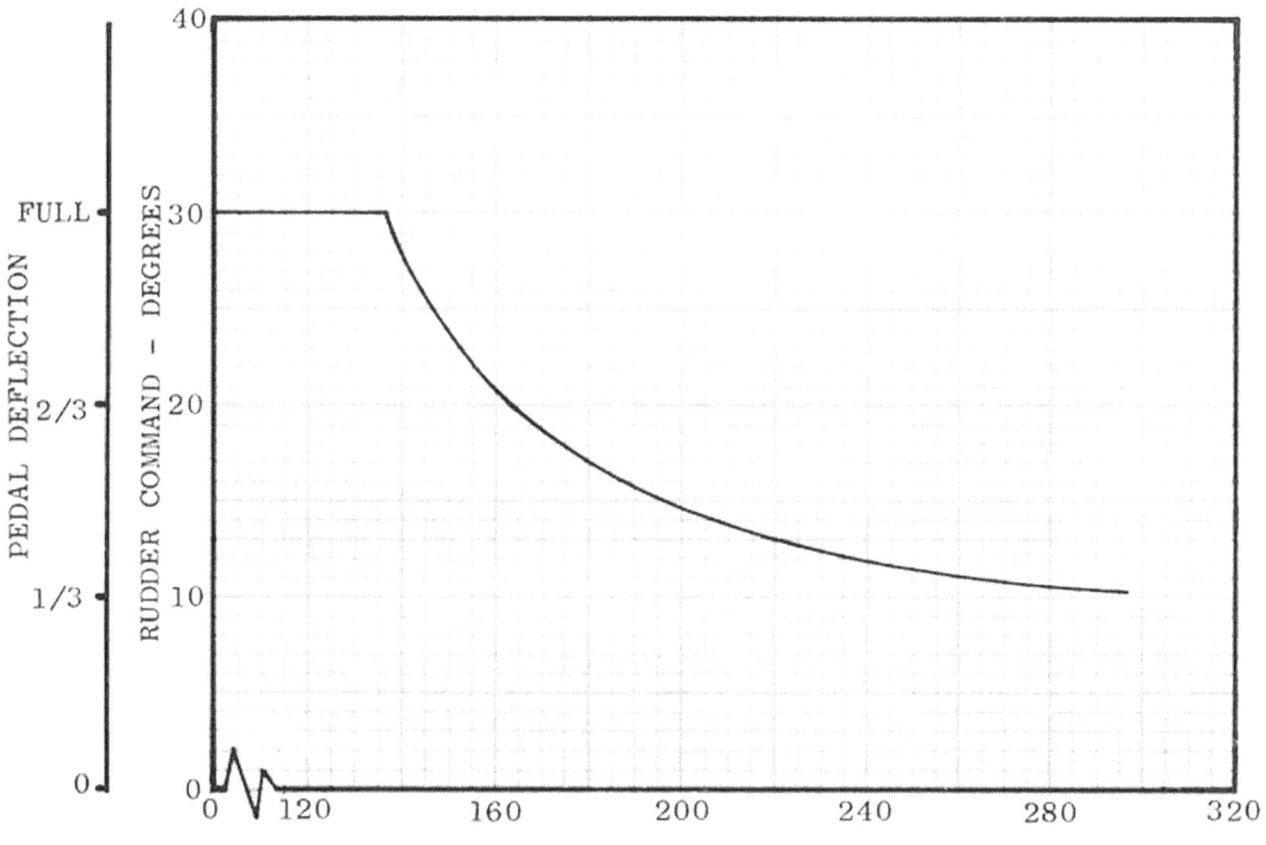

Figure 5-7.

Section V
Operating Limitations

T.O. 1F-111A-1

ANGLE OF ATTACK AND SIDESLIP.

The angle of attack and sideslip limitations presented in figure 5-8 must be observed.

WARNING

Maneuvers resulting in uncoordinated flight should not be performed above 15 degrees angle of attack. Because the rudder required to maintain coordinated flight increases, increased attention should be given to coordinating rudder and lateral control when maneuvering at angles of attack above 10 degrees.

PROHIBITED MANEUVERS.

The following maneuvers are prohibited:
- Spins
- Stalls
- Flight into heavy buffet.
- Rolls in excess of 360 degrees.

- Zoom climbs to above 35,000 feet pressure altitude at subsonic speeds, and above 50,000 feet pressure altitude at supersonic speeds.
- **19** ↓ **30** Flight in icing conditions.

Note

Icing is possible under the following conditions:

Ground operation.
- In visible moisture—Temperature between 35°F and −10°F.
- In Clear air—Relative humidity above 70 percent and dew point temperature 25°F to 35°F.

Inflight operation.
- In visible moisture—Ambient temperature between 35°F and −10°F.
- In Clear air—No limitations related to icing.

Angle of Attack and Sideslip Limitations

WING SWEEP (Degrees)	CONFIGURATION (With or without weapons)	ANGLE OF ATTACK	RUDDER PEDAL LIMIT Applicable for all angles of attack.
16-26	Gear and flaps down.	18 degrees	Sideslip angle is limited by the rudder pedal deflection limits presented in figure 5-7. With the yaw damper off, do not make abrupt rudder inputs.
16-45	Gear and flaps up.	15 degrees or moderate buffet (±.25 g) whichever occurs first.	Yaw damper on: ½ pedal deflection sideslip. Yaw damper off: No intentional pedal deflection sideslip.
46-72	Gear and flaps up.	18 degrees.	Yaw damper on: ½ pedal deflection sideslip. Yaw damper off: No intentional pedal deflection sideslip.

Figure 5-8.

CENTER-OF-GRAVITY LIMITATIONS.

Figure 5-9, "External Stores and Weapon Loading Configurations," is provided to determine the specific chart to be used to locate the aft center of gravity limit for store loading. Figure 5-10, sheets 1 through 4, presents the aft center of gravity limits based on wing sweep angle and mach number for all gross weights. Each sheet contains a low speed and a high speed section. The "Low Speed" section locates the aft center of gravity limits for low speed inflight operation and takeoff and landing operations. The "High Speed" section locates the aft center of gravity limits for longitudinal stability and directional stability. Both low speed (flaps and gear up or down) and high speed limits are presented under the following considerations:

(1) The low speed limits are applicable up to flap limit speeds and are set to maintain at least one percent static margin.

(2) The high speed aft limits for wing sweep angles of 16 through 50 degrees are based on maintaining a one percent static margin at mach 0.8 at sea level.

(3) The high speed aft limits for wing sweep angles of 50 through 72.5 degrees are based on maintaining a minimum level of directional stability.

Example: Determine the aft center of gravity limit for store loading, wing sweep, and airspeed for specific phases of flight with MK-43 weapons loaded.

Given: Stations 4 and 5, 3 and 6—MK43 weapons for each of the following:
  a. Takeoff: Low speed, flaps and gear down, 16 degree wing sweep, auxiliary flap extended.
  b. Low Speed: Flaps and gear up, 16 degree wing sweep, slats extended.
  c. Low Speed: Flaps and gear up, 26 degree wing sweep, clean airplane.
  d. High speed: 26 degree wing sweep.
  e. High speed: 72.5 degree wing sweep, mach 2.2.
  f. Landing: Low speed, flaps and gear down, 26 degree wing sweep, auxiliary flap retracted.

Find: Aft center of gravity limit for the following:
  a. Takeoff.
  b. Low speed, flaps and gear up, 16 degree wing sweep, slats extended.
  c. Low speed, flaps and gear up, 26 degree wing sweep, clean airplane.
  d. High speed, 26 degree wing sweep.
  e. High speed (mach 2.2), 72.5 degree wing sweep longitudinal and directional aft limits.
  f. Landing.

Refer to "External Stores and Weapons Loading Configurations," figure 5-9. Locate the MK 43 weapons loadings on pylon stations 4 and 5, and 3 and 6. To determine the correct chart to be used for determination of the longitudinal and directional aft center of gravity limits, read to the right and note:

(1) The chart to be utilized is figure 5-10, sheet 2.

(2) The longitudinal limit is depicted by longitudinal index "B".

(3) The directional limit is depicted by directional index "G". (An asterisk indicates no directional limit applicable for that store loading configuration).

Follow the example lines on figure 5-10, sheet 2 in the appropriate speed regime for the particular configuration specified above to determine the following:

	Aft Limit	
a. Takeoff	29.0 percent	❶
b. Low Speed, flaps and gear up, 16 degree wing sweep, slats extended	39.0 percent	❷
c. Low Speed, flaps and gear up, 26 degree wing sweep, clean airplane	54.0 percent	❸
d. High Speed, 26 degree wing sweep	39.5 percent	❹
e. High Speed (mach 2.2) 72.5 degree wing sweep:		
(1) Longitudinal	60.0 percent	❺
(2) Directional	48.5 percent	❻

Note

The aft limit for directional stability is less than the aft limit for longitudinal stability; therefore it would determine the center of gravity limit for flight in this regime.

f. Landing	42.5 percent	❼

If weapons are jettisoned with wing sweeps of 16 through 26 degrees, center of gravity shifts will be negligible and within the limits presented in figure 5-10, sheet 1.

After determining the aft center of gravity limit, either longitudinal or directional, refer to "Center of Gravity Envelope (Typical)", Section VI, to determine the gross weight ranges within which the aircraft should be operated to maintain the center of gravity limits.

Section V
Operating Limitations

T.O. 1F-111A-1

External Stores And Weapon Loading Configurations

(For use in determining center of gravity limits. Applicable to all weapon bay loadings. Bay loading does not effect the limit. Bay loading effects the center of gravity of the aircraft).

PYLON STATIONS				CHART AND INDEX DETERMINATION		
4 & 5	3 & 6	2 & 7	1 & 8	Figure 5-10	Longitudinal Index	Directional Index
None	None	None	None	Sheet 1	A	E
Pylons	Pylons	None	None	Sheet 1	A	E
Pylons	Pylons	Pylons	Pylons	Sheet 1	A	*
Pylon	A/B-45Y-1			Sheet 2	B	*
Pylon	5 MK-82 QRC			Sheet 3	C	*
Pylon	5 M-117			Sheet 3	C	*
Pylon	QRC			Sheet 2	B	F
Pylon	Pylon	A/B-45Y-1	A/B-45Y-1	Sheet 2	B	*
Pylon	Pylon	TMU-28B	TMU-28B	Sheet 3	C	*
AIM-9B	2 AIM-9B			Sheet 2	B	F
MK-43	MK-43			Sheet 2	B	G
MK-57	MK-57			Sheet 2	B	F
6 MK-82	5 MK-82 QRC			Sheet 3	C	*
MK-84	QRC	MK-84	MK-84	Sheet 3	C	*
3 M-117	3 M-117			Sheet 3	C	*
3 M-117	3 M-117	3 M-117	3 M-117	Sheet 4	D	*
6 M-117	6 M-117	3 M-117	3 M-117	Sheet 4	D	*
6 M-117	5 M-117 QRC			Sheet 4	D	*
M-118	QRC			Sheet 3	C	*
M-118	QRC	M-118		Sheet 4	D	*
M-118	QRC	M-118	M-118	Sheet 4	D	*
2 BLU-1/B	2 BLU-1/B	2 BLU-1/B	2 BLU-1/B	Sheet 4	D	*
3 BLU-14/B	3 BLU-14/B	3 BLU-14/B	3 BLU-14/B	Sheet 4	D	*
BLU-34	QRC	BLU-34	BLU-34	Sheet 3	C	*
3 CBU-7/A	3 CBU-7/A			Sheet 3	C	*
3 CBU-7/A	3 CBU-7/A	3 CBU-7/A	3 CBU-7/A	Sheet 4	D	*
3 CBU-24/B	2 CBU-24/B QRC			Sheet 3	C	*
3 CBU-24/B	2 CBU-24/B QRC	3 CBU-24/B	3 CBU-24/B	Sheet 4	D	*
3 CBU-29/B	2 CBU-29/B QRC	3 CBU-29/B	3 CBU-29/B	Sheet 4	D	*
3 LAU-3/A	3 LAU-3/A	3 LAU-3/A	3 LAU-3/A	Sheet 4	D	*
3 LAU-18/A	3 LAU-18/A	3 LAU-18/A	3 LAU-18/A	Sheet 4	D	*
3 MLU-10/B	3 MLU-10/B	3 MLU-10/B	3 MLU-10/B	Sheet 4	D	*
SUU-20/A	Pylon			Sheet 2	B	*
SUU-20/A	QRC			Sheet 2	B	*
TDU-11/B	Pylon			Sheet 2	B	*
TDU-11/B	TDU-11/B			Sheet 2	B	*
TMU-28B	TMU-28B			Sheet 3	C	*
TX-61	TX-61			Sheet 2	B	F

*Not carried to critical mach/altitude conditions; therefore directional aft limits are not applicable.

Figure 5-9.

Changed 18 August 1967

For any wing sweep, airspeed, or aircraft configuration, there is no inflight forward center of gravity limitation within the loading capabilities of the aircraft.

Note

Current loading of the aircraft does not result in center of gravity positions forward of 23 percent MAC at takeoff. If future loadings result in center of gravity positions forward of 23 percent MAC, increase rotation speed one knot for each one percent forward of 23 percent MAC.

Figure 5-11 presents the forward center of gravity limits for landing. The limits for landing are set forth as a result of structural considerations during the landing phase rather than longitudinal controllability during the approach phase.

Note

Loadings which result in an aft center of gravity in excess of 60 percent MAC can cause the aircraft to tip back when brakes are released with A/B power.

For crew module center of gravity limitations, refer to "Miscellaneous Operational Limitations" this section.

GROSS WEIGHT—CENTER OF GRAVITY LIMITATIONS FOR TAXI AND GROUND OPERATION.

The center of gravity limits for taxi and ground operation, based on gross weight, are presented in figure 5-12.

Note

At light gross weights, forward wing sweep angles will prevent nose wheel steering difficulties.

GROSS WEIGHT LIMITATIONS.

Maximum Taxi and Takeoff Gross Weight.

The maximum gross weight for taxi and takeoff is 90,000 pounds. Taxi and takeoff operations at weights above 72,000 pounds shall be confined to well prepared runways until completion of structural certification tests.

Maximum Flight Gross Weight.

The maximum gross weight for flight is 90,000 pounds.

Maximum Landing Gross Weight.

The maximum gross weight for landing is 80,000 pounds. The allowable sink rate at touchdown for various gross weights is shown in figure 5-13.

This page intentionally left blank.

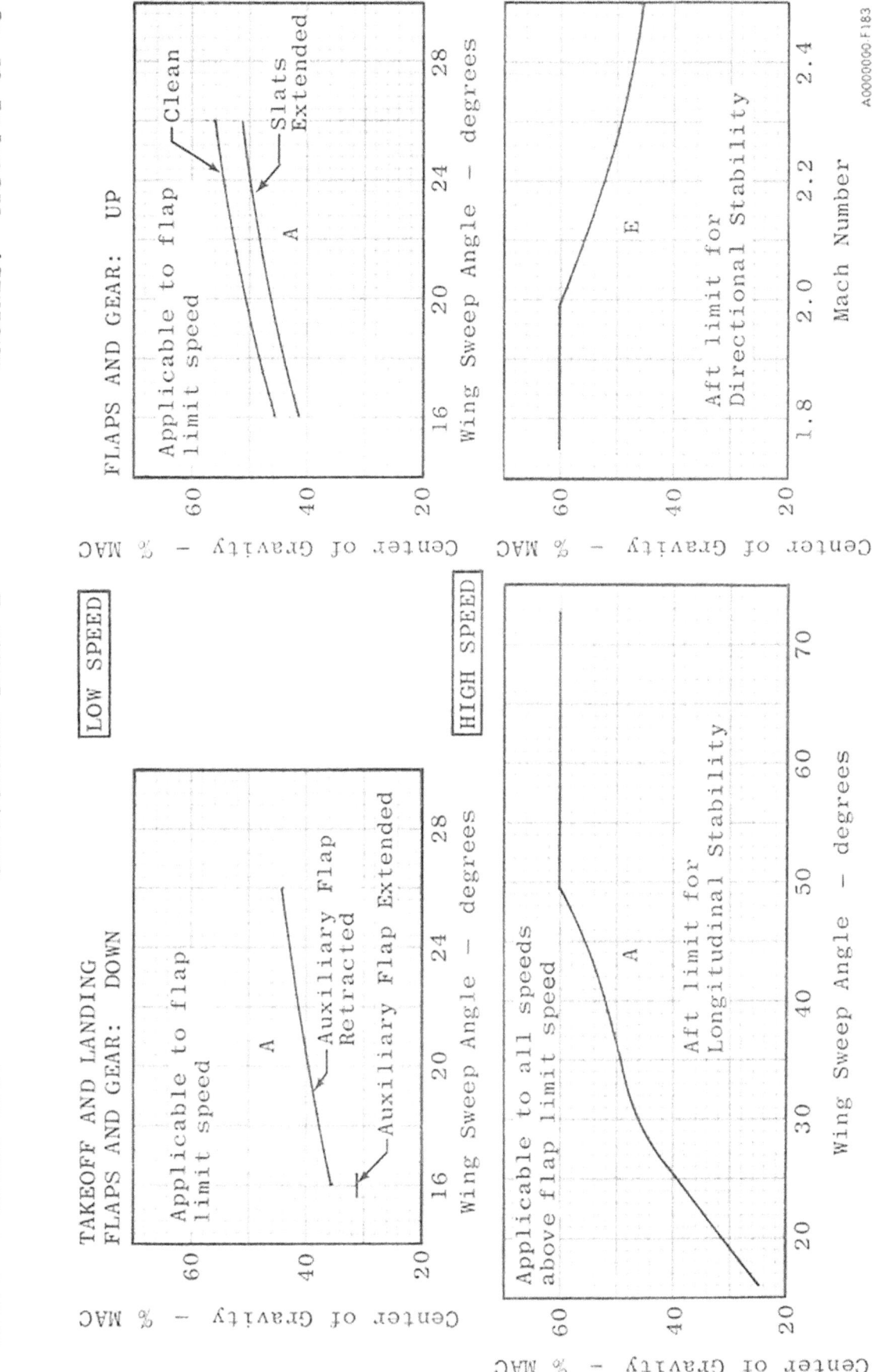

Figure 5-10. (Sheet 1)

Section V
Operating Limitations

T.O. 1F-111A-1

Aft Center of Gravity Limitations

DATA BASIS: ESTIMATED
DATE: 7 APRIL 1967

Longitudinal Index B -
Directional Index F and G

FUEL GRADE: JP-4
ENGINES: TF30-P-1 or -3

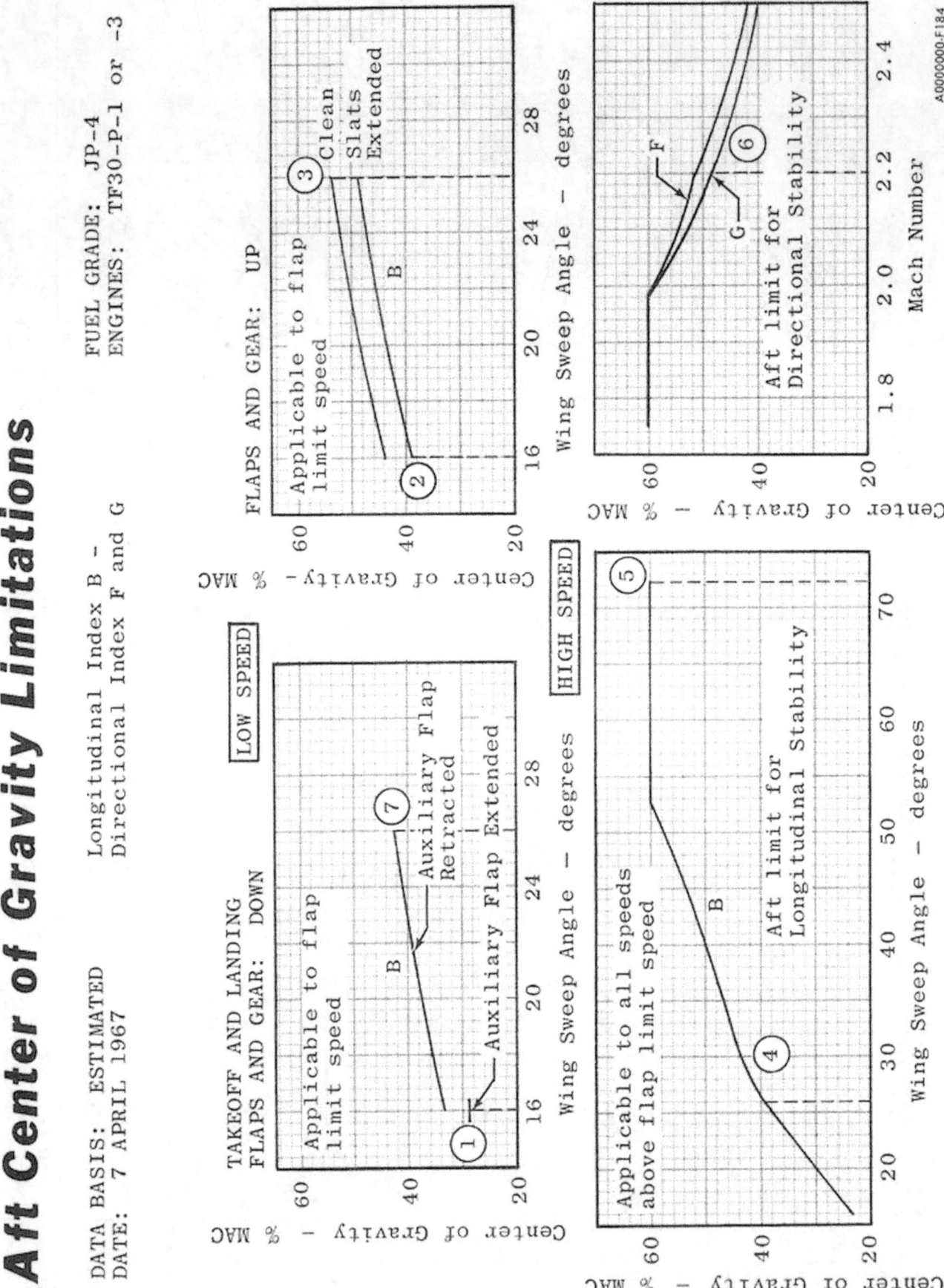

Figure 5-10. (Sheet 2)

5-14   Pages 5-14A thru 5-14B deleted.   Changed 18 August 1967

Aft Center of Gravity Limitations

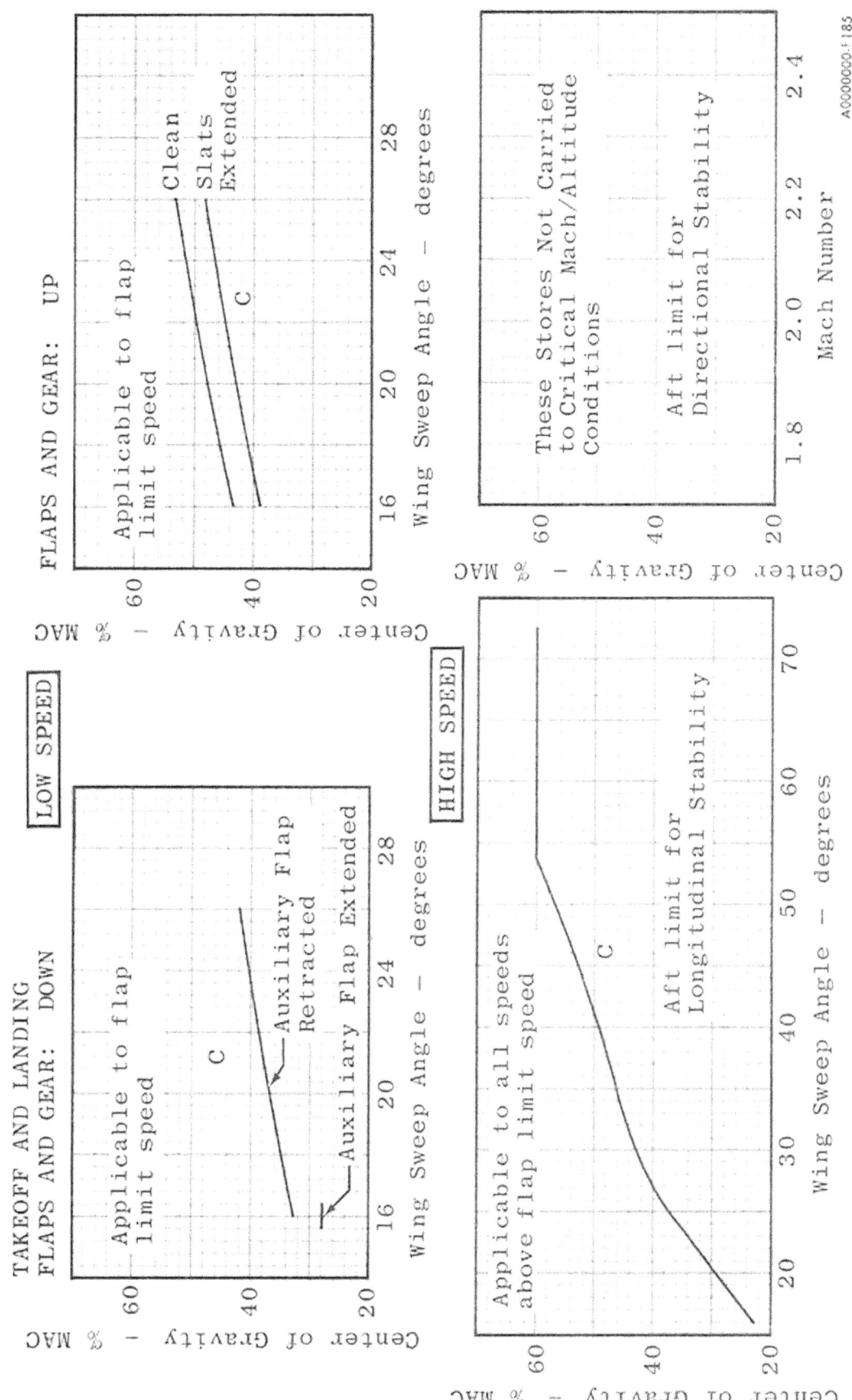

Figure 5-10. (Sheet 3)

Section V
Operating Limitations

T.O. 1F-111A-1

Aft Center of Gravity Limitations

DATA BASIS: ESTIMATED
DATE: 7 APRIL 1967

Longitudinal Index D –
Directional Index (not applicable)

FUEL GRADE: JP-4
ENGINES: TF30-P-1 or -3

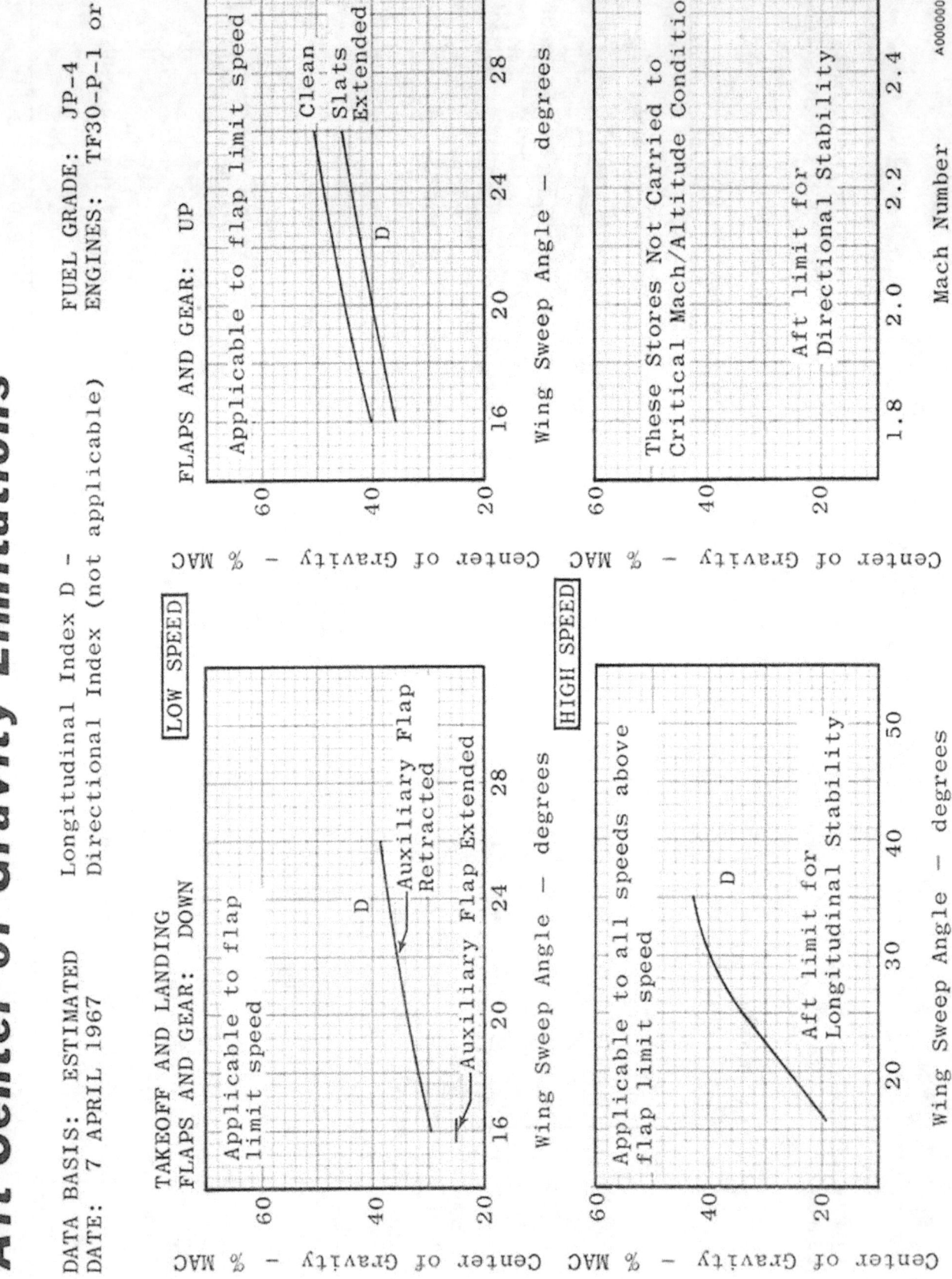

Figure 5-10. (Sheet 4)

5-16

Changed 18 August 1967

Section V
Operating Limitations

Foward Center of Gravity Limitations for Landing

DATA BASIS: ESTIMATED FLAPS AND GEAR DOWN FUEL GRADE: JP-4
DATE: 18 AUGUST 1967   ENGINES: TF30-P-1/P-3

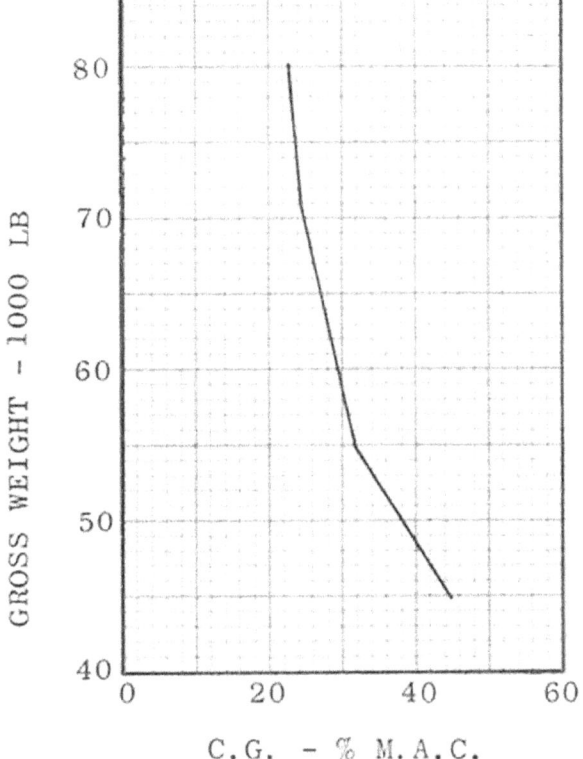

Figure 5-11.

Section V
Operating Limitations

T.O. 1F-111A-1

Gross Weight - C. G. Limitations for Taxi and Ground Operation

DATA BASIS: ESTIMATED
DATE: 7 APRIL 1967

FUEL GRADE: JP-4
ENGINES: TF30-P-1 or -3

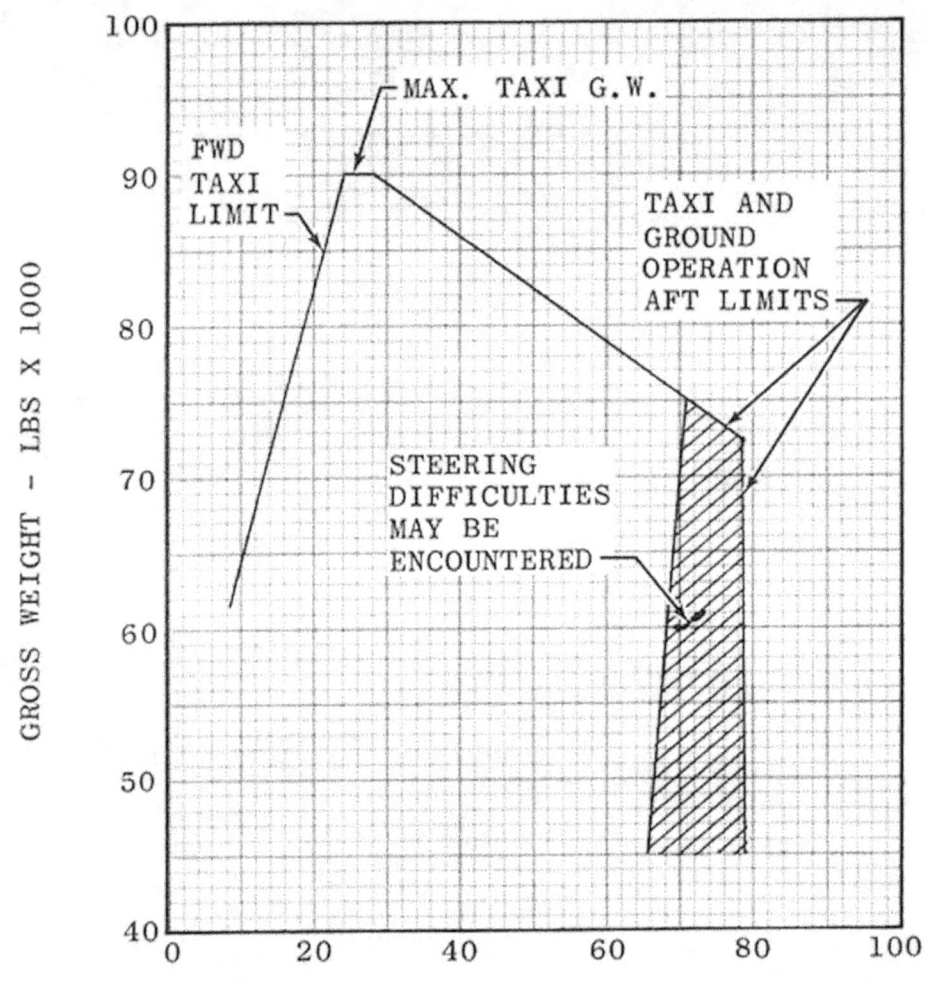

Figure 5-12.

Pages 5-18A thru 5-18D deleted.

Changed 18 August 1967

Allowable Sink Rate at Touchdown

DATA BASIS: ESTIMATED
DATE: 11 NOVEMBER 1966

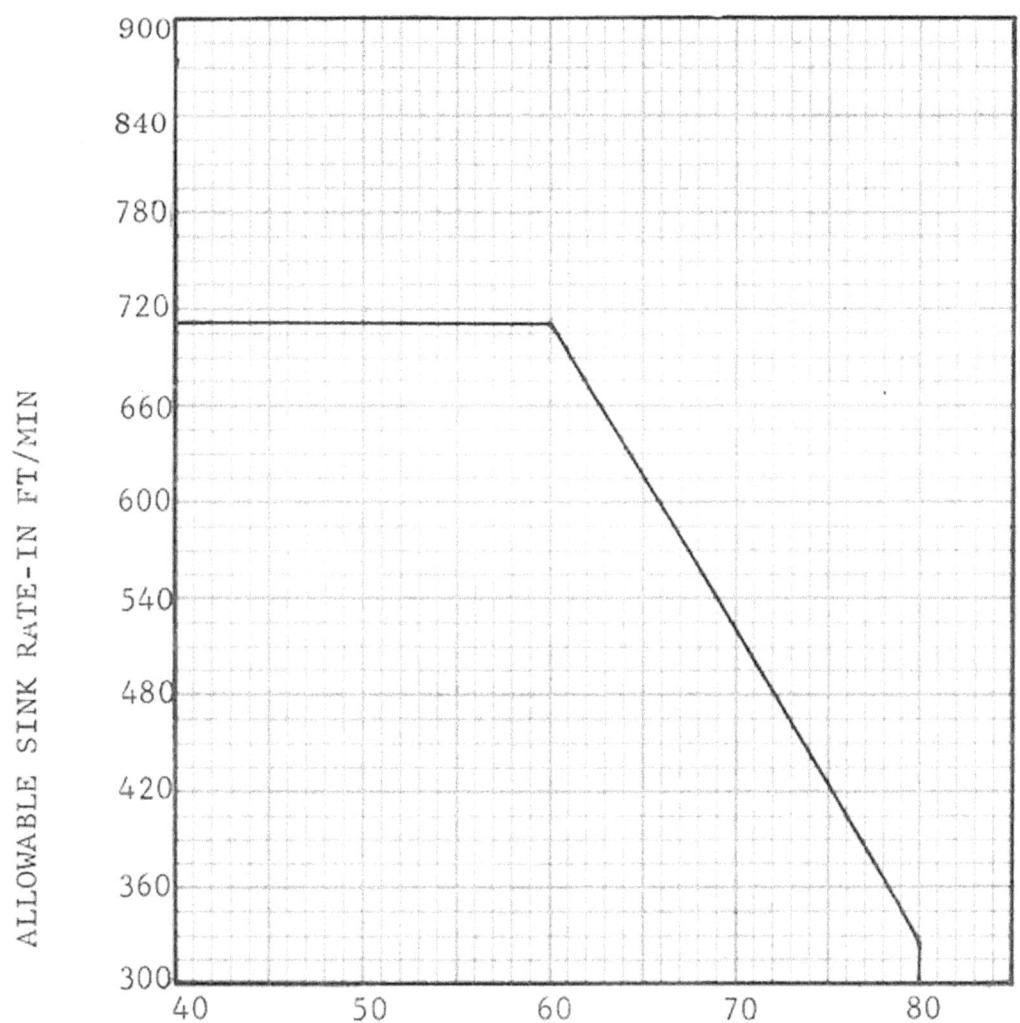

Figure 5-13.

Section V
Operating Limitations

T.O. 1F-111A-1

FLIGHT WITH AUGMENTATION OFF.

Figure 5-14 presents the augmentation off operating limits. For a complete discussion, refer to "Flight with Augmentation Off", Section VI.

WARNING

For landing with pitch and/or yaw damper off, approach at 10 degree angle of attack (approach indexer setting).

Augmentation Off Operating Limits

DO NOT EXCEED THE FOLLOWING AIRSPEEDS/ALTITUDES:		
PITCH DAMPER OFF		
Wing Sweep	Altitude	Airspeed
16 Degrees	All	Mach 0.40
26-45 Degrees	All	400 KCAS or Mach 0.75 whichever is less
46-72.5 Degrees	Sea Level to 20,000 feet / Above 20,000 feet	Mach 0.70 / None
ROLL OR YAW DAMPER OFF		
Wing Sweep	Altitude	Airspeed
16-45 Degrees	All	None
45-72.5 Degrees	All	Mach 1.5

Figure 5-14.

BRAKE LIMITATIONS.

BRAKE APPLICATION SPEED LIMIT.

Brake energy limits with slats, flaps and spoilers extended are presented in figure 5-15, sheet 1. The example lines explain how to determine the amount of energy absorbed by the brakes during a stop.

Note

Subtract 50 percent of the headwind component, measured by the tower, from the IAS. A tailwind component must be added to the IAS.

Example: Full Stop Landing.

Given: Gross weight = 60,000 pounds.
Airspeed when brakes applied = 95 knots IAS.
Tower reported wind velocity = 5 kt tailwind.
Pressure Altitude = 1000 feet.
Outside air temperature = 80 degrees F.

Find: Brake Energy Absorbed.

Solution:

Following example lines on figure 5-15, sheet 1, the brake energy absorbed is 13.4 million foot-pounds per brake.

CAUTION

If maximum braking capacity is utilized (danger zone), wheel blowout plugs will relieve tire pressure within 3 to 15 minutes after the stop. Provisions should be made to cope with possible wheel fires which may start shortly after blowout plug release.

Note

When figure 5-15 is used to determine values of brake energy absorbed, it is assumed that the airplane is brought to a complete stop with a single continuous application of the brakes.

Brake energy limits with slats, flaps and spoilers retracted are shown in figure 5-15, sheet 2.

Changed 18 August 1967

T.O. 1F-111A-1

Section V
Operating Limitations

Brake Energy Limits

DATA BASIS: ESTIMATED
DATE: 18 AUGUST 1967

SLATS-FLAPS-SPOILERS EXTENDED

FUEL GRADE: JP4
ENGINES: TF30-P-1/P-3

The following information explains action to be taken when a stop in the DANGER, CAUTION, or NORMAL ZONES is performed:

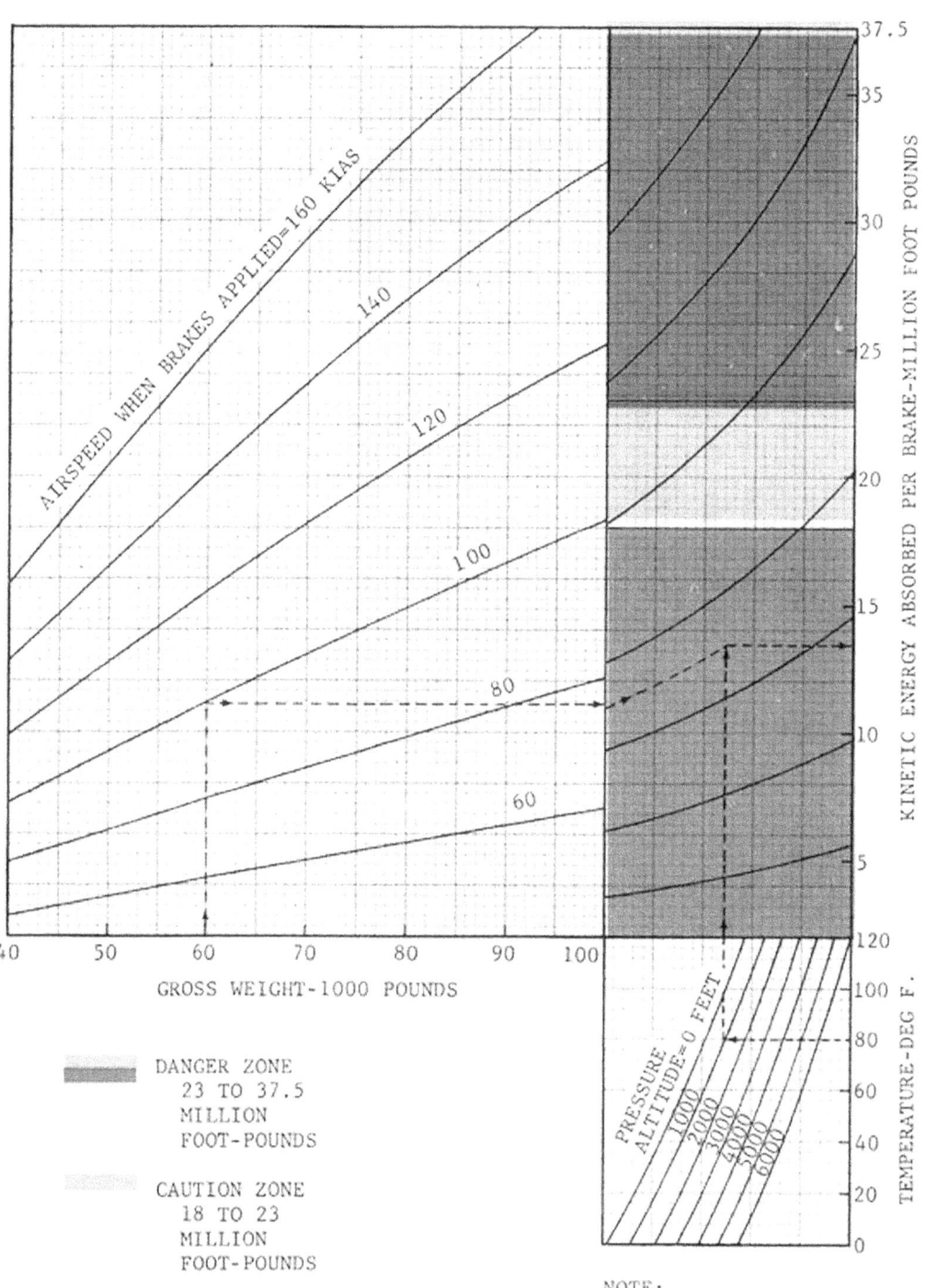

DANGER ZONE

1. Use moderate braking below 25 knots until taxi speed of 5-10 knots is obtained. Release brakes, if possible, and maintain forward motion.

CAUTION

Applying maximum brake pressure below 25 knots may cause brake rotors and stators to fuse together.

2. Proceed to the nearest parking area clear of other airplanes and personnel without stopping and as quickly as possible. Do not set parking brakes.

3. Request fire fighting equipment. Hydraulic fluid fire is imminent. Approach main landing gear from front or rear for fire fighting purposes only.

4. Extinguishing agents shall be applied as a fog or foam on the tires and directly to the brakes. Do not spray liquid directly on the wheels.

5. Evacuate aircraft immediately. Leave immediate vicinity keeping forward of the aircraft.

CAUTION ZONE

1. The area in the vicinity of the main landing gear within 50 ft. of any brake should be regarded as unsafe during the first one hour and 15 minutes after the stop, unless the thermal release plugs have blown allowing the tires to be deflated.

2. Do not set parking brakes. Request fire fighting equipment. Hydraulic fluid fire is possible.

3. Do not attempt takeoff until the brake housings and tires are cool to the bare hand to prevent possible tire failure during takeoff or in flight.

NORMAL ZONE

1. Parking brakes may be set.

2. If stop does not exceed 14 million foot pounds per brake, subsequent takeoff may be performed immediately. However, brake application is restricted to speeds and gross weights in the CAUTION ZONE or below in the event a subsequent takeoff is aborted.

3. Unrestricted subsequent takeoff may be performed only after brake housings and tires are cool to the bare hand.

4. If stop exceeds 14 million foot pounds per brake, subsequent takeoff may be performed only after brake housing and tires are cool to the bare hand.

DANGER ZONE
23 TO 37.5
MILLION
FOOT-POUNDS

CAUTION ZONE
18 TO 23
MILLION
FOOT-POUNDS

NORMAL ZONE
0 TO 18
MILLION
FOOT-POUNDS

NOTE:
For aborted takeoff, if brake application speed is 100 knots or above, add four million foot pounds to charted value to account for residual engine thrust.

Figure 5-15. (Sheet 1)

Section II
Normal Procedures

T.O. 1F-111A-1

Brake Energy Limits

DATE BASIS: ESTIMATED
DATE: 18 AUGUST 1967

FLAPS - SLATS - SPOILERS RETRACTED

FUEL GRADE: JP4
ENGINES: TF30-P-1/P-3

DANGER ZONE

1. Use moderate braking below 25 knots until taxi speed of 5-10 knots is obtained. Release brakes, if possible, and maintain forward motion.

The following information explains action to be taken when a stop in the DANGER, CAUTION, or NORMAL ZONES is performed:

CAUTION

Applying maximum brake pressure below 25 knots may cause brake rotors and stators to fuse together.

2. Proceed to the nearest parking area clear of other airplanes and personnel without stopping and as quickly as possible. Do not set parking brakes.

3. Request fire fighting equipment. Hydraulic fluid fire is imminent. Approach main landing gear from front or rear for fire fighting purposes only.

4. Extinguishing agents shall be applied as a fog or foam on the tires and directly to the brakes. Do not spray liquid directly on the wheels.

5. Evacuate aircraft immediately. Leave immediate vicinity keeping forward of the aircraft.

CAUTION ZONE

1. The area in the vicinity of the main landing gear within 50 ft. of any brake should be regarded as unsafe during the first one hour and 15 minutes after the stop, unless the thermal release plugs have blown allowing the tires to be deflated.

2. Do not set parking brakes. Request fire fighting equipment. Hydraulic fluid fire is possible.

3. Do not attempt takeoff until the brake housings and tires are cool to the bare hand to prevent possible tire failure during takeoff or in flight.

NORMAL ZONE

1. Parking brakes may be set.

2. If stop does not exceed 14 million foot pounds per brake, subsequent takeoff may be performed immediately. However, brake application is restricted to speeds and gross weight in the CAUTION ZONE or below in the event a subsequent takeoff is aborted.

3. Unrestricted subsequent takeoff may be performed only after brake housings and tires are cool to the bare hand.

4. If stop exceeds 14 million foot pounds per brake, subsequent takeoff may be performed only after brake housing and tires are cool to the bare hand.

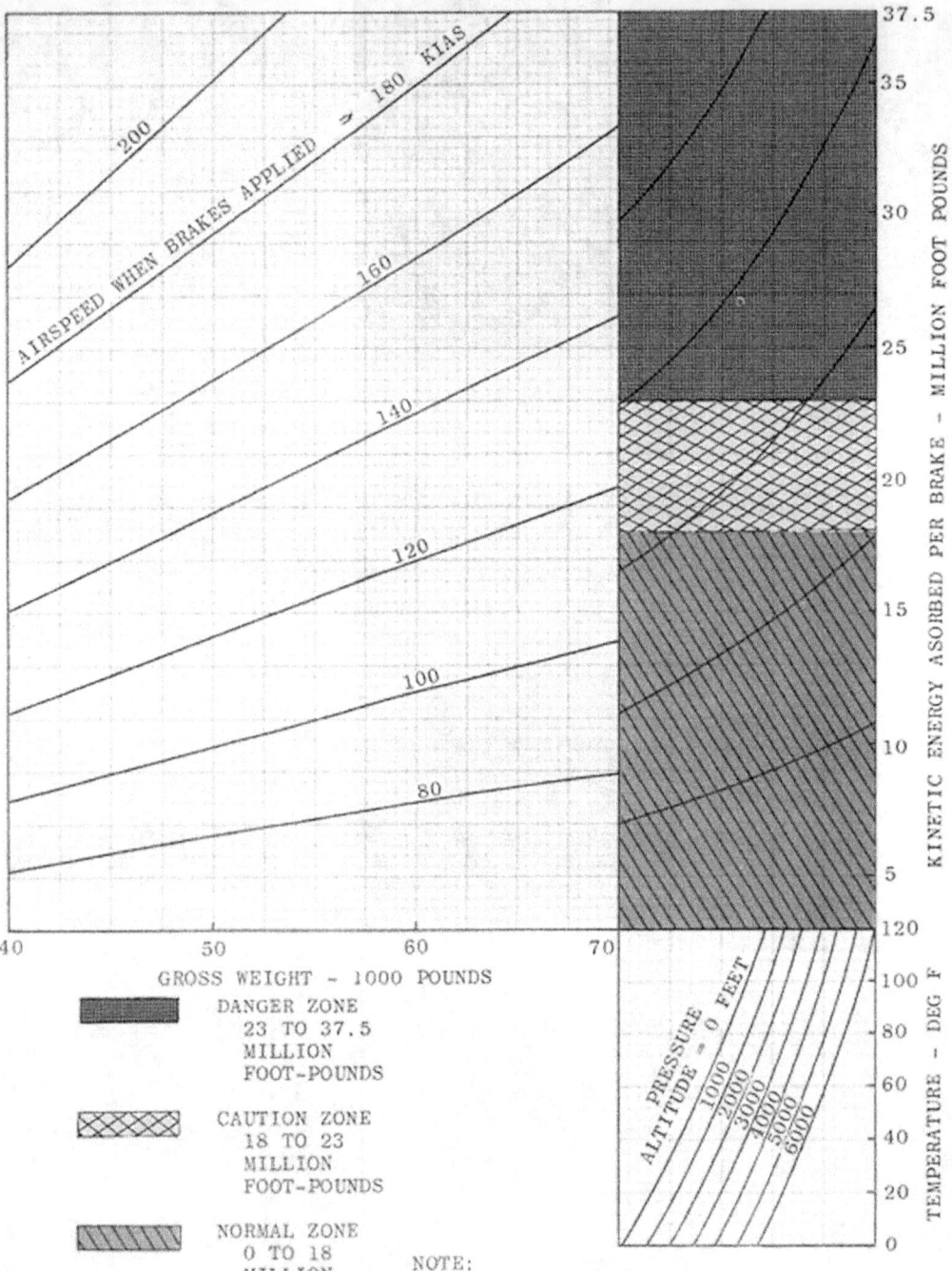

DANGER ZONE
23 TO 37.5 MILLION FOOT-POUNDS

CAUTION ZONE
18 TO 23 MILLION FOOT-POUNDS

NORMAL ZONE
0 TO 18 MILLION FOOT-POUNDS

NOTE:
For aborted takeoff, if brake application speed is 100 knots or above, add four million foot pounds to charted value to account for residual engine thrust.

Figure 5-15. (Sheet 2)

Tail Bumper Contact Limits

DATA BASIS: ESTIMATED
DATE: 18 AUGUST 1967

FUEL GRADE: JP-4
ENGINES: TF30-P-1/P-3

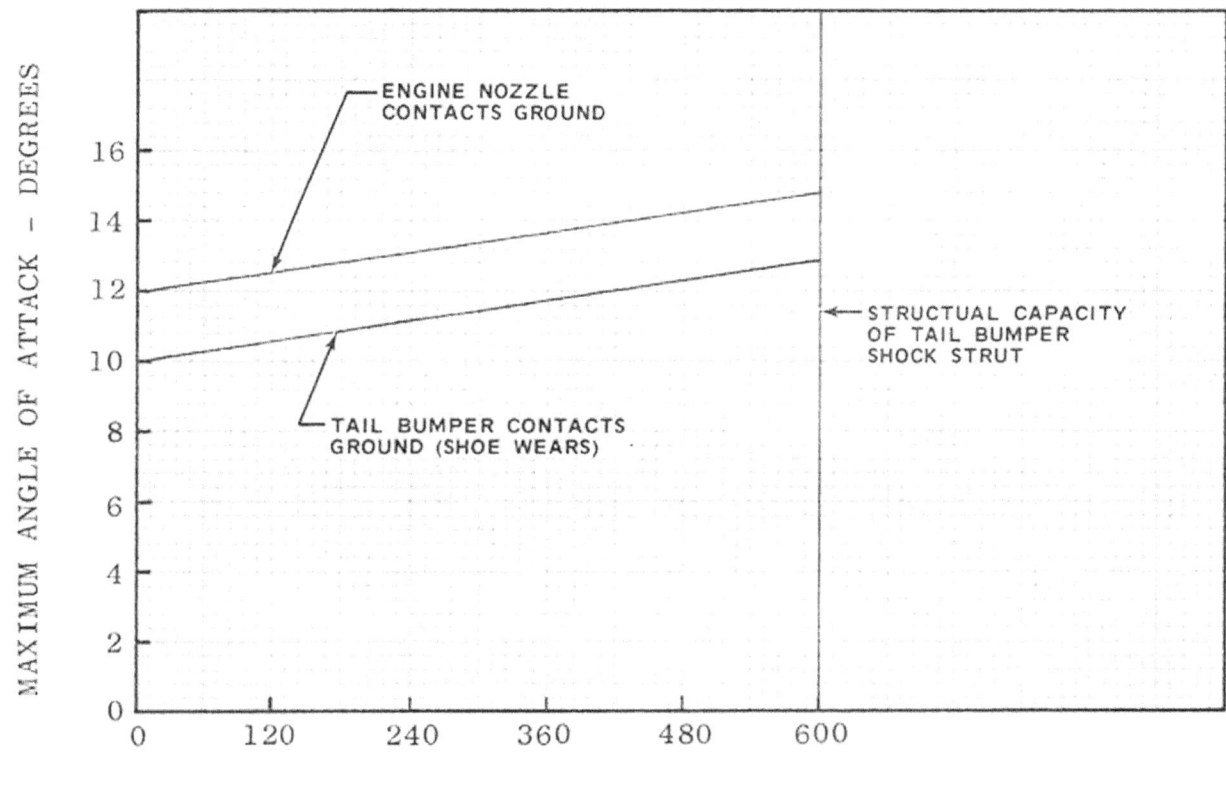

Figure 5-16.

Section V
Operating Limitations

T.O. 1F-111A-1

Speed Brake Limits

DATA BASIS: ESTIMATED
DATE: 18 AUGUST 1967

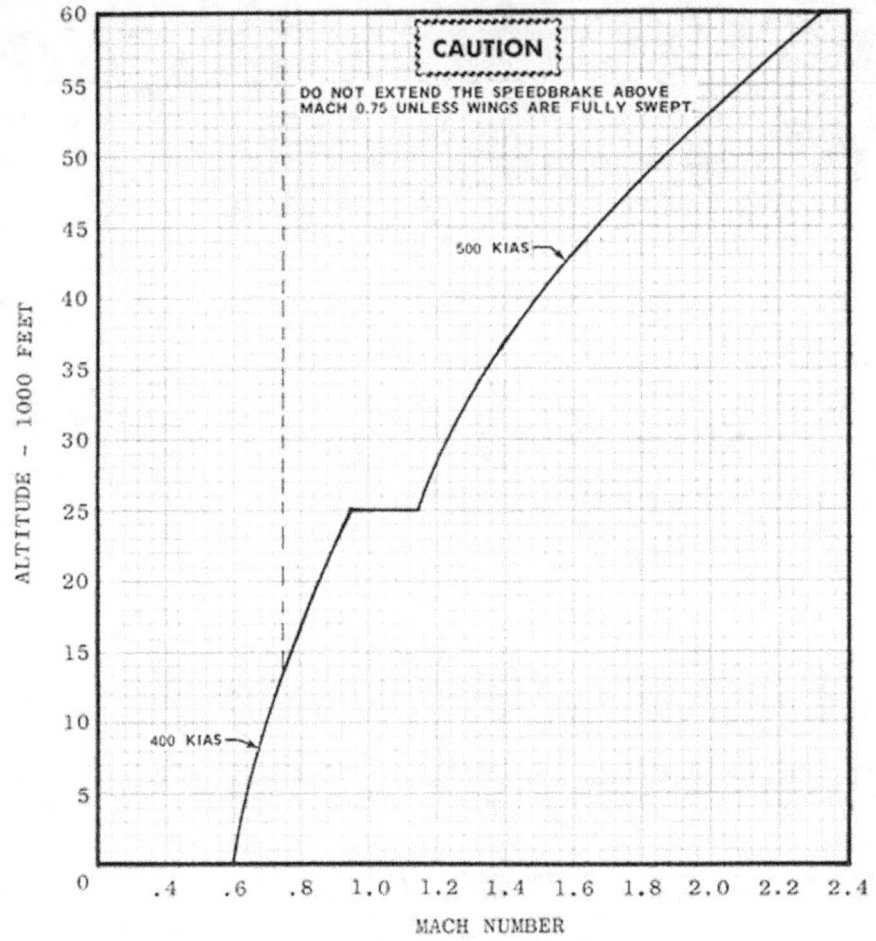

Figure 5-17.

MINIMUM ANTI-SKID CONTROL SPEED.

Minimum anti-skid control speed—20 knots.

Employ only light to medium braking below this speed.

MISCELLANEOUS OPERATIONAL LIMITATIONS.

SPEED BRAKE LIMIT.

Refer to figure 5-17 for speed brake limits.

TAIL BUMPER CONTACT LIMITS.

See figure 5-18 for maximum angle of attack versus sink rate for tail bumper contact limits.

CANOPY HATCH OPERATING SPEED.

Do not open canopy hatch when relative wind is in excess of 60 knots.

CREW MODULE.

WARNING

- The crew module should not be considered flyable without its full crew and complement of survival equipment, or the equivalent ballast to maintain center of gravity. Personal belongings or additional heavy equipment shall not be carried in the cockpit without compensation for cg effect. To assure stability of the module in event of ejection, it must be loaded in accordance with T.O. 1-1B-40.

- [19] ♦ [25] The self righting bags and/or aft flotation bag may be damaged during the ejection sequence; therefore, flight over open water is prohibited.

SLIP-ON FERRY WING TIPS.

For aircraft with slip-on ferry wing tips installed, observe the following limitations:

1. Wing sweep 26 degrees or less.
2. Do not exceed 330 KIAS/mach 0.95 whichever is less.
3. Refer to figure 5-18 for limit maneuver factors with slip-on ferry wing tips installed.

Limit Maneuver Factors- Slip-On Ferry Tips Installed

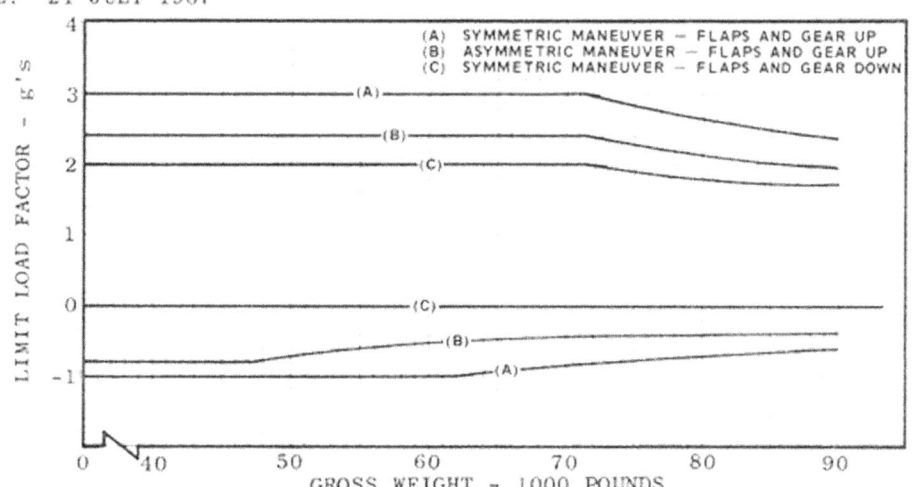

Figure 5-18.

This is the last page of Section V.

This page intentionally left blank.

SECTION VI
FLIGHT CHARACTERISTICS

Note

The airspeed indicated on the airspeed mach indicator has been calibrated for pitot-static system errors by the CADC and therefore is actually KCAS (knots calibrated airspeed). However, this air speed is referred to as KIAS (knots indicated airspeed) throughout this manual since it is read directly from the instrument.

TABLE OF CONTENTS.

	Page
Introduction	6-1
Flight Control System	6-1
Level Flight Characteristics	6-3
Maneuvering Flight Characteristics	6-5
Engine Stall Characteristics	6-7
Flight with Augmentation Off	6-8
Recommended Minimum Flying Speeds	6-9
Dive Recovery	6-12
Stalls	6-12
Spins	6-17
Flight with External Stores	6-18
Flight with Speedbrake Extended	6-18
Center-of-Gravity Envelope	6-18

INTRODUCTION.

The flight characteristics information presented in this section is based primarily on estimations supplemented by flight experience. Detailed stability and control flight testing has not been completed. Utilization of the variable sweep concept has not resulted in unusual flight characteristics. The main features of the flight control system (self adaptive gain changing and command augmentation) significantly minimizes variations in stability and control characteristics over the large mach-altitude operating spectrum of the aircraft. The low friction and breakout forces associated with the flight control system enhance ease of handling and maneuverability. Wing sweep transition will not be reflected to the pilot in the form of a trim change due to the series trim feature of the flight control system which acts as an automatic trim system. At a fixed mach-altitude condition, wing sweep transition will be noticed only by the increase in aircraft angle of attack and attitude for an aft movement of the wing. For a forward movement of the wing, a decrease in angle of attack and attitude will occur.

FLIGHT CONTROL SYSTEM.

A detailed description of the flight control system appears in Section I. A short summary is presented herein of those features pertinent to flight characteristics.

LONGITUDINAL CONTROL.

Longitudinal control is accomplished by means of symmetrical (elevator) motion of the horizontal stabilizers. A direct mechanical linkage is provided between the control sticks and the horizontal stabilizer servo actuators. Artificial feel is provided by a fixed spring which reflects a force of 10.8 pounds per inch of stick deflection, measured at the stick grip. The elevator deflection per inch of stick is varied throughout the flight envelope by the command augmentation feature to maintain a relatively constant stick force per "g." The command augmentation feature compares commanded normal acceleration and pitch rate with actual aircraft normal acceleration and pitch rate, and generates a pitch damper command proportional to the error. The pitch damper input is summed mechanically with the stick input, and if the actual aircraft response is less than commanded, the damper will produce an elevator deflection in a direction to aid the stick input. Conversely, if the actual aircraft response is greater than commanded, the pitch damper input will oppose the stick input. This action tends to maintain relatively constant aircraft response throughout the flight envelope.

Stability Augmentation.

The stability augmentation gains in the pitch channel is automatically set by the self-adaptive gain system. This system sets the pitch gain automatically throughout the flight spectrum as a function of the aircraft dynamics to maintain essentially constant longitudinal short period and damping characteristics. At low speed, however, with the slats extended, the pitch gain remains at a fixed value. The stability augmentation system is provided automatically whenever power is supplied to the flight control system. The stability augmentation system is redundant from the sensors to the damper servos. Caution lamps are provided on the caution panel to indicate a failure in one of the redundant branches. The procedures to be followed when any flight control system caution lamp is lighted are discussed in Section III.

Changed 18 August 1967

Manual Trim.

Manual trim inputs are commanded from the trim button on either of the control stick grips when the auxiliary trim switch is in the stick position. Manual trim inputs can also be commanded by the switch on the auxiliary flight control panel in case of a stick trim button failure. During normal operation the manual trim commands the pitch parallel trim actuator. Manual trim commands move the stick and elevator linkage unless restrained by the pilot. If the pitch damper is turned off, the parallel trim actuator will be driven to stick neutral, and the trim buttons will then drive the series trim actuator. Under normal operations in high speed flight when the pitch damper is on, the pitch series trim actuator relieves the steady state load carried by the pitch damper servo. This action relieves the damper from carrying one "g" trim and minimizes damper disengage transients. In low speed flight with the flaps and slats extended the series trim actuator is locked during normal operation. The series trim commands are added in series with the stick inputs and as such, the manual trim commands using the pitch series trim are not reflected to the pilot's stick.

Low Speed Trim Compensation. 31

At lift-off and when slats are extended prior to landing, low speed trim compensation is provided so that a positive stick force variation with speed (i.e., angle of attack) is reflected to the control stick (increasing pull force with decreasing speed from the trim point and increasing push force with increasing speed from the trim point). An angle-of-attack signal is sent from the angle-of-attack probe through the feel and trim system to the pitch damper so that to the pilot a positive speed stability gradient in stick force is apparent. This same function also augments the aircraft longitudinal dynamics (short period and damping) characteristics. Low speed trim compensation is available only when the pitch damper is on.

LATERAL CONTROL.

When the wings are forward of 45 degrees, lateral control of the aircraft is provided by two spoiler segments on each wing panel in addition to the asymmetrical (aileron) motion of the horizontal stabilizers. Lateral control of the airplane with the wings aft of 45 degrees is achieved using only asymmetrical motion of the horizontal stabilizers. A direct mechanical linkage from the control stick to the horizontal stabilizer servo actuators is provided. Mixing of the aileron and elevator control to the actuators is also accomplished mechanically. The spoilers are connected to the control stick by redundant electrical circuits. A force detent occurs at approximately one-half maximum lateral stick deflection. With the roll damper on, full normal control is achieved when the stick is moved to the detent. The detent should not be exceeded for normal operation. With the roll damper off, full spoiler deflection (for wing sweeps less than 45 degrees) and one-fourth asymmetrical horizontal stabilizer deflection are provided when the stick is moved to the detent. Full asymmetrical horizontal stabilizer deflection can be obtained, for emergency operation only, by overpowering the force detent and displacing the stick to the physical stops. Roll rate command augmentation is provided when the roll damper is on. The command augmentation feature compares commanded roll rate with actual aircraft roll rate and generates a roll damper command proportional to the error. If the actual airplane response is greater than commanded, the roll damper will reduce the commanded roll rate and if it is less it will increase the commanded roll rate. This feature tends to maintain a relatively constant roll rate per pound of force throughout the flight envelope. Roll damping is also provided through the roll damper and is available only when the damper is on.

Stability Augmentation.

The stability augmentation gain in the roll channel is automatically set by the self-adaptive gain system. This system sets the roll gain automatically throughout the flight spectrum as a function of the aircraft dynamics to maintain essentially constant lateral short period and damping characteristics. At low speed, however, with the slats extended, the roll gain remains at a fixed value. The stability augmentation system is provided automatically whenever power is supplied to the flight control system. The stability augmentation system is redundant from the sensors to the damper servos. Caution lamps are provided on the caution panel to indicate a failure in one of the redundant branches. The procedures to be followed when any flight control system caution lamp is lighted are discussed in Section III. Stability augmentation is available only when the roll damper is on.

Manual Trim.

Manual trim inputs are commanded through the roll damper from the trim button on either of the control stick grips when the auxiliary trim switch is in the stick position. When the roll damper is off or the auxiliary trim switch is out of the stick position, no roll trim is provided and the aircraft should be trimmed laterally with the rudder.

DIRECTIONAL CONTROL.

Directional control is achieved using direct mechanical linkage between conventional rudder pedals and the servo actuator of the rudder.

Stability Augmentation.

The stability augmentation gains in the yaw channel are fixed values of yaw rate and lateral acceleration feedbacks. These feedbacks serve to augment the aircraft yaw damping and directional stability. The stability augmentation system is provided automatically whenever power is supplied to the flight control system. The stability augmentation system is redundant from the sensors to the damper servos. Caution lamps are provided on the caution panel to indicate a failure in one of the redundant branches. The procedures to be followed when any flight control system caution lamp is lighted are discussed in Section III. Stability augmentation is available only when the yaw damper is on.

Manual Trim.

Direction manual trim is actuated by displacing the rudder trim switch, located on the auxiliary flight control panel, to the right or left. Rudder trim is added in series with the rudder pedal inputs and is not reflected to the pedals.

Adverse Yaw Compensation.

At lift-off and when the slats are extended prior to landing, adverse yaw compensation is provided so that in low speed flight the sideslip angle developed during turning flight and rolling flight are significantly reduced. An angle of sideslip signal is sent from the angle of sideslip probe, together with a roll rate signal, through the feel and trim system to the yaw damper which effectively improves turn coordination during low speed flight. This same function also augments the aircraft directional dynamics (short period and damping) characteristics. Adverse yaw compensation is available only when the yaw damper is on.

LEVEL FLIGHT CHARACTERISTICS.

TAKEOFF.

Takeoff is normally accomplished with the wings in the 16 degree wing sweep position with full flaps. Adequate longitudinal control is available to lift the nose gear and obtain lift-off attitude prior to attaining lift-off velocity. During normal performance takeoffs, aft stick forces of approximately 15 to 20 pounds will be required for nose gear lift-off. Immediately after lift-off a forward stick movement is required to arrest the rotation of the aircraft. During climbout, trim changes associated with retraction of the gear and slats and flaps are small. A noticeable increase in angle of attack will occur as the slats and flaps are retracted. This is a result of the loss in lift as the slats and flaps are retracted. Slats and flaps should not be fully retracted until such time that the minimum recommended flying speeds for the clean airplane are attained. It is recommended that the flaps and slats be raised in two steps to prevent rapid increases in angle of attack after takeoff. Upon completion of slat and flap retraction, the wing should be swept to 26 degrees.

SUBSONIC FLIGHT.

Operation of the aircraft at subsonic speeds up to mach 0.8 should normally be accomplished with a wing sweep of 26 degrees. Generally, response and damping about all axes in this speed range is considered excellent based on flight experience to date. Flight at wing sweeps aft of 45 degrees for subsonic flight is not recommended due to the fact that the spoilers are locked out and as a result roll control is significantly reduced. For wing sweeps aft of 45 degrees, rolling maneuvers should not exceed 60 degrees of bank to prevent excessive sideslip angles from being developed. However, all other characteristics of the aircraft are considered good at the aft sweep angles. The angle-of-attack limits presented in Section V should not be exceeded in either 1"g" or maneuvering flight. Based upon these angle-of-attack limits, recommended minimum flying speeds for 1"g" and limited maneuvering flight are presented for nominal center-of-gravity positions (associated with automatic fuel sequence) and no external stores. (See "Recommended Minimum Flying Speeds" this section). The recommended minimum flying speeds will vary as much as one knot from these values for each one percent MAC center-of-gravity deviation from the quoted values. These recommended minimum flying speeds are for operational planning purposes only, and the angle-of-attack limits should not be exceeded in either 1"g" or maneuvering flight.

WARNING

Under no circumstances should the angle-of-attack limits be exceeded. Possible inadvertent stall and post-stall gyrations will result from exceeding these limits.

At subsonic speeds and altitudes below 20,000 feet, a high frequency rudder buzz may occur due to structural coupling through the lateral accelerometer and yaw damper. This has occurred only occasionally and appears to be aggravated by turbulence. If rudder buzz is encountered, accomplish the following:

1. Turn yaw damper OFF.
2. Change flight conditions by decreasing speed or increasing altitude or both, avoiding turbulence if possible, to permit returning the yaw damper switch to ON.
3. Turn yaw damper ON.
   If buzz returns, turn yaw damper OFF and observe yaw damper off operating limitations.

TRANSONIC FLIGHT.

During operation of the aircraft at transonic mach numbers (mach 0.80 to 1.1) wing sweep angles of 45 to 72.5 degrees should be utilized. At 20,000 feet and above, sweep angles of 45 degrees are recommended to keep the aircraft angle of attack low which will result in better acceleration characteristics. At the lower altitudes, more aft sweep angles are recommended to optimize acceleration. Although the spoilers will be locked out with the more aft sweeps, roll performance will be improved due to the lower angle of attack. During transonic flight above 25,000 feet a relatively small directional trim change occurs just prior to achieving supersonic flight. As altitude is decreased in this speed regime, the trim change is more noticeable and below 10,000 feet may be exhibited as a small Dutch roll transient accompanied by mild buffet. No trim changes occur longitudinally or laterally. The exact cause of this characteristic is not known at this time, but will be investigated further. Predicted longitudinal short period characteristics for a wing sweep of 50 degrees at low altitude-high transonic and low supersonic speeds indicate that the short period will have a frequency of approximately 1.0 to 1.2 cycles per second. Operation in these flight conditions should be avoided through the utilization of sweep angles at or near the maximum sweep angle until flight evaluation of this high longitudinal short period characteristic has been completed.

SUPERSONIC FLIGHT.

Flight in the supersonic flight spectrum (mach 1.1 and above) should normally be accomplished with the wings fully swept. Some external store loadings preclude full aft sweep and as such are limited to 65 degrees. Flight can be performed in the supersonic speed range with wing sweep angles as low as 50 degrees; however, such sweep angles are detrimental to optimum performance. Deceleration at high altitudes from supersonic speed can be enhanced through use of 50 degree wing sweep due to the increased drag. Throughout the supersonic flight spectrum covered to date, response and damping characteristics have been good.

LANDING.

Slats and Flaps Extended.

Landing should normally be accomplished with the wing at 26 degrees. This sweep is compatible with that associated for subsonic flight and as such the slats and flaps can be extended without further wing sweep operation. A change in angle of attack will be evident as the slats and flaps are extended. As the slats are extended, a small increase or decrease in angle of attack will occur depending on the initial angle of attack at extension. As the flaps extend, a decrease in angle of attack will occur. Trim changes reflected to the pilot will be small. Approach power should be maintained until initiation of the flare. At such time, power should be reduced so that at touchdown, IDLE power is attained. On 31, in order to provide the pilot with a positive stick force variation with speed (increasing pull forces with decreasing speed from the trim point and increasing push forces with increasing speed from the trim point), a low speed trim compensation has been incorporated in the longitudinal flight control system. The pilot will find that airspeed and angle-of-attack control is easily maintained during approaches with the low speed trim compensation operating. If the low speed trim compensation should fail, a satisfactory landing can still be accomplished; however, airspeed control on final will be more difficult and increased pilot attention to maintaining angle of attack will be required. Angle-of-attack control will be even more degraded if pitch damper is inoperative. It is recommended that if a landing approach is required with the pitch damper off, the final approach should be flown at an angle of attack of 10 degrees. Turn coordination is less than optimum at slow speeds and "adverse yaw" may be noticed when lining up on final approach. It is recommended that no abrupt lateral control inputs be made in order to prevent large sideslip angles from developing. On 31, an adverse yaw compensation is incorporated in the flight control system to improve turn coordination. However, some "adverse yaw" may still be noticed during rolling maneuvers at low speed. If the adverse yaw compensation or yaw damper is inoperative, it is recommended that a "straight-in" approach be accomplished and that lateral control inputs be made as smoothly as possible. The maximum angle of attack permitted with the slats and flaps extended is 18 degrees in 1"g" and maneuvering flight. Based upon this angle-of-attack limit, recommended minimum flying speeds in 1"g" flight are presented for 16 and 26 degree wing sweep angles with no external stores for nominal center-of-gravity positions associated with automatic fuel sequencing. (See "Recommended Minimum Flying Speeds" this section). The recommended minimum flying speeds will vary as much as one knot for each one percent MAC center-of-gravity deviation from the quoted values. These recommended minimum flying speeds are for operational planning purposes only, and the 18 degree angle-of-attack limit should not be exceeded in either 1"g" or maneuvering flight. On 31, a rudder pedal shaker is activated at 18 degrees wing angle of attack.

WARNING

Under no circumstances should the 18 degree angle-of-attack limit be exceeded. Possible inadvertent stall and post-stall gyrations will result from exceeding this limit.

Slats Extended and Flaps Retracted.

The characteristics described above for the aircraft with the slats and flaps extended apply to the aircraft with only the slats extended. It is recommended that if the aircraft must be landed in this configuration that the approach be made at an angle of attack of 10 degrees.

Slats and Flaps Retracted.

The characteristics described above for the aircraft with the slats and flaps extended apply to the aircraft with the slats and flaps retracted with the exception that a maximum angle of attack of 15 degrees in 1"g" and maneuvering flight must be observed. It is recommended that if the aircraft must be landed in this configuration that the approach be made at an angle of attack of 10 degrees.

Note

On 31 ♦, with the low speed trim compensation and adverse yaw compensation, place the flight control system switch in the TO & LAND position to activate these functions.

Crosswind Landing.

Although crosswind landing experience has been relatively limited to date, landings have been accomplished in up to 25 knots effective crosswind conditions and have required no unusual techniques. In general, it is recommended that a wing-low crab approach be conducted.

Landing With Forward Wing Sweep (16 Degrees).

It is possible at certain fuel loadings to utilize the maximum forward wing sweep of 16 degrees, slats and flaps extended, for landing. In such cases, improved landing performance, i.e., lower approach speed and less ground roll distance, can be achieved for the same gross weight.

WARNING

Before use of 16 degree sweep for landing, aft center of gravity should be checked against aft center-of-gravity limit to establish minimum fuel loading permissable.

MANEUVERING FLIGHT CHARACTERISTICS.

LONGITUDINAL FLIGHT.

Wing sweep angles for maneuvering flight are compatible with those previously described for level flight characteristics. During flight with the slats and flaps extended, longitudinal maneuvering should not be allowed to exceed an angle of attack of 18 degrees to preclude the entrance to a stall. Stall is expected to occur at an angle of attack of 24 to 25 degrees. On 31 ♦, the rudder pedal shaker will activate at an angle of attack of 18 degrees with the slats and flaps extended. During pullups or turns at high speed with slats and flaps retracted, the stick force per "g" is relatively independent of wing sweep and altitude. A mild variation with mach number, however, does exist. Stick deflection per "g" also exhibits the same basic characteristics. (See figure 6-1.) Flight test results obtained to date essentially confirm the basic levels and trends of the predicted maneuver gradients. During supersonic flight at altitudes above 30,000 feet with aft wing sweeps, full back longitudinal control maneuvers can result in some stick "talkback" being detected. This characteristic is a result of the pitch damper and mechanical input attaining full noseup surface authority. Excessive rate of longitudinal control application will make this characteristic more apparent; therefore, smooth application of control is recommended. Loss of pitch damping in one direction will result but may be restored by relieving the back pressure being held. This same characteristic is exhibited at negative load factors for the aft sweep throughout its operational flight envelope.

BUFFET.

Refer to Section VI, T.O. 1F-111A-1A.

Refer to Section V, T.O. 1F-111A-1A, for further discussion on longitudinal maneuverability considerations as related to buffet onset and heavy buffet.

WING SWEEP/MANEUVERABILITY EFFECTS.

Refer to Section VI, T.O. 1F-111A-1A.

ROLLING FLIGHT.

Throughout the operational envelope of the aircraft, rolling maneuvers should be accomplished with the wing sweeps recommended under "Level Flight Characteristics", this section. During flight with the slats and flaps extended, large rolling maneuvers should be avoided to preclude buildup of excessive adverse sideslip. Rolling maneuvers with wing sweeps of more than 45 degrees at subsonic flight (below mach 0.8) should be avoided due to the decreased roll control when the spoilers are locked out. During 1"g"

Section VI
Flight Characteristics

T.O. 1F-111A-1

Longitudinal Maneuver Gradients

DATA BASIS: ESTIMATED
DATE: 18 AUGUST 1967

WING SWEEPS =
26 TO 72.5 DEGREES
NO EXTERNAL STORES
STABILITY AUGMENTATION
SYSTEM ON

FUEL GRADE: JP-4
ENGINES: TF30-P-1/P-3

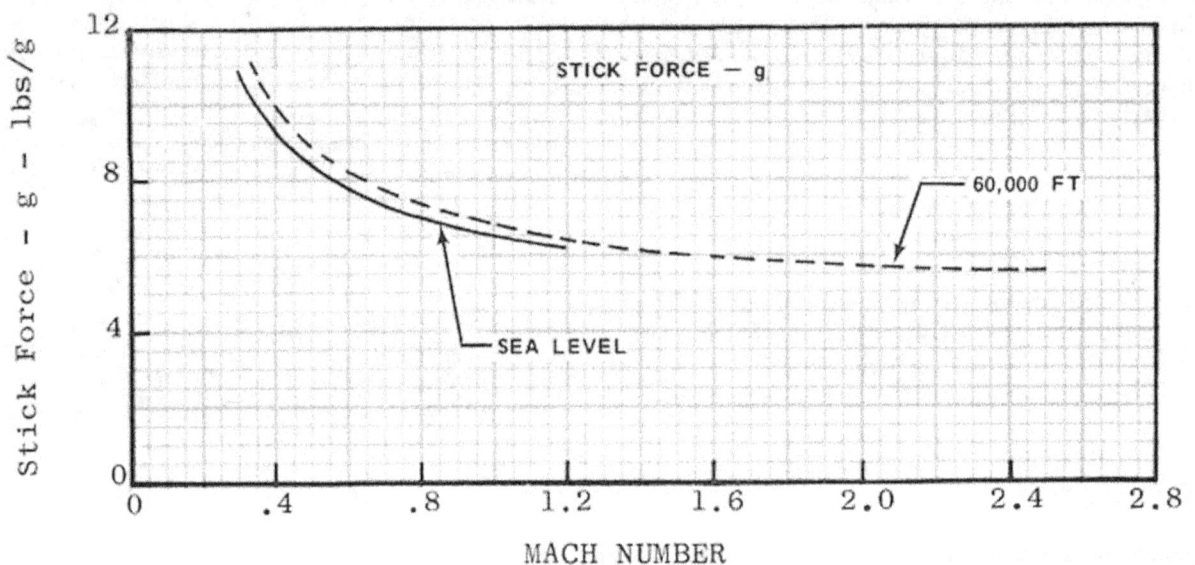

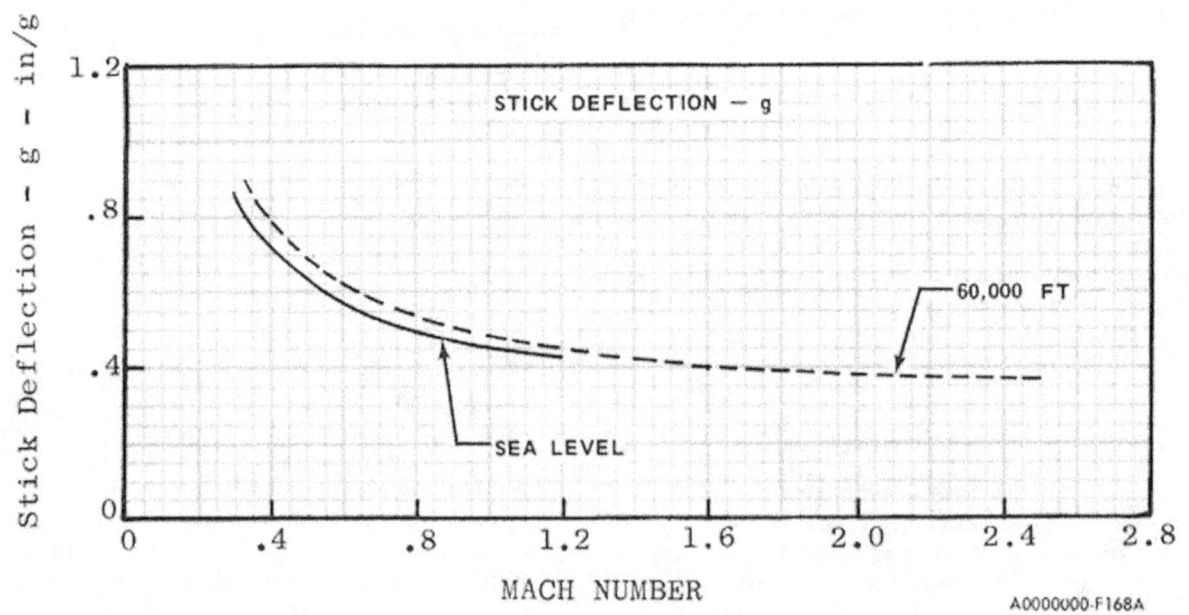

Figure 6-1.

360 degree rolls, the aircraft tends to roll about the fuselage; therefore, as the aircraft rolls, the angle of attack becomes sideslip. To the pilot, this appears as adverse yaw. For a given wing sweep angle, the slower the airspeed, the higher the angle of attack and this will result in a higher angle of sideslip during the roll.

WARNING

At high speeds during maximum rolling maneuvers, abrupt forward stick motion should not be made to preclude rapid buildup in roll rate.

ENGINE STALL CHARACTERISTICS.

Stalls are caused by an aerodynamic disruption of the airflow through the engine resulting in a breakdown of airflow in the engine compressor similar to the disruption in flow encountered during a wing stall. Engine stalls may be classified into two types of stalls: fan stalls and compressor stalls. Fan stalls usually occur when selecting or while in the afterburner range of operation. Compressor stalls are possible at any power setting.

ENGINE OPERATING ENVELOPE.

It is possible for the engine to flame out due to an engine stall; however, no flameouts have been experienced to date. The engine operating envelopes specified in figure 6-2 have been defined to minimize engine stalls. A mach-altitude operating envelope and angle of attack envelope for fixed throttle settings are shown. A/B blowouts are not expected in the flight envelope represented by curve ①. A/B lights may be accomplished in the envelope up to the altitudes shown by curve ②. The envelope where throttle retard can be accomplished without possible compressor stall is represented by curve ③. It is possible for engine stalls to occur within this envelope. Engine stalls may occur more frequently at angles of attack near those specified in the angle-of-attack envelope shown in figure 6-2, or during A/B light at altitude. Throttle should not be reduced below MIL power during flight above mach 1.6 to prevent inlet buzz and/or engine stall. During flight above mach 0.80 the throttle should not be positioned lower than halfway from MIL to IDLE to prevent the engine from entering the off-idle stall regime which will require aircraft deceleration to clear.

Engine Operating Envelope

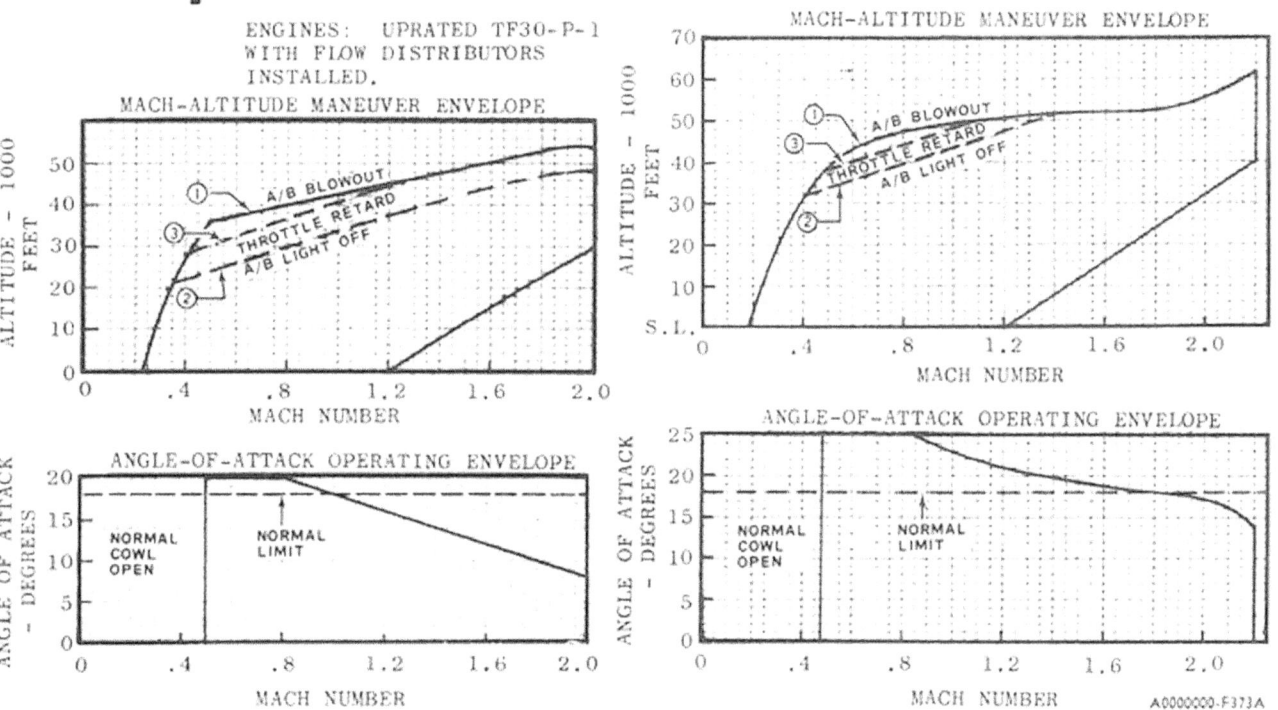

Figure 6-2.

STALL RECOGNITION.

Fan stalls result in an audible "bang" with an almost immediate recovery to military power and in some cases to afterburner power (with the throttle in A/B). These stalls occur and recover too quickly to be detected by observing any engine instrument except nozzle position, to determine which engine stalled. The nozzle will end up in a closed position, if recovery is to the military power range, or will be transitioning from closed to open if it recovers to afterburner. Compressor stalls are noted by the audible "bang" and in most cases, at supersonic speeds, are preceded by a period of inlet rumble. The engine intruments react as follows during a compressor stall:

- EPR—quickly drops to 1.0.
- RPM—decreases at a moderate rate to below a normal idle speed and then is slowly unstable until stall recovery.
- TIT—flashes to a high TIT followed by an unstable decrease to some base level where it remains unstable until the engine recovers.
- Fuel flow—decreases at a moderate rate towards that required for the RPM and then is unstable until stall recovery.
- Nozzle position—closes; sometimes fast, sometimes slow, and sometimes appears to remain in an intermediate position for a period of time.

The best indicator of a stalled engine is its TIT—it will be significantly and abnormally different from the unstalled engine. The peak-out TIT will depend on airspeed and altitude. For example, the peak-out TIT will be higher at mach 1.2/50,000 feet than at mach 2.0/50,000 feet or at mach 1.2/30,000 feet.

STALL RECOVERY.

Engine stalls may occur either during ground operation or inflight. During ground operation, if an engine stalls during A/B light, the air source selector knob may be positioned to the affected engine and A/B operation reattempted. If the engine still stalls with air conditioning on the affected engine, A/B operation may be reattempted by rapidly advancing the throttle into A/B from approximately 85 percent rpm.

Note

- During ground operation the engine susceptibility to stall is decreased by the increase in engine bleed airflow.
- Stalls during A/B lights are somewhat more prevalent with tailwind or crosswinds.

If the engine stalls during throttle retard, clear the stall by retarding the throttle to IDLE. Inflight compressor stalls may be induced by engine or inlet control malfunction, excessive angle of attack or yaw causing poor inlet air distribution, rapid throttle reversal (high power to low power and return), or speedbrake deflection. There is an increased probability of compressor stall as the maximum speedbrake deflection is approached. Compressor stalls may be self clearing, or may result in a steady state fully developed stall. In the first case the engine will stall and immediately recover with the only evidence of a stall being a moderate "bang" and no action is required. The second case requires recognition and corrective action to restore power and prevent damage to the engine from overtemperature. Experience has shown that it is impossible to constrain the TIT from its peak-out temperature by throttle action. Although the stalled engine's throttle position should be reduced quickly it is better to determine which engine is stalled than to snap both throttles to some reduced level. A snap reduction of both throttles can induce the other engine to stall. Whenever an engine stall is experienced the throttle should be retarded to approximately one-half way from idle to military to minimize the possibility of an overtemperature condition. If the engine does not show response toward recovery then the throttle should be maintained slightly above idle and still low enough to prevent excessive TIT. Stall recovery is aided by returning the aircraft to a steady-state flight condition within the parameters of the operating envelopes shown in figure 6-2.

FLIGHT WITH AUGMENTATION OFF.

Flight experience to date has indicated that flight without the basic stability augmentation systems in either of the pitch, roll, or yaw channels is extremely remote. Basic redundancy, failure monitoring, and self-test of the system enhance the full time operation of the system. However, if such a case should arise, the following discussion is presented to point out those pertinent characteristics of the aircraft that the pilot should know.

SLATS AND FLAPS EXTENDED.

Loss of the pitch damper will result in degraded damping chacteristics and on aircraft **31**, loss of low speed trim compensation also. As a result, airspeed control on final approach will become more difficult and increased pilot attention to maintaining angle of attack will be required. Reduced speed stability will be noticed by the pilot with attendant lower maneuver force gradients. Loss of the yaw damper will result in degraded damping characteristics and on aircraft **31**, loss of the adverse yaw compensation also. As a result, excessively large sideslip angles can be developed during abrupt lateral inputs. Such inputs should be avoided. Loss of the roll damper will result in slightly degraded damping and loss of roll trim.

Degraded roll damping is not considered serious. Loss of roll trim can be compensated for by trimming the aircraft with the rudder.

WARNING

In the event the pitch damper or yaw damper is off at landing, perform a "straight-in" approach at an angle of attack of 10 degrees. Avoid abrupt longitudinal and/or lateral control inputs.

SLATS AND FLAPS RETRACTED.

Figure 6-3 presents the mach-altitude limitations imposed on the aircraft for various wing sweeps considering the damper in each axis (these data are presented in Section V, but are repeated here for continuity). Loss of the pitch damper will result in degraded damping characteristics as well as the loss of the command augmentation system. Much larger variations in stick force per "g" will be reflected to the pilot. Flight in given portions of the operating spectrum is restricted due to low stick force per "g" (less than 3 pounds per "g"). With the degraded damping and low maneuver gradients and attendant high short period frequency, the pilot/airframe combination may be susceptible to pilot induced oscillations. Loss of the yaw damper will result in degraded Dutch roll dynamics, the most significant of these being the reduced damping. This is most pronounced at high supersonic speeds above mach 1.5. Aileron inputs should be minimized to preclude excitement of the Dutch roll mode. Attempts to damp the Dutch roll mode through pilot rudder inputs should be minimized to prevent getting in-phase with the oscillations and causing the aircraft to enter a sustained oscillation. Loss of the roll damper will result in degraded damping as well as the command augmentation system. Aileron inputs with aft wing sweeps at supersonic speeds should be minimized. Basic aircraft roll damping can be augmented by sweeping the wings forward to 50 degrees at supersonic speeds.

RECOMMENDED MINIMUM FLYING SPEEDS.

SLATS AND FLAPS EXTENDED.

For the aircraft with the slats and flaps extended, the recommended minimum flying speed is based on a wing angle of attack of 18 degrees. Figure 6-4 presents these speeds for 1"g" flight and a bank angle of 30 degrees. A variation with center of gravity is presented for gross weights below 60,000 pounds, since at approximately this gross weight the center of gravity moves aft as the remaining fuel is used from the forward tank. For variations in center of gravity from the nominal 30 percent MAC presented, with weights above 60,000 pounds, the speed may vary approximately 1 knot per 1 percent MAC, i.e., 1 knot increase for each 1 percent forward of 30 percent MAC.

Augmentation Off Operating Limits

DO NOT EXCEED THE FOLLOWING AIRSPEEDS/ALTITUDES:		
PITCH DAMPER OFF		
Wing Sweep	Altitude	Airspeed
16 Degrees	All	Mach 0.40
26-45 Degrees	All	400 KIAS or Mach 0.75 whichever is less
46-72.5 Degrees	Sea Level to 20,000 Feet	Mach 0.70
	Above 20,000 Feet	None
ROLL OR YAW DAMPER OFF		
Wing Sweep	Altitude	Airspeed
16-45 Degrees	All	None
45-72.5 Degrees	All	Mach 1.5

Figure 6-3.

SLATS AND FLAPS RETRACTED.

For the aircraft with the slats and flaps retracted, the recommended minimum flying speed is based on a wing angle of attack of 15 degrees for wing sweeps of 16 through 45 degrees and a wing angle of attack of 18 degrees for a wing sweep of 72.5 degrees. Figure 6-5 presents these speeds for 1"g" flight and 2"g" flight (60 degree bank). These speeds are based on a nominal center-of-gravity position indicated for each wing sweep. For variations in the center of gravity, the speeds will vary approximately 1 knot for each percent MAC, i.e., 1 knot increase for each 1 percent forward of the center of gravity indicated for each wing sweep on figure 6-5.

WARNING

Under no circumstances should the angle-of-attack limits be exceeded. Possible inadvertent stall and post-stall gyrations will result from exceeding these limits.

This page intentionally left blank.

Recommended Minimum Flying Speeds

DATA BASIS: ESTIMATED GEAR UP AND FLAPS UP FUEL GRADE: JP-4
DATE: 18 AUGUST 1967 SLATS RETRACTED ENGINES: TF30-P-1/P-3
NO EXTERNAL STORES

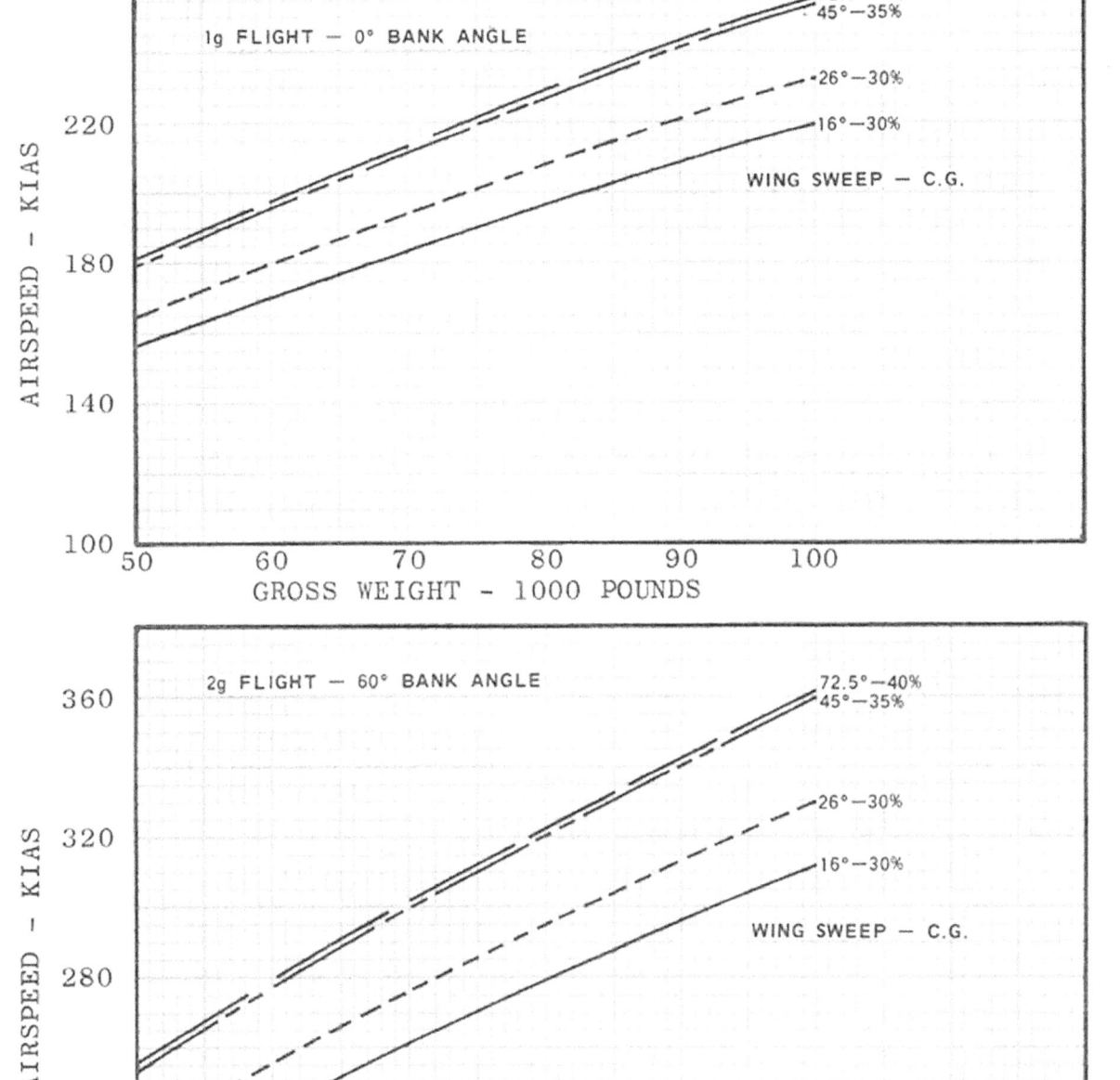

Figure 6-5.

DIVE RECOVERY.

This section presents data necessary to determine the fuselage angle during various conditions of dive and the altitude required to recover from the dive. Data are based on the clean airplane for sweep angles of 26, 50 and 72.5 degrees. Dive recovery charts are presented in figures 6-6, 6-7, and 6-8 and may be used as follows:

Given:

Wing Sweep — 26 degrees
Dive Angle — 30 degrees
Airspeed — 500 KIAS
Ambient Temperature — 0°C
Start Recovery — 6000 feet
Desired Load Factor — 3.0"g's"
Gross Weight — 60,000 lbs

Find:
Altitude required to recover

Solution:
Enter figure 6-6 at 500 KIAS (A), proceed horizontally to the right to 6000 feet pressure altitude (B), move vertically down to 0°C (C), proceed horizontally to the right to 30 degrees dive angle (D), move vertically upward to the 3.0"g" load factor line (E), and project horizontally to the right and read 2000 feet required to recover (F). To check the capability of the airplane to attain the desired load factor within set angle-of-attack limits, enter figure 6-6 at 500 KIAS as before (A), proceed horizontally to the left to the 60,000 pound gross weight line (G), then project down to read 6.6"g's" as the load factor (H). Thus the desired 3.0"g" pullout can be accomplished without exceeding the temporary 15 degree angle-of-attack limitations on which the 26 degree sweep load factors are based. The angle-of-attack limits shown on the charts of 26, 50, and 72.5 degree sweep are as called out.

Drag Effect on Dive Recovery.

Figure 6-9 presents the altitude loss in dive recovery due to weapons drag effect. The chart indicates that a clean airplane requires a larger altitude to recover from a dive than an airplane with increased drag. As drag is increased the altitude to recover is decreased. An example in the use of the chart is not presented since the chart is self-explanatory.

STALLS.

LOW SPEED (SLATS AND FLAPS EXTENDED).

The stalling characteristics with flaps and slats extended are expected to be as follows: There should be no increase in lift with increased angle of attack, possible roll and yaw oscillations and a sharp reduction in roll power due to a decrease in spoiler effectiveness. There is no natural warning of an impending stall in the form of airframe buffet or "g break." On aircraft 31♦, a rudder pedal shaker is set to be activated at 18 degrees angle of attack. Angle-of-attack increases are prohibited after rudder pedal shaker is felt to preclude a stall. Stabilator power is adequate to recover from a stalled condition by applying full forward stick. If roll angle starts to diverge at a high angle of attack, do not attempt to maintain wings level or else sideslip angle will also rapidly increase.

WARNING

- If roll angle divergence or oscillations are encountered at high angles of attack, immediately apply forward stick to unload the airplane and do not attempt to correct the divergence or oscillations until the angle of attack is below 15 degrees.

- Flight into heavy buffet or intentional stalls are prohibited.

HIGH SPEED (SLATS AND FLAPS RETRACTED).

Accelerated stalls are expected to be preceded by adequate stall warning in the form of airframe buffet. For wing sweeps of 26 through 45 degrees, stall characteristics should be similar to those described above. For wing sweeps of 45 through 72.5 degrees, no stall, in the usual sense of the word, is encountered. At all wing sweeps, for most flight conditions, there will be a tendency to diverge or oscillate in roll and yaw. To preclude entering these conditions, the angle-of-attack limits presented in Section V should not be exceeded. Normal recovery techniques (neutral lateral stick, while applying forward longitudinal stick) are expected to provide adequate recovery from all stall conditions.

WARNING

- If roll angle divergence or oscillations are encountered at high angles of attack, immediately apply forward stick to unload the airplane and do not attempt to correct the divergence or oscillation until the angle of attack is below 15 degrees.

- Flights into heavy buffet or intentional stalls are prohibited.

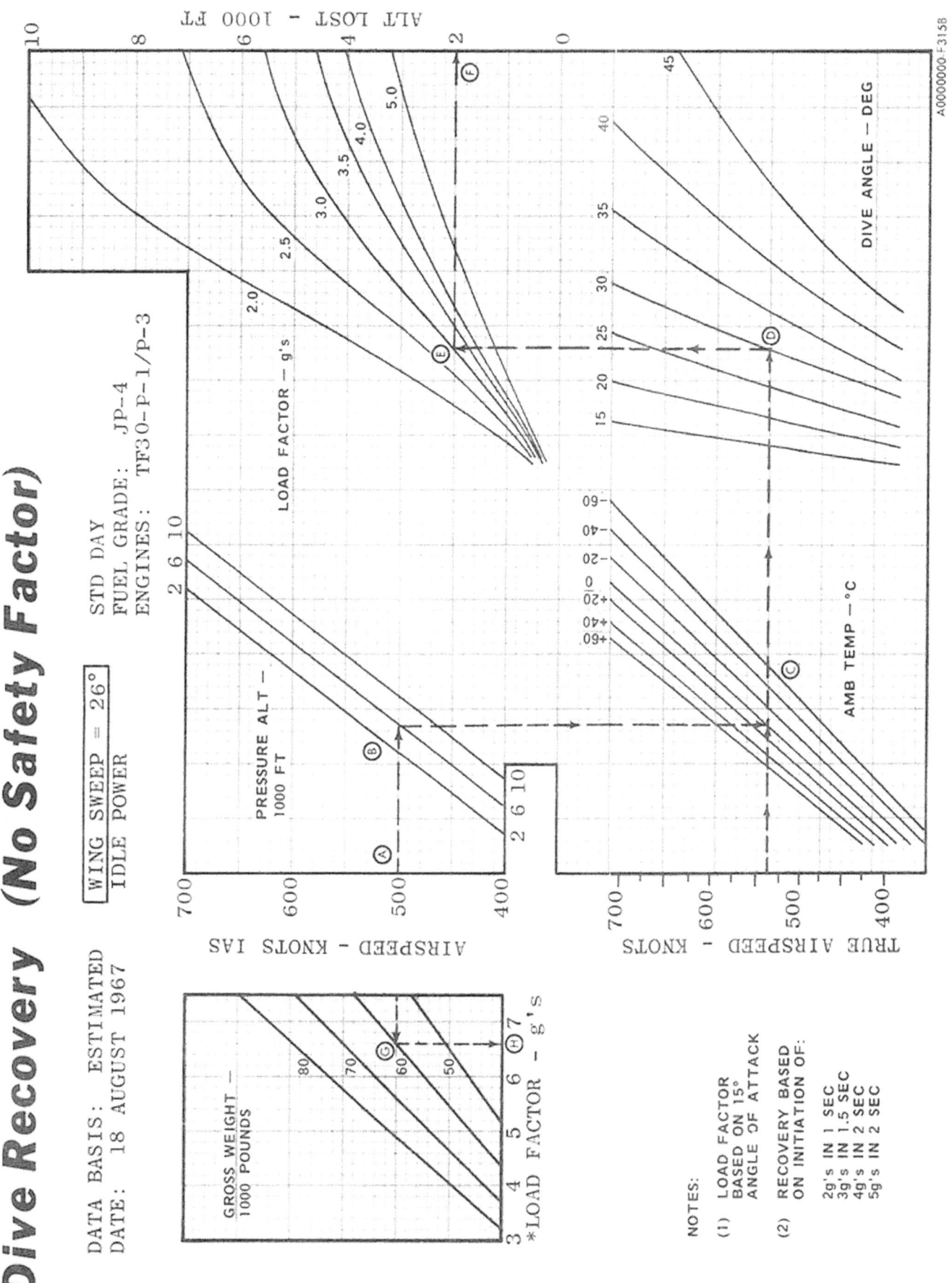

Figure 6-6.

Section VI
Flight Characteristics

T.O. 1F-111A-1

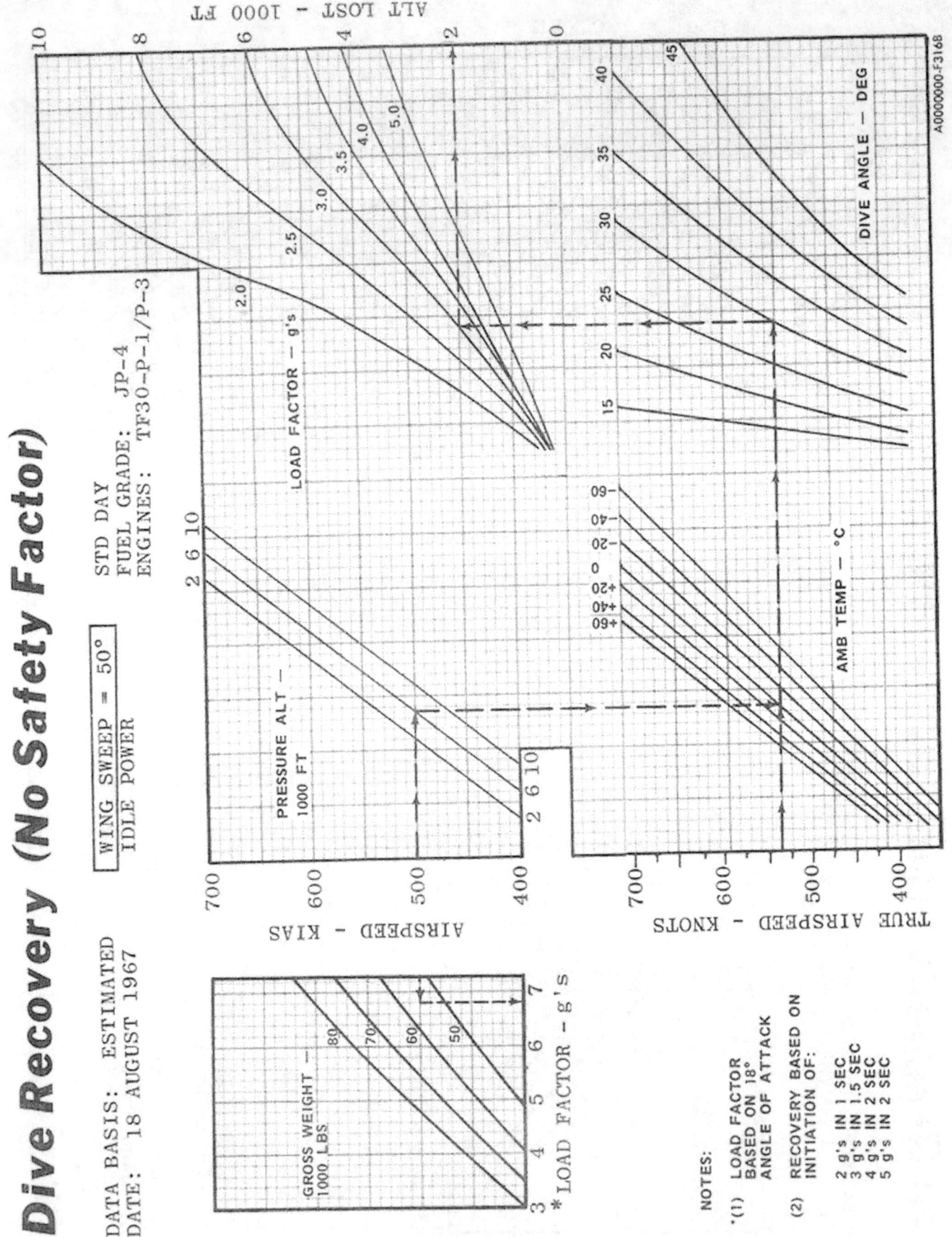

Figure 6-7.

T.O. 1F-111A-1

Section VI
Flight Characteristics

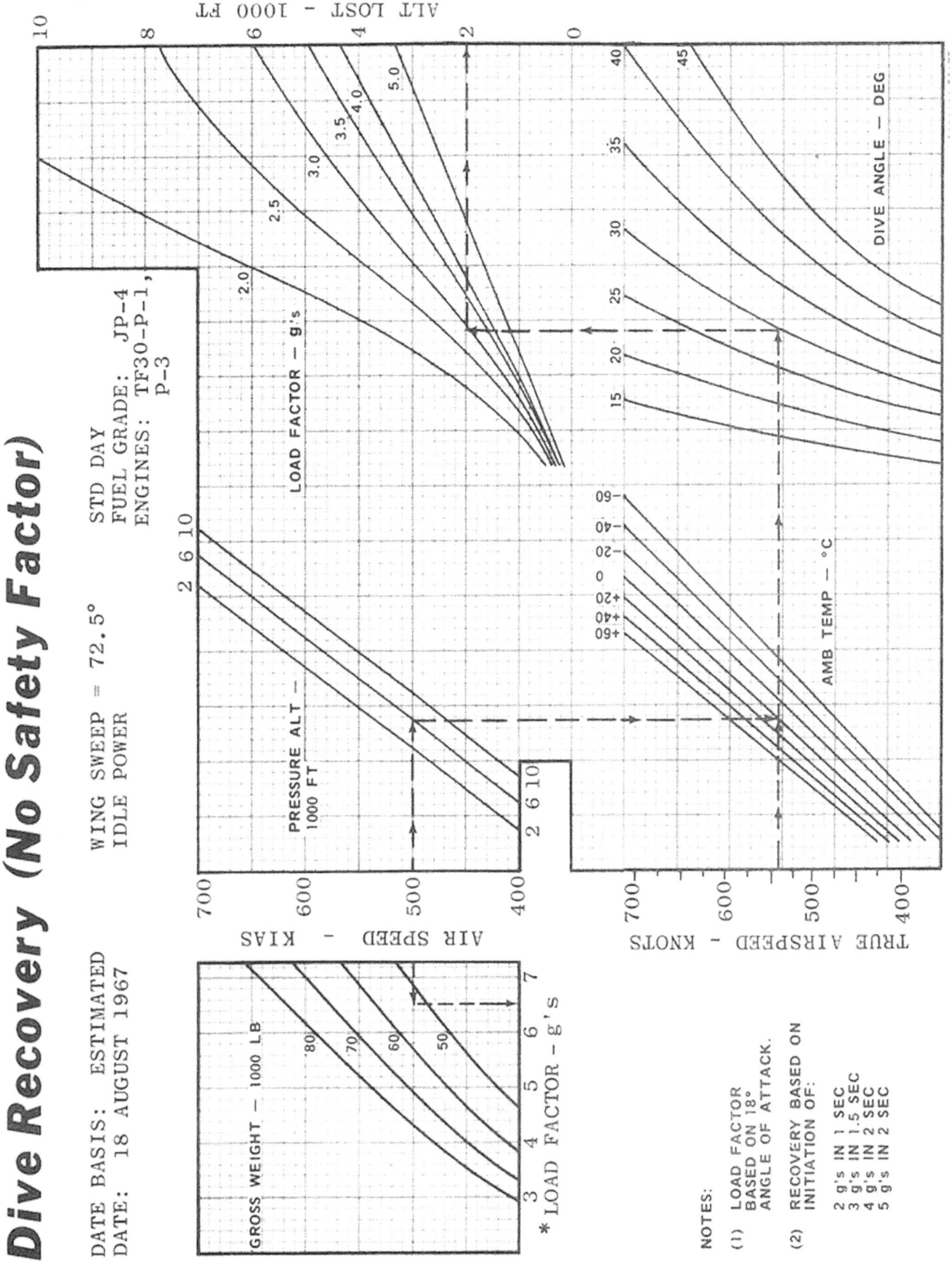

Figure 6-8.

Changed 18 August 1967

6-15

Section VI
Flight Characteristics

T.O. 1F-111A-1

Drag Effect on Dive Recovery

DATA BASIS: ESTIMATED
DATE: 18 AUGUST 1967

WING SWEEP = 26° AND 50°

STD DAY
FUEL GRADE: JP-4
ENGINES: TF30-P-1/P-3

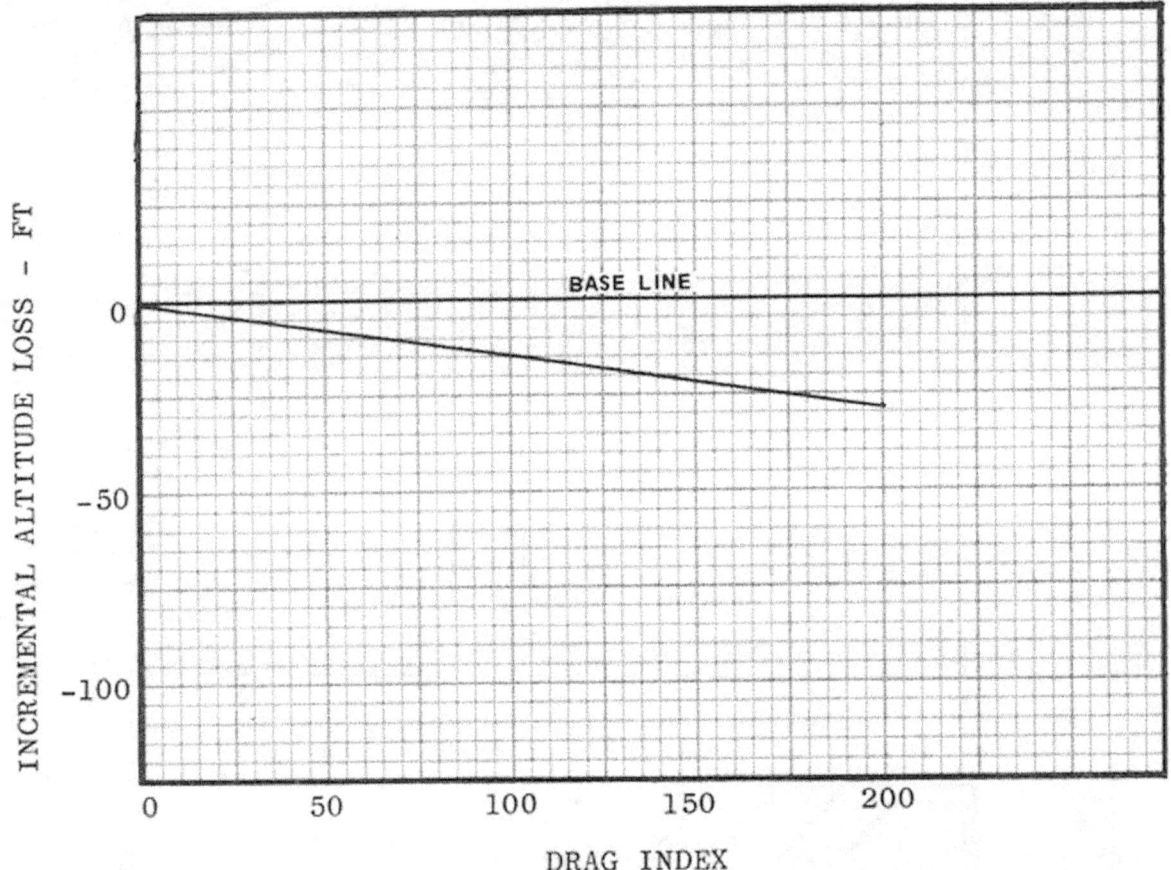

Figure 6-9.

SPINS.

Spin tests have not been conducted on the airplane and consequently, its exact spin characteristics are unknown. However, spin investigations conducted during wind tunnel testing have indicated a tendency for the airplane to enter a spin in any configuration and wing sweep. Spin entry from 1"g" stall with symmetrical controls has been possible in some instances. However, when asymmetric rudder and/or lateral control is supplied at stall, spin entries should be expected for all configurations. Crossed controls at or before accelerated stalls should likewise produce abrupt entries into erect or inverted spins. It should be possible to enter spins at all altitudes and at mach numbers up to supersonic speeds. Engine stall or flameout should occur prior to or at spin entry.

Intentional spins and flight into heavy buffet and/or stall are prohibited.

UPRIGHT SPINS.

Upright spins are expected to be primarily oscillatory in nature with excursions up to ± 25 degrees in pitch and ± 35 degrees in roll. The spin rates can vary from 10 to 4 seconds per turn. A flat spin mode has also been noted for wing sweeps of 50 degrees and less. This mode is relatively free from oscillations about any axes and spins at 4 to 2.3 seconds per turn. The latter could produce pilot loads of up to 5"g's" forward. This mode should rarely be encountered and would develop only after a spin has been permitted to build up for several turns.

UPRIGHT SPIN RECOVERY.

Lateral control is the primary spin recovery system and it is imperative that the stick be held into the spin until recovery is obtained. Under no circumstances should an attempt be made to oscillate the airplane out of spin. Immediately upon recognition of the direction of rotation (turn indicator should be used to verify direction) apply the following procedure:

1. Throttles—IDLE.
2. Opposite rudder (switch to full rudder authority when in clean configuration).
3. Roll into spin using full stick throw (longitudinally keep stick full aft).
4. Maintain full aft stick.

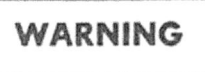

Do not move stick around as this will deplete the hydraulic supply and reduce possibility of recovery.

5. Do not make any configuration changes to flaps, gear, speedbrake or wing sweep.
6. Neutralize controls upon recovery.
7. Throttles — As required.
8. Switch back to normal rudder authority.

The airplane is expected to recover from spins in a near vertical attitude. Unless a pullup is initiated immediately, ground clearance can become critical.

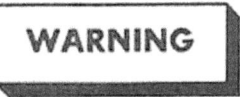

If the airplane has not recovered by the time 15,000 feet has been reached — EJECT.

INVERTED SPINS.

An inverted spin is similar to erect oscillatory spin and relatively easy to terminate.

INVERTED SPIN RECOVERY.

Immediately upon recognition of inverted spins (turn indicator should be used to verify direction), use the following procedure:

1. Throttles — IDLE.
2. Apply opposite rudder (switch to full rudder authority when in clean configuration).
3. Apply full aft stick.
4. Neutralize rudder upon recovery and obtain normal flight attitude.
5. Throttles — As required.
6. Switch back to limited rudder authority.

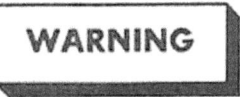

If the airplane has not recovered by the time 15,000 feet is reached — EJECT.

FLIGHT WITH EXTERNAL STORES.

Testing of all of the external store loadings currently planned for the aircraft has not been completed. Testing has covered some single store loadings on the pivoting pylons, limited TER rack loadings on the four pivoting pylons and four fixed pylons, and limited tests of the MER rack loadings on the pivoting pylons. The most predominant effect of the loadings other than performance effects is the obvious results of increased inertia and weight. Abrupt control inputs should be avoided to preclude exceeding structural limitations associated with the various loadings.

FLIGHT WITH SPEEDBRAKE EXTENDED.

Extension of the speedbrake will result in excessive aircraft buffet and a random pulsating motion in the lateral-directional axes. In addition, extension of the speedbrake at speeds above mach 0.75 with the wings at 26 degree wing sweep will result in inadequate nosedown longitudinal control for 1"g" flight. For full aft wing sweeps, adequate longitudinal control is available.

Do not extend the speedbrake above mach 0.75 unless wings are fully swept. Inadequate nosedown longitudinal control exists for resulting trim change.

CENTER-OF-GRAVITY ENVELOPE.

Figure 6-10, sheets 1 and 2, present a typical center-of-gravity envelope for the aircraft with and without internal stores. Because of the variance in basic weight and center-of-gravity conditions between aircraft, the weight and balance handbook, T.O. 1-1B-40, must be used to determine the actual weight and balance conditions of a specific aircraft. Fuel sequencing (pounds used) for an 8200 pound differential between the forward and aft tanks is identical regardless of stores loading if AUTO engine feed is selected.

T.O. 1F-111A-1

Section VI
Flight Characteristics

Center of Gravity Envelope (Typical)

DATA BASIS: ESTIMATED
DATE: 18 AUGUST 1967

LOADING WITH STORES

FUEL GRADE: JP-4
ENGINES: TF30-P-1/P-3

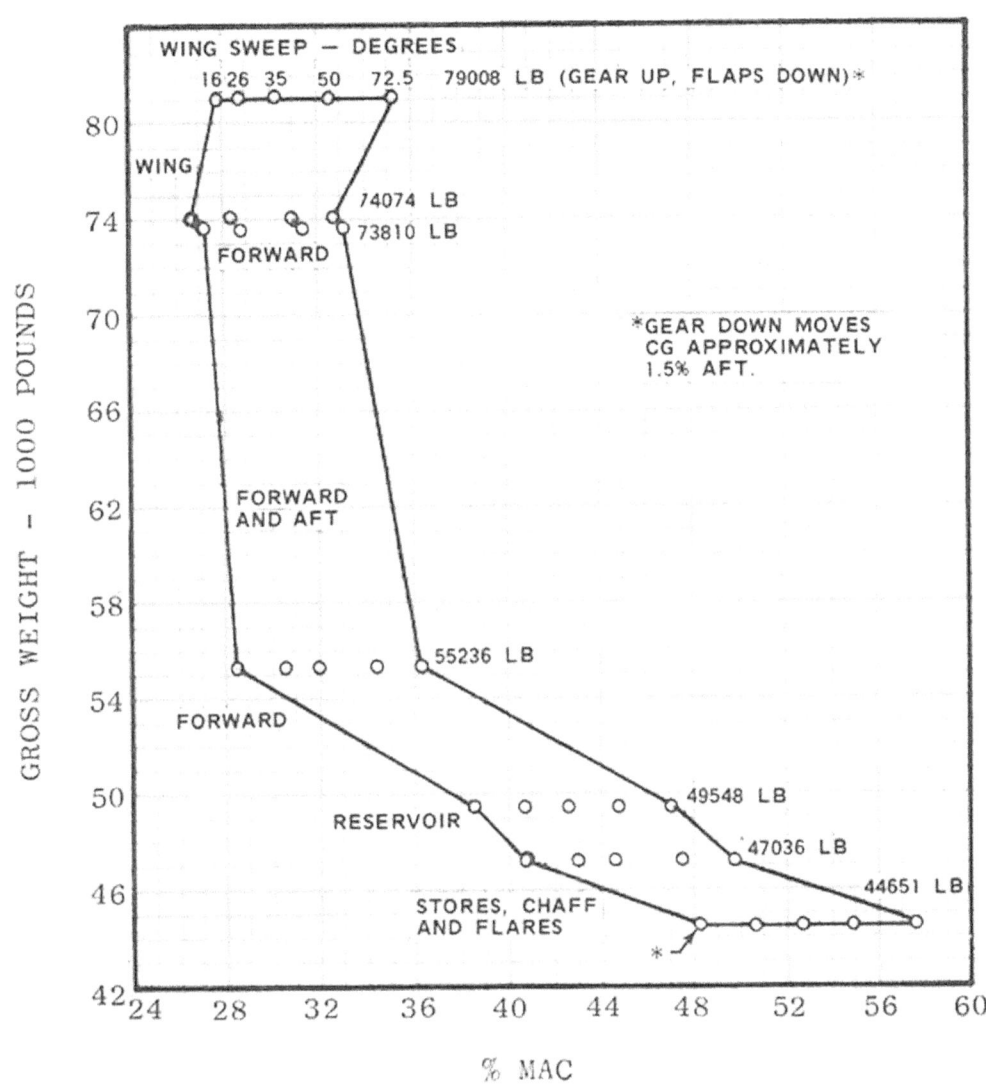

Figure 6-10. (Sheet 1)

Changed 18 August 1967

6-19

Section VI
Flight Characteristics

T.O. 1F-111A-1

Center of Gravity Envelope (Typical)

DATA BASIS: ESTIMATED
DATE: 18 AUGUST 1967
LOADING WITHOUT STORES
FUEL GRADE: JP-4
ENGINES: TF30-P-1/P-3

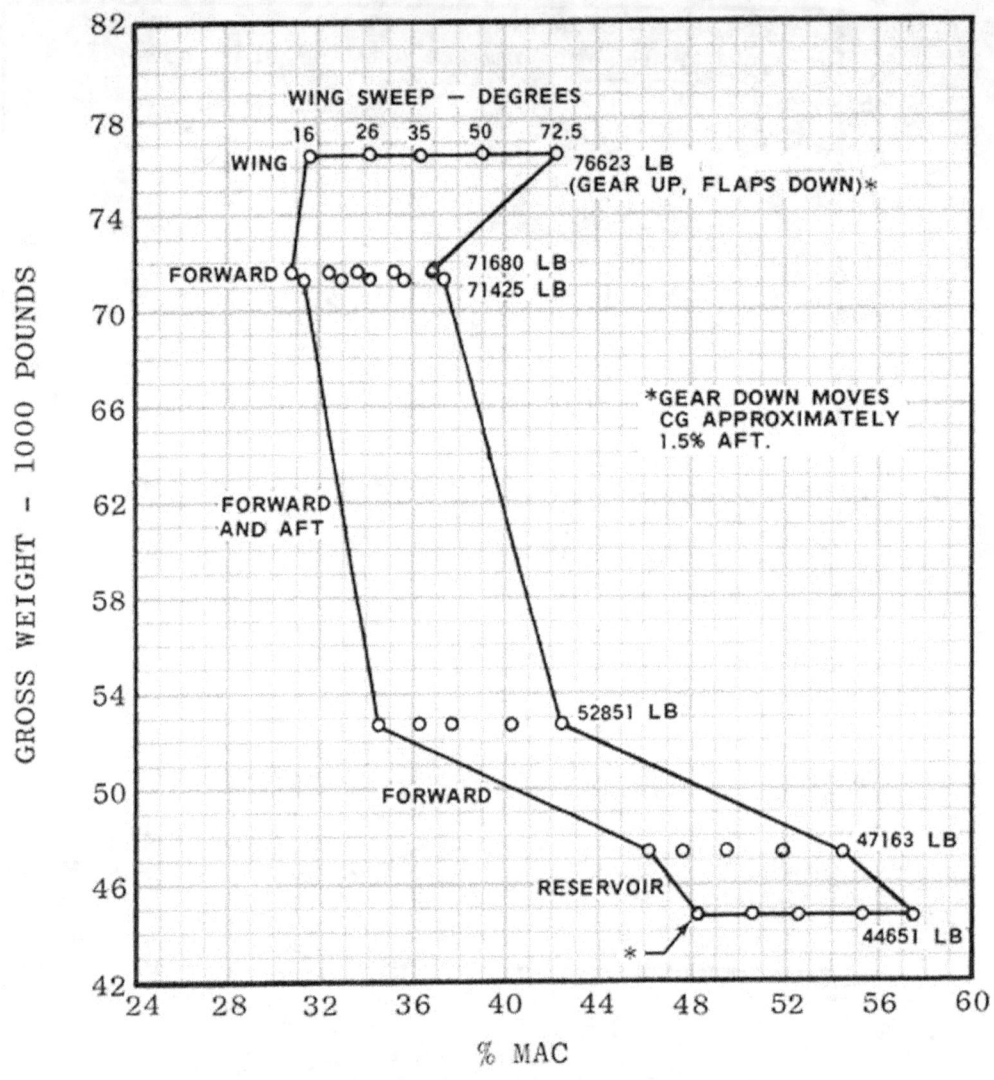

FUEL SEQUENCE (8200 LB DIFFERENTIAL)	
TANK	POUND
WING	4934 LB
FORWARD	264 LB
FORWARD & AFT	9287 LB EACH
FORWARD	5688 LB
RESERVOIR	2512 LB
TOTAL FUEL	31972 LB

Figure 6-10. (Sheet 2)

This is the last page of Section VI.

SECTION VII
ALL WEATHER OPERATION

TABLE OF CONTENTS.

Instrument Flight Procedures	7-1
Ice and Rain	7-4
Turbulence and Thunderstorms	7-5
Night Flying	7-5
Cold Weather Procedures	7-6
Hot Weather and Desert Operation	7-7

Note

- In general, this section consists of procedures and information which differ from, or are supplementary to, the normal operating procedures in Section II. In some cases, however, repetition has been necessary for emphasis, clarity, or continuity of thought.

INSTRUMENT FLIGHT PROCEDURES

This airplane is designed to perform operational missions in all extremes of weather. On instrument flights, delays in departure and descent, and low climb rates to altitude are often required in high density control areas. These factors may increase fuel consumption, reduce flight endurance and dictate that all flight under instrument conditions be carefully planned and that due consideration be given to the additional time and fuel which may be required.

BEFORE TAKEOFF.

1. Line up visually with center line of runway.
2. Instrument system coupler mode selector knob — MAN HDG.
3. HSI heading set knob — Set runway heading.
4. Attitude indicator — Adjust to indicate 2.5° nose down position.
5. Pitot heat — Climatic.

INSTRUMENT TAKEOFF.

Make normal takeoff.

INSTRUMENT CLIMB.

After lift off, maintain **10** degrees pitch attitude until reaching climb speed and then establish climb configuration and climb schedule. The optimum thrust climb schedule recommended in Appendix I is suitable for instrument flight.

INSTRUMENT CRUISING FLIGHT.

Thrust settings and configuration for optimum cruise schedule recommended in Appendix I are satisfactory while using standard instrument techniques. Maximum bank angle of 30 degrees is normally used.

HOLDING.

Holding should be accomplished at 280 KIAS. Maximum bank angle of 30 degrees is normally used.

JET PENETRATION.

Prior to beginning penetration ascertain the weather conditions and the availability of radar or ILS. If ceiling or visibility is below published minimums,

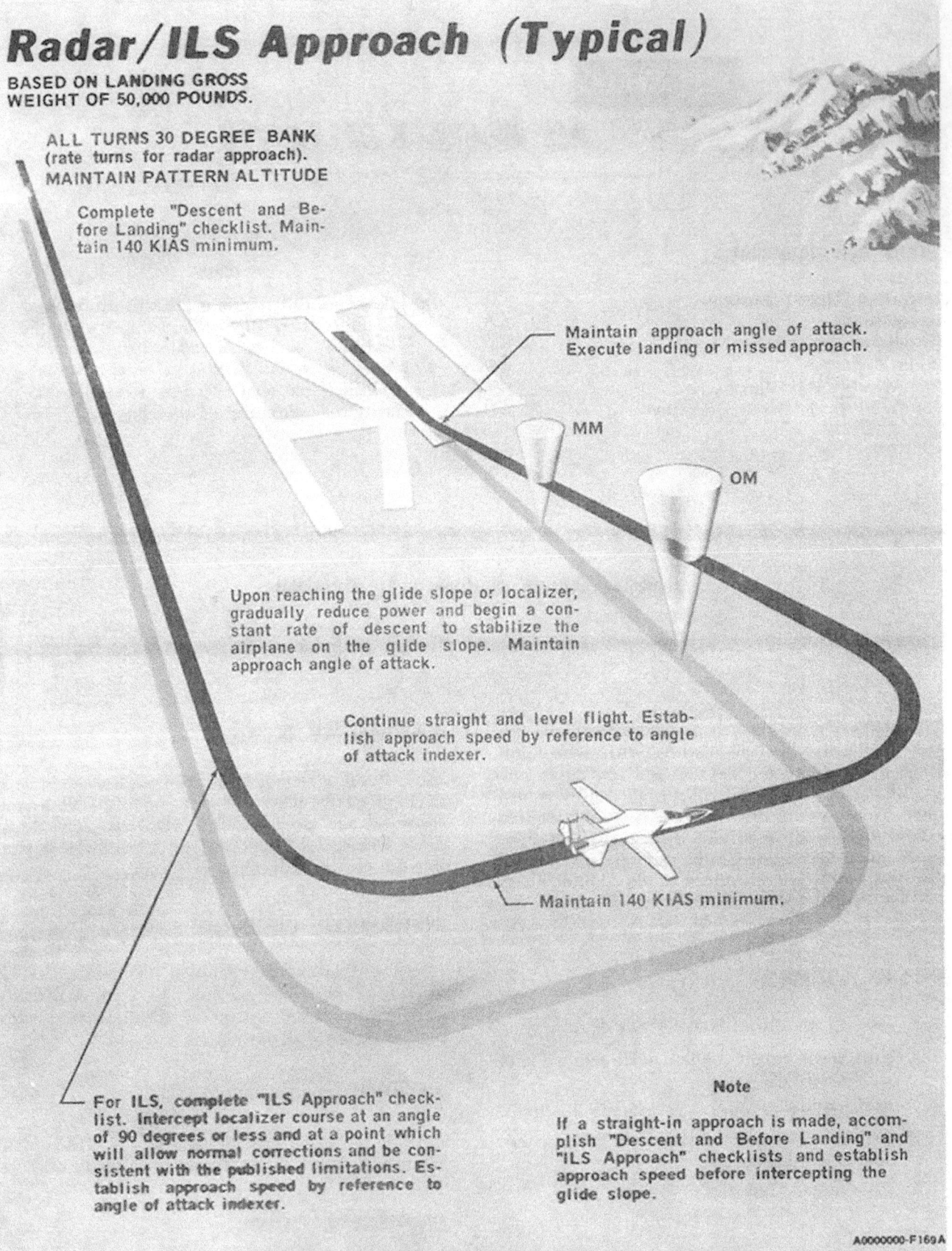

Figure 7-1.

make the decision to proceed to an alternate while still at altitude. Refer to the descent charts in Appendix I for appropriate airspeeds and airplane configuration. For maximum range an idle power descent at 225 KIAS, with 26 degree wing sweep and speed brakes retracted is recommended. For minimum time in descent, mach .80 or 300 KIAS, whichever is less, at a 26 degree wing sweep and speed brake extended is recommended.

PAR/ASR APPROACH.

Refer to descent charts in Appendix I for appropriate airspeeds. Figure 7-1 illustrates a typical Radar/ILS approach.

ILS APPROACH.

Refer to descent charts in Appendix I for appropriate airspeeds. Figure 7-1 illustrates a typical Radar/ILS approach.

1. ILS power switch — POWER.
2. ILS frequency selector knob — Set.
    Set the ILS frequency selector knob to the frequency of the localizer to be used for the approach and adjust volume control for identification.
3. Instrument system coupler mode selector knob — ILS.
4. Horizontal situation indicator — Set.
    Set the inbound heading of the localizer in the course selector window.
5. Radar altimeter — On and set to minimum approach altitude.
6. Instrument system coupler pitch steering mode switch — ALT REF.
    When at glide slope interception altitude, place the instrument system coupler pitch steering mode switch to ALT REF and keep the pitch steering bar centered until glide slope is intercepted.
7. Before Landing Checklist — Complete.
8. Localizer course — Intercepted.
    Intercept the localizer, by centering the bank steering bar, at an angle of 45 degrees approximately 10 miles from touchdown.
9. Glide slope — Intercepted.
    Intercept the glide slope by centering the pitch steering bar. Check that the instrument system coupler pitch steering mode switch goes to OFF when the glide slope is intercepted.
10. Minimum altitude fly-up — Checked.
    Upon reaching minimum altitude, the radar altitude low warning lamp will light and the pitch steering bar will indicate a fly-up command.

AIRBORNE INSTRUMENT LOW APPROACH (AILA).

The bomb-nav system, in conjunction with the attack radar, can be used for making approaches to runways not equipped with ground based letdown facilities and as a backup for monitoring TACAN, ILS and Radar approaches. Airplane altitude should be calibrated and the position should be updated by the most accurate means available immediately prior to starting the letdown.

1. Altitude calibration — Completed.
    Calibrate altitude over a point of known elevation, preferably the landing runway.

WARNING

Altitude calibration is critical. AILA glide slope angle to desired touchdown point is computed on the basis of ground range and altitude. Altitude calibration errors will cause the glide slope to be computed to a point short of or over the desired touchdown point.

2. Attack radar mode selector knob — GND VEL.
3. Bomb nav mode selector knob — SHORT RANGE.
4. Target fix mode selector button — Depressed.
5. Destination position counters — SET.
    Set the destination position counters to the coordinates of the touch down point on the approach end of the runway. When in range, synchronize and maintain the radar crosshairs on the touchdown point.
6. Fixpoint elevation counter — Set.
    Set the fixpoint elevation counter to the elevation of the runway.
7. Glide/dive angle counter — Set.
    Set the glide/dive angle counter to the glide slope angle for the approach runway.
8. Radar altimeter — On and set to minimum approach altitude.
9. Instrument system coupler mode selector knob — AILA.
10. Horizontal situation indicator — Set.
    Set inbound heading of the runway in the course indicator window and set the heading marker to the runway heading on the compass card.
11. Instrument system coupler pitch steering mode switch — ALT REF.
12. Before Landing Checklist — Complete.
13. Runway heading — Intercepted.
    Intercept the runway heading, by centering the bank steering bar at an angle of 45 de-

Changed 18 August 1967

7-3

Section VII
All Weather Operation

T.O. 1F-111A-1

grees approximately 10 miles from touchdown.
14. Glide slope — Intercepted.
   Intercept the glide slope by centering the pitch steering bar. Check that the instrument system coupler pitch steering mode switch goes to OFF when the glide slope is intercepted.
15. Minimum altitude fly-up — Checked.
   Upon reaching minimum altitude, the radar altitude low warning lamp will light and the pitch steering bar will indicate a fly-up command.

MISSED APPROACH PROCEDURE.

Refer to Go-Around, Section II, for missed approach procedure.

ICE AND RAIN

The airplane is equipped with engine anti-icing, pitot heat, and windshield rain removal provisions. Refer to "Anti-Icing and Defogging Systems", Section I. There are no provisions for surface anti-icing. Flight through areas of sustained heavy icing is not recommended. The performance capabilities of the airplane should be utilized to avoid extreme icing conditions. When moderate to heavy icing is encountered, a change in altitude, course, or airspeed should be made to prevent ice accumulation on the wings and empennage. Engine anti-icing capabilities should be utilized whenever icing conditions are anticipated.

WARNING

In the event of the pitot tube icing, the airspeed and mach indicators may drop to zero or remain fixed. All systems that receive intelligence based upon pitot pressure through the central air data computer, and the standby airspeed instruments, will be affected. The loss of airspeed indication during climb or descent is an extremely dangerous safety of flight hazard. The attitude indicator, vertical velocity indicator, altimeter and power setting can be used during the emergency flight condition.

Substantial ice buildups can necessitate increased power setting for maintaining airspeed and could cause distortions in the shape of air foil surfaces, thus affecting the lift and handling characteristics of the airplane. Either of these conditions tends to reduce total range. Flight can be safely accomplished during light to moderate icing by using normal flight procedures. Rain has little or no appreciable effect on the flight characteristics.

OPERATION IN RAIN OR ICING CONDITIONS.

Note
Icing is possible under the following conditions:
Ground operation.
- In visible moisture — Temperature between 35°F and —10°F.
- In clear air — Relative humidity above 70 percent and dew point temperature 25°F to 35°F.
Inflight operation.
- In visible moisture — Ambient temperature between 35°F and —10°F.
- In clear air — No limitations related to icing.

GROUND OPERATION.

Operate the airplane and systems as indicated in the "Cold Weather Procedures" in this section. Rain removal should be used when needed to improve visibility.

TAKEOFF AND INITIAL CLIMB.

Accomplish takeoff in the normal manner. Refusal speed will be considerably lower and the emergency stopping distance greater on wet or icy runways.

CRUISE.

WARNING

⑲ ♦ ㉚ Flight in icing conditions is prohibited.

Operate the airplane as necessary to avoid icing conditions whenever possible. When ice is encountered,

7-4

Changed 18 August 1967

pitot heat and engine anti-icing should be used. Do not operate in rain, sleet, or hail longer than absolutely necessary. If it becomes necessary to fly in these conditions, constantly check the aircraft leading edges, including radome, for indications of peeling or other structural deterioration of the airplane surfaces. In the event deterioration of surfaces is observed, maintain airspeed as low as practicable and land at the nearest suitable airfield as soon as possible. If heavy precipitation conditions of the above type are encountered at any speed or light to moderate conditions exist at high airspeeds, an entry must be made in Form 781.

WARNING

To minimize impact damage from rain or sleet, do not exceed 450 KIAS.

TURBULENCE AND THUNDERSTORMS

WARNING

Flight through thunderstorm activity or known severe turbulence is not recommended and should be avoided if at all possible. Careful judgment must be exercised by the pilot in determining capability to safely enter or circumnavigate areas of such weather activity. The appropriate corrective action to be taken if moderate or greater turbulence is forecast will be preplanned with assistance of the weather forecaster during the weather briefing.

The use of attack radar, ground mode, provides an excellent means of navigating between or around storm cells and the airplane is capable of climbing over the top of most developed thunderstorms. If circumstances should force the flight into a zone of severe turbulence, establish throttle setting and pitch attitude. Recommended thunderstorm penetration airspeed is **275-300 KIAS**.

Note

When using terrain following radar, the back scatter from drizzle or rain and other forms of precipitation will often be visible on the scope. It should be quite apparent to the operator that if the precipitation is so heavy that he cannot determine visually where the terrain ends and the precipitation begins, the automatic signal detection circuitry will also be incapable of this discrimination and a climb command will result.

Note

The following factors, singly or in combination, may cause engine flameout:

- Flight in cumulus buildups containing a high moisture content.
- Engine icing of inlet guide vanes.
- Turbulence associated with penetration of thunderstorms can result in excessively high angles of attack with resultant marginal engine performance.

NIGHT FLYING

Night flight necessitates a high degree of instrument proficiency and more dependence on flight instruments than would be expected for normal day VFR operations. Otherwise, techniques used in night flying do not differ appreciably from those used in daylight operation. Cockpit lighting has been designed to enhance night flying capability.

WARNING

The anti-collision lights should be turned OFF during flight through actual instrument conditions to avoid spatial dis-orientation resulting from the rotating reflections on the clouds. The navigation lights may be set to flash unless this becomes distracting in clouds.

Changed 18 August 1967

COLD WEATHER PROCEDURES

Most cold weather operating difficulties are encountered on the ground. The following instructions are to be used in conjunction with the normal procedures given in Section II when cold weather operation is necessary.

BEFORE ENTERING AIRPLANE.

WARNING

- All accumulated ice and snow must be removed from the airplane before flight is attempted. For complete ice and/or snow removal procedures, refer to T.O. 1F-111A-2-1. Takeoff distance and climb out performance can be adversely affected by ice and snow accumulations. The degree of roughness and distribution of these accumulations can vary stall speeds and alter flight characteristics to a degree hazardous to safe flight.

- Ensure that water does not accumulate on control surfaces or other critical areas where refreezing may cause damage or binding.

CAUTION

To avoid damage to airplane surfaces, do not permit ice to be chipped or scraped away.

Remove all protective covers and duct plugs; check to see that all surfaces, ducts, struts, drains and vents are free of snow, ice and frost. Ice and encrusted snow may be removed by using de-icing fluid or by direct air flow from a portable ground heater. Inspect the airplane carefully for fuel and hydraulic leaks caused by the contraction of fittings or by shrinkage of packings. Inspect areas behind the airplane to ensure that water or snow will not be blown onto personnel and equipment during engine start.

STARTING ENGINES.

Use normal procedures for starting engines. The throttles may be advanced to allowable power settings as long as engine instruments register within the engine operating limits. Refer to "Engine Operating Limits", Section V.

BEFORE TAXIING.

Check flight controls, flaps and slats for proper operation. Cycle flight controls to circulate warm fluid throughout the systems and check control reaction and operation.

TAXIING.

WARNING

Nose wheel steering may not be completely effective when taxiing on ice or hard packed snow. A combination of nose wheel steering and braking is recommended. Exercise care and taxi at reduced speed while operating on these surfaces. Increase the normal interval between airplanes to insure safe stopping distance and to prevent icing of airplane surfaces by melted snow and ice in the jet blast of preceding airplanes. Insure that all instruments have warmed sufficiently to insure operation. Check for sluggish instruments during taxiing.

CAUTION

Painted areas on runways, taxiways and ramps are significantly more slippery than on unpainted areas, particularly when wet. In addition, painted areas sometimes serve as condensation surfaces and it is possible to have wet, frosty or even icy conditions on those areas when the overall weather condition is dry.

TAKEOFF.

Insure that takeoff data accounts for reduced braking capability due to ice and snow on runway in event of an abort. Make normal takeoff. Care should be exercised to avoid exceeding climb schedule speeds due to additional thrust available at low temperatures.

AFTER TAKEOFF.

After takeoff from a wet snow-covered or slush-covered field, operate the landing gear through several complete cycles to prevent gear freezing in the retracted position.

DESCENT.

Follow normal procedures.

LANDING.

Follow normal procedures.

ENGINE SHUTDOWN.

Follow normal procedures.

BEFORE LEAVING AIRPLANE.

Leave the canopy partly open; this will allow circulation within the cockpit to reduce windshield and canopy frosting.

HOT WEATHER AND DESERT OPERATION

Hot weather and desert operation requires that added precautions be taken against damage from dust, sand, and high temperatures. Particular attention should be given to those components and systems (engine, fuel, oil, hydraulic, pitot-static, etc.) which are susceptible to contamination, malfunction, or damage from sand and dust. All the filters on the airplane should be checked frequently. Components containing plastic or rubber parts should be protected as much as possible from blowing sand and extreme temperatures. During conditions of blowing sand and dust, the canopies should be closed and sealed and all protective covers installed when the airplane is not in use.

> **CAUTION**
>
> Do not attempt takeoff or engine operation in a sand storm or dust storm if avoidable. Park airplane crosswind and shut down engine to prevent damage from sand or dust.

EXTERIOR INSPECTION.

Inspect the exposed areas of the shock strut and actuator pistons on the landing gear and have them cleaned as required. Check engine inlet ducts for sand accumulation. Check tires for signs of blistering, and check for overinflation of tires and struts due to high ambient temperatures. Check for fuel or hydraulic leakage due to thermal expansion of sealing materials. Inspect the area aft of the airplane to make sure that engine exhaust will not cause sand or dust to be blown onto personnel or equipment when engines are started.

INTERIOR INSPECTION.

Inspect the crew compartments for excessive dust accumulation.

ENGINE START.

Follow normal procedures.

BEFORE TAXIING.

Ground testing should be complete but accomplished as expeditiously as possible.

TAXIING.

Follow normal procedures.

TAKEOFF.

Allow for longer takeoff distances in hot weather. Refer to Appendix I for recommended takeoff speeds and required takeoff distances.

> **CAUTION**
>
> It is imperative that takeoff not be made at lower than recommended speeds. When outside air temperature is high, do not rotate too soon, as more than usual takeoff distance will be required to obtain takeoff speed.

APPROACH AND LANDING.

Maintain recommended approach and landing speeds as shown in Appendix I. Allow for longer landing rolls resulting from increased true airspeeds.

> **CAUTION**
>
> Hot weather operation requires the pilot to be cautious of gusts and wind shifts near the ground.

ENGINE SHUTDOWN.

Follow normal procedures.

BEFORE LEAVING THE AIRPLANE.

Follow normal procedures.

This is the last page of Section VII.

Appendix I
PERFORMANCE DATA

Performance Data is contained in Appendix I of Classified Supplement T.O. 1F-111A-1A.

ALPHABETICAL INDEX

— A —

	Page
Abandoning the Airplane on the Ground	3-2
Abort	3-3
AC Electrical Power Supply System	1-26*
AC Voltmeter	1-29
Acceleration Limitations	5-14
Acceleration, Engine	1-16
Accelerometer	1-65
Accumulators, Hydraulic	1-32
Adverse Yaw Compensation	6-3
Aerodynamic Deceleration Equipment	1-41
Aft Center of Gravity Limitations	5-13*
After Landing	2-14
After Takeoff	2-12
Afterburner Control Malfunction	1-16
Afterburner Failure During Takeoff	3-3
Afterburner Fuel System	1-7
Afterburners, Engine	1-7
Aiming Reticle and Steering Bar Presentations	1-105*
Air Conditioning and Pressurization System Failure	3-12
Air Conditioning and Pressurization Systems	1-116*
Air Conditioning Control Panel	1-118*
Air Conditioning System	1-115
Air Conditioning System Alternate Operation	1-119
Air Refueling	1-24, 2-13
Normal Operation	2-13
Alternate Operation	2-13
Air Refueling System	1-20
Aircraft Arresting System	1-40
Airplane, The	1-1
Dimensions	1-1
Flight Crew	1-6
Weight	1-6
Airplane Position Updating	1-80
Airplane Upset Limit at Brake Release	5-18B*
Airspeed Limitations	5-3
Airstart	3-4
Airstart Envelope	3-4A*
Alignment to Stored Magnetic Variation	1-80B
Allowable Differences Between Primary and Standby Instruments	1-61*
Allowable Rudder Command	5-9*
Allowable Sink Rate At Touchdown	5-19*
Alpha/Beta Probe Heat Caution Lamp	1-120A
Alternate Operation of Weapon Bay Doors and Trapeze	1-87
Alternate Platform Alignment Procedures	1-80B
Alternating Current Power Supply System	1-24

	Page
Altimeter	1-62A
Altimeter, Radar	1-92
Altitude Calibration	1-79
Altitude Hold Mode	1-55
Angle-of-Attack Indexer	1-65
Angle-of-Attack Indicating System	1-65
Anti-Icing and Defog Systems	1-120
Anti-G Suit	1-133
Anti-Skid System	1-40
Antenna Locations	1-99*
Antenna Select Panel	1-98*
Arm Rests	1-134
Armament Select Panel	1-82*
Armament System	1-81
Artificial Stall Warning System	1-49
Assembly, Maximum Safe Mach	1-58
Attack Radar (AN/APQ-113)	1-98
Attack Radar Control Panel	1-101*
Attack Radar Scope Panel	1-103*
Attack Radar Tracking Control Handle	1-101*
Attitude Stabilization Mode	1-55
Augmentation Off Operating Limits	6-9*, 5-20*
Automatic Direction Finder Operation	1-111
Automatic Fuel System Management	1-23
Autopilot Damper Panel	1-52*
Autopilot Operation	1-56B
Disengaging the Autopilot	1-57
Engaging the Autopilot	1-56B
Selecting the Autopilot Control Modes	1-57
Autopilot Release Lever	1-56A
Autopilot System	1-55
Altitude Hold Mode	1-55
Attitude Stabilization Mode	1-55
Heading Navigation Mode	1-56
Control Stick Steering	1-56
Controls and Indicators	1-56
Mach Hold Mode	1-55
Auxiliary Flight Control Panel	1-51*
Auxiliary Flight Reference System (AFRS)	1-58
Auxiliary Flight Reference System Operation	1-60
Auxiliary Gage Panel	1-36*
Auxiliary Mode Operation	1-80

— B —

	Page
Before Landing	2-15
Before Leaving Airplane	2-18
Before Starting Engines	2-7
Before Takeoff	2-13
Before Taxiing	2-10
Bomb Nav Control Panel	1-74*
Bomb/Nav Distance-Time Indicator	1-78
Bomb Nav System Operation	1-78

*Denotes Illustration

	Page
Bombing and Launching Equipment	1-81
Bombing-Navigation System (AN/AJQ-20)	1-71
Bombing Procedures	1-81
Brake Energy Limits	5-21*
Brake Hydraulic Hand Pump	1-40
Brake Limitations	5-20
Brake, Speed	1-41
Brake System	1-39
Buffet	6-5
Bumper System, Tail	1-39
Buttons	
AFRS Gyro Fast Erect	1-59
Aiming Reticle Cage	1-107
Air Start	1-12
Attack Radar Manual Photo	1-101
Attack Radar Range Search	1-101
Bomb Nav Fix Mode Selector	1-73
Damper Reset	1-52
Damper Servo	1-53
Emergency Generator Indicator/Cutoff	1-28A
Engine Oil Quantity Indicator Test	1-16A
External Stores Jettison	1-84
Flight Control Master Test	1-52A
Fuel Quantity Indicator Test	1-22
Hot Microphone	1-111
Instrument Test	1-70D
Interphone Call	1-112
Landing Gear Handle Lock Release	1-37
Malfunction and Indicator Lamp Test	1-71
Nose Wheel Steering/Air Refuel	1-22, 1-39
Oxygen Quantity Indicator Test	1-124
Present Position Correction	1-73
Present Position Hold	1-74
Pylon Weapon Selector	1-83
Rate Gyro Test	1-53
Reference Engage	1-56A
Release System Test	1-83
Spike Test	1-14B
Spoiler Reset	1-53
Takeoff Trim Test	1-51
Tone	1-110
Trim	1-50
Weapon Bay Control	1-86
Weapon Release	1-84

— C —

	Page
Cabin Air Distribution Control Lever	1-115
Cabin Overheat, Uncontrolled	3-12
Cabin Pressure Schedule	1-120*
Canopy	1-114
Canopy Hatch Operating Speed	5-25
Canopy, Left Removal	3-8
Caution Lamps	
Anti-Skid	1-40
Arresting Hook	1-41
Auxiliary Attitude (AUX ATT)	1-60
Engine Icing	1-122
Engine Oil Hot	1-15
Equipment Hot	1-119
Equipment Low Pressure	1-120
Flight Control Spoiler	1-54
Foreign Object Damage (FOD) Prevention Door	1-15
Fuel Distribution	1-23
Fuel Low	1-23
Fuel Manifold Low Pressure	1-23
Fuel Tank Pressurization	1-23
Generator	1-29
Heading Malfunction	1-60
Hydraulic Fluid Overheat	1-33
Inlet Hot	1-122
Low Pressure	1-33
Master	1-70D
Oil Low	1-16A
Oxygen	1-125
Pressurization	1-120
Primary Attitude/Heading	1-75
Reference Not Engaged	1-56A
Roll and Pitch Gain Changer	1-55
Roll, Pitch, and Yaw Channel	1-54
Roll, Pitch, and Yaw Damper	1-54
Rudder Authority	1-55
Spike	1-15
TF Fly-Up Off	1-95
TFR Channel Fail	1-95
Total Temperature	1-62
Translating Cowl	1-15
Turbine Inlet Temperature (TIT) Hot	1-15
Windshield Hot	1-123
Caution Lamp Analysis	3-17*
Center-of-Gravity Envelope	6-19, 6-19*
Center-of-Gravity Limitations	5-11
Central Air Data Computer System (CADC)	1-57
Chaff Dispenser Control Lever	1-131
Channel, Pitch	1-45
Channel, Roll	1-48
Channel Set Pushbutton	1-111
Channel, Yaw	1-48
Check, Preflight	2-2
Circuit Breaker Panel	1-32*
Climb	2-15
Cold Weather Procedures	7-6
Command Augmentation	1-48A
Command Steering Bars	1-106
Communication Equipment	1-107
Communications and Avionics Equipment	1-109*
Compass Control Panel	1-60*
Compressor Bleed Valve Position Indicator	1-14B
Compressor Stall	3-5
Computer, Navigational	1-72
Control	
Directional	6-2
Lateral	6-2
Longitudinal	6-1
Control Levers, Oxygen	1-124

*Denotes Illustration

	Page
Control Malfunction, Afterburner	1-16
Control Stick Steering	1-56
Control Sticks	1-50, 1-50*, 1-131
Control Surface Position Indicator	1-53
Controls and Indicators, Engine	1-11
Controls and Indicators, Fuel System	1-20
Controls, Wing Sweep Handle Lockout	1-43
Cooling System, Hydraulic	1-32
Correction Card Holders	1-133
Counters	
Attack Radar Cursor Range	1-104
Destination Distance/Time	1-77
Destination Position	1-76
Fixpoint Elevation	1-76
Glide/Dive Angle	1-77
Groundtrack and Groundspeed	1-77
Magnetic Variation	1-76A
Offset Range and Offset Bearing	1-77
Present Position	1-76
Rounds	1-89
Time-of-Fall	1-77
Trail/Range	1-77
True Heading	1-76
Wind Speed and Wind From	1-77
Crew Entrance Ladders and Steps	1-131
Crew, Flight	1-6
Crew Module Ejection Sequence	1-128, 1-129*
Crew Module Escape System	1-125
Crew Module General Arrangement	1-126*
Crew Module	5-25
Crew Module Seats	1-125, 1-127*
Crew Requirements, Minimum	5-1
Crew Station General Arrangement	1-4*
Cruise	2-15
Crosswind Landing	6-5

— D —

	Page
Danger Areas	2-8*
DC Electrical Power Supply System	1-30*
Defog System, Windshield	1-122
Descent	2-15
Destination Set Procedure, Bomb Nav System	1-78
Destination Storage, Bomb Nav System	1-79
Dimensions, Airplane	1-1
Direct Current Power Supply System	1-29
Directional Control	6-2
Disengaging the Autopilot	1-57
Ditching Escape Sequence	1-130
Dive Recovery	6-12
Double Engine Failure During Flight	3-4
Double Generator Failure With Both Engines Operating	3-10
Dual Bombing Timer	1-85, 1-85*
Dump System, Fuel	1-20
Dumping, Fuel	1-24

— E —

	Page
Ejection	3-6
Ejection Equipment	1-127
Ejection Handles	1-130
Ejection Procedures	3-7*
Electrical Control Panel	1-28*
Electrical Power Supply System	1-24
Electrical Power Test Panel	1-29*
Emergencies, Ground Operation	3-2
Abandoning the Airplane on the Ground	3-2
Emergency Entrance	3-2
Engine Fire During Start	3-2
Wheel Brake System Emergency Operation	3-2
Emergencies, Inflight	3-3
Air Conditioning and Pressurization System Failure	3-12
Airstart	3-4
Caution Lamp Analysis	3-3
Complete Hydraulic System Failure	3-9
Compressor Stall	3-5
Double Engine Failure During Flight	3-4
Double Generator Failure With Both Engines Operating	3-10
Ejection	3-6
Emergency Generator Operation With One Engine Shutdown	3-10
Emergency Wing Sweep Operation	3-3
Engine Fire During Flight	3-5
Flight Control System Malfunctions	3-9
Fuel Pressure Caution Lamp Indication	3-11
Fuel System Operation on Emergency Electrical Power	3-10
Glass Panel Failure	3-6
Oil System Malfunctions	3-12
Primary or Utility Hydraulic System Failure	3-8
Single Engine Failure	3-4
Single Generator Failure	3-10
Smoke and Fume Elimination	3-5
Spike System Failure	3-12
Unlock Canopy Indication	3-6
Emergencies, Landing	3-12A
Caution Lamp Analysis	3-17*
Emergency Extension of Flaps and Slats	3-14
Emergency Landing Airspeeds and Ground Roll Distances	3-16*
Landing Gear Emergency Extension	3-12A
Landing With a Blown Tire	3-14
Landing With Both Translating Cowls Closed	3-15
Landing With Main Gear Up or Unlocked and Nose Gear Down or Landing With All Landing Gear Up or Unlocked	3-13
Landing With Nose Gear Up or Unlocked, Main Gear Down	3-13

*Denotes Illustration

Index

Emergencies, Landing (Cont)

	Page
Landing With One Translating Cowl Closed	3-14
Landing With Primary or Utility Hydraulic System Failure	3-12A
Landing With Unsafe Gear Indication	3-13
Landing With Wings at 26 Degrees or Greater and No Flaps	3-15
Main Landing Gear Failure To Extend and Lock After Releasing From Uplock	3-12A
Single Engine Landing and Go-Around	3-14

Emergencies, Takeoff ... 3-3
- Abort ... 3-3
- Afterburner Failure During Takeoff ... 3-3
- Engine Failure During Takeoff ... 3-3
- Engine Fire During Takeoff ... 3-3
- Tire Failure During Takeoff ... 3-3

Emergency Entrance ... 3-2
Emergency Entrance ... 3-21*
Emergency Extension of Flaps and Slats ... 3-14
Emergency Generator Indicator/Cutoff Push Button ... 1-28A
Emergency Generator Operation With One Engine Shutdown ... 3-10
Emergency Landing Airspeeds and Ground Roll Distances ... 3-16*
Emergency Oxygen Pressure Gage ... 1-125
Emergency Oxygen System ... 1-125
Emergency Pressurization System ... 1-120
Emergency Pressurization System Gage ... 1-120
Emergency Wing Sweep Operation ... 3-3
Engine Acceleration ... 1-16
  Acceleration Limits ... 5-3
Engine Fire During Flight ... 3-5
Engine Fuel System ... 1-8*
Engine Panel ... 1-13*
Engine, The ... 1-6*
Engines ... 1-6
- Afterburners ... 1-7
- Anti-Icing Systems ... 1-121
- Before Starting ... 2-7
- Controls and Indicators ... 1-11
- Failure During Flight, Double ... 3-4
- Failure During Flight, Single ... 3-4
- Failure During Takeoff ... 3-3
- Fire Detection and Extinguishing System ... 1-16
- Fire During Flight ... 3-5
- Fire During Start ... 3-2
- Fire During Takeoff ... 3-3
- Fuel Control System ... 1-7
- Fuel System Emergency Operations ... 3-10
- Fuel Supply System ... 1-17
- Ignition System ... 1-11
- Inlet Spikes ... 1-10
- Limitations ... 5-1
- Operation ... 1-16

	Page
Engine Stall Characteristics	6-7
Engine Stall Recognition	6-8
Engine Stall Recovery	6-8
Starting	2-7
Starting System	1-11
Tachometers	1-14B
Throttles	1-11
Translating Cowls	1-10
Variable Exhaust Nozzles	1-10
Equipment Aerodynamic Deceleration	1-41
Exterior Inspection	2-3*
Exterior Interphone Stations	1-112
Exterior Lighting	1-112
External Stores and Weapon Loading Configuration	5-12*
External Stores, Flight With	6-18

— F —

	Page
Fire Detection and Extinguishing System, Engine	1-16
Fixed Pylon Jettison Procedure	1-85
Flaps and Slat Handle	1-42
Flaps, Wing	1-41
Flight Characteristics	2-15
Flight Characteristics, Level	6-3
Flight Characteristics, Maneuvering	6-5
Flight Control Switch Panel	1-51*
Flight Control System	1-43, 6-1
Flight Control System Controls and Indicators	1-50
Flight Control System Malfunctions	3-9
Flight Control System Schematic	1-46*
Flight Crew	1-6
Flight, Preparation for	2-1
Flight Procedures, Instrument	7-1
Flight With Augmentation Off	6-8, 5-20
Flight With External Stores	6-18
Flight With Speed Brake Extended	6-18
Forward Center of Gravity Limitations for Landing	5-17*
Frequency Meter	1-29
Fuel, Alternate	5-3
Fuel Control Panel	1-21*
Fuel Control Unit	1-7
Fuel Control System, Engine	1-7
Fuel Dump System	1-20
Fuel Dumping	1-24
Fuel Pressure Caution Lamp Indication	3-11
Fuel Pressurization and Vent System	1-17
Fuel Pumps	1-17
Fuel Quantity Data	1-16B*
Fuel Supply System	1-18*
Fuel Supply System	1-16A
Fuel Supply System, Engine	1-17
Fuel System Controls and Indicators	1-20
Fuel System Management, Automatic	1-23
Fuel System Management, Manual	1-23

*Denotes Illustration

	Page		Page
Fuel System Operation	1-23	Headrest Adjustment Lever	1-130
Fuel System Operation on Emergency Electrical Power	3-10	HF Radio (AN/ARC-123)	1-111
		Horn, Landing Gear Warning	1-37
Fuel Tank Pressure Gage	1-23	Hot Weather and Desert Operation	7-7
Fuel Tanks	1-17	Hydraulic Accumulators	1-32
Fuel Transfer	1-17	Hydraulic Cooling System	1-32
		Hydraulic Fluid Overheat Caution Lamps	1-33
		Hydraulic Fluid Reservoirs	1-32
		Hydraulic Hand Pump, Brake	1-40

— G —

		Hydraulic Isolation Valve	1-33
Gage, Fuel Tank Pressure	1-23	Hydraulic Power Supply System (Primary)	1-32*
Gate, Wing Sweep Handle 26 Degree Forward	1-43	Hydraulic Power Supply System (Utility)	1-34*
Gear, Main	1-33	Hydraulic Power Supply System	1-32
Gear, Nose	1-36	Hydraulic Pressure Indicators	1-33
Gear System, Landing	1-33	Hydraulic Pumps	1-32
General Arrangement	1-2*	Hydraulic System Failure	3-8
Generator Decouple Pushbuttons	1-28		
Generator Failure, Double	3-10		
Generator Failures	3-10	— I —	
Generator Operation With One Engine Shutdown, Emergency	3-10	Ice and Rain	7-4
		IFF Control Panel	1-97*
Gloves, Rotating	1-42	IFF System (AN/APX-64)	1-97
Go-Around	2-18, 2-19*	Ignition System, Engine	1-11
Gravity Refueling	1-20	ILS Control Panel	1-91*
Gross Altimeter	1-66	Indicators	
Gross Weight—C. G. Limitations for Taxi and Ground Operation	5-18*	Airspeed	1-62, 1-65
		Airspeed Mach	1-64
Gross Weight Limitations	5-12B	Altitude-Vertical Velocity	1-66
Ground Check Panel	1-54*	Angle-of-Attack	1-65
Ground Operation Emergencies	3-2	Attitude	1-62A
Ground Roll Spoilers	1-41	Attitude Director	1-66
Ground Safety Locks	1-38*	Bearing-Distance-Heading	1-64
Gunnery Equipment	1-89	Bomb/Nav Distance—Time	1-78
Gyrocompass Alignment Procedure	1-80A	Cabin Altitude	1-120
		Compressor Bleed Valve Position	1-14B
		Control Surface Position	1-53
— H —		Electrical Power Flow	1-28
Handles		Engine Fuel Flow	1-14B
Arresting Hook	1-41	Engine Nozzle Position	1-14B
Attack Radar Tracking Control	1-100	Engine Oil Pressure	1-14B
Auxiliary Brake	1-40	Engine Oil Quantity	1-16
Auxiliary Flotation	1-130	Engine Pressure Ratio	1-14B
Canopy External Emergency Release	1-115	Engine Turbine Inlet Temperature	1-15
Canopy External Latch	1-114	Flap and Slat Position	1-42
Canopy Internal Emergency Release	1-115	Flight Control System Controls and	1-50
Ejection	1-130	Fuel System Controls and	1-20
Emergency Oxygen	1-125	Fuselage Fuel Quantity	1-22
Emergency Pressurization	1-120	Horizontal Situation	1-68
Flap and Slat	1-42	Hydraulic Pressure	1-33
Inertial Reel Control	1-130	Landing Gear Controls and	1-36
Internal Canopy Latch	1-114	Mach	1-65
Landing Gear	1-36	Magnetic Heading Synchronization	1-76A
Landing Gear Emergency Release	1-37	Oxygen Quantity	1-124
Left Canopy Detach	1-114	Synchronization	1-60
Recovery Parachute Deploy	1-130	TFR Control and	1-93
Recovery Parachute Release	1-130	Total/Select Fuel Quantity	1-22
Severance and Flotation	1-131	Total Temperature	1-62
Wing Sweep Control	1-43	Translating Cowl Position	1-15

Index

Indicators (Cont)
Landing

	Page
Indicators (Cont)	
True Airspeed	1-62
Unused Film	1-104
Vertical Velocity	1-62A, 1-66
Wing Sweep Position	1-43
Inflight Emergencies	3-3
Inflight Glass Panel Failure	3-6
Inlet Spikes, Engine	1-10
Inspection, Before Exterior	2-2
Inspection, Interior	2-2
Power Off	2-2
Power On	2-4
Instrument Flight Procedures	7-1
Instrument Landing System	1-90
Instrument Markings	5-2*
Instruments	1-62
Integrated Flight Instrument System	1-64
Integrated Flight Instrument System	1-67*
Integrated Flight Instruments	1-113
Internal Lighting	1-111
Interphone (AN/AIC-25)	1-111
Interphone Control Panels	1-112*
Isolation Valve, Hydraulic	1-33

— K —

Knobs

	Page
AC Meter Selector	1-29
Aiming Reticle Brightness	1-107
Air Refueling Receptacle Lights Control	1-113
Air Source Selector	1-118
Altitude/Test Selector	1-75
Antenna Tilt Control	1-95, 1-102
Attack Radar Frequency Control	1-100
Attack Radar Function Selector	1-100
Attack Radar Mode Selector	1-100
Attack Radar Range Selector	1-103
Attack Radar Scope Intensity Control	1-102
Bezel/Range Marks Intensity Control	1-102
Bomb Nav Mode Selector	1-72
Code Selector	1-98
Command Bar Brightness	1-107
Communications Monitor	1-111
Compass Mode Selector	1-59
Delivery Mode Selector	1-82
Engine Feed Selector	1-20
Fuel Quantity Indicator Selector	1-22
Fuel Transfer	1-21
Heading Set	1-60
IFF Master Control	1-97
ILS Frequency Selector	1-91
ILS Volume Control	1-91
Instrument System Coupler Mode Selector	1-68
Intermediate Frequency Gain	1-101
Internal Lighting Control	1-114
Intervalometer Counter and Set	1-83
Latitude Correction	1-60
LCOS Mode Select	1-107
LCOS Reticle Depression Set	1-106
Master Volume Control	1-111
Missile Step Selector	1-88
Mode 4 Code Control	1-98
Nuclear Weapons Arm	1-83
Nuclear Weapons Monitor and Release	1-83
Platform Alignment Control	1-74
Radar Scope Control	1-95
Range and Azimuth Cursor Intensity Control	1-102
Range Selector	1-95
Ride Control	1-94
Sensitivity Time Control	1-102
Tacan Function Selector	1-89
Tacan Volume Control	1-90
Temperature Control	1-118
Terrain Clearance	1-94
TFR Channel Mode Selector	1-93
Transmitter Selector	1-111, 1-112
True Airspeed Set	1-106
UHF Radio Function Selector	1-108
UHF Radio Manual Frequency Selector	1-110
UHF Radio Preset Channel Selector	1-110
UHF Radio Volume Control	1-110
Video/Transmitter Tuning Control	1-102
Weapon Mode Selector	1-82, 1-88

— L —

Lamps

	Page
Alpha/Beta Probe Heat Caution	1-120A
Antenna Cage Pushbutton Indicator	1-104
Attack Radar Range Lock Indicator	1-104
Bomb Release	1-78
Canopy Unlock Warning	1-115
Emergency Generator Indicator	1-29
Fire Pushbutton Warning	1-16
Fuel Dump Low Pressure Indicator	1-23
Go	1-76
Landing Gear Position Indicator	1-37
Marker Beacon	1-91
Nose Wheel Steering/Air Refueling Indicator	1-23, 1-39
Nuclear Weapons Monitor	1-84
Nuclear Caution	1-84
Photo Malfunction Indicator	1-104
Platform Indicator	1-75
Pressurization Warning	1-120
Radar Altitude Low Warning	1-92
Reference Not Engaged Caution	1-56A
Reduced Speed Warning	1-62
Takeoff Trim Indicator	1-54
Test	1-98
TFR Failure Warning	1-95
Translating Cowl Caution	1-15
Translating Cowl Warning	1-15
Trapeze Extend	1-86
Warning, Caution and Indicator	1-70D
Weapons Bay Door Open	1-87
Landing	2-16

*Denotes Illustration

	Page		Page
Landing and Go-Around With One Engine Out	3-14	Liquid Containers	1-134
Landing, After	2-18	Longitudinal Control	6-1
Landing, Before	2-15	Longitudinal Maneuver Gradients	6-6*
Landing, Crosswind	6-5	Low Pressure Caution Lamps	1-33
Landing Emergencies	3-12A	Low Speed Trim Compensation	1-48A, 6-2
Landing Gear Control Panel	1-36*		
Landing Gear Controls and Indicators	1-36	**— M —**	
Landing Gear Emergency Extension	3-12A		
Landing Gear Handle	1-36	Magnetic Compass	1-62A
Landing Gear System	1-33	Magnetic Variation Updating	1-80
Landing Gear Warning Horn	1-37	Main Gear	1-33
Landing on Slippery Runways and/or Minimum Run Landings	2-16	Main Landing Gear Failure To Extend and Lock After Releasing From Uplock	3-12A
Landing, Spike System Failure	3-12	Maneuvering Flight Characteristics	6-5
Landing Pattern	2-17*	Maneuverability Limitations	5-7
Landing, Touch and Go	2-18	Manual Trim	6-2
Landing With a Blown Tire	3-14	Manual Fuel System Management	1-23
Landing With Both Translating Cowls Closed	3-15	Manual Present Position Fix	1-80A
Landing With Main Gear Up or Unlocked and Nose Gear Down or Landing With All Landing Gear Up or Unlocked	3-13	Map Stowage	1-133
		Master Caution Lamp	1-70D
Landing With Nose Gear Up or Unlocked, Main Gear Down	3-13	Maximum Arresting Hook Engaging Speed Based on BAK12 Barrier	5-8*
Landing With One Translating Cowl Closed	3-14	Maximum Safe Mach Assembly	1-58
Landing With Primary or Utility Hydraulic System Failure	3-12A	Meter, Frequency	1-29
		Minimum Crew Requirements	5-1
Landing With Unsafe Gear Indication	3-13	Mirrors	1-133
Landing With Wings at 26 Degrees Sweep or Greater and No Flaps	3-15	Miscellaneous Equipment	1-131
		Miscellaneous Operational Limitations	5-25
Lateral Control	6-2	Miscellaneous Switch Panel	1-92*
LCOS Aiming Reticle	1-105	Missed Approach Procedure	7-4
LCOS Mode Select Knob Positions Versus Indications	1-108*	Missile Trapeze	1-86
		Missile Trapeze Controls	1-86
Lead Computing Optical Sight System	1-105, 1-106*	Missile Trapeze Operation	1-86
Left Main Instrument Panel	1-14*, 1-14A*	Missiles	1-88
Left Sidewall	1-45*	AIM-9B (GAR-8)	1-88
Letdown Chart Holder	1-134	Modes	
Level Flight Characteristics	6-3	Altitude Hold	1-55
Lever, Autopilot Release	1-56A	Attack Radar Air	1-98A
Lever, Headrest Adjustment	1-130	Attack Radar Ground	1-99
Lever, Seat Forward and Aft Adjustment	1-130	Attitude Stabilization	1-55
Lighting Control Panel	1-113*	Constant Track	1-56
Lighting System	1-112	Ground Mapping (GM)	1-93
Limitations		Heading Navigation	1-56
Airspeed	5-3	Mach Hold	1-55
Angle of Attack and Sideslip	5-10	Manual	1-119
Augmentation Off, Operating	6-9*	Ram Air	1-119
Brake	5-20	Selecting the Altitude Hold	1-57
Center-of-Gravity	5-11	Selecting the Autopilot Control	1-57
Engine	5-1	Selecting the Constant Track	1-57
Gross Weight	5-12A	Selecting the Heading Nav	1-57
Maneuverability	5-7	Selecting the Mach Hold	1-57
Miscellaneous Operational	5-25	Situation (SIT)	1-93
Oil Temperature	5-3	Terrain Following (TF)	1-92
Roll	5-7		
Starter	5-3	**— N —**	
Wing Sweep	5-7	Navigational Computer	1-72
Yaw	5-7	Night Flying	7-5
		Normal Mode Operation	1-78

Changed 18 August 1967   *Denotes Illustration

	Page
Normal Oxygen System	1-123
Nose Gear	1-36
Nose Wheel Steering System	1-39
Nose Wheel Steering/Air Refuel Buttons	1-22, 1-39
Nose Wheel Steering/Air Refueling Indicator Lamp	1-23, 1-39
Nuclear Caution Lamp	1-84
Nuclear Weapons Arm Knob Lock Lever	1-83
Nuclear Weapons Control Panel	1-84*

— O —

	Page
Oil Supply System	1-16
Oil System Malfunctions	3-12
Oil Temperature, Excessive With Normal Oil Pressure	3-12
Operation, Auxiliary Flight Reference System	1-60
Operation, Engine	1-16
Operation, Fuel System	1-23
Oxygen Control Levers	1-124
Oxygen Duration	1-123*
Oxygen—Suit Control Panel	1-124*
Oxygen System	1-123
Oxygen System Alternate Operation	1-125
Oxygen System, Emergency	1-125

— P —

	Page
Pedals, Rudder	1-50
Penetration Aids	1-107
Pitch Channel	1-45
Pitch-Roll Mixing	1-48
Pitch Trim	1-49
Pitot-Static Probe Anti-Icing	1-120
Pitot-Static System	1-61
Pneumatic Power Supply Systems	1-33
Pneumatic Servicing Requirements Table	2-22*
Power Supply System, Electrical	1-24
Alternating Current	1-24
Direct Current	1-29
Power Supply System, Hydraulic	1-32
Power Supply Systems, Pneumatic	1-33
Precheck Selector Valves	1-22
Preflight Check	2-2
Before Entering Cockpit	2-2
Before Exterior Inspection	2-2
Exterior Inspection	2-2
Interior Inspection	2-2
Preparation for Flight	2-1
Checklists	2-1
Entrance	2-2
Flight Planning	2-1
Flight Restrictions	2-1
Takeoff and Landing Data Cards	2-1
Weight and Balance	2-1

	Page
Pressurization and Vent System, Fuel	1-17
Pressurization System	1-115, 1-119
Primary or Utility Hydraulic System Failure	3-8
Prohibited Maneuvers	5-10
Pumps, Fuel	1-17
Pumps, Hydraulic	1-32
Pushbuttons, Generator Decouple	1-28

— R —

	Page
Radar Altimeter	1-92
Radar Altimeter System (AN/APN-167)	1-91
Radar Fix	1-80A
Radar/ILS Approach (Typical)	7-2*
Radar Target Position Determination Procedure	1-80A
Ram Air Mode Limits	5-6*
Range Bomb (Direct Sighting) Procedure	1-81
Rapid Alignment to Stored Gyrocompass Heading	1-80B
Recommended Minimum Flying Speeds	6-9
Recovery and Landing Equipment	1-127
Recovery, Dive	6-12
Refueling, Air	1-24, 2-15
Refueling, Gravity	1-20
Refueling, Single Point	1-24
Refueling System, Air	1-20
Refueling System, Single Point	1-20
Reservoirs, Hydraulic Fluid	1-32
Right Main Instrument Panel	1-63*
Right Sidewall	1-121*
Roll Channel	1-48
Roll Limitations	5-7
Rolling Flight	6-5

— S —

	Page
Seat Forward and Aft Adjustment Lever	1-130
Self-Adaptive Gain System	1-49
Servicing Diagram	1-132*
Side Curtains	1-131
Simulated Single Engine Landing	2-18
Single Engine Failure During Flight	3-4
Single Generator Failure	3-10
Single Point Refueling	1-24
Single Point Refueling System	1-20
Slats, Wing	1-42
Slippery Runways and/or Minimum Run Landings, Landing on	2-16
Smoke and Fume Elimination	3-5
Speed Brake	1-41
Speedbrake Extended, Flight With	6-18
Speed Brake Limit	5-25
Spike System Failure	3-12
Spins	6-17
Spoilers, Ground Roll	1-41
Stability Augmentation	1-49, 6-3

*Denotes Illustration

	Page		Page
Stabilization Platform	1-71	Emergency Generator	1-28
Stalls	6-12	Engine Ground Start	1-11
Standby Instruments	1-62	Engine/Inlet Anti-Icing	1-121
Starter Cartridge Stowage Container	1-134	Entrance Ladder	1-133
Starter Limitations	5-3	External Power	1-28A
Starting Engines	2-7	Fire Detection System Ground Test	1-16
Starting System, Engine	1-11	Flap and Slat	1-42
Steering, Control Stick	1-55	Flight Control System	1-52A
Steering System, Nose Wheel	1-39	Flight Instrument Reference Select	1-59
Sticks, Control	1-50	Foreign Object Damage (FOD) Prevention Door	1-14B
Stored Destination Recall Procedure	1-79	Formation Lights	1-113
Stores Release System	1-85	Fuel Dump	1-21
Stowage		Fuel Tank Pressurization Selector	1-21
Chart	1-133	Fuselage Lights	1-113
Chart Board	1-133	Generator	1-25
Checklist	1-133	Ground Roll Spoiler	1-41
Data Case	1-133	Gun Selector	1-89
Ejection System Safety Pin	1-133	Gun Trigger	1-89
Food Compartment	1-133	Hemisphere Selector	1-60
Hood Compartment	1-133	Identification-of-Position	1-97
Relief Container	1-133	IFF Antenna Selector	1-98
Spare Lamp and Fuse Holder	1-133	Ignition Cutoff	1-12
Strange Field	2-20	ILS Power	1-91
After Landing	2-20	Instrument System Coupler Pitch Steering Mode	1-68
Delayed Takeoff	2-22	Landing and Taxi Lights	1-113
Postflight	2-22	LCOS Test	1-107
Supply System, Fuel	1-16A	Mach Trim Test	1-13, 1-120A
Supply System, Oil	1-16	Malfunction and Indicator Lamp Dimming	1-71
Survival Equipment	1-128	Master Power	1-82
Switches		Microphone	1-111, 1-112
Agent Discharge/Fire Detect Test	1-16	Mode 4 Control	1-98
Air Conditioning System Mode Selector	1-118	Mode 4 Monitor Control	1-98
Air Refueling	1-21	Mode Select/Test	1-98
Altitude Hold/Mach Hold Selector	1-56A	Nuclear Consent	1-83
Antenna Polarization	1-100	Pitot Heater	1-120A
Anti-Collision Lights	1-113	Pitot/Probe Heater	1-120A
Anti-Skid Control	1-40	Position Light	1-113
Attack Radar Beta	1-102	Position Lights/Stores Refuel Battery Power	1-22, 1-113
Attack Radar Fast Time Constant	1-100	Pressurization Selector	1-120
Attack Radar Sector	1-101	Rad Test/Monitor	1-98
Attack Radar Side Lobe Cancellation	1-100	Radar Altimeter Bypass	1-92
Attack Radar Sweep Control	1-102	Radar Altimeter Channel Selector	1-92
Attack Radar Test	1-102	Radar Bomb Scoring (RBS) Tone	1-78
Autopilot Emergency Override	1-56A	Ram Area Control	1-119
Autopilot/Damper	1-51, 1-56	Rudder Authority	1-52
Auto Terrain Following	1-52, 1-93	Rudder Trim	1-51
Auxiliary Flight Reference System Power	1-59	Seat Adjustment	1-130
Auxiliary Pitch Trim	1-50	Speed Brake	1-41
Battery	1-29	Spike Control	1-14B
Bomb Arming Selector	1-83	Spoiler Test	1-53
CADC Power	1-58	Squelch	1-110
CADC Test	1-58	Stability Augmentation Test	1-53
Compressor Bleed Valve Control	1-13	TACAN Antenna Selector	1-90
Computer Power	1-53, 1-56	Translating Cowl	1-12
Constant Track	1-56		
Destination/Present Position Selector	1-100		
Emergency Flap and Slat	1-42		

*Denotes Illustration

Switches (Cont)

	Page
Emergency Override Switch	1-13
UHF Radio Antenna Selector	1-111
UHF Radio Mode Selector	1-110
Utility Hydraulic System Isolation	1-33
Weapons Bay Auxiliary Control	1-87
Weapons Bay Door	1-87
Windshield Selector	1-122
Windshield Wash/Rain Removal Selector	1-122
System, Aircraft Arresting	1-40
System, Anti-Skid	1-40
System, Autopilot	1-55
System, Auxiliary Flight Reference	1-58
System, Brake	1-39
System, Central Air Data Computer (CADC)	1-57
System, Engine Fuel Control	1-7
System, Flight Control	1-43, 6-1
System, Fuel Supply	1-16A
System, Oil Supply	1-16
System, Wing Sweep	1-43

— T —

	Page
TACAN Channel Selector	1-90
TACAN Control Panel	1-90*
TACAN Operation	1-90
Tachometers, Engine	1-14B
Tactical Air Navigation System (AN/ARN-52)	1-89
Tail Bumper Contact Limits	5-23*, 5-25
Tail Bumper System	1-39
Takeoff	2-13, 2-14*
Takeoff, After	2-13
Takeoff, Before	2-13
Takeoff Emergencies	3-3
Tanks, Fuel	1-17
Taxiing	2-12
Taxiing, Before	2-10
Terrain Following Radar (AN/APQ-110)	1-92
Terrain Following Radar Operation	1-95, 5-6
TFR Control Panel	1-94*
TFR Scope Panel	1-94*
Thermal Radiation Protection	1-131
Throttle Panels	1-12*
Tire Failure During Takeoff	3-3
Touch and Go Landing	2-18
Trail Bombing (Direct Sighting) Procedures	1-81
Transfer, Fuel	1-17
Translating Cowls, Engine	1-10
Caution Lamp	1-15
Emergency Override Switch	1-13
Malfunction	3-14
Switches	1-12
Test Switches	1-13
Warning Lamp	1-15

	Page
Trim	1-49
Trim, Pitch	1-49
Trim, Roll	1-49
Trim, Yaw	1-49
Trim, Low Speed Compensation	1-48A
Turbulence and Thunderstorms	7-5
Turn Radius and Ground Clearance	2-13*

— U —

UHF Radio Control Panel	1-110*
UHF Radio Frequency Indicator Window	1-111
Unlocked Canopy Indication	3-6
Utility Hydraulic System Isolation Switch	1-33

— V —

Valves, Precheck Selector	1-22
Variable Exhaust Nozzles, Engine	1-10
Vent System, Fuel Pressurization and	1-17
Vernier Altimeter	1-66
Vertical Velocity Indicator	1-66
Voltmeter, AC	1-29
Vortex Destroyers	1-10

— W —

Warning, Caution and Indicator Lamps	1-70*, 1-70B*, 1-70D
Weapon Bay Gun Module	1-89
Weapons Bay Doors	1-86
Weight, Airplane	1-6
Weight and Balance	2-1
Wheel Brake System Emergency Operation	3-2
Windshield Defog System	1-122
Windshield Wash and Rain Removal System	1-122
Windshield Wash/Anti-Icing Control Panel	1-122*
Wing Flaps	1-41
Wing Flaps and Slats	1-41
Wing Slats	1-42
Wing Sweep and Pylon System	1-44*
Wing Sweep Control Handle	1-43
Wing Sweep Handle 26 Degree Forward Gate	1-43
Wing Sweep Handle Lockout Controls	1-43
Wing Sweep Position Indicator	1-43
Wing Sweep System	1-43

— Y —

Yaw Channel	1-48
Yaw Limitations	5-7
Yaw Trim	1-49

Aircraft At War DVD Series

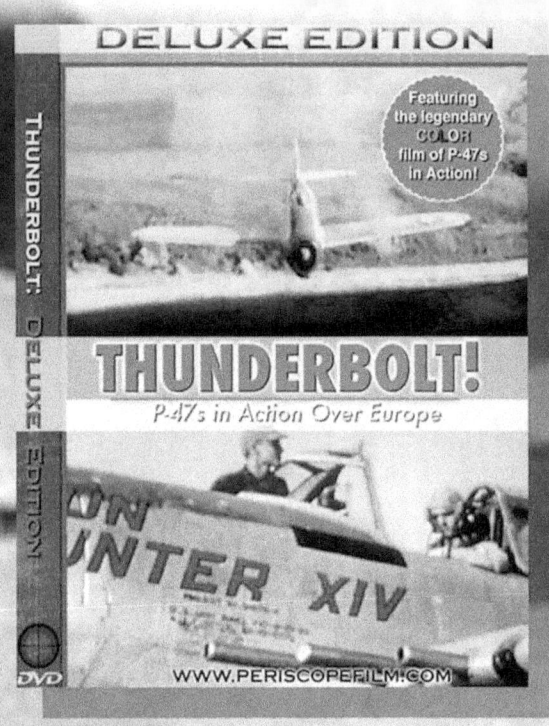
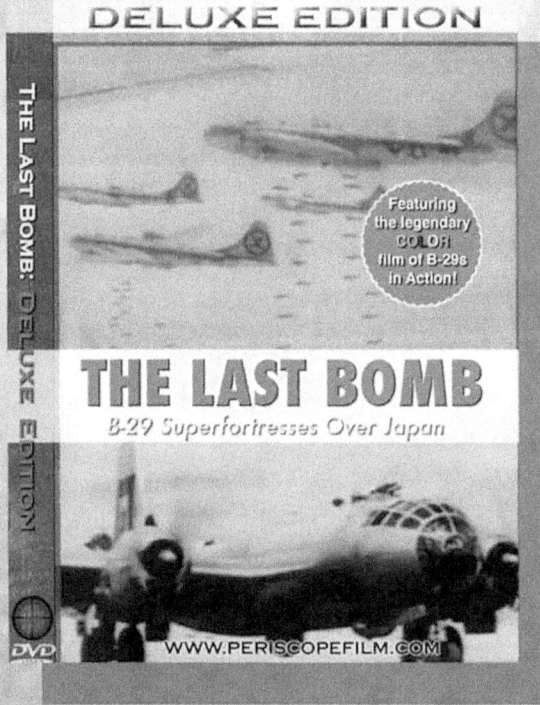
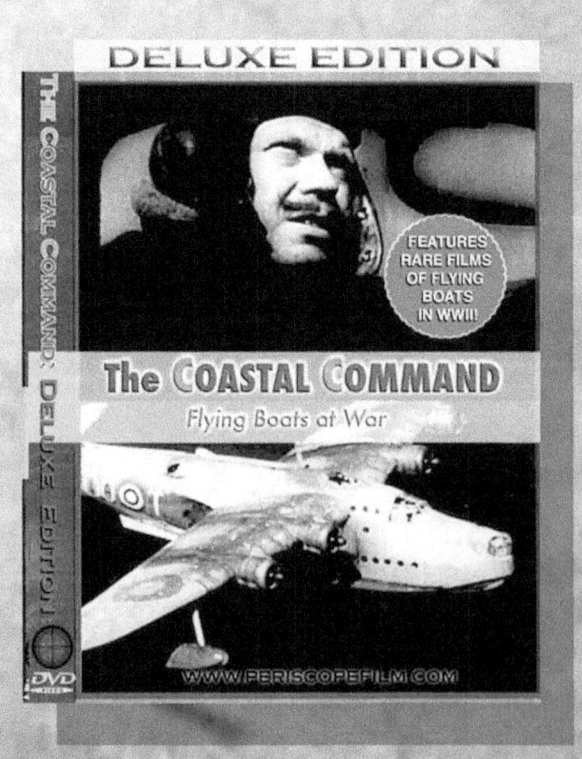

Now Available!

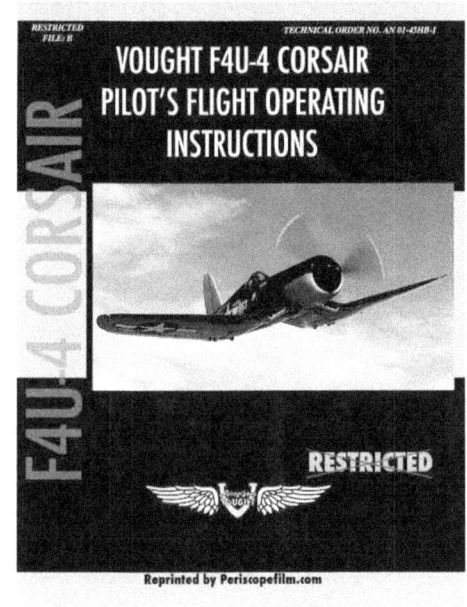

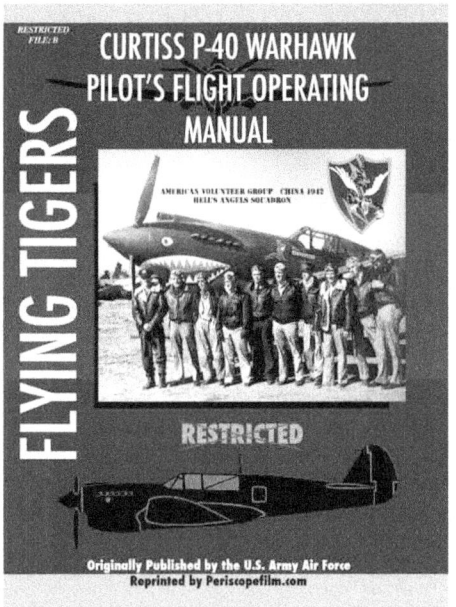

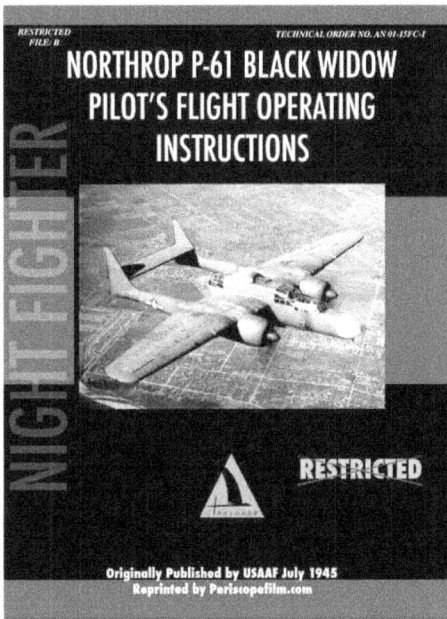

ALSO NOW AVAILABLE
FROM PERISCOPEFILM.COM

F-111 Aardvark Pilot's Flight Operating Instructions
ISBN #9781940453316
Copyright ©2014 Periscope Film LLC
www.PeriscopeFilm.com

www.ingramcontent.com/pod-product-compliance
Lightning Source LLC
Chambersburg PA
CBHW080726230426
43665CB00020B/2633